Micro

a Lonely Planet travel survival kit

Glenda Bendure
Ned Friary

Micronesia - a travel survival kit

3rd edition

Published by
  Lonely Planet Publications
  Head Office: PO Box 617, Hawthorn, Vic 3122, Australia
  Branches: 155 Filbert St, Suite 251, Oakland, CA 94607, USA
                  10 Barley Mow Passage, Chiswick, London W4 4PH, UK
                  71 bis rue du Cardinal Lemoine, 75005 Paris, France

Printed by
  Colorcraft Ltd, Hong Kong

Photographs by
  All photos by Ned Friary & Glenda Bendure

  Front cover: The Village Hotel in Pohnpei, Federated States of Micronesia (Douglas Peebles)

First Published
  April 1988

This Edition
  October 1995

**Although the author and publisher have tried to make the information as
accurate as possible, they accept no responsibility for any loss, injury or
inconvenience sustained by any person using this book.**

National Library of Australia Cataloguing in Publication Data

Bendure, Glenda.
  Micronesia.

  3rd ed.
  Includes index.
  ISBN 0 86442 310 1.

  1. Micronesia – Guidebooks. I. Friary, Ned. II. Title.
  (Series: Lonely Planet travel survival kit).

919.6504

text & maps © Lonely Planet 1995
photos © photographers as indicated 1995
Climate charts compiled from information supplied by Patrick J Tyson, © Patrick J Tyson, 1995

Glenda Bendure & Ned Friary

Glenda grew up in California's Mojave Desert and first travelled overseas as a high school AFS exchange student to India. A few years later a Chuukese exchange student lived with Glenda's family, introducing her to Micronesia.

Ned grew up near Boston, studied Social Thought & Political Economy at the University of Massachusetts in Amherst and upon graduating headed west.

They met in Santa Cruz, California, where Glenda was completing her university studies. In 1978, with Lonely Planet's first book *Across Asia on the Cheap* in hand, they took the overland trail from Europe to Nepal. The next six years were spent exploring Asia and the Pacific, with a home base in Japan where Ned taught English and Glenda edited a monthly magazine.

Since that time they've made many lengthy trips to Micronesia. On their last journey, to update the current edition of this book, they chalked up nearly 30,000 miles on a total of 38 flights and dozens of boat rides.

Ned and Glenda have a particular fondness for islands and tropical climates. They are the authors of Lonely Planet's guides to *Hawaii*, *Honolulu* and the *Eastern Caribbean*. They also write the Norway and Denmark chapters of LP's *Scandinavian & Baltic Europe on a shoestring*.

They now live on Cape Cod in Massachusetts – at least when they're not on the road.

From the Authors

A special thanks to Francis X Hezel, of the Micronesian Seminar; Samuel McPhetres, of the former Trust Territory archives; Alfred Capelle, of Alele Museum; John Engbring, of US Fish & Wildlife; Lisa King, marine biologist at the Micronesian Mariculture Demonstration Center; Jack Niedenthal, trust liaison for the people of Bikini; Randall Cherry, FSM staff attorney; Kay Henderson, of the College of Micronesia; Roman Yano, special assistant to the president of Palau; Yvette Manger-Cats, United Nations development counselor; Lori Colin, of the Chuuk Atoll Research Laboratory; Melinda Mailhot, of the Centers for Disease Control; Mary Lanwi, of the Marshall Handicraft Co-op; Patricia Loftus Lee, of the Guam Visitors Bureau; and Gloria from the Palau Visitors Bureau.

A heartfelt thanks to the Peace Corps volunteers who shared their time and insights with us on various islands: Chris

Arthur, Lisa Wandke, Marla Steinhoff, Harry Biddulph, Dale McKay-Naholowaa and director Jamie Fouss.

We'd also like to thank Beverly Battaglia, Ted Brattstrom, Klaus Benke, Captain Benny, John Enloe, Margie Falunruw, Sarah Freund, Jim & Barbara Kershner, Mellanie Lee, Richard Macaranas, Judah Rekemesik, Koichy Sana, Harvey Segal, Raphaela Simon, William Stewart, Joe & Poorly Suka, Jeffer Wright and Kelly Wyatt.

From the Publisher

This 3rd edition of *Micronesia – a travel survival kit* was edited in Oakland, California, by Kim Haglund and Greg Mills. Hugh D'Andrade designed the cover and the colour section and Richard Wilson kept us all on our toes with his speedy layout. Jane Hart, Kay Dancey, Michelle Stamp and Tamsin Wilson of the Melbourne office drew the maps and Alex Guilbert, Cyndy Johnson, Scott Summers and Wayne Heiser assisted with mapping in the US office. Jane Hart, Mark Butler and Hayden Foell all contributed illustrations. Mark Rosen and Adrienne Costanzo proofed the book and Adrienne prepared the index. Special thanks to Carolyn Hubbard and Sue Galley for their advice and assistance.

Thanks also to the following travellers who wrote in with information and helpful suggestions:

Raymond Brennan (USA), Brian Kressin (USA), Christopher Chardon (J), Dr Christopher Herron (Guam), Captain Sandra Sundin (Guam), Frederique Willard (Pohnpei), Russell Hill (AUS), Michael & Kate Quinlan (AUS), Beverly Battaglia (Tinian), Jerome Temengil (Palau), John Higham (J), Steve Frlan (AUS), Roy & Ann Gillette (USA), Chris Hazel (USA), Steve Fox (USA), Ronald H Wolff (USA), Kaye Couickshank (AUS), Tom & Yoshiko Burger (J), Allison Asher (USA), Jeff Herrin (USA), Mr & Mrs Alex McKasson (USA), Harry Biddulph (USA), Suzie Geermans (AUS), Heather Stanton (J), Vicki Pauli (AUS), Keren Haynes (HK), Raymond Smith (HK), Andrew Sharpe (HK), Donna Marchetti (USA), James Gallagher (USA), Shirley Dye (USA), Theresa San Pedro (Saipan), Jennifer Wilson (Saipan), Giovanna Petrone (USA), Marino Segnan (USA), Cherie Predmore, Mark C Blackham, Sola J Freeman, Ralf Leutz (D), Zoe E Butler (USA), Susan Atkinson (USA)

AUS – Australia, D – Germany, HK – Hong Kong, J – Japan, USA – United States of America

Warning & Request

Despite clocks running on Micronesian time, not everything moves slowly in the islands. Things change – prices go up, schedules alter, good places go bad and bad places go bankrupt. So if you find things better or worse, recently opened or now closed, please write and tell us so we can make the next edition better.

Your letters will be used to help update future editions and, where possible, important changes will also be included as a Stop Press section in reprints.

We greatly appreciate all information that is sent to us by travellers. Back at Lonely Planet we employ a hard-working readers' letters team to sort through the many letters we receive. The best ones will be rewarded with a free copy of the next edition or another Lonely Planet guide if you prefer. We give away lots of books, but, unfortunately, not every letter or postcard receives one.

Contents

Map Legend

BOUNDARIES

—··—··—··— International Boundary

—·—·—·—·— Internal Boundary

ROUTES

————————— Major Road

————————— Paved Road

———————— Unpaved Road or Track

========== Major City Street

========== City Street

··············· Foot Trail

— — — — — Ferry Route

AREA FEATURES

Park

Beach or Desert

Ancient or City Wall

HYDROGRAPHIC FEATURES

Coastline

Reef

Water

River, Creek

Swamp, Spring

Rapids, Waterfalls

SYMBOLS

◉ **State Capital**

● **City**

● Town

■ Hotel, B&B

⚑ Youth Hostel

▲ Campground

⌺ RV Park

⌂ Hut or Chalet

▼ Restaurant

🍺 Pub, Bar

🏛 Museum

🏛 Stately Home

✛ Hospital

★ Police Station

✈ Airport

✛ Airfield

✉ Post Office

❶ Tourist Information

☎ Telephone

$ Bank

P Parking

⛽ Gas Station

⛴ Bus, Ferry Station

❖ Shopping Center

⊥ Buddhist Temple

▭ Cathedral

† Church

⚒ Hindu Temple

⚓ Mosque

Ⅱ Shinto Shrine

⚐ Monument

▲ Mountain or Hill

⌒ Cave

Cliff or Escarpment

▣ Tomb

∴ Archaeological Site, Ruins

⌂ Observatory

⚘ Lighthouse

✳ Lookout

⌣ Shipwreck

◣ Dive Site/Shop

⊓ Picnic Site

❖ Gardens

🐘 Zoo

⚑ Golf Course

▱ Swimming Pool

← One Way Street

Note: not all symbols displayed above appear in this book

Introduction

All the idyllic island clichés fit Micronesia perfectly: warm aqua waters lapping at pristine bleached sands, swaying coconut palms, lush tropical jungles, tumbling waterfalls and traditional thatched huts.

Micronesia's 2100 islands lie scattered in the North Pacific between Hawaii and the Philippines. Although they cover an ocean expanse the size of the continental USA, their total land mass is less than Rhode Island, the smallest US state. Many world maps don't even bother dotting them in.

Four colonial powers have used these tiny specks of land as stepping stones between continents, first as provision ports on trade routes and later as military bastions. Following WW II, the USA took over the administration of Micronesia. The island groups have only recently emerged as 'island nations', each with some sort of political identity of its own, yet all still firmly locked into a future with the USA.

Not only are they spread out over a great distance but each of the island groups has its own culture and character. The inhabited areas vary from idyllic villages with no cars or electricity to the high-rise resort developments of Guam and Saipan.

Steeped in a rich yet largely unknown history, the ruins of the great stone cities of Pohnpei's Nan Madol and Kosrae's Lelu are on an archaeological par with the stone statues of Easter Island and the Mayan ruins of Central America. You can still get a glimpse of these abandoned worlds by navigating the canals of Nan Madol or walking Lelu's coral rock pathways.

Unfrequented Yap has giant stone money, grass skirts, men's houses and Micronesia's most traditional lifestyle. With only a few small hotels and no developed tourist sights Yap offers the sort of unspoiled earthy attractions that independent travellers yearn for.

All the district centres are now linked by air. Mountainous Kosrae, the least populated, is a friendly backwater that still seldom sees more than a handful of visitors at

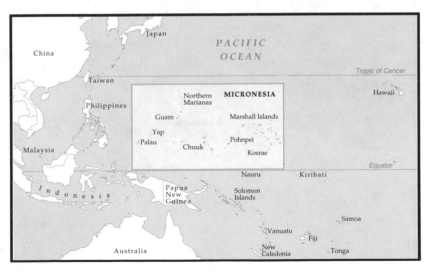

9

any one time, although it may awaken a bit as its first small dive resort has recently opened.

With more ocean than land, some of the region's top sights are underwater. Micronesia's clear 80°F (27°C) waters with coral gardens and zillions of tropical fish offer unsurpassed snorkelling and diving. Around Palau, three ocean currents converge to bring in some of the most varied and dazzling marine life in the world – and it's all accessible from your own private beach on one of Palau's Rock Islands.

In Chuuk (formerly Truk), the lagoon bed holds an entire Japanese fleet, frozen in

time where it sank in February 1944. Complete with sake cups and skeletons, jeeps and tanks tied on board and fighter planes still waiting in the holds, the wrecks have been declared an underwater museum.

Some of the bloodiest battles of WW II were fought in Micronesia. On Peleliu, Saipan and Tinian, Japanese and Americans killed each other by the thousands. These days the battle scars and WW II ruins have been turned into sightseeing attractions, and both US and Japanese war veterans and relatives of war dead make up a sizable (though dwindling) portion of Micronesia's visitors. Not a lot of people

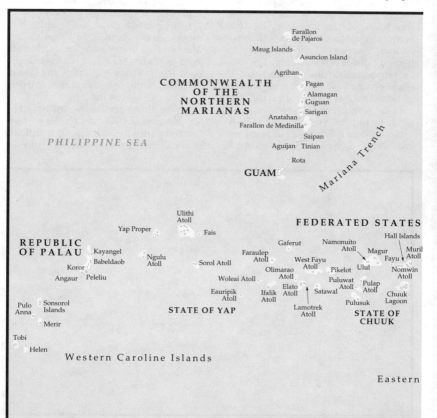

live on these islands, the saying goes, but a lot of people died here.

The Marshall Islands include more than a thousand flat coral islands with white sand beaches and turquoise lagoons. To some it's a tropical paradise but many Marshallese are struggling with some of the nastier effects of 20th-century technology. Some of the Marshall Islands served as testing sites for atomic bombs and as a consequence many Marshallese have suffered radioactivity poisoning and some islands still remain too contaminated to be re-settled.

Micronesia is caught between past tradi-tions and present realities. Many islanders who still make their homes of coconut fronds and sail outrigger canoes now also have electric generators and VCRs; visiting neighbours to watch the latest video is a popular pastime. Some islanders have moved away from subsistence farming and fishing only to find hard times and high unemployment in district centres such as Weno and Majuro. As elsewhere, it's a society in a state of flux.

Still, outside the larger towns, many of Micronesia's more remote islands remain refreshingly distant from the pollution and problems of the modern world.

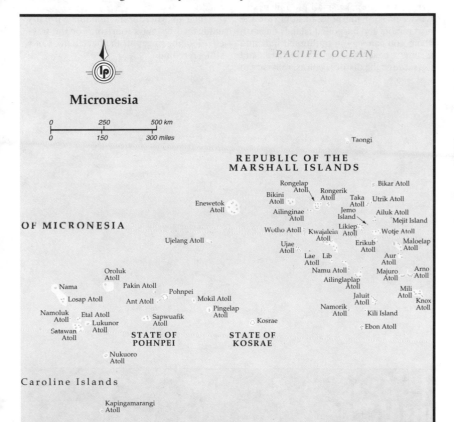

Micronesia Defined

The boundaries of Micronesia are not cut and dried. In this guidebook we include the Mariana, Marshall and Caroline island chains. The islands covered are: the US territory of Guam, the Commonwealth of the Northern Marianas (Saipan, Rota, Tinian), the Republic of the Marshall Islands, the Federated States of Micronesia (Yap, Chuuk, Pohnpei and Kosrae) and the Republic of Palau.

These islands (with the exception of Guam) were grouped together after WW II as the Trust Territory of the Pacific Islands – officially a United Nations territory, but for all practical purposes a US colony, which has only recently been dissolved. Because these islands have in many ways been thought of as a single unit since the end of the war, they have become for most purposes synonymous with the term Micronesia. ■

Micronesia can be explored in depth or taken in small chunks; there is plenty of variety. You can take small prop planes or two-week ship journeys to some of the most remote and unspoiled islands on earth where you can stay in traditional huts and become a beachcomber; or you can island hop through the district centres, rent cars to drive around and spend sunset hours on a beach lounge chair with a tropical drink in hand.

Much of Micronesia remains virtually untouched by mass tourism. For the traveller looking to get off the beaten track, it's still a rare find.

Facts about the Region

HISTORY

In the most commonly accepted theory of Micronesian origins, the first settlers of the region canoed across the Pacific from the Philippines and Indonesia to settle on the high western islands of the Marianas, Yap and Palau.

Although carbon dating of the earliest artefacts found thus far in the western part of Micronesia shows them to date back only to 1500 BC, most historians speculate that this region was first settled between 2000 and 4000 BC.

Much later, so the theory goes, voyagers from Melanesia settled the eastern islands of the Marshalls and then worked their way west to Kosrae, Pohnpei and Chuuk. In time they continued still farther west, settling the outer atolls of Yap and Palau. Although spread over an enormous expanse of ocean, the islands settled by these Melanesian descendants still share related cultures and languages. Micronesians themselves have no legends of a life outside Micronesia.

In 1986 an American archaeologist studying the nuclear-bombed Bikini Atoll in the Marshall Islands discovered bone fragments and the remains of a village. These artefacts have been carbon dated to 1960 BC, making Bikini the site of the earliest human settlement yet discovered in all of Micronesia.

Pre-European Contact

Micronesia's inhabited island groups had thriving cultures and well-established societies long before the arrival of the Europeans.

As the islands had no metals, the most impressive archaeological remains of early Micronesians are achievements in stone. While Europe was lost in the Dark Ages, Micronesia was flourishing with

Ancient latte stones were common in the Mariana Islands and are thought to have been used as building pillars

Early European settlers in the Mariana Islands

civilisations that built the great stone cities of Nan Madol in Pohnpei and Lelu in Kosrae.

Hundreds of years before the birth of Christ, the Chamorro people of the Marianas were quarrying large *latte* stones to use as foundation pillars for their buildings.

The Yapese, who quarried immense circles out of the limestone found on Palau to use as money, carried the stones back to Yap on barges behind their canoes. They were superb ocean navigators and built an empire that stretched across hundreds of miles of ocean.

In Palau, on the northernmost point of the main island of Babeldaob, there are two rows of large basalt monoliths. Their original use remains a mystery but their size and layout suggest they may have been part of a structure that held thousands of people. There are also elaborately terraced hillsides

nearby that date back to 100 AD though no one knows who built them or why.

Most of what is known today about ancient Micronesian societies comes from village remains or archaeological digs, since prior to European contact the islanders had no written languages and passed down all information through oral histories.

Western influences, such as the diseases that killed off most of the population and the missionaries that converted the rest, shredded the traditional social fabric of the islands. The missionaries, by discouraging talk of the early religions and gods, contributed to the loss of oral traditions. In many places the old stories have been forgotten completely, resulting in a sort of cultural amnesia.

The First Europeans

In the late 1400s Portuguese explorers, in a quest for spices, established a trade route around Africa and across the Indian Ocean to the Spice Islands, or the Moluccas, which are part of present-day Indonesia. The Spanish, who were denied use of this Portuguese trade route by a decree from the pope, were forced to sail west to get to the East.

The search for an alternate route to the Spice Islands led to a flurry of exploration, beginning with Christopher Columbus, who discovered parts of the Americas while floundering around the Atlantic looking for a route to the Pacific. The Americas were, however, just a pain in the arse for Columbus and the next few explorers, posing a massive obstacle en route to the Spice Islands.

The first Europeans to actually set foot in Micronesia were with the Spanish expedition of Portuguese explorer Ferdinand Magellan in 1521. It had taken 30 years to successfully find a way around the Americas. Magellan became the first navigator to lead his ships around the tip of South America into the Pacific and the expedition was the first to circumnavigate the globe.

It is an indication of the vastness of the Pacific and the smallness of its islands that

Magellan managed to sail across the entire ocean from South America's Cape Horn to the Mariana Islands, close to the Asian mainland, without encountering any of the thousands of scattered islands along the way.

By the time they arrived in the Marianas, Magellan and his scurvy-ridden crew were eating rats and boiled leather to ward off complete starvation. Although the islanders provided the starving crew with food, drink and shelter, they also helped themselves to whatever they could carry off the ships. This led to retaliation by the Spanish.

Antonio Pigafette, one of Magellan's crew, wrote the following about the first encounter between Europeans and Micronesians.

... the people of these islands boarded the ships and robbed us, in such a way that it was impossible to preserve oneself from them. Whilst we were lowering the sails to go ashore, they stole away with much address and diligence the small boat called the skiff, which was made fast to the poop of the captain's ship, at which he was much irritated, and went on shore with forty armed men, burned forty or fifty houses, with several small boats, and killed seven men of the island; they recovered their skiff.

This was just the first of many confrontations between explorers and Micronesians.

Spanish Period

Numerous explorers soon followed in Magellan's path, beginning with the Spanish expedition under Juan Garcia Jofre de Loaysa in 1526. The tiny islands of Micronesia, devoid of cloves or gold, held little interest for the explorers other than as a quick stopover to replenish water and food. Certainly no one ever set out to 'discover' Micronesia and it took more than 300 years for all of the islands to get added to the charts.

In 1565 Spanish trade ships started making annual trips between Mexico and the Philippines. These 'Manila Galleons' picked up silk, spices and tea from Chinese traders in Manila and took them to Acapulco, where they loaded newly mined silver and carried it back to the Philippines.

The 'new' transpacific shipping corridors, established by the Spanish traders to take advantage of favourable trade winds, actually followed routes the ocean-going Micronesians had been sailing for centuries. Because the ships attempted to stick to these precise routes very few Micronesian islands outside these corridors were discovered during the 16th and 17th centuries.

In one notable exception, after a mutiny in 1565, the Spanish ship *San Lucas* dropped a few degrees from the usual route to avoid other Spanish ships. In doing so it was the first European vessel to come upon Chuuk Lagoon and a number of Marshallese atolls.

Spain's interest in Micronesia at this time was centred almost entirely on the Marianas, where the galleons made regular stops to replenish supplies. Spanish missionaries arrived in the Marianas in 1668, accompanied by the military and government authorities sent to establish colonial rule. Spanish culture, language and Catholicism were forced upon the native Chamorros.

The Caroline Islands got their first Spanish missionaries in the early 1700s, but they had only a nominal presence. Outside the Marianas there were no significant European influences in Micronesia until the late 1700s when British, American and European traders began plying the waters for commercial purposes.

Whalers, Traders & Missionaries

Beginning in 1817 with Otto Kotzebue, Russian and French explorers began carefully exploring and mapping Micronesia's islands. They also wrote and sketched some colourful accounts of the island people and their lifestyles.

The first British whalers began to arrive in the early 1800s, and American whale ships out of New England arrived a couple of decades later in much greater numbers. During the whaling boom, which peaked in the 1840s, there were as many as 500 ships hunting whales in the Pacific.

The whale ships were virtual factories which could stay at sea for years on end, boiling down blubber into oil and storing it in tanks on board. The Micronesian islands were used by the whalers to replenish food, water and wood. Desertion was common.

Traders were also infiltrating Micronesia at this time, setting up posts to deal in copra and beche-de-mer (sea cucumbers).

Whalers and traders were not usually the cream of civilised society. The sailors picked fights, taunted the islanders and spurred massacres, although quite often it was the islanders who would do away with the crews. Kosrae had so much trouble with the 'degenerate Whites' who jumped ship that the chief initiated a policy of putting deserters back out to sea on the next ship that pulled into port.

When the sailors came into port, usually after many months at sea, they were ready to carouse and they wanted women. In the process they brought venereal and other contagious diseases to which the islanders, with no natural immunities, were particularly susceptible.

Foreign diseases such as syphilis, smallpox, measles and influenza had devastating effects and caused a rapid depopulation of the islands. A single smallpox epidemic in 1854 killed approximately 50% of Pohnpei's population.

Prior to the arrival of the whaling ships, Kosrae's population was estimated to be about 6000. By the time the whalers had left the population had dropped to 300 and the Kosraeans were ripe for the prudish morality the Congregationalists were about to lay on them.

The American Board of Commissioners for Foreign Missions began sending missionaries to eastern Micronesia in 1870, after two decades of Protestant work had proven successful in Hawaii.

The Protestant missionaries in the east, like the Catholic priests in the west, brought more than religion. They brought Western clothing for the scantily clad islanders, as well as Western laws and values. They were the first to put the native languages into a written form, primarily so the Bible could be translated, and they set up schools to teach the people to read and write.

The 19th century was a time of major change in Micronesia with the introduction of alcohol, firearms, new animals, new tools and new ideas all having a dramatic effect upon the islands.

German Period

Disregarding Spanish claims in the region, the Germans arrived in Micronesia in the 19th century to develop the copra trade. The start of the German period in Micronesia was more of a commercial venture than a fully fledged attempt to colonise.

The first German company to set up operations in Micronesia was Godeffroy & Sons who, from their headquarters in New Guinea, opened an office in Yap in 1869. Meanwhile, 2200 miles to the east, the Germans were negotiating a treaty with the chiefs of Jaluit Atoll in the Marshall Islands. In 1878 Germany established a protectorate over the Marshalls.

Spain grumbled about German activity in the Carolines but did little else until 1885 when the dispute was taken to Pope Leo XIII for arbitration. The pope ruled that Spain owned the land and had administrative rights, but that Germany had a right to establish plantations and commerce. For Spain, it was largely a face-saving decision as her period as a major colonial power was clearly on the wane.

In 1898 the USA, looking to get in on the action, abruptly declared war on a reluctant Spain. As an outcome of the Spanish-American War, the USA was ceded Spain's Pacific possessions of Guam, the Philippines and Wake Island (as well as Puerto Rico and Cuba). As part of the deal, the USA paid US$20 million to Spain.

Not particularly keen on selling her remaining Micronesian possessions to gunboat diplomats, Spain went into secret negotiations with Germany for the sale of the Carolines and the remaining Marianas. In 1899 the Germans, now eager to become established as a colonial power, agreed on a purchase price of 25 million pesetas, or about US$4.25 million.

The period of German administration therefore began with a simple real estate transaction. It was to last a mere 15 years. Commercial development was mainly in terms of copra production, though there were also some phosphate mining operations. German interests, led by the Jaluit Company, controlled the copra trade in the Marshalls and eastern Carolines; governance of the islands was through local chiefs. In Yap and Palau the copra market was largely in the hands of Japanese traders.

To support the copra trade, the Micronesians were encouraged to grow coconuts and were given seeds, tools and long-term contracts. To increase the labour supply for German mines and plantations, outer islanders were sometimes forcibly removed from their atolls. Communally held land, often seemingly idle, was redistributed to the new arrivals or leased by the government to private businesses. Germany's main legacy in Micronesia rests in the social disruptions caused by forced relocations and altered land-use policies.

German presence, however, was limited to a small group of government officials, businessmen and missionaries. The total population of Germans in all Micronesia numbered well under 1000. Some businesses such as the German South Seas Phosphate Company in Angaur and the Jaluit Company made money, but in the overall picture German government subsidies to faltering businesses outweighed the total profits taken in Micronesia.

With the onset of WW I German forces fled Micronesia, allowing the Japanese fleet to sail in without resistance.

Japanese Period

Japan had control of the whole of Micronesia, with the exception of Guam, between the two world wars, a period of about 30 years.

Throughout Germany's occupation, Japan had been tightening its economic ties with Micronesia and just prior to WW I maintained more than 80% of all trade with 'German Micronesia'. The Japanese imported turtle shell, mother-of-pearl, beche-de-mer and other products from the islands.

With the outbreak of hostilities in Europe, Japan made her move to strengthen her ties to Micronesia even further and in October 1914 the Japanese Navy seized possession of the German colonies under the pretext of alliance obligations with Britain. The Japanese then proceeded to occupy the islands, starting in the east with the Marshalls and moving westward.

Japan wasted no time developing the infrastructure and administration necessary for the complete annexation of Micronesia. The League of Nations formally mandated control of Micronesia to Japan in 1920.

By this time Saipan, the nearest island to Japan, was already home to a growing number of Japanese colonists and entrepreneurs who had sugar cane production underway. A Japanese conglomerate, the South Seas Development Company, bought them out in 1921 and rapidly became the dominant force in Micronesia's development and exploitation.

The Japanese left no doubt they were there to stay. Micronesia was an extension of the empire's boundaries, an expansion of its horizons. Their intent was to make Micronesia as Japanese as possible. They built Buddhist temples and Shinto shrines, geisha houses and public baths. Each administrative centre became a little Tokyo.

The building of roads, harbours, hospitals and water systems were followed by seaplane ramps, airfields and other fortifications, the latter in violation of the League of Nations mandate. The Japanese withdrew from the League of Nations in 1935 but remained firmly in control of Micronesia.

Administrative buildings were constructed of heavy concrete capable of withstanding not only typhoons but also direct aerial bombings. Many of these buildings, with their 20-inch thick walls and steel reinforcements, were to weather both.

Although the League of Nations mandate had called for the economic and social development of Micronesia, the Japanese geared such development not toward benefiting the local population but rather toward supporting and fortifying their own settlements. Expatriates came to outnumber the Micronesians – by 1940 the Japanese population in the Marianas, Carolines and Marshalls was more than 70,000, compared to about 50,000 Micronesians.

In the Marianas, railroads were built to carry sugar cane from the plantations to harbourside refineries; from there the sugar and alcohol were shipped to the Japanese homeland. Throughout Micronesia, fisheries projects, copra and tapioca production, phosphate and bauxite mining and trochus shell production were developed and began to thrive.

The Japanese, drawing from their own experiences of life on their resource-scarce home islands, created an astonishing level of agricultural activity in Micronesia. With exports exceeding imports, they achieved an economic viability that would never be remotely approached under the Americans. In terms of production it was Micronesia's heyday.

Not that all that necessarily made it the most pleasant of times for the Micronesians themselves, whose place in this profitable system was clearly at the bottom. There was a two-tier system of education which saw Japanese children attending excellent schools, while the three years of compulsory education for Micronesians was primarily geared to teaching them a servant's form of the Japanese language. This subordination prevailed in wage scales and social treatment as well.

Although the economy was an impressive one, for the Micronesians it was a trickle-down economy and during wartime, when the trickle stopped, it was the local islanders who were the first to feel hard times and hunger.

The Japanese not only made the islands more productive than they had ever been before, they also set Micronesia on a shifting course from a traditional subsistence lifestyle to a moneyed economy. In boom towns like Garapan and Koror, the sudden development awed many locals who acquired a taste for the imported goods in the store windows. Many wanted a piece of the pie, or more precisely, they wanted the rice, canned food and sugar candies that only money could buy.

WW II

The war in the Pacific was launched with the Japanese air attacks on Honolulu's Pearl Harbor on 7 December 1941, and against the US territory of Guam on the same day, 8 December across the International Date Line.

Undefended, Guam surrendered two days later, just hours after Japanese forces came ashore. With its capture, the Japanese possessed all of Micronesia and it was two years before any serious counteroffensive was launched by the USA.

On 1 February 1944, US Admiral Chester Nimitz, Commander in Chief of the Pacific Fleet, started his drive across the Pacific with an attack on Kwajalein Atoll, a major Japanese air and naval base in the Marshall Islands. By 4 February the USA had captured Kwajalein and the undefended Majuro Atoll to the south, and from these two outposts the Americans began air raids on Japanese bases in the western Carolines.

On 17 February the USA made a surprise attack on a fleet of Japanese warships and commercial vessels harboured in Chuuk Lagoon (then called Truk Lagoon). This supposedly impenetrable fortress was the Imperial Japanese Fleet's most important base in the central Pacific. The USA destroyed more than 200 planes on the ground and sent nearly 60 ships to watery graves. The 200,000 tons of equipment sunk in the two days of fighting was to be a record for WW II. After the raid the few surviving Japanese ships evacuated Chuuk, leaving behind 30,000 Japanese troops who had little to do but wait out the war.

With the Chuuk base neutralised and no longer able to provide support to other Pacific bases, the USA continued moving west from Majuro, capturing Enewetok and other smaller atolls and islands in the Marshalls.

In June 1944, US forces moved west from the Marshalls with their Fifth Fleet, the largest armada ever assembled. Nearly 600 battleships, carriers, cruisers and destroyers carried a quarter of a million American troops across the Pacific.

The fight for the Marianas began with the US invasion of Saipan on 15 June. Tinian and Guam were invaded in July and all three islands were 'liberated' by the beginning of August. These battles were some of the war's most brutal and costly. They marked a major turning point in the war as they gave the USA air bases that were within striking distance of Japan.

With the Marianas secured, only Palau was left, and in retrospect it would have been better off bypassed. Although it was earlier feared that air raids from Palau would threaten a planned US invasion of the Philippines, Japanese air power in the western Pacific had nearly collapsed and the Palau bases had little significance in the declining days of the war.

Nevertheless, the USA attacked the Palauan island of Peleliu on 15 September. It was secured after a month of even bloodier battles than those witnessed in the Marianas.

With planes taking off from Micronesian airstrips, the air bombing of Japan began in force in November 1944. In August 1945 two planes, leaving from Tinian, dropped the first atomic bombs ever used in warfare on the industrial ports of Hiroshima and Nagasaki. The devastation of those cities, and the awesome death toll, was followed days later by the unconditional surrender of the Japanese.

The Micronesians had watched the impressive Japanese construction of fortified command posts, communications buildings, hospitals, airports and harbours. Caught in the crossfire, they watched as the USA turned it all into rubble. Whole towns such as Koror, Garapan and Sapou were levelled, some of them never to be rebuilt. For Micronesia, the Rising Sun had set.

In the months following the end of the war, thousands of Japanese were shipped home, most of them civilians or soldiers from uninvaded islands. The USA took few military prisoners since most Japanese soldiers chose to fight to the death or commit suicide rather than surrender. Many Japanese civilians killed themselves as well, rather than risk the torture which they had been indoctrinated into believing that the Americans would inflict upon them.

Thousands of Americans and tens of thousands of Japanese died fighting in Micronesia. Thousands of Micronesians died too, though no one paid much attention to Micronesian body counts. In all the volumes written about WW II they are scarcely mentioned. Their islands were the stage but the islanders were not the players, merely the victims.

The Americans Move In

Even though Micronesians played no role in the Pacific conflict, the US government immediately began to treat Micronesia as its 'spoils of war'. The occupying forces were suddenly American instead of Japanese and when the war ended, the occupation continued.

The US Navy took command of the islands in 1945 and effectively sealed Micronesia off to visitors. Some areas remained closed until 1962.

The remoteness of the islands, and the fact that the Micronesian people were so few in number, left them unseen, unheard and isolated to all beyond their shores. It was an isolation that the US military took measures to maintain.

The Nuclear Age

Throughout Micronesia, islanders had been rocked by two military superpowers battling on their shores. Yet for the Marshallese, the destruction did not cease with the end of the Pacific conflict; for them the most fearsome display of firepower still lay ahead.

Soon after the end of the war, the USA took over sections of the Marshalls to test

---

Operation Crossroads

Operation Crossroads, a dual-bomb test which took place at Bikini Atoll, was the first peacetime explosion of atomic bombs. Nearly 100 decommissioned and captured warships were anchored in the lagoon as target subjects to test the effectiveness of the nuclear bomb in sinking an enemy fleet. The first bomb was detonated on 1 July 1946 directly above the lagoon while the second bomb was exploded underwater from the lagoon floor on 25 July. It all took place with the bizarre fanfare of a gala international event and rates as the biggest public relations coup of the early Cold War.

Scores of congressmen, foreign dignitaries and scientists were invited to witness the event, a blitz of media personnel were brought in and over 200 movie cameras were used to shoot 18 tons of film, equal to half the world's film supply at the time. It's little wonder that the sickening mushroom cloud that resulted from the explosion has since been used as a backdrop in hundreds of programmes and movies.

Back in the USA, radio programmes were interrupted to broadcast the event. The media reporting was replete with such patronising sound bites as 'The islanders aren't exactly sure what the atom bomb means but at least they admit it' and blurbs from congressional observers comparing it to a huge firecracker and complaining they weren't allowed to get closer to the explosion.

Of those present at the testing, more than 1000 veterans, including the military newscaster, later filed disability claims for radiation-induced cancer. ■

---

nuclear weapons and the little-understood effects of radiation.

On 1 July 1946 the first nuclear bomb explosion, part of a perversely theatrical testing programme dubbed 'Operation Crossroads', took place at Bikini Atoll, with dignitaries and military officials from around the world brought in to witness the event. Without any fanfare, nuclear testing was expanded to a second Marshallese atoll, Enewetok, in 1948. There would be 66 nuclear tests altogether that would leave some atolls uninhabitable and hundreds of islanders victims of radiation poisoning.

The most powerful bomb ever tested by the USA was detonated over Bikini's lagoon in 'Operation Bravo' on 1 March 1954. The 15-megaton hydrogen bomb had a tonnage of TNT greater than the total tonnage of explosives used during the entire course of WW II. Operation Bravo's H-bomb was 1000 times more powerful than the bomb dropped on Hiroshima.

Pulverised coral from Bikini's reef was scattered, along with radioactive fallout, over an area of about 50,000 sq miles. It filtered down as ash upon the Marshallese on the islands of Rongelap and Utrik, upon US weather station personnel on Rongerik and upon the unlucky crew of the Japanese fishing vessel *Lucky Dragon*. Hundreds of people and their offspring were affected. The USA evacuated the Rongelapese 48 hours later, but by that time many had already suffered severe radiation burns from 'Bikini snow'. Although the USA downplayed the extent of the contamination, it's now believed that nearly two dozen Marshallese atolls were affected by the fallout.

Nuclear experiments ended in 1958 with an international test-ban treaty, just prior to US plans to blast nuclear warheads into space from Bikini Atoll. The warheads were instead launched from Johnston Island in 1961.

Trust Territory

In 1947 the UN established a trusteeship in Micronesia. Called the Trust Territory of the Pacific Islands, it had six districts: the Northern Marianas, Pohnpei (including Kosrae), Chuuk, Yap, the Marshalls and Palau. The USA was given exclusive rights to administer the islands.

The UN designated the area a 'strategic trust', allowing the USA to establish and maintain military bases in Micronesia and to prevent other nations from doing the same.

In 1951 the US Department of the Interior took over from the US Navy, moving the Trust Territory headquarters from Honolulu to Guam. The Northern Marianas was the only district not to come under Interior Department jurisdiction; it remained under military control until 1962.

Under UN guidelines, the USA was obliged to foster the development of political and economic institutions with the goal of helping the Micronesians achieve self-government and self-sufficiency. Instead, 20 years of neglect were followed by 20 years of promoting welfare dependency.

Instead of developing an economic infrastructure and promoting industry, the USA pumped in money for government-operated services. Instead of encouraging farming and fishing, they passed out USDA food commodities. They built airports, schools, old age centres and other projects, creating an abundance of government jobs with no internal base capable of bankrolling it all. It was an economy reliant on imported greenbacks.

With anticolonial sentiment high in the '60s, the USA found itself, with its Micronesian possessions, coming under mounting criticism.

Yielding to Micronesian aspirations, steps were taken for the islanders to assume a degree of self-government. In 1965 the USA agreed to the formation of the Congress of Micronesia as a forum for islanders to deliberate their future political status. The congress was a two-house legislature made up of elected representatives from all island groups.

Executive authority in the Trust Territory, however, remained under the control of the US High Commissioner. Just to make sure nothing got out of hand, the CIA kept tabs on island legislators by bugging the offices of the Congress of Micronesia.

Peace Corps

The Peace Corps arrived in Micronesia in 1966. The US government saw the Peace Corps as a way of spreading American influence and for a while there was one volunteer for every 100 Micronesians. By putting a volunteer on every inhabited island, they brought English as a unifying language to the distant corners of Micronesia. What they hadn't calculated on was the idealism and the critical outlook on US policies that the volunteers would also bring.

Volunteers worked in community development projects and as legal advisors. Peace Corps lawyers taught the Micronesians that they had certain legal rights, including the right to challenge US government policies. The US Defense Department became particularly concerned with challenges to land policies. In response to the volunteers' activities in Micronesia, the Nixon administration dismantled the Peace Corps' legal services programme.

Emerging States

When negotiations for self-government were first started, the USA had initially expected that the six Trust Territory districts would join together as one Micronesian nation, but this was not to be.

In January 1978 the people of the Northern Marianas opted to become US citizens under US Commonwealth status.

In July 1978 the remaining six districts (Kosrae had become a separate district in 1977) voted on a common constitution. It failed to pass in the Marshalls and Palau.

The four central districts which had voted in favour – Pohnpei, Kosrae, Chuuk and Yap – became the Federated States of Micronesia (FSM). Their constitution went into effect in May 1979.

The Marshalls became a separate political entity, the Republic of the Marshall Islands. Their constitution also became effective in May 1979.

The Palauans, opting to become the Republic of Palau, voted for a constitution that went into effect in January 1981. That constitution included a provision which totally banned the use, testing and storage of nuclear weapons on Palauan land and in its surrounding waters.

The internal governments of each of these emerging nations are based on the US system of executive, legislative and judicial branches, with the exception of the government of the Marshall Islands, which also incorporates elements of the British parliamentary system. In all three nations, traditional village councils and high-ranking chiefs retain some powers through advisory boards.

In 1982 each of the new nations – the FSM, Marshalls and Palau – signed separate Compacts of Free Association with the USA, all striking their own economic deal. In theory the compacts allow the new nations to manage their internal affairs, although their relationships with other nations are subject to US restrictions. In return for an aid package to the fledgling governments worth about three billion dollars in total, the compacts allow the USA to maintain sweeping military rights throughout Micronesia.

As part of the process for dissolving the Trust Territory, each compact had to be approved by four separate groups in turn: by the peoples of each new nation in a general election, by the legislatures of those nations, by the US Congress and by the UN Security Council.

The compacts of the FSM and the Marshalls were approved in plebiscites in 1983, and then ratified by their respective congresses. Finally the US Congress approved the two compacts, with the provisions going into effect in November 1986.

However, over the next few years, unresolved issues in Palau stalled not only Palau's own political process, but the dissolution of the Trust Territory as well.

The compact between the USA and Palau permitted the USA to transfer and store nuclear materials in the area, a clear violation of Palau's constitution. In vote after vote, Palauans consistently approved the compact by the simple majority which was required to ratify the compact, but with less than the 75% majority necessary to simultaneously overturn the anti-nuclear provision in their constitution. The compact and the constitution, both legally approved by Palauans, were in legal conflict with one another. As a result Palau's status, and consequently the rest of Micronesia's, hung in limbo throughout the 1980s.

Under veto power by the USSR, which called the compacts 'virtual slavery' for Micronesians, the UN Security Council had maintained throughout the 1980s that it would make only one vote to dissolve the trusteeship, rather than disband it a portion at a time.

With the thawing of the Cold War, the USSR dropped its objection to the Trust Territory's piecemeal disbandment and in December 1990 the UN Security Council voted (with only Cuba dissenting) to terminate the trusteeship for the Commonwealth of the Northern Mariana Islands, the Federated States of Micronesia and the Republic of the Marshall Islands. The council allowed Palau to be dealt with separately.

In 1993, following a vote to amend their constitution, Palauans ratified the Compact of Free Association with the USA by a simple majority. In October 1994, Palau became an independent nation and later that year it became the 185th member of the UN.

With Palau's independence, the last of the 11 UN-mandated trusteeships of former colonial possessions was finally abolished. Most of the others had run their course decades earlier; Papua New Guinea, the last non-US trusteeship, gained its independence in 1975.

GEOGRAPHY

It's no easy task counting the islands of Micronesia – there are more than 2100 of them. Some are just small flat specks that disappear and reappear with the tides; some are still growing, through coral build-up or volcanic flows; most are uninhabited. With the vast majority of these islands covering less than one sq mile each, they are aptly named Micronesia – 'small islands'.

Micronesia's islands are scattered over three million sq miles of the western Pacific between Hawaii and the Philippines. They are divided geographically into three archipelagoes – the Marshalls, Carolines and Marianas.

All are in the tropics, except two of the Marianas which poke up just north of the Tropic of Cancer. The southernmost island is Kapingamarangi, one degree north of the equator.

Together the islands have a total land mass of 919 sq miles. In comparison Hawaii totals 6450 sq miles, Bali is 2147 and Tahiti is 402.

The islands of Micronesia are classified as 'high' or 'low'. The main islands in western Micronesia are high types and are actually the exposed peaks of a volcanic mountain ridge that runs from Japan through the Northern Marianas, Guam and Palau on down to New Guinea. The Northern Marianas have Micronesia's only active volcanoes.

While basically of volcanic formation, some of the western Micronesian islands are partly or wholly capped with a layer of limestone. Pohnpei, Kosrae and Chuuk, in the eastern Carolines, are also high volcanic islands, while Yap is a raised part of the Asian continental shelf.

High islands, which make up the vast majority of Micronesia's land area, usually have good soil, abundant water and lush vegetation. Guam is the largest island, followed by Babeldaob in the Republic of Palau.

The highest point in Micronesia is 3166 feet above sea level, on Agrihan Island in the Northern Marianas. A canyon, known as the Mariana Trench, runs for 1835 miles alongside the Mariana Islands and has the world's greatest known ocean depth. The canyon is more than seven miles deep, so, if measured from the bottom of the canyon, the Mariana Islands would be the highest mountains in the world!

All of the more than 1100 islands that comprise the Marshalls are low coral islands, as are the hundreds of small islands of the central Carolines between Yap Proper and Chuuk Lagoon, and the outer islands of Pohnpei and Palau.

Some of these low coral islands are like the archetypal cartoon island – just a patch of white sand with a single coconut tree – while other islands are grouped together on the rims of atolls. Micronesia features the world's first, second and fourth largest atolls: Kwajalein in the Marshalls, Namonuito in Chuuk, and Ulithi in Yap,

Coral Atolls

Charles Darwin was the first to recognise that atolls are made from coral growth which has built up around the edges of a submerged volcanic mountain peak.

In a scenario played out over hundreds of thousands of years, coral first builds up around the shores of a high island producing a fringing reef. Then, as the island begins to slowly sink under its own weight, the coral continues to grow upwards at about the same rate. This forms a barrier reef which is separated from the shore by a lagoon. By the time the island has completely submerged, the coral growth has become a base for an atoll, circling the place where the mountain top used to be.

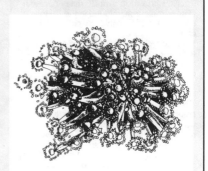

The classic atoll shape is roughly oval, with islands of coral rubble and sand built up on the higher points of the reef. There are usually breaks in the reef rim large enough for boats to enter the sheltered lagoon.

The coral is made up of millions of tiny rock-like limestone skeletons. These are created by tentacled coral polyps which draw calcium from the water and then excrete it to form hardened shells to protect their soft bodies. Only the outer layer of coral is alive. As polyps reproduce and die, the new polyps attach themselves in successive layers to the empty skeletons already in place. ■

respectively. Together Micronesia accounts for 23% of all the atolls in the world.

Low islands have practically no topsoil and the sand has a high salt content, so vegetation is limited. Though the islands have no springs or rivers, many sit atop freshwater lenses that can be tapped by wells.

CLIMATE

Micronesia has a tropical oceanic climate that is consistently warm and humid, with some of the most uniform year-round temperatures in the world. Temperatures range between 70°F and 90°F (21°C to 32°C), with the average daily temperature for all of Micronesia about 81°F (27°C). Humidity averages about 78%.

Generally the more comfortable months are December through March. These months usually see less rainfall, somewhat lower humidity, slightly cooler weather and refreshing north-easterly trade winds.

The average annual rainfall is about 85 to 150 inches, but this varies from place to

place. Some of the northern Marshalls get only 20 inches a year, while Pohnpei's rainforest interior gets over 400 inches per year. Rainfall decreases in the Carolines from east to west.

FLORA & FAUNA
Fauna

The closer an island group is to the Asian land masses, the more numerous its birds and animals. High islands have a greater variety and support larger populations than coral atolls. Therefore the isolated Marshall Islands have few creatures other than seabirds and shorebirds while Palau, predictably, has Micronesia's greatest variety of fauna.

The only land mammals native to Micronesia are bats. Fruit bats, with wingspans of up to three feet, are found on all island groups except the Marshalls. They are common at dusk in Palau's Rock Islands and on Chuuk, Pohnpei and Yap. Because of a Chamorro penchant for eating the furry flying beasts, they are now on the endangered list in Guam and are rare in the Northern Marianas. Despite being a protected species, poaching continues to threaten remaining fruit bat populations and imported fruit bats sell for a premium on Guam.

Animals that have been introduced into the islands include dogs, cats, mice, rats, pigs, cattle, horses and goats. Angaur in Palau has monkeys. Sambar deer are found on Pohnpei, Rota, Guam and Saipan, though they are seldom seen.

Guam has carabao (water buffalo), which were probably brought in by Jesuit missionaries in the 1600s. Carabao are most often seen in the southern part of Guam where they are used on small farms as beasts of burden. They are large, clumsy animals and not always good-tempered with strangers.

Palau has estuarine crocodiles (and a few New Guinea crocodiles) that frequent both saltwater and freshwater areas, favouring muddy mangrove swamps. They are primarily nocturnal, but sometimes bask in the sun during the day. Adult crocodiles aver-

---

Typhoons

A typhoon is a tropical storm in the western Pacific with winds over 75 miles per hour. (The same storm, if found in the Atlantic or eastern Pacific, would be called a hurricane.)

While typhoons can occur in any month, they are most frequent in Micronesia between August and December. Guam and the Northern Marianas are particularly susceptible, being directly in the main storm track.

For travellers staying in modern hotels, being caught in a typhoon mostly means enduring heavy winds and rains, damp rooms and the loss of a day or two outdoors. Most of the serious damage affects thatched huts and tin-roofed shanties that easily get blown apart or wrecked by downed trees. Typhoons which sweep across low coral islands have been known to destroy every home and wipe out most of the trees and vegetation.

Supertyphoons are those with winds in excess of 150 miles per hour. At the other end of the scale are 'banana typhoons', those with winds that do little more than knock down banana trees. ■

Brown Tree Snake

The brown tree snake, which is native to the Solomon Islands and was accidentally introduced to Guam with military cargo in the late 1940s, has wiped out virtually all of Guam's forest birds. In the 1960s it was noted that the number of Guam's birds was declining and by the late 1970s many species survived only in a small forested area in the north. At first pesticides and avian disease were suspected and it wasn't until the 1980s that the snake was identified as the culprit. For most birds it was too late. Nine of the island's endemic species, including the Guam flycatcher and the Guam broadbill, are now extinct, and others survive only in precariously low numbers.

Meanwhile there are millions of brown tree snakes living without predators on Guam, roaming the forest trees at night and polishing off birds and eggs, or at least what's left of them. With so few birds left to eat, the snakes are resorting to chicken eggs, rodents and lizards.

Adult snakes can reach up to eight feet in length and though they'll take a threatening stance when cornered, they pose little danger to humans (other than infants), as their toxin is mild and is injected through chewing rather than a strike.

In addition to the devastation of the native ecology, the snakes commonly climb around electrical lines, causing frequent power outages on Guam. So far little has been done to address the problem, though other Pacific islands are very worried that the snake may slink onto their islands via cargo from Guam; it's already been sighted on Saipan, Wake and Oahu. ■

age about nine feet in length and can be dangerous. After a spearfisherman (who was hunting fish, not crocs) was eaten in the late 1960s, Australian hunters were brought in to pick off Palau's largest crocodiles. The one that killed the fisherman was captured and part of the man's arm and flashlight were found in its stomach.

On several islands you might come across monitor lizards sunning themselves on the roads or hanging out in caves or muddy swamps. They can reach up to six feet in length but are more commonly half that size.

Other than venomous but non-aggressive sea snakes and worm-sized blind snakes, Micronesia's only snakes are on Guam and Palau. Palau has the Pacific Island boa in its forests; the Palau tree snake in its small trees and shrubs; and the dog-faced water snake in its mangrove swamps. None pose a threat to people. The infamous brown tree snake found in Guam has spelled extinction for most of that island's forest birds, but is generally not a danger to people.

Micronesia has a number of native skinks, including a green variety which can grow up to one foot in length, and others with bright iridescent blue tails. The endearing gecko, a small common house lizard that scampers along walls and ceilings by means of suction-cup-like feet, has a loud call. It prefers to live indoors with people, paying its way by eating mosquitoes and other pesky insects.

Micronesia has a variety of crabs, including coconut crabs and mangrove crabs which both make good eating. Coconut crabs are sometimes caught by islanders and kept in cages while they grow to a meatier size, which can be up to three feet long. They are strong enough to tear open a metal rubbish bin and pry apart the bars of a steel barbecue grill. And yes, they can also rip through coconut husks and shells!

Micronesia has about 7000 varieties of insects. Mosquitoes, beach gnats and cockroaches are the most common annoyances. Great numbers of butterflies are particularly noticeable on Guam, largely because the birds and skinks that once preyed on the caterpillars have been greatly diminished by the brown tree snake.

Marine Life Micronesia has an abundance of marine life, including a wide range of hard and soft corals, anemones, sponges and many varieties of shellfish, the best known among them being the giant tridacna clam.

Sea turtles, including hawksbills, green turtles and leatherbacks, which are all endangered species, lay eggs on uninhabited sandy beaches throughout Micronesia.

They've been an important native food source for centuries and both turtles and their eggs are still eaten, especially by outer islanders.

Micronesian waters hold porpoises, sperm whales and beaked whales. Palau has the rare dugong, or sea cow, which is an herbivorous, seal-like mammal, about nine feet in length.

Sea cucumbers, particularly common in the Marianas, dot the bottom of shallow waters near shore. Their entrails squish underfoot if you happen to step on one, but they're harmless. One variety of these creatures is the beche-de-mer that traders were after in the 1800s. When boiled, dried and smoked they are considered delicacies and aphrodisiacs in China and South-East Asia.

Birds More than 200 species of birds have been recorded in Micronesia and about 85 species breed in the area.

The cardinal honeyeater, a small bright red and black bird, is endangered in Guam but easily seen elsewhere. It's found in gardens and forests, poking its curved bill into the centres of hibiscus and other flowers. The Northern Marianas have a beautifully plumed golden honeyeater.

The white or grey Pacific reef heron is common on reefs and in shallow water, where it uses its long beak to hunt for fish and small crabs. Cattle egrets are sometimes seen in open grassy areas and are par-

Megapodes are ground-dwelling birds that incubate their eggs by building mounds of sand and compost around them

ticularly common in western Micronesia during the winter.

Kingfishers in Micronesia seldom fish. These pretty blue and white birds, with cinnamon-coloured touches, are found on Pohnpei, Palau and in the Marianas, and their diet consists mainly of insects and lizards.

Micronesian starlings are common and widespread. Starlings like to eat papayas and some islanders like to eat starlings.

The best place to see the endangered Micronesian megapode is in Palau's Rock Islands, where some of these ground-living birds have built their nests on the picnic beaches. The megapode does not incubate its eggs, but lays them in the ground, warming them with dirt and decaying matter. Endemic to Micronesia, this species is now extinct on Guam and Rota, though there is a small group near Saipan's Suicide Cliff.

The Guam rail, a flightless bird indigenous to Guam but wiped out on that island by the brown tree snake, was introduced on Rota in 1990 and 1991 after a successful captive breeding programme saved the bird from total extinction. Unfortunately the 50 birds that were released on Rota haven't been spotted since; there is some doubt that the captivity-bred birds have the skills to survive in the wild. Palau has a banded rail.

Some of the more commonly seen shorebirds in Micronesia, especially during spring and autumn migrations, include the lesser golden plover, wandering tattler, whimbrel and ruddy turnstone. Common seabirds include the brown noddy, black noddy and white tern.

White-tailed tropicbirds, distinguishable by two long white tail feathers, are often seen riding the air currents around the cliffs where they build their nests.

Serious birdwatchers should get hold of the 12-page *Checklist of the Birds of Micronesia* by Peter Pyle & John Engbring. It's available for a nominal fee from the Hawaii Audubon Society, 1088 Bishop St, Suite 808, Honolulu, HI 96813. For a suggested reference book, see Books in the Facts for the Visitor chapter.

Flora

The coconut palm tree is Micronesia's most important plant. Copra, the dried meat of the nut from which coconut oil is made, is the region's most important export and the main source of revenue for outer islanders. The nut also provides food and drinking liquid, while the flowers provide sap for making a wine called tuba. Rope is made from the green coconut husks and fuel and charcoal are made from mature husks. The wood is used for lumber and carving, the fronds for thatch and baskets.

Breadfruit trees provide timber and their large green globular fruits are a major food source. Timber also comes from tropical mahogany and other trees including the betel nut tree (Areca palm), although the latter is more treasured for its nuts. Pandanus is eaten and the leaves are used for making mats, baskets and fans.

Other traditional food plants include taro, yams, tapioca and bananas. The lush heart-shaped leaves of the taro plant, which is cultivated in mud flats, are big enough to use as umbrellas.

Mangrove swamps are common along the shores of many of the high islands. The most unique thing about mangrove trees are their looping prop roots that arch above the water before reaching down into the mud. Mangrove trees help to expand the shoreline as their roots extend away from shore and sediments build up around them, creating new soil.

Colourful tropical plants and flowers are abundant in Micronesia, especially on the high islands. Common varieties include hibiscus, bougainvillea, beach morning glories, plumeria, lilies, lantana and crotons. The Marianas are especially noted for their flame trees (royal poinciana) which have scarlet blossoms.

Plants such as coleus, caladium and philodendron, which in colder climates are painstakingly nurtured indoors in pots, grow in wild abandon in Micronesia, reaching huge proportions.

Two of the more peculiar plants found in Micronesia are the low-growing insectivorous pitcher plant and the 'sensitive plant', a small green ground cover with thin compound leaves that close up when touched.

National Parks & Reserves

With so little land area, it's not surprising that Micronesia has few public parks. Under traditional Micronesian land ownership patterns not only the land, but also the reef and waters surrounding it, are part of an extended family or clan's property. Consequently there are no vast tracts of public land for parks on traditional islands such as those of the FSM and the Marshalls. On Guam and Saipan, where colonial powers eroded traditional land ownership patterns, there is more public domain space, but even there parks are limited.

Guam has a few hundred acres of land under US National Park Service jurisdiction, called the War in the Pacific National Historical Park, which have been set aside to preserve WW II battle sites. In addition, the territorial government has established a conservation preserve in south-western Guam which has hiking trails up to a couple of mountain ridges and down to a secluded bay that once held a Chamorro village. In 1993 Ritidian Point, the northern tip of Guam, was transferred from the US Navy to the US Fish & Wildlife Service as a new national wildlife refuge intended to restore native wildlife and plant species; there's no public access to it.

On Saipan, the Marpi Commonwealth Forest, in the northern part of the island, is an upland forest large enough to provide visitors with an hour of so of hiking. The only presence the US National Park Service has on Saipan is in the form of a small war memorial park in Garapan.

Palau has set aside a group of its uninhabited Rock Islands, known as 70 Islands, as a marine preserve, prohibiting public access so as not to disturb nesting turtles and seabirds.

GOVERNMENT

Guam is an incorporated US territory. The Commonwealth of the Northern Marianas is a commonwealth of the USA. The Federated States of Micronesia, the Republic

---

District Centres

The term 'district centre' refers to the main centre within a cluster of islands. This is generally the place where services are centred, including the international airport, main medical facility, government offices and tourist facilities.

The main district centres in Micronesia are: Majuro (Marshall Islands), Koror (Palau), Saipan (Northern Marianas) and, in the Federated States of Micronesia, Pohnpei Island (Pohnpei), Weno Island (Chuuk), Yap Proper (Yap) and Kosrae. Guam, the largest island in Micronesia, acts as a district centre for the entire Micronesian region and has the most developed commercial, medical and educational facilities.

A few of the more expansive island groups, such as the Marshalls, further designate domestic district centres (sometimes referred to as sub-districts) within their own political unit. ■

---

of the Marshall Islands, and the Republic of Palau are now independent nations.

ECONOMY

The economy of Micronesia is heavily dependent upon US appropriations, which makes it possible for island governments to employ roughly 60% of the total work force. On many islands their payrolls form the backbone of the entire economy.

By and large the whole moneyed economy is an artificial one bankrolled by the USA. It has no local base and no way of sustaining itself. Exports are generally limited to copra, handicrafts and a few marine products. The total value of all exports doesn't generate enough income to pay even Micronesia's fuel bills.

Actually, with the exception of those in the subsistence economy, Micronesians produce very little. Many of the private sector jobs that do exist deal largely in imported goods. Few, if any, of the products found in the department stores, markets, bars, office suppliers, petrol stations or Toyota dealers are produced in Micronesia.

The nature of US expenditures in Micronesia has created dependency, rather than fostering self-sufficiency. Micronesians still have little to barter except their water and their land, the latter for US military bases and Japanese resorts, the former to foreign tuna fleets who want fishing rights within their 200-mile economic zones.

At the end of the trusteeship, the USA undertook extensive capital improvement projects in Micronesia which included new airports, docks, water and sewerage systems, paved roads and hospitals. However, with their multi-million dollar annual maintenance and operation costs, many of these capital improvements represent yet another economic liability. Despite all the funding, most district centres still lack potable water, a result of poor initial design, half-executed plans and local mismanagement.

Ironically, some of the facilities that were successfully completed have turned into mixed blessings. For example, the new ice plants and docks that were supposed to provide the infrastructure for a Micronesian fishing industry are now crowded with foreign fishing boats that are choking out local fishing operations, polluting waters and contributing to political corruption.

The per capita Gross Domestic Product (GDP) varies greatly in Micronesia. Guam has the highest GDP at $14,000, followed by the Commonwealth of the Northern Marianas at $11,812, the Republic of Palau at $5750, the Federated States of Micronesia at $2516 and the Republic of the Marshall Islands at $1922.

POPULATION & PEOPLE

Micronesia's population is about 375,000, with 145,000 of those living on Guam. Micronesia has high birth rates and one of the world's highest per capita populations of people under the age of 18.

The people of the eastern and central islands of Micronesia are thought to be predominantly of Melanesian descent, while the people of the western islands of Micronesia are thought to be of South-East Asian descent. For the most part Micronesian societies evolved in relative isolation and maintained fairly undiluted indigenous cultures. The Chamorro people of the Mariana Islands have the only notable admixture of Western blood, a result of 17th-century Spanish conquest in those islands and a policy of cultural absorption.

For more information see the individual island chapters that follow.

EDUCATION

Free public education is provided in Micronesia through high school, but on most islands it's mandatory only through the 8th grade or to the age of 14.

There are colleges in the Marshalls, the FSM, Palau, Saipan and Guam. The only university in the region is the University of Guam, which has a high enrollment of students from other Micronesian islands.

ARTS
Dance

Traditional dancing is important on many Micronesian islands, especially those less affected by Westernisation such as Yap and the outer Carolinian islands. Micronesian dancers wear colourful native costumes and commonly accompany their movements with unison chanting. Dancing is done in groups, with the women and men customarily dancing separately. Dances can be performed marching, sitting or standing. One form, known as stick dancing, involves beating bamboo poles together to create a rhythm.

Most dancing in the outer islands takes place only on special occasions or village events, such as the opening of a new community centre. But in a few of the district centres, notably Pohnpei and Koror, visitors can arrange to watch a show of native dancing. Indeed, the tourist trade may help to buoy the art on these more developed islands, in the same way hula dancing has seen a revival in Hawaii; it offers a source of income for dancers and an incentive for young people to continue the tradition.

Traditional thatched-roof houses

Traditional Architecture

While Western ways now prevail in architectural styles, some islands still have traditional community buildings constructed in the centuries-old manner using planks of native mahogany and roofs of thatched nipa palm, bound by hand-twisted coconut sennit. On Pohnpei, these traditional buildings are called *nahs* and are used as ceremonial houses. On Palau, they're called *bai* and serve as men's meeting houses, while Yap has *pebai*, which are community meeting houses, and *faluw*, or men's houses.

Canoes

While speedboats are more common, traditional outrigger canoes are still found throughout Micronesia. The canoes have a single outrigger and are generally made from a breadfruit tree trunk that's hollowed out and crafted using simple hand tools. Model versions of the canoes are handcrafted on a few islands including the Marshalls and Pohnpei.

Stone Money

There were many forms of indigenous money in Micronesia, including those made of beads, turtle shell and rare clams. Still, the most notable was Yapese stone money, called *rai*, which was made of a single stone that could reach up to 12 feet in diameter and weigh as much as five tons. It was carved into a round disc shape and carried by boring a hole through the centre, which gave it the appearance of a giant wheel. Although the stones are no longer 'minted', Yap still has many impressive stone money banks, as village paths lined with rai are called.

Tattooing

Before the arrival of missionaries, tattooing was a common practice on many Micronesian islands. It was considered a rite of passage to adulthood and the extent and design of tattoos often signified one's place within the social hierarchy. Chiefs, for instance, were often the only ones permitted to have facial tattoos.

Tattoos were generally simple repetitive patterns that either extended horizontally or formed a triangular design. Women were generally tattooed less extensively than men. On the Marshalls for example, only the shoulders, arms and thighs of a woman could be tattooed unless she was royalty, in which case the hands were also tattooed. These days traditional tattooing is a dying art. Some of the elderly on the remote outer Caroline Islands are still tattooed, but younger people have all but abandoned the practice.

Handicrafts

Some items traditionally used in daily Micronesian life are still made by islanders, sometimes for practical use, other times for sale as souvenirs. Occasionally something functions both ways, such as the finely woven hibiscus-fibre skirts known as *lava-lava* that are worn by Yapese women and which also make lovely wall hangings.

In some cases the souvenir market has kept the traditional art alive, such as with Marshallese stick charts that were once used to teach traditional navigation methods and carved Palauan storyboards which are smaller versions of the legends that once decorated traditional structures.

Other common handicrafts in Micronesia

are baskets woven of pandanus or coconut fibres, some of the finest of which are found in the Marshall Islands, and detailed wood carvings such as the dolphins, manta rays and sharks created by the Kapingamarangi people in Pohnpei.

SOCIETY & CONDUCT
Traditional Lifestyle

Traditional Micronesian societies can be divided into two groups: those on the high islands and those on the low islands.

On the high islands, people developed a land-based subsistence livelihood and tended to be homebodies. Food sources were reliable and it was a fairly easy lifestyle that supported relatively large populations. Because life wasn't a constant struggle for survival, the high islanders were able to develop stable and elaborate societies, some of which became highly stratified with caste hierarchies, chiefs, royalty and the like.

Low atoll islanders had a more challenging life, eking their living out of the sea rather than the land. They became expert navigators, sailors and fishers. They travelled great distances and though their next door neighbours were sometimes hundreds of miles away, visits were not infrequent.

Canoe journeys between islands brought trade, warfare and new ideas. Islands near each other share cultural elements and their inhabitants can often understand each other's languages, whereas islands at opposite ends of Micronesia are culturally quite different and their languages mutually unintelligible. Commonalities of culture and language are spread over the greatest distances among the low islands due to the extensive travels of low islanders.

Micronesian societies are made up of clan groupings descended matrilineally (except Yap, which is patrilineal) from a common ancestor. The head clan on each island can trace its lineage back to the original settlers of the island and members of that clan usually retain certain privileges.

Extended families are the norm and it's not uncommon for grandparents, cousins, children and adopted clan members to live

Ancient Chamorro village in the Mariana Islands

under the same roof. If one family member gets a good job, other relatives may well move in and live off the income. In general, when people visit other islands they simply look up a member of their clan to stay with.

Traditional Canoes & Navigation

Some of the greatest navigators in the Pacific have come from the resource-scarce low islands of Micronesia. With their sandy soil offering limited food supplies, the low islanders took to the oceans. In general, the smaller the island, the more ocean-going the islanders.

Without compasses or maps, Micronesians used a combination of natural aids to navigate around the Pacific.

The long Marshallese atolls, which are fairly close together in north-south lines, interrupt the large swells that move across the Pacific from east to west. Marshallese navigation depended largely on learning to feel and interpret the patterns of the currents and waves that were deflected around their islands.

The Carolinians' main navigational focus was on the sky. Because most travel was in an east-west line, they could keep on course by watching the sun and by identifying individual stars that would rise or set over particular islands. They memorised ancient chants which contained information on star patterns and other navigational directions.

In addition to swell interpretations and celestial compasses, the Micronesians also keyed into other natural phenomena. For instance, to see if land was nearby they would watch for birds returning home to their island nests in the evening. A single stationary cloud off in the distance was often moist ocean air hovering over a high island, and, although coral atolls are too flat to be seen from far away, their shallow aqua-coloured lagoons reflect a pale green light onto the underside of clouds.

Micronesian canoes have a single outrigger. In protected areas islanders used simple dugout canoes made from a single tree trunk. On the open ocean they used huge canoes, up to 100 feet long, constructed of planks tied together with cord made from coconut husk fibres. These ocean-going vessels were often larger and faster than the ships of the early European explorers and could hold 100 passengers or more.

Dos & Don'ts

Outside Guam, Saipan or the beaches of resort hotels, skimpy swimsuits are apt to get you more attention than you'll want.

In most parts of the FSM short skirts and even shorts are deemed inappropriate for women. In Yap, Kosrae and some of the outer islands it's considered offensive for women to expose their thighs. In those places, although it's OK to wear a swimsuit in the water, women are expected to put on a skirt when they get out.

Though skimpy clothing is not appropriate anywhere in Micronesia, things are a bit more relaxed on the more developed parts of Palau and in Guam and the Northern Marianas, where longer shorts don't pose a problem for women. Always follow local custom.

For the most part it's acceptable for men to wear shorts throughout Micronesia, even on islands like Pohnpei and Weno where just about all the local men seem to be sweating it out in long pants.

RELIGION

Micronesia has been almost completely Christianised. Spanish Catholics got to the Marianas and the western islands first and New England Protestants converted the Marshalls and the eastern islands. They met somewhere in the middle, with Chuuk and Pohnpei turning out about half Catholic and half Protestant.

LANGUAGE

Micronesian languages are in the Austronêsian language group. The major native languages are: Marshallese in the Marshall Islands; Palauan in Palau; Chamorro in Guam and the Northern Marianas; Yapese, Ulithian and Woleaian in Yap; Pohnpeian and Kapingamarangi-Nukuoro in Pohnpei; Chuukese and Mortlockese in Chuuk; and Kosraean in Kosrae. In addition there are numerous minor dialects on the outer islands, some spoken by fewer than 100 people.

English is spoken throughout Micronesia and serves as the linking language connecting the far-flung states. Not only is it the main language of inter-island trade and business, but it's the most common language of instruction in schools. Elderly people often have a limited command of English, but many speak Japanese.

Facts for the Visitor

PLANNING
Maps

Local tourist offices throughout Micronesia often have simple island maps that they distribute free to visitors. The quality varies from simple hand-drawn sketches on most of the more remote islands to fold-out public highway maps on Guam. There are no commercial road maps of Micronesia.

USGS maps with topographical details have been made for many Micronesian islands, though they're not available for some islands, including the entire Marshalls chain. The maps were last updated in the early 1980s, so they don't show many of the new roads and developments. USGS maps can be purchased from some larger bookshops or ordered in advance from the US Geological Survey, Box 25286, Denver Federal Center, Denver, CO 80225. Prices for the maps are generally around $4 each. Upon request, USGS will send a free map catalogue.

When to Go

By and large, when you decide to visit Micronesia should be determined by when it's most convenient for you. Being in the tropics, the temperature is not a major variable, though it's a tad more comfortable in the drier and less humid months of December to March (see Climate in the Facts about the Region chapter) and consequently those are generally the busiest months.

If you're visiting Guam, Saipan or Palau, it may be wise to avoid traditional Japanese holiday seasons when most of the mid- and top-end hotels get solidly booked up. These seasons include: Christmas through the first week of January, Golden Week (the last week of April and the first week of May) and Obon (August). Travel to these islands is not impossible during these periods, but advance reservations are certainly advis-able and you may need to stay in a more obscure business or low-end hotel.

The rest of Micronesia still lies well off the package tourist track and doesn't tend to see seasonal flocks of visitors.

If you're planning to visit around Christmas keep in mind that far-flung Micronesian families like to return home for the holidays, so booking flights in the weeks around Christmas can be a challenge. Pre-Christmas flights to Guam can get particularly overbooked as many islanders head there to fill their shopping lists.

There are small-town holidays and festivities occurring throughout the year on various islands that can be fun to catch (see the Holidays & Festivals sections in each chapter), but there are no grand region-wide festivities, such as Carnival in the Caribbean, to plan your trip around.

What to Bring

Travelling light, a good policy anywhere, is easier in the tropics as sleeping bags, heavy jackets and bulky clothing are totally unnecessary.

Dress is definitely casual. For men, dressing up means wearing a Hawaiian-print shirt; for women, a lightweight cotton dress is as formal as it gets.

Ideal clothes are made of cotton, which breathes best in hot, humid weather; are loose fitting and don't need to be tucked in; and can be hand washed in a sink and hung up to dry without wrinkling.

One long-sleeved shirt, lightweight cotton jacket or windbreaker might be useful against air-con and insects. There are mosquitoes in Micronesia so if you use insect repellent, bring some.

Most islanders walk in the warm rain unprotected, but you could bring an umbrella or rain jacket if it bothers you.

Footwear in Micronesia is predominantly rubber thongs, which are sold everywhere, or other casual sandals. Sneakers can be useful for hiking off the beaten path and for walking along rough coral reefs.

A flashlight is good to have on hand for the occasional power blackout and is essential if you want to fully explore caves. A Swiss Army knife is worth its weight in gold. If you plan to do a lot of snorkelling, it's a good idea to bring your own gear.

You might want to consider a passport pouch or money belt to wear around your neck or waist.

Zip-lock plastic sandwich bags in a couple of sizes are indispensable for keeping things dry. You can use them to protect your film and camera equipment, to seal up airline tickets and passports, and to keep wet bathing suits away from the rest of your luggage.

A one-cup immersion heater, usually available for a few dollars from hardware or department stores, and a durable lightweight cup can come in handy. Not only can you sterilise your own water and make coffee and tea in your room but you can use it to make up a quick meal if you carry a few packets of instant oatmeal, ramen, soup or the like.

Medical supplies and toiletries are available in most places, though outside Guam and Saipan the selection may be limited. Contact lens cleaning solutions and supplies can be found in Guam, but may be unavailable elsewhere. Bring sunscreen.

You may well be able to travel lightly enough to take carry-on luggage only. In addition to one piece of luggage, you're also allowed to carry on a handbag, camera bag or daypack.

TOURIST OFFICES

All the island groups give out brochures, maps or other standard tourist information that you can pick up once you're there. You can also write in advance and have the information mailed to you, but give yourself extra time as the responses can be slow. For information on the FSM, contact each state individually.

Tourist Offices in Micronesia

Local tourist offices can be found on the following islands:

Chuuk
    Chuuk Visitors Bureau, Box FQ, Weno, Chuuk, FM 96942 (☎ 691-330-4133, fax 691-330-4194)
Guam
    Guam Visitors Bureau, Box 3520, Agana, GU 96910 (☎ 671-646-5278, fax 671-646-8861)
Kosrae
    Kosrae Tourism Office, Box C&D, Tofol, Kosrae, FM 96944 (☎ 691-370-2228, fax 691-370-2066)
Marshall Islands
    Tourism Office, Box 1727, Majuro, MH 96960 (☎ 692-625-3206, fax 692-625-3218)
Northern Marianas
    Marianas Visitors Bureau, Box 861, Saipan, MP 96950 (☎ 670-234-8325, fax 670-234-3596)
Palau
    Palau Visitors Authority, Box 256, Koror, PW 96940 (☎ 680-488-2793, fax 680-488-1453)
Pohnpei
    Pohnpei Tourist Commission, Box 66, Kolonia, Pohnpei, FM 96941 (☎ 691-320-2421, fax 691-320-2505)
Yap
    Division of Tourism, Box 36, Colonia, Yap, FM 96943 (☎ 691-350-2298, fax 691-350-2571)

Tourist Offices Abroad

For advance information on Guam and the Marshall Islands, contact:

Hong Kong
    Guam Visitors Bureau, 7th Floor West, Savoy Court, 101 Robinson Rd, Hong Kong (☎ 540-6456, fax 559-0083)
Japan
    Guam Visitors Bureau, Kokusai Building 2F, 3-1-1 Marunouchi, Chiyoda-ku, Tokyo 100 (☎ 3212-3630, fax 3213-6087)
Korea
    Guam Visitors Bureau, 5th Floor, Baeksuk Building, 432-3, Shindang-dong, Choong-ku, Seoul 100-450 (☎ 2-253-0020, fax 2-253-1185)
Taiwan
    Guam Visitors Bureau, 68 Chung Shan North Rd, Sec 2, Taipei (☎ 2-571-6594, fax 2-531-7915)

USA
　　Guam Visitors Bureau, 1150 Marina Village
　　Parkway, Suite 104, Alameda, CA 94501
　　(☎ 800-873-4826, fax 510-865-5165)
　　Marshall Islands Tourist Representative,
　　Hilary Kaye & Associates, 4000 Westerly
　　Place, Suite 210, Newport Beach, CA 92660
　　(☎ 714-851-5150, 800-846-3483, fax 714-
　　851-3111)

VISAS & DOCUMENTS

US citizens don't need a passport to visit
Micronesia, though it makes things simpler
to carry one. Without a passport, some
other proof of US citizenship, such as an
official birth or naturalisation certificate
combined with a driving licence or similar
photo ID, is required. All other nationalities must carry a valid passport.

Apart from your passport there are a few
other documents to consider. Bring your
home driving licence, and if it's in a language other than English it's a good idea to
also bring an International Driving Permit.

If you're coming from an area infected
with cholera or yellow fever, such as South
America, you should also carry an International Health Certificate. Divers of course
will need to make sure they are in possession of their certification cards.

It's wise to obtain any visas you need for
onward travel before arriving in Micronesia, as there are only a few embassies in
the region and some of those have very
limited operations.

Visas & Visa Extensions

US citizens don't need a visa to visit any of
the islands. For other nationalities; those
visiting Guam (except Canadians and those
travelling on a visa waiver) must obtain a
US visa in advance. Non-US citizens visiting the Marshalls must purchase a visa
upon arrival, but no visas are required for
tourist visits to other Micronesian islands.
Further details are in the destination sub-
headings that follow.

Note that immigration officials in Micronesia commonly ask how long you're planning to stay and then stamp that exact
number of days into your passport. It's a
good idea to go for the maximum or at least

give yourself a buffer, so you won't have to
bother about getting (or paying for) an
extension if you decide to stay on a bit
longer.

Officially, most island groups require
visitors to have return or onward tickets,
though you're not always asked to show
them.

Republic of the Marshall Islands US
citizens and Micronesian residents do not
need visas to enter the Marshall Islands.
Everyone else will be asked by the immigration officer to pay $25 for a 'visa' upon
arriving at the airport. It's valid for 30 days
and can be extended twice, up to a
maximum of 90 days, for $10 per exten-
sion. This new port-of-entry fee has taken a
lot of travellers by surprise – when you add
on the $15 departure tax required to leave
the country, it certainly makes a quick stop
in the Marshalls a costly experience.

Federated States of Micronesia Visas
are not required for tourist visits of up to 30
days. Each of the four FSM states (Kosrae,
Pohnpei, Chuuk, Yap) has its own immigration process, so you automatically get a
new entry permit, good for up to 30 days,
each time you fly into a new district centre.
Entry permits can be extended through the
immigration offices without fee for up to 90
days, or up to 365 days for US citizens.

Republic of Palau All tourists may stay in
Palau for 30 days without a visa. After that,
two extensions of 30 days each may be
granted by the immigration office. Extensions should be applied for seven days prior
to the expiration of your current visa. The
cost is $50 for each extension.

**Commonwealth of the Northern Mari-
anas** US citizens need no visa and can stay
as long as they like. Non-US citizens don't
need a visa for tourist stays of up to 30
days. Tourists can get an extension of up to
two months by applying to the immigration
office at the airport and paying a $25 exten-
sion fee.

Guam All non-US citizens need a US visa to visit Guam, except Canadians and those eligible for Guam's visa waiver programme.

Under Guam's visa waiver programme, citizens of certain countries may enter Guam for up to 15 days for business or pleasure without obtaining a US visa. Those countries are Australia, Brunei, Myanmar, Hong Kong, Indonesia, Japan, Malaysia, Nauru, New Zealand, Papua New Guinea, Singapore, Solomon Islands, South Korea, Taiwan, the UK, Vanuatu and Western Samoa.

One disadvantage of the visa waiver programme is that it's not possible to extend your stay.

EMBASSIES
Micronesian Embassies Abroad
The following are Micronesian embassies and consulates abroad:

China
    Republic of the Marshall Islands Embassy, 2-14-1 Ta Yuan Diplomatic Office Building, Beijing, PRC 100600 (☎ (1-532-5904)
Fiji
    FSM Embassy, Box 15439, Suva (☎ 304-180)
    Republic of the Marshall Islands Embassy, 41 Borron Rd, Box 2038, Suva (☎ 387-130)
Japan
    FSM Embassy, 2nd Floor, Reinanzaka Building, 1-14-2, Akasaka 1-chome, Minato-ku, Tokyo 107 (☎ 3585-5456)
    Republic of the Marshall Islands Embassy, 12-1 3-chome, Motoazabu, Minato-ku, Tokyo 106 (☎ 5411-0972)
USA
    FSM Embassy, 1725 N Street NW, Washington, DC 20036 (☎ 202-223-4383)
    FSM Consulate, 3049 Ualena St, Suite 408, Honolulu, HI 96819 (☎ 808-836-4775)
    Republic of the Marshall Islands Embassy, 2433 Massachusetts Ave NW, Washington, DC 20008 (☎ 202-234-5414)
    Republic of the Marshall Islands Consulate, 1357 Kapiolani Blvd, Suite 1240, Honolulu, HI 96814 (☎ 808-942-4422)

Foreign Embassies in Micronesia
The following countries have diplomatic representation in Micronesia:

Australia
    Australian Embassy, Box 5, Kolonia, Pohnpei, FSM (☎ 320-5448)
China
    Embassy of the People's Republic of China, Airport Rd, Majuro, Republic of the Marshall Islands (☎ 247-3275)
    Embassy of People's Republic of China, Box 1530, Kolonia, Pohnpei, FSM (☎ 320-5575)
Japan
    Consulate of Japan, ITC Building, Marine Drive, Tamuning, Guam (☎ 646-5220)
Korea
    Consulate of Republic of Korea, 305 GCIC Building, Agana, Guam (☎ 472-3097)
Nauru
    Consulate of Nauru, Pacific Star Hotel, Tumon, Guam (☎ 649-8300)
Philippines
    Consulate of the Philippines, ITC Building, Marine Drive, Tamuning, Guam (☎ 646-4620)
USA
    US Embassy, Airport Rd, Majuro, Republic of the Marshall Islands (☎ 247-4011)
    US Embassy, Box 1286, Kolonia, Pohnpei, FSM (☎ 320-2187)
    US Embassy, Topside, Koror, Republic of Palau (☎ 488-2920)

CUSTOMS
Sometimes Micronesian customs officers carry out baggage checks. These are usually brief and cursory, except in Palau where they're commonly quite thorough and where consequently the queues move slowly.

As elsewhere, Micronesian nations prohibit the entry of drugs, weapons, large quantities of alcohol, and fruits and plants that might carry insects or diseases harmful to local crops.

MONEY
There are commercial banks on Majuro, Ebeye, Kosrae, Pohnpei, Weno, Yap, Koror, Saipan, Rota, Tinian and Guam. On the outer islands you should always bring enough cash to get you through your stay.

Plastic addicts will be pleased to know that major credit cards (particularly MasterCard and Visa) are accepted all over Guam; at most hotels and large restaurants on Saipan and Palau; at most hotels and a few restaurants on Pohnpei and Kosrae; by most car rental companies and dive shops throughout the islands; and by travel agents and Continental Micronesia agents everywhere. Credit cards are also beginning to catch on in a few places on Majuro, Chuuk and Yap.

Currency
The US dollar is the official currency throughout Micronesia and is the only practical currency for travellers to carry.

Except in the remote outer islands, US dollar travellers' cheques are accepted everywhere. You'll rarely have to wait in a bank queue to change them since most hotels, restaurants and larger stores will accept them as cash.

Exchange Rates
At press time, exchange rates were:

A$1	=	US$0.74
¥100	=	US$1.17
C$1	=	US$0.75
DM1	=	US$0.72
NZ$1	=	US$0.68
UK£1	=	US$1.62
HK$10	=	US$1.34

Costs
In part because the islands are so spread out, and in part because the economy is reliant upon imported items, Micronesia can be an expensive place to travel.

For most people the biggest cost will be airfare. Depending on where you're coming from, and which islands you choose to visit, that cost could reach as high as a few thousand dollars. It's certainly an area worth researching well before you go.

Although it varies between islands, accommodation is generally on the high side. Expect to pay about $45 a night for a simple low-end room, $75 for a business-style hotel and nearly double that for a beach resort.

Food prices vary a bit between islands but if you stick to local foods, including fresh fish, it's generally quite reasonable. On most islands you could get by eating on

$15 a day, though it would be easy to spend double that without any big splurges.

In terms of getting around, public transport is limited and most visitors opt to rent a car for at least part of their stay. Expect to pay about $50 a day including petrol.

Most visitors to Micronesia are scuba divers. If you're one of them, a full day of diving will generally add another $65 to $100 to your budget.

Tipping
Tipping of 10% to 15% is expected in restaurants on Guam and in the Northern Marianas. Tipping is beginning to catch on in Palau and Pohnpei, but is generally not the custom elsewhere in Micronesia.

Bargaining
Most things in Micronesia are sold from stores and prices are fixed. There are a few fruit markets on the islands where you can try your knack at some low-keyed bargaining, but the first price quoted is generally the last.

Consumer Taxes
There are no value-added taxes in Micronesia, but some islands have a nominal sales tax. Of more significance to travellers is the popularity of hotel room taxes: 5% on Kosrae, 6% on Pohnpei, a flat $2 per night in the Marshalls and 10% on all the other islands.

POST & TELECOMMUNICATIONS
Postal Rates
All of Micronesia is under the umbrella of the US Postal Service, which handles Micronesia's international mail. US postage rates apply.

Airmail rates from Micronesia are 32 cents for a one-ounce letter and 20 cents for a postcard to the USA or within Micronesia; 40 cents for a one-ounce letter and 30 cents for a postcard to Canada; 35 cents for a half-ounce letter and 30 cents for a postcard to Mexico; and 50 cents for a half-ounce letter and 40 cents for a postcard to any other foreign country.

Guam and the Northern Marianas use US

stamps, but the Marshalls, FSM and Palau print their own stamps which can only be used from those particular island groups.

Micronesia is in US Postal Zone 8 (the same as Hawaii) for calculating parcel rates to US destinations.

Sending Mail

Service is reasonably efficient between major islands and the outside world. International mail to Micronesia goes through either Honolulu or Guam and generally takes a week to 10 days to arrive, depending on the district centre.

Mail delivery to and from the outer islands depends on the frequency of field trip ships and/or commuter flights and can be very slow. If you're writing to someone on an outer island, you need to include their island's name, in addition to the district centre's address and zip code.

In accordance with US postal regulations, each area in Micronesia has a zip code and its own two-letter 'state' abbreviation – MH for the Marshall Islands, PW for Palau, GU for Guam, FM for the Federated States of Micronesia and MP for the Northern Marianas. However, since these abbreviations are not well-known outside the region, it's a better idea to write out the country name instead of the abbreviation. When sending mail from outside the USA, also add 'via USA' below the address.

The following are the zip codes for the main postal areas in Micronesia, excluding Guam (which has zip codes from 96910 to 96931).

Chuuk
    Federated States of Micronesia 96942
Ebeye
    Republic of the Marshall Islands 96970
Koror
    Republic of Palau 96940
Kosrae
    Federated States of Micronesia 96944
Majuro
    Republic of the Marshall Islands 96960
Pohnpei
    Federated States of Micronesia 96941
Rota
    Commonwealth of the Northern Marianas 96951

Saipan
    Commonwealth of the Northern Marianas 96950
Tinian
    Commonwealth of the Northern Marianas 96952
Yap
    Federated States of Micronesia 96943

Receiving Mail

You can have mail sent to you c/o General Delivery at any district centre post office. While Guam has numerous post offices, general delivery is only available at the general post office (GPO) so all mail should be addressed to General Delivery GMF, Barrigada, Guam 96921.

Stamp Collecting

The Micronesian islands issue some colourful commemorative stamps. Collectors can order Marshall Islands or FSM stamps from the Philatelic Center (☎ 307-771-3000, 800-443-3232), One Unicover Center, Cheyenne, WY 82008. Palau stamps can be ordered from the Palau Philatelic Bureau, GPO Box 7775, New York, NY 10016.

Telephone

All district centres have phone systems. Outer islands can be reached by radio, which are sometimes solar-powered.

Guam and Saipan have pay phones readily available in public places. On smaller islands if you want to make a local call, it's common practice to just ask to use the phone at a store or hotel front desk.

The FSM has debit card phones for which you purchase a $10 plastic card that you insert whenever you make a phone call. When $10 worth of calls have been made, the service is cut off and you have to insert another card to keep talking. However it's still a half-baked system, as there are very few card phones around the islands. Most islanders who don't have a home phone tend to use a friend's phone or go directly to the telecommunications office. Each district centre has a telecommunications office where you can make both local and long-distance calls and pay in cash.

Calling from Micronesia To make direct international calls from Micronesia, dial 011 to get an international line, followed by the country code of the country you're calling (for instance, 1 for the USA, 61 for Australia), and the area code and local number.

Long-distance telephone services are available in the major district centres 24 hours a day. Specific rates are given in individual island chapters, but average $3 to $4 per minute to most places outside Micronesia, usually with a three-minute minimum. Calls from Guam and Saipan, however, are significantly cheaper, so you might want to wait until you get to those islands to call home.

Calling Micronesia When calling direct to Micronesia from overseas, dial the overseas access code for the country you're in, followed by the Micronesian country code for the island you're calling and the seven-digit local number. Collect calls are not accepted in the FSM and Palau.

Micronesian country codes are:

FSM	– 691
Guam	– 671
Marshall Islands	– 692
Northern Marianas	– 670
Palau	– 680

Fax, Telex & Telegraph
Fax, telex and telegraph services are available on the district centres through the telecommunications offices. More information is given in individual island chapters.

BOOKS
Travel & Guidebooks
Kosrae: The Sleeping Lady Awakens (Kosrae Tourist Division, Kosrae, 1989) by Harvey Gordon Segal is an insightful and comprehensive book on the human and natural history of Kosrae. It also covers sights and general information of interest to visitors.

A Guide to Pohnpei – An Island Argosy (Rainy Day Press, Pohnpei, 1987) by Gene Ashby covers Pohnpei's history, government, culture, flora, fauna and island sights.

Making Tracks in the Mariana Islands (Marine Images, Barrigada, Guam, 1992) by Dave Lotz, a Guam parks administrator, details hiking trails on Saipan, Tinian, Rota and Guam, with simple maps and write-ups that include time, difficulty and distance.

Yachters considering a voyage to Micronesia should take a look at *Landfalls of Paradise: Cruising Guide to the Pacific Islands* (University of Hawaii Press, Honolulu, 1993) by Earl Hinz. It has information on ports of entry, suggested anchorages and data on oceanographic phenomena for islands throughout Micronesia, Melanesia and Polynesia.

History
The First Taint of Civilization (University of Hawaii Press, Honolulu, 1983), by Francis X Hezel SJ is an excellent anecdotal history of the Caroline and Marshall Islands during the pre-colonial era from 1521 to 1885. Hezel, a long-time resident in Micronesia and head of the Micronesian Seminar, presents some poignant insights into the culture and history of the islands.

Micronesia: Winds of Change (Government of the Trust Territory of the Pacific Islands, 1980), edited by Francis X Hezel SJ & M L Berg, is a colourful history taken from the accounts of early explorers, missionaries and others involved in Micronesia between 1521 and 1951. It contains wonderful old etchings and photos.

History of Micronesia (University of Hawaii Press, Honolulu, 1994), edited by Rodrigue Levesque, is a comprehensive two-volume history of the region covering the period from 1521 to 1595, complete with colourful passages by 16th-century explorers.

Lee Boo of Belau (University of Hawaii Press, Honolulu, 1987) by Daniel J Peacock covers the events surrounding Captain Wilson's voyage to Palau in 1783, his return to Britain with the young Prince Lee Boo of Palau, and Lee Boo's adventures in London before succumbing to smallpox in 1784.

Nan'yo: The Rise & Fall of the Japanese in Micronesia, 1885-1945 (University of

Hawaii Press, Honolulu, 1988) by Mark R Peattie, is one of the best books about the Japanese colonial empire in Micronesia.

Politics

For some current insights into Micronesian society, pick up *The Edge of Paradise* (University of Hawaii Press, Honolulu, 1993) by P F Kluge, a perceptive account of the effects of cultural imperialism on Micronesians written by a former Peace Corps volunteer.

Operation Crossroads: The Atomic Tests at Bikini Atoll (Naval Institute Press, Annapolis, Maryland, 1994) by Jonathan M Weisgall, the lawyer for the Bikini islanders, explores the inner workings of the agencies responsible for the atomic bomb tests over Bikini and the various cover-ups that were made by US officials to avoid embarrassing investigations and lawsuits.

Eyes of Fire: The Last Voyage of the Rainbow Warrior (Lindon Publishing, Auckland, New Zealand, 1987) by David Robie gives the account of the *Rainbow Warrior*'s 1985 evacuation of the Rongelapese from their radioactivity-contaminated atoll in the Marshall Islands. This was the last voyage the Greenpeace ship made before being blown up in New Zealand by French agents.

Micronesia: A Trust Betrayed (Carnegie Endowment for International Peace, New York, 1975) by Donald McHenry is an insightful history of the Trust Territory and the events leading up to the Compacts of Free Association.

The American Touch in Micronesia (W W Norton & Co, New York, 1977) by David Nevin, looks at fumbling American colonialism and the effects of power, money and corruption in Micronesia.

Culture

There are a good number of scholarly anthropological works about Micronesian culture, many written by individuals who have lived on remote islands and studied a single group of people in depth. The following books about Micronesian culture are geared more to the general reader.

An Introduction to the Peoples & Cultures of Micronesia (Addison-Wesley Publishing Co, Redding, Massachusetts, 1972) by G Alkire is a comprehensive study resulting from Alkire's 3½ years of field work in the islands. Alkire is an authority on Micronesian societies and this book is a bible of sorts on Micronesian cultural anthropology.

Prehistoric Architecture in Micronesia (University of Texas Press, Austin, 1988) by William N Morgan is a study of the unique traditional architecture found on Kosrae, Pohnpei, Yap, Palau and the Marianas, including the stone cities of Lelu and Nan Madol.

The Lelu Stone Ruins (University of Hawaii Press, Honolulu, 1994) by Ross Cordy documents life in ancient Lelu, using archaeological and historical information gathered during research of the Kosraean ruins in the 1980s.

We, the Navigators: The Ancient Art of Landfinding in the Pacific (University of Hawaii Press, Honolulu, 1994) by David Lewis is a comprehensive work which traces the navigational routes and methods of early Micronesian and Polynesian sailors.

Micronesia: The Land, the People & the Sea (Mobil Oil, Micronesia, 1981) by Kenneth Brower covers the relationship between the Micronesians and the sea. There are good sections on navigation, canoes and ruins, accompanied by colour photos.

Micronesian Customs & Beliefs and *Never & Always: Micronesian Legends, Fables & Folklore* (Rainy Day Press, Pohnpei, 1989), compiled by Gene Ashby, are collections of legends and stories written by the students at the College of Micronesia.

Man This Reef (Micronitor News & Printing Co, Majuro, 1982) by Gerald Knight is a translated collection of tales and legends as told by an elderly Marshallese storyteller. Knight is the former curator of the Alele Museum in Majuro.

Book of Luelen (University of Hawaii Press, Honolulu, 1977) is an account of

Pohnpei's history and traditions by an elderly Pohnpeian man who wanted Pohnpei's stories to remain alive. It was translated and edited by John L Fischer, Saul H Riesenberg & Marjorie G Whiting.

Islands Islands: A Special Good (Caulderwood-McCandless Publishing, Newport Beach, California, 1986) by Bernadette V Wehrly, is a collection of poems, songs, stories and legends from the FSM, with a separate section by poet Petrus Martin of the Mortlock Islands.

Decorative Marshallese Baskets (University of Hawaii Press, Honolulu, 1991) by Judy Mulford describes in detail the technique of preparing and weaving the pandanus and coconut fibres used in making Marshallese baskets and wall hangings. It has more than 100 photos and illustrations.

Language Books

The PALI Language Texts, published by the University of Hawaii in Honolulu, is the most comprehensive Micronesian language series, although the approach tends to be scholarly. The series includes the following:

Marshallese-English Dictionary (1986) by Takaji Abo, Byron W Bender, Alfred Capelle & Tony DeBrum

Spoken Marshallese (1978) by Byron W Bender; an intensive language course with grammatical notes and glossary

Ponapean-English Dictionary (1979) by Kenneth L Rehg & Damian G Sohl

Kapingamarangi Lexicon (1974) by Michael D Lieber & Kalio H Dikepa

Mokilese-English Dictionary (1977) by Sheldon P Harrison & Salich Y Albert

Mokilese Reference Grammar (1976) by Sheldon P Harrison

Kusaiean-English Dictionary (1976) by Kee-Dong Lee

Kusaiean Reference Grammar (1975) by Kee-Dong Lee

Woleaian-English Dictionary (1976) by Ho-min Sohn & Anthony F Tawerilmang

New Palauan-English Dictionary (1991) by Lewis S Josephs

Spoken Chamorro (1980) by Donald M Topping

Chamorro Reference Grammar (1973) by Donald M Topping

Chamorro-English Dictionary (1975) by Donald M Topping, Pedro M Ogo & Bernadita C Dungca

Carolinian-English Dictionary (1991) by Frederick H Jackson & Jeffrey C Marck; covers the three dialects spoken by islanders who migrated from the central Caroline Islands to Saipan

The University of Guam (Mangilao, Guam) also has a series on the more prominent Micronesian languages. It, however, is aimed at helping English-speaking teachers who are instructing young non-English-speaking children. Each book starts with a bit of history and culture, incorporates a long word list and ends with native language songs. The series is as follows: *The Palauan Child* (1994), *The Yapese Child* (1993), *The Pohnpeian Child* (1993), *The Marshallese Child* (1994), *The Chuukese Child* (1994) and *The Chamorro Child* (1991).

Diving & Marine Life

The *Diver's Guide to Guam & Micronesia* (Marine Images, Agana, Guam, 1990) by Guam journalist Tim Rock describes in detail 47 dive and snorkelling locations in Guam; 22 in Palau; 15 in Chuuk; and a half dozen dives each in Yap, Saipan and Rota.

Tim Rock also has individual books for specific islands, including the *Diving & Snorkelling Guide to Truk Lagoon*, *Diving & Snorkelling Guide to Palau* and *Diving & Snorkelling Guide to Guam & Yap*, all by Pisces Books (Houston, Texas, 1994).

Micronesian Reef Fishes (Coral Graphics, Barrigada, Guam, 1991), by Robert F Myers, is a comprehensive book with 975 quality colour photos. This superb book identifies more than 1250 of the most common reef fishes found in Micronesian waters, as well as 150 pelagic fish.

This Living Reef (Quadrangle/The New York Times Co, New York, 1974) by environmentalist Douglas Faulkner is a beautiful book, heavy on colour photographs of coral, fish and underwater life.

Ghost Fleet of the Truk Lagoon (Pictorial Histories Publishing Co, Missoula, Montana, 1985) by William H Stewart is an account of the American attack on the Japanese naval base in Chuuk Lagoon during WW II. Stewart includes maps and photographs showing how and where the more than 60 ships were sunk.

WW II Wrecks of Palau (North Valley Divers Publications, Redding, California, 1991) by Dan E Bailey is a coffee table book on the various war wrecks to be found in Palauan waters. It includes colour photos of wrecks and period black & white photos of the war era. Bailey also has a similar book on central Micronesia called *WW II Wrecks of the Kwajalein and Truk Lagoons* (1992).

The informative *Hailstorm over Truk Lagoon* (Pacific Press Publications, 1989) by Klaus Lindemann has a historical survey of the WW II battle in Chuuk Lagoon, including maps with the location of the lagoon wrecks and a description of each ship.

General

The classic *A Reporter in Micronesia* (W W Norton & Co, New York, 1966) by E J Kahn is a very readable log of Kahn's travels around the islands. His journeys were mostly by field ship, as Micronesia then had no jet traffic, no tourist hotels and very few visitors.

A Field Guide to the Birds of Hawaii & the Tropical Pacific by H D Pratt, P L Bruner & D G Berrett (Princeton University Press, Princeton, New Jersey, 1987) is the best general bird guide to the area.

Micronesia: The Breadfruit Revolution (East-West Center Press, Honolulu, 1971) by Byron Baker features black & white photographs by Robert Wenkam offering glimpses of Micronesian life in days past.

Bookshops

The only real bookshops in Micronesia are in Guam and Saipan. On other islands, some gift shops sell a few souvenir-style picture books about the islands.

Ordering Books by Mail

A select collection of books about Micronesia is available from the Alele Museum (Box 629, Majuro, Marshall Islands 96960). You can either get them while you're in Majuro or write for a book list and order by mail.

The University of Hawaii Press (2840 Kolowalu St, Honolulu, HI 96822) prints a catalogue detailing books they publish about the Pacific, including Micronesia, which can be sent out upon request for mail orders.

The Cellar Book Shop, 18090 Wyoming, Detroit, MI 48221, is a mail-order book company specialising in the Pacific. A catalogue is sent upon request

Serendipity Books, PO Box 340, Nedlands, WA 6009, Australia, has a mail-order service and a comprehensive selection of books on Micronesia and the rest of the Pacific. Catalogues are sent upon request.

MEDIA
Newspapers

Micronesia's only daily newspaper is Guam's *Pacific Daily News* (Box DN, Agana, Guam 96910), which is flown to capital towns all around Micronesia. PDN, as the paper is commonly called, is a member of the Gannett group of newspapers and provides a good mix of regional and international news.

The Marshalls has a weekly newspaper, the *Marshall Islands Journal* (Box 14, Majuro, Marshall Islands 96960). Palau has a biweekly newspaper, *Tia Belau* (Box 477, Koror, Palau 96940). In the Northern Marianas, the *Marianas Variety* (Box 231, Saipan, MP 96950) is published five days a week, and three other newspapers come out less frequently.

If you're contemplating an extended stay in Micronesia, ordering copies of the local newspaper in advance will help you get a feel for island happenings and politics.

Magazines

A good news magazine for Micronesian events is *Pacific Magazine* (Box 25488, Honolulu, HI 96825), published six times a year. Although it covers all the Pacific, it gives a fair weight to Micronesia, with an emphasis on politics, business and new developments. Subscriptions cost $15 a year for surface mail; add $12 for airmail to the USA or $24 overseas.

Two other Pacific-region magazines that have less coverage of Micronesia are *Pacific Islands Monthly* (GPO Box 1167, Suva, Fiji) and *Islands Business Pacific* (Box 12718, Suva, Fiji). Each costs $45 a year to overseas destinations and is published monthly.

Guam Business News (Box 3191, Agana, Guam 96910) is a substantial monthly magazine geared for the business community in Guam and the Northern Marianas. Annual subscriptions cost $36 for surface mail and $60 for airmail sent to the USA, $46/130 outside the USA.

Continental Micronesia's glossy inflight magazine, titled *Pacifica*, is published quarterly and has interesting feature articles in both English and Japanese.

The University of Guam's *Isla: A Journal of Micronesia Studies* (Graduate School & Research, UOG Station, Mangilao, Guam 96923) is a scholarly journal devoted exclusively to Micronesia and published twice a year. An annual subscription costs $15.

Newsletters

The Micronesia Institute (☎ 202-842-1140), 1275 K St NW, Suite 360, Washington, DC 20005, was founded to provide an independent link between Micronesian countries and funding resources in the USA. The institute helps formulate educational, cultural, health, social and small-business development programmes, with the primary focus on self-help and self-sustaining projects. It prints an annual newsletter about its activities in the islands.

The *Micronesian Investment Quarterly* (☎ 301-279-2647), Box 3867, North Potomac, MD 20885, is a free quarterly newsletter which promotes business investment in the FSM, Marshall Islands and Palau, attempting to link up investors with local partners.

Radio & TV

All the district centres have radio stations with local broadcasting.

All the main islands, with the exception of Kosrae, have cable TV. Most have live CNN news, but beyond that the coverage varies. In the Marshalls and the FSM, the mainstay is pre-recorded US network broadcasts complete with California commercials. In Guam there are three local TV stations and the full range of standard US cable connections including HBO, live news from the US mainland and the Disney and Playboy stations. The Northern Marianas also have an extensive selection of channels on cable TV.

PHOTOGRAPHY

The high temperatures in the tropics, coupled with high humidity, greatly accelerate the deterioration of film. The sooner you have exposed film developed, the better the results. Sending off your film in pre-paid mailers is a good way to avoid carting it around. Print film and some slide films can be professionally processed on Pohnpei, Palau and Guam.

Don't leave your camera in direct sunshine any longer than necessary. A locked car can heat up like an oven in just a few minutes.

Another problem that often arises is moisture condensing on film and lenses that have been taken from air-con rooms into the warm, moist outside air. One way to avoid this is to keep your camera in an area of the room less affected by the air-con, such as a closet or the bathroom. Or try keeping it wrapped inside a camera case or carry-bag for an hour or so after leaving a place with air-con.

Sand and water are intense reflectors and in bright light they'll often leave foreground subjects shadowy. You can compensate by adjusting your f-stop (aperture) or attaching a polarising filter, or both, but the most effective technique is to take photos in the gentler light of early morning and late afternoon.

Print film is available on the main islands, though it takes more searching to find slide film. Film is a bit more expensive in Micronesia than in the USA and you should check the expiry dates carefully.

Photo Etiquette

You should never take pictures of Micronesians without first asking permission. As a rule, it's much easier to photograph children, especially groups of children, as they often enjoy posing. On some islands, notably Yap, staring at people is considered highly offensive and the very act of randomly pointing a camera is perceived as being so invasive as to warrant an angry response.

While there are no places of military or religious significance where photography is forbidden, if a *bai* or other culturally significant sight is on private land you may be asked to pay a fee to photograph it – this situation is most common in Palau.

TIME

The International Date Line runs between Hawaii and the Marshalls. Going from the USA to Micronesia you lose a day, while on the return you gain a day.

Micronesia has four time zones. Guam is 10 hours ahead of GMT/UTC. When it's noon in Guam, the Northern Marianas, Yap and Chuuk it is: 1 pm in Pohnpei and Kosrae; 2 pm in Majuro; and 11 am in Palau. It is also noon in Port Moresby, Sydney and Melbourne; 11 am in Tokyo; 10 am in Manila and Hong Kong; 2 am in London; 4 pm the day before in Honolulu; 6 pm the day before in San Francisco; and 9 pm the day before in Boston.

ELECTRICITY

Electricity is 110/120 volts, 60 cycles, and a flat two-pronged plug is used, the same as in the USA.

WEIGHTS & MEASURES

Micronesia, like the USA, uses the imperial system of measurement. Distances are in inches, feet, yards and miles; weights are in ounces, pounds and tons. For those accustomed to the metric system of measurement, there is a conversion table at the back of this book.

LAUNDRY

There are self-service coin laundries in each of the main district centres. Rates vary, but $1 to wash a load of clothes and $1 to dry will generally cover it.

HEALTH

In general, Micronesia is not an unhealthy place to visit. Still, sunburn, fungal infections, diarrhoea and other gut infections all warrant precautions.

If you're new to the heat and humidity you may find yourself easily fatigued and more susceptible to minor ailments. Acclimatise yourself by slowing down your pace. The climate is one of the reasons Micronesia is so laid-back, so learn to go with the flow.

Most of the district centres throughout Micronesia have small hospitals built in recent times with American aid. With but a couple of exceptions, they are modern and competently staffed, although services may be limited. Still, the best medical treatment is generally found on Guam and Saipan, though costs are high there, on par with the rest of the USA.

Many outer islands have no health services available so if you're going somewhere remote, it's a good idea to take along a first aid kit with some of the more common medical supplies.

Travel Health Guides

There are a number of books on travel health. Three of the more useful are:

Travellers' Health, Dr Richard Dawood, Oxford University Press, 1992. This book is comprehensive, easy to read, authoritative and highly recommended, although it's rather large to lug around.

Where There is No Doctor, David Werner, Macmillan, 1994. This is a very detailed guide intended for those going to work in an undeveloped country, rather than for the average traveller.

Travel with Children, Maureen Wheeler, Lonely Planet Publications, 1995. This book includes basic advice on travel health for younger children.

Predeparture Preparations

Health Insurance A travel insurance policy to cover theft, loss and medical problems may be a wise idea. There are a wide variety of policies and your travel agent should have recommendations. Check the small print. For instance, some policies specifically exclude 'dangerous activities' which can even include scuba diving. Check if the policy covers an emergency flight home or a medivac (medical evacuation) flight to Honolulu. If you have to stretch out you will need two seats and somebody has to pay for them! It's a good idea to keep all receipts and, should anything happen, contact the insurance carrier immediately to find out what the proper procedures are.

Medical Kit A small, straightforward medical kit is a wise thing to carry. A possible kit list includes:

- Aspirin or Panadol – for pain or fever.
- Antihistamine (such as Benadryl) – useful as a decongestant for colds, allergies, to ease the itch from insect bites or stings or to help prevent motion sickness.
- Antibiotics – useful if you're travelling well off the beaten track, but they must be prescribed and you should carry the prescription with you.
- Kaolin preparation (Pepto-Bismol), Imodium or Lomotil – for stomach upsets.
- Rehydration mixture – for treatment of severe diarrhoea; this is particularly important if travelling with children, but is recommended for everyone.
- Antiseptic and antibiotic powder or similar 'dry' spray – for cuts and grazes.
- Calamine lotion – to ease irritation from bites or stings.
- Bandages and Band-aids – for minor injuries.
- Scissors, tweezers and a thermometer (note that mercury thermometers are prohibited by airlines).
- Insect repellent, sunscreen, suntan lotion, lip balm and water purification tablets.

Health Preparations Make sure you're healthy before you start travelling. If you intend to be in Micronesia a long time make sure your teeth are OK; many outer islands have no dentists and outside of Saipan and Guam dental care varies.

If you wear glasses take a spare pair and your prescription. If you require a particular medication take an adequate supply, as it may not be available on many islands. If you might need refills while in Micronesia, bring a prescription with the generic rather than the brand name; this will make getting replacements easier. Even if you don't intend to refill your prescription, it's a wise idea to bring it with you to show you legally use the medication – it's surprising how often over-the-counter drugs from one place are illegal without a prescription or even banned in another.

Immunisations The only immunisations required to enter Micronesia are for cholera and yellow fever, but that's only if you're coming from an infected area. Although not required, you should be up to date on your tetanus vaccination (a booster is necessary every 10 years) and if you're going to the Marshalls or Chuuk a typhoid shot is sometimes recommended. All vaccinations should be recorded on an International Health Certificate, which is available from your physician or government health department.

Basic Rules

Care in what you eat and drink is the most important health rule; stomach upsets are the most likely travel health problem but the majority of these upsets will be relatively minor. Don't become paranoid; trying the local food is part of the experience of travel, after all.

Water Tap water is not always safe to drink. There are a lot of parasites in Micronesia, including giardia and amoeba, and unclean water is a great way to discover them.

Often the problem derives not so much from impure water as from poor water distribution. On many islands ageing sewer and water pipes are laid alongside each other, and when the water is turned off for more than a few hours for rationing purposes, cross-seepage can occur.

When in doubt stick with readily available canned beverages or bottled water. Tea or coffee should also be OK, since the water should have been boiled.

To avoid dehydration, you should make a conscious effort to drink an ample supply of liquids to replace the body fluids you quickly lose in the heat and humidity of the day. Always carry a water bottle with you on long trips. Drinking coconuts, which are readily available in many places, are not only a good source of uncontaminated water but they're also excellent for re-hydration, being full of vitamins and minerals.

Water Purification The simplest way of purifying water is to boil it thoroughly for five minutes.

Simple filtering will not remove all dangerous organisms, so if you cannot boil water it should be treated chemically. Chlorine tablets (Puritabs, Steritabs or other brand names) will kill many but not all pathogens, including giardia and amoebic cysts. Iodine is very effective in purifying water and is available in tablet form (such as Potable Aqua), but follow the directions carefully and remember that too much iodine can be harmful.

If you can't find tablets, tincture of iodine (2%) can be used. Four drops of tincture of iodine per quart or litre of clear water is the recommended dosage; the treated water should be left to stand for 30 minutes before drinking. Flavoured powder will disguise the taste of treated water and is a good idea if you are travelling with children. Iodine loses its effectiveness if exposed to air or damp so keep it in a tightly sealed container.

Food Food in Micronesia is usually sanitarily prepared and requires no unusual precautions, but avoid pre-cooked foods that are sold in the marketplace on smaller islands. As a general rule, places that look clean and well run are a safer bet than those that look run down. Restaurants busy with customers are apt to be fine, while empty restaurants are more questionable.

Make sure your diet is well balanced and that you get enough protein. Rice and fish are plentiful in Micronesia, so this shouldn't be much of a problem. Fruit is a good source of vitamins.

Poisonous Fish Ciguatera fish poisoning is a problem throughout the Pacific and is most common in areas, such as the Marshalls, where coral reefs are well developed.

More than 300 species of fish can be toxic when eaten. Sometimes the same species can be safe in some areas and poisonous in others, so get local advice before eating your catch. Cooking the fish doesn't destroy the toxin.

Reef fish served in restaurants pose little risk as restaurateurs know which species to avoid; and tuna, which is the most common fish served in Micronesia, is an unaffected deep-water fish.

The symptoms, if you do eat the wrong fish, can include nausea, stomach cramps, diarrhoea, paralysis, tingling and numbness of the face, fingers and toes, and a reversal of temperature feelings so that hot things feel cold and vice versa. Extreme cases can result in unconsciousness and even death. Vomit until your stomach is empty and get immediate medical help.

Climatic & Geographical Considerations

Sunburn Sunburn is a definite concern in Micronesia because the islands are so close to the equator, where fewer of the sun's rays are blocked by the atmosphere. Don't be fooled by what appears to be a hazy overcast day – the rays still get through.

Fair-skinned people can get first and second degree burns in the hot Micronesian sun, so wearing a hat for added protection is a good idea. The most severe sun is between 10 am and 2 pm.

Sunscreen with a SPF (sun protection factor) of at least 10 to 15 is recommended. If you're going into the water, use one that's water-resistant. You may want to wear a T-shirt (or even light cotton pants)

Everyday Health
A normal body temperature is 98.6°F or 37°C; more than 2°C higher is a 'high' fever. A normal adult pulse rate is 60 to 80 per minute (children 80 to 100, babies 100 to 140). As a general rule the pulse increases about 20 beats per minute for each degree Celsius rise in fever.

Respiration (breathing) rate is also an indicator of illness. Count the number of breaths per minute: between 12 and 20 is normal for adults and older children (up to 30 for younger children, 40 for babies). People with a high fever or serious respiratory illness (like pneumonia) breathe more quickly than normal. More than 40 shallow breaths a minute usually means pneumonia.

The common cold is alive and well in tropical Micronesia. Probably the most effective way to avoid susceptibility is to be in prime condition before you travel. Over-zealous air-conditioning can be a particular problem. In a restaurant you may have to position yourself in a corner away from the blast; and at night you should adjust the air-con vent so it's not aimed directly at your bed and keep a blanket within reach.

Many health problems can be avoided by taking care of yourself. Clean your teeth with purified water rather than straight from the tap. Keep out of the sun when it's hot. Seek local advice: if you're told the water is unsafe due to jellyfish or crocodiles, don't go in. In situations where there is no information, discretion is the better part of valour. ■

---

while snorkelling, especially if you plan to be out in the water for a long time. You'll not only be protecting against sunburn but also against premature ageing of the skin and potential skin cancer. Calamine lotion is good for mild sunburn.

Prickly Heat Prickly heat is an itchy rash caused by excessive perspiration trapped under the skin. It usually strikes people who have just arrived in a hot climate and whose pores have not yet opened sufficiently to cope with greater sweating. Keeping cool by bathing often or resorting to air-con may help until you acclimatise.

Heat Exhaustion Dehydration or salt deficiency can cause heat exhaustion. Take time to acclimatise to high temperatures and make sure you get sufficient liquids. Salt deficiency is characterised by fatigue, lethargy, headaches, giddiness and muscle cramps. Salt tablets may alleviate these symptoms. Vomiting or diarrhoea can deplete your liquid and salt levels.

Heat Stroke This serious, sometimes fatal, condition can occur if the body's heat-regulating mechanism breaks down and the body temperature rises to dangerous levels. Long, continuous periods of exposure to high temperatures can leave you vulnerable to heat stroke. You should avoid excessive alcohol or strenuous activity when you first arrive in a hot climate.

The symptoms are feeling unwell, not sweating very much or at all and a high body temperature (39°C to 41°C). Where sweating has ceased the skin becomes flushed and red. Severe, throbbing headaches and lack of coordination will also occur, and the sufferer may be confused or aggressive. Eventually the victim will become delirious or convulse. Hospitalisation is essential, but meanwhile get patients out of the sun, remove their clothing, cover them with a wet sheet or towel and then fan continually.

Fungal Infections The same climate that produces lush tropical forests also promotes a prolific growth of skin fungi and bacteria. Hot weather fungal infections are most likely to occur on the scalp, between the toes or fingers (athlete's foot) or in the groin.

To prevent fungal infections, keeping your skin cool and allowing air to circulate is essential. Choose cotton clothing rather than artificial fibres and sandals instead of shoes.

If you do get an infection, wash the infected area daily with a disinfectant or medicated soap and water, and rinse and dry well. Apply an antifungal powder like the widely available Tinaderm. Try to expose the infected area to air or sunlight as much as possible. Wash all towels and underwear in hot water as well as changing them often.

Motion Sickness Eating lightly before and during a trip will reduce the chances of motion sickness. If you are prone to motion sickness try to find a place that minimises disturbance – near the wing on an aircraft or close to amidships on boats. Fresh air usually helps; reading or cigarette smoke doesn't. Commercial antimotion-sickness preparations, which can cause drowsiness, have to be taken before the trip commences; when you're feeling sick it's too late. Ginger is a natural preventative and is available in capsule form.

Jet Lag Jet lag is experienced when a person travels by air across more than three time zones. It occurs because many of the functions of the human body (such as body temperature, pulse rate and emptying of the bladder and bowels) are regulated by internal 24-hour cycles called circadian rhythms. When we travel long distances rapidly, our bodies take time to adjust to the 'new time' of our destination, and we may experience fatigue, disorientation, insomnia, anxiety, impaired concentration and loss of appetite. These effects will usually be gone within three days of arrival, but there are ways of minimising the impact of jet lag:

- Rest for a couple of days prior to departure; avoid late nights and a rush of last-minute travel preparations before you commence a long flight.
- Try to select flight schedules that minimise sleep deprivation; arriving late in the day means you can go to sleep soon after you arrive. For very long flights, try to organise a stopover.
- Avoid excessive eating (which bloats the stomach) and alcohol (which causes dehydration) during the flight. Drink plenty of non-carbonated drinks such as fruit juice or water.
- Avoid smoking, as this reduces the amount of

oxygen in the airplane cabin even further and causes greater fatigue.
- Make yourself comfortable by wearing loose-fitting clothes and perhaps bringing an eye mask and ear plugs to help you sleep.

Diseases of Poor Sanitation

Diarrhoea A change of water, food or climate can all cause the runs; diarrhoea caused by contaminated food or water is more serious. Despite all your precautions you may still have a bout of mild travellers' diarrhoea but a few rushed toilet trips with no other symptoms is not indicative of a serious problem.

Dehydration is the main danger with any diarrhoea, particularly for children, so fluid replenishment is the number one treatment. Weak black tea, bottled water or coconut liquid are all good. With severe diarrhoea a rehydrating solution is necessary to replace minerals and salts. Commercially available ORS (oral rehydration salts) is very useful; add the contents of one sachet to a litre of boiled or bottled water. In an emergency you can make up a solution of eight teaspoons of sugar to a litre of boiled water and provide salted cracker biscuits at the same time. You should stick to a bland diet as you recover.

Lomotil or Imodium can be used to bring relief from the symptoms, although they do not actually cure the problem. Only use these drugs if absolutely necessary – eg, if you *must* travel. For children Imodium is preferable. Under all circumstances fluid replacement is the main message. Do not use these drugs if the person has a high fever or is severely dehydrated.

Giardiasis The parasite causing this intestinal disorder is present in contaminated water. The symptoms are stomach cramps, nausea, a bloated stomach, watery, foul-smelling diarrhoea and frequent gas. Giardiasis can appear several weeks after you have been exposed to the parasite. The symptoms may disappear for a few days and then return; this can go on for several weeks. Tinidazole, known as Fasigyn, or metronidazole (Flagyl) are the recommended drugs for treatment. Either can be used in a single treatment dose. Antibiotics are of no use.

Dysentery This serious illness is caused by contaminated food or water and is characterised by severe diarrhoea, often with blood or mucus in the stool. There are two kinds of dysentery. Bacillary dysentery is characterised by a high fever and rapid onset; headache, vomiting and stomach pains are also symptoms. It generally does not last longer than a week, but it is highly contagious.

Amoebic dysentery is often more gradual in the onset of symptoms, with cramping abdominal pain and vomiting less likely; fever may not be present. It is not a self-limiting disease: it will persist until treated and can recur and cause long-term health problems.

A stool test is necessary to diagnose which kind of dysentery you have, so you should seek medical help immediately. In case of an emergency the drugs norfloxacin or ciprofloxacin can be used as presumptive treatment for bacillary dysentery, and metronidazole (Flagyl) can be used for amoebic dysentery.

Cholera Cholera is spread through poor sanitation conditions. The minimum precautions where cholera is suspected include drinking only bottled liquids and not eating raw fish. Also avoid swimming in polluted lagoons, especially near populated areas. In the early 1980s, Chuuk Lagoon had a cholera epidemic but at present there is no cholera in Micronesia.

The cholera vaccine is not very effective. The bacteria responsible for this disease are waterborne, so attention to the rules of eating and drinking are the primary protection for travellers.

Outbreaks of cholera are generally widely reported, so you can avoid such problem areas. The disease is characterised by a sudden onset of acute diarrhoea with 'rice water' stools, vomiting, muscular cramps and extreme weakness. You need medical help – but treat for dehydration,

which can be extreme, and if there is an appreciable delay in getting to hospital then begin taking tetracycline. The adult dose is 250 mg four times daily. It is not recommended in children aged eight years or under nor in pregnant women. An alternative drug would be Ampicillin. Remember that while antibiotics might kill the bacteria, it is a toxin produced by the bacteria which causes the massive fluid loss. Fluid replacement is by far the most important aspect of treatment.

Typhoid Typhoid fever is a gut infection that travels the faecal-oral route – ie, contaminated water and food are responsible. Vaccination against typhoid is not totally effective and since it is one of the most dangerous infections, medical help must be sought.

In its early stages typhoid resembles many other illnesses: sufferers may feel like they have a bad cold or flu on the way, as early symptoms are a headache, a sore throat and a fever which rises a little each day until it is around 40°C or more. The victim's pulse is often slow relative to the degree of fever present and gets slower as the fever rises – unlike a normal fever where the pulse increases. There may also be vomiting, diarrhoea or constipation.

In the second week the high fever and slow pulse continue and a few pink spots may appear on the body; trembling, delirium, weakness, weight loss and dehydration are other symptoms. If there are no further complications, the fever and other symptoms will slowly go during the third week. However you must get medical help before this because pneumonia or peritonitis (perforated bowel) are common complications, and because typhoid is very infectious.

The fever should be treated by keeping the victim cool and dehydration should also be watched for.

Insect-Borne Diseases
Dengue Fever While there's no malaria in Micronesia, there are incidences of dengue

fever. There is no prophylactic available for this mosquito-spread disease; the main preventative measure is to avoid mosquito bites. A sudden onset of fever, headaches and severe joint and muscle pains are the first signs before a rash starts on the trunk of the body and spreads to the limbs and face. After a further few days, the fever will subside and recovery will begin. Serious complications are not common.

Cuts, Bites & Stings

Cuts & Scratches Skin punctures can easily become infected in hot climates and may be difficult to heal. Treat cuts with an antiseptic such as Betadine. Where possible avoid bandages and Band-aids, which can keep wounds wet.

Insect Bites & Stings Other than mosquitoes and sand gnats, there are very few pesky insects in Micronesia that bite.

Cone Shells

Cone shells should be left alone unless you're sure they're empty. There is no safe way of picking up a live cone shell, as the animal inside has a long stinging tail that can dart out and reach any place on its shell to deliver a puncture wound. Stings can result in numbness at the wound site, breathing distress and sight and speech disturbances. A few species, such as the textile cone, have a venom so toxic that the sting could prove fatal. If you should get stung by such a shell, seek immediate medical attention. ■

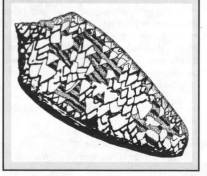

Calamine lotion will give relief for those that do.

Lice All lice cause itching and discomfort. They make themselves at home in your hair (head lice), your clothing (body lice) or in your pubic hair (crabs). You catch lice through direct contact with infected people or by sharing combs, clothing and the like. Powder or shampoo treatment will kill the lice and infected clothing should then be washed in very hot water.

Coral Cuts Coral cuts are notoriously slow to heal, as the coral injects a weak venom into the wound.

Most coral cuts occur when swimmers are pushed onto the coral by rough waves and surges. It's a good idea to wear diving gloves when snorkelling over shallow reefs and suitable footwear when walking on reefs. Clean any cut thoroughly, with sodium peroxide if available.

Learn to identify fire coral, which is usually in the form of vertical sheets of brown coral rimmed in a light green color. Touching the rim can give you a stabbing pain as severe as a jellyfish sting.

Fish Stings Encounters with venomous sea creatures in Micronesian waters are pretty rare. You should, however, learn to recognise such venomous varieties as the turkey fish, lionfish, scorpion fish and stonefish. The latter two are sometimes seen in quite shallow water and all can inject venom through their dorsal spines.

The sting causes a sharp burning pain, followed by numbness around the area, nausea and headaches. Immediately stick the affected area in water as hot as bearable (be sure not to unintentionally scald the area due to numbness) and go for medical treatment.

Sea Urchins & Starfish Sea urchins and crown of thorns starfish have long spines that can puncture the skin and break off, causing burning and possible numbness. You can try to remove the spines with tweezers or by soaking the area in warm water and Epsom salts, although more serious cases may necessitate surgical removal.

Jellyfish Take a peek into the water before you plunge in, to make sure it's not jellyfish territory. These gelatinous creatures with stinging tentacles are fairly common around Guam, for example, where even the dangerous sea wasps and Portuguese man-of-war have occasionally been sighted.

The sting of a jellyfish varies from mild to severe, depending on the variety. A man-of-war sting is very painful, similar to a bad bee sting except that you're likely to get stung more than once from clusters of long tentacles. Even touching a man-of-war a few hours after it's washed up on shore can result in a burning sting.

You can at least partly neutralise the venom of a sting by dousing the skin with vinegar, or even urine. Calamine lotion, antihistamines and analgesics may reduce the reaction and relieve the pain. For serious stings, which are usually followed by swelling, bleeding, stomach spasms, difficulty in breathing or chest pains, seek immediate medical attention.

Women's Health
Poor diet, lowered resistance through the use of antibiotics and even contraceptive pills can lead to vaginal infections when travelling in hot climates. Maintaining good personal hygiene and wearing skirts or loose-fitting trousers and cotton underwear will help to prevent infections.

Yeast infections, characterised by a rash, itch and discharge, can be treated with a vinegar or even lemon-juice douche or with yoghurt. Nystatin suppositories are the usual medical prescription.

WOMEN TRAVELLERS
Although most places in Micronesia shouldn't be a hassle, women travelling alone may occasionally get some unwanted attention. Duly earned or not, Chuuk seems to have the worst reputation. Although it's largely their demeanor, some young Chuukese males may seem to have surly macho stares. Women travelling alone are particularly likely to hear a few come-ons and under-the-breath innuendoes. The women of Chuuk have their own defence, which largely consists of remaining aloof and pretending they don't hear. Although this little macho game doesn't make a very favourable impression, women are not necessarily any more likely to be in physical danger here than elsewhere.

Nonetheless, in most parts of Micronesia, women should use standard precautions and avoid walking alone in out-of-the-way places after dark.

DANGERS & ANNOYANCES
Marine Dangers
Most underwater experiences in Micronesia are safe, and while you shouldn't miss out for fear of monsters lurking in the depths, it's important to be aware of potential dangers.

There are a few venomous varieties of fish in Micronesian waters, including scorpion fish and stonefish which inhabit shallow waters and can inject venom through their dorsal spines. Refer to Cuts, Bites & Stings in the Health section earlier for more details on these and other marine dangers.

Sharks The probability of shark attacks on humans has been greatly exaggerated. Still, there are plenty of sharks in Micronesian waters and it doesn't hurt to have a healthy respect for them.

The few attacks that do occur in Micronesia usually happen while the victim is spearfishing. When the shark tries to chomp down on a bloody, just-speared fish, the spearer sometimes gets in the way. Still, even these incidents are rare. And just for the record, the Yap Institute of Natural Science notes that people eat sharks 600,000 times more often than sharks eat people!

Sharks are attracted by shiny things and by anything bright red or yellow, which might influence your choice of swimsuit colour. Those popular day-glo orange life jackets are said to be known as 'yummy orange' in shark circles.

Strong Currents & Riptides Be careful of water funnelling off the reefs into channels when the tide's going out as it can have a very strong pull.

You can quickly use up all your energy and lose ground if you try to fight a strong current. It's easier to swim across a current than against it. If you do find yourself being carried out through a reef passage, once outside the reef you should be able to move down along the reef and cross back over it to a calmer area.

Property
In Micronesia, most things are shared, and individual property in the Western sense is a rather foreign concept. If you don't want visitors, particularly when you're out, be careful to leave your doors locked. The more remote the place you're staying, the more likely you'll have the village kids just walking in.

Don't tempt anyone. If you have anything that looks appealing, lock it up in your bags. The old adage 'out of sight, out of mind' holds true in Micronesia. Two-way zippers on soft luggage and backpacks allow for use of a small lock, which might be enough to deter the overly curious.

The simplest way to feel at ease is to not bring anything you don't mind parting with. Keep your passport and air tickets on you and if you have a camera you might want to bring a day pack to carry it around with you.

Privacy
The concept of privacy is also a different affair in Micronesia compared to most Western societies. You can often tell which house in a village has a VCR by the crowds standing outside looking in the windows; it's an acceptable way to watch a movie. If you stay with a local family and are given your own room it won't be uncommon for groups of the extended family to come by and join you for impromptu visits. You should see this not as an intrusion, but as an indication that you're being honoured and accepted as part of the family.

Payday Weekends
Throughout most of Micronesia every other Friday is payday. From payday until Sunday a number of Micronesian males go on a drinking binge and, for the most part, they don't make happy-go-lucky drunks. Many islanders have a low tolerance for alcohol and it often acts as a key that unleashes suppressed feelings. Domestic violence, suicide and the desire to settle up pent-up accounts all tend to come to a head on this weekend. A few places have responded by enacting prohibition, though most of Micronesia just sits it all out. The problem tends to be worse in district centres.

BUSINESS HOURS & HOLIDAYS
Business hours vary throughout the islands, but 8 am to 4.30 pm Monday to Friday is fairly common. Banking hours also vary, though 10 am to 3 pm Monday to Thursday and 10 am to 5 pm on Fridays is average.

The last weeks of the year are very difficult for doing business. Not only do Christmas and New Year holidays and parties interfere, but many government employees have leftover annual leave that must be taken by the end of the year or lost, so lots of people scoot off for a quick vacation.

ACTIVITIES
Diving & Snorkelling
What Micronesia lacks in land, it makes up for in water. Some of the region's most spectacular scenery is underwater and the traveller who never looks below the surface is missing out on some incredible sights.

Micronesia has an abundance and variety of fish in every imaginable, and some quite unimaginable, colour and shape. There are hundreds of types of hard and soft corals, anemones, colourful sponges and many varieties of shellfish, including giant tridacna clams. There are also lots of reef sharks and manta rays.

Micronesia's water temperature is about 80°F (27°C). Wet suits are not required for warmth, although some divers wear them as protection against coral cuts.

Divers the world over know about Chuuk's underwater wreck museum and Palau's great drop-offs. These are the finest diving spots in Micronesia and among the very best locales in the world.

There are many other superb, though less famous, diving opportunities in Micronesia, including unspoiled reefs, forests of towering sea fans, coral gardens, underwater caves and the scattered wrecks of whaleboats and WW II ships and planes.

There are dive shops in Majuro, Kosrae, Pohnpei, Chuuk, Yap, Palau, Guam, Saipan, Rota and Tinian. Specific information on dive shops, as well as diving and snorkelling locales, is given under Activities in each island section.

It's recommended that you bring your own buoyancy compensator and other personalised equipment with you, not only to save on the added rental charge, but to avoid the uneven quality that can be encountered when renting these particular items. A dive computer can be very useful, as can some advance training in decompression diving, especially if you plan to dive Chuuk's wrecks. Know your limits and make them clear to the divemaster, as a few shops tend to pay less attention to depth and a diver's level of experience than they should.

If you've never been scuba diving before, here's your chance to learn. Some dive shops offer non-divers an introductory dive down to about 30 feet, which costs anywhere from $60 to $100. You can also take an intensive three or four-day course to become fully certified at several places in Micronesia.

On the other hand you could just pack a mask and snorkel and enjoy it all for free. It's nice to have your own flippers too, though they are a bit heavier to carry around. If you prefer to travel light, snorkelling gear can be rented at many places for about $10 a day.

For information on diving holiday packages, refer to the Tours section in the Getting There & Away chapter.

Other Water Sports

While diving is clearly the major attraction to the region, there are a handful of other water sports that can be enjoyed. Kayak rentals are available on Saipan and Palau. Windsurfing is quite popular in Saipan, and although conditions aren't as good it's also possible to windsurf in Guam. Guam is the only island where board surfing enjoys any popularity. Both Saipan and Guam have beach huts offering recreational water activities such as outrigger canoe rides, banana boats, jet skis etc, although these are geared for Japanese tourists so are priced on the high side.

Hiking

On some of the smaller islands, it takes but two minutes to walk from one side to the other, so hiking is obviously limited to a stroll down the road. Most of the larger high islands have at least a couple of tracks to scenic points or waterfalls that can make for a bit of exercise. Outside Guam and the Northern Marianas, most trails cross private land so hikers will often have to consult with the local municipal office to get permission to cross or to arrange a guide.

An interesting option is to join one of the Hash House Harrier groups that lead guided 'harrier' walk/runs on most of the larger islands on Saturdays. The Hash House Harriers are an internationally affiliated organisation with a large expat membership and their outings are as much social event as exercise, ending with beer and good company. The Hash House Harriers welcome visitors; a contribution of a few dollars covers the cost of the beer.

Tennis

There is at least one tennis court on most of the larger islands. Guam and Saipan have the best public facilities. A few of the larger resort hotels have courts, as well as tennis racquets that guests can rent, but you can't count on finding rentals elsewhere and true tennis buffs might want to bring their own.

Golf

The islands of Guam and Saipan both have a number of 18-hole golf courses, while Rota is opening its first nine-hole golf course. More information is given in those island chapters.

Other Activities

There are bowling alleys on Guam, Saipan and Majuro. Deep-sea fishing is available on a charter basis in many places, but is most popular in Guam, the Marshalls and Yap. On the smaller islands, such as those of the FSM, there are few conventional recreational activities, but there are a couple of uniquely local ones, such as a canoe journey through the mangrove swamps on Kosrae.

As Guam has the largest and most diverse population, it's not surprising that it

also has the largest range of activities and facilities, including a running course and public swimming pool in the capital of Agana, and a local sailing club.

ACCOMMODATION

Camping

Throughout Micronesia most of the land, including the beaches, is privately owned and uninvited campers are about as welcome as they would be if they walked into your backyard at home and started pitching a tent. So if you want to camp, you'll need to get permission from the landowners first.

In any case, camping is very uncommon in many places, especially throughout the FSM, and you're likely to collect a crowd of curious onlookers.

While there are no established camping grounds in Micronesia, there are some possibilities for roughing it. The best are on the Rock Islands and Peleliu in Palau, on Tinian in the Northern Marianas, at Bechiyal village in Yap and on the uninhabited islands off Pohnpei. Details on camping are given in each island section.

If you decide it's worth your while to carry camping gear, you won't need a sleeping bag but you'll sleep more comfortably with some sort of covering that is gnat and mosquito-proof.

Hotels

All islands where Continental Micronesia flies have Western-style hotels. In the overall picture Micronesian hotels tend to be a bit pricey for what you get and there aren't a lot of real cheapies.

Depending on the island, hotel rates usually start between $35 and $50. What you get for the lowest rate varies quite a bit from island to island. A few are rock-bottom places where the mattresses sag, the walls arc dirty and thc bathroom is down the hall, though many others are clean and comfortable, with private bathrooms, air-con and a friendly atmosphere.

Hotels with Micronesian influences are far too few in number, though the Pathways Hotel in Yap and the Village Hotel and Hotel Pohnpei in Pohnpei are pleasant

---

Highlights

In terms of activities, diving is overwhelmingly the main highlight in Micronesia, and virtually every island has top-notch dive possibilities. Still, for underwater wrecks Chuuk Lagoon is tops, while for variety Palau is unsurpassed.

As for archeological highlights, Micronesia has the ruins of two impressive stone cities – Nan Madol on Pohnpei and Lelu on Kosrae – which were once the centre of island kingdoms.

In terms of traditional culture, no island group has held on so strongly to its old ways as Yap, which is known to the outside world largely for its giant stone money. It's a special place for independent travellers.

For scenic beauty, there are lovely atolls and lagoons throughout Micronesia. Palau with its strikingly lovely Rock Islands is singularly unique. ∎

exceptions. Each has traditionally designed thatched cottages that attempt to balance native aesthetics with modern conveniences.

Outside the district centres, you can experience Micronesian hospitality in some nice island-style accommodations for $15 to $25 a night. These include the men's house in the traditional village of Bechiyal on Yap, family guesthouses on the Palauan islands of Angaur and Peleliu and beach huts on Pohnpei's lagoon islands.

All the main islands have a few midrange hotels with standard comforts at rates in the $60 to $90 range.

Guam, Saipan and Palau have luxurious beachside resort hotels, though rates are a good $125-plus. A couple of these are tastefully laid out while others resemble bustling inner-city highrises and process package tourists in one end and out the other.

Some hotels offer discounts to government employees, Peace Corps volunteers, the military and business people.

Outer Islands
Few of the outer islands have hotels or guesthouses for visitors. It's generally best to make some sort of arrangement for accommodation in advance through the island's mayor or chief magistrate. Although you could try doing it by mail before you go, it's often less confusing to just radio ahead through the governor's office in the district centre. Local airlines can also be helpful in arranging a place to stay on islands they service.

If you do just fly out to one of the islands or get off a boat somewhere, the local school principal might allow you to stay in the schoolhouse, especially if school's not in session. You could also approach the local mayor or chief or perhaps a Peace Corps volunteer.

Usually people are warm and friendly and will help you out. However, because islanders feel obligated to provide for visitors, foreigners can sometimes impose without realising it. Be careful not to take advantage of Micronesian hospitality.

While islanders readily welcome each other into their homes, it's a long-established system founded on reciprocity and kinship obligations and the casual visitor should not expect the same rights.

If you stay with a family you should offer them something, but unless money is requested, giving coffee, rice or other gifts is probably a more appropriate way to pay for your stay.

FOOD
Considering the geographic spread, it's surprising how similar the food is throughout Micronesia.

Western foods like hamburgers, sandwiches, fried chicken and steak are found on most menus. Almost equally as common is Japanese food, such as fresh sashimi, teriyaki and ramen. Breakfasts are typically Western style, with toast, eggs, bacon (or Spam!) and French toast.

Fish is plentiful, fresh and delicious throughout the islands. Grilled tuna is often one of the best and cheapest meals available.

On most of the islands restaurants are quite simple local eateries – don't expect to find quaint cafes, pastry shops or coffee bars.

Island Dishes
Fish, shellfish, coconuts, breadfruit, taro, tapioca and bananas are Micronesian staples. Traditional local dishes are not often served in restaurants, however, although mangrove crab and fried breadfruit find their way onto a few menus.

Breadfruit is prepared much like potatoes – either boiled, fried, mashed, roasted or baked. Preserved (fermented) breadfruit, which was traditionally a provision food for long canoe journeys, is definitely an acquired taste. Taro root is eaten baked or boiled, rather than smashed up into a Hawaiian-style poi.

Turkey tails are a really hot item, particularly in Chuuk and the Marshalls. You'll often see them amidst the hot dogs and reef fish on picnic barbecue grills.

Micronesians developed a taste for rice

The taro plant has broad leaves and a large
edible rootstock

during the Japanese era and it remains the
single largest imported food. Canned fish
and high-salt, high-fat canned meats are
other popular imported foods, as are chocolate chip cookies and candy bars. In grocery stores, banana cake mix may be easier
to find than bananas.

Dog is a popular food in Pohnpei, but
you don't have to worry much about having
it thrust upon you by surprise. It's regarded
as a speciality food, served primarily at
occasions such as funeral feasts.

Some of Micronesia's more exotic dishes
include crocodile (Palau), fruit bat, mangrove crab and coconut crab.

There's more food variety in Guam and
Saipan than in the rest of Micronesia. On
those islands it's easy to find spicy Chamorro food, good salad bars, Mexican food
and Korean, Chinese, Thai and other Asian
cuisines.

Fruit & Vegetables

If you've imagined a wild abundance of
exotic tropical fruits, you'll probably be
disappointed. You can buy bananas,
papayas and coconuts in local markets and
on a lucky day you might find citrus,
passion fruit, soursop or mangoes. But
despite year-round sun, many fruits in
Micronesia are seasonal and, unfortunately,
fresh fruit is rarely served in restaurants.
Families often grow just enough for their
own use and feed the surplus to their pigs,
so those sweet papayas you were hoping to
see on the breakfast menu might well be
going to the family porker instead.

Fresh vegetables, especially crisp salad
types, are scarce, as they're not part of the
typical Micronesian diet. Most vegetables
are imported, so the more remote the
island, the scarcer they are. What you do
find often looks ready for composting.

In Micronesia 'green salad' usually
refers to a small clump of shredded cab-
bage and occasionally some cucumber
slices, with a dribble of Thousand Island
salad dressing.

Self-Catering

There are grocery stores where you can buy
packaged and canned Western foods on all
the main islands. Although the selection
varies widely, on the larger islands it's generally quite extensive. Some islands also
have simple farmer's markets where you
can pick up fresh fruits and limited local
produce. When buying groceries, watch out
for wormy food and check the expiry dates.

DRINKS
Nonalcoholic Drinks

Tap water is safe in Guam and the Northern
Marianas, but it's more risky elsewhere in
Micronesia and it's a good idea to boil it
when you're unsure, or avoid it altogether.

Bottled water is usually available in
grocery stores throughout the islands. Soft
drinks, coffee and tea are easy to get almost
everywhere.

Although coconuts are plentiful, not
many travellers carry a machete with them
so they can whack one open any time they
find one! If you buy a coconut from a fruit
stall the vendor will open it for you. Otherwise, if you have a coconut that's already
husked, look for the three dots that resemble a face with two eyes and a mouth. It's
easy to poke a hole through the 'mouth'
with a pointy object to get to the juice
inside.

Alcohol

There are bars serving alcohol almost everywhere in Micronesia. Budweiser is truly the king of beers in Micronesia, though its reign is being challenged by Japanese and Australian beers. Most exciting of all is the new German-run micro-brewery on Saipan producing Taga beer, Micronesia's first native brew.

Among island drinks, *tuba*, which is labouriously made from coconut sap, is the most common.

Then there's *yeast*, which is coconut water or fruit juice mixed with sugar and baker's yeast. The fermenting takes place in the stomach and the high continues until the fermenting stops – up to 24 hours later. It's a cheap way to get drunk, though apparently not always a pleasant one.

OTHER HIGHS

Sakau, extracted from the roots of a pepper plant, is a mild narcotic that can give the drinker a mellow high. For the most part the mind stays clear and the body numbs up. These days in Micronesia it's only available in Pohnpei, where sakau bars still outnumber alcohol bars two to one.

Betel nut is readily available in Yap and Palau and anywhere else there are Yapese and Palauans. Unlike places in Asia where it's chewed dry and brown, Micronesians like it green, mixed with a little lime and wrapped in a pepper leaf. It produces a very mild short-lived high.

There's still debate as to whether Peace Corps volunteers introduced marijuana to Micronesia or whether Micronesian students returning home from school in the USA brought the first seeds. One way or the other its cultivation is now common on some islands. Attitudes toward marijuana use vary from place to place, but the possession of marijuana is illegal everywhere.

THINGS TO BUY

Micronesia has less of a variety of handicrafts than you'd probably expect, although there's some fine basketwork and weaving to be found on many of the islands.

Yap has some of the most interesting traditional crafts, including hibiscus fibre skirts and other functional items still used by the Yapese. The Marshall Islands have stick charts and high-quality baskets; Palau has intricately carved wooden storyboards; and Chuuk has carved love sticks and masks. The Northern Marianas and Guam are devoid of any real native handicrafts.

Things Not to Buy

Sea turtle shells make beautiful jewellery – too beautiful, in fact, for the welfare of the turtles. Although the islanders have taken turtles for subsistence purposes for centuries, a combination of driftnetting and worldwide demand for the ornamental shells has thrown sea turtles onto the endangered species list. Tortoise shell jewellery, as well as the whole shells, are prohibited entry into the USA, Canada, Australia and most other countries.

The importation of black coral is likewise banned in more than 100 countries. The purchase of other corals, which are often dynamited from their fragile reef ecosystem and sold in chunks or made into jewellery, should also give pause to the environmentally conscious. ■

Some of the best wood carvings in Micronesia are those of marine animals made by the Kapingamarangi islanders on Pohnpei. Gourmet pepper and island-made coconut soaps and oils are other Pohnpeian specialities. The Marshalls, FSM and Palau sell their own colourful postage stamps, which make lightweight souvenirs.

Getting There & Away

AIR

The main air gateways into Micronesia are Honolulu and Guam but there are also direct flights to the Marshall Islands and Pohnpei from the South Pacific, and to Saipan and Palau from Asia.

Air Passes

The standard Circle Pacific and Round the World air passes are of limited value in exploring Micronesia as the only Micronesian island that is currently included in any of those passes is Guam.

Continental Micronesia, which maintains a monopoly on flights between most of the islands, offers a Circle Micronesia airfare and a Visit Micronesia pass. Neither are an exceptional value, so check your desired itinerary carefully to determine the best airfare option. If you're travelling with a spouse, for example, discounts offered under Continental Micronesia's family plan may well work out better and have fewer restrictions.

Circle Micronesia Circle Micronesia airfares are round-trip tickets that originate in Los Angeles or San Francisco and allow travel on Continental Micronesia's island-hopper route through Micronesia.

The base fare depends on your turn-around point; if it's Guam, the base fare is $1230; if it's Saipan, it's $1280; if it's Yap, it's $1500; and if it's Palau, it's $1650.

On all routes, intermediate stops can include Honolulu, Majuro, Kwajalein, Kosrae, Pohnpei, Chuuk and Guam. Four stopovers are allowed for the base fare. Additional intermediate stops are $50 per stop. The tickets are valid year round and are applicable for a maximum stay of six months. Reservations and ticketing must be made seven days prior to departure. There are restrictions and fees for changes and cancellations.

Visit Micronesia Continental Micronesia offers a Visit Micronesia pass, which starts and ends in Guam and allows travel to Saipan, Palau, Chuuk and Yap for a set fee; Pohnpei can be added for an additional charge.

The pass must be purchased outside Guam in conjunction with an international ticket to Guam; purchasers cannot be citizens of Guam. Travel on the pass must commence within 60 days of arrival in Guam, while the pass itself is valid for 30 days.

The price is the same throughout the year, but differs according to the originating country. The cost for the four-island pass is $625 for passengers coming from Australia, New Zealand, Asia, Europe or Africa and $655 for those coming from North or South America. If you want to add on Pohnpei, the cost is $775 or $812 respectively.

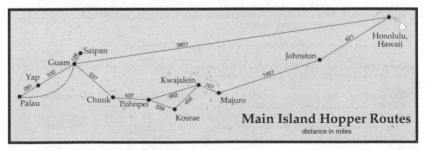

Main Island Hopper Routes
distance in miles

Air Travel Glossary

Apex Apex ('advance purchase excursion') is a discounted ticket which must be paid for in advance. There are penalties if you wish to change it.

Baggage Allowance This will be written on your ticket: usually one 20 kg item to go in the hold, plus one item of hand luggage.

Bucket Shop An unbonded travel agency specialising in discounted airline tickets.

Bumped Just because you have a confirmed seat doesn't mean you're going to get on the plane – see Overbooking.

Cancellation Penalties If you have to cancel or change an Apex ticket there are often heavy penalties involved; insurance can sometimes be taken out against these penalties. Some airlines impose penalties on regular tickets as well, particularly against 'no show' passengers.

Check-In Airlines ask you to check in a certain time ahead of the flight departure (usually two hours on international flights). If you fail to check in on time and the flight is overbooked the airline can cancel your booking and give your seat to somebody else.

Confirmation Having a ticket written out with the flight and date you want doesn't mean you have a seat until the agent has checked with the airline that your status is 'OK' or confirmed. Meanwhile you could just be 'on request'.

Discounted Tickets There are two types of discounted fares – officially discounted (see Promotional Fares) and unofficially discounted. The lowest prices often impose drawbacks like flying with unpopular airlines, inconvenient schedules, or unpleasant routes and connections. A discounted ticket can save you other things than money – you may be able to pay Apex prices without the associated Apex advance booking and other requirements. Discounted tickets only exist where there is fierce competition.

Full Fares Airlines traditionally offer 1st class (coded F), business class (coded J) and economy class (coded Y) tickets. These days there are so many promotional and discounted fares available from the regular economy class that few passengers pay full economy fare.

Lost Tickets If you lose your airline ticket an airline will sometimes treat it like a travellers' cheque and, after inquiries, issue you another one. In the USA, airlines often require you to purchase a new ticket and then if your old ticket hasn't been used within a certain number of months they will refund your ticket price minus an administrative fee. Legally, however, an airline is entitled to treat the ticket like cash and if you lose it then it's gone forever. Take good care of your tickets.

No Shows No shows are passengers who fail to show up for their flight, sometimes because of unexpected delays or disasters, sometimes because they simply forget, sometimes because they made more than one booking and didn't bother to cancel the one they didn't want. Full fare passengers who fail to turn up are sometimes entitled to travel on a later flight. The rest of us are penalised (see Cancellation Penalties).

On Request An unconfirmed booking for a flight (see Confirmation).

Open Jaws A return ticket where you fly out to one place but return from another. If available this can save you backtracking to your arrival point.

Overbooking Airlines hate to fly empty seats and since every flight has some passengers who fail to show up (see No Shows) airlines often book more passengers than they have seats. Usually the excess passengers balance those who fail to show up but occasionally somebody gets bumped. If this happens guess who it is most likely to be? The passengers who check in late.

Promotional Fares Officially discounted fares like Apex fares which are available from travel agents or direct from the airline.

Reconfirmation At least 72 hours prior to departure time of an onward or return flight you must contact the airline and 'reconfirm' that you intend to be on the flight. If you don't do this the airline can delete your name from the passenger list and you could lose your seat. You don't have to reconfirm the first flight on your itinerary or if your stopover is less than 72 hours. It doesn't hurt to reconfirm more than once.

Restrictions Discounted tickets often have various restrictions on them – advance purchase is the most usual one (see Apex). Others are restrictions on the minimum and maximum period you must be away, such as a minimum of 14 days or a maximum of one year. See Cancellation Penalties.

Standby A discounted ticket where you only fly if there is a seat free at the last moment. Standby fares are usually only available on domestic routes.

Tickets Out An entry requirement for many countries is that you have an onward or return ticket, in other words, a ticket out of the country. If you're not sure what you intend to do next, the easiest solution is to buy the cheapest onward ticket to a neighbouring country or a ticket from a reliable airline which can later be refunded if you do not use it.

Transferred Tickets Airline tickets cannot be transferred from one person to another. Travellers sometimes try to sell the return half of their ticket, but officials can ask you to prove that you are the person named on the ticket. This is unlikely to happen on domestic flights, but on an international flight tickets may be compared with passports.

Travel Agencies Travel agencies vary widely and you should ensure you use one that suits your needs. Some simply handle tours while full-service agencies handle everything from tours and tickets to car rental and hotel bookings. A good one will do all these things and can save you a lot of money but if all you want is a ticket at the lowest possible price, then you really need an agency specialising in discounted tickets. A discounted ticket agency, however, may not be useful for other things, like hotel bookings.

Travel Periods Some officially discounted fares, Apex fares in particular, vary with the time of year. There is often a low (off-peak) season and a high (peak) season. Sometimes there's an intermediate or shoulder season as well. At peak times, when everyone wants to fly, not only will the officially discounted fares be higher but so will unofficially discounted fares or there may simply be no discounted tickets available. Usually the fare depends on your outward flight – if you depart in the high season and return in the low season, you pay the high-season fare. ■

There's also a variation of the pass that allows travel beginning and ending in Saipan for the same price.

Micronesian-Based Airlines

The phone numbers for the main airlines based in Micronesia are:

Continental Micronesia
    Canada (☎ 800-231-0856)
    Guam (☎ 647-6453)
    Hong Kong (☎ 852-525-7759)
    Indonesia (☎ 361-287774)
    Japan (☎ 03-3592-1631)
    Korea (☎ 773-0100)

    Philippines (☎ 2-818-8701)
    Taiwan (☎ 2-719-5947)
    USA (☎ 800-231-0856)
Air Marshall Islands (AMI)
    Fiji (☎ 72-2192)
    Kiribati (☎ 28088)
    Marshall Islands (☎ 625-3733)
    Tuvalu (☎ 20737)
    USA (☎ 800-543-3898; in Honolulu ☎ 949-5522)

To/From the USA

Island Hopping Continental Micronesia is the only airline that island hops between Honolulu and Guam. The route is as follows: Honolulu, Johnston, Majuro, Kwajalein, Kosrae, Pohnpei, Chuuk and Guam.

The island hopper flights leave Honolulu for Guam at 6.30 am on Mondays, Wednesdays and Fridays, crossing the International Date Line before arriving at Majuro, the first destination where civilians can disembark. Coming from Honolulu, you lose a day, arriving one day later than you leave. (The island hopper going east to Honolulu leaves Guam at 8.20 am on Mondays, Wednesdays and Fridays.)

The plane refuels on Johnston but no stopovers are permitted on this small, flat coral island which is shaped like an aircraft carrier. Nuclear testing was carried out on Johnston Island after WW II and it now serves as a site for the destruction of chemical munitions. With its incinerators and drab barracks, it has quite a foreboding appearance.

Kwajalein is another military base and home to the airfield visitors use if they're going to Ebeye Island.

The one-way island hopper fare that allows all stopovers between Honolulu and Guam costs $651. Continental Micronesia's family plan allows an accompanying spouse to pay $480.

The same ticket between Los Angeles or San Francisco and Guam costs about $140 more, allows a stopover in Honolulu and is valid for one year. These island hopper tickets are unrestricted so you can leave your departure dates open or change them at will.

It costs about $30 more to have Saipan added on to the island hopper tickets.

If you're going the full distance you'll definitely save money by buying the island hopper as opposed to point-to-point tickets. For example, Honolulu to Majuro costs $577, just $74 less than the whole island hopper route to Guam.

For non-Micronesia residents, the only discount fares on the one-way tickets are through the family plan, which allows a 25% discount for an accompanying spouse and a 33% discount for children.

For people who reside in Micronesia,

there are hefty discounts on most point-to-point routes, some as high as 50%. For example, the regular one-way fare between Guam and Pohnpei is $370, though Micronesia residents pay only $180. The regular one-way fare between Guam and Palau is $320, while locals pay $166.

Many of Continental's overseas agents aren't all that familiar with Continental Micronesia's various fares and may tell you there is no family plan on the island hopper etc so you need to be persistent. If you're not satisfied with the answers you get, call back and get another agent.

Once you're finally flying with Continental Micronesia you'll find a certain down-home quality quite in touch with Micronesian flavour. If you island hop you'll see the same faces over and over again, and half the people on the flights always seem to know each other.

Honolulu to Majuro In addition to Continental Micronesia flights, Air Marshall Islands (AMI) flies between Honolulu and Majuro on Tuesdays, Thursdays and Sundays, stopping in Kwajalein on the way.

The Honolulu-Majuro fare is a bit cheaper with AMI: $563 one way, or $597 return with a seven-day advance purchase.

Direct to Guam Continental flies nonstop between Honolulu and Guam at least once a day. One-way tickets cost $459 Monday to Thursday and $495 on the weekend. Using the family plan, an accompanying spouse pays $344. Direct flights from Los Angeles to Guam cost from $709 one way. With the family plan, the spouse pays $549.

Northwest flies from Honolulu to Guam, via Tokyo or Nagoya, for $465 one way, and from Los Angeles for $709 one way.

United Airlines flies daily between Honolulu and Guam via Osaka with a one-way fare of $511 from Honolulu and $743 from Los Angeles or San Francisco.

Continental, Northwest and United offer round-trip excursion tickets to Guam for around $825 from Honolulu and $1100

Flight Times

Honolulu-Johnston	2 hours 5 minutes
Johnston-Majuro	3 hours 10 minutes
Majuro-Kwajalein	50 minutes
Kwajalein-Kosrae	1 hour 10 minutes
Kosrae-Pohnpei	1 hour
Pohnpei-Chuuk	1 hour 10 minutes
Chuuk-Guam	1½ hours
Guam-Yap	1 hour 25 minutes
Yap-Koror	50 minutes
Guam-Koror	1 hour 55 minutes
Guam-Saipan	35 minutes
Guam-Honolulu (direct)	7½ hours ∎

from the US West Coast. The tickets are valid for up to one year and return dates can be kept open.

Although the tickets originating on the West Coast allow a stopover in Honolulu, these excursion tickets don't allow for any island hopping through Micronesia. If you want to island hop one way and return on a direct flight, you need to piece together two one-way tickets.

Between Guam & Palau

You can continue from Guam to Yap and Palau (Koror) via Continental Micronesia.

The regular economy fare on a return ticket from Guam to Palau, with a stopover in Yap, is $544, while the full one-way fare from Guam to Palau, with a stopover in Yap, is $320.

As the main discount fares on these routes are now restricted to Micronesia residents, the best way for foreign visitors to beat these prices will probably be to have Yap and Palau added on to their original ticket to Micronesia.

In this scenario, Palau would be the final destination of a longer routed ticket, such as one starting from Los Angeles or Honolulu. As an example, the island hopper from Honolulu to Guam costs $651, while the same ticket ending in Palau is $804. On the return, a direct flight from Palau to Honolulu (en route Yap stopover allowed) would cost $668, versus the Guam-Honolulu direct fare of $459. When ticketed this way the additional airfare to Yap

and Palau would cost $362, as opposed to purchasing a separate $544 excursion ticket from Guam.

To/From Indonesia

Continental Airlines flies between Bali and Guam four days a week. The one-way fare is $463. An excursion ticket allowing a stay of up to 90 days costs $584 in the low season and $699 in the high.

To/From Hong Kong

Continental Airlines flies from Hong Kong to Guam three days a week. The one-way fare is $424, the return fare $672. For the same fare you can also fly from Hong Kong to Saipan.

Northwest Airlines flies daily from Hong Kong to Guam via Tokyo for $481 one way, or $667 with a 45-day excursion ticket.

To/From the Philippines

Continental Airlines flies daily from Manila to Guam; on Tuesdays, Thursdays and Saturdays the flight stops en route in Palau. The one-way fare from Manila to Guam is $422. An excursion ticket, valid for two to 45 days, costs $520. Both tickets allow a stopover in Palau.

Continental flies between Cebu City and Guam on Mondays, Wednesdays and Fridays with a one-way fare of $446 and a return fare of $542 to $671, depending upon the season.

For flights between Manila and Palau, Continental charges $210 one way, double that return.

Continental flies nonstop Manila-Saipan flights four days a week, with a one-way fare of $457 and an excursion fare of $551.

Air Nauru has a once a week red-eye flight between Guam and Manila for $430 return. The flight continues on to Pohnpei, with the Pohnpei-Manila fare $383 each way.

To/From Japan

There are numerous daily flights from Japan to Saipan and Guam.

There are daily flights from Tokyo on Japan Air Lines, Northwest Airlines and Continental; from Osaka on Japan Air Lines, Continental and United Airlines; and from Nagoya on Continental and Japan Air Lines. There's also regular but less frequent service from other ports in Japan including Sapporo, Sendai and Fukuoka.

Return fares from Japan begin around $700 for midweek travel with a 14-day advance purchase and a 30-day stay. The one-way fare with no restrictions is $686. Travel in the opposite direction is much cheaper – $331/430 one way/return from Saipan or Guam to Tokyo, Osaka or Nagoya.

If you're travelling around Asia and want to stop in Japan on your way to Guam (or elsewhere in Micronesia), try to get a through ticket before you arrive in Japan so you don't get stuck having to buy a ticket at inflated prices there.

Reservations are almost impossible to make around the time of Japan's New Year's vacation (Christmas through the first week of January), the Golden Week period (the last week of April and the first week of May) and during Obon (August), as almost all the seats are pre-booked for package tours during these holiday times.

If you're heading to the USA from Japan, or vice versa, island hopping through Micronesia is a great alternative to a nonstop transpacific flight!

To/From Korea

Continental Airlines flies daily between Seoul and Guam. The fare is $353 one way, or $586 for a 45-day excursion ticket.

Continental also flies from Seoul to Saipan four days a week for $329 one way and from $586 for a 45-day excursion ticket.

Korean Air Lines flies from Seoul to Guam daily with a one-way fare of $402 and a 45-day excursion ticket for $586.

To/From Taiwan

Continental Airlines flies between Taipei and Guam daily except on Tuesdays. The one-way fare is $365, while a 45-day excursion ticket costs $551 in the low season and $679 in the high. The Sunday flight stops in Palau en route to Guam. Continental also flies twice a week from Kaohsiung to Guam.

To/From the South Pacific

Air Marshall Islands flies to Majuro from Nandi (Fiji) via Funafuti (Tuvalu) and Tarawa (Kiribati) on Thursdays and Saturdays. The fare between Tarawa and Majuro is $193 one way, or $321 on an excursion ticket. The fare between Funafuti and Majuro is $459 one way, or $738 on an excursion ticket. The fare between Nandi and Majuro is $647 one way, or $894 on an excursion ticket. Excursion tickets require a seven-day advance purchase and allow a maximum stay of 23 days.

Air Nauru has on-again-off-again routes to a few Micronesian islands from Nauru. Currently there's a once a week flight between Nauru and Pohnpei for $217. You can also fly via Nauru between Pohnpei and Fiji for $444 one way.

To/From Australia

Continental Airlines flies nonstop between Guam and Sydney on Sundays, Tuesdays and Thursdays. The fare from Sydney is A$972 one way and A$1150 return on an excursion ticket that's valid for a stay of up to 90 days.

Air Nauru flies between Guam and Sydney, with an excursion fare of US$921.

SEA

Although there are inter-island boats within Micronesia, it's rare to find any sort of passenger vessel going to Micronesia from other countries, save for the occasional private yacht.

TOURS

Conventional sightseeing package tours in Micronesia are largely limited to tours from Japan geared for Japanese tourists.

There are a number of diving and

Banana stalk

Plumeria

Torch ginger

Hibiscus

Heliconia

Wild orchid

Schoolchildren at Lelu Ruins, Kosrae

Chuukese children

Bathing in the Winchon River in Weno, Chuuk

Produce seller in Weno Market, Chuuk

Mwaramwar head wreath, Kosrae

Yapese boys

speciality tours to Micronesia, however. If diving is your main focus, some of the dive holiday packages might work out a bit cheaper than if you were to piece together the dives and hotels by yourself, especially if you want to stay in more upscale hotels. The following prices do not include airfare, except where noted, and are based on double occupancy.

Tropical Adventures (☎ 206-441-3483, 800-247-3483, fax 206-441-5431), 111 Second Ave North, Seattle, WA 98109, arranges dive vacations in Chuuk, Palau, Pohnpei and Yap. For $749 you can have five days of diving with Fish 'N Fins in Palau, including six nights at the Palau Marina Hotel, or five days of diving with Blue Lagoon in Chuuk, staying six nights at the Truk Continental Hotel. For $1355 there's a trip that takes in both Palau and Chuuk, with nine days of diving.

The PADI Travel Network offers dive trips to Palau, Chuuk and Yap. Three days of diving in Palau and four nights at the Palau Pacific Hotel cost $629, while a week at the Truk Continental Hotel in Chuuk and six days of diving costs $848. The tours can be booked through PADI offices worldwide, including those in the USA (☎ 800-729-7234, fax 714-540-2983) and Australia (☎ 2-417-2800, fax 2-417-1434).

Sea Safaris (☎ 310-546-9299, 800-545-9524), 3770 Highland Ave, Suite 102, Manhattan Beach, CA 90266, and See & Sea Travel Service (☎ 415-434-3400, 800-348-9778, fax 415-434-3409), 50 Francisco St, Suite 205, San Francisco, CA 94133, also offer dive packages in Micronesia.

Oceanic Society Expeditions (☎ 415-441-1106, 800-326-7491), Fort Mason Center, Building E, San Francisco, CA 94123, the travel arm of the environmental group Friends of the Earth, leads a nine-day tour to Palau each summer, with an emphasis on Palauan culture, snorkelling and boat tours of the Rock Islands. The cost is $2390, including airfare from Honolulu, accommodation at the Palau Marina Hotel and picnic lunches.

University Research Expeditions (☎ 510-642-6586, fax 510-642-6791), University of California, Berkeley, CA 94720, has a programme each September in which participants assist biologists in field work in Palau's marine lakes. The cost is $1695 for an 11-day outing, which includes camping on the Rock Islands.

Valor Tours (☎ 415-332-7850), Box 1617, Schoonmaker Building, Sausalito, CA 94965, plans guided tours for WW II veterans who want to revisit islands and battle sites where they fought during the war.

Live-Aboard Dive Boats

The SS *Thorfinn* and the *Truk Aggressor*, based in Chuuk Lagoon, and the *Sun Dancer* and *Palau Aggressor*, based in Palau, are live-aboard dive boats with set rates that include diving, accommodation and meals. They can be booked directly or through Tropical Adventures, Sea Safaris and travel agents. Details on the boats are in the Chuuk and Palau chapters.

LEAVING MICRONESIA

Departure taxes are $5 in Pohnpei, $10 in Palau, Kosrae and Chuuk and $15 in Majuro. Guam and the Commonwealth of the Northern Marianas have no departure taxes.

WARNING

The information in this chapter is particularly vulnerable to change: prices for international travel are volatile, routes are introduced and cancelled, schedules change, special deals come and go, and rules and visa requirements are amended. Airlines and governments seem to take a perverse pleasure in making price structures and regulations as complicated as possible. You should check directly with the airline or a travel agent to make sure you understand how a fare (and ticket you may buy) works.

The upshot of this is that you should get opinions, quotes and advice from as many airlines and travel agents as possible before you part with your hard-earned cash. The details given in this chapter should be regarded as pointers and are not a substitute for your own careful, up-to-the-minute research.

Getting Around

AIR

Continental Micronesia links Micronesia's eight major district centres of Majuro, Kosrae, Pohnpei, Chuuk, Guam, Saipan, Yap and Palau.

Some island groups have domestic airlines connecting the district centres with their outer islands. The government-supported Air Marshall Islands (AMI) is by far the most extensive, linking every inhabited Marshallese atoll. One-way fares range from $24 to $261.

Pacific Missionary Aviation (PMA) links Pohnpei with the outer islands of Pingelap and Mokil. On Yap, PMA flies between Yap Proper and the outer islands of Ulithi, Fais and Woleai. One-way fares range from $60 to $150.

On Palau, Paradise Air flies a six-seater Cessna from Koror to the outer islands of Peleliu and Angaur. Their fares are very reasonable ($24 and $30 respectively) and they provide one of the best views in Micronesia, as they overfly the Rock Islands on the way.

In the Marianas, two small commuter airlines, Freedom Air and Pacific Island Aviation, fly between Guam, Rota, Saipan and Tinian, charging from $25 to $55 a flight.

More detailed information on these flights is provided in the respective island sections.

Island Airlines

The following airlines have services within Micronesia:

Air Marshall Islands (AMI)
Majuro	☎ 625-3733
Kwajalein	☎ 2416
Ebeye	☎ 329-3036

Continental Micronesia
Majuro	☎ 625-3209
Kosrae	☎ 370-3024
Pohnpei	☎ 320-2424
Chuuk	☎ 330-2424
Yap	☎ 350-2127
Palau	☎ 488-2448
Guam	☎ 647-6453
Saipan	☎ 234-6491
Rota	☎ 532-0397

Freedom Air
Guam	☎ 646-6527
Saipan	☎ 234-8328
Rota	☎ 532-3800
Tinian	☎ 433-3288

Pacific Island Aviation
Guam	☎ 647-3600
Rota	☎ 532-0397
Saipan	☎ 288-0770
Tinian	☎ 433-3600

Pacific Missionary Aviation (PMA)
Pohnpei	☎ 320-2796
Yap	☎ 350-2360

Paradise Air
Koror, Palau	☎ 488-2348

LAND

Most of the major islands have fairly extensive road systems. Usually the main drag around town and the road out to the airport are paved but beyond that it varies, and unpaved roads are as common as not.

In some places you can just cruise along, while in others roads are little more than pitted washed-out obstacle courses, challenging you to get through without bottoming out. To challenge you even further, car agencies often rent low-riding compact cars in dubious mechanical condition.

Bus

A fledgling public bus system operates on Guam. The next closest thing to a public bus system in Micronesia is on Yap, where the school buses will take visitors between Colonia and outlying villages twice a day on a space-available basis.

Taxi

Majuro gets the prize for its inexpensive system of shared taxis that cruise up and down the main road, making it one of the easiest places in Micronesia to visit without having to rent a car. As long as the taxi is not full, it can be waved down and another passenger taken on. Rates are charged for each person according to their own destination, and are as low as 30 cents.

Weno Island (Chuuk) also has an efficient shared taxi system, with rides usually given in the back of pick-up trucks. You can go anywhere around the island on the main roads for a dollar or less.

Pohnpei has a taxi system of minivans, though fares are not a bargain. It costs $1 for in-town rides and up to $30 for rides to out-of-the-way places.

Yap, Koror (Palau), Saipan and Guam have private taxis. Rates are quite reasonable in Yap and a bit more expensive in Palau, while those in Saipan and Guam are comparable to fares in the USA or Australia.

Car & Motorbike

Rental cars are available on the major islands, though they occasionally book out completely during busy times.

The minimum rates range from $35 to $45 per day and there's usually no mileage charge. The cars are seldom more than three years old but then again, between the salt air and the rough roads, that's about their average life expectancy.

Because most cars are rented on a 24-hour basis, you can get two days usage by renting at midday and driving around all afternoon, then heading out in a different direction the next morning before the car is due back.

Major car rental chains operate in Guam and the Northern Marianas and cars can easily be booked in advance from their overseas offices. This is a good idea as otherwise you may find the cheaper cars already rented out when you arrive. Unless you have a pre-paid deal, there are no cancellation penalties.

Upon renting a car you should check it over carefully and note on the contract any major scratches, dents or other damage before you drive away, to avoid hassles when you return the car. Also check the condition of the tyres – it's common to get

a car with dangerously bald tyres (and there are often contract clauses that hold you responsible for tyre damage!).

On some on the lesser developed islands it's hard to find cars with collision insurance. It's a mixed bag – you save a few bucks, but as the person at one rental booth told us: 'you hit it, you buy it'.

Motorbike The only Micronesian island that consistently has had motorbike rentals over the years is Saipan, but unfortunately they're generally at exorbitant hourly rates that surpass those of car rentals.

Road Rules Throughout Micronesia, driving is on the right side of the road, as it is in the USA. Other US traffic laws generally apply, including stopping for school buses (for traffic in both directions) when the bus lights are flashing.

Throughout Micronesia your home driving licence is acceptable for at least 30 days, although if your licence is not in English it's a good idea to also bring an international driver's licence.

Bicycle

Cycling is not a common way for visitors to get around in Micronesia. The only island that currently has any bicycle rental shop is Guam, but unfortunately Guam also has some of the worst traffic conditions.

Guesthouses on Peleliu and Angaur occasionally have bicycle rentals available, which is a great way to get around those islands.

Hitching

Hitching is never entyrely safe in any country in the world, and we don't recommend it. Travellers who decide to hitch should understand that they are taking a small but potentially serious risk. People who do choose to hitch will be safer if they travel in pairs and let someone know where they are planning to go.

All the usual hitchhiking safety precautions apply, especially for women, but with the exception of Guam, getting lifts in Micronesia is not terribly difficult.

SEA

Field Trip Ships

Field trip ships link several of Micronesia's district centres with the outer islands, carrying both supplies and passengers and loading copra for the return journeys. Few travellers take them, but they're a fantastic way to meet local people and to travel to the remote corners of Micronesia where the most traditional lifestyles prevail. They're also one of the cheapest ways of travelling in Micronesia.

Ships leave from Majuro in the Marshalls and from the FSM islands of Weno (Chuuk), Pohnpei and Yap Proper.

Some of the routes have the ships out for weeks, while the shorter routes, such as Pohnpei to Pingelap, take only a few days. You can get lists of departure dates in advance, but they shouldn't be taken too seriously as the ships often run behind schedule. Occasionally they'll skip a sailing altogether or even go into dry dock for months at a time.

Be prepared for a hardy and rugged travel experience – these are working ships, not cruise ships, and the boats tend to get grubby after a few days of crowded human habitation.

The field trip ships have both deck class and a handful of simple cabins. Priority for the cabins is generally given to government officials, village elders and those with medical needs. Even if you manage to book a cabin, you may get bumped if someone with more authority decides they need it at the last moment.

Deck class passengers should board the boat early and mark out a spot on deck as soon as they get on the ship. Guard your spot until the boundaries are established with your new neighbours, as extended families travelling together will have no qualms about moving unattended gear out of the way.

It's a good idea to befriend all sorts of passengers, as Micronesians are generally quite hospitable once they get to know you and can be incredibly helpful if they learn that you're travelling to their island.

The meals served on board usually consist of monotonous dishes of rice, canned fish and canned meat so you'll probably want to bring at least some of your own food, as well as an adequate supply of water.

For more details, see the respective island sections.

Commuter Boats

Chuuk is unique for its extensive weekday system of commuter boats which bring people to Weno from the other islands in Chuuk Lagoon in the morning and return them to their home islands in the late afternoon.

Chuuk also has fishing boats that double as passenger carriers, running sporadically between Weno and some of the islands outside Chuuk Lagoon. These fishing boats don't really run on any schedule, so you have to catch them when they're in port.

Palau has government boats that take passengers from Koror to Peleliu and Angaur a few times a week and to Kayangel and various points on the island of Babeldaob less frequently.

The fares for all these public boats are quite reasonable, generally just a few dollars.

In addition, there's a private ferry service that runs daily between Saipan and Tinian for $20.

Speedboats

There are lots of private speedboats in Micronesia which commute back and forth between islands within the same lagoon. Depending on how rough the seas are, traffic sometimes crosses open ocean to neighbouring islands as well.

Hitching a ride on one of these boats is not all that difficult if you're friendly and offer a few dollars to help pay for the petrol. Just go down to the docks and ask around.

Republic of the Marshall Islands

The Marshalls consist of more than a thousand small coral islands. They are particularly narrow and they are all, without exception, flat. Most can be walked across in a couple of minutes.

The Marshall Islands have little fertile topsoil and are devoid of rivers. Aside from coconuts, pandanus and breadfruit, few crops grow in the salty sand of most atolls, so the Marshallese long ago turned to the sea for their resources. They became, by absolute necessity, expert fishers and navigators.

The Marshalls had little to tempt Western settlers or conquerors and because they hadn't much food, water or wood to offer, even whalers and explorers never stayed long.

It wasn't until the 20th century that the outside world found that the remoteness of these scattered islands fit their own designs. Between the two world wars the Japanese used the Marshall Islands as an anchor to lay claim to the central Pacific. After ousting the Japanese, the Americans found the isolation of the Marshalls ideally suited for the testing of nuclear weapons. In the 67 nuclear bomb tests that took place in the post-war years, islands were vaporised, entire atolls contaminated and scores of Marshallese became nuclear guinea pigs.

Although the bomb tests have stopped, the Marshallese are still grappling with the lingering effects of radiation, and entire communities remain isolated from their homelands.

Majuro, the capital of the Marshall Islands, is quite Westernised, rather overcrowded and by no means a resort area. Most of the outer islands, however, still

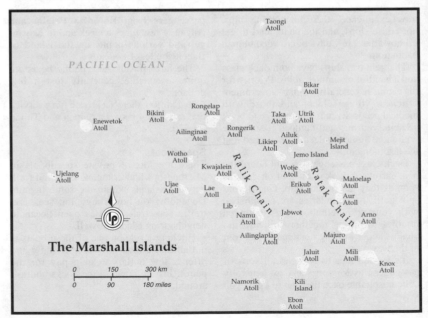

The Marshall Islands

Stick Charts

The low elevation of the Marshalls and the distances between the atolls make them particularly difficult to sight from the sea. In travels between islands, early inhabitants learned to read the patterns of the waves by watching for swells which would show when land was ahead.

Stick charts were used to teach the secrets of navigation. They were made by tying flat strips of wood together in designs which imitated the wave patterns. Shells were then attached to these sticks to represent the islands.

Three kinds of charts were used. The *mattang* showed wave patterns around a single island or atoll and was used first to teach the basic techniques. The *medo* showed patterns around a small group of atolls and the *rebillit* mapped an entire chain, showing the relationships between the islands and the major ocean swells.

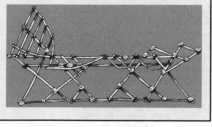

All the information contained on the stick charts was memorised and the charts themselves were not actually taken on journeys. Not many present-day Marshallese understand how to read stick charts, though due to their popularity as souvenirs many islanders can still make them. ■

retain the more pristine nature you'd expect to find in the tropical Pacific.

HISTORY

The Marshalls were never unified under a single leader, however one chief often controlled several atolls and at times the entire Ralik chain came under the reign of a single chief. Chiefs had absolute authority, although their wealth and power depended upon the loyalty and tribute payments made by commoners.

Living on such narrow stretches of sand, land control has always been an extremely important issue for the Marshallese. They married for land, went to war for land and, when all else failed, employed magic to get land.

Pandanus was an important food in the northern islands, breadfruit equally so in the south, while coconut production and fishing were important everywhere.

Because their islands are so widely scattered, the Marshallese developed some of the finest canoe-building and navigational skills in the Pacific.

European Contact

The Marshall Islands were off the main trade routes and consequently received few visits from early European explorers.

In 1525 a Spaniard named Alonso de Salazar became the first European to sight one of the islands. Although other Spanish expeditions landed in the Marshalls during the 1500s, Spain took little interest in the islands and did nothing to colonise the area.

The islands were named after the English sea captain John Marshall, who, in 1788, sighted Arno, Majuro, Aur, Maloelap, Wotje and Ailuk, and docked at Mili. His visit was probably the first made by Europeans in 200 years and the brief exchange between the British and the 'Marshallese' was friendly.

The Russian explorer Otto von Kotzebue made more thorough expeditions in the early 1800s and drew up the first detailed maps of the islands.

Whalers, Traders & Missionaries

Traders and whalers first showed up in the region in the early 1800s but they began to avoid the Marshalls after contact with the islanders turned violent. The 30-year period from the mid-1820s was a time of especially brutal attacks on European and American traders.

In case after case, ship officers putting into port at various atolls in the Marshalls recorded the death of a captain or crew members. Sometimes the scouting parties that went ashore completely disappeared and in the early 1850s the entire crews of three trading ships were massacred, one each at Namorik, Ebon and Jaluit.

Some of the fighting was prompted by the stealing of island women, while other incidents were essentially acts of revenge that followed earlier hostile encounters.

Violence was on the decline when the first Protestant missionaries to the Marshalls arrived on Ebon in 1857. The missionaries were at first welcomed, or at least tolerated, by the chiefs. Schools and churches were opened side by side and conversions came quickly. By the time the chiefs realised their traditional authority was being usurped by Western values and the Christian god, the missionaries had become well entrenched. Within a couple of decades Marshallese graduates of the mission schools were running most of the churches themselves.

German Period

Germany annexed the Marshalls in 1885, but didn't place government officials on the islands until 1906. Instead, island affairs were left to the Jaluit Gesellschaft, a group of powerful German trading companies.

Coconut plantations and copra facilities had been set up as far back as the 1860s, including a coconut oil factory on Ebon in 1861 and trading stations on Mili, Ebon, Jaluit, Namorik, Majuro and Aur atolls. These outposts were never highly lucrative for the Germans, but they did manage to make a narrow profit.

Japanese Period

The Japanese took control from 1914 and colonised the Marshalls extensively, developing and fortifying large bases on many of the islands.

They also took over the copra business, but unlike the Germans the Japanese sold copra directly to traders instead of going through local chiefs. This policy undermined, even further, the traditional authority of island chiefs.

WW II

The first Micronesian islands captured by the Americans in WW II were at Kwajalein Atoll in February 1944. The atoll's Roi-Namur Island, the main Japanese air base in the Marshalls, fell first, followed by Kwajalein Island with its almost-completed airstrip.

Majuro Atoll, which had been left undefended, was taken next and quickly developed into a base for aircraft carriers. From Majuro and the air base at Kwajalein, the USA staged attacks on the Caroline Islands.

The USA bypassed four Marshallese atolls still in Japanese hands, but within weeks had captured Enewetok Atoll and about 30 more Marshallese islands before continuing their westward naval assault across the central Pacific.

Americans & Atomic Bombs

After the war, the Americans immediately moved in and started atomic bomb experiments on Bikini and Enewetok atolls. Kwajalein Atoll was later established as a missile testing site.

Some of the islanders who breathed radioactive air or lived on contaminated land have since died from radiation-related ailments while others have lingering health problems. Many suspect that they were deliberately used as test subjects for monitoring radiation's long-term effects on humans.

Bikini Atoll Bikini, which was home to the earliest known habitation in Micronesia, was selected by President Truman, without the knowledge of a single Micronesian, as the site for the first peacetime explosion of the atomic bomb.

Early in 1946 the US military governor of the Marshalls met with the fervently religious Bikini islanders, following church services, to inform them that their islands were needed for 'a greater good'. After deliberations, Bikini's Chief Juda responded that if the USA wanted to use Bikini for the 'benefit of all mankind' his people would go elsewhere. Still awed by the US firepower which had recently defeated the Japanese Imperial Navy, the Bikinians felt in no position to baulk. The Americans were also well aware that challenging authority was contrary to the very fibre of Marshallese custom.

Bikini's 161 residents were relocated on the assurance they could move back once the tests were over. A few months later the USA exploded a nuclear device 500 feet over Bikini's lagoon, the first of 23 nuclear tests that would leave the islands uninhabitable, the Bikinians displaced and their society irreparably disrupted.

The Bikinians were first moved to Rongerik Atoll, a place of ill omen in Marshallese legend. They got sick from eating poisonous fish in the lagoon and nearly starved from inadequate food supplies. Two years later they were moved to Kwajalein Atoll and then later to Kili Island.

In the 1970s the Bikinians were told it was safe to move back home and a resettlement programme began. The Bikinians, who had been awaiting the day they could return, were shocked to find two entire islands blown away and most of the others treeless, blasted apart and covered with wreckage and debris. Nevertheless, they remained on Bikini and tried to get their lives back in order.

In 1978 US tests showed that by eating food grown in the caesium-contaminated soil the Bikinians had collected high levels of radioactivity in their bodies, so they were moved off Bikini again.

Scientists from the Lawrence Livermore Laboratory in California are using Bikini as a study in ways to clean up radiation. So far they've successfully used potassium fertiliser to block the uptake of caesium in plants, but there are still long-term problems with eating anything grown on the island.

The US Department of Energy currently has a couple dozen construction workers involved in cleaning up the main atoll islands, Eneu and Bikini. Eneu, which they use as a base, is currently considered safe, both by the Department of Energy and by independent scientists from Germany who

were hired by the Bikinians to test for radiation. Bikini Island, on the other hand, remains eight times more radioactive than Eneu and the final clean-up there will probably require removing all the current soil and replacing it with imported soil. The cost of that procedure alone is estimated to be about $200 million, nearly double the amount of money allocated for the entire clean-up project.

Eneu now looks like a construction site and has accommodation for the clean-up crews, but no houses. The Bikinians are reluctant to return if it means living on Eneu Island, as it's the far more appealing Bikini Island, with its beautiful beaches, that was always their primary settlement. They also feel the USA should be responsible for cleaning up the entire atoll, not just two islands.

Ironically, as the USA proceeds with the costly clean-up, the Marshallese government is considering the atoll as a possible dump site for nuclear waste! Nam Island, which is at the opposite end of the atoll from Eneu, is one proposed site, but there's even talk of utilising Bikini Island itself as a repository for commercial radioactive waste.

There are two award-winning documentary films on Bikini that are real eye-openers. *Radio Bikini*, produced by the Corporation for Public Broadcasting in 1988, is a compilation of historic footage on the events surrounding the exile of the Bikinians and the actual bomb tests. *Bikini: Forbidden Paradise*, produced by the ABC

Bikini

According to legend Bikini was the favourite island of Loa, creator of the Marshalls. Loa used the words *lia kwe!*, 'You are a rainbow', to describe Bikini. Eventually the term grew to describe anything lovely and is said to be the source of the current greeting *yokwe*.

In case you're wondering, the bikini swimsuit was originally named *atome* by its French designer, a year after the first atomic bomb tests at Bikini. ■

TV network in 1993, gives a contemporary account of conditions on Bikini, including some interesting underwater footage of the decommissioned warships sunk in the lagoon during the testing.

The ships, which include the US aircraft carrier *Saratoga* (complete with planes and racks of bombs), the battleships *Nagato* and *Arkansas* and several destroyers and cruisers, have in recent years been targeted as an exotic dive site. Logistics have thus far kept commercial diving proposals from materialising, but there's a keen interest; for the latest information contact the Bikini Liaison Office (☎ 625-3177), Box 1096, Majuro, MH 96960.

Enewetok Atoll Enewetok islanders were evacuated to Ujelang Atoll before atomic bomb tests began in 1948. Over a 10-year period 43 atomic bombs were detonated from Enewetok.

In 1980, after a $120 million clean-up programme, the islanders were allowed to return to Enewetok Island, in the southern part of the atoll.

Ten miles north of Enewetok is Runit Island, where contaminated items from the atoll were stashed under a huge 18-inch-thick concrete dome nicknamed Cactus Crater. The radiated debris and soil will supposedly be safe in 50,000 years. The concrete may last 300!

A 9.8-megaton hydrogen bomb which was exploded in 1958 on Enewetok was the focus of an extensive geological study conducted in the 1980s which showed the bomb had blasted a mile-wide, 200-foot-deep crater in the lagoon and fractured the rock to a depth of 1400 feet beneath the crater's surface. The geological impact of such massive bending and breaking of the earth's crust remains unknown.

Rongelap Atoll The immensely powerful hydrogen bomb 'Bravo' that exploded on Bikini in March 1954 sent clouds of deadly radioactivity toward inhabited Rongelap Atoll, 100 miles to the east. The fallout came down as powdered ash six hours after the blast.

Signs of radiation sickness including nausea, hair loss and severe burns occurred within hours, yet it wasn't until three days after the blast that the US military evacuated the 253 inhabitants of Rongelap to Kwajalein for decontamination. The Rongelapese were returned to their atoll in 1957.

The Rongelapese have continuing health problems that include high rates of mental retardation, leukemia, stillbirths and miscarriages. Almost 75% of the people who were under the age of 10 on the day of the blast have had surgery for thyroid tumors.

Despite an aerial survey showing that some of the islands of Rongelap were as 'hot' as islands in Bikini, and despite a ban placed on eating shellfish because of accumulated radiation, the USA insisted that Rongelap was safe and refused to help resettle the islanders.

In 1985 the Greenpeace ship *Rainbow Warrior* moved the Rongelapese to a new home on Mejato Island in Kwajalein Atoll, 110 miles to the south. (The boat was later sunk in New Zealand by French agents who hoped to stop the *Rainbow Warrior*'s activities aimed at ending nuclear testing in the South Pacific.)

Half Life, a film by Australian director Dennis O'Rourke, tells the plight of the islanders and convincingly presents a picture of the Rongelapese being used as nuclear guinea pigs. Some argue that the exposure to radioactivity was deliberately allowed for the purpose of experimentation, while others feel that US officials were simply so caught up in proceeding on schedule that the Rongelapese were more victims of expediency than intentional subjects.

In 1994 a US Congressional Committee reexamined the Bravo test and discredited the previously held US position that the Rongelapese were irradiated only because of an unexpected last-minute change in wind direction. Testimony by atomic energy officials revealed that the day before the bomb test US meteorologists reported that the winds had shifted in the direction of Rongelap and a warning had been issued

MARSHALL IS

that contamination of the islands would occur if the test were to proceed.

Utrik Atoll Although their plight is not as well known, the islanders of Utrik Atoll also received fallout from the Bravo test on Bikini and have similar radiation-related medical problems.

GEOGRAPHY
Of the 1225 islands and islets that comprise the Marshalls, only five are single islands. The rest are grouped into 29 coral atolls, which together comprise more than one-tenth of all atolls in the world.

The atolls run roughly north-south in two nearly parallel chains about 150 miles apart and 800 miles long. The eastern chain is called *Ratak* which means 'toward dawn' and the western chain is *Ralik*, 'toward sunset'.

Although the total land area is only 70 sq miles, the Marshall Islands are scattered across 750,000 sq miles of ocean. True to classic atoll form, the islands are narrow and low and encircle large central lagoons. The widest island, Wotje, is less than a mile across; the highest elevation, just 34 feet, is on the island of Likiep.

The southern islands have more vegetation than those in the north. Virtually all of them have gorgeous white sand beaches.

CLIMATE
In Majuro, the average daily temperature is 81°F (27°C). As the lowest temperatures occur during heavy rains, and most heavy rains fall during the day, night-time temperatures actually average a couple of degrees higher than daytime temperatures.

The northern Marshalls are quite dry, averaging just 20 inches of rain each year. Rainfall increases as you head south, with some islands getting up to 160 inches a year.

On Majuro, the wettest period is September through November, which averages about 14 inches of rain per month, while the driest period is January through March, which sees about eight inches of rain a month.

Full-blown tropical storms or typhoons are rare, but can be devastating when they whip across these low unprotected islands.

GOVERNMENT
Desiring to be politically independent of other Micronesian islands, the Marshallese took the initial steps of withdrawing from the Congress of Micronesia in 1973. Their constitution became effective on 1 May 1979.

As with other Trust Territory districts, the Marshallese signed a Compact of Free Association with the USA. The compact with the USA was not overwhelmingly popular, however. Almost 90% of the Bikinians voted against it, afraid the USA would use conditions of the compact to limit compensation and deny further responsibility for cleaning up Bikini. The compact passed in September 1983 with the approval of 58% of Marshallese voters and went into effect in 1986.

The Marshallese government is modelled after a combination of both the British

Marshall Islands Flag
The flag of the Republic of the Marshall Islands has a deep blue background which represents the sea. In the upper left is a star with 24 points representing the 24 municipalities. The four longest points represent the four district centres of Majuro, Ebeye, Jaluit and Wotje, and are also intended to symbolise the Christian cross.

The two-colour diagonal ray depicts the Marshalls' two parallel island chains: the sunrise chain Ratak in white and the sunset chain Ralik in orange. ∎

and US systems. The unicameral 33-member parliament, called Nitijela, meets in Majuro in January and August for a total of about 50 days each year. The Nitijela elects one of its members as president of the Marshall Islands. The current president, Amata Kabua, has held the office since 1979.

In addition to the elected offices there's a national Council of Iroij, comprised of hereditary tribal chiefs, which acts as an advisory board.

The Marshall Islands are divided into 24 municipalities, each of which has its own mayor and is represented by at least one senator in the Nitijela. The major district centres are Majuro, Ebeye, Wotje and Jaluit.

ECONOMY

The Marshallese economy is largely reliant on US funding; almost $40 million in annual compact grants accounts for about two-thirds of the island government's gross receipts. In addition the USA is paying $170 million rent for Kwajalein bases and $80 million for development projects on Kwajalein Atoll over a 30-year period.

In recent years the US Congress has also allocated $240 million to compensate victims of nuclear testing in return for their pledge to drop lawsuits against the US government. Some of the money was paid directly to individual victims via a special claims tribune that met in 1992, some is being distributed as an annual stipend to the still-displaced Bikinians and other money is set aside as an investment trust.

With a GDP of just $1922, the per capita income in the Marshalls remains the lowest in Micronesia and many islanders, particularly in Majuro, live in conditions of poverty.

What domestic industry does exist is small scale. Some locally generated income comes from copra production and handicrafts, though with little land available, the Marshallese are looking to the sea for a source of income.

Aquaculture projects are now underway on several islands. Giant clams obtained from Palau are being cultivated on Majuro, Likiep and Mili atolls. Oyster and black pearl cultivation are also being developed.

Less environmentally sound is an agreement with a Shanghai fishing operation that has about 75 long-line fishing boats harvesting tuna in Marshallese waters, taking about 750 tons annually. Ironically, the arrival of the Chinese might hurt the Marshallese economy more than help it, as the fledgling domestic fishing fleet, which consists of seven boats, has seen its own catches drop 50% since the Chinese arrived in late 1993.

Since independence, the government of the Marshall Islands has entertained a number of schemes for accepting waste from industrial nations. Some of the proposals have involved importing municipal garbage from the US West Coast, others toxic industrial waste from Asia, but none have yet to materialise.

In 1994 the government raised the ante by announcing its willingness to serve as a nuclear waste site, utilising islands already contaminated by nuclear testing as depositories. In exchange the Marshalls would receive an estimated $75 million a year, more than the nation's current annual budget. It appears to be the most calculated and serious dump site proposal yet made and has divided the Marshallese, who already have the world's highest incidence of nuclear-induced illnesses. It has also drawn the protest of scores of regional neighbours, including the FSM, who feel their own safety would be at stake since the nuclear waste would be transported by ship across the typhoon-prone Pacific and an accident could very well deposit the waste on their own shores.

Tourism remains very low-key in the Marshalls. Only about 6000 visitors arrive each year, and nearly half of those are business travellers. Some initial efforts are being made to expand tourism, especially among divers, but the government has instituted a new policy of greeting visitors at the airport with an on-the-spot $25 'visa' charge, which is giving mixed messages at best.

POPULATION & PEOPLE

The population of the Marshall Islands is approximately 52,000, with the majority of islanders living on Majuro and Kwajalein atolls.

Population growth has been a major problem, with the number of Marshallese doubling over the past 20 years, although family planning programmes seem to be slowing down the trend. Half of the population is under the age of 15.

More than 95% of the people living in the Marshalls are Marshallese. Many of the foreign residents are Americans, including quite a few former Peace Corps volunteers. There are also a number of Australians, including a small naval contingent that assists the Marshallese Coast Guard.

SOCIETY & CONDUCT

The Marshallese are a soft-spoken, good-natured people with a rich oral tradition of chants, songs and legends.

Marshallese society has always been a stratified one, and despite increasing Westernisation and the introduction of a moneyed economy, social status still comes as much from the kinship group a person is born into as it does from an individual's own economic achievement. Chiefs continue to wield a great deal of authority over land ownership and usage.

Men and young people generally wear Western-style clothing such as T-shirts and pants, while older women often wear loose-fitting floral print muu-muu dresses. Both women and girls keep their knees covered; most skirts are calf-length. On Majuro schoolchildren wear T-shirts of specific colours that identify their school.

Basketball is the most popular sport on Majuro. Children commonly play street versions of other Western games with rudimentary equipment like a stick and tennis ball substituting for a baseball and bat.

RELIGION

The Protestant 'Boston Mission' that started converting the Marshallese in the mid-1800s effectively wiped out the ancient religion of the islanders.

There are many Protestant sects in the Marshalls, including Congregationalist, Assembly of God, Baptist and Seventh-Day Adventist. There's also a large Catholic church, a Bahai centre, a Salvation Army mission and a rapidly growing Mormon presence.

LANGUAGE

Marshallese is the official language, but English is taught in schools and is widely understood. The islanders' gentleness is reflected in their traditional greeting *Yokwe yuk*, which means 'Love to you'. 'Thank you' is *Kommol tata*.

HOLIDAYS & FESTIVALS

Public holidays in the Marshalls include:

New Year's Day
  1 January
Nuclear Victims Day
  1 March

Health Problems

Much of Micronesian society has been traumatised by its exposure to Western culture. Dietary health problems in the Marshalls are among the most blatant examples.

Although the Marshallese eagerly took to a new diet heavy in processed sugars, genetically they have been unable to assimilate it. The sugar-laced cereals and soft drinks and the extensive variety of packaged junk food that crams supermarket shelves have left 35% of the population prone to diabetes. At Majuro's hospital, 75% of inpatients are diabetic. Other health problems of epidemic proportions include high blood pressure, alcoholism and radiation-related thyroid tumors.

Malnutrition is also severe. There have been cases of blindness from vitamin A deficiency, even though vitamin A-rich pandanus, papaya and pumpkins are locally grown. Rather than eating the produce, some families cart it off to the market and sell it to get money to buy more tantalising junk food. ■

Constitution Day
    1 May
Fisherman's Day
    1st Friday in July
Labor Day
    1st Friday in September
Culture Day
    last Friday in September
Independence Day
    21 October
President's Birthday
    17 November
Gospel Day
    1st Friday in December
Christmas
    25 December

Majuro school children celebrate Constitution Day by participating in numerous sporting events.

On Christmas Day people gather at the churches for a day of singing, dancing and skits.

Majuro has a number of fishing tournaments each year with the largest ones held on the weekend before the fourth Thursday in November and on the weekend closest to the 4th of July. Lots of islanders, expats and a growing number of international sports-fishing enthusiasts participate; yellowfin tuna commonly top out around 125 pounds and the record for Pacific Blue marlin is 407 pounds. For more information write to the Marshalls Billfish Club, Box 1139, Majuro, Marshall Islands 96960, or call Bill Graham at 625-7491.

Majuro Atoll

Most travellers to the Marshalls get only as far as Majuro Atoll, the nation's political and economic centre. The name Majuro means 'many eyes' and it has always been one of the more heavily settled Marshallese atolls.

The atoll has 57 small islets curving 63 miles in an elongated oval shape. The larger islets have been connected by a single 35-mile stretch of paved road, making it appear that most of Majuro is one long narrow island. The highest elevation is a mere 20 feet.

When author Robert Louis Stevenson visited Majuro in 1889 he called the atoll

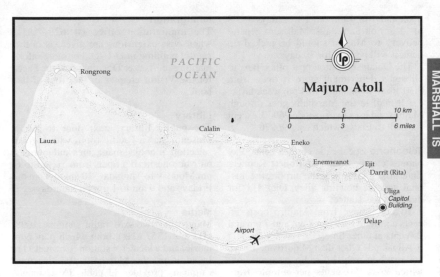

Map: Majuro Atoll showing Rongrong, Laura, Calalin, Eneko, Enemwanot, Ejit, Darrit (Rita), Uliga, Capitol Building, Delap, Airport, and the Pacific Ocean.

the 'Pearl of the Pacific', but it's a far less pristine Majuro that one sees today.

One of the problems with 20,000 people living on such a narrow sandbar is that there's just no place to dispose of the packaging of Western culture. Tin cans, junked cars and disposable diapers pile up by roadside dumping stations and spill into the lagoon.

Although Majuro is the most populated and the most Westernised of the Marshall Islands, there's still a simple island flavour to it all. Even in the main municipality of D-U-D you might wake to crowing roosters or see pigs rooting through fallen coconuts.

And there's a lot that can be learned about life in the Marshalls just from visiting Majuro. You can grasp what it's like to live on a ribbon of land so thin that as often as not you can see the ocean on both sides, and by visiting Laura Village you can find a rural lifestyle somewhat similar to the outer islands.

INFORMATION
Tourist Office
The Marshall Islands Tourism Office occupies a room in the Resources & Development Office (☎ 625-3206); it's essentially a bureaucratic office, although you're free to stop by and you might be able to pick up a few brochures if there are any lying around. This office isn't really set up for visitors, but it's all there is – there's no tourist information booth at the airport.

Details on obtaining tourist information in advance by mail is under Tourist Offices in the Facts for the Visitor chapter in the front of the book.

Money
The Bank of Guam is on the 1st floor of the RRE Hotel building, the Bank of the Marshall Islands is next to the main post office and the Bank of Hawaii is at the side of Gibson's. Banking hours are from 10 am to 3 pm Monday to Thursday and from 10 am to 5 pm on Fridays, except for the Bank of Hawaii which stays open until 6 pm on Fridays.

Post & Telecommunications
Sending Mail Majuro's main post office, next door to Robert Reimers Enterprises in Uliga, is open from 8 am to noon and 1 to 4 pm on Tuesdays and Thursdays, 8.30 am to

noon and 1 to 4 pm other weekdays and 8 to 11 am on Saturdays. Mail sent general delivery to Majuro should be picked up here; it will be held for 30 days.

The Delap substation post office next to Gibson's department store is open from 8.30 am to noon and 1 to 4 pm weekdays.

All mail to the Marshalls goes through Majuro and uses the zip code 96960, except for mail to Ebeye which uses 96970.

Telephone Local calls cost 25 cents. Pay phones can be found at Robert Reimers Enterprises, Gibson's, the airport, the hospital and the bowling alley. Dial 411 for directory assistance.

To call Ebeye from Majuro costs 75 cents a minute between 7 am and 7 pm and 25 cents at other times.

All islands other than Majuro and Ebeye are reached only by radio transmission, which costs 50 cents per minute from Majuro. Calls are made from Outer Islands Radio (KUP-65) in the unmarked, white concrete building along the lagoon road in Rita. It's a good idea to call ahead (☎ 625-3363) to see if the island you're trying to reach is currently on-line, as some outer islands only staff their radios specific hours.

Fax, Telex & Long-Distance Calls Long-distance calls, faxes and telexes can be made 24 hours a day from the new two-storey building behind the National Tele-communications Authority's satellite dish in Delap. Calls to the USA cost $2.50 per minute between 3 am and 9 pm and $2 per minute at other times. Calls to Guam cost $3 per minute between 3 am and 9 pm and $2.50 at other times. Calls to other countries cost the same at all hours: $3 per minute to the FSM, Palau, Australia and Japan; $3.50 to New Zealand, Canada and Saipan; and $4 to most other destinations. Guests at the RRE Hotel can make overseas calls from the hotel at these rates plus a $2-per-call service charge.

When calling the Marshalls from overseas, add 692 to the seven-digit local number.

Immigration
The immigration office (☎ 625-3181), where visa extensions are given, is in the capitol building in D-U-D. For more information see Visas & Documents in the Facts for the Visitor chapter in the front of the book.

Library
The public library, next door to Alele Museum, has a Pacific room with a good selection of books, magazines and journals on Micronesia. It's open from 10 am to 6 pm Monday to Thursday, 10 am to 5 pm on Fridays and 9 am to 1 pm on Saturdays.

Media
Majuro has two AM radio stations (1098 kHz and 1557 kHz), both which play pop music, and a local TV station (Channel 11). In addition, the Marshalls Broadcasting Company provides 11 cable TV channels of American programming, including the three major US networks (ABC, CBS and NBC), HBO, CNN and Fox. The network news usually comes on at 5.30 pm but it's pre-recorded and generally about a week late.

The *Marshall Islands Journal*, which has interesting coverage of the islands, is published on Fridays, costs 50 cents and is easy to find in stores around town. Guam's *Pacific Daily News* is available at the RRE Hotel, Quik Stop Coffee Stop and at larger stores.

Medical Services
Majuro's 80-bed hospital (☎ 625-4144 for emergencies, 625-3480 for the switchboard) in Delap is relatively modern and is adequate for routine medical procedures. The emergency room has a flat fee of $17 that includes everything from seeing the doctor to X-rays and drugs. For nonemergency situations, the hospital clinic opens at 1 pm on weekdays and visitors join the queue with everyone else. There are no private doctors.

Other Information
There's a coin laundry on the main road in

Traditional decorative motifs

Delap about a third of a mile west of Gibson's. For weather information call 625-3079.

ACTIVITIES
Diving & Snorkelling

Majuro is a good place to find rare varieties of tropical fish as well as lots of white-tipped and grey reef sharks. In addition there are a couple of plane wrecks off the airport and scuttled ships and barges in the waters off Rita.

Diving is possible throughout the year, though the best months are May to October when the water is calmest. A popular dive is the Calalin Channel, which has a fairly good reef and enough shark activity to be dubbed 'Shark Alley'. There's also good diving and snorkelling along the lagoon side of the islands north-west of Rita. The farther from Rita you go, the clearer the water gets. Enemwanot has good snorkelling and Calalin, the last island before the channel, is even better, but beware of currents.

If you want to snorkel without having to find boat transportation, there's a shallow coral reef at Laura Beach, at the west end of Majuro.

Dive Operations Marshalls Dive Adventures (MDA; ☎ 625-5131, ext 215), Box 1, Majuro, MH 96960, is a new dive operation run by the RRE Hotel. Situated in a waterfront hut at the south side of the hotel, it's open from 9 am to 6 pm daily except on Mondays. MDA charges $75 for a two-tank dive in Majuro Atoll and $100 for a two-tank dive in neighbouring Arno Atoll, which has a nicer reef with more pristine coral but takes about 1¼ hours by speedboat from Majuro. Dive prices include tanks and weights; add about $25 more if you need to rent complete gear. MDA also sells and rents snorkelling gear; complete sets cost $10 a day.

Matthew Holly (☎ 625-3669) of Marshall Islands Aquatics, Box 319, Majuro, MH 96960, also runs a small dive operation out of an unmarked trailer near the old dock in Uliga. As Matt is a jack-of-all-trades who sometimes takes on other projects and is not always available, his services are more geared to island residents than to walk-in customers.

Tennis & Bowling

There are two public tennis courts lighted for night use in Uliga.

The six-lane Majuro Bowl, the island's first bowling alley, is the busiest place in town. It opens at 10 am (Sundays at 2 pm) and stays open late, locking its doors once the customers finally thin out. The cost is $2 a game.

D-U-D MUNICIPALITY

Three of Majuro's islands – Delap, Uliga and Darrit (Rita) – are joined into one municipality with the unappealing moniker 'D-U-D'. (Pronounce each letter separately, rather than spitting out the single syllable 'dud'.)

D-U-D is the nation's capital and the majority of Majuro's residents are concentrated there. It's certainly not the type of place one conjures up when imagining a tropical paradise. The lagoon around D-U-D is awash with pollution and not suitable for swimming. Poor sanitation conditions are compounded by causeways and bridges that close up the lagoon and block water circulation.

Delap

The community of Delap begins as you cross over the Majuro Bridge coming from the airport. The pink house with the spiffy tennis courts just past the bridge is the home of President Amata Kabua.

The Marshall Islands government offices are spread around Delap, with the centre of it all being the $9 million **capitol building** – an incongruous modernistic structure of bright reflective glass, which looks like no other building this side of Guam. The capitol building has a circular parliamentary hall for the Nitijela, a meeting room for the House of Iroij and a 200-seat spectator gallery.

Next to the new dock where the field trip ship pulls in is the **Tobolar Copra Processing Plant**. The field trip ship, which carries supplies to the outer islands, returns loaded with the copra that's then piled high in the processing plant warehouse. It's hard to believe that mountain of gritty brown coconut meat is what gets transformed into pure transparent oil! If you're interested in looking around, someone will probably offer to give you a little tour.

If you walk out to the dock behind the copra plant you may feel like you've suddenly landed in another country. It's not unusual to find over a dozen **Chinese fishing boats** lined up three deep along the dock, crowded with people playing mahjong and cooking over open fires. The scene is made even more bizarre by the condition of the boats; the old wooden hulls look barely seaworthy, let alone capable of crossing the open Pacific. The boats have become a source of contention among islanders because of the waste they release into Majuro's already polluted lagoon.

Uliga

Most of Majuro's businesses and services are in Uliga.

The **Alele Museum** and the public library are housed in a two-storey building next to the courthouse. The museum is small but has quality exhibits of early Marshallese culture, including stick charts, model canoes and shell tools. One highlight is the collection of photographs of the Marshalls taken at the turn of the century by Joachim deBrum, the son of a Portuguese whaler who lived on Likiep Atoll. There's also a display of hundreds of different seashells collected in the Marshall Islands. The museum is open from 8 to 11 am on Mondays, from 11 am to noon and 5 to 7 pm Tuesday to Friday and from 10 am to 1 pm on Saturdays. There's no entrance fee, though donations are appreciated.

Darrit (Rita)

US forces stationed on Majuro during WW II gave the island of Darrit the nickname 'Rita', after pin-up girl Rita Hayworth, and the name has stuck. (They also named Laura after another Hollywood favourite, Lauren Bacall.)

Die-hard sightseers may want to seek out the Japanese bunker, which is Majuro's only remaining WW II fortification, or the overgrown Action Wave Memorial raised after a tidal wave destroyed the area in November 1979. Neither is particularly interesting nor easy to find. The bunker is beyond the high school and is reached by tramping through people's yards.

Islands beyond Rita People commonly wade across the reef to and from the islands north of Rita – it's such a well-trodden

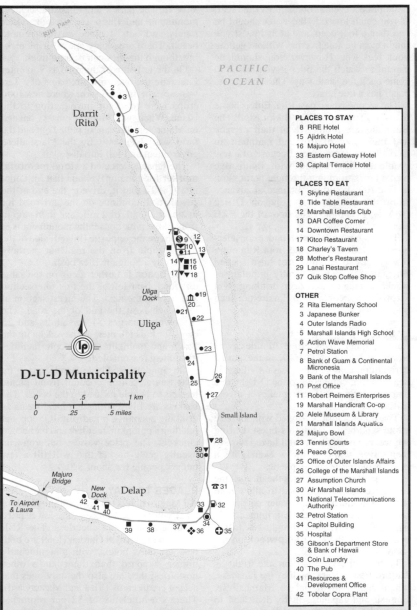

PACIFIC
OCEAN

Darrit
(Rita)

Uliga
Dock

Uliga

D-U-D Municipality

0   .5   1 km
0   .25   .5 miles

Small Island

Majuro
Bridge

New
Dock

Delap

To Airport
& Laura

PLACES TO STAY
8   RRE Hotel
15 Ajidrik Hotel
16 Majuro Hotel
33 Eastern Gateway Hotel
39 Capital Terrace Hotel

PLACES TO EAT
1   Skyline Restaurant
8   Tide Table Restaurant
12 Marshall Islands Club
13 DAR Coffee Corner
14 Downtown Restaurant
17 Kitco Restaurant
18 Charley's Tavern
28 Mother's Restaurant
29 Lanai Restaurant
37 Quik Stop Coffee Shop

OTHER
2   Rita Elementary School
3   Japanese Bunker
4   Outer Islands Radio
5   Marshall Islands High School
6   Action Wave Memorial
7   Petrol Station
8   Bank of Guam & Continental
    Micronesia
9   Bank of the Marshall Islands
10 Post Office
11 Robert Reimers Enterprises
19 Marshall Handicraft Co-op
20 Alele Museum & Library
21 Marshall Islands Aquatics
22 Majuro Bowl
23 Tennis Courts
24 Peace Corps
25 Office of Outer Islands Affairs
26 College of the Marshall Islands
27 Assumption Church
30 Air Marshall Islands
31 National Telecommunications
    Authority
32 Petrol Station
34 Capitol Building
35 Hospital
36 Gibson's Department Store
    & Bank of Hawaii
38 Coin Laundry
40 The Pub
41 Resources &
    Development Office
42 Tobolar Copra Plant

route there's even a footpath over the reef. If you catch low tide the water should be less than a foot deep, and at its lowest you might even be able to cross without getting your feet wet. However you should be careful to watch the tides if you intend to come back the same way. The local newspaper has a tide chart.

The second island past Rita, **Ejit**, is home to about 250 people from Bikini Atoll. The Bikinians are protective of their privacy and their way of life and maintain an alcohol-free community. Because of a few problems they've had with inquisitive media types tromping through, permission to visit Ejit should be obtained in advance from the Bikini Trust Liaison Office (☎ 625-3177) on the 2nd floor of the RRE Hotel in Uliga.

There's currently a plan under consideration to continue the road from Rita out a few islands to **Enemwanot** (also spelled Enemanit), which is locally popular for weekend picnics and beer drinking. Not surprisingly, people from Ejit are not keen on the plan.

LAURA

Laura, a quiet green refuge 30 miles away from the bustle of D-U-D, is the atoll's agricultural centre. This pleasant village is neat as a pin compared to the D-U-D area and the outing to Laura makes a lovely drive.

The tip of Laura is fringed with a pretty white sand beach, Majuro's finest. During the week, visitors may well have Laura to themselves, while on the weekends it's a popular place for family picnics.

The road to Laura passes the airport, the runway of which is sloped to allow it to serve as Majuro's main water catchment source. A dirt path to the left, immediately past the runway, goes straight out to the beach, where there's a **shipwreck** on the shore.

Farther up the road on the right is **Majuro Peace Park**, built by the Japanese, which has a memorial in Marshallese, English and Japanese that's dedicated to those who died in the East Pacific during

WW II. The park's amphitheatre, cement monument and flagpoles all look rather lonely and out of place on this remote beach. There are shady spots for picnicking, though the flies can be a bit thick.

On the left side of the road as you enter Laura are the overgrown remains of a Taiwanese experimental farm where new food crops were tried for introduction to the island. When the Chinese Embassy opened on Majuro the Taiwanese pulled out and the farm was taken over by the Marshallese government and fell into disrepair.

The Japanese erected a **stone memorial marker** for a major typhoon that hit Laura in 1918. To find it, drive to the end of the paved road, continue on the dirt road for just over a tenth of a mile and then stop in front of the pink house; the monument is in the yard on the opposite (inland) side of the road, visible from the road but partially shaded by a bougainvillea bush.

The **beach** is farther along on the same dirt road; bear left at the first intersection and right at the next. The nicest section of the beach is at the end of the road. The landowner charges $1 for adults and 25 cents for kids to enter; as they clean up the beach and maintain some picnic facilities it's quite a reasonable fee.

On Sundays, roadside stands spring up near Laura, selling coconut frond picnic baskets to people headed to the beach. The baskets are filled with such local treats as drinking coconuts, breadfruit, IQ (coconut pudding), pumpkin, reef fish and barbecued chicken. The price varies, but you can usually get a basket that will fill a few hungry people for about $20.

PLACES TO STAY

All Majuro hotels tend to be high priced for what you get, and those at the lower price range are plain and cheerless. The RRE Hotel and the Royal Garden Hotel are both business-class hotels, with a significantly higher standard than the island's other hostelries; they are also the only ones that accept credit cards (Visa and MasterCard). There's a hotel tax of $2 per room per night.

Bottom End

The *Ajidrik Hotel* (☎ 625-3171, fax 625-3712), Box E, Majuro, MH 96960, tucked behind the Downtown Restaurant in Uliga, has 15 air-con rooms with mini-refrigerators, TV and private bathrooms with showers. Singles/doubles cost $47/52. It's quite basic, but adequate, which gives it an edge on other bottom-end hotels. Isaac, the hotel's Fijian clerk, is friendly and helpful. Free airport transportation is provided.

Just a minute's walk of the Ajidrik Hotel is the ramshackle *Majuro Hotel* (☎ 625-3324), Box 185, Majuro, MH 96960, on the 2nd floor above a restaurant in Uliga. It has about a dozen spartan rooms and could be considered as a last resort. Singles/doubles cost $42/47, though you can sometimes get one without air-con for a few dollars less.

Best not considered at all is the *Capital Terrace Hotel* (☎ 625-3831), Box 107, Majuro, MH 96960, a dingy place above a little grocery store in Delap, which has small bug-infested rooms that are terribly overpriced at $47/52 for singles/doubles.

Less than a mile east of the airport is the motel-style *Elten Hotel* (☎ 625-3858), Box 5039, Majuro, MH 96960, which has seven adequate rooms. The hotel is within walking distance of Blue Lagoon snack shop and the new RRE Store, so getting something to eat shouldn't be a problem. Singles/doubles cost $30/45. You'll probably need a car, as taxis are few and far between in this area. Because visitors tend to stay in the D-U-D area the long-term outlook for this little hotel is in doubt; be sure to call in advance if you're interested.

Over the years other attempts to open airport-area hotels have all been short-lived, with the customers never materialising and the owners eventually converting the places into local housing.

If you're looking for a long-term place to stay, Brian & Nancy Vander Velde (☎/fax 625-3811), Box 1603, Majuro, MH 96960, have a couple of simple studio and one-bedroom apartments that might be available. Known as *Garden Apartments*, they're south of the high school in Rita.

Each has air-con, hot water and cooking facilities and costs from $100 to $250 a week, depending on current demand.

Top End

RRE Hotel (Hotel Robert Reimers) (☎ 625-3250, fax 625-3505), Box 1, Majuro, MH 96960, is a comfortable, modern 18-room hotel in the centre of town that's popular with business travellers. Rooms have a refrigerator, thermostatic air-con, cable TV and rattan furnishings, including a table, chairs and a settee. There's purified water and room phones with free local calls. Rooms on the inside corridor are larger, have bathtubs and cost $75/80 for singles/doubles, while rooms with balconies and views of the lagoon cost $90/95 for singles/doubles. There are also a dozen duplex ground-level trailers between the hotel and the lagoon with small rooms that cost as much as the hotel rooms but are not as appealing.

A slightly more up-market option is the *Royal Garden Hotel* (☎ 247-3701, fax 247-3705), Box 735, Majuro, MH 96960, two miles west of D-U-D across the Majuro bridge, which has 24 large rooms in a two-storey complex overlooking a little white sand beach. Rooms have TVs, bathtubs, phones, air-con, carpeting, refrigerators and ocean views. The rates are $78 for a single room, $95 for a double with two queen beds and $103 for a suite. Single rooms have one queen bed and cost the same if occupied by a single person or a couple. Transportation is one drawback here; if you don't have a car it can be a long wait between taxis.

Opposite the capitol building is the multistorey *Eastern Gateway Hotel* (☎ 625-3259, fax 625-3512), Box 106, Majuro, MH 96960. Financed by the Republic of Nauru, the hotel was erected during a decade of on-and-off construction and then mothballed just prior to completion. If it ever comes out of its long hibernation, it'll be the island's largest hotel, with 65 rooms. In the meantime there are six older concrete bungalows on the lagoon that are small and run down for $57 and seven motel-style rooms that are larger and a bit nicer for $67. All have small refrigerators and private baths. Rates are $5 less for singles.

PLACES TO EAT
Food in Majuro is reasonably priced and fresh fish is found in most restaurants. Water is not safe to drink from the tap; you can find bottled water in grocery stores. Tipping is not customary.

Budget
From the outside, the *Kitco Restaurant*, in the centre of D-U-D, looks like nothing more than a windowless cinder-block garage, but in fact it's a good place for inexpensive food and the most popular eatery in town. Pancakes cost $1, breakfast combos $2 to $3, and there are inexpensive sandwiches and a full chalkboard of dishes from ramen to teriyaki steak for $2.50 to $5. It's open from 6 am to 8 pm.

Charley's Tavern, next to Kitco Restaurant, has the island's best pizza – $8 for a small, $10 for a medium. It's open from 5 pm till late.

Quik Stop Coffee Shop is a little diner next to Gibson's that has a sizable following. The food is good, the place clean and the Filipino cook, who used to be the chef at Tide Table, is one of the island's best. Sandwiches with salad and fries cost $3 while a wide variety of dishes, including a recommendable fresh tuna in garlic butter and pancit canton (a tasty Filipino noodle dish with meat and vegetables), cost around $5. It's open for three meals a day from 7.30 am to 9 pm.

Mother's Restaurant, next to Momotaro's store at Small Island, has eight cosy tables in a non-smoking environment. It's a favourite lunch spot among American expats. Recommended are the grilled tuna on salad greens and the teriyaki chicken plate, each $4. There are also sandwiches and vegetarian tofu dishes. At breakfast you can get 75-cent banana pancakes or various omelettes from $3. It's open from 6 am to 2 pm daily except on Sundays.

The *Skyline Restaurant* in Rita is a rather pleasant place with a bit of East Indian influence. French toast and other breakfast items cost around $3, while lunch and dinner, which includes tuna, Indian curry and fried chicken meals, is priced mostly from $4 to $5. It's open daily from 6.30 am to 11 pm.

The Deli attached to the RRE store has ordinary burgers and sandwiches for $2 to $3, and simple, cheap breakfast items; there are picnic tables at the side where you can sit and eat. Similar but better quality food can be found on the back street at *DAR Coffee Corner*, which is simple, clean and locally popular for its 25-cent pancakes. It's open from 6 am to 2 pm and 5 to 10 pm daily.

Of the numerous grocery stores in D-U-D, *Gibson's* has the freshest food and best prices; it's open from 8 am to 8 pm (9 am to 6 pm on Sundays).

Top End
Tide Table Restaurant, upstairs at the RRE Hotel, is a popular place with ordinary food and fine views of the lagoon. Standard breakfast fare, such as eggs, pancakes and the like, costs $3 to $5 and is served until 11 am. Lunch features burgers and sandwiches with fries and salad for $4 and a few hot dishes for a bit more. Seafood and steak dinners cost $10 to $15, including soup, salad and rice. It's open daily from 7 am to 2 pm and from 5 to 9.30 pm.

The *Lanai Restaurant*, on the lagoon at Small Island next to the Air Marshall Islands office, has a Chinese cook and a varied menu that includes good Chinese food. At lunch everything on the menu is $5, including satay beef, Peking stir fry and chicken curry – all served with rice. At dinner seafood and meat dishes are priced from $10 to $13 and vegetarian tofu dishes average $7. Lunch is from 10 am to 2 pm weekdays and dinner from 5 to 10 pm Monday to Saturday.

Royal Garden Restaurant, at the Royal Garden Hotel, has sandwiches with fries for around $3, reef fish or a nice spaghetti with shrimp for $6.50 and good steaks for around $12. It's a pleasant setting with a good ocean view and it's not uncommon to find President Kabua, whose daughter owns the hotel, dining here in the evening. There's a happy hour from 5 to 7 pm.

ENTERTAINMENT

The drinking age in the Marshalls is 21. Majuro is on the verge of getting its first locally produced brew, under the guidance of an Australian venture called Republic Brewery.

PJ's Lounge, above Majuro Bowl in Uliga, is open from 4 pm to 2 am and has a live band playing rock, reggae, jazz or soul from 10 pm. The cover charge of $2 for women and $3 for men is waived on Mondays and Tuesdays.

The Pub, a blue and white building at the side of Ace International in Delap, is the more popular early-evening spot and has both a bar and disco.

The *Lanai Restaurant* at Small Island has a live band from 10 pm to 2 am on Thursdays, Fridays and Saturdays.

The *Tide Table Restaurant* at the RRE Hotel has a bar that's open from 4 pm daily and there's a good sunset view, as the restaurant faces west across the lagoon.

Charley's Tavern in the centre of Uliga has live music from 10 pm to 2 am on Fridays and is a popular spot to knock back a beer. Another popular drinking spot is the open-air *Marshall Islands Club*, on the back road in Uliga, which has a nice ocean view and simple eats.

THINGS TO BUY

Marshallese handicrafts are among the best in Micronesia, and include stick charts, carved models of outrigger canoes and intricately woven items such as baskets, wall hangings and purses made from pandanus leaves, coconut fronds and cowrie shells.

The Marshall Handicraft Co-op, behind the museum, is open from 9 am to noon and 1 to 5 pm Monday to Friday, and is a good place to watch women weaving. Busy Hands, on the road near the Assumption Church, is open more sporadically. There are also two handicraft booths at the airport, the larger of which is operated by a Laura group and carries unique outer island handicrafts.

Prices are reasonable; you can get a stick chart, a fan or a small basket for about $10.

Locally made coconut oil soap is sold in Majuro stores. You can get colourful commemorative postage stamps at the post office and first day covers at the Alele Museum. The Alele Museum sells stick charts, T-shirts and cassette tapes of Marshallese chants and stories. The library next to the museum sells books on Micronesia.

The *Marshall Islands Guidebook* (Micronitor News & Printing Co), largely written by Marshall Islands Journal editor Giff Johnson, covers lots of topics of interest for long-term visitors. It's available at the library and major stores for around $10.

GETTING THERE & AWAY
Air

Majuro is a free stopover on Continental Micronesia's island hopper route between Honolulu and Guam. Otherwise, Continental's Honolulu-Majuro ticket costs $577 one way, or $600 return with a seven-day advance purchase and a one-year maximum stay.

Air Marshall Islands (AMI) flies from Honolulu to Majuro three days a week and costs $563 one way, $597 return.

AMI also flies twice a week from Nandi (Fiji) to Majuro for $647 one way or $894 return; the flight stops en route at Funafuti in Tuvalu and Tarawa in Kiribati. The Funafuti-Majuro fare is $459 one way, $738 return. The Tarawa-Majuro fare is $193 one way, $321 return. These return fares require a seven-day advance purchase and allow a maximum stay of 23 days.

Airport The airport has a simple restaurant where you can get drinks and snacks, two handicraft shops that open at departure times, a couple of car rental booths and a pay phone (opposite the restaurant entrance).

Airline Offices Air Marshall Islands (☎ 625-3733), located in the Small Island section of D-U-D, is open from 8 am to 6 pm Monday to Friday, from 8 am to 2 pm on Saturdays and from 8 am to noon on Sundays.

Continental Micronesia (☎ 625-3209) is on the ground floor of the RRE Hotel building and is open from 8.30 am to noon and 1 to 4.30 pm Monday to Friday.

Leaving Majuro
Majuro has a $15 airport departure tax for all visitors over the age of 12.

GETTING AROUND
To/From the Airport
Most hotels provide a free minivan service to and from the airport. A few may meet the flights whether they have guests or not, but most show up only when there's a reservation. Still, if you call from the airport to book a room, most hotels will send someone out to get you. Otherwise, a taxi from the airport to D-U-D costs $2. The drive takes about 15 minutes.

Taxi
Majuro has a fine, inexpensive shared taxi system. Most taxis are sedans, clearly marked with taxi signs. You stand at the side of the road and wave them down and as long as they're not full they'll stop and pick you up. It costs just 30 cents to go anywhere within D-U-D.

There are also 15-passenger minivan taxis. Whereas car taxi routes are determined by wherever the passengers want to go, including side roads and residential areas, the vans generally stick to the main road. Some make a straight run between the RRE Hotel and Laura, though most turn around at Majuro Bridge. The cost is 25 cents within D-U-D and varying amounts beyond.

If you're going all the way to Laura ($2) it's best to pick up the minivan from the parking lot of the RRE Hotel in Uliga, as only certain vans do the entire route.

If you're outside D-U-D you may have to wait well over an hour before a taxi comes by, but in town they're quite frequent.

Car
Car rentals on Majuro are for a 24-hour period and include unlimited mileage.

Hertz (☎ 625-3321, fax 625-3293), the only internationally affiliated car-rental company in Majuro, has rates from $50, plus $12 for optional insurance.

The other company with a booth at the airport is DAR (☎ 625-3174, fax 625-3344), which charges $47 per day for an air-con sedan, plus $6 for insurance. They also have an office next to DAR Coffee Corner on the oceanside road in Uliga.

The RRE Hotel (☎ 625-3250, fax 625-3505) rents cars for $45; add on another $13 if you want insurance coverage. Other companies with similar rates include the Royal Garden Hotel (☎ 247-3701, fax 247-3705), Deluxe Rent A Car (☎ 625-3665, fax 625-3663) and HER Car Rental (☎ 625-3271, fax 625-3872). Both RRE and Royal Garden give priority to their hotel guests.

Road Rules Visitors are allowed to drive in Majuro for 30 days with a valid driving licence from their home country.

The speed limit is 25 miles per hour in the D-U-D area and 45 miles per hour between the airport and Laura, except for school and church zones which are 15 miles per hour.

Petrol costs $2.10 a gallon; there are several stations in the D-U-D area and one a mile east of the airport.

Boat
Hotels can arrange boat rentals or you can try to save money by cutting out the intermediaries and making arrangements yourself with someone who has a speedboat. Ask around at the docks and bargain the price. Marshallese are generally very fair and won't cheat you, but if you throw money around they'll take it.

Kwajalein Atoll

Nowhere in Micronesia is the US military presence so ominous as on Kwajalein Atoll, a missile testing range operated by the US Department of Defense.

Kwajalein is the world's largest coral atoll. Its 97 islands have a total land mass of just 6.5 sq miles but they surround an immense 1100-sq-mile lagoon.

The lagoon, sometimes called 'the world's largest catcher's mitt', is the target and splashdown point for intercontinental ballistic missiles (ICBMs) fired from the Vandenberg Air Force Base in California, 4200 miles away.

The missile tests, which generally occur at night, often light up the sky with a brilliant display of explosions, burning debris and sonic booms.

Kwajalein's $2 billion facility is cur-rently a test range for anti-ballistic missiles and Strategic Defense Initiative (SDI) systems, on the cutting edge of the 'Star Wars' programme.

The Kwajalein Missile Range (officially called US Army Kwajalein Atoll, or USAKA) includes Kwajalein Island in the southern part of the atoll, Roi-Namur Island in the north and some smaller islands between the two. It's a world of radiation shields, radar systems, microwave dishes and sophisticated computers and tracking equipment.

The Americans stationed on Kwajalein Island include an active group of divers whose main function is diving for missile pieces after a splashdown.

KWAJALEIN ISLAND
About 3000 American civilian contract workers and their families live on Kwajalein Island, which is commonly referred to as 'Kwaj' by islanders.

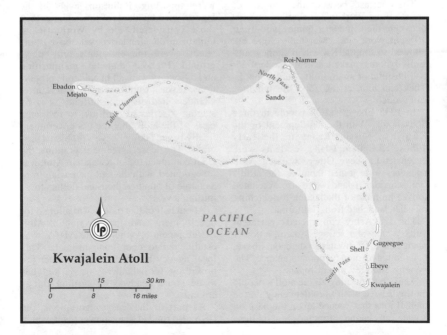

Recreational facilities include two swimming pools, three baseball diamonds, a golf course, tennis courts, movie theatres, handball and basketball courts, a bowling alley and a dart league. Everything is free to residents, including taxi vans to get around.

There's also a dinner club, restaurants and snack bars, a chapel, schools from kindergarten through high school, a supermarket and a modern department store. As much as possible, it is American suburbia transplanted.

The whole island is off-limits to unofficial visitors except as a transit point to neighbouring Ebeye.

EBEYE ISLAND

About 1500 Marshallese labourers work on Kwajalein Island and live on 78-acre Ebeye Island, three miles to the north. They support an additional 7500 relatives and friends in inadequate, overcrowded conditions.

The contrasts between the two islands are startling. Workers are shuttled by boat between their meagre homes and their affluent work sites. Marshallese are not allowed to shop at Kwajalein's fancy subsidised stores, make use of its modern 25-bed hospital or swim in its 'public' pools. They can look at the good life but they can't touch.

In 1935 Ebeye had 13 people in three households. With the development of the Kwajalein Missile Range in the early 1960s, Kwajalein Island residents were evacuated to Ebeye. Other Kwajalein Atoll islanders soon joined them, as the atoll's 'mid-corridor' islands were also evacuated to free up most of the lagoon for catching missiles launched from California.

The US Army constructed apartment units, a saltwater sewage system, a power plant and a freshwater system on Ebeye, but allotted no money for maintenance. The systems soon fell into disrepair.

As if concentrating all the atoll's people on tiny Ebeye wasn't problem enough, the menial jobs that opened up on the base on Kwajalein Island attracted Marshallese

from other atolls, particularly those who had relatives on Ebeye. With traditional Marshallese custom dictating that members of each extended family take in relatives in need, the neat little apartments built by the military were on their way to becoming Micronesia's most overcrowded ghetto.

In 1968 Marshallese workers at Kwajalein began receiving the US minimum wage, which was much higher than the average salary elsewhere in the Marshalls. By 1970 Ebeye had 4000 people and by 1978 the population had swelled to 8000 – on an island just one mile long and less than 200 yards wide. One-room shacks and lean-tos of plywood, tin, cinder block and plastic sheeting were jammed side by side. The island came to be known as the 'Slum of the Pacific'.

A new sewage system built in 1979 broke down soon after its completion, electrical power was out more often than not, running water was restricted to as little as 15 minutes a day and sanitation conditions were appalling. Pollution levels in the lagoon were hundreds of times higher than those considered safe by World Health Organisation standards, yet those same waters were the children's only playground. Typhoid, diabetes, malnutrition and dysentery were all in epidemic proportions. It wasn't until the early 1980s, after islanders had disrupted military tests by staging a series of 'sail-ins' to restricted parts of the atoll, that the US government finally began taking Ebeye's problems seriously. The lease agreement granting the USA continued use of Kwajalein Atoll was renegotiated, with the rent increasing from a couple of hundred thousand dollars to $9 million a year.

About half of that money was allotted for development and the Kwajalein Atoll Development Authority (KADA) was established to coordinate projects. This local agency has done a much better job providing for islanders' needs and has made some headway in turning things around.

As part of the lease negotiations, the USA also funded a new power plant, which came on line in 1987. It is combined with an Israeli-designed water desalination plant that innovatively uses waste heat from the power plant to produce as many as 300,000 gallons of fresh water daily – enough to meet Ebeye's needs.

As part of KADA's projects, Ebeye's dusty potholed roads have been paved, sidewalks built and the sewage system rebuilt.

A recently completed causeway now stretches six miles northward from Ebeye to neighbouring islands, joining half a dozen of them in an effort to relieve Ebeye's overcrowding.

Gugeegue, the island at the far end of the causeway, is under development in what is being promoted as the Marshalls' first planned urban community. With 59 acres, Gugeegue is the largest of these islands and is expected to eventually house up to 3000 people.

Though some things are obviously getting better, Ebeye is still saddled with enormous problems. Infant mortality and suicide rates are high and alcoholism is rampant. And though new buildings are replacing the old, the island still has little greenery and few trees – there simply isn't room.

Needless to say, Ebeye is not a big tourist spot, but it is a real eye-opener. The people are generally very friendly, especially the children.

Diving

Kwajalein Atoll has more than 30 WW II-era Japanese ships at the bottom of the lagoon that until recently have been the exclusive playground of American divers stationed on Kwajalein Island. However, Ebeye now has a new dive operation, Kwajalein Atoll Dive Resort, which is opening up the area to civilian divers. The operation is being set up by divemaster Steven Gavagan, who moved here from the Caribbean. Dives are currently underway and a dive resort is in the making; until it opens, Steven can be reached through the Anrohasa Hotel (see Places to Stay). The dive sites include coral pinnacles, a dozen ships

at the south end of the atoll and an aeroplane graveyard off Roi-Namur.

Places to Stay

The only recommendable place to stay is the two-storey *Anrohasa Hotel* (☎ 329-3161, fax 329-3248), Box 5039, Ebeye, MH 96970, a pleasant family-owned hotel run by Fountain and Ann Inok. The 26 rooms have thermostatic air-con, refrigerators, phones and TVs. There are six small rooms in an older wing for $65. The newer, spiffier rooms cost $85, $95 with limited cooking facilities. Visa and MasterCard are accepted.

Kwajalein Atoll Dive Resort plans to build duplex bungalows in native thatch style on Shell Island, just south of Gugeegue. The resort, geared for divers, will be capable of accommodating 32 people.

In the USA, reservations for the Anrohasa Hotel and information on the dive resort can be obtained from Hilary Kaye & Associates (☎ 714-852-5150, 800-846-3483, fax 714-851-3111).

Other options are the *DSC Hotel* (☎ 329-3194), Box 5097, Ebeye, MH, 96970, which has seven rooms with double beds, TV and refrigerator for $52, and the *Midtown Hotel* (☎ 329-3199), Box 159, Ebeye, MH, 96970, which has 10 simple rooms at $45.

Places to Eat

Bob's Island Restaurant, a block from the Anrohasa Hotel, has a little balcony with a water view, good prices and the best food on Ebeye. They make great French toast and good baby back ribs.

The *Anrohasa Hotel Restaurant* has a varied menu with American-style food as well as Chinese and Japanese dishes. They make their own pastries and sometimes have fresh hydroponic-grown vegetables from the atoll's North Loi Island. It's open for three meals a day, prices are moderate and there's a bar.

For local food try *Juanita's Jeli Diner*,

next to the Bank of Guam, which has reef fish, tuna and other inexpensive Micronesian fare.

RRE Store has the regular line of groceries as well as takeaway deli foods.

Getting Around

Taxi From Ebeye's dock you can get a taxi to anywhere on the island for 30 cents, though it only takes 20 minutes to walk from one end of the island to the other. Most taxis are extended-cab pick-up trucks and you ride in the cab or hop in the back, wherever there's room.

Boat It's possible to rent boats on Ebeye to visit islands around the atoll, but you'll have to bargain the price. Ask around and be sure to talk directly to the boat owner. Before setting off to any of the other islands you need to get permission from the landowner on Ebeye first, but this shouldn't be hard to do. Avoid military installations around the lagoon, as you may be arrested for trespassing.

ROI-NAMUR & SANDO ISLANDS

Fifty miles north of Ebeye, Roi-Namur houses radar and other tracking equipment. Like Kwajalein, it's a restricted military facility and another 'little America' with modern amenities available to Americans only.

Sando is the home of Marshallese workers commuting to Roi-Namur, much like Ebeye is to Kwajalein. The Japanese had communications facilities on Sando and large bomb shelters still stand, though they were damaged by heavy bombing during WW II. Live shells are still occasionally found on Roi-Namur and Sando.

Sando is so close to the missile touchdown site that the USA built a modern bomb shelter for the 400 residents. But the islanders, who once dutifully practised drills, no longer bother to go to the shelter when US missiles are shot their way.

MEJATO ISLAND

Mejato, in the north-west part of the atoll, is home to 350 Rongelapese, many of

whom were irradiated in US nuclear testing.

After years of US failure to respond to the islanders' concerns about radioactive contamination on Rongelap, Greenpeace helped the Rongelapese relocate to Mejato in 1985. During their first few years on Mejato, the Rongelapese suffered food shortages as a result of problems in bringing in enough supplies from Ebeye, 70 miles to the south. One of the obstacles was the waters around Mejato, which are too shallow for most cargo boats to land.

Greenpeace came to the rescue again in 1988, providing the islanders with $50,000 to build a 40-foot catamaran to transport food and supplies.

GETTING THERE & AWAY

Although Kwajalein Island is a closed military base, it is the transit point if you're entering Ebeye by air. Visitors have long needed to go through the formality of getting a permit in advance before entering Ebeye. That system is in flux and there's some debate as to whether a permit is still essential. However, as both Air Marshall Islands and Continental Micronesia agents often won't let you on the flight without the permit, you should still plan on getting one or at least confirm in advance with the airline that it's not going to be required to board the flight. Permits can be picked up at the Office of the Chief Secretary on the 3rd floor of the capitol building in Majuro between 8 am and 5 pm Monday to Friday.

Continental Micronesia stops on Kwajalein Island as part of the island hopper flight. Air Marshall Islands flies between Majuro and Kwajalein daily for $125 one way.

Once you're on Kwajalein, you'll be escorted to the dock and ferried to Ebeye. The boat, a US Army catamaran, is free and takes just 15 minutes.

Field trip ships stop at Ebeye. The one-way deck fare is $30.50. For more information, see Getting There & Away at the end of the Outer Islands section.

Outer Islands

Something of Marshallese traditional island life still remains in the quiet village communities away from Majuro and Kwajalein. The pace on the outer islands is relaxed and very s-l-o-w.

Usually a few people on each island speak English and nearly everyone is friendly. Because of the language barrier some people may appear shy while others will strike up a conversation just to practise their English.

If you're visiting somebody special you might even rate a real Marshallese welcome. On these occasions a group of women singing in harmony and bearing baskets piled with food will surround the visitors. The women give the guests flower headbands and leis and then everybody stands around exchanging compliments.

One Peace Corps volunteer, describing a visit by her brother, told how some of the older village women welcomed him by rubbing baked breadfruit on his stomach and chanting about how good-looking he was. For better or worse, this isn't something the average traveller will encounter!

Although some outer islanders still use the *korkor*, a dug-out fishing canoe made from a breadfruit log, 'boom-booms', or motorboats, are steadily gaining in popularity. Both kinds of boats are used for frequent *jambos* (trips or picnics) to uninhabited atoll islands.

ACCOMMODATION

The Marshallese in the islands and atolls away from Majuro and Kwajalein are used to weekly flights dropping off the occasional visitor now and again. Although most atolls do not have formal arrangements for visitors, the Marshallese are generally hospitable to those who approach them kindly and you should be able to find a family to stay with or a place to camp. Needless to say, you need to get permission before setting up a tent, as all land belongs to someone.

In addition to private homes there's sometimes a public service commission house for visitors on official business where the local mayor might let you stay – and every now and then someone attempts to start up a guesthouse on one of the islands.

If you have a lot of time before your arrival to the Marshalls, you could try writing in advance. Just direct the letter to, for example: Mayor of Wotje, Wotje Atoll, Marshall Islands 96960. However, you won't necessarily get a response; the most common procedure is simply to radio ahead to the mayor of the atoll you wish to visit once you arrive on Majuro (see Telecommunications at the start of this chapter).

The Air Marshall Islands office in Majuro is another potential resource and can be helpful in filling you in on the latest developments on the islands, including any new accommodation possibilities.

If there's a Peace Corps volunteer on the island (you can find out from their Majuro office), they might welcome the company or at least be able to help you find a place to stay.

Don't expect this to be a freebie. Many islanders are quite fond of money so you should be prepared to pay; it's wise to establish what the cost will be before jumping on a plane.

Trade items are sometimes more useful than cash, especially if they are things not readily available from the field trip ships. Coffee, printed T-shirts, D-size batteries and cassette tapes of Western music are popular items.

Most outer islands do not have electricity, running water or flush toilets. Some houses are of concrete and others are made of thatch with coral rock floors. Instead of beds, pandanus mats are piled on the floor. The Marshallese take excellent care of guests and will share what they have.

FOOD & DRINK

Restaurants don't exist outside the major atolls. You can make do with local store provisions, eat with the family you stay with or bring food with you from Majuro which you can then either eat or trade for local fresh foods.

Usually you will find a couple of small stores with a very limited inventory of staples, such as rice, flour, tea and canned meats. Island meals generally consist of a combination of those items and local foods like breadfruit, pandanus, pumpkin, taro and fish.

Most of the outer islands are dry. Although alcohol is often illegally made and consumed, visitors who drink are not usually appreciated.

To be safe, all water should be boiled, even if it's from catchments – and without fail if it's not.

MILI ATOLL

Mili can be a good choice for travellers who want to visit one of the outer atolls, as it has friendly people and beautiful beaches and, as it's not far from Majuro, is relatively cheap to get to.

After Kwajalein, Mili has the most land area of the Marshallese atolls – just over six sq miles. The population is about 850.

In 1937 famed US aviator Amelia Earhart disappeared in this part of the Pacific in the midst of a flight around the world. Although the mysterious circumstances surrounding her death remain unknown, she was reportedly seen in Mili under Japanese custody long after her disappearance.

Toward the end of the war, some 17,000 Japanese soldiers were isolated on Mili. As a result of a US blockade, near-starvation conditions existed and the execution of Mili islanders who failed to turn their food over to the Japanese were so commonplace that the people of Mili are now suing the Japanese government for war crime compensation.

As a major WW II Japanese base, Mili has many abandoned weapons, Japanese and US war planes and bombed-out buildings still scattered around.

The plane lands on Mili Island, the atoll's main island. It's a pleasant quarter-mile walk to the village from the airstrip.

Mutiny in Mili

Mili played a part in one of the bloodier and most famous mutinies of the whaling years. In 1824 the captain and officers of the Nantucket whaleship *Globe* were murdered and the mutineers, led by Samuel Comstock, chose Mili as their hideout. Other crewmen, however, stole the ship and abandoned the mutineers on the island. A US naval ship that came ashore two years later learned that Comstock and all but two of his crew had been killed by the islanders, apparently in retaliation for their cruelty. ■

Along the way you'll see large bomb craters now covered with vines and coconut trees. Mili has a mosquito problem as these bomb craters make perfect spawning grounds. Bring mosquito repellent or coils or both with you. (Mosquito coils and coffee also make nice gifts for people on Mili.)

The whole lagoon side of Mili Island is trimmed with sandy white beaches, while shell collecting is good on the ocean side. At low tide you can easily walk along the reef to the neighbouring islands, some of which have only a single house upon them.

In the past there have been thatched cottages for rent on the beach on Mili Island, though currently the only established place to stay is on Wau Island which is diagonally across the lagoon from Mili Island. Wau makes a great place to play Robinson Crusoe. This tiny island has a giant-clam hatchery owned by Robert Reimers Enterprises, lots of coconut trees and three cottages geared for divers looking for a getaway vacation. The surrounding waters have pristine diving.

Places to Stay & Eat

Marshalls Dive Adventures (see Activities in the Majuro section) maintains the three thatched cottages on Wau Island. Each has a private bathroom, one queen-size and one single bed, running water and solar power. For $750 and with a six-person minimum, divers can spend a week on the island, which includes air fare from Majuro, dives, food and accommodation. Depending on availability, shorter stays may be possible. A three-day stay would cost $460.

Getting There & Away
Air Marshall Islands flies between Majuro and Mili on Mondays and Fridays for $48 one way.

There's also a 50-foot schooner that makes the four-hour ride from Majuro to Mili on occasion for about $5 one way. To make arrangements, call Kejjo Bien at Downtown Restaurant in Majuro (☎ 625-3145). He may also be able to tell you if there are any new accommodation options.

MALOELAP ATOLL
Taroa (Tarawa) Island, in Maloelap Atoll, was the main Japanese airbase in the eastern Marshalls during WW II and most visitors these days come to see war relics. There are numerous twisted wreckages of Zeros and Betty bombers, pillboxes, guns and the remains of an airfield, narrow-gauge railroad and a radio station. The southern tip of the island has coastal defence guns, including a 127 mm anti-aircraft gun and a Howitzer on wheels.

You can stumble across some of the stuff on your own, but a lot of it is hidden under thick jungle foliage and is difficult to find. A few islanders are willing to trek with visitors and show them the sites, so if you're interested just ask around.

Off Taroa's lagoon beach the Japanese freighter *Toroshima Maru* lies half submerged where it was sunk by US bombers. Periscopes and the mast can still be seen, but it's pretty well stripped, except for some live depth charges. If you swim out around it, watch for the grouper (a type of sea bass) that is said to be as large as a human. The lagoon also has its share of sharks, so watch out for them too! After the war ended, Taroa was not settled again by Marshallese until the 1970s. Now it's the centre of atoll activity because of its airport, stores and copra cooperative.

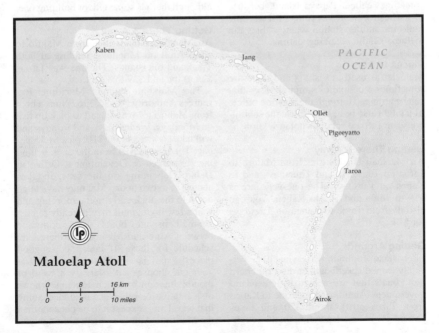

Legend has it that Taroa used to be in the centre of the lagoon in a spot where it was easy for all canoes to sail to. But the legendary figure L'etao, who demanded food from each of the atoll islands, got irritated with the stingy offerings given by the Taroa islanders and kicked Taroa to where it is now.

Maloelap Atoll, with a population of 800 people, has four other inhabited islands. Airok is 16 miles south of Taroa; and Ollet, Jang and Kaben are respectively six, 18 and 32 miles to the north-west. Not many Japanese were stationed on the other islands so they don't have the same amount of war junk as Taroa does.

Maloelap has two chiefs. One is head of Taroa, Ollet, Jang and Kaben islands, as well as the northern atolls of Wotje, Utrik and Ailuk, while the other presides over Maloelap's Airok Island and parts of Aur Atoll.

Just a few miles from both Taroa and Ollet is uninhabited Pigeeyatto, which is sometimes called 'Papaya Island' because of its fresh fruit. It has ruins of a wartime radio transmitter station where cables ran to Taroa's radio receiving station.

Places to Stay

Maloelap is used to visitors and there are sometimes a couple of simple houses that can be arranged through the mayor's office. You might also be able to stay at the schoolhouse on Taroa if school's not in session.

Getting There & Away

Air Marshall Islands flies from Majuro to Taroa on Tuesdays and Thursdays and to Kaben on Tuesdays. The one-way fare is $59 to Taroa and $62 to Kaben. You can also fly from Taroa to Kaben on Tuesdays for $24.

Getting Around

Inter-island commuting is via either privately owned speedboats or diesel inboard motorboats that are owned by the island government. An inboard boat ride to Kaben from Taroa costs about $20 and takes around 4½ hours, depending on the roughness of the water in the lagoon. From Taroa to Airok it takes about one hour by speedboat or just over two hours by diesel inboard, and costs about $20 one way.

ARNO ATOLL

Arno is the closest atoll to Majuro, just nine miles away. It has 133 islands, two airstrips and nearly 1700 people.

The Longar area in Arno is famous for its 'love school' where young women were once taught how to perfect their sexual techniques.

The waters off Longar Point are known for superb deep-sea fishing where yellowfin tuna, marlin, mahi-mahi and sailfish abound.

About 10,000 pounds of tuna and reef fish caught near Arno are sold on Majuro each month, thanks in part to a Japanese-funded fishing project on Arno Island, which paid for fishing boats, a cold storage facility and an upgrade of the dock.

Currently there isn't a hotel on Arno, although there is some talk of building one.

Getting There & Away

Air Marshall Islands flies from Majuro to Arno Atoll on Mondays, landing at both Tinak and Ine islands. The one-way fare is $24 to Ine and $29 to Tinak.

The Marshall Islands Maritime Resources Authority (☎ 625-3262) runs a boat from Majuro to Arno Island to pick up fish on Mondays, Wednesdays and Fridays and will take passengers for $10, plus $1.75 per bag. The boat leaves from the dock behind the Resources & Development Office in Delap. Depending on the seas, it takes about 1½ to two hours. You may have to go down to the dock early in the morning and wait a few hours until they're ready to go.

Small private boats often commute between Arno and Majuro, but there's no schedule for these. If interested, a good place to start is simply to ask around at your guesthouse – it's largely a word of mouth situation in which someone knows of a relative or other acquaintance going that way. Don't expect it to be cheaper than the Maritime Authority boat, although you

Basket maker at a handicraft co-op in Majuro, Marshall Islands

Hanging out on Long Island, Majuro

Lagoon sunset seen from Uliga, Majuro

might be able to negotiate passage for a reasonable price.

LIKIEP ATOLL

Likiep Atoll is made up of about 60 islands around a shallow lagoon and has a population of 500.

Likiep houses are unusual for the Marshalls in that they're built in a sort of Western style with porches and railings. Because of this Likiep has been dubbed by some islanders as 'The Williamsburg of the Pacific', although it does take a bit of imagination.

In 1877, during the German era, Jose deBrum, a Portuguese harpooner who arrived aboard an American whaleship, and Adolf Capelle, a German trader from a Honolulu-based company, bought Likiep Atoll from the high chief who owned it. They both married Marshallese women and settled in, planted coconuts and fruit trees and started profitable copra and ship-building companies.

Descendants of deBrum and Capelle still own Likiep and operate it as a copra plantation. The sale of the island is still a source of contention 120 years later as current traditional leaders question its validity, claiming the document of sale was written in a foreign language that the high chief wasn't able to read.

Jose deBrum's son Joachim designed ships and homes and the mansion he built for his family still stands on Likiep. Joachim was also a photographer with a keen historian's perspective. More than 2300 glass plate negatives, taken between 1885 and 1930, and hundreds of documents and diaries have been recovered from the mansion and were catalogued and reprinted for display in Majuro's Alele Museum.

Getting There & Away

Air Marshall Islands flies from Majuro to Likiep on Tuesdays and Fridays. The cost is $108 one way.

WOTJE ATOLL

Wotje, the main island in Wotje Atoll, is literally covered from one end to the other with remnants of WW II. Huge Japanese-built structures loom out of the jungle, some bombed to pieces but others still habitable.

Large portions of the island were once paved in concrete, and machinery, fuel tanks and all sorts of unidentifiable war junk stick out everywhere. Right in the centre of the village is a large Japanese gun that can still be moved on its pivot. The lagoon is also full of wreckage, including a few ships which would probably make interesting diving.

The lagoon beaches of Wotje Island are quite beautiful and relatively clean. The nearby small islands are even better as they're mostly deserted and at low tide you can walk right over to them.

Wotje, known as the 'Marshallese garden centre', is a sub-district centre with about 650 people. It's said that its abundant produce is due to topsoil the Japanese shipped over from Japan.

Places to Stay

There's a council house on Wotje where visitors may be able to stay, and sometimes families are willing to put people up as well. Mayor Tony Philips may be able to help you find a place to stay.

Another possibility is to contact Charles Domnick through DAR Car Rentals (☎ 625-3174) in Majuro. His family has a two-bedroom house with an ice box, kitchen and living room on Wotje that is sometimes available for rent.

Getting There & Away

Air Marshall Islands flies from Majuro to Wotje on Tuesdays and Thursdays. The cost is $84 one way.

MEJIT ISLAND

Mejit is a single coral island, about three-quarters of a sq mile, with a population of about 450 people. It's a beautiful island, with lush taro patches in the centre, and an abundance of coconut, breadfruit and pandanus trees.

Since Mejit does not have a protective lagoon, fishing and the unloading of field trip ships can be quite perilous. This is particularly true in November and December, months which also have pleasantly cooling winds. From May to July it's very humid and the mosquitoes are out in full force.

Mejit has a small freshwater lake, a rarity in the Marshalls, which even attracts a few wayward migrating ducks in the winter. If you can ignore the fact that it has quite a bit of algae, the lake is a nice place to swim.

California Beach, a beautiful beach on the north-west side of the island, is the best beach for swimming. Snorkelling is good north of California Beach.

Mejit has lots of seasonal tuna, as well as lobster and octopus and, unlike other islands, no poisonous fish. Fishing is still very traditional on Mejit. The men go out fishing every morning, except Sundays, in dugout canoes called *korkor*. They are hesitant to take foreigners out fishing and consider it plain bad luck to have a woman on board.

The island is known for its beautiful quality mats which the women weave from pandanus leaves.

Mejit has one of the best outer island schools and quite a few islanders speak fluent English. The people of Mejit are friendly and used to visitors as Peace Corps training sessions sometimes take place here.

Places to Stay
There's a government council house where you might be able to stay, but you should offer to pay something to the council for the privilege.

Getting There & Away
Air Marshall Islands flies from Majuro to Mejit on Tuesdays and Fridays. The cost is $106 one way. The field trip ship usually takes about eight days from Majuro, though it can take twice that long on the return as it loads up with copra on the way back.

JALUIT ATOLL
Traditionally Jaluit was the home of the high chief of the southern Ralik islands. Today it's a sub-district centre with a population of 1700 people; it's the only outer island with a public high school.

Jaluit's main island, Jabwor, was the headquarters of Jaluit Gesellschaft, a powerful group of German copra traders. It later became the German capital and Marshallese from other islands moved in, attracted by the schools, churches and higher standard of living.

When the Japanese took over they fortified the islands and started a fishing industry; the ruins of Japanese buildings and bunkers still remain. The USA captured the atoll during WW II but then mostly ignored it. In the 1950s Catholic and Protestant missions were set up and Jabwor began to prosper again.

In 1958 Typhoon Ophelia swept waves and wind over Jaluit, flooding the islands with water several feet deep, washing away most of the homes and coconut trees and killing 16 people. Jaluit is not a good place to be during typhoons; one in 1904 swept away at least 60 people.

You can see the wreck of the ship *Alfred* still on the reef at Jabwor Pass where it sank in 1899.

Jaluit Atoll has some of the best diving in the Marshalls, with lots of plane and shipwrecks, and as a consequence there are plans to build a small dive resort here. For the latest information, check with Marshalls Dive Adventures in Majuro.

Places to Stay & Eat
On Jabwor Island, there's a little coffee shop selling doughnuts and noodles, and an air-con public service commission house where visitors can sometimes stay.

Getting There & Away
Air Marshall Islands flies from Majuro to Jaluit on Mondays and Fridays. The cost is $72 one way.

KILI ISLAND
In 1948, the US government resettled the displaced Bikinian people on 200-acre Kili, a single isolated island which was uninhabited before they arrived.

The Bikinians soon learned that the canoes they had brought with them to Kili were useless as the island has no easy access to the sea; there is no lagoon, no port – not even a nice beach. The surf is so rough that nearly half of the year it's inaccessible by boat. Once a society of famed navigators, their seafaring skills are dying with the older Bikinian men.

Kili is now home to about 900 of the 2050 Bikinians (nearly as many live in Majuro). Despite the fact that a Bikinian trust fund distributes a $2000 annual stipend to each islander, most people still live in the ramshackle shacks that the Americans built for them in 1948, albeit now furnished with TVs and VCRs.

The biggest annual event on Kili is still Bikini Day, held in March on the anniversary of the day in 1946 that the Bikinians became 'nuclear nomads'. There are sporting events and feasts, but much of the day is taken up by wistful speeches from the elders about returning to their homeland.

Getting There & Away
Air Marshall Islands flies from Majuro to Kili on Mondays and Saturdays. The cost is $84 one way.

AUR ATOLL
Aur Atoll has a population of 450 people who are equally divided between Tobal and Aur islands. The atoll is 75 miles north of Majuro and just a few miles south of Maloelap. The other islands in the atoll are officially uninhabited, though they're used for copra production and families sometimes live on these islands for stretches of a month or two.

Aur is a scenic atoll with a beautiful lagoon and excellent snorkelling. Not only is there a good variety of tropical fish and corals, but it's not uncommon to see turtles and small sharks.

Aur is a fairly traditional atoll and a good place to see both men and women making handicrafts. The people of Aur specialise in making model canoes and large wall hangings.

Getting There & Away
Air Marshall Islands flies from Majuro to Aur on Tuesdays. The one-way fare is $41.

AILINGLAPLAP ATOLL
Ailinglaplap is the Marshall Islands' third largest atoll, with the land area measuring 5.67 sq miles. It is home to over 1700 people, surpassed in population only by Majuro and Kwajalein. Ailinglaplap is also one of the biggest copra producers in the Marshalls.

Woja, one of the main islands, is about seven miles long and has approximately 600 people. Though there are few 'sights' as such, Woja is a lovely, lush island with white sand beaches. The large protected lagoon offers good snorkelling, swimming and fishing. The island has a good school with some US-educated teachers; many people speak English and are friendly to visitors. There's an abundance of local food, particularly in the summer, and a couple of stores, though no restaurants or hotels. A few pick-up trucks act as taxis.

Getting There & Away
Air Marshall Islands flies to three islands in the atoll: to Airok on Wednesdays and to Jeh and Woja on Saturdays. The one-way fare from Majuro is $65 to Jeh, $79 to Airok and $84 to Woja.

Small private boats can take you across the expansive lagoon from one island to another for about $50 one way, and sometimes there are government boats around which can do the same at nominal cost.

OTHER ATOLLS
Many Marshallese claim that **Wotho**, with a population of 120, is the most beautiful atoll in the world. It has a pretty lagoon full of giant clams that are harvested by the islanders. Wotho is a traditional place and it helps if visitors speak a little Marshallese, though the mayor knows some English.

Although flying fish are caught throughout the Marshalls, they are especially associated with **Ailuk Atoll**, figuring in Ailuk's music, dance and legends. The fish are caught at night using lights and scoop nets, and Ailuk is known for its delicious flying fish cuisine. The atoll has a population of about 500 people. Many of the finer woven baskets sold in Majuro are made in Ailuk.

Namorik is a lovely diamond-shaped atoll with about 800 people and a plan to build a little two-storey hotel in the centre of the village. If you want to know more about Namorik, inquire at the Ajidrik Hotel in Majuro, whose owner is the mayor of Namorik.

Bikar Atoll, **Taka** and **Taongi** atolls and **Jemo Island** are uninhabited by people, but are home to birds, coconut crabs and sea turtles.

Researchers from the East-West Center in Honolulu and the South Pacific Regional Environment Programme inspected atolls in the Marshalls a few years ago and recommended designating Taongi and Bikar as National Preservation Areas. The team called Taongi (also known as Bokaak) 'possibly the only example of a completely natural, unaltered, semiarid atoll ecosystem remaining in the world today'. Taongi has an abundance of shearwaters, a kind of seabird which burrows into the sand to nest. Bikar has an especially large population of green sea turtles.

GETTING THERE & AWAY
Air
The government-owned Air Marshall Islands (☎ 625-3733 in Majuro) operates services to about two dozen islands, touching down at every inhabited atoll.

From Majuro, AMI flies daily to Kwajalein and at least once a week to every other atoll. Some flights hop across a couple of islands at a time, so it can be possible to visit a few different islands without returning to Majuro each time.

The flight schedule changes periodically, so if you're intent on using AMI write ahead for a schedule (Box 1319, Majuro, MH 96960) or pick one up at the Majuro office. AMI flies 48-passenger HS748s and 20-passenger Dornier 228s to the outer islands and a Saab 2000 jetprop on its Fiji route.

Boat
The Marshalls have four field trip ships – *Micro Pilot, Micro Palm, Micro Chief* and the M/V *Juk Ae* – which service the outer islands about once a month, dropping off supplies and picking up copra. The first three boats are 179 feet long, the latter 100 feet long.

There are a number of different routes. Typically two or three days are spent at each stop. The longest run is the western field trip which goes to Kwajalein, Lae, Ujae, Wotho, Enewetak and Ujelang, a round-trip distance of 1510 miles that takes about three weeks. The eastern route takes in nine islands on Arno Atoll and six on Mili Atoll, covering 175 miles in two to three weeks. The southern route takes two weeks and goes to Jaluit, Kili, Ebon and Namorik, a trip of 680 miles. The remaining atolls are covered in the northern and central routes.

The fare is 13 cents per mile on deck. Cabins, when available, cost 40 cents per mile and are basic, with two bunk beds and a sink. There's no air-con and bathrooms are usually shared. Meals cost about $10 per day.

Scheduling information is available from the Transportation Office (☎ 625-3469, fax 625-3486), Box 1079, Majuro, MH 96960, at Uliga Dock in Majuro. The boats, however, leave from the new dock near the copra processing plant.

Yachties should radio ahead from Majuro before visiting outer islands and should check in with the mayor of each atoll upon arrival in the lagoon. This is more than a simple courtesy, as failure to notify the mayor is likely to make you an unwelcome guest.

GETTING AROUND
Some islands have vehicles – such as a pick-up truck that doubles as an inexpensive taxi – but most of the time people just walk.

Outer islands usually have at least one motorboat and trips to other islands within the atoll can generally be arranged if visitors are willing to pay for petrol and maybe a little extra. Each situation is different, but the price to an island one hour away by motorboat might be about $25.

Sometimes the uninhabited atoll islands are used for copra production or to raise livestock. The more remote islands often have the best beaches and occasionally have thatched shelters for overnight stays.

For a price, it should be fairly easy to get someone to take you fishing, lobstering, coconut-crab hunting and the like. Check with the mayor to see if there is a local fishing ordinance or a fee.

Federated States of Micronesia

The Federated States of Micronesia (FSM) consists of the four states of Kosrae, Pohnpei, Chuuk and Yap. All are part of the Caroline Islands, and all have similar colonial histories under Spain, Germany, Japan and the USA, yet the four states have their own distinctive cultures, traditions and identities.

The 110,000 residents of the FSM have eight major indigenous languages between them and no two states have the same native tongue. They communicate with each other in English, the language of their most recent colonial administrator.

The main thread that ties these widely scattered islands together is their new political affiliation as the FSM.

POLITICAL BEGINNINGS

In July 1978, the Trust Territory districts of Pohnpei, Kosrae, Chuuk (formerly Truk), Yap, the Marshalls and Palau voted on a common constitution. The Marshalls and Palau rejected it, along with the concept of a single unified Micronesian nation, and went on to establish separate political futures. What was left became, by default, the Federated States of Micronesia.

National and state governments were then elected. Tosiwo Nakayama of Chuuk became the first FSM president under the new FSM constitution which took effect on 10 May 1979.

In October 1982 the FSM signed a 15-year Compact of Free Association with the USA which guaranteed annual funding to the islands in exchange for granting the USA exclusive military access to the region. The compact was approved by FSM voters in a 1983 plebiscite and officially imple-

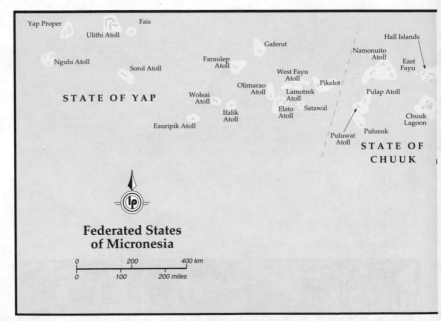

Federated States of Micronesia

mented in November 1986. In 1991 the FSM was admitted to the UN.

While the compact pretty much gives the US military carte blanche to do anything it wants in the FSM, with the winding down of the Cold War the only US military presence currently in the region are a couple of Civic Action Teams that construct schools and roads.

GEOGRAPHY

The FSM has 607 islands sprinkled across more than a million sq miles of the Pacific and extends 1800 miles from east to west. About 65 islands are inhabited.

The total land area is 271 sq miles. Pohnpei has nearly half the land area, with the rest almost equally divided between the other three states.

GOVERNMENT

The FSM has three levels of government: national, state and municipal.

The national government is divided into executive, legislative and judicial branches. The FSM Congress is unicameral, with 14 senators. Each state elects one senator-at-large and the other 10 are elected based on population apportionment (five from Chuuk, three from Pohnpei, one each from Kosrae and Yap). The president and vice president, who cannot be from the same state, are elected by Congress from among its members. The national capital is in Palikir on Pohnpei.

Each state has its own governor elected by popular vote for a four-year term, an elected state legislature and a state court.

On a municipal level, the traditional village leaders play an active role in government. They often select candidates for political office, and whether the village leaders approve or disapprove legislation usually determines how people vote. It's common for the mayor of a municipality to be a local chief.

FSM

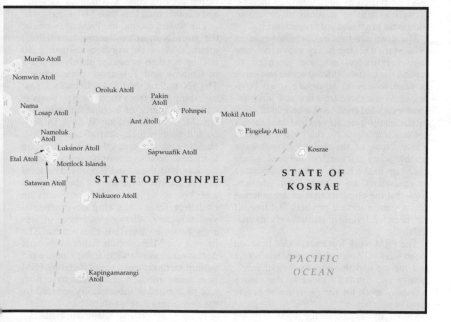

Murilo Atoll

Nomwin Atoll

Oroluk Atoll

Pakin Atoll

Nama
Losap Atoll

Pohnpei   Mokil Atoll

Ant Atoll

Namoluk Atoll

Pingelap Atoll

Lukunor Atoll

Sapwuafik Atoll

Kosrae

Etal Atoll

Mortlock Islands

Satawan Atoll   **STATE OF POHNPEI**

STATE OF KOSRAE

Nukuoro Atoll

PACIFIC OCEAN

Kapingamarangi Atoll

Constitution of the Federated States of Micronesia
PREAMBLE

WE, the people of Micronesia, exercising our inherent sovereignty, do hereby establish the Constitution of the Federated States of Micronesia.

With this Constitution, we affirm our common wish to live together in peace and harmony, to preserve the heritage of the past, and to protect the promise of the future.

To make one nation of many islands, we respect the diversity of our cultures. Our differences enrich us. The seas bring us together, they do not separate us. Our islands sustain us, our island nation enlarges us and makes us stronger.

Our ancestors, who made their homes on these islands, displaced no other people. We, who remain, wish no other home than this. Having known war, we hope for peace. Having been divided, we wish unity. Having been ruled, we seek freedom.

Micronesia began in the days when man explored seas in rafts and canoes. The Micronesian nation is born in an age when men voyage among stars; our world itself is an island. We extend to all nations what we seek from each: peace, friendship, cooperation and love in our common humanity. With this Constitution we, who have been the wards of other nations, become the proud guardian of our own islands, now and forever. ■

ECONOMY

The FSM economy is still buoyed by US funding. During the 15 years of its compact with the USA, the FSM will receive a total of $1.34 billion in direct compact monies, as well as tens of millions of dollars in additional grant and aid programmes.

The compact funding, which began in 1986, started off top-heavy with a five-year capital infusion that was intended to expand the islands' infrastructure and serve as seed money to stimulate small businesses. While there are a few new airstrips, some extended roads and a couple of electrification projects, all said and done there's not much to show for the capital infusion phase. None of the district islands have potable water and much of the seed money ended up in the hands of foreign investors or squandered on corrupt local schemes. Now that the compact monies are tapering down, public service projects that haven't yet been undertaken are unlikely to materialise.

The FSM work force is divided between those who rely on subsistence agriculture and fishing and those in the labour force. Nearly two-thirds of those in the money economy work for the government in one form or another.

Under the Japanese the FSM was not only self-sufficient, but actually exported food. Now, however, the cost of imported food and beverages in the FSM is largely responsible for a huge trade imbalance in which imports total $75 million annually and exports total less than $10 million.

The waters around the FSM are some of the world's most productive tuna-fishing grounds. A catch worth more than $250 million is taken annually, mainly by fleets of Chinese and Taiwanese purse seiners. The $20 million the FSM collects each year as fishing fees from these foreign boats is its largest source of income following US aid. Most of the fishing is done in anti-quated boats which, despite coming from cholera-endemic areas, have no sanitation facilities and commonly dump waste directly into the island lagoons. The local papers are rife with stories about junkets and bribes to government officials in exchange for overlooking environmental violations and allowing hundreds of foreign boats to overfish the waters. The impact on Micronesian fishers has been devastating, as islanders using century-old fishing methods and a small fledgling FSM fleet using modern equipment have both had their catches substantially reduced by the competing foreign ships.

Efforts are being made to build up

tourism in the FSM, but it remains small-scale on all the islands, in large part due to their remoteness and the high cost of air travel to them.

Kosrae

Kosrae is a casual, unpretentious backwater, where people consistently return a smile. This is one of the least spoiled and least developed areas in Micronesia, an unhurried place that retains a certain air of innocence.

A high volcanic island whose peaks are draped in lush tropical greenery and sometimes shrouded in clouds, Kosrae is rich in natural beauty. It has an interior of uncharted rainforests, a pristine fringing reef and a coast which is a mix of sandy beaches and mangrove swamps. Flowering hibiscus, bananas and coconuts are abundant and the island is known for its citrus fruit, especially oranges, tangerines and limes.

The ruins of Kosrae's ancient stone city, Lelu, while not as well known as Pohnpei's Nan Madol ruins, are nearly as impressive and more easily accessible.

The introduction of the first jet service to Kosrae in the late 1980s has had a surprisingly limited impact. Having more than a dozen visitors on the island at any one time is still quite unusual and, in a friendly way, people take note when someone new is in town.

Kosrae, pronounced ko-SHRYE (last syllable rhymes with 'rye'), was formerly called Kusaie.

HISTORY
Kosrae once had the most stratified society in Micronesia. By the year 1400 Kosrae was unified under one paramount chief, or *tokosra*, who ruled from the island of Lelu. Essentially a handful of high chiefs owned the land, low chiefs managed it and the

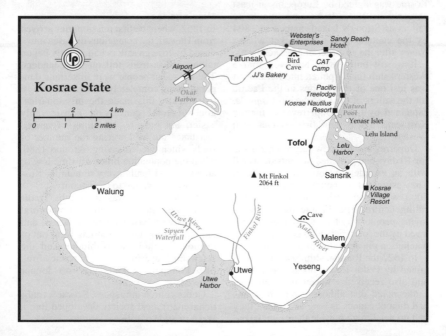

mass of commoners worked it. It was a feudalistic system with each group passing a percentage of their produce up the ladder.

While the commoners lived on the main island, which was then called Ualang, the royalty and their retainers lived inside more than 100 basalt-walled compounds on Lelu and the nearby islets of Pisin, Yenyen and Yenasr. With its canal system and coral streets, the fortressed island of Lelu would have rivalled its medieval counterparts in Europe.

There are indications that Kosrae once was an important power in the region. Pohnpeian legend says that around the 14th century Kosraean warriors sailed to Pohnpei and overthrew the tyrannical *saudeleur* dynasty that ruled that island. Chuukese legends also suggest cultural influences from Kosrae around the same time.

European Contact

Kosrae was sighted by Europeans at least as early as 1801. It became known to sailors as Strong's Island, named in 1804 by the captain of the Nantucket whaler *Nancy* after the governor of Massachusetts.

It wasn't until 1824, however, that a Western ship finally pulled into harbour. It was just one of many stops in the Pacific for the sailors of the French ship *Coquille*, captained by Louis Duperrey, but for the Kosraeans it was their first contact with Westerners.

Duperrey and his crew stayed on Kosrae for 10 days and provided the outside world with an excellent account of the island. They estimated the population to be about 5000, with about 1500 living on Lelu, the ruling centre. The Kosraeans, a peace-loving people who had no weapons, were awed by the foreigners who gave them iron hatchets, a pig and other presents.

In 1827 the Russian ship *Senyavin*, captained by Fedor Lutke, docked at Kosrae and also received a hospitable welcome. Lutke noted that although the Kosraeans had dugout canoes as long as 30 feet, they had no need to go outside their own island and had no boats equipped for the open ocean.

Whalers and traders started calling at Kosrae in the early 1830s, attracted by deep-water harbours and reports of plentiful supplies of food, water, wood and women.

Not all early confrontations were peaceful ones, however. In 1835 Kosraeans torched the Hawaiian ship *Waverly* and massacred the entire crew, apparently as revenge against the sailors who had boldly bedded island women without first getting permission from Kosraean men. The Boston trading ship *Honduras* was similarly attacked the same year, with only two of its crew managing to escape.

In the early 1840s relations again became harmonious under the reign of chief Awane Lapalik I, who was known as 'Good King George' by visiting Westerners. From then until the decline of whaling in the Pacific in the mid-1860s, whale ships visited Kosrae by the dozens each year.

Missionaries

In 1852, when the first missionaries arrived from Hawaii, the contagious diseases introduced by foreign sailors had already begun taking a disastrous toll on the islanders. The Kosraean people were in serious danger of being completely obliterated.

Ironically this made the missionaries' goal of total conversion considerably easier, not only by lessening organised resistance but by lowering the number of souls which needed saving. Around 1880, when the population hit an all-time low of about 300, virtually every remaining Kosraean was converted to Christianity.

The conversion was thorough. Traditional songs, dances, myths and other oral histories were discouraged or banned and ultimately forgotten. Tattooing went out of fashion, alcohol was forbidden and the ceremonial use of *seka*, a narcotic drink like Pohnpei's sakau, was no longer allowed.

Under church influences, Kosrae's traditional matrilineal society developed into a Western-style patrilineal system.

Traders

Traders started arriving in full force in the 1870s. One of Kosrae's most famous visitors during this time was the American 'Bully' Hayes, a notorious swindler and trader who roamed the Pacific after years of involvement in the China opium trade. He was a frequent visitor to Kosrae, where he traded in beche-de-mer, copra and coconut oil.

In March 1874 Hayes' 218-ton brigantine *Leonora* sank in Utwe Harbor during a sudden storm, becoming Kosrae's most famous shipwreck. Hayes was murdered at sea three years later in a brawl with his ship's cook, Dutch Pete.

Some believe that at the time of his death, Hayes was on his way back to Kosrae to recover the treasure he had rescued from the sinking *Leonora* and reputedly buried somewhere on the island. These rumours have inspired many a treasure hunt on Kosrae.

Japanese Period

The Japanese, who arrived in 1914, exploited Kosrae's natural resources and took over three of the island's four coastal villages, forcing the Kosraeans to move inland.

Developments in agriculture, forestry, fishing and copra helped support the Japanese war effort during WW II, as well as provide for the 7000 Japanese living on the island. Kosrae was never invaded by Allied forces during the war.

Post WW II

After the war, when the USA took over and the Trust Territory was set up, Kosrae was included in the Pohnpei district. For three decades thereafter Kosrae played only a secondary role as development was centred on Pohnpei, 350 miles to the north-west.

In 1977 Kosrae broke away from Pohnpei, becoming a separate district within the Trust Territory and later a separate FSM state. Although Kosrae gets more funding this way than it would as an appendage of Pohnpei State, a desire for a bigger slice of the pie was not the only motive. Kosraeans

and Pohnpeians had never before considered themselves one political unit until lumped together at the whim of the US administration.

GEOGRAPHY

Kosrae is roughly triangular, covering an area of 42 sq miles. It's one-third the size of Pohnpei, an island it resembles in shape and topography.

Kosrae has a rugged interior of mountain ridges and river valleys. A full 70% of the island is mountainous and another 15% is given over to mangrove swamps. Mt Finkol, the highest point, rises to 2064 feet.

Lelu, Utwe and Okat are the main deepwater harbours and all villages are along the coast.

Kosrae is the easternmost island of both the Federated States of Micronesia and the Caroline Island chain. It is the only state in the FSM with no outer islands.

CLIMATE

Temperatures on Kosrae average 80°F year round. Rainfall averages 185 to 250 inches per year and is heaviest in summer, with more falling on the west coast than on the east. Trade winds come mainly from the north-east and are weakest from May to November. Kosrae is fortunate to lie outside the main typhoon tracks and even strong storms are relatively rare.

ECONOMY

Most people still rely on subsistence farming and fishing for their livelihood. Less than 15% of the population works in the money economy and 75% of those work for the government. Cutbacks in the local budget have recently resulted in scaling back working hours and as a consequence visitors will find many government offices, including the tourist office and museum, closing in mid-afternoon.

Some produce is exported to Majuro, Pohnpei and Guam, the main crops being bananas, limes, tangerines and taro. The FSM Aquaculture Center in Lelu grows giant clams for export to restaurants in

Pohnpei and Chuuk. Fruit bats caught in Utwe are exported to Saipan.

While the Chinese fishing company Ting Hong is active in Kosraen waters, Kosrae is the only one of the four FSM states that doesn't allow the company to use purse seiners and instead restricts the boats to using long-line methods. In part due to a shipwreck off Sandy Beach that spilled oil, there's a growing movement to push Ting Hong out of Kosraean waters and replace it with a local fishing fleet.

POPULATION & PEOPLE
Kosrae is home to 8100 people, which accounts for just 7.3% of the FSM's total population. Approximately 3000 people live in the Lelu and Tofol areas, 1670 in greater Malem, 1300 in the Utwe area, 1900 in Tafunsak and 230 in Walung.

SOCIETY & CONDUCT
In Kosrae when you talk about the culture, you talk about religion – the most essential part of modern Kosraean society. About 90% of all Kosraeans are Congregationalists.

The religious beliefs and practices of the late 1800s that so totally overtook the islanders have changed little over the years, though today the ministers are Kosraean.

The church has a firm grip on most aspects of Kosraean life and while it no doubt helps to make Kosrae a homogenous, law-abiding society it also tends to foster intolerance. Conversion to another faith, even another Protestant faith, is usually seen as a disgrace to the rest of the family. As a consequence, the convert is commonly ostracised and disinherited from family land.

RELIGION
Although most Kosraeans are Congregationalist, there's also a Baptist church in Malem and a Mormon church in Utwe.

LANGUAGE
English is the official language of the government and is widely spoken, though Kosraean, the native language, is more commonly used in everyday conversation.

'Good morning' is *tu wo*, 'good afternoon' is *lwen wo*, 'good evening' is *ekwe wo* and 'good night' is *fong wo*. 'Thank you (very much)' is *kulo (na maluhlap)*.

It is said that early whalers used the expression 'ah shit' so often that the islanders picked up on it and identified the whalers as *ahset*. This is still the common word for 'foreigner' today.

HOLIDAYS & FESTIVALS
Kosrae celebrates these holidays:

New Year's Day
    1 January
Kosrae Constitution Day
    11 January
FSM Constitution Day
    10 May
Kosrae Liberation Day
    8 September
FSM Independence Day
    3 November
Thanksgiving
    last Thursday in November
Christmas
    25 December

Liberation Day, which commemorates the day the Americans liberated Kosrae from the Japanese at the end of WW II, is marked by spirited sports competitions and canoe races between village teams. A sincere effort is made to include everyone in the festivities and there's usually an 'ahset' team that visitors are welcome to join.

Christmas features formation marching and singing competitions between church choirs, a memorable experience as Kosraeans are outstanding singers. The events include a grand feast that is open to all.

Another way to experience Kosraean singing is to just head for the nearest village church on any Sunday. The hymns are sung in four-part harmony and the whole congregation joins in.

ORIENTATION
Kosrae is divided into four districts, called municipalities, which are named after the main village in each: Lelu, Malem, Utwe

and Tafunsak. Kosrae's administrative centre is in Tofol, two miles south of the causeway to Lelu Island.

Historically Kosrae's population was dispersed around the coast in about 70 villages and many of the names of now-uninhabited villages are still used to designate sites.

The airport is on an artificial island off the north-west side of Kosrae. From the airport, the main road runs clockwise around the coast, ending in Utwe. The road between the airport and Tofol is paved, and there are plans to eventually pave the section between Tofol and Utwe.

Walung, a major village on the west coast, can only be reached by boat.

ACTIVITIES
Diving
Kosrae has unspoiled coral reefs close to shore and both walk-in and boat diving. The confluence of two currents makes for prolific and varied marine life. Underwater visibility can easily be 100 feet, and in summer as much as 200 feet!

There's an American PBY search plane in about 60 feet of water at the mouth of Lelu Harbor. Also in Lelu Harbor are two Japanese boats, including a 300-foot freighter, which were skip-bombed and blown apart, and the remains of a whaling ship. All these dives are best done during a spell of clear weather, as rain can substantially cut harbour visibility.

The Blue Hole in Lelu is also good for diving and harbours coral heads, lionfish, sting rays and lots of big fish including barracuda.

In the south, a nice dive spot is Hiroshi's Point, which is a drift dive that goes over beautiful soft corals and in summer often takes you past hammerhead sharks.

Bully Hayes' ship, the *Leonora*, remained untouched in Utwe Harbor for more than 90 years. After a diving team from the Scripps Oceanographic Institute in California and a private group from Kwajalein stripped artefacts from the wreck, the site was officially designated off-limits to sport divers. Now the wreck is

protected under law and can only be visited with advance notice and when accompanied by a guide authorised by the Historic Preservation Office.

There's good diving between Utwe Harbor and Walung, where large groupers, barracuda and hump-headed parrotfish can be seen. At several places you can just step into the water at high tide, swim out 50 to 100 feet and start diving.

The most shark activity, including tiger sharks and small docile whitetips, is between Walung and Okat. Kosraeans say there hasn't been a shark attack in three generations.

Dive Shops There are two good dive operations on the island. The fees given for both include tanks and weights; other gear can be rented.

The Australian-run Kosrae Nautilus Divers (☎ 370-3567, fax 370-3568), Box

---

Never on Sunday

It is Kosraean custom to be quiet on Sunday. Not only are stores and businesses closed on Sundays, but even recreational activities are frowned upon. US Civic Action Team (CAT) soldiers building roads on the island caused quite a sensation a few years back by water-skiing in the harbour on Sunday.

The official government tourist brochure advises visitors as follows:

On Sundays:
- DO wear long pants and a shirt with a collar (men) or a dress (women)
- DO feel free to attend church (the Kosraeans are noted for their choral singing), visit friends, read and relax
- DO NOT cook, work, collect seashells, snorkel, water-ski or scuba dive
- DO NOT fish or obtain any other marine life (Category One misdemeanor)
- DO NOT drink alcoholic beverages (Category One misdemeanor)

Please understand that this list of suggested behavior is not meant to limit your enjoyment or recreational opportunities while visiting Kosrae. Instead, it is intended to help you appreciate both the culture and spectacular beauty of our island. ■

135, Kosrae, FM 96944, at Kosrae Nautilus Resort, caters to English speakers. The resort has a 27-foot boat that can carry up to 10 divers. A two-tank boat dive costs $85, including lunch. An escorted shore dive to the Blue Hole costs $45 and you can also rent tanks alone for $10.

Phoenix Marine Sports Club Kosrae (☎ 370-3100, fax 370-3509), Box PHM, Kosrae, FM 96944, a third of a mile south of the CAT Camp, is a branch of the Japanese dive operation of the same name based in Pohnpei. Although they cater predominantly to Japanese divers on packaged tours, they'll take English-speaking divers as well. You'll have more flexibility if you go out independently with Phoenix rather than join a group, as Japanese pack-tour divers prefer to plan their diving destinations in advance and stick to the schedule. Rates are $65 for a two-tank dive if there are two or more people and $100 if you go out alone. For $5 more you can have lunch included.

Snorkelling & Swimming

The best spots for snorkelling and swimming change with the seasons and the trade winds. Conditions are usually good between Malem and Utwe in the winter, though there are treacherous currents and rogue waves around Malem itself. The areas near Tafunsak, around the bridge to the airport and off Kosrae's north-east point are usually good in the summer, but can be rough from December to February. Amongst these, the north-east side of the airport runway is a favourite snorkelling spot, with 15- to 20-foot walls, lobsters, giant clams, sting rays and good visibility, but be cautious of currents in the channel.

The natural swimming hole formed in the reef alongside Lelu causeway is good for swimming. Because it tends to silt up, it's not well suited for snorkelling. However, farther out on the reef, near Yenasr Islet, there's another natural pool, the Blue Hole, that's larger and deeper and harbours lots of marine life and coral. This is where the early Kosraeans deposited the bones of

their kings. Snorkelling is good . . . if you dare!

Snorkellers who go out with the dive companies are often taken to Walung, which has coral gardens.

Local women go swimming in clothes that cover their knees.

Kosrae Nautilus Divers rents snorkel sets for $15 and usually also has reef walkers for rent.

Hiking

For a short hike in Tofol, there's an easy walk up to the radio tower which offers a nice view of the surrounding area and Lelu. For something a bit more substantial, the hike up the Tafunsak Gorge (see the Tafunsak section) makes for a pleasant little afternoon outing.

The most rewarding and challenging hike on the island, however, is the hike from Utwe to the top of Mt Finkol. The whole trip takes eight to 10 hours and hikers should be in good shape as it's a strenuous climb. Much of the trail follows the Finkol River; expect to get wet as the route jumps across river rocks and sloshes through mud. At the top you'll be rewarded with an incredible view that includes all three of the island's harbours.

The Mt Finkol hike requires a guide. Hanson Nena of Utwe does a great job and charges $50 for a group of one to four people, or $15 each for five people or more. He can be reached at the power plant in Tofol during weekday working hours; give him as much notice as possible.

Other Activities

Kosrae has a big gym, behind the high school in Tofol, that doubles as a meeting hall for special events. There's also an adjacent athletic field and a tennis court, all open to the public.

TOFOL

Tofol is the state administrative centre, though it's so small that it seems odd to think of it as the centre of anything. It's just a few buildings scattered here and there along a couple of dusty roads.

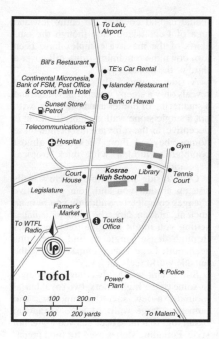

To Lelu,
Airport

Bill's Restaurant

TE's Car Rental

Continental Micronesia,
Bank of FSM, Post Office
& Coconut Palm Hotel

Islander Restaurant

Bank of Hawaii

Sunset Store/
Petrol

Telecommunications

Hospital

Gym

Kosrae
High School

Library

Tennis
Court

Court
House

Legislature

Farmer's
Market

Tourist
Office

To WTFL
Radio

Tofol

Power
Plant

Police

0   100   200 m

0   100   200 yards

To Malem

KOSRAE

You can get an excellent view of Tofol and Lelu Island by following the narrow dirt road up to the radio station. Though it's possible to drive up (carefully, in first gear!), it takes just 10 minutes to walk up and by walking you'll be able to take a closer look at Kosrae's lush flora, including a stand of painted eucalyptus trees with rainbow-coloured bark.

Information

Tourist Office The tourist office (☎ 370-2228, fax 370-2066), housed in a traditional-style Kosraean building with a high-pitched thatched roof, has basic brochures, can arrange guided tours and sells a few handicraft items. It's open from 7.30 am to 2.30 pm Monday to Friday, closed on weekends.

Money The island's two banks, the Bank of the FSM and the Bank of Hawaii, are both in Tofol and are open from 9.30 am to 2.30 pm Monday to Friday. Credit cards are accepted by most hotels, Continental Micronesia and the telephone company, but expect other transactions on the island to be in cash.

Post The post office is open from 8 am to 3.30 pm Monday to Friday and from 8 to 11 am on Saturdays.

Telecommunications Local and long-distance telephone calls can be made 24 hours a day from the FSM Telecommunications building in Tofol. Local calls are free; simply pick up the phone in one of the two booths and tell the operator who you want to call. The office will send long-distance faxes for the cost of a phone call; telex and telegram service is available when the equipment is working.

The rate to call between FSM states is $1 a minute between 6 am and 6 pm on weekdays, and 50 cents a minute at all other times. Phone calls to all parts of the world except the FSM have a three-minute minimum charge – the per-minute rate is $2.50 to the USA or Guam ($2 on Sundays); $3 to the Marshall Islands, Palau, Saipan or Australia; $4 to Canada, the UK or Germany; $5 to most everywhere else.

Library You can read the *Pacific Daily News* and browse magazines and books about Micronesia at the library, which is at Kosrae High School. It's open from 8 am to 2.30 pm weekdays and occasionally on Saturday mornings.

Media Kosrae's only radio station is at 1500 AM. Kosrae doesn't have its own newspaper, but Guam's *Pacific Daily News* is sold at Bill's Restaurant.

Airline Office The Continental Micronesia office (☎ 370-3024) is open from 8 am to 4 pm on Mondays and Wednesdays and from 9 am to 4 pm on Tuesdays, Thursdays and Fridays.

Other Information The island's small hospital (☎ 370-3012) is in Tofol. The Peace

Corps has a small office at Kosrae High School.

LELU ISLAND

Lelu (also spelled Leluh) is a separate island connected to the rest of Kosrae by a causeway.

The early Kosraeans artificially extended the low part of Lelu by piling stones and packing coral upon the surrounding reef. They then used the new land to build a massive walled city for Kosraean royalty.

Lelu Hill, the island's high point, has a scattering of caves and tunnels used by the Japanese during WW II. There's a good view of the harbour from the top of the hill, which once held a Japanese observation tower and gun emplacements. A trail goes up the hill, but as it's across private land, it's best to find a local guide; inquire at the museum.

Museum

The state museum is housed in the oldest Western-style building on the island – a small cement warehouse built at the turn of the century. The museum has charts and drawings detailing different aspects of Lelu's history and photos of the archaeological work done at the ruins. There are also a few artefacts such as ancient basalt food pounders and adzes made from giant clam shells.

The museum is a good place to start a visit to Lelu ruins. Not only can you get a free brochure to a self-guided walk through the ruins, but if the museum staff is not busy they can provide a guide to go through the ruins with you. While there's no charge for the guide service a donation to the museum is appreciated.

The museum is open from 9 am to 3 pm Monday to Friday, closed on weekends and holidays. There's no admission fee for the museum or the ruins.

Lelu Ruins

The construction of Lelu dates back at least as far as 1400 AD, and probably as early as 1250 AD. In its heyday this royal city and feudal capital covered the entire lowland area of Lelu Island, and though the outskirts of the massive complex have been torn down the remaining ruins still cover a third of the island.

A ride around Lelu's perimeter road reveals only a sleepy waterfront village and a smattering of homes and businesses, with not a single stone wall in sight. But Lelu is deceptive, as the ruins are just behind these homes, beyond their backyards, almost completely hidden with thick tropical vegetation.

Once inside the complex, Lelu's walls rise up around you and your perspective changes completely. Suddenly you're in an ancient, hidden city, the kind of isolated setting you might imagine trekking hours through dense jungle to find. The ruins seem quite large and encompassing and the outside world feels far away.

Still extant are the dwelling compounds of some of the high chiefs, two royal burial mounds, a few sacred compounds and numerous large walls of huge hexagonal basalt logs that have been stacked log-cabin style. Pounding stones used for food preparation or making seka are identifiable by their smooth, indented surfaces.

To enter the ruins, take the driveway between the two houses directly across the road from the museum. Follow the path past the houses and continue walking straight back along the right side of the pigpen; within a minute you'll be within the ruins. Continue straight ahead through the complex and just before crossing the canal take the stone footpath on the left to get to **Kinyeir Fulat**, one of the most impressive sections of the ruins. Kinyeir Fulat, which has stacked prismatic basalt walls reaching 20 feet high, is believed to have served as both dwelling compound and meeting house.

The compounds opposite Kinyeir Fulat are known as **Pensa**. The walls at Pensa are mostly of medium-sized round basalt stones, with some brain coral added in, a later-day architectural feature. The high chief's feast house occupied the south-east compound, and the adjacent areas of Pensa,

KOSRAE

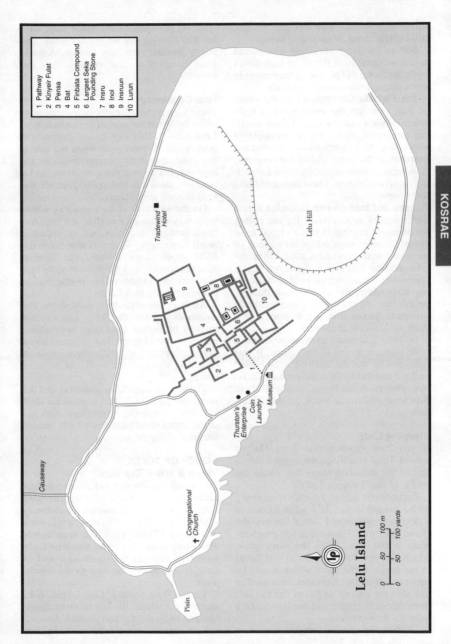

Lelu Island

1 Pathway
2 Kinyeir Fulat
3 Pensa
4 Bat
5 Finbata Compound
6 Largest Seka Pounding Stone
7 Insru
8 Inol
9 Insrunn
10 Lurun

Tradewind Hotel

Lelu Hill

Insrunn

Inol

Insru

Lurun

Bat

Pensa

Finbata Compound

Kinyeir Fulat

Museum

Thurston's Enterprise

Coin Laundry

Causeway

Congregational Church

Pisin

0   50   100 m
0   50   100 yards

which were once used for food preparation, still contain about 20 pounding stones.

Bat is the large dwelling compound across the canal from Pensa. Its high basalt walls are thought to be among the newest in town, dating from around 1600 AD.

The **Finbata Compound**, to the south of Bat, contains the remains of a feast house, while **Lurun**, a high-walled dwelling compound, offers another example of impressive stacked prismatic architecture. **Insruun**, at the north end of the complex, is thought to have originally been a dwelling compound that was later converted into other uses.

Insru and **Inol** contain mounded tombs which served as temporary resting places for deceased royalty. It was a sacred area, closed to commoners except for a group of wailing female mourners who, from the time the king was laid in the crypt, kept a continuous watch over his tomb and decaying body. After the king's flesh decomposed, the bones were ceremoniously carried to Yenasr Islet and dropped into a deep, natural hole in the reef.

In 1910 a German excavation found a male skeleton in one of the tombs. It was presumed he was the last king to be buried on Lelu and that in the whirlwind of Christian conversion his bones, and with them Kosraean traditions, were quickly abandoned.

Sleeping Lady
If you look south across Lelu Harbor toward Tofol you'll see the rugged ridgeline of the mountain range that forms the profile of the 'Sleeping Lady'.

According to legend the gods were angry with a woman so they laid her in the sea in a sleeping position and turned her into the island of Kosrae. The woman was menstruating at the time, or so the story goes, which accounts for the rich red soil found in the jungle at the place which would be between her thighs. Kosraean men used to trek into the interior to gather the red soil from this sacred place and use it to make a paint for their canoes.

To view the profile, imagine a woman lying on her back facing south-east, with her hair flowing out behind her head. The pointy 'breasts' are easy to spot. A good place to enjoy a clear view is from the church.

Lelu Causeway
There's a natural saltwater swimming pool off to the left at the start of the causeway to Lelu Island. This expansive, deeply cut pool is full of water even when the tide is low and the flats surrounding it are exposed. It's a good place to swim, and a concrete platform and stairs just off the road provide easy access.

On the west side of the causeway where there was once a tiny airstrip, the land has been dredged and reshaped to create a small boat marina. This area also holds the FSM Aquaculture Center, the Marine Resources office and a couple of stalls that were intended to be used as a public market but never really took hold.

At low tide islanders walk from the causeway across the reef (about 500 metres) to Yenasr Islet (see Snorkelling earlier in this chapter), but visitors should not attempt the walk without reef walkers or canvas shoes as the coral can be quite sharp.

The area between Lelu causeway and the north-east point of Kosrae is good for shell collecting when the tide is low. On full moon nights some islanders go out 'moon-shelling' along the reef.

SOUTH OF TOFOL
Views & WW II Remains
The rusted remains of two Japanese midget tanks sit at the water's edge on the west side of the thatched-roofed elementary school in the village of Sansrik, a bit over a mile beyond Tofol. From this area there's also a very good view of the Sleeping Lady mountain ridge to the south-west and of Lelu Island across the bay to the north-west.

Viewed from Sansrik, Lelu Island looks much like a whale, the hill resembling the humped body, the flat part the tail. According to legend, the island of Lelu was formed from a whale that got trapped inside the reef.

About two-tenths of a mile east of the school, partly hidden behind a small concrete block house on the right side of the road, are 115 overgrown concrete steps heading skyward. It's a climb to nowhere these days, but a Japanese weather station and lookout tower once commanded the hilltop above the stairs.

Malem

Malem, five miles south of Tofol, is the third largest village in Kosrae. The village sits at the mouth of the Malem River.

Behind the municipal building in Malem there's a small stone monument put up by the Kosraean-Japanese Friendship Society to honour the island's 700 WW II dead.

The first road to the right past the municipal building goes by the Malem Congregational Church and up to a small dam that marks the beginning of a short, overgrown trail leading to the old Japanese command post. Nothing remains of the commander's house, but you can see the cave that served as his bunker by walking up the right side of the river for a few minutes. Look carefully for a cave opening on the right.

If you want to see the cave, you should seek permission from the landowner, Milton Timothy, who lives directly behind the municipal office – someone in the office can arrange this for you.

Yeseng, the next village, has several concrete WW II bunkers scattered along the beach behind people's homes.

Utwe

The village of Utwe (also called Utwa) is five miles past Malem, at the mouth of the Finkol River.

This is a pleasant village to stroll around. People can often be seen sitting outside their homes cooking over an open fire while naked children play nearby. For a quick bite, there's a little bakery in the centre of the village with coffee and 10-cent doughnuts.

If you want to hike, there's a pretty walk from Utwe up the Finkol River. After about

45 minutes or so walking across rocks and through mud, you'll come to some nice pools. You can do this first section on your own; ask anyone in Utwe how to get started.

With a guide you could continue walking upriver all the way to the top of Mt Finkol. It's a strenuous all-day walk which will reward you with a splendid view that includes all three of the island's harbours (see the Hiking section).

Inland Road

Some 4.5 miles beyond Malem, at the eastern outskirts of Utwe, there's a wide dirt road leading inland opposite a utility pole marked with an 'X', which is just before the Mormon church. This is the start of a new road along the southern part of the island that's intended to eventually complete the circle-island route. It currently ends after about six miles. Driving along this road gives an easy passage into the island's jungle interior.

If you're searching for sights, you might want to visit the **Sipyen Waterfall**, which is 3.5 miles up the inland road. After the road climbs through a cut in the mountains it descends steeply. Park off to the right side of the road at the bottom of the descent, where the guardrail stops. From the road you can hear (but not see) the falls It's a five-minute walk up the river, though there's not a real trail and you must walk along the stream bed rocks, some of which are mossy. The waterfall, about 25 feet high and four to five feet wide, is pleasant enough but by no means spectacular and the shallow pool beneath the falls is not deep enough for swimming.

TAFUNSAK

The municipality of Tafunsak stretches along the entire west flank of Kosrae. It includes the remote Walung Village, Okat Harbor, the airport, Tafunsak Village and several smaller villages on the north side of the island.

Airport to Lelu

The drive between the airport and Lelu is

the prettiest on the island, offering views of both the mountains and the coast, as well as a close-up look at Kosrae's luxuriant greenery.

The bridge which connects the airport with the main island crosses a reef channel whose striking turquoise waters are popular with snorkellers. Just beyond the bridge there's a mangrove swamp where you might spot a grey Pacific reef heron *(noklap)* scenically perched on one of the swamp's bleached white logs.

As you get closer to Lelu, there are picturesque white sand beaches lined with coconut palms. Along the shallow reefs fronting the beach you can sometimes watch fishers casting thrownets in the reef pools.

Bird Cave

A large swampy cave at the west side of the rock quarry in the Wiya area is home to a sizable colony of swiftlets *(kalkaf)* who cling to the cave walls by their claws and build nests of dried saliva and moss. When flying they look like small bats.

Islanders collect the bird droppings in the cave bottom to use as a rich fertiliser. Like lots of other places in Kosrae, this big swampy cave is thought to be haunted. In this case the belief is spurred on by rumours of Kosraean bodies left in the back of the cave by the Japanese.

Although the tourist bureau promotes the cave as an attraction, if you're not keenly interested in caves and swiftlets this is a good site to be viewed from a distance. The cave can readily be seen from the road and the swiftlets can often be spotted circling just outside the entrance. If you must go closer, tread gently. Swiftlets are vulnerable to disruption by humans and may abandon a cave that is visited too often. At any rate the cave itself is not particularly attractive up close and smells of decaying matter.

Tafunsak Gorge

There's a steep gorge with 70-foot walls in Tafunsak Village which could be an interesting place to explore on a sunny day. As the gorge is extremely narrow, just eight to 10 feet wide in places, it has the potential to flash flood so it can be dangerous during a downpour.

To get there, take the path running southeast from JJ's Bakery/Thurston's Enterprise at the crossroads in Tafunsak Village. It's a 45-minute walk up the gorge, following an old steel water pipe. Be careful crossing the pipe as it perspires and can be quite slippery under foot. A few minutes up the trail there's a shallow pool where neighbourhood kids swim, the first of a number of waterfalls and pools along the way.

Circle-Island Rd

The section of a new road that will eventually circle the island leads south off the main road at the east side of the bridge to the airport. The road construction was abandoned by the last governor, but it is expected to resume as the governor who originally undertook the project returned to office at the end of 1994. Currently the road runs about three miles, passing above mangrove swamps and through jungles thick with bananas, tapioca and wild ginger. Stone ruins of residential compounds and canoe platforms uncovered during road construction can be seen a short way down on the left side of the road.

Walung

The new circle road will eventually connect Walung on the west coast with the rest of the island. Walung is the island's most traditional village and not everyone there is happy about ending their isolation. For now it's a quiet place with few visitors.

Walung is lined with lovely sandy beaches that stretch intermittently for a couple of miles. Just inland, craggy green peaks poke their heads up above the mist, creating a scenic backdrop.

Walung has a church and elementary school as well as the foundations of an old mission. The village is cut by tidal channels that are spanned by log footbridges.

The only way of getting to Walung is by boat. The tourist office can arrange for an outrigger canoe equipped with an outboard motor to take you on a fascinating trip through the mangrove channel from Utwe to Walung. You'll pass by some of the largest and oldest mangrove trees to be found in all Micronesia and see herons and scurrying monitor lizards. The trip takes about 45 minutes and costs $40. The boat ride within the channel can only be made at high tide, though it's also possible to make a quicker, less scenic journey outside the reef. You can get tide information from the Marine Resources office (☎ 370-3031) in Lelu.

The other way to get to Walung is by private speedboat from Okat Dock. The ride takes about 15 minutes, but it's not nearly as interesting. There's no scheduled service, but you can usually find someone willing to take you over for a reasonable fee by inquiring at the Okat Marina kiosk.

If you want to spend more than a day in Walung, the tourist office can arrange for you to stay with a family. Inquire about the 'mansion', a large house that was built by an American and which sometimes has rooms for $5 a night; it has a great location, right up against breakers on one side, the lagoon on the other.

PLACES TO STAY
Camping
Camping remains a fairly foreign concept in Kosrae but people are generally accommodating, so if you want to set up a tent, check with the mayor of the village you want to camp in and something can probably be arranged.

Hotels
Kosrae has only a handful of small hotels. The few places that formerly comprised the island's bottom-end accommodation are no longer available for travellers, as they have been taken over as barracks by Ting Hong, the Chinese company that leases the fishing grounds throughout the FSM.

A tax of 5% will be added to the rates listed below. Except for Tradewind, hotels accept MasterCard and Visa and a couple also accept the JCB card.

Coconut Palm Hotel (☎ 370-3181), Box 87, Kosrae, FM 96944, is in the middle of Tofol on the upper floor of a small business centre. The hotel has 11 straightforward rooms that are clean and commodious with comfortable beds, a sofa, desk, refrigerator and air-con. A long-time favourite with businesspeople, the hotel is a relatively good value at $40 for a single person in a room with a queen bed, $45 for a couple in the same room and $50 for two people in a room with two beds.

Sandy Beach Hotel (☎ 370-3239, fax 370-2109), Box 6, Kosrae, FM 96944, on the beach between Tafunsak and Lelu, has 10 adequate rooms in two-storey duplex and fourplex buildings. Rooms have two double beds, air-con, a desk, refrigerator and an oceanfront porch. All have private bathrooms, most with bathtubs as well as showers. Although the buildings are made of concrete, there's a thatch facade on the exterior that lends a nice element to the beachfront location. Rates are $45/60 for singles/doubles in the upstairs rooms and $5 less for the ground-level rooms. There's also a single cottage that's smaller and costs $35/50 for singles/doubles.

Tradewind Hotel (☎ 370-3991), Box TE, Kosrae, FM 96944, on Lelu Island, has five older free-standing concrete cottages with refrigerators, private bathrooms and air-con. Rates are $30/50 for singles/doubles. There are often room and car packages available as it belongs to the same family that owns TE car rentals.

Pacific Treelodge (☎ 370-2102, fax 370-3060), Box 51, Kosrae, FM 96944, has a dozen modern rooms in new duplex cottages that are nicely spread around a mangrove pond. Rooms have a queen and twin bed, private bathroom with shower, air-con, carpeting, phone and a mini-refrigerator. Singles/doubles cost $55/75. It's opposite the beach, half a mile north of Kosrae Nautilus Resort, and there's a restaurant and a small store on site.

The island's most up-market option is the *Kosrae Nautilus Resort* (☎ 370-3567, fax 370-3568), Box 135, Kosrae, FM 96944, a cosy new hotel run by two friendly Australian couples. The 16 rooms are very comfortable and modern, each with two double beds, ceramic tile floors, a mini-refrigerator, bathroom with tub, aircon and a TV that shows video movies on two channels. There are other nice touches, including complimentary tea and coffee. The hotel, which is a few minutes' walk from the Lelu causeway and the natural swimming hole, has a restaurant, a dive shop and Kosrae's only swimming pool. Singles/doubles cost $75/95; it's an additional $25 each for a third and fourth person.

A second small hotel geared for divers, the *Kosrae Village Resort* (☎ 370-3483, fax 370-5839) Kosrae, FM 96944, is being built between the mangrove channel and the ocean a few miles south of Tofol on the road to Malem. It will initially have half a dozen traditional style bungalows and costs are expected to be about $150 a day for lodging, meals and diving. The two Californian owners, Katrina Adams and Bruce Brandt, are both PADI instructors.

PLACES TO EAT

Bill's Restaurant in Tofol has good food and is a popular spot for Peace Corps volunteers and other expats. Beef teriyaki, chicken in peanut sauce and a recommendable sweet and sour fish are all priced from $5 to $6 at lunch and dinner. Bill's also has good sashimi with rice for $3.75, moderately priced sandwiches and ramen, and breakfasts for $2 to $5. Though it's not on the menu, with a little advance notice Bill's can usually send someone out to fetch a local mangrove crab and serve it up for about $10. It's open from 6.30 am to 2 pm Monday to Saturday and from 6 to 8.30 pm daily.

The *Pacific Treelodge Restaurant*, at the hotel of the same name, is in a thatched-roof open-air building with a charming setting. You reach the restaurant via a 75-metre-long wooden-plank footbridge that winds above a mangrove swamp. The food is good, but come when you have time to linger as the service can be slow. At breakfast you can get pancakes for 50 cents each or various egg combinations from $3. At

lunch or dinner a cheeseburger or grilled tuna sandwich with fries cost $3, while various meat dishes, including a nice chicken teriyaki, are priced around $5. It's open from 6.30 am to 2.30 pm Monday to Saturday and 4.30 to 9.30 pm daily.

The restaurant at the *Kosrae Nautilus Resort* has a pleasant air-con dining room that's smoke free. At breakfast, pancakes, French toast and omelettes are priced from $2 to $3, while a bottomless cup of coffee costs a dollar. At lunch, burgers with fries, or fried rice with fish, cost under $5. Dinners include a meaty lasagna with salad, grilled tuna or chicken teriyaki for $6 to $8. The house dessert is a scrumptious crepe a la mode. Beer, spirits, wine and champagne are available; the margaritas, which are made with Kosraean limes and cost $4.50, are a speciality. It's open daily from 7 to 9 am, from 11.30 am to 1.30 pm and from 6 to 8.30 pm.

The *Islander Restaurant* in Tofol is a popular spot for breakfast, which is served from 6 am daily except on Sundays. The restaurant has a pleasantly local atmosphere and reasonable prices. Pancakes cost $1.50, eggs, toast and ham $3.25 and various fish and meat dishes are about a dollar more. It's open until 2.30 pm on weekdays, until noon on Saturdays. On Sundays it does a reversal of its hours, opening at 6 pm for dinner only.

The *Sandy Beach Hotel* also has a small waterfront restaurant but the hours are unreliable and the food isn't notable.

Tropical Breeze, on the coastal road just east of the CAT Camp, is a small store with a bakery that makes a tasty banana bread, chocolate-frosted doughnuts (40 cents) and pretty good breads. It's open daily from 7 am to 9 pm (from 10 am on Sundays).

Webster's Enterprises in Tafunsak and *Thurston's Enterprise* in Lelu are Kosrae's largest grocery and general stores. There are no real grocery stores in Tofol, but you can pick up bottled water ($1.85 for 1.5 litres), canned stew and a few snack items at the small store below Coconut Palm Hotel and at the more sparsely stocked *Sunset Store*.

You can get fresh fish and live lobster and mangrove crabs at the little dock at Okat Harbor, just before crossing the causeway to the airport.

On Fridays, the FSM Aquaculture Center on the causeway to Lelu sells mango-size giant clams for $2 each – a popular sashimi item. When they're not busy, staff at the centre will gladly give visitors a little tour.

There's a farmer's market opposite the tourist office in Tofol that's generally open on weekday mornings. If there's something you're looking for that you don't see, inquire, as some items are in a separate cold storage area. In addition to locally grown bananas, citrus and the occasional watermelon, you might also be able to buy local foods such as boiled breadfruit, boiled taro or baked bananas. A real treat would be *fafa*, a sweet poi made from pounded taro with a coating of sugar caramel, a Kosraean delicacy made on special occasions.

Drink
Water is not safe to drink from the tap in Kosrae as it comes down from the mountains untreated and can be contaminated by wild pigs and rats that live in the interior. Although it's not terribly common, leptospirosis can be transmitted from these animals to humans via fresh water.

Most islanders drink catchment water and, although few people bother, it's not a bad idea to treat or boil catchment water as not all catchment systems are equally sanitary. Most hotels and restaurants serve catchment water.

Visitors officially need a drinking permit to purchase alcoholic beverages in Kosrae. Kosrae Nautilus Resort, which has the only restaurant serving alcohol, can issue diners the permit for $3. Valid for 30 days, the permit can also be picked up at the police station. Webster's Enterprises in Tafunsak sells beer and a few spirits.

ENTERTAINMENT
Entertainment in the conventional sense is limited on Kosrae. There are no discos or staged cultural shows and even the movie theatre closed down when video rentals came in.

THINGS TO BUY
Typical Kosraean crafts include wooden taro pounders, carved wooden canoes, woven bags and purses and wall hangings of fibres and shells.

For a nice memento consider *Kosrae: The Sleeping Lady Awakens*, a comprehensive book covering Kosrae's history, culture and flora and fauna written by Harvey Segal, an American educator who's been around Kosrae for a few decades.

The book, as well as a small selection of handicrafts and T-shirts, are sold at the tourist office and Kosrae Nautilus Resort.

GETTING THERE & AWAY
Air
All of Continental Micronesia's island-hopper flights between Guam and Honolulu stop in Kosrae.

Flights between Pohnpei and Kosrae cost $130 one way, $208 return. Flights between Kosrae and Majuro are $272 one way or $454 return. Return tickets require a three-day advance purchase and are good for a stay of up to 30 days. For travellers who are island hopping between Guam and Honolulu, Kosrae is a free stopover.

Airport Kosrae has an open-air airport terminal with a snack bar, restrooms, car rental booths for TE's and Webster's, and a small handicraft stand that's sometimes open. Although there's a debit-card phone in the lobby, there's also a regular telephone in the nook opposite the car rental booths that you can use to make free local calls.

Sea
SeAir Transportation sometimes takes passengers on its cargo runs between Pohnpei and Kosrae, but the schedule is very irregular. See Getting There & Away in the Pohnpei section for more details.

Yachties should get advance permission to enter the state or they risk being asked to leave soon after arrival. Lelu Harbor, which is an official port of entry, has a couple of mooring buoys where visiting yachts can tie up. Okat Harbor is also a port of entry, but it's primarily geared for commercial shipping.

Leaving Kosrae
Kosrae has a $10 departure tax.

GETTING AROUND
There are no taxis or public buses on the island, so the only practical way to explore Kosrae is to rent a car.

To/From the Airport
The airport is about a 20-minute drive from Tofol or Lelu. The hotels provide free airport transportation for their guests. Most send a van to meet all arriving flights – if there's not one there, give the hotel a call from the airport and they'll usually send someone out to fetch you.

Otherwise, getting a ride from someone going into Lelu or Tofol shouldn't be too difficult, as most people head that way and few will be put out if you ask for a ride.

Car
TE's (Thurston's Enterprise) Car Rental (☎ 370-3226), Box TE, Kosrae, FM 96944, opposite Coconut Palm Hotel in Tofol, has cars for $40. Webster George Car Rental (☎ 370-3116), Box 164, Kosrae, FM 96944, in Tafunsak rents cars for $45. Car rentals can also be arranged through the hotels or from Thurston's Enterprise (☎ 370-3047) on Lelu.

The cheapest place to get petrol is at Okat Harbor ($1.70 a gallon); there's also a new pump station on the north side of the Lelu causeway. Most other places on the island store petrol in drums and sell it a gallon at a time, pouring it into your tank via a funnel – no fire hazard here!

Outside of built-up areas, the speed limit is 35 miles per hour, but most people drive a bit slower than that.

Hitching
It's generally fairly easy to get rides around Kosrae and you may find people stopping to offer you a ride in the back of their pick-up truck if you're just walking down the road. At other times, you may have to make a more concerted effort and give an eager wave at passing vehicles.

Tours
Kosrae doesn't have enough tourism to support organised sightseeing tours. With a little notice the tourist office and a few of the larger hotels can usually arrange a personalised tour, but expect it to be more expensive than renting your own car.

Pohnpei

Pohnpei, with its lush vegetation, jungle hillsides and flowering hibiscus, fits the typical South Sea island image, albeit a wet one. The abundant rainfall feeds a multitude of streams, rivers and tumbling waterfalls. The damp rainforest interior, which is uninhabited and difficult to reach, has soft, spongy ground and moss-covered trees.

Pohnpei's boldest landmark is the scenic Sokehs Rock, a steep cliff face often compared to Honolulu's Diamond Head. The ancient stone city of Nan Madol, abandoned on nearly 100 artificial islets off the south-east coast, is Micronesia's best known archaeological site.

The main town of Kolonia is relatively large by island standards, yet despite a spurt of growth in recent years it still retains an unhurried small-town character. Outside the Kolonia area it's largely unspoiled and undeveloped, with small villages scattered around the island.

Kolonia is the capital of Pohnpei state while Palikir, five miles outside Kolonia, is the new capital of the Federated States of Micronesia.

Pohnpei was spelled 'Ponape' until 1984 and many schools and businesses still retain the old spelling.

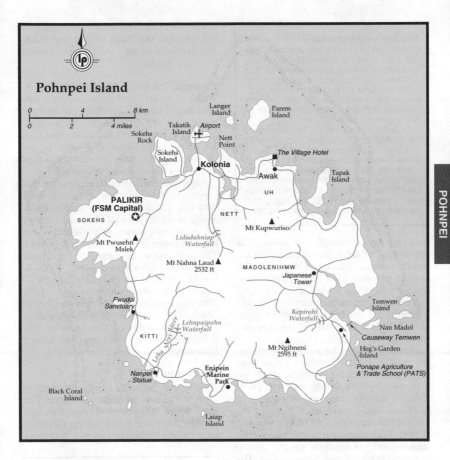

Pohnpei Island

HISTORY
Pre-European Contact
Although Pohnpei was inhabited at least as early as 200 AD, virtually nothing is known of Pohnpeians prior to the saudeleurs. The saudeleurs were a tyrannical royal dynasty which ruled from Nan Madol, an elaborate city of stone fortresses and temples; they apparently reached their peak of power in the 13th century.

The most common story of the demise of the saudeleurs tells of conquests from Kosrae. The Thunder God, who had been severely punished for having an affair with the wife of a saudeleur on Pohnpei, set out for Kosrae in his canoe. The canoe sank, but the Thunder God was able to continue on when a floating taro flower changed into a needlefish and guided the god to the island. On Kosrae he made a woman of his own clan pregnant, and the child, Isokelekel, was raised on the stories about the cruel saudeleurs back on Pohnpei. After reaching adulthood Isokelekel gathered an army of 333 men and went to Nan Madol. He conquered the saudeleurs and established a new system of royalty.

Pohnpei was divided into districts, each

The Tattooed Irishman
One of Pohnpei's more colourful early visitors was James O'Connell, an ex-convict from Australia, who became known as 'The Tattooed Irishman' after enduring Pohnpeian tattooing rites. O'Connell was shipwrecked on Pohnpei around 1830 and was captured by Pohnpeian islanders whom he thought were cannibals.

In order to save his life he entertained the islanders by dancing an Irish jig – over and over again apparently, as the Pohnpeians were quite impressed with his antics. He not only managed to save his own life but he earned the respect of one of the chiefs and gained a 14-year-old wife as well. When the American ship *Spy* pulled into port in 1833, O'Connell escaped. ■

---

with two separate families of nobles. The senior man of the highest ranking family was the *nahnmwarki*, or district chief. The head of the other royal line was the *nahnken*, or secondary leader. The victorious Isokelekel became nahnmwarki of the region called Madolenihmw, the highest ranked district on Pohnpei and the one which included Nan Madol.

Sometime before the arrival of Westerners in the 1820s, Pohnpei Island was divided into the five districts of Madolenihmw, Uh, Kitti, Sokehs and Nett. These districts are the same municipalities in existence today, with the addition of the town of Kolonia, which previously was part of Nett. Each municipality still has its own nahnmwarki and nahnken, and the system of ranked titles remains largely intact. The current nahnmwarki of Madolenihmw, Ilden Shelten, traces his lineage back to Isokelekel.

European Contact
In 1528 a Spaniard, Alvaro de Saavedra, became the first known European to sight Pohnpei, but it wasn't until 1595 that the island was actually claimed for Spain by Pedro Fernandez de Quiros. Even then, like most of the Carolines, Pohnpei was virtually ignored by the Spanish who were concentrating their efforts in the Marianas.

In 1828 Fedor Lutke, of the Russian sloop *Senyavin*, christened the island of Pohnpei and the atolls of Ant and Pakin 'the Senyavin Islands' and for quite a while the name stuck.

Whalers, Traders & Missionaries
Whalers, traders and Protestant missionaries began arriving in Pohnpei around the mid-1800s. During each of the peak whaling years of 1855 and 1856 more than 50 whale ships dropped anchor in the island's lagoon. Pohnpei was known as Ascension Island during this period.

As in other Micronesian islands, the diseases spread by visiting Westerners took their toll. The worst was the smallpox epidemic of 1854, introduced by the crew of the American whale ship *Delta*, which killed between 2000 and 3000 Pohnpeians. The indigenous population dropped from an estimated 10,000 in the early 1800s to less than 5000 by the end of the century.

In 1870 the naval cruiser USS *Jamestown* pulled into Pohnpei and forced island chiefs to sign a treaty which, among other things, allowed foreigners to buy Pohnpeian land. Kolonia was then named Jamestown.

Spanish Period
The Spanish began to occupy Pohnpei in 1886, following the papal arbitration that gave Spain authority over the Caroline Islands. They did not, however, receive a hospitable welcome in Pohnpei. Just three

---

The Shenandoah
One bizarre event of the whaling era took place in 1865 during the US Civil War. The Confederate ship *Shenandoah*, on a mission to destroy the Union whaling business in the Pacific, pulled into Madolenihmw Harbor alongside four Yankee whale ships, took the officers as prisoners and set the ships on fire. The news that the Confederate South had surrendered to the Union just one week after this event did not reach the crew of the *Shenandoah*, who managed to destroy almost 40 Union whale ships throughout the Pacific before returning home. ■

months after his arrival, the island's first Spanish governor was killed in a rebellion by Pohnpeians who were protesting against the use of forced native labour to build a Spanish fort in Kolonia.

Spain's occupation of Pohnpei continued to be plagued by a series of uprisings, quite a few of which concerned the Catholic missions that the Spanish were trying to introduce into communities that were by now staunchly Protestant.

German Period
The Germans arrived in 1899 after buying the Carolines from the Spanish. Their interest was in copra and other commercial products and they were rather heavy-handed in going about their development projects, relying upon forced labour for much of the work.

The infamous 1910-1911 Sokehs Rebellion was sparked when a Pohnpeian working on a labour gang on Sokehs Island was given a beating by a German overseer. The Pohnpeians killed the overseer, and the revolt was on. The Germans promised revenge, though it took more than four months for ships with reinforcements to arrive from Melanesia. The Germans then blockaded Kolonia and sent troops of Melanesians charging up Sokehs Ridge. The uprising was suppressed and 17 rebel leaders were executed and thrown into a mass grave. Not wanting to see the incident repeated, the Germans exiled 426 Sokehs residents to Palau and then brought in people from other Micronesian islands to settle on Sokehs.

Japanese Period
The Japanese took over in 1914. As elsewhere in Micronesia, Pohnpei became a site of intense commercial and agricultural development. The Japanese cultivated trochus shells and set up a sugar plantation to make alcohol.

At the beginning of WW II there were nearly 14,000 Japanese, Okinawans and Koreans living on Pohnpei and only about 5000 Pohnpeians.

Although Japanese military fortifications on Pohnpei were hit by US aerial bombings throughout 1944 and Kolonia was virtually levelled, Pohnpei was not invaded.

GEOGRAPHY
Pohnpei Island is high, volcanic and roughly circular, edged with coves and jutting peninsulas. The interior has rugged mountain ridges and deep valleys. Averaging 13 miles in diameter and with a land mass of 129 sq miles, it's the largest island in the FSM and the third largest island in Micronesia.

The centre of Pohnpei Island is Mt Nahna Laud but the highest peak is the 2595-foot Ngihneni. The coastline, devoid of natural sandy beaches, is mainly tidal flats and mangrove swamps. In between the island and its surrounding circular reef is a 70-sq-mile lagoon containing dozens of small islands, many with lovely white sand beaches.

Pohnpei State also includes eight outlying atolls, each covering less than one sq mile of land. To the south-east, almost like stepping stones down to Kosrae, are the atolls of Mokil and Pingelap – 80 and 140 miles from Pohnpei Island. To the south-west are Sapwuafik (formerly Ngatik) Atoll, 90 miles away; Nukuoro Atoll – 250 miles; and Kapingamarangi Atoll – 445 miles. Oroluk Atoll is 180 miles to the north-west and Pakin and Ant atolls are a few miles west of Pohnpei Island.

CLIMATE
The town of Kolonia has an average annual rainfall of 192 inches and Pohnpei's interior often gets a whopping 400 inches, making it one of the rainiest places on earth. The lowest rainfall occurs between January and March, while the wettest months are April and May. A typical Pohnpei day is cloudy with intermittent showers and the sun breaking through now and then.

Temperatures average 81°F (27°C) and during most of the year there are north-easterly trade winds. However, from July to November the winds die down, the

POHNPEI

POHNPEI

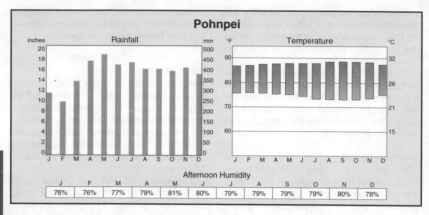

Pohnpei

Rainfall

| inches | mm |
| J | F | M | A | M | J | J | A | S | O | N | D |

Temperature (°F / °C)

| J | F | M | A | M | J | J | A | S | O | N | D |

Afternoon Humidity

J	F	M	A	M	J	J	A	S	O	N	D
76%	76%	77%	79%	81%	80%	79%	79%	79%	79%	80%	78%

humidity inches up and the nights can be especially oppressive.

Pohnpei is within typhoon spawning grounds, although outside the major tracks.

ECONOMY

As the FSM government is centred in Pohnpei, the majority of workers in the moneyed economy are on the government payroll. These include 24 American lawyers, most of whom act as advisers to FSM officials.

Agriculture is important on Pohnpei and subsistence farming is still widespread; the island is home to PATS, Micronesia's only agricultural trade school.

Pohnpei also has a sprinkling of pepper plantations. Pepper grows on climbing vines which in the wild sometimes reach to the top of full-grown trees. When cultivated, the vines are usually trained up posts six to eight feet high for easy picking. Pohnpei pepper, which is shipped overseas to gourmet food shops, is a leading export crop, along with copra.

Other exports include trochus shell buttons and coconut oils, soaps and shampoos.

POPULATION & PEOPLE

The state population is 35,000. About 90% of the people live on Pohnpei Island and of those 20% are Kapingamarangis, Mort-lockese, Pingelapese, Mokilese and, in smaller numbers, Kosraeans, Palauans, Filipinos, Americans, Japanese and Australians.

The people of the remote Pohnpeian islands of Nukuoro and Kapingamarangi are the only Polynesians in Micronesia.

SOCIETY & CONDUCT

Traditionally Pohnpeian society has been a stratified one, with a person's status being derived from membership in a particular clan. Each clan had its own chief, its own territory and a 12-tiered ranking system. Although Pohnpeian society is more Westernised today, about 90% of Pohnpeians still have a title related to the clan system.

Sakau

In Micronesia the use of sakau, a drink made from *Piper methysticum*, the roots of a pepper shrub, is unique to Pohnpei, although the Kosraeans enjoyed it before the missionaries came along.

In ancient times, the drinking of sakau had a religious significance and generally was restricted to times when the nahnmwarki was present. There were strict rules governing how it was passed from hand to hand, with the highest chief served first.

Sakau is called a mild narcotic, but it can be quite potent. It has a sedative effect, with

Sakau making

your tongue and lips going numb first. You then feel quite mellow and while your thinking seems clear your body doesn't always respond quite as you think it should. F W Christian, an Englishman who did archaeological research at Nan Madol in the 1890s, perhaps described it best in his book *The Caroline Islands*: 'After four cups of sakau, one leg struggles south while the other is marching due north.'

Sakau is a bit slippery and slimy going down. Some people liken the taste to a mud milkshake, and whether it's the sakau itself or impure water sometimes used to rinse the roots, it may give the novice a case of the runs.

In the traditional method, the pepper roots are pounded on a stone and the pulp squeezed by hand through hibiscus bark. The juices are then mixed with a little water and poured into a coconut shell which is passed around communally. Nowadays many shops use machines to do the work and serve sakau in a glass, though connoisseurs claim the hand-squeezed sakau is more potent and less bitter. The traditional

method is certainly a more theatrical experience.

Sakau is perfectly legal and still somewhat ceremonial. Sakau bars are as thick in Kolonia as those that serve alcohol. These days you don't need a chief present to turn on to sakau and most bars welcome foreigners (see Sakau Bars under Entertainment).

Incidentally, sakau is the same drink that in Polynesia is known as 'kava'.

Food
Pohnpeians are big on yams and yams can be big on them. Sometimes it takes 12 men just to carry one yam, as they can grow up to 10 feet in length and weigh as much as 1500 pounds!

Yams take on almost mystical qualities in Pohnpeian society and there's a lot of prestige attached to growing the biggest yam in the village. You've heard of the Inuit having dozens of words for 'snow' – well, the Pohnpeians have more than 100 words for yam.

Pohnpeians can eat yams day after day

after day. Oddly (or is it?), yams are rare on restaurant menus.

Breadfruit and seafood are other island staples.

Funeral feasts are important social events that can last three days, and everyone brings gifts of food and sakau. Dog is a traditional feast food, but the casual visitor is unlikely to come across it.

RELIGION

Reflecting its history, Pohnpei's population is pretty evenly divided between Catholics and Protestants, the latter most strongly represented by the United Church of Christ. There are also Assembly of God, Bahai, Baptist, Catholic, Jehovah's Witnesses, Mormon and Seventh-Day Adventist churches.

LANGUAGE

Pohnpeian is the main indigenous language. Other Micronesian languages spoken on Pohnpei are Mokilese, Pingelapese, Ngatikese and Nukuoro-Kapingamarangi, , as well as Mortlockese, a Chuukese dialect. English is widely spoken, and is the language of instruction in schools from the 4th grade up. Some older people speak Japanese.

The common greeting, *kaselehlia*, is a melodic word used for both 'hello' and 'good-bye' in a manner similar to the Hawaiian *aloha*. Thank you is *kalahngan*. Foreigners are called *mehnwhi*.

HOLIDAYS

Pohnpei celebrates these public holidays:

New Year's Day
  1 January
Sokehs Rebellion Day
  24 February
Cultural Day
  31 March
FSM Constitution Day
  10 May
Pohnpei Liberation Day
  11 September
United Nations Day
  24 October
FSM Independence Day
  3 November

Pohnpeian Constitution Day
  8 November
Christmas Day
  25 December

Each municipality in Pohnpei has its own constitution and thus its own constitution day holiday: 27 February in Kitti, 1 May in Madolenihmw, 26 May in Uh, 2 August in Sokehs, 25 August in Nett and 20 September in Kolonia.

ACTIVITIES
Diving & Snorkelling

Pohnpei has pretty coral reefs, manta rays and lots of fish. If the sea is rough, divers may have to stay inside the barrier reef, which lies one to five miles offshore, and be content to explore the lagoon waters. However, visibility is much better outside the reef. Night diving is available and it's also possible to dive Nan Madol.

While snorkelling is not good on Pohnpei Island itself, there are a number of small nearby islands accessible by short boat rides that have clear waters and good coral and marine life.

Ant and Pakin atolls are favourite diving spots. Ant has sheer coral drop-offs, schools of barracuda and lots of reef-shark action. Pakin has virgin reefs with gorgonian fans and other coral as well as abundant marine life. The one-way boat ride takes one hour to Ant and two hours to Pakin. Spring, summer and autumn are the best times for diving. From December to February the waters between Pohnpei and Pakin are rough.

Dive Shops Phoenix Marine Sports (☎ 320-5678, fax 320-2364), Box 387, Kolonia, Pohnpei, FM 96941, is a Japanese dive operation, with the latest equipment, comfortable boats, a friendly staff and a good reputation. Two-tank boat dives cost $65 inside Pohnpei reef, $75 outside, including lunch. For Ant or Pakin, add $10. Weight belts and tanks are included in the rate; other equipment can be rented. Snorkelling tours that include a visit to Nan Madol and Kepirohi Waterfall cost $55, lunch included.

Iet Ehu (☎ 320-2959, fax 320-2958), Box 559, Kolonia, Pohnpei, FM 96941, is a good local operation that's extremely knowledgeable and has a following among expats on Pohnpei – small boats (and bumpy rides) but fun people. Two-tank boat dives within Pohnpei reef cost $60, to Ant and Pakin $75. They also offer a one-tank manta ray dive that's combined with a tour of Nan Madol for $65. Prices include weights, tanks and lunch.

Joy Ocean Service (☎ 320-2447, fax 320-2478), Box 484, Kolonia, Pohnpei, FM 96941, behind Joy Hotel, is a small operation run by dive-master Yukio Suzuki. Unlike Phoenix, very little English is spoken, so it's not a practical option if you don't speak Japanese. Joy charges $100 for two-tank boat dives around Pohnpei, including lunch. Snorkellers can go out with divers for $50. Snorkel sets rent for $6.

For other snorkelling options, see Tours in the Getting Around section.

Hiking
The two main hikes in the greater Kolonia area are on Sokehs Island, one an easy hike up the ridge and the other a difficult one up the rock face. Both offer great views and are detailed elsewhere in the chapter.

You can also make hardy hikes into Pohnpei's jungle interior though you'll need a guide; one can be arranged through the tourist office or Iet Ehu Tours.

The island has a Hash House Harriers group that meets every other Saturday, usually at 3 pm at the Spanish wall. Schedules are posted on bulletin boards at Kolonia grocery stores. There's a $5 donation to cover drinks and transportation.

Tennis
There are two busy tennis courts at the south side of Kolonia Town Hall, a building originally constructed during the Japanese era and marked only in Japanese script. If you want to play, there's usually somebody from the local tennis club around who can explain the proper protocol.

Other Activities
Pohnpei waters have a good variety of fish, including yellowfin tuna, mahimahi, marlin, barracuda and numerous reef fish. Trolling, bottom fishing and spearfishing trips can be arranged through most tour companies. For a listing of companies, see Tours in the Getting Around section.

KOLONIA
With a population of 7000, Kolonia is the largest town in the FSM.

Although it used to be likened to an American frontier town, Kolonia's appearance is rapidly changing. Modern buildings are replacing ramshackle shops and the broad main street now fills with 'rush hour' traffic.

Still, once you get into the town's back streets, a rural character surfaces. Dogs laze on the side of the roads and it seems that every other yard, no matter how small, contains a pen of squealing pigs.

Main St is the town centre. About midway down the street, beside the tourist office, there's a small Japanese tank painted in camouflage splotches. A few blocks south, the state legislature buildings sit on the highest hill in Kolonia.

Along the waterfront road on the east side of town you'll find old warehouse-style businesses, a public market, new retail stores and the island's largest Protestant church, built in the early 1930s. The most colourful church in town is the new Kosrae Kolonia Congregational Church, near the college, which has a unique design and is the place of worship for the island's 500 Kosraeans.

Information
Tourist Office The tourist office (☎ 320-2421, fax 320-2505), on Main St, is open from 8 am to noon and 1 to 5 pm Monday to Friday. They have a few brochures on Pohnpei, including a detailed one of Nan Madol that's free here but sold for $2 elsewhere.

Money The Bank of Guam and the Bank of Hawaii are together with a couple of

POHNPEI

POHNPEI

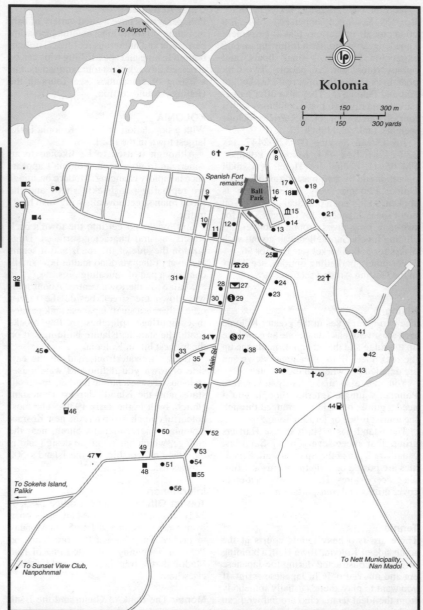

To Airport

Kolonia

0 ··· 150 ··· 300 m
0 ··· 150 ··· 300 yards

1

6 † ● 7

● 8

Spanish Fort
remains

Ball
Park

17 ● 19
16 ★ 18 ■
15 ▥
13 ● 14

2 ■

5 ●

3

4 ■

9 ▼

10 ▼
11 ■   12 ●

25 ■

☎ 26

32 ■

31 ●

28 ▣   27 ✉
30 ▼   29 ⓘ

24 ●
23 ●

22 †

34 ▼   ⓢ 37

45 ●

33 ●   35 ▼

38 ●

41 ●

42 ●

39 ●   † 40

43 ●

36 ▼

44

⛽ 46

50 ●

52 ▼

49 ▼
47 ▼

48 ■   51 ●

53 ▼
54 ●
55 ■

56 ●

To Sokehs Island,
Palikir

Main St

To Sunset View Club,
Nanpohnmal

To Nett Municipality,
Nan Madol

PLACES TO STAY		OTHER		28	The Pharmacy
2	South Park Hotel	1	Sokehs Rebels Grave	29	Tourist Office
4	Cliff Rainbow Hotel	3	Across the Street	30	J&T Store
11	Joy Hotel	5	German Cemetery	31	Phoenix Marine Sports
18	Sea Breeze Hotel	6	Catholic Church	33	Scooter Rentals
25	Yvonne's Hotel	7	German Bell Tower	37	Banks & Travel Agencies
32	Hotel Pohnpei	8	Iet Ehu Tours	38	State Legislature
48	Palm Terrace Hotel	12	SeAir Transportation	39	College of Micronesia
55	Penny Hotel	13	Immigration	40	Kosrae-Kolonia
		14	Peace Corps		Congregational Church
PLACES TO EAT		15	Pohnpei Lidorkini Museum	41	Hervis Rent-A-Car
9	Cafe Ole & Ambros Store	16	Police Station	42	Penny Rent-A-Car
10	Joy Restaurant	17	Australian Embassy	43	Yamaguchi Store
34	Namiki Restaurant	19	Chinese Embassy	44	Petrol Station & Coin
35	Town's Mini-Mart & Bakery	20	Ponape Coconut Products		Laundry
36	Fruit Stand	21	Public Market	45	Kapingamarangi Village
47	PCR Restaurant	22	Protestant Church	46	Paradise Cove
49	Palm Terrace Store	23	GP Car Rental & Tennis	47	PCR Car Rental
52	Linn's Fruit Stand		Courts	50	Coin Laundry
53	Sei Restaurant	24	Kolonia Town Hall	51	Library
		26	FSM Telecommunications	54	US Embassy
		27	Post Office	56	Agricultural Station

travel agencies in a small complex in the centre of Kolonia. The Bank of Hawaii is open from 9 am to 3 pm Monday to Thursday and 9 am to 5 pm on Fridays, while the Bank of Guam has slightly shorter hours.

Post Pohnpei's main post office, on Main St, is open from 8 am to 4 pm Monday to Friday, 10 am to noon on Saturdays. Pohnpei's only other post office is in the new FSM capitol complex in Palikir.

Telecommunications Local and long-distance telephone calls can be made and telex, faxes and telegrams can be sent from the FSM Telecommunications building on Main St. It's open 24 hours a day. Faxes can be received free of charge at ☎ 320-2745 and can be sent for the price of a phone call.

The rate to call between FSM states is $1 a minute between 6 am and 6 pm on weekdays, and 50 cents at all other times. Phone calls to all parts of the world except the FSM have a three-minute minimum charge – the per-minute rate is $2.50 to the USA or Guam ($2 on Sundays); $3 to the Marshall Islands, Palau,

Saipan or Australia; $4 to Canada, the UK or Germany; $5 to most everywhere else.

Local calls on Pohnpei cost 25 cents for three minutes.

Immigration The immigration office is near the museum and is open from 8 am to 5 pm weekdays.

Laundry There's a coin laundry north of the Palm Terrace Store that's open from 8 am to 10 pm daily, and another behind the Mobil petrol station on the road to Nett. Both cost $1 to wash and $1 to dry.

Library The public library, at the side of the agricultural station, is open from 8 am to 5 pm Monday to Friday. The library carries current *Time* and *Newsweek* magazines as well as the *Pacific Daily News*.

Media The two local radio stations are at 1300 AM and 103 FM.

There are 14 cable TV stations, including local Channel 6 that consists largely of pre-recorded speeches by island politicians. The other stations include live CNN and one-week delayed programming of the major US networks.

Anti-litter sign, Pohnpei

The *FSM-JTPA News* is a quality little monthly newspaper replete with political analysis and investigative stories on island affairs. The *Pohnpei Advertiser* is a free monthly with a few local articles and lots of ads. These local papers and Guam's *Pacific Daily News* can be picked up at larger Kolonia stores. The Australian Embassy on the waterfront road has Australian newspapers that visitors can drop by to read.

Film & Photography Phoenix of Micronesia, next door to Phoenix Marine Sports, does quality one-day film processing, with a 24-exposure roll of prints costing $8. They also sell print and slide film and make nice 70-cent postcards, each one a mounted photo.

Airline Office The Continental Micronesia office (☎ 320-2424) is at the airport. It's open from 9 am to 3.30 pm, but they're not always at the counter; if no-one is out front knock on the door behind the counter. Air Nauru (☎ 320-5963) also operates from the

office in back of its airport counter and an agent can generally be found there during the day.

Medical Services The hospital is a mile south-east of Kolonia, on the main road heading down the east coast. Fees are usually only a couple of dollars for simple treatments, but it's a rudimentary and somewhat dirty facility and people who can afford it usually fly to Guam or Honolulu for major medical services. The Pharmacy, on Main St in Kolonia, sells prescription and over-the-counter drugs.

Emergency For police emergencies, dial 320-2221; for medical emergencies, dial 320-2213.

Pohnpei Lidorkini Museum
This worthwhile little museum has well-presented displays, including one with shell adzes, coral pounders, pottery shards and beads found at Nan Madol. Another display has a sakau pounding stone housed in a little ceremonial nahs. There are also model outrigger canoes, handicraft weavings, traditional fibre clothing and a few items from the Japanese occupation. Located on the side road south of the police station, the museum is open from 10 am to 5 pm Monday to Friday and admission is free.

German Tower & Spanish Fort
Pohnpei's original Catholic mission was founded at the north end of town in the late 19th century by Capuchin missionaries. Additions during the German administration include a bell tower built in 1907. Today that tall grey tower is the only structure which survived the WW II bombing raids that took down the rest of the mission.

Also in this area are the moss-covered remains of Spanish stone walls, which were built around 1887 and once enclosed Fort Alphonse and large sections of the Spanish colony. One notable section of the old wall is at the side of the ball park, while another starts across the street and runs along the road leading down to the waterfront.

POHNPEI

Cemeteries

The cemeteries where the casualties from the Sokehs Rebellion were laid to rest are both in the north-west part of Kolonia. The German cemetery, behind the church that's down the hill from the South Park Hotel, holds the remains of sailors from the German cruiser *Emden* who died fighting the Sokehs rebels. It also has the grave of Victor Berg, the German governor who died suddenly in 1907 after excavating a grave in Nan Madol. Unfortunately, the cemetery is overgrown and enclosed by a fence, so it's hard to make out the gravestones.

The mass grave site for the executed Pohnpeian rebels is in a residential area to the north-east of the German cemetery. Look for the small unmarked cement enclosure that's at the left edge of the road shortly before it dead ends.

Kapingamarangi Village

This village, on the west side of town in an area called Porakiet, is home to the Polynesians who moved to Pohnpei from Kapingamarangi and Nukuoro atolls following typhoon and famine disasters earlier in the century. They live a more open and outdoor lifestyle than other Kolonia residents. Their breezy thatched homes with partially open-air sides are built on raised platforms a couple of feet off the ground.

The Kapingamarangi people are easygoing and don't mind sensitive visitors strolling around the village and poking into the craft shops. The men make wood carvings while the women create the weavings which are sold in island gift shops. You can purchase things directly from the craftspeople, and there's generally no hard sell.

Agricultural Station

An agricultural station, started by the Germans and expanded by the Japanese, is in the southern part of town. While not a formal botanical garden, there are some nice old trees on the grounds, including a breadfruit grove near the road, tall royal palms flanking the driveway, traveller's palms and a big fern-draped monkeypod tree. Many of the trees originally came from Borneo or Sumatra.

The three-storey building on the grounds once had a weather station on top. It was one of the few structures left standing in Kolonia after WW II but the building is now abandoned and condemned.

SOKEHS ISLAND

To get to Sokehs Island, take the road to the right at the fork past the PCR Restaurant. Once you cross the causeway onto the island the road divides, following the coast in both directions. Both ways finish in a dead end, as the island road doesn't connect around the northern tip.

It's possible to walk around Sokehs Island, but it takes half a day. The northern part, where there's no driveable road, is made up of large rough rocks, so sturdy shoes are essential. This is the road the Germans ordered to be built with forced labour in 1910, prompting the labourers to resist; that incident touched off the armed Sokehs Rebellion.

After the rebellion, all Pohnpeians living on Sokehs Island were exiled and the land resettled by people from the Mortlocks in Chuuk and from Pingelap, Mokil and Sapwuafik atolls. Their descendants still live on Sokehs Island today.

Sokehs Ridge

The 900-foot Sokehs Ridge is loaded with anti-aircraft guns, naval guns, pillboxes and tunnels and affords an excellent view of Kolonia and the surrounding reef from the top. Naturalists should be able to spot

POHNPEI

The fruit bat, of the suborder *Megachiroptera*, is a protected species in Micronesia

nesting tropicbirds and fruit bats. The walk up to the ridge takes about 45 minutes and is not difficult. The trail starts on a 4WD road behind the municipal office, the yellow building just to the right after coming over the causeway. If you come by car, you can park at the municipal office. The trail doesn't cross private property and you can do this walk on your own.

Sokehs Rock

The steep 498-foot Sokehs Rock can be climbed by those who like a challenge. After crossing the causeway, take the road to the right, which ends 1.75 miles down. The trail begins shortly before the end of the road, near the Danpei United Church of Christ. The climb up takes 45 minutes to an hour and a local guide is advisable – this can be arranged at the aforementioned municipal office.

The trail can be fairly intense as it climbs the rock's sheer basalt face, and it can be very slippery when wet. Along the steepest part of the trail there's a wrapped cable you can use to pull yourself along. The reward is the good view of Kolonia and the reef from the top.

PALIKIR

The 135-acre FSM capitol complex in Palikir Valley, built on the site of a Japanese WW II airfield, is five miles south-west of Kolonia.

The complex incorporates traditional Micronesian architectural designs. The building roofs are peaked, like those of ancestral Kosraean homes. Supporting pillars cast of black concrete resemble the basalt columns of Nan Madol. The ends of the beams on the 1st storey are in the shape of Yapese stone money, whereas those on the 2nd storey look something like the bow of a Chuukese outrigger canoe.

The complex, built in 1989 to the tune of $13 million, has four legislative and judicial buildings grouped together, including an attractive Congressional chamber with a pyramidal roof topped by a huge skylight. A second cluster contains five buildings used for the executive branch, which administers day-to-day government operations.

The paved road to Palikir heads uphill to the left just before the causeway to Sokehs Island. This is also the start of the circle-island road. This section of the road is in excellent condition, though it has no shoulders and you'll need to watch out for children who walk along the road oblivious to cars. The entrance to Palikir is 3.5 miles down.

Pwusehn Malek

Legend says this high volcanic cone formation in Palikir was created during the defeat of Pohnpei's saudeleur dynasty. The ruler of Palikir changed himself into a giant rooster to fly to Nan Madol and along the way he left a huge pile of droppings.

Pohnpeians call the hill Pwusehn Malek. The English translation so stumped Pohnpei's tourist office that their brochure simply lists it as 'Mount' followed by a long blank space. The popular translation is 'Chickenshit Mountain'.

A trail up Pwusehn Malek starts by the telephone pole on the right side of the road, a little over 1.5 miles south of the FSM capitol complex. It's about a 10-minute walk on a grassy and overgrown trail up to the first ridge. It's an easy trail, though when it's wet it can be muddy and slippery.

NETT MUNICIPALITY
Liduduhniap Waterfall

Liduduhniap Waterfall, a popular swimming spot on the Nanpil River, is a 15-minute drive from Kolonia. To get there, take Kolonia's waterfront road heading south and half a mile past Yamaguchi Store turn right onto the paved road that starts just before the tyre shop. After 2.75 miles up this riverside road there's a small power plant; continue for another six-tenths of a mile to where the road forks, turn left at the fork and stop at the kiosk two-tenths of a mile in.

The trail to the waterfall begins at the small village that's directly opposite the kiosk. One of the villagers will collect $1 from you as you enter. It's but a five-minute walk to the falls along a pleasant hibiscus-lined path. The falls, which drop about 50 feet, have nice wide pools both above and below them. The one at the base of the falls is about 35 feet across. It's a moderate scurry down to the base of that pool, but it only takes two minutes.

Nahs About halfway between the tyre shop and the waterfall, on the east side of the road, there's a beautiful ceremonial *nahs* owned by the local nahnken that's well worth a look.

The nahs, which has been restored to showpiece condition, is made of native materials in the traditional manner. Split reeds and thatch make up the roof and sides, hand-twisted coconut sennit rope ties the beams, and all the wood pillars are set on stones so as not to touch the ground.

A black granite plaque on the grounds, presented by the Oomoto Foundation of Japan, waxes poetic:

Into the dim reaches
Beyond cloud haze
I make my way
Toward Ponape.

Nett Point

Nett Point is another popular place for swimming and picnics, though the area does have a noticeable number of rats. As in most places, it's safe if there are families around, but you might want to avoid the area if just drinkers are hanging out.

To get there, turn left onto the dirt road immediately after crossing Dausokele Bridge, a half mile past the hospital. The road leads two miles down to an old dock which offers good views of the lagoon islands and a distant glimpse of the thatched cottages of the Village Hotel to the east. From the pier, there are steps leading down into clear waters, good for swimming, though be cautious of boat traffic in the channel.

The drive itself is nice too, passing both modern and thatched homes, and providing

excellent views of Sokehs Rock across the bay.

AROUND THE ISLAND

A 54-mile road circles Pohnpei, but except for about 10 paved miles around Kolonia it's a rutted dirt road and a lot of the driving can only be done at about 10 to 15 miles per hour. The less-developed west side of the island doesn't get as much traffic and the road on that side is usually in better condition. While plans call for the entire road to eventually be paved, with the scaling down of compact funding it seems doubtful it will happen anytime soon.

For now, it takes about 1¼ hours to go the 22 miles from Kolonia to the Ponape Agriculture & Trade School (PATS) and the Madolenihmw municipal building, and about three hours to circle the entire island. Give yourself a few hours more to take in the sights or, better still, work in a visit to Nan Madol or one of the reef islands and make a full day of it.

East Pohnpei

The circle-island road, taken clockwise, leads south out of Kolonia, through small villages in Nett, Uh and Madolenihmw municipalities.

You'll see a nice cross-section of village life on this drive. The men walk along carrying machetes, and sometimes a stalk of bananas or a basket of yams as well, naked children play at the roadside and women gather in the streams to do laundry.

A mile out of Kolonia the road crosses the **Dausokele Bridge**, which spans a wide river. The turn-off to the Village Hotel is 3.5 miles beyond the bridge, on the left.

A half-mile past the Village Hotel, you'll cross a bridge and enter **Awak Village** in Uh Municipality. The church on the right, with a picturesque mountain backdrop, is worth a look.

Six miles past Awak Village there's a nice **hillside view** looking down onto lagoon islands that somewhat resemble Palau's Rock Islands.

Six miles farther, in the village of **Nami-shi**, an old Japanese lookout tower covered with vines is visible on the right side of the road.

This side of the island is Pohnpei's wetter, windward side and there's an abundance of tropical flora, including plumeria, bougainvillea, beach hibiscus, African tulip trees, breadfruit, pandanus, mangoes and bamboo.

Kepirohi Waterfall You'll likely have seen Kepirohi Waterfall before you get there, as this is the impressive waterfall pictured in tourist brochures. The broad 70-foot falls cascade over a basalt rockface into a pool that's good for a refreshing midday dip.

The waterfall is at the far end of the village of Sapwehrek. One-third of a mile past Sapwehrek Elementary School, you'll cross a river followed by a small church on the right side of the road. Park at the church and walk back about 50 feet to the trail, which begins on the north side of the church property. It takes about 15 minutes to walk up to the falls. The property owner charges visitors $3.

Ponape Agriculture & Trade School Just a few hundred yards past the church there's a road junction. You get three choices and as usual nothing's marked.

If you're planning to visit the Ponape Agriculture & Trade School (better known as PATS) or are on your way to Nan Madol, then go straight ahead at this intersection rather than taking the sharp left or veering right. (If you want to continue around the island, take the road to the right.)

PATS is a private Jesuit-run high school that offers four-year courses in agriculture, construction and mechanics to boys from all over Micronesia. The school is surrounded by about 200 acres of land, some of which has been developed as an experimental farm.

Students give free tours of the school by appointment. Call a day or two in advance (☎ 320-2991) to schedule a time. The tours last about an hour and are generally offered between 1 and 3.30 pm. You could also have lunch at the school if you happen to be there at noon.

To get to the Madolenihmw municipal building, or to go over to Temwen Island, drive straight through the PATS complex. Across from the municipal office is Ponape Coconut Products, a small business started by PATS but now independent, which makes the coconut-oil soaps and shampoos sold in gift shops around Kolonia.

South-West Pohnpei

Back on the circle-island drive, continuing clockwise, the road goes through a eucalyptus grove and then up and down a series of hills, the steepest of which offers a beautiful ocean view.

This back side of Pohnpei remains largely in a natural state, with only a few clusters of houses here and there, many made of thatch and mangrove wood. This side is also drier, with less jungle and more open vistas into the interior. On the south coast of Pohnpei is **Enipein Marine Park** which can be toured by canoe (see Tours in the Getting Around section).

A bronze **statue of Henry Nanpei** (1860-1928), an influential Pohnpeian nationalist involved in the struggle against the Spanish colonists, is one of the few conventional 'sights' in the area.

The dirt road to the statue leads off to the left 12.5 miles from the turn-off to PATS and a quarter mile before reaching the cement bridge that crosses Lehn Mesi River, the widest on Pohnpei's south side. The statue is almost half a mile down the side road, off to the right in a small grassy clearing. Nanpei was buried a little farther down the road, in a **church cemetery**. Also in this area is the Lehnpaipohn Waterfall (see below).

As the cross-island road continues it edges along mangrove swamps, winds inland and back to the coast, crosses dozens of streams and goes through a run of small villages.

The most interesting place along this coast is picturesque **Pwudoi Sanctuary**, where a long boardwalk meanders above a mangrove swamp. The site has a freshwater eel pond, a refreshment stand and a sakau bar. It's all quite pleasant – there's a $5 continue on the dirt road for another 1.5 miles. After going over a rise look for a stand of bamboo; the unmarked trail starts on the left side of the road opposite the bamboo. Road conditions vary with the rain, but you can usually reach the trailhead by car.

The trail is well defined, beginning down carved clay steps, and takes about 15 minutes in all. It's a neat walk through a jungle of ferns and tropical trees. There's a stream crossing about 10 minutes down, but unless the water is high you can usually make it across the rocks without getting your feet wet. The trail ends at a hillside ledge above the falls. If you walk about 15 yards to the south-east there's a short but steep trail that scurries down the hillside to the edge of the pool. Watch your footing and take your time.

Henry Nanpei was one of the leading figures in the struggle against the Spanish occupation of Pohnpei

admission fee, which is used for the boardwalk maintenance.

The distinctive conical mountain called Pwusehn Malek marks the beginning of the Palikir area and Sokehs Municipality. The FSM capitol complex is just ahead and the road continues back to Kolonia.

Lehnpaipohn Waterfall This pleasant 30-foot fall drops into a wide, deep pool that's ideal for swimming.

To get to the trailhead coming from Kolonia, continue 10 miles south of Palikir, at which point you'll cross the wide bridge that spans the Lehn Mesi River. Exactly a mile farther turn inland at the school bus stop, pass the Pohn Alamwahu Church and

POHNPEI

NAN MADOL

Nan Madol was an important political, social and religious centre built during the saudeleur dynasty. It was a place for ritual activity and the homes of royalty and their servants.

Nan Madol is comprised of 92 artificial islets which were built on the tidal flats and reef off the south-east side of Pohnpei, near Temwen Island. The islets extend nearly a mile in length and a half-mile in width.

Basalt pillars, which had formed naturally into hexagonal columns, some of them 25 feet in length and 50 tons in weight, were quarried on Pohnpei Island and hauled to the site by raft.

The columns were stacked horizontally around the edges of the islets to serve as retaining walls, which were then filled with coral rubble and rock. In this manner the islets were eventually raised and the twisting canals shaped into what is sometimes referred to as the 'Venice of Micronesia'. On the level surfaces were built temples, burial vaults, meeting houses, bathing areas and pools for turtles, fish and eels.

The eastern half, Madol Powe (upper town), was the section for priests and rituals. The western half, Madol Pah (lower town), was the administrative section.

The construction of Nan Madol began in force between 1100 and 1200 AD and continued for another 200 to 300 years. Nan Madol was uninhabited when the first Westerners came ashore in the 1820s, but it was a recent abandonment. In 1852 missionaries recorded that elderly Pohnpeians could still remember when Nan Madol was densely populated.

The best time to visit is at high tide, when small boats can easily navigate the twisting mangrove-lined channels which wind through the complex.

Although many of the ruins have collapsed, it just adds to the dramatic impact, especially as you round a sharp corner in the canal and suddenly find yourself in the shadow of the massive Nan Douwas.

Nan Douwas is the largest structure still standing and the most impressive sight. The outer walls of the compound stand 25 feet high. The inner compound contains four crypts which were burial places for the saudeleurs and later the nahnmwarkis. The largest crypt is rectangular and is in the centre of two sets of enclosing walls, covered by basalt stones about 18 feet long and weighing a ton each.

The islet of **Kariahn islet** also has high walls surrounding a tomb.

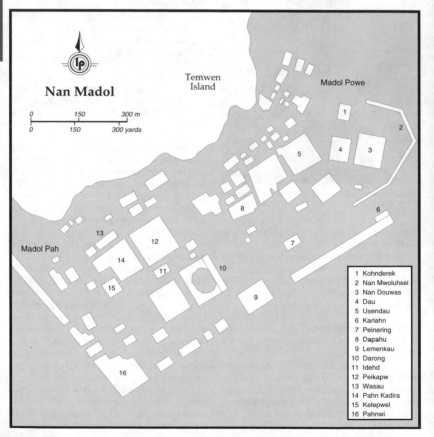

Nan Madol

1 Kohnderek
2 Nan Mwoluhsei
3 Nan Douwas
4 Dau
5 Usendau
6 Kariahn
7 Peinering
8 Dapahu
9 Lemenkau
10 Darong
11 Idehd
12 Peikapw
13 Wasau
14 Pahn Kadira
15 Kelepwel
16 Pahnwi

Pahn Kadira was probably the administrative centre of Nan Madol and also featured the temple of the Thunder God. A large, low platform is all that remains of the temple.

The islet of **Idehd** was the religious centre of Nan Madol. An annual ritual performed here by high priests culminated with the offering of cooked turtle innards fed to Nan Sanwohl, the 'holy eel' that was kept in the compound pool. The ritual was part of a two-week religious ceremony which included canoe-building competitions, feasting, singing, dancing and sakau drinking.

Darong, also an important ritual area, has a natural reef pool in its centre which may have been used for raising clams. Near one wall is a large stone once used for pounding sakau.

Other major islets are **Usendau**, an area where priests lived; **Nan Mwoluhsei** ('where the voyage stopped'), the ocean entrance to Nan Madol; **Pahnwi**, a multipurpose islet that included burial tombs; **Kelepwel**, a residential islet for servants and visitors; **Wasau**, an area where food was prepared; **Kohnderek**, a site for funeral services; **Dapahu**, an islet where canoes were made; **Dau**, a place where warriors lived; **Peikapw**, an islet which had two pools for turtles; **Lemenkau**, the medical centre; and **Peinering**, a coconut processing centre.

Getting There & Away
The best way to visit Nan Madol is via boat through the canals. This is not only the traditional method, but also the most scenic approach and the most practical way to see the majority of the islets.

There are several companies that provide boat tours of Nan Madol from Kolonia for $40, including Joy Hotel and Iet Ehu Tours (see Tours under Getting Around at the end of this Pohnpei section). You could also pre-arrange with the management of Heg's Garden Island (☎ 320-2088) for a $13 tour leaving from the Madolenihnw municipal building.

Another option is to wade across to Nan

> **Mysteries of Nan Madol**
> Although Nan Madol is Pohnpei's foremost sightseeing spot for foreigners, not all Pohnpeians feel comfortable there and the local belief that people shouldn't disturb the ruins may be more than mere superstition. In 1907, Pohnpei's German governor died of a mysterious ailment immediately after excavating a burial tomb on Nan Madol. The German administration claimed it was heat exhaustion but a lot of older Pohnpeians still doubt that diagnosis.
>
> Nan Madol holds its mysteries well. Some believe that the legendary lost continent of Mu, or Lemuria, may lie off its waters and that Nan Madol was built as a mirror image of a sunken city which at the time of construction could still be seen lying beneath the water's surface. ■

Madol. From the Madolenihmw municipal building, go across the causeway to Temwen Island. From the south side of Temwen you can wade over the reef to Nan Madol and explore the ruins on foot, though you'll want to coordinate this with low tide. (There's a tide chart in the *Pohnpei Advertiser*.) Because Nan Madol is so spread out, you will probably be able to explore only a part of the complex this way.

If you walk over, expect to pay the nahnmwarki of Madolenihnw $3 to visit Nan Madol; you don't need to hunt him down – he'll generally find you. If you take a boat tour, the permit fee is usually included in the tour price.

PLACES TO STAY
Camping
Camping is not a custom on Pohnpei Island and because of crime issues, it's not advisable. Camping can sometimes be arranged, however, on the uninhabited islands of Ant and Pakin atolls for a modest fee, though you'll also have to pay for the boat ride. Iet Ehu Tours or the tourist office are generally willing to make arrangements.

Hotels
Pohnpei has a 6% hotel tax. With the exception of Hotel Pohnpei and Pwomeria

Resort, the following hotels accept Master-Card and Visa.

Kolonia *Hotel Pohnpei* (☎ 320-2330, fax 320-5983), Box 430, Kolonia, Pohnpei, FM 96941, near the Kapingamarangi Village, has 19 rustic thatch and wood cottages, with walls of woven split bamboo, built in native Pohnpeian style. Although it's in a residential area, it has a garden setting with tropical flowers and views across the water to Sokehs Rock. The cottages are screened all the way round and rooms have fans, refrigerators and bottled water. The bathroom showers are sun-lit and draped with ferns. Thatch doesn't block sound well, however, so be sure to get a cottage away from the road, and even then you may hear music blaring late into the night from one of the neighbourhood bars. Singles/doubles cost $35/45.

Yvonne's Hotel (☎ 320-4953), Box 688, Kolonia, Pohnpei, FM 96941, consists of four rooms on the ground floor of a four-storey apartment building. The rooms have air-con, phones, TVs, refrigerators and private bathrooms. It's a few minutes' walk from the centre of town and a reasonable value at $45/50 for singles/doubles. You can also get a room/car package for $80; check at the GP Car Rental booth at the airport.

Palm Terrace Hotel (☎ 320-2392, fax 320-2567), Box 310, Kolonia, Pohnpei, FM 96941, has 11 large rooms with air-con, ceiling fans, cable TV and bathrooms with tubs. Once a favourite with business travellers, the hotel has declined over the years and is a bit run down and overpriced at $51/58 for singles/doubles.

A much better option in this price range is the newer *Sea Breeze Hotel* (☎ 320-2065, fax 320-2067), Box 371, Kolonia, Pohnpei, FM 96941, which is on the harbour road near the Australian Embassy. Rooms are good-sized with two double beds, private bathroom, table and chairs, refrigerator, phone and remote-control TV. Singles/doubles cost $55/65 for oceanview rooms and $5 less for backside rooms that are a bit quieter as they don't front the road.

The 18-room *South Park Hotel* (☎ 320-2255, fax 320-2600), Box 829, Kolonia, Pohnpei, FM 96941, has a fine hillside location on the west side of Kolonia. The new wing has pleasant rooms, each with tile floors, a mini-refrigerator and a sliding glass door opening to a veranda with a clear-on view of Sokehs Rock. Rates are $75/85 for singles/doubles. The old wing also has good water views but with a more cottage-like atmosphere. Those rooms are basic but also have TV, air-con and private baths and are a good value at $40/45.

The *Cliff Rainbow Hotel* (☎ 320-2415, fax 320-5416), Box 96, Kolonia, Pohnpei, FM 96941, has 33 rooms with air-con, TV and phones. Rates range from $40 to $85 for singles and $48 to $95 for doubles. The cheaper rooms are in an older section that's quite ordinary and overall it's not one of the island's cheerier accommodation options.

Joy Hotel (☎ 320-2447, fax 320-2478), Box 484, Kolonia, Pohnpei, FM 96941, is a pleasant in-town hotel with 10 nicely furnished rooms, each with a phone, air-con, ceiling fan, cable TV, desk and small balcony. Rooms with one double bed cost $66/70 for singles/doubles and rooms with two double beds are $90 for doubles.

Penny Hotel (☎ 320-5770, fax 320-2040), Box 934, Kolonia, Pohnpei, FM 96941, is a newer 16-room hotel adjacent to the US Embassy, about a 10-minute walk from the centre of town. The rooms are comfortable with air-con, phones, refrigerators, remote-control cable TV, bathtubs and either a king bed or two twins. All rooms have large balconies, but ask for one of the rear-facing ones, as they are not only quieter but they have pleasant garden-like views. Singles/doubles cost $71.50/82.50, tax included.

Airport Area The *Pwomeria Resort Club* (☎ 320-5941, fax 320-2391), Box 1416, Kolonia, Pohnpei, FM, 96941, consists of a run of beachside cottages squeezed between the commercial dock and the backside of the airport. Considering that Pohnpei has a number of late night flights, the runway proximity could certainly disrupt sleep. The cottages themselves have a certain rustic appeal with wood interiors, wicker furniture, ceiling fans, phones and refrigerators. Singles/doubles cost $65/70. This under-utilised hotel, which caters largely to Japanese tourists, is a five-minute walk north-west of the airport terminal.

The *Harbor View Hotel* (☎ 320-5244, fax 320-5246), Box 1328, Kolonia, Pohnpei, FM 96941, is also within walking distance from the airport. Despite the name the views leave much to be desired, as the hotel is oddly situated at a commercial dock. The 40 rooms are lacklustre but adequate, with refrigerators, air-con and private baths. Singles/doubles cost $45/60. There's a restaurant on site.

Outside Kolonia The *Nantehlik Hotel* (☎ 320-4981, fax 320-4983), Box 225, Kolonia, Pohnpei, FM 96941, on the river opposite Nett Point, has a pleasant local flavour. The hotel nicely balances island touches, including thatched roofing, with modern amenities. The rooms have air-con, cable TV, refrigerators, desks, phones and tubs, and room balconies that are literally perched over the river bank. It would be an idyllic setting if the river weren't so trashed. The staff is friendly and there's a restaurant and bar. Singles/doubles cost $65/85. To get there from Kolonia, go south-east on the circle-island road; one-third of a mile past the hospital, turn left diagonally opposite Ambros Last-Stop Grocery.

The *Village Hotel* (☎ 320-2797, fax 320-3797), Box 339, Kolonia, Pohnpei, FM 96941, has 21 native-style thatched cottages perched on a hillside in a natural setting five miles south of Kolonia. The rooms have two queen waterbeds, wicker furniture, private baths and ceiling fans. This is the trendy place to stay for Kwajalein contract workers on R&R and tends to have a heavier volume of American tourists than the in-town hotels. Rates are $70 to $90 for singles and $75 to $95 for doubles, with the higher priced rooms having better views. Airport transfers cost an additional $8 return.

The new *Snow Land Hotel* (☎ 320-3533, fax 320-3537), Box 418, Kolonia, Pohnpei, FM 96941, on a hillside in Palikir, two miles south of the capitol, has eight rooms with air-con, ceiling fans, TVs (showing videos only), refrigerators and verandas with fine views of Ant Atoll. While the rooms are quite nice, they're too pricey to recommend at $85/90 for singles/doubles.

If you're looking for a long-term rental, one of the easier places to book is *C-Star Apartelle* (☎ 320-3460, fax 320-3399), Box 279, Kolonia, Pohnpei, FM 96941, on the road to Nanpohnmal, a couple of miles south of Kolonia. This modern apartment complex has 25 units, with cooking facilities, living room, air-con, phone and cable TV. Rates begin at $700 a month. Units can also be rented by the day for $60/75 for singles/doubles.

For accommodation options on offshore islands, see the Langer Island, Heg's Garden Island and Black Coral Island sections.

PLACES TO EAT

Pohnpei has excellent fresh tuna. Sashimi is often the cheapest dish on the menu and grilled or fried fish dishes are not much more. Most restaurants offer a combination of Japanese and Western food.

Tap water is only sporadically chlorinated and is not safe for drinking unless it's been treated or boiled. Bottled water is available in grocery stores for about $2 a gallon.

Kolonia

Cafe Ole, a simple cafe at the side of Ambros Store, makes good milkshakes and has reasonably priced breakfast fare. There are also burgers with fries for $3, plate lunches from $5. It's open from 7 am to 4 pm on weekdays, 7 am to 3.30 pm on weekends.

Joy Restaurant, at the north side of Kolonia, is a perennial favourite with excellent Japanese food. Fresh fish is the speciality, though they also have beef and chicken dishes. The 'Joy Lunch' of fried tuna, rice, sashimi, soup and salad is the most popular lunch in Kolonia and costs just $4.50. You can also get inexpensive sashimi and fried fish burgers. It's open for lunch from 11 am to 3 pm Sunday to Friday, and for Sunday dinner (same menu) from 5.30 to 9 pm.

Joy Hotel Restaurant, not to be confused with the nearby Joy Restaurant, is off the lobby of the Joy Hotel. It has a variety of Japanese and Western foods. The tuna dinner is good and includes a big piece of fish, soup, salad and French fries for $6.50. Chicken teriyaki plates are $7.25. At lunch they have sandwiches for around $4 and oyako donburi and other dishes for not much more. At breakfast, French toast, pancakes and egg dishes cost around $3. It's open from 7 am to 3 pm and 5.30 to 9 pm daily.

Namiki Restaurant on Main St is a clean local eatery serving mostly Western fare, with breakfasts averaging $4, lunch $5 or $6. It's open from 7 am to 3 pm Monday to Saturday.

PCR Restaurant, up from the Palm Terrace Hotel on the way to Sokehs, offers a varied menu and the island's best sushi. Their Napolitan spaghetti is loaded with fish, octopus and green peppers and comes on a sizzling platter with garlic bread for $7.25. Sashimi and rice cost $5, fish and chicken dishes start at $7. It's a popular and pleasant place and the seafood is consistently fresh. It's open from 11 am to 9 pm Monday to Saturday, from 5 to 9 pm on Sundays.

Sei Restaurant, at the south end of Kolonia, has a very pleasant setting and excellent food. At lunch there are sandwiches, including a good cheeseburger for $4, and various full meals for a couple of dollars more. At dinner the chicken teriyaki ($8) and the tuna steak ($7) are both recommendable and come with rice and miso soup. You can also cook teppanyaki-style at your own table – the standard is a $16 plate of tenderloin slices with a few vegetables. For a second dish, consider ordering the $6.50 sashimi plate and grill it too – it's delicious seared on the outside and raw inside. Sei is open from 11 am to 2 pm Sunday to Friday, and from 5 to 10 pm daily.

The *South Park Restaurant* at the South Park Hotel has a nice view of Sokehs Rock through glass louvred windows. The varied menu includes oyako donburi and various fish, chicken and pork dishes for $7 to $10 at dinner. At lunch there are some good-value specials, including a fried fish and sashimi meal, for $5. Western-style breakfasts also cost around $5. It's open from 7 am to 2 pm Monday to Saturday and 5 to 9 pm daily.

The fruit stand near the weather station on Main St has fresh island produce, including bananas, tangerines, limes, breadfruit and yams. *Linn's*, a smaller fruit stand on the same road, has chilled drinking coconuts for 50 cents. You can also buy produce and drinking coconuts at the public market on the waterfront road.

Town's Mini-Mart has a bakery that makes a nice banana bread for $1.

The modern *Palm Terrace Store*, the island's best and largest grocery store, is open until 8 pm on weekdays, to 6 pm on Saturdays and to 5 pm on Sundays. It has a small bakery section, a deli with fresh roasted chickens by the pound and a small wine and spirits section. At the opposite end of Kolonia is *Ambros Store*, another well-stocked grocery store, which is open to 9.30 pm.

Outside Kolonia

The *Village Hotel's* open-air thatched restaurant has an unbeatable hillside setting, with a distant view of Sokehs Rock across the lagoon. This is a good place to stop for breakfast if you're on your way around the island. If you have a sweet tooth, try the Pohnpei hot cakes topped with thick fruity syrup for $3.75. At lunch there are sandwiches and omelettes for around $5. Dinners, which aren't particularly notable, range from chicken ($11) to steak ($18) and come with soup and salad. On Sundays, there are some nice brunch items, including Caesar salad and eggs Benedict as well as $2 glasses of champagne.

Restaurant Asaka at the Snow Land Hotel in Palikir is a simple place serving ordinary food. Oyako donburi costs $3.50, fried rice or spaghetti $5.50. It's open from 11 am to 2 pm and from 5.30 to 9.30 pm daily. Of more interest is the adjacent open-air thatch-roofed bar which has a splendid view of Ant Atoll.

ENTERTAINMENT
Alcohol Bars
Drinking scenes in Pohnpei can sometimes get a bit rough, with fist fights breaking out and the like, particularly in those places where there's dancing. The bars listed below have the better reputations, although it's wise to become increasingly cautious as the night wears on.

Paradise Cove, at the south side of Kapingamarangi Village, is one of the mellowest bars on the island, with a mahogany interior, easy jazz and New Age music and a beautiful jungle view. It opens around 5 pm.

Across the Street, a bar opposite Cliff Rainbow Hotel, is in a large open-air thatched-roof building with a great hilltop view of Sokehs Rock. It's open from noon to midnight weekdays, until 2 am on weekends. Beer costs $1.50, mixed drinks $2 to $4.

Rumors, an open-air bar at the side of the marina, half a mile past PCR Restaurant, has a pleasant harbourside locale that attracts a nice mix of islanders and younger expats. There's a happy hour from 4 to 6 pm on weekdays with $1 beers and $2 mixed drinks.

The *Palm Terrace Bar*, at the side of the Palm Terrace Hotel, is a watering hole favoured by older American expatriates, but it occasionally has a live rock band on weekends.

When there's a good sunset, the open-air *Sunset View Club* is the place to be. There's dancing to recorded music from 6 pm nightly, to midnight on weekdays and to 2 am on weekends. To get there head past the PCR Restaurant and where the road forks, take the left branch. Just short of a mile from the fork, turn right onto the paved road that leads past the old telecommunications building; six-tenths of a mile down

this road you'll come to a three-way fork. Bear right here, and the drive will end shortly at the cliffside bar.

The *Ocean View Bar*, on the road to Sokehs, has a good hillside view looking across Pohnpei's main harbour. There's sometimes live music and dancing in the evenings.

If you're looking for an unusual setting and don't mind going out of your way, the *Pwudoi Sanctuary* in Kitti, tucked in the mangroves, has live music and dancing most nights.

The *Tattooed Irishman*, the bar at the Village Hotel's open-air restaurant, has a more genteel atmosphere. For a breathtaking view, order up a tropical drink and head for the thatched gazebo.

Sakau Bars
Sakau bars are prolific around Kolonia. Every neighbourhood has one, though most are small, casual and inconspicuous. Most commonly they are a simple thatched-roof, open-air structure in someone's backyard. If you see a sign hung on a shack saying *mie sakau pwongiet* it means sakau is being served there that night.

The best way to find a sakau bar is just to ask around. However, one that's popular with the foreign community is the sakau bar behind the Bahai church, on the road to Nanpohnmal, about a mile south of Kolonia.

Unlike alcohol drinkers who tend to be boisterous and temperamental, sakau drinkers are quiet and relaxed. Sakau partakers generally sit in a circle sharing stories, passing the sakau bowl and gradually falling into quiet contemplation.

If you prefer to drink sakau in your own room, bring a container and most sakau bars will fill it for you and you'll have 'sakau to go'. Either way it generally costs $3 to $4 for your fill of sakau.

Cultural Shows
Pohnpei's cultural centres offer shows of traditional dances, songs and demonstrations of coconut husking and crafts. Shows usually include ritual sakau making, with

POHNPEI

samples handed around to the audience. There are two cultural centres, one in Nett Municipality and the other in Uh Municipality by the Village Hotel.

Each centre gives a slightly different show. The one in Uh generally demonstrates more crafts and gives more detailed explanations, while the one in Nett usually prepares a wonderful sampling of traditional Pohnpeian foods roasted in an earthen oven.

In the past, the cultural centres have tried to hold performances on a schedule, but there simply haven't been enough tourists for that to be workable and they now do it on demand. Performances can be arranged whenever at least five people have booked, so reservations must be made in advance through the tourist office or hotels. The cost is $10 per person for the performance in Nett, $15 in Uh.

THINGS TO BUY

Pohnpei has the highest quality wood carvings found in Micronesia, virtually all made by Kapingamarangi islanders who live in Kolonia. Most common are dolphins, sharks with real shark teeth, turtles and outrigger canoe models with woven sails, all carved of mangrove or ironwood. A new item being made by the Kapingamarangi people are finely carved amulets of manta rays and dolphins that are made from the nut of the ivory palm, a hard seed that resembles real ivory.

Other local handicrafts that make good souvenirs include fans, woven fibre pocketbooks, baskets, trochus shell buttons and brightly coloured appliqued skirts.

Packages of gourmet Pohnpei pepper make nice lightweight presents to carry back home. A three-ounce pack of black or white peppercorns costs about $3.50 in a small plastic bag, while five ounces that's attractively bottled and packaged in a woven basket costs around $12. If you're curious to see how the pepper is packaged, you can go down and watch the operation at Island Traders, adjacent to the public market.

Pohnpei soap, massage oil, suntan lotion and shampoo that are made from coconut oil are sold separately in stores for local use or gift-packaged in woven boxes at the handicraft shops. Or, for slightly cheaper prices, go to the Ponape Coconut Products office, just north of the public market.

Good places to pick up general handicrafts include the gift shop at Joy Restaurant and the one adjacent to PCR Restaurant. J&T Store, opposite the post office, has a pretty good collection of weavings, baskets and wood carvings, including some larger pieces priced up to $400. J&T also has one of the better selections of Pohnpei design T-shirts.

You can also purchase items directly from craftspeople at the workshops in Kolonia's Kapingamarangi Village.

GETTING THERE & AWAY
Air
Continental Micronesia flies to Pohnpei on its island-hopper route, with flights coming from Honolulu three days a week and from Guam four days a week.

The regular one-way fare is $179 between Chuuk and Pohnpei and $370 between Guam and Pohnpei, though FSM residents pay only $97/180 on those routes.

The regular one-way fare from Kosrae to Pohnpei is $130, while an advance-purchase return ticket costs $208. From Majuro, it's $355 one way, or $591 for the round-trip excursion.

For travellers who are island hopping between Guam and Honolulu, Pohnpei is a free stopover. Otherwise, Honolulu to Pohnpei costs $557 one way, or $933 round-trip.

Air Nauru flies into Pohnpei at 1.30 am on Tuesdays en route to Guam and Manila. The one-way Pohnpei-Guam fare is $259, the Pohnpei-Manila fare $383. On Thursdays, Air Nauru flies into Pohnpei at 4.30 am coming from the opposite direction. The one-way Pohnpei-Nauru fare is $217. There's also a Pohnpei-Fiji ticket for $444 one way, $710 for a 30-day excursion.

Airport Pohnpei's airport is on Takatik Island, connected to Kolonia by a mile-long causeway. The terminal has a snack bar (which also sells Pohnpei pepper and coconut soap), GP and Hervis car rental booths and restrooms. Sometimes a handicraft stall sets up at departure times.

Sea

Kolonia Harbor is the official port of entry in Pohnpei. Yachts dock at the marina near Rumors bar.

SeAir Transportation (☎ 320-2866), Box 96, Kolonia, Pohnpei, FM 96941, is a private company that operates the MS *Caroline Islands*, a boat similar to the government field trip ship. It runs on an irregular basis between Pohnpei and Kosrae, and sometimes also goes to Chuuk and on rare occasions to Yap, depending upon its cargo schedules. Fares are calculated on a per-mile basis. The one-way fare to Kosrae costs $18 on deck, $63 for a cabin. There's limited meal service on board, but it's best to bring your own food. The SeAir office is on Main St in Kolonia.

Information on the field trip ship to Pohnpei's outer islands is under Getting There & Away at the end of the Outer Atolls section.

Leaving Pohnpei

Pohnpei has a departure tax of $5.

GETTING AROUND
To/From the Airport

Most hotels will provide free airport transfers on request and some occasionally run their minivans out to meet incoming flights just to see if there are any potential customers.

Taxis generally don't run out to the airport, as it's off their main route. It's about a two-mile walk to the town centre, so if you don't have somebody coming to pick you up, it's a good idea to catch a ride from someone heading into town – you might try one of the car rental agents.

Taxi

Pohnpei has a system of radio-dispatched shared taxis. The taxis are marked; some are sedans, others are minivans. You can call to have a taxi pick you up, or you can flag them down. Either way, the fare is $1 anywhere within greater Kolonia, including Palikir, as long as you don't go off the paved road. To go onto dirt roads there's an extra $1 charge.

It costs $2 to go from Kolonia to the Village Hotel and $30 to the Madolenihmw municipal office. These fares are per person, and taxis will stop and pick up other passengers along the way. Two of the biggest of Pohnpei's taxi companies are Penny's (☎ 320-2940) and Kaselehlia (☎ 320-4911).

Car & Scooter

Of the two car rental companies at the airport, the more reliable is GP Car Rental (☎ 320-5648), which has sedans for $45 including insurance with a $500 deductible. The other company, Hervis Rent-A-Car (☎ 320-2784), has similar rates but doesn't always staff the booth. Both also have offices in town.

Two other key car rental companies are PCR Car Rental (☎ 320-5252), behind PCR Restaurant, which rents Mazda 323s from $45, and Penny Rent-A-Car (☎ 320-5770), on the waterfront road, which rents sedans for $42. Cars can be delivered to your hotel. Penny's offers no insurance, while at PCR the collision damage waiver costs an additional $4.

Hotels can also arrange car rentals for their guests and the tourist office keeps a list of a few other car rental agencies, mostly mom-and-pop operations that come and go. Car rental companies tack on a 6% fee if you pay by credit card.

You can rent scooters for $20 a day from the small store that's a couple of minutes' walk west of Town's Mini-Mart.

If you plan to drive around the entire island or explore a lot of rutted back roads, try to avoid renting a low-riding sedan, as lost oil pans are not uncommon and the rental companies will hit you up for the repair costs.

Petrol costs $1.70 a gallon in Pohnpei.

Hitching

Hitching has mixed results. If you've got your thumb out it will often be one of the taxis that stops to pick you up – and they expect payment. On the other hand, when you're just walking along the road, people who have had some passing contact with you, such as a customs officer, will often stop and offer you a ride. The usual safety precautions apply, especially for women.

Tours

Recommended for tours of all sorts is Iet Ehu Tours (☎ 320-2959), a flexible and friendly small tour operation run by Emensio Eperiam. He offers dozens of customised sightseeing tours, everything from a sakau bar tour for $15 to overnight trekking outings in the jungle for $80. One particularly nice tour is the $40 trip to Nan Madol, which includes snorkelling, a dip under Kepirohi Waterfall, and a lunch of freshly speared fish. Iet Ehu can also take you to any of Pohnpei's nearshore islands, including Langer and Black Coral.

Other tour companies have more limited options and include the following:

Blue Oyster Tours (☎ 320-5117)
C-K Tours (☎ 320-3448)
Joy Hotel (☎ 320-2477)
Micro Tours (☎ 320-2888)
Village Hotel Tours (☎ 320-2797)

For a real Pohnpeian experience, consider a guided tour by outrigger canoe through the winding mangrove channels of the **Enipein Marine Park**. This small community-run business is in the Enipein ('Ghost Lady') area of Kitti Municipality, on the sparsely populated south side of the island. Tours start from a canoe landing and thatched-roof visitor centre 3.5 miles east of the Lehn Mesi River.

The tours start at 9 am and include a canoe ride through the swamp, a trip to a nearby reef for snorkelling, a lunch of fruit, fish and mangrove crab, plus sakau tasting for those who care to indulge. The cost is $35, and transportation from Kolonia can be provided for another $7.50. Regularly scheduled tours are only on Saturdays but

can be arranged on other days if there's a minimum of four people and at least one day's notice. Arrangements should be made in advance through the tourist office (☎ 320-2421).

Micronesian Aviation Corporation (☎ 320-2000, fax 320-4920) offers 45-minute **flight tours** that overfly the island's jungle interior, Nan Madol and the near-shore reef islands surrounding Pohnpei. The cost is $100 with one passenger, $120 with two and $150 with three.

ISLANDS IN POHNPEI LAGOON

The number of islands in Pohnpei's lagoon depends on the tide and how you make the count. Not including the artificial islets of Nan Madol, there are about 24 basalt islands, 30 coral islets on the barrier reef and some islands of alluvial sands.

Langer Island

The basaltic island of Langer figures in colonial history. German traders had copra operations there and the Japanese built a seaplane base on the island which survived US bombings in 1944. After WW II the seaplane ramp was used as Pohnpei's only runway, with all air travel by Grumman SA-16 amphibian, until 1970 when the current airport was built on Takatik.

Today Langer Island is a popular place for weekend family picnics and has clear waters with good swimming and snorkelling.

There are simple cottages on the island where visitors can stay for $15, bedding included; the short boat ride over can be arranged for $5. For more information, contact Jerry Barbosa (☎ 320-2769) at Jerry's Enterprises, next to the Chinese Embassy.

Heg's Garden Island

Heg's Garden Island is a quiet little island with a white sand beach and a dozen unfurnished rough-wood cottages with thatched roofs, back-to-basics style. Small groups sometimes come to Heg's for picnics, but most of the time it's near-deserted except for the caretaker, some pigs and an amorous goose.

Overnight lodging costs $10, plus $2 to rent a sleeping mat. There's an electric generator and lights in the huts. Bring your own food. Be sure to specify a hut as far away as possible from the toilets and pigpens.

If you don't want to stay overnight, you can also visit Heg's for sun and snorkelling for a $5 landing fee. A boat ride can be arranged from Madolenihnw municipal building, just beyond PATS, for $5. Tours to nearby Nan Madol can be arranged for $13. For more information call 320-2088 or write Herbert Gallen, Box 175, Kolonia, Pohnpei, FM 96941.

Black Coral Island

Black Coral Island, a small island on Pohnpei's south-western barrier reef, is owned by a friendly Pohnpeian family and makes a fine place for either a day outing or an overnight getaway.

There's nice coral around the island and splendid marine life on the ocean side. Be careful of strong tidal currents in the channel. In addition to swimming and snorkelling, the island can be a fun place for shell searching or just lying on the beach.

The island has 11 simple but suitable huts that cost $13 per person with mattresses, pillows and sheets. You can bring your own food or make arrangements in advance to buy meals there; prices range from $5 for a fish and sashimi dinner to $15 for lobster or crab.

There's no boat or transport service from Kolonia. You must instead make advance arrangements to be picked up behind the Seinwar Elementary School in Kitti, which is less than a mile south of the Pwudoi Sanctuary. The 15-minute boat trip costs $35 for one to four people, $7.50 each for more than four. For those on day trips, there's a $5 landing fee. Arrangements are made through Dakio Paul (☎ 320-4869 or 320-3533), Black Coral Island, Box 1519, Kolonia, Pohnpei, FM 96941.

OUTER ATOLLS
Ant Atoll

Ant, a beautiful atoll with a palm-fringed lagoon, lies a few miles south-west of Pohnpei Island. It has pristine white sand beaches and aqua waters with abundant coral and fish, and is one of Pohnpei's most popular dive destinations.

Ant has a large seabird colony, including brown noddies, great crested terns, sooty terns and great frigate birds.

The atoll is part of Kitti Municipality and belongs to descendants of Pohnpeian nationalist Henry Nanpei.

The largest of the atoll islands, Nikalap Aru, once had a little thatched-cottage resort under development, but a typhoon nipped the project in the bud and the island remains uninhabited.

Pakin Atoll

Pakin is a small atoll about 25 miles off Pohnpei Island's north-west coast. Its half-dozen islands are inhabited by a single family. It has good beaches and, like Ant, is a popular dive spot.

Oroluk Atoll

Oroluk has a sizable population of hawksbill and Pacific green turtles, as well as a dozen people. Although its 19 islands total less than a quarter sq mile of land it has a large lagoon.

Mokil Atoll

Mokil (also called Mwoakilloa) was once commonly visited by Marshallese and Gilbertese and later became a popular stop with whalers.

Mokil Atoll's three islets total about half a sq mile. Fewer than 300 people live on Kahlap, the largest and only inhabited islet. The other two, Urak and Mwandohn, are farmed.

Mokil is a tidy little place, with friendly people, a pretty lagoon and a 1000-foot airstrip served by Pacific Missionary Aviation (PMA). With advance notice, PMA can arrange through their agent on Mokil for visitors to stay in homes with island families.

POHNPEI

Pingelap Atoll

Pingelap has three islands but all of the atoll's 750 people live on Pingelap Island. Sukoru and Deke islands are visited for gathering coconuts and crabs.

Early foreigners did not find a ready welcome in Pingelap until about the 1850s when the first whaling ships arrived. In the 1870s, Congregationalist missionaries trained two Pingelapese teachers on Pohnpei and sent them back to their home islands. In just two years they had not only converted practically the entire population, but had adults and children alike all wearing Western clothing.

Pingelap is known for *kahlek*, a kind of night fishing which uses burning torches to attract flying fish into hand-held nets. Kahlek means 'dancing' and refers to the way the men holding the torches have to sway to keep their balance when they're standing up. This sort of fishing is done from January to April.

Unfortunately, there's a lot of poverty in Pingelap, the island's not very clean and the flies and mosquitoes can be thick. Like Mokil, Pingelap has a 1000-foot airstrip serviced by Pacific Missionary Aviation.

Sapwuafik (Ngatik) Atoll

With the drawing up of its municipal constitution in 1986, Ngatik Atoll renamed itself Sapwuafik Atoll, correcting an inaccuracy it had been carrying for 150 years as a result of careless European cartographers. The name Ngatik now, as in pre-European times, refers solely to the largest and only populated island in the atoll.

Sapwuafik is well known for its outrigger sailing canoes, made from breadfruit logs and assembled using wooden pegs and coconut fibre twine. Unlike on other Pohnpeian atolls where islanders have switched to speedboats or have attached small outboard motors to their canoes, Sapwuafik's traditional canoes are powered solely by the wind using sails lashed to bamboo poles.

The FSM government is currently building an airstrip on Sapwuafik.

Nukuoro & Kapingamarangi Atolls

The people of Nukuoro and Kapingamarangi atolls are physically, linguistically and culturally Polynesian. Both atolls are beautiful, with good beaches.

Nukuoro has 42 tiny islets formed in a near-perfect circle around a lagoon four miles in diameter. The total land area is just six-tenths of a sq mile. Most of the population of about 400 live on the largest island, a third of which is covered by taro. Subsistence comes largely from taro farming and fishing.

Nukuoro is a real haven, with welcoming Polynesian hospitality, and would be a fine place to spend some time just lazing around on beaches, picking up seashells and playing with island children. There is a guesthouse on the pier available for overnight or longer stays and the local senator has a traditional wooden house on stilts that is

---

Bloody Hart

A visit to Ngatik by the British ship *Lambton* in 1837 left an indelible mark on the island. Charles 'Bloody' Hart, the Australian captain of the ship, was after fine pieces of tortoise shell he had seen on an earlier excursion. However, the shells had religious significance to the Ngatikese and they refused to trade. In fact, during the first visit trading negotiations were halted by a group of armed islanders who attacked the crew and forced them to run for their lives back to the ship.

Hart was a swindler accustomed to getting his own way, and although his crew had escaped unharmed they went back for revenge. The Ngatikese, armed only with clubs and slings, had little defence against the muskets of the *Lambton*'s crew, and the sailors massacred all the island men.

As a result, the 600 people of Sapwuafik Atoll are largely descended from a mix of Ngatikese women and British, American, Pohnpeian and Gilbertese men, many of them crew members of the *Lambton*. ■

sometimes available; to make advance arrangements call 320-2750 in Kolonia and ask for the Nukuoro senator, or radio Nukuoro Atoll via the FSM Telecommunications office.

Kapingamarangi Atoll is just one degree, or 65 miles, north of the equator. Its 33 islets total just over half a sq mile, with a lagoon seven miles across at its widest point. The population is about 500. There are no arrangements for visitors to stay on Kapingamarangi, and overall the island is not terribly welcoming to outsiders.

Both Nukuoro and Kapingamarangi are hit from time to time by severe droughts, which result in food shortages on the islands.

Getting There & Away

Air The only airstrips on Pohnpei's outer atolls are on Mokil and Pingelap, although one is underway on Sapwuafik. Division among islanders on Nukuoro has stalemated plans for building an airstrip there.

Pacific Missionary Aviation (☎ 320-2796, fax 320-2592), Box 517, Kolonia, Pohnpei, FM 96941, flies to Mokil and Pingelap on Mondays and Fridays, provided there are enough passengers. PMA's one-way fare from Pohnpei Island is $60 to Mokil, $70 to Pingelap. Return fares are double.

Flights leave Pohnpei from PMA's two-storey cement building on the west side of the main airport terminal.

Sea The government field trip ship, *Micro Glory*, usually schedules at least one trip a month to the outer islands, though it doesn't stick to the schedule and the boat has been known to be dry docked for months at a time. The ship holds 125 passengers and has eight cabins. Fares are calculated on a per-mile basis.

The eastern islands trip goes to Mokil and Pingelap, returning in about five days. The round-trip fare is $12 on deck, $62 for a cabin. The southern islands trip goes to Sapwuafik, Oroluk, Nukuoro and Kapingamarangi and takes about 10 days. The round trip costs $30 on deck, $155 for a

cabin. As a rule, one day is spent at each island. You can take along your own food or pay $4 for breakfast, $5 for lunch and $6 for dinner.

The field trip ship leaves from the commercial dock on Takatik Island. For more information, contact the Office for Island Affairs (☎ 320-2710, fax 320-2505), Pohnpei State Government, Kolonia, Pohnpei, FM 96941. If you go in person, it's the first building on the left (marked Office of Public & Governmental Relations) as you go up the hill toward the legislature building in Kolonia.

Chuuk (Truk)

Chuuk is colourful, lively and rough around the edges. Houses are commonly painted in several bright contrasting colours. On hot days village women sit bare-breasted in streams doing laundry and young children run around naked. Speedboats zip back and forth across the lagoon and from Weno you can watch the sun set behind the Faichuk Islands, often with a brilliant light show.

Chuuk's biggest drawing card is its sunken wrecks and its most enthusiastic visitors are divers. A whole Japanese fleet rests on the lagoon floor – a moment in time captured in an underwater museum. Most of the wrecks lie off the islands of Dublon, Eten, Fefan and Uman, and together they represent the largest naval loss in history.

The waters of Chuuk Lagoon are clear and calm and you don't have to be an experienced diver to take a look at its underwater attractions. A couple of the shipwrecks are only a few feet under the water's surface and can readily be snorkelled.

With the passing of its state constitution in 1989, Truk officially renamed itself Chuuk (pronounced 'chuke'). It is a change which will take some getting used to by divers, WW II veterans, Micronesia residents and visitors alike, who have long

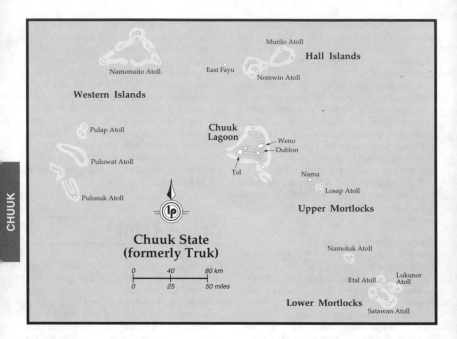

known the island as Truk. You'll see both names in use.

HISTORY
Pre-European Contact
Legend says that at a time estimated to be about the 14th century the great leader Sowukachaw came by canoe to Chuuk with his son Sowooniiras. Where they really came from is anybody's guess but most people put their money on Kosrae since in Chuuk (as in Pohnpei) there are many legends relating to Kosrae.

The arrival of these leaders represented something analogous to the end of medievalism. They are credited with introducing new varieties of breadfruit as well as a method of fermentation used to preserve breadfruit. That's important because at the time breadfruit was the main staple food crop. The arrival of Sowukachaw also represented the beginning of clan history and some sort of social ranking system. When

the Chuukese trace their ancestry they go back as far as that time, but never any further.

European Contact
The first Europeans to sight Chuuk Lagoon were with the Spanish ship *San Lucas*, captained by Alonso de Arellano, in 1565. The Chuukese came after them with hundreds of canoes filled with armed warriors. The Spaniards stayed only long enough to fire a few cannon shots and make their way across the lagoon and out another passage.

When Manuel Dublon, captaining the *San Antonio*, came to Chuuk in 1814 to collect beche-de-mer he became the first European to enter the lagoon in 250 years.

The Germans took possession of Chuuk from the Spanish in 1899 and developed a copra trade, with their headquarters on Dublon Island.

Japanese & WW II
The Japanese Navy began building bases

on Dublon immediately after occupying the islands in 1914.

During the war, Chuuk Lagoon became the Japanese Imperial Fleet's most important central Pacific base. The fortification of the islands was so great and thought to be so impenetrable that the lagoon earned the nickname 'Gibraltar of the Pacific'. As the huge sheltered lagoon had only a few passageways it could be easily defended against naval invasion, making for a perfect, calm anchorage. Unfortunately for the Japanese, these same conditions also made it easy to trap their fleet.

On 17 February 1944, the US Navy launched an air-bomb attack, code-named 'Operation Hailstone', against the Japanese Fourth Fleet which was docked in the lagoon. Like sitting ducks, they were bombed nonstop for two days and by the finish some 60 ships had sunk to the bottom. The islands of Chuuk Lagoon, however, were never invaded by Allied forces.

When the US military moved in after the war, Dublon was crowded with the 30,000 Japanese soldiers who had survived the air raids but had no means of leaving the island. Since it was easiest to keep them on Dublon until they could be repatriated to Japan, the USA established its headquarters on Weno, which has been the administrative centre ever since.

GEOGRAPHY
Chuuk State includes 192 outer islands in addition to the 15 main islands and more than 80 islets that make up Chuuk Lagoon. All in all, about 40 of the state's islands are inhabited.

Chuuk Lagoon
The whole lagoon area was once one large volcanic island but over the millennia most of the island has sunk. The 15 high islands in Chuuk Lagoon are the tallest peaks of that original island. The lagoon formation is similar to an atoll although, strictly defined, an atoll no longer contains high volcanic islands.

There are also numerous small low coral islands inside Chuuk's enormous lagoon, which is enclosed by 140 miles of barrier reef. At its widest point, the 822-sq-mile lagoon is almost 40 miles from one reef to another. It has five main passages.

The main populated islands in the lagoon are Weno, Dublon, Fefan, Uman, Eten, Param, Udot, Pata, Polle and Tol; most of them are mountainous and wooded. The islands in Chuuk Lagoon have a combined land area of about 46 sq miles.

CLIMATE
The average annual temperature is a fairly constant 81°F (27°C). Annual rainfall averages 143 inches in Chuuk Lagoon. Humidity is high year round and can get particularly uncomfortable between July and November when the north-easterly trade winds die down. The most agreeable time of the year is the dry season from January to March.

Although Chuuk lies outside the main typhoon belt, it has been hit by a number of severe storms in recent years. In November 1990, Typhoon Owen struck the Hall and Western Islands, levelling most buildings and crops, and leaving thousands of islanders homeless and without food or water.

ECONOMY
As elsewhere in the FSM, Chuuk's moneyed economy is largely dependent on US compact monies. Chuuk currently gets the

---

From Truk to Chuuk
To outsiders, the name change from Truk to Chuuk may be confusing, but Chuukese have always called the islands in the main lagoon 'Chuuk' when speaking in their native language. The pronunciation of 'Truk', a Germanic corruption of the name, was used only when speaking in English. *Chuuk* means 'mountain'. The outer islands are *fanabi* – *fanu* is 'island', *bi* is 'sand'. ■

lion's share of FSM funding, about $43 million annually. This money is intended for government operational expenses and social and economic development. Much of it is squandered, however, on a bloated government bureaucracy of about 3000 employees. Chuuk is commonly the target of criticism by other FSM states who feel that Chuuk is draining the FSM by misappropriating its funding and failing to pay legitimate bills. As a result of Chuuk's growing budget problems there's not always enough fuel to run government boats and the school year has been shortened.

Subsistence farming and fishing are still widespread on Chuuk. The main subsistence crops are breadfruit, coconuts, bananas and taro. Copra production provides some local income.

Chuuk has a small state-owned fishing fleet that provides fresh fish for the local market, but the biggest players are now foreign fishing boats, mainly Chinese and Taiwanese.

POPULATION & PEOPLE
Chuuk is the most populated Micronesian island group outside Guam, with about 55,000 people. Approximately one-third live on the island of Weno.

SOCIETY & CONDUCT
In Chuuk, each island has a predominant clan, the members of which are generally the descendants of the first people to settle that island. While the head clan no longer owns all the island's land, the members still enjoy limited privileges. For instance, other people on the island are often obliged to present the clan with some token of respect, such as the fruits from the first harvest.

Today the chief of the predominant clan's actual power over those outside his own clan is only nominal, though he is still occasionally called on to mediate disputes between other clans on the island.

Many Chuukese women wear *nikautang*, a dress with puffed sleeves, a dropped waist with lace trim and a gathered skirt that hangs below the knee. Also popular are brightly coloured appliqued skirts called *uros*.

Occasionally around Weno you see men from Chuuk's Western Islands wearing the bright cotton loincloths that are typical of those outer islands.

RELIGION
Chuuk is pretty evenly divided between Catholics and Protestants, although there's also a congregation of Jehovah's Witnesses.

Love Sticks
In the days of thatched houses, love sticks were used by courting males to get a date for the evening. These slender sticks of mangrove wood were each intricately notched and carved in a design unique to its owner.

A young man would show his love stick to the object of his desire, so she would be able to recognise the carving at the appropriate time.

If all went well the suitor would wait until the young woman had gone to bed and then push the love stick in through the side of the thatched house and entangle it in her long hair. She would be woken by his gentle tugging, feel the carving to determine who was outside and, if tempted, would sneak out into the night for a secret rendezvous.

It seems like a system with a built-in potential for disaster, like poking the loved one in the eye or tangling the stick in her mother's hair, but perhaps there was more to it than is usually told. When thatched houses went out of fashion, so did love sticks. Replicas make popular souvenirs. ■

LANGUAGE

The native language is Chuukese, but there are also several minority dialects, the most widely spoken being Mortlockese. English is widely understood throughout the islands.

Many native words and place names have more than one spelling. This is due not only to inconsistencies among Westerners who transcribed the native language into the Roman alphabet, but also because most people living in Chuuk Lagoon pronounce 'l' as 'n'.

'Good day' is *ran annim* for Chuukese from the lagoon, or *ran allim* for outer islanders. 'Thank you' is *kini so* or *kili so*. Add *chapur* for 'very much'.

Itang, a specialised and highly metaphorical language taught only to chiefs and people of high rank, has been in use since the 14th century. It is used to pass down secret knowledge and to call on supernatural powers.

HOLIDAYS

Chuuk has the following public holidays:

New Year's Day
  1 January
FSM Constitution Day
  10 May
Chuuk State Constitution Day
  1 October
United Nations Day
  24 October
FSM Independence Day
  3 November
Christmas Day
  25 December

ACTIVITIES
Diving

Chuuk Lagoon is a wreck diver's dream. On its bottom rest about 60 Japanese ships, including oil tankers, submarines, cruisers, tugboats and cargo ships, as well as scores of US and Japanese planes.

The ships lie just as they sank in 1944 – some upright, some intact, some in pieces strewn across the lagoon floor. Each is a separate time capsule. The holds are full of guns and trucks and fighter planes, the

> **Chuukese Magic**
>
> Believers say Chuukese magic is powerful and they take it very seriously. It takes many forms – as a curse, a love potion, a way to remove evil spirits or a form of protection. Satawan Atoll is said to have the strongest magic.
>
> Perfumed love potions, called *omung*, may contain such exotica as centipede teeth and stingray tail mixed with coconut oil. If a beautiful woman falls in love with a plain-looking man, people will joke and say he used omung. Magic aside, Chuukese say that nowadays money is a more effective way to win someone's heart. ■

dining areas are littered with dishes, silverware and sake bottles and the skeletal remains of the perished crews lie 'buried' at sea.

The wrecks have become artificial reefs for hundreds of species of vividly coloured corals, sponges and anemones that have attached themselves to the metal. These shelters also attract large schools of fish. The water is warm, about 85°F, and visibility is generally 50 to 100 feet.

The largest wreck in the lagoon is the *Heian Maru*, a 535-foot passenger and cargo ship lying on its port side at 40 to 110 feet. Divers can see the ship's name and telegraph mount on the bow, as well as large propellers, periscopes and a torpedo.

The *Fujikawa Maru*, an aircraft ferry that landed upright in 40 to 90 feet of water, is one of the most popular dives. Until recently the stern mast stuck up out of the water, but damage caused by local fishers using dynamite near the wreck caused the mast to collapse. The main deck is 60 feet below the surface, while the hold, which contains four Zero fighters, is at 90 feet.

Underwater photographers like the *Sankisan Maru* for its excellent soft coral formations. This half-destroyed munitions freighter is upright at 50 to 100 feet and still has a cargo of trucks, machine guns and ammunition.

Although it's the wrecks that make Chuuk special, the walls on the outside of the lagoon reef also make for good diving.

CHUUK

Visibility outside the lagoon can be up to 200 feet.

Although strictly illegal, some islanders tear the shipwrecks apart looking for stores of explosives, which they then use to dynamite the reefs for an easy catch of fish. Unfortunately there's a ready market for fish caught this way.

Dive Shops To keep souvenir hunters at bay, the wrecks in Chuuk Lagoon have been declared an underwater historical park and can't be visited without a guide. All three of the dive operations on Weno are competitively priced and currently charge $65 for a two-tank dive, including tanks, backpacks and weight belts. Other equipment can be rented at an additional cost. Lunch is extra, or bring your own.

The Blue Lagoon Dive Shop (☎ 330-2796, fax 330-4307), Box 429, Chuuk, FM 96942, in Weno centre, was Chuuk's first dive operation, started in 1973 by Kimiuo Aisek and now managed by his son Gradvin.

Highly regarded is Micronesia Aquatics (☎ 330-2204, fax 330-4096), Box 57, Chuuk, FM 96942, which is run by former Peace Corps volunteer Clark Graham and his Chuukese wife, Chineina. The office is just inside the gate of the Truk Continental Hotel. Graham, who specialises in underwater photography, runs the most conservation-oriented operation and gives divers a full-day outing that generally includes snorkelling and a lunch break on one of the lagoon islands in between dives.

The newest operation is Sundance Tours & Dive Shop (☎ 330-4234, fax 330-4451), Box 85, Chuuk, FM 96942, which is located at the side of Truk Stop hotel.

Dive Boats Two live-aboard dive boats are based in Chuuk Lagoon. The busiest is the SS *Thorfinn*, which has a Sunday-to-Sunday package that includes six days of diving wrecks and reef walls (up to five dives a day), along with meals and accommodation, for $1700. There's also a plan sans the dive package that costs $850 a week, plus $40 for each dive you opt to

make. The *Thorfinn*, which is a converted whaler, holds 26 passengers in 13 air-con rooms, with shared showers and toilets. Although the ship is not new, it's quite comfortable and even has a hot tub on deck, and the food is good. Divers can also arrange to go out on a flexible schedule, with accommodation and meals at $150 a day, plus $40 a dive. Reservations can be made direct through Seaward Holidays (☎ 330-4302, fax 330-4253), Box DX, Chuuk, FM 96942.

The *Truk Aggressor* has weekly trips, from Sunday to Sunday, which include 5½ days of diving. The cost is $1895 per person which, like the *Thorfinn*, includes everything except the airfare to and from Chuuk and alcoholic beverages. This modern boat holds 20 people in 10 double cabins, each with a double and single bunk, a shower and toilet. Reservations can be made through Live/Dive Pacific (☎ 808-329-8182, 800-344-5662; fax 808-329-2628), 74-5588 Pawai Place, Building F, Kailua-Kona, HI 96740. If you're already in Chuuk and have a couple grand burning a hole in your pocket, you could check with the captain, who anchors off the Truk Continental Hotel on Saturday nights, to see if there's space available.

Both dive boats can also be booked through travel agents abroad.

Snorkelling

Boat trips for snorkellers usually include a visit to the *Dainihino Maru*, a small coral-encrusted transport ship that lies on its starboard side in 40 feet of water off Uman. It has a bow gun just three feet underwater and its deck is about eight feet down. Other wrecks visited for snorkelling are a Zero fighter in shallow waters off Eten and the *Susuki Maru*, a sub-chaser off the coast of Dublon, with its deck about 10 feet underwater.

Blue Lagoon Dive Shop charges $40 for its snorkelling tour. If three or more snorkellers are going out, they'll usually take a separate boat and snorkel around the shallow wrecks described above, but otherwise snorkellers go out with divers.

Sundance Tours & Dive Shop can arrange a snorkelling trip and picnic island tour for $50. Yasu Mori, who operates from a desk in the lobby of the Truk Continental Hotel, also offers snorkelling tours for about $50.

Micronesia Aquatics can arrange snorkelling tours as well, with the cost depending on whether you go out with divers or on a special trip, and how many people are in the group.

Micronesia Aquatics and Yasu Mori both rent snorkel sets for $10 a day.

Hiking

Virtually all land on Chuuk is privately owned, which puts a dent in hiking opportunities. If you want to do a fairly substantial hike into the interior, consider the guided hike to the top of Mt Witipon offered by Micronesia Aquatics. The hilltop has a panoramic view as well as the remains of a Japanese radar base, antiaircraft guns and some explorable caves.

It's a moderately difficult half-day outing and the cost is $25 per person.

WENO (MOEN) ISLAND

Weno, formerly Moen, is the capital and commercial centre of Chuuk. At just over seven sq miles, it is the second largest island in the lagoon. Tropical forests make up much of the interior, with the highest point, the 1214-foot Mt Tonoken, nearly in the centre.

Villages circle the outer edges of Weno; the district centre, government offices and airport are on the north-west side of the island. A coastal road extends most of the way around Weno, broken by a narrow gap of mangrove swamp between the tiny villages of Nukunap and Winipis on the east side of the island.

Many outer islanders come to Weno in search of job opportunities, of which there are few for those without political connections, and thus they end up living in poverty. As one of the most densely populated

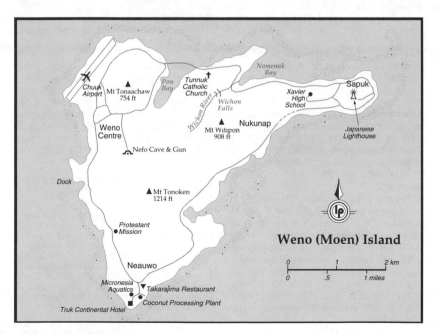

Weno (Moen) Island

islands in Micronesia, Weno has its share of pollution problems, including sewerage that runs into the lagoon and streets littered with trash.

Information

Tourist Office The Chuuk Visitors Bureau (☎ 330-4133, fax 330-4194), tucked back off the road at the south side of the post office, is open from 8 am to 5 pm Monday to Friday.

Money The Bank of Guam has a branch next to Susumu's Store that's open from 10 am to 3 pm Monday to Thursday, to 5 pm on Fridays, and another next to Shigeto's Store that's open from 9.30 am to 2.30 pm on Tuesdays and Thursdays and 9 am to 1 pm on Saturdays. The Bank of the FSM is open from 9.30 am to 2.30 pm Monday to Thursday, to 3 pm on Fridays. On payday Fridays, you can expect long queues at the counters.

Credit cards are not widely accepted on Weno, though larger hotels such as the Truk Continental and Truk Stop accept them.

Post Chuuk's only post office is in Weno centre. It's open from 8 am to 4 pm Monday to Friday and 9 to 11 am on Saturdays.

Telecommunications Telephone calls can be made and faxes, telex and telegrams can be sent 24 hours a day from the FSM Telecommunications building, east of the airport. Local calls are free and faxes can be received at the office (fax 330-2777) at no charge.

The rate to call between FSM states is $1 per minute between 6 am and 6 pm on weekdays, and 50 cents per minute at all other times. Phone calls to all parts of the world except the FSM have a three-minute minimum charge – the per-minute rate is $2.50 to the USA or Guam ($2 on Sundays); $3 to the Marshall Islands, Palau, Saipan or Australia; $4 to Canada, the UK or Germany; $5 to most everywhere else.

Immigration The FSM Immigration Office (☎ 330-2335) is opposite the high school and adjacent to Nantaku Loop Restaurant.

Laundry There's a coin laundry (50 cents to wash, 50 cents to dry) on the inland side of the road about midway between Truk Trading Co and the Truk Stop hotel.

Media There's no Chuukese newspaper, but Guam's *Pacific Daily News* is sold at larger grocery stores, including Shigeto's Store and Stop & Shop. Weno has two radio stations and cable TV that includes live CNN and prerecorded network broadcasts from San Francisco.

Weather You can get a 24-hour recorded weather forecast, including temperatures, tides and winds, by calling 330-4349.

Medical Services The hospital (☎ 330-2216) is in Weno centre, up from the government offices.

Emergency For police emergencies, dial 330-2223, and for medical emergencies, 330-2444.

Mt Tonaachaw

When the legendary Sowukachaw arrived on Chuuk he brought a lump of basalt rock with him, stuck it on the summit of Mt Tonaachaw and built a meeting house on the mountaintop, from which he ruled all of Chuuk Lagoon.

The steep-sided 754-foot mountain, with

Paper Prohibition

In response to political pressure from Chuukese women, tired of alcohol-related domestic violence, Weno is officially dry, though the state of Chuuk is not. As all imports are first unloaded at Weno, however, alcohol has always been available on the island, at least at black market rates. For practical purposes, prohibition now exists only on paper, as the empty Budweiser cans strewn along the roadsides readily attest. ■

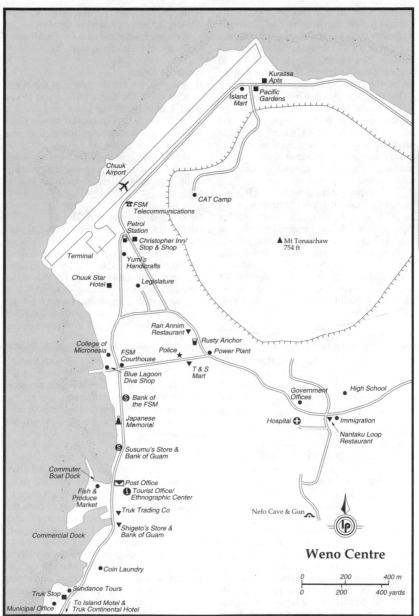

CHUUK

Kurassa Apts

Island Mart

Pacific Gardens

Chuuk Airport

CAT Camp

FSM Telecommunications

Petrol Station

Christopher Inn/ Stop & Shop

Yumi's Handicrafts

Terminal

Chuuk Star Hotel

Legislature

Mt Tonaachaw 754 ft

Ran Annim Restaurant

Rusty Anchor

College of Micronesia

FSM Courthouse

Police

Power Plant

Blue Lagoon Dive Shop

T & S Mart

Government Offices

High School

Bank of the FSM

Japanese Memorial

Hospital

Immigration

Nantaku Loop Restaurant

Susumu's Store & Bank of Guam

Commuter Boat Dock

Fish & Produce Market

Post Office

Tourist Office/ Ethnographic Center

Truk Trading Co

Nefo Cave & Gun

Commercial Dock

Shigeto's Store & Bank of Guam

Weno Centre

Coin Laundry

0   200   400 m

0   200   400 yards

Truk Stop

Sundance Tours

Municipal Office

To Island Motel & Truk Continental Hotel

its lone tree on the knobby top, is the backdrop for the airport and harbour. Although there's a trail to the top, Chuukese are wary of climbing this mountain because Neawacha, the ghost of an old woman who lives there, is believed to have the power of curses.

The US Air Force Civic Action Team (CAT) has a barracks on the side of the mountain above Weno centre, at an elevation of 250 feet. The CAT crew is made up of a dozen people who make eight-month stints on the island doing public works projects such as road and school construction.

The narrow dirt road to the CAT camp begins just east of Island Mart and ends a half mile up at the barracks, where there's a lagoon view that's particularly nice at sunset. You can see the Faichuk Islands straight ahead past the runway and the flat island of Param to the left.

A trail that goes to the top of Mt Tonaachaw begins at the left side of the main CAT building. Follow the trail past the small house above the CAT camp and continue on up. The path starts out well defined and then becomes less so, but it's not hard to follow. The walk can be slippery when wet but otherwise, if you avoid the midday sun, it's not too strenuous. It takes about 30 minutes to get to the top where there's a Japanese bunker and good panoramic views.

Ethnographic Center

A little one-room museum at the tourist office, known as the Ethnographic Center, has love sticks, outrigger canoe models and a few other interesting traditional items, such as the *ulong*, a special food bowl that was used to present the season's first harvest to the high chief.

There are also artefacts from the lagoon shipwrecks, including the compass, a ship lantern and a coral-encrusted machine gun from the bridge of the *Fujikawa Maru*. A display of photos taken during the two-day US bombing assault on the Japanese fleet shows all the ships in the lagoon during the attack, the layout of Weno's South Field

with its seaplane ramps and the then densely developed island of Dublon.

It's open from 8 am to 4.45 pm Monday to Friday and admission is $1.50.

Coastal Views

If you look toward the beach at the north side of the FSM Loan Office you'll see what looks like a big black marble. It's actually a Japanese memorial to war dead with the kanji character for peace, *wa*, carved into the pedestal.

This is also a vantage for viewing some of the nearshore shipwrecks and rusting hulls that have been abandoned in the lagoon.

Nefo Cave & Japanese Gun

A large cave above the town holds a Japanese naval gun and offers a good view of Weno centre. To get there, head east from downtown Weno, take the paved road to the right after the hospital and follow the road up the hill to where it dead-ends at a big water tank. The second house from the end, incidentally, is the governor's official residence, though not all governors opt to live there.

Directly across the street from the driveway of the last house there's a path leading up the hill. It's a two-minute walk to the cave. Go straight through the cave, which is 75 feet long, to get to the gun.

If you step out a few feet beyond the gun, you can also get a good view of Mt Tonaachaw to the right.

South Field

South Field, at the southern tip of Weno, was once a large Japanese seaplane base. The three-mile drive from Weno centre to South Field offers pretty views of both the lagoon islands and Weno's west coast, with intermittent patches of taro, mangroves, bananas and breadfruit trees.

The **Truk Coconut Processing Plant** is in the corrugated tin building to the left just before the gate to the Truk Continental Hotel. If you want to see how soap is made from copra, go inside.

One of the old **Japanese seaplane**

Coconut meat drying for copra

ramps, now used to unload copra, is behind the soap factory, as is a beached ferro-concrete boat, the result of a failed government-funded small industries project.

At the head of the seaplane ramp is the **Chuuk Atoll Research Laboratory**, which collects marine algae and marine invertebrates for cancer and AIDS research. American marine biologists Lori and Patrick Colin run the facility and welcome interested visitors, although there's not much to see per se.

At the southernmost point of South Field is the **Truk Continental Hotel**, which has the only easily accessible sandy beach on Weno and a splendid lagoon view. There's another seaplane ramp here, as well as grass-covered Japanese bunkers and a few other war artefacts on the hotel grounds. There's also a traditional outrigger canoe from the Western Islands, made from a breadfruit tree.

The road heading east from South Field gets rougher as it goes along, with only about a mile of it negotiable in a sedan.

East of the Airport
From the airport heading east, the road edges along the coast and passes through small villages. After the Bethesda church comes up on the right, the road goes across Pou Bay. The attractive church with red trim on the hill to the right is the Tunnuk Catholic Church.

Wichon Falls
Wichon Falls are not very big, but the walk up the river is pleasant and will get you a little closer to village life. On sunny mornings, the stream is busy with women doing laundry and after school lets out kids play in the water holes.

To reach the falls go 1.25 miles past Tunnuk Church to the innermost part of Nomenuk Bay, where the Wichon River empties into the lagoon. Just before a very small bridge, you'll see a rough dirt road to the right which leads into Wichon Village.

Walk one-third of a mile up this road, turn on the first drive to the left, go behind the house and begin walking up the river. There's a crossing over rocks in the stream not far from the house and from there the falls are just a couple of minutes up. As you are crossing private property, you should ask permission to continue if you see anyone along the way.

Ancient petroglyphs in the shape of triangles, parallel lines and other geometric shapes have been carved into the smooth rock both above and near the base of the falls. Most are quite weathered, but can be made out with a determined eye.

The Wichon area figures into many Chuukese legends. One story tells of a ghost who scooped up part of nearby Mt Witipon, creating the Wichon Valley, and then flew to the Mortlocks where he dropped the land in the sea to form Losap Atoll.

Xavier High School

The Jesuit-run Xavier High School opened in 1953 as the first four-year high school in Micronesia and maintains a reputation as the region's best.

Originally the site of a German chapel, the land was taken by the Japanese in 1940 and a fortress-like wartime communications centre was constructed. The main building, with two-foot-thick reinforced concrete walls and vault-like steel doors and windows, survived two direct hits by US bombers, amazingly requiring only a patch job on the roof. The building now houses the school's classrooms.

Visitors are welcome to climb the roof for a panoramic view of Chuuk Lagoon and to walk around the grounds, provided they don't disturb classes. Cars should be parked under the big mango tree at the far right of the main building.

Go quietly through the centre doorway of the main building, past the study hall and up the stairs on the left. At the top of the stairs go through the door on the left, then turn right to get outside, where there are stairs up to the roof. You can see many of the lagoon islands from the rooftop. There's an especially attractive view of the Faichuks and in the opposite direction you can see the old Japanese lighthouse on the hill in Sapuk.

A display cabinet at the top of the stairs on the 2nd floor holds objects from sunken ships, including dishes, sake bottles and a porthole. The landing below has a collection of Chuukese seashells.

The windmill on the grounds runs the school's computers, and a network of Japanese-built tunnels is burrowed into the hill, alongside the driveway leading up to the school.

Japanese Lighthouse

There's a fine view from the Japanese lighthouse in Sapuk. The lighthouse, which was built in the early 1930s, sits atop Newech Hill at an elevation of 348 feet. It's on private property, however. The best way to visit is to contact the property owner, Rively Walter (☎ 330-2222), who can arrange to pick visitors up at their hotel and take them to the top for $10 per person. The whole thing takes about two hours.

PLACES TO STAY

All hotels, other than the Truk Continental Hotel, are in town or in residential neighbourhoods. Chuuk has a 10% room tax.

The *Island Motel* (☎ 330-2928, fax 330-2926), Box 728, Chuuk, FM 96942, is a friendly, locally owned hotel with 10 rooms – unpretentious but quite sufficient, and Weno's cheapest accommodation option at $40 a double. Rooms are clean and have refrigerators, cable TV, air-con and private bathrooms. There are no room phones, but you can use the one at the front desk. There's no restaurant on site but Truk Stop Restaurant is just a five-minute walk to the north and the staff will drive you to and from any restaurant you like. Free airport transfers are also provided.

Kurassa Apartments (☎ 330-4415, fax 330-4355), Box 64, Chuuk, FM 96942, three-quarters of a mile east of the airport, has nine one-bedroom and studio apartments, though some are rented on a monthly basis. Those apartments rented by the day cost $48 ($280 by the week) and have air-con in the bedroom, a ceiling fan in the living room, a kitchenette, TV, VCR, phone and daily cleaning service. Manager Vicky Mori is quite helpful and can provide free airport transfers. The little grocery store below the apartments is convenient for picking up supplies and it is a pretty easy area for catching taxis. There's also a room and car package for $80 a day, tax included.

The *Pacific Gardens* (☎ 330-2334, fax 330-2606), Box 494, Chuuk, FM 96942, is a 20-room local hotel opposite Kurassa Apartments. The units have a small separate kitchen-like area with a table, sink and refrigerator but no cooking facilities, and a small bedroom with a double and single bed, TV, phone and air-con – all OK but not special. Singles/doubles cost $45/55. There's a simple restaurant and bar downstairs from the hotel.

The *Christopher Inn* (☎ 330-2652, fax 330-2207), Box 37, Chuuk, FM 96942, in central Weno, has 19 rooms that cost $44/52 for singles/doubles. All rooms have air-con, mini-refrigerators and private bathrooms. TVs are available for an additional $3 a day. It's a simple place that's adequate but overpriced. There's a restaurant at the side and a store below. The airport is a three-minute walk away.

The *Chuuk Star Hotel* (☎ 330-2040), Box 235, Chuuk, FM 96942, is a new 30-room hotel just south of the airport. The rooms have two double beds, phones, remote-control cable TV, balconies with water views and bathrooms with tubs. The cost is $65 for either singles or doubles, $95 for a suite with a little sitting area.

Truk Stop (☎ 330-4232, fax 330-2286), Box 546, Chuuk, FM 96942, is a 23-room hotel about a mile south of the airport. Most rooms are in a modern three-storey complex and are spacious and comfortable with two double beds, cable TV, table and chairs, air-con, mini-refrigerators and phones. There are fine lagoon views from the balconies of the oceanfront units ($80), while the standard units ($65) are without a view but have the same decor. As long as the hotel sticks with these new rates, rather than reverting to its old rates which were about 30% higher, it's a recommendable value. Truk Stop also has a couple of basic studio-style rooms with cooking facilities for $55, but they're older and a bit musty.

The *Truk Continental Hotel* (☎ 330-2727, fax 330-2439), Box 340, Chuuk, FM 96942, the only hotel on Weno with a beachside setting, sits at the island's southernmost point. Chuuk's top hotel, it has 56 rather standard tourist-class rooms in several two-storey buildings, each with a balcony facing the lagoon. Rooms have air-con, phones, small refrigerators and two beds. It's not particularly fancy, though it's comfortable enough and the setting, on Weno's nicest beach, is hard to beat. There's a restaurant and a gift shop. Singles/doubles cost $106/118.

If you're looking for long-term rentals, the *Tradewind Hotel* (☎ 330-2277), Box 520, Chuuk, FM 96942, has modern apartments with air-con and kitchens above the KS Store. It's in a quiet residential area on the coastal road, 1.5 miles east of the airport.

See also *Falos Beach Resort* under Picnic Islands.

PLACES TO EAT
Most restaurants offer a combination of American and Japanese foods, while the public market offers the opportunity to sample a few traditional Chuukese items.

Stay clear of unboiled tap water. You can get juices and bottled water in grocery stores.

The best place to eat on Weno is the *Truk Stop Restaurant* at the Truk Stop hotel, which has a pleasant lagoon setting and good food at moderate prices. At breakfast you can get a nice serving of banana pancakes for $2.15 or bacon and eggs for $3.50, plus a cup of coffee (free refills) for a dollar more. Skip the orange juice and order a fresh drinking coconut for half the price. At lunch and dinner there are sandwiches with fries from $4, fried fish or chicken meals for around $6, kebabs and pizzas for $7.50. Breakfast is served from 6.30 to 10.30 am, lunch from 11 am to 2 pm and dinner from 6 to 10 pm.

T&S Fast-Food, next to T&S Mart, is a cafeteria-style snack bar serving breakfast and lunch from steamer trays. These are not overly tempting but they are cheap enough. Pancakes are $1.25, burgers or pieces of fried chicken are $1.50, while other dishes are about double that. You can get a glass of distilled water for a quarter. It's open from 7 am to 5 pm daily.

CHUUK

Truk Trading Co also has a simple snack bar with inexpensive sandwiches, fried chicken by the piece and ice cream.

The unmarked *Ran Annim Restaurant*, just north of the Rusty Anchor, is an inexpensive favourite of Peace Corps volunteers. It's a simple hole-in-the-wall, but a friendly place, serving good sashimi or large burgers for $1.50, fried chicken or fish plates for $4, cinnamon rolls for a mere dime and the cheapest coffee in town at 30 cents. It's open from 6.30 am to 8 pm, on Sundays to 2 pm.

Nantaku Loop Restaurant, next to the immigration office and directly opposite the high school, has cheap Filipino and local food – mostly pre-cooked and served out of trays but otherwise good. A full meal costs between $3 and $5. It's open from 7 am to 2.30 pm Monday to Saturday.

The Christopher Inn's *Rainbow Coffee Shop* has formica tables and standard Western fare. You can get eggs, toast and coffee for around $4 and chicken or fish plates for $5. It's open from 6 am to 9 pm daily.

Takarajima Restaurant, just a few minutes' walk from the Truk Continental Hotel, has the best Japanese food on Weno. The oyakodon, sweetened chicken and egg atop rice, comes with miso soup and is one of the better deals at $6.50. A flavourful dish is the pork ginger for $8.50, while tempura dishes cost $15 and mangrove crab and lobster are about double that. It's open from 11 am to 2 pm weekdays and from 5 to 10 pm daily. Saltwater aquariums spread around the restaurant add a nice touch; when the restaurant is busy, service can be very slow.

The *Truk Continental* has the island's best setting but the food is disappointingly ordinary and on the pricey side. Breakfasts start around $5 and a cup of weak coffee is a whopping $1.75. A cheeseburger or club sandwich with fries is $6 at lunch, while the reef fish is one of the cheaper dinner dishes at $10.25. There are good views from the dining room of the Faichuks, Fefan and Dublon.

The fruit stalls opposite the post office sell drinking coconuts for 50 cents, or a tad less to those with a knack for bargaining. Other items include pounded taro wrapped in green taro leaves, boiled breadfruit, preserved breadfruit, sea cucumber in vinegar and fresh produce such as bananas, mangoes and cucumbers, most of which comes from Fefan. You can also pick up a fragrant *mwaramwar* (head wreath) for $1. Booths behind the fruit stalls sell inexpensive fried reef fish and barbecued chicken for take-away.

Truk Trading Co, *Shigeto's Store* and *T&S Mart* are Chuuk's largest grocery stores and have the freshest food. T&S, while not the spiffiest, has the best prices, including bottled water at $1.50 a gallon.

ENTERTAINMENT

Though Weno is officially dry, you'd never know it. Beer sells for $2.50 a can at the *Truk Continental Hotel* gift shop as well as at a number of restaurants.

Nightlife is limited, but there is a bar, the *Rusty Anchor*, that opens from 8 pm to 2 am nightly, serves beer and mixed drinks and has loud music and a small dance floor. The staff are pleasant, the crowd is a mix of locals and expats, and it's considered safe for non-Micronesian visitors.

Chuuk has no movie theatre, but there's many a video shop.

THINGS TO BUY

Popular souvenirs include love sticks, hibiscus fibre fans, wood carvings, wooden masks, baskets, seashells and shell jewellery.

Preserved Breadfruit

One customary Chuukese food speciality, *oppot*, is made by filling a pit with alternating layers of ripe cut breadfruit and banana leaves, then covering the top with rocks and leaving it for months, or even years. Uninitiated noses might think it rotten, but preserved breadfruit is highly valued and has traditionally served as an important staple that carried islanders through long canoe journeys or during months when fresh breadfruit was not in season. ■

Northside beach, Kosrae

Sleeping Lady in profile, Kosrae

Pwusehn Malek (Chickenshit Mountain), Pohnpei

Boatman among the Nan Madol ruins, Pohnpe

Ceremonial nahs in Nett Municipality, Pohnpei

German Tower in Kolonia, Pohnpei

Yumi's Handicrafts, opposite the airport, and Sundance Tours, next to Truk Stop hotel, have the widest selections of quality handicrafts. There's a gift shop at Truk Continental Hotel that also sells handicrafts and T-shirts and carries a few books about Micronesia, including a dive guide to the island by Tim Rock.

Body oils and bath soaps made from coconut oil at the Truk Coconut Processing Plant are sold in shops around town.

Combs, jewellery and other items made from the shells of endangered sea turtles are sold all around Chuuk, but cannot be imported into most Western countries, including the USA and Australia.

GETTING THERE & AWAY
Air
Continental Micronesia is the only airline which flies to Chuuk, connecting Weno with Pohnpei and Guam on the island-hopper routes. The one-way fare is $242 between Guam and Chuuk, while the return fare is $406. From Pohnpei to Chuuk it's $184 one way and $294 return. Return tickets require a three-day advance purchase and are good for a stay of up to 30 days.

Airport Chuuk's open-air airport terminal has a tourist information booth that usually opens briefly at flight times, car rental booths that are seldom staffed, a simple snack bar and restrooms that are boarded shut.

Airline Offices Continental Micronesia's only office (☎ 330-2424) is at the check-in counter in the airport. It's open from 8 am to 4 pm daily, but avoid going there for business within two hours of flight time or there will be lines to contend with.

Leaving Chuuk
Chuuk has a $10 departure tax.

GETTING AROUND
To/From the Airport
Weno's airport is smack in the centre of town. You can catch a taxi right out front.

Many hotels provide airport transport, so if you know in advance where you're staying give them a call or look around to see if they already have a representative at the airport.

Car
Truk Stop Car Rentals (☎ 330-4232), at the Truk Stop hotel, rents older cars for $35 a day and newer cars for $45, plus 13% tax. VJ Car Rental (☎ 330-2652) at the Christopher Inn has cars for $39.50 including tax. Kurassa Apartments (☎ 330-4415) has a few cars for $45 including tax. Petrol costs $1.60 a gallon.

Taxi
Shared taxis, which are usually pick-up trucks but can also be sedans or minivans, can be identified by signs in their front windows and will stop when flagged down. They cruise the main road in the town centre every few minutes during the day. It costs 50 cents to go anywhere around the downtown area or as far as Truk Continental Hotel, and $1 to Xavier High School. However, the farther you are from downtown Weno, the fewer the taxis. Note that most taxis stop running around 6 pm. If you do get stuck, try calling BNS Taxi Service (☎ 330-4119) which will pick up on request at double the usual rate.

Tours
Yasu Mori (☎ 330-2438), who operates from a desk in the lobby of the Truk Continental Hotel, offers 2½-hour land tours of Weno for $18 per person and four-hour lagoon boat tours for $50 per person.

Sundance Tours & Dive Shop (☎ 330-4234), next to the Truk Stop hotel, can arrange a variety of sightseeing tours. A land tour of Weno, including Nefo Cave, Xavier High School and the Japanese lighthouse, costs $20.

In addition, the tourist office can arrange local tour guides at negotiable fees. See the Activities section for snorkelling and diving tours.

Caroline Pacific Air (☎ 330-4457) offers air sightseeing tours for $240 an hour for up to six people, and $40 more for each additional person, with a maximum of nine passengers.

ISLANDS IN CHUUK LAGOON

Outside Weno, the most easily accessible populated islands in Chuuk Lagoon are Dublon, Eten and Fefan. Uman and Param are not particularly receptive to visitors and the Tol islanders have a reputation for being a bit rough and rowdy. Many of these islanders commute by boat to jobs on Weno while others have subsistence farms or earn money through fishing or copra.

It's a more traditional Chuukese lifestyle on the islands in the outer lagoon. On some islands people still live under thatched roofs and cook outdoors over open fires. Roads are scarce and vehicles are few.

There's no established accommodation for visitors on any of the following lagoon islands, except for Falos.

Dublon (Tonoas) Island

Dublon is also called Tonoas, which was the island's original name until 1814 when Manuel Dublon landed there and humbly renamed it.

Dublon is a peaceful island today, with a

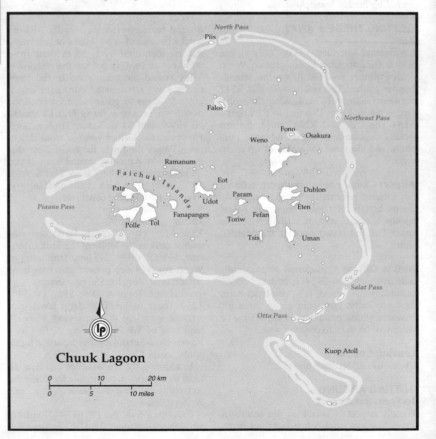

Chuuk Lagoon

population of only about 3000, but there are many remnants of its colonial past that reveal its former importance under occupying powers. Both the Germans and Japanese made Dublon their administrative centres; the Japanese military headquarters there included submarine, seaplane and coastal defence bases. Intense US bombings left nearly all of them in ruins.

After the war Dublon became sleepy and overgrown. Although it recently got a cut of development funding, which brought electricity to the island, Dublon still provides a good glimpse of rural Chuukese life.

There are docks at Sapou, in the northeast corner of the island, and in the south at the fisheries plant. A road runs around the island and there are private pick-up trucks, but no taxis.

Sapou Overgrown vegetation in Sapou Village partly conceals the remains of what was once a city. The wooden buildings are long gone, but the cement footings they were built upon are still there. Broad cement sidewalks, once covered with tin awnings to shelter the Japanese against sun and rain, are now shaded by breadfruit trees. The remains of the **Japanese naval hospital** can be explored on the hill above the youth centre.

Sapou's colourful village **church**, which is dark grey trimmed with bright primary colours, sports a sign in Old English lettering reading *kinamue*, which means 'peace'.

South Dublon If you drive anticlockwise from Sapou to the south side of Dublon, you'll see a large Japanese dome-like **concrete bunker** on the right side of the road. An iron pipe protruding from the top served as an air vent.

Ahead, where the road splits in two, you can take the right fork which takes you to a **fortified Japanese building** with heavy metal doors and windows.

A little farther on is the junior high school, built on the concrete airfields of the old **Japanese seaplane base**. There's a seaplane ramp leading down into the water.

Back on the main road, on the left, are the remains of a collapsed Japanese **oil storage tank**, now used by a local family as a garage. Ahead, up a grade to the left, an aluminium geodesic dome covers a large **freshwater reservoir**. The concrete water tank was built by the Japanese, who secretly placed a steel tank in the centre to serve as a hidden fuel reserve.

Turn right at the next road to get to Dublon's **deepwater dock** and multi-million dollar fisheries complex and freezer, which was built with Japanese aid and now serves as a dock for Chinese fishing boats.

East-Central Dublon Continuing on the main road, you'll see more burned-out **oil storage tanks** on the right. At the crossroads, turn left and you'll pass a small **Japanese memorial**. Just past the municipal building turn left, then keep an eye out to the left for the entrance to a massive **cement tunnel** built under the mountain. The tunnel looks big enough to run a subway through and did in fact hold a fleet of military vehicles. It ran under the Japanese governor's residence and still has a rusted electric generator inside.

Farther down on the left, a sign in Japanese announces a **naval cemetery**. Steep stairs lead up to the site but this is private property so you should ask permission if you want to climb up, and the owner may charge you a few dollars.

Down the road on the left look closely to see the narrow overgrown entrance to the **general's cave**, one of five openings to an interconnecting network of tunnels. The road finishes in a dead end a little farther on at a Protestant church.

Go back the way you came and take the road diagonally opposite the municipal building. After passing a school on the left, you'll come to the ruins of the **Japanese civil hospital** at the crossroads. What remains of the hospital is basically just the arched concrete entrance hall, now covered in graffiti. Straight ahead are the stairs to a former Shinto shrine.

CHUUK

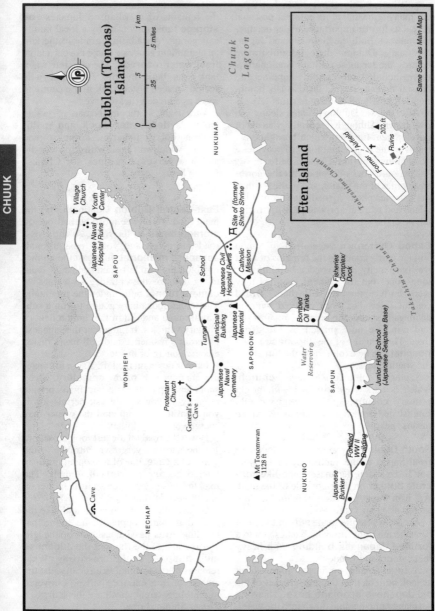

Dublon (Tonoas) Island

Eten Island

Eten Island

From a distance Eten looks like a huge aircraft carrier which, in effect, it was. The Japanese used Chuukese labour to tear down the mountaintops and carry away half the island to turn Eten into an airfield.

If you dock on Eten's north-west side, directly opposite the fisheries complex on Dublon, then it's a 10-minute walk inland to a complex of bombed-out concrete and steel buildings.

From the dock you pass a couple of houses, then walk up to the right through the village and follow the path to the right of the Catholic church. It's a well-defined trail, much of it on the pavement still left from the old airstrip.

The path leads directly to a massive two-storey concrete structure, which islanders say was hit by 15 to 20 bombs. The roof and 2nd floor are partly caved in, with twisted steel reinforcement rods hanging down, but one room is amazingly still intact.

Beyond are three more two-storey Japanese buildings with two-foot-thick concrete walls and vault-like steel windows and doors. There's a demolished tower and a big gun on top of the hill as well as wrecked planes in the water around the island.

Fefan Island

Fefan is known for its abundance of fresh produce and for its high-quality basketry woven of banana and hibiscus fibres. Mangrove swamps line much of the shoreline, while the forested interior reaches an elevation of 984 feet. Pieces of pottery found in archaeological digs on Fefan date back 1500 years.

Mesa Wharf is on the east side of Fefan and you can take in the whole village of Mesa, such as it is, in a 10-minute stroll. The municipal office and elementary school are both visible to the left from the wharf. The village church is a few minutes walk to the right of the wharf.

On Fefan, kids come up and touch you to see if you're for real. They smile, ask your name, follow you around for a minute or

two and then go back to whatever they were doing.

Most war relics are inland on the hills and difficult to reach. The hike up to some anti-aircraft guns which are spread out on top of a hill directly up from Mesa Wharf would take about 30 minutes, but there's no real trail.

A couple of pick-up trucks drive the rough circle-island road, charging $2 per person. However, they don't run on a very regular basis and as the trip around takes about 1½ hours there's no guarantee there'll be one on your side of the island at the right time.

Faichuk Islands

The Faichuk Islands, in the western part of Chuuk Lagoon, include Tol, Polle, Pata, Udot, Eot, Ramanum and Fanapanges.

Tol, the largest and most populated of the Faichuks, is about a one-hour boat ride from Weno. Tol's Mt Tumuital, which rises 1453 feet, is the tallest mountain in Chuuk. The island's high jungle forest is the sole habitat of the Truk greater white-eye, a rare bird with one of the most restricted ranges of any in Micronesia.

The Japanese once had vehicles on Tol but the roads took a beating during the war bombing and today there are no cars.

In the 1970s, when Chuuk's political future was being debated, most Faichuk islanders wanted Chuuk to opt for commonwealth status with the USA, similar to that of the Northern Marianas. When the majority of Chuukese voted instead to become a state in the FSM, the Faichuks started statehood attempts of their own.

In the late 1970s, the FSM Congress actually approved the Faichuks as a new FSM state after 98% of Faichuk voters chose by referendum to break away from the rest of Chuuk. The movement failed with a veto by the FSM president, who was incidentally from Chuuk.

With one-third of Chuuk's population, the Faichuk islanders feel they're entitled to one-third of the state budget, but they only get a trickle of that. They want electricity and paved roads, and perhaps most importantly, they want a reliable water system, as during severe droughts they sometimes run out of water completely and have to rely on drinking coconut milk.

Picnic Islands

There are numerous small uninhabited coral islets scattered around the lagoon which the Chuukese use as fishing grounds and picnic or drinking spots. Many of them have white sand beaches and small stands of coconut palms.

The waters are generally clear and snorkelling can be excellent, though in some spots dynamiting has damaged the coral and near the shore you'll often see as many empty beer cans as fish.

Deserted or not, all the islands are owned and you're supposed to get permission from the owners to visit. However, the person who takes you out generally arranges that.

Falos Island

Falos is a tidy little island circled with soft white sand beaches and thickly shaded with coconut palms. For the casual visitor to Chuuk, this is the easiest of the Picnic Islands to visit, as it's been set up for both day trips and overnight stays.

Coral close to the shore makes for good snorkelling, and the deeper waters just a short way out have larger fish and even an occasional shark or two. From the beach you can see Weno, Dublon, Fefan and the Faichuks.

If you visit on weekdays you may well have the beach to yourself, while on weekends it's usually a bit livelier with people from Weno coming over to picnic. A family lives on the island as caretakers, with other 'staff' coming over on the boat when there are overnight visitors.

Places to Stay *Falos Beach Resort* (☎ 330-2606, fax 330-2334), Box 494, Chuuk, FM 96942, has 10 simple concrete, tin-roofed cottages with linoleum floors, electric lights and plywood platforms topped with futons. Ask for cottage Nos 1,

5, 6 or 7, as each one is free-standing with screened, louvred windows on all four walls to catch the breeze. Toilets and showers are outside and shared. The only drawback here is the price: $40/50 for singles/doubles, plus 10% room tax and the boat fare. Meals can sometimes be arranged, but it's best to plan on bringing your own food to cook.

Getting There & Away

Commuter boats leave the main lagoon islands for Weno on weekday mornings and return from Weno in the early afternoons. They're obviously convenient for islanders commuting to Weno to work, shop or sell their produce, but the schedules are backwards for anyone planning a day trip from Weno.

Boats from Fefan tie up at the Weno dock, on the side opposite the post office, where the Fefan women market their vegetables. Boats from Dublon and Tol are usually moored on the other side of the dock. The cost is $1 to $2 each way, depending on the island.

Many private speedboats cross the lagoon daily. If you ask around you might find someone to take you to another island in exchange for petrol money. Like the commuter boats however, most speedboats come to Weno in the morning and return to home islands in the afternoon.

Sundance Tours & Dive Shop (☎ 330-4234) can arrange outings to Dublon, Fefan and Uman for $50, and tours to Tol for $65. In addition, the tourist office can arrange boat rentals, though don't expect any bargains.

Arrangements to visit Falos Island should be made in advance at Island Mart (☎ 330-2606), on the main road opposite the north-east end of the airport runway.

There's no schedule to Falos Island, but boat rides can be arranged for $10 per person if you're staying overnight, or $60 return for up to four people if you're just going over for the day. The ride takes about 30 minutes one way when the lagoon waters are calm.

CHUUK'S OUTER ISLANDS

Outside Chuuk Lagoon are the far-flung Mortlocks, Hall Islands and Western Islands. Together they comprise 11 atolls and three single islands. All are flat coral formations, some just wisps of sand barely rising above the surface of the ocean.

In their isolation, the outer islands maintain a more traditional lifestyle than can be found in Chuuk Lagoon. They have footpaths but virtually no cars or roads. A day's work might include fishing, cultivating the taro patch, preparing copra or making sleeping mats and coconut fibre ropes.

The Mortlocks

The Mortlocks stretch about 180 miles in a south-easterly direction from Chuuk Lagoon.

The Upper Mortlocks include the single island of Nama, and Losap Atoll with its main islands of Losap and Piis. The Mid-Mortlocks include Etal and Namoluk atolls, as well as Kuttu and Moch, the northernmost islands in Satawan Atoll. The Lower Mortlocks incorporate Lukunor Atoll with its islands of Lukunor and Oneop as well as the southernmost Satawan Atoll islands of Satawan and Ta.

The Mortlockese are a gentle, easy-going people and are more Westernised in their dress than other outer islanders. They also tend to be a more religious bunch overall, perhaps because it was in the Mortlocks that Christian missionaries established Chuuk's first church, in 1875, long before they reached Chuuk Lagoon. Many religious prohibitions, such as those against building fires on Sunday, have only recently been abandoned.

The Mortlockese still make traditional masks of hibiscus wood. Once worn by men during battle and to ward off evil spirits, they are now carved for Chuuk's tourist trade.

For visitors, the handiest destination in the Mortlocks is **Satawan Atoll**, which has both boat and air connections to Weno. It is the largest of all Chuuk's outer island groups, though its four populated islands and 45 islets cover a total of only 1.8 sq miles.

The main island, **Satawan**, is a sub-district centre with about 500 people. The island is fringed with white sand beaches and has lots of coconut palms and breadfruit trees, two churches (one Catholic, one Protestant), a regional high school and a couple of small stores. There's a single pick-up truck that's used to haul cargo from boats to the village and an electric generator that tends to only be operational for the couple of weeks prior to Chuukese elections. You can find half a dozen rusting Japanese tanks in the village centre and a fairly intact Japanese Zero in a banana patch.

Ta Island is separated from Satawan Island by about 200 yards of shallow reef that can readily be walked across at low tide. Home to about 300 people, Ta is just a couple of hundred yards wide, though it extends for five miles. It's a lovely

Dance mask of the Mortlock Islands

unspoiled place with empty beaches, good for relaxing. Unlike on many of Chuuk's other islands, the Satawanese welcome outsiders and even come to greet the plane. A nice way to meet people is simply to walk the wide road that goes down the middle of the island.

The swimming and snorkelling is great off Satawan and Ta islands, with lots of turtles, fish and coral, and sometimes dolphins as well. The lagoon waters are usually placid and have excellent visibility. You can walk along the fringing reef for miles at low tide and find all sorts of seashells.

Places to Stay & Eat Binte and Reiko Simina have a few simple cottages on Ta. Known as *Simina's Sunset Bungalows*, they're located on a white sand beach within walking distance of the runway. The cottages are suitably simple and perfectly adequate, with comfortable mattresses, clean sheets and towels, mosquito netting and generator-powered electricity. All in all, it makes a wonderful getaway if you're looking for a quiet place on a remote tropical island. The cost is $30/$40 for singles/doubles. Activities, including traditional net or spearfishing outings and motorboat tours, can be arranged at reasonable costs. Reservations can be made through Caroline Pacific Air (☎ 330-4457), Box 960, Chuuk, FM 96942.

There's a small reasonably priced restaurant on site that serves predominantly local food, including fresh fish, sashimi, taro, breadfruit and a few Western items such as ham and eggs.

If you want to stay on Satawan Island, Representative Harper, who can usually be contacted through his office on Weno (☎ 330-2666), has a four-bedroom house and sometimes rents out a room to visitors.

The Hall Islands
The Halls, north of Chuuk Lagoon, include the single island of East Fayu, Murilo Atoll with its islands of Murilo and Ruo, and Nomwin Atoll with its islands of Nomwin and Fananu. Fananu Island, where an

airstrip is under construction, is one of the most attractive of all the Halls.

These islands are, in a sense, a satellite community of Chuuk Lagoon. They were once allied with Weno and with islands on the Chuuk Lagoon reef, with whom they share a common dialect.

The Western Islands
The Western Islands, Chuuk's most remote and traditional, share close ties with the outer islands of Yap. Though political distinctions divvy them up into two separate states, outer islanders in the central Carolines have more in common with each other than they do with the high islands of Yap or Chuuk Lagoon to which they belong.

On these islands the men still wear bright loincloths and the women wear only woven fibre or grass skirts. Houses are made of thatch, subsistence comes from the sea and men continue to sail single-hulled outrigger canoes carved from breadfruit logs, relying on centuries-old navigational methods.

Young women from the Western Islands who attend the University of Guam have been known to enter classrooms crawling on their knees if any of their male relatives are in the room. This would be expected of

Fabric made of banana fibre

them in their home islands, but university teachers, not too keen on the custom, eventually get them to make some concessions to Western culture.

The Western Islands include Namonuito, Pulap, Pulusuk and Puluwat atolls. As a group, the latter three are also called Pattiw.

Namonuito is a huge triangular atoll, so large that all the islands are widely separated and it's a very long boat ride between them. The main island, Ulul (also called Onoun), is at the west side of the lagoon. Ulul is a rather traditional place with as much Japanese influence as American. Caroline Pacific Air now provides air service to Ulul; don't let the wreck off the runway unnerve you – it's just a wartime Japanese plane! There's no established accommodation on Ulul, although elderly Japanese sometimes return here to visit old friends, with the chief arranging a hut for them to stay in; if the idea tempts you, make arrangements through the airline.

The people of Pulap Atoll, which has two small and lightly populated islands, Pulap and Tamatam, are said to be Chuuk's best navigators. They also hold on to other traditions and if you're lucky enough to arrive on a special occasion, you can expect to see the young women performing custom dances and the village men performing stick dances, both wearing beaded necklaces and colourful ceremonial dress.

Pulusuk Atoll has just one island, Houk, but it's fairly large for the Westerns, covering a little over one sq mile. The island has Chuuk's only freshwater pond. There's an airstrip under construction.

Puluwat's five islands almost surround its small lagoon, leaving just one passageway and an excellent anchorage with a safe refuge from storms. The Japanese had an airstrip and lighthouse on one of the now uninhabited islets.

Outer islanders used to have a reputation for being tough fighters, and the people of Puluwat were probably once the most feared people in all the central Carolines. However, around the late 1800s they took to religion and became as gentle as lambs.

Places to Stay

There are no guesthouses on any of the outer islands, but the governor's office on Weno can sometimes make arrangements with island magistrates to help accommodate visitors. For any island with air service, arrangements can be made through the airline. Take food as gifts for those who help you.

Getting There & Away

Air Caroline Pacific Air (☎ 330-4457), Box 960, Chuuk, FM 96942, flies two nine-seater Beechcraft E18s from Weno to Ta in the Mortlocks and Ulul in the Western Islands. The flight to Ta is on Mondays, Wednesdays and Fridays, and on other days if there's a demand. The cost for the 1¼ hour flight is $70. The Weno-Ulul flight is on Fridays only, takes a bit over an hour and costs $63. You're allowed 35 pounds of baggage.

Boat Two field trip ships, the *Micro Trader* and the *Micro Dawn*, together aim to make a total of about 60 trips a year, each trip an average of one week long. Separate trips are scheduled to the Lower (and Mid) Mortlocks, the Upper Mortlocks, the Halls and Namonuito, and to Pattiw. The ships commonly leave late (occasionally they skip a sailing completely) and don't have a reputation for sticking to schedules, so you should have an ample amount of flex time worked in. The ships, which can carry 150 people, generally spend at least a few hours unloading supplies at each island where they stop.

It costs eight cents per mile on deck or 26 cents per mile plus $2 per night for a cabin. There are only seven two-bunk cabins, however, and they are often reserved for government officials. The Chuukese aren't known for their tidiness, so expect deck passage to be in disarray. From Weno it's 170 miles to Satawan, 160 miles to Pulusuk and 80 miles to Murilo.

It's recommended that you take your own food and water, although you can buy breakfast ($3.50), lunch ($4.50) and dinner ($5) on board. With a little persistence, you can get a copy of the latest schedule from the Transportation Office (☎ 330-2592), Chuuk State Government, Chuuk, FM 96942, which is at the north side of Weno's commercial dock.

If you are considering a field trip ship journey, you should note that in part because of government funding problems, the ships were running particularly irregularly as we went to press, and some areas such as the Lower Mortlocks had been going without a field trip ship visit for months at a time.

In addition to the field trip ships, there are also a couple of government boats that make trips to the Mortlocks. One boat runs between Weno and the Mid-Mortlocks about once a week for $7 one way. The boat generally leaves Weno at 8 pm and arrives at 10 am the next day.

Another boat goes to the Upper Mortlocks about twice a week. It makes extra trips between May and August, when the water is calmest. Nama Island, 48 miles and a couple of hours from Chuuk Lagoon, costs $3 one way. Losap and Piis, about 60 miles away, cost $4.

Yap

Yap, the land of giant stone money, is Micronesia's most traditional district.

You know you're in a unique place as you catch your first glimpse of Yap at the airport. Most people dress in Western clothes but a fair number of men and boys wear bright coloured loincloths and some of the women wear only woven hibiscus skirts. Everyone, including the very official-looking customs officers, has a bulge of betel nut in their cheek. The dirt floors of the old airport were so deeply stained with betel nut juice that the designers of Yap's new airport terminal decided to go with the flow and painted the cement floors betel-nut red!

Out in the villages, which are connected by centuries-old stone footpaths, men's houses are still built in the elaborate, tradi-

tional style of wood, thatch, rope and bamboo. It's a society where the caste system survives and where village chiefs still hold as much political clout as elected public officials.

The Yapese are a shy yet proud people. They are offended by the occasional tourist who brazenly points a camera at them as if they were subjects in an anthropological museum, yet at the same time they're receptive to travellers who respect their customs and culture.

As the tourist brochure says:

It takes patience, good manners and plenty of understanding to see Yap and observe some of its traditions. Yap is not a world built for tourists, but a world that welcomes visitors.

If you visit Yap on its own terms you won't be disappointed. For the traveller who treads gently, it's still a rare place to see.

HISTORY
Pre-European Contact
Pottery and other archaeological finds on Map Island date the earliest known Yapese settlement at around 200 AD.

The Yapese once reigned over a scattered island empire, extending as far north as the Mariana Islands and encompassing Chuuk to the east. In ancient times, lengthy ocean-going voyages were not uncommon.

The Yapese empire was built upon magic, rather than conquest. The high chiefs of Yap Proper employed sorcerers who were believed to have powers to induce famine, sickness and typhoons. Fearful of this sorcery, the outer islanders offered the high chiefs annual tributes in the hope of remaining in good favour.

European Contact
The first contact with Europeans was in 1526 when the Portuguese explorer Dioga da Rocha landed on Ulithi. The islanders were 'without malice, fear or cautiousness' and da Rocha and his crew remained on the island for four months. Over the next 300 years the rest of Yap's islands were gradually 'discovered' and added to the charts.

Early attempts to settle Yap were half-hearted at best. In 1731 a Spanish Jesuit mission was established on Ulithi but when a supply ship returned a year later they found that all 13 people of the colony had been killed by the islanders.

Apparently Europeans got the hint and for the next 100 years their visits to Yap were few and far between. Strangely, however, Dumont d'Urville, the only European known to have visited the main Yap islands in the early 1800s, found a people who spoke enough Spanish to request cigars and brandy. It's largely thought that the islanders' knowledge of Spanish was the result of their own inter-island commerce with places as distant as the Marianas.

In the 1830s two Spanish ships came to gather beche-de-mer in Yap but at some point during the operation the crews were attacked and brutally murdered. In 1843 the English captain Andrew Cheyne made a similar attempt for a cargo of beche-de-mer. Yapese chiefs seemed cooperative at first, but a brush with would-be assassins and contact with an enslaved survivor of the Spanish massacre convinced Cheyne to drop the venture before suffering a similar fate. It wasn't until the 1860s that regular trade with the West was gradually established. The Germans opened the first permanent trading station in 1869.

Spanish & German Periods

Although Spain had long held claim to Yap, it wasn't until the Germans attempted to annex the islands in 1885 that the Spanish established a permanent garrison. Formal colonial occupation of Yap was to continue in one form or another for the next 100 years.

In 1899, in the aftermath of the Spanish-American War, Spain sold Yap to Germany, whose interest in the islands was primarily commercial. Concerned about the shortage of labourers to work their plantations and mines, the Germans developed health and sanitation services in hopes of stemming the rapid depopulation. The Germans were the first to use forced Yapese labour, both in Yap and in the phosphate mines on Angaur in Palau.

Japanese Period

The Japanese took control of Yap in 1914 when the outbreak of WW I forced the Germans to quickly withdraw from the islands.

YAP

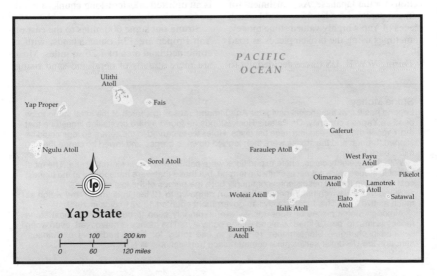

A Land Called Wa'ab

According to one story, when early European explorers first arrived, the natives paddled out to meet them. The explorers pointed and asked the name of the island but the islanders, with their backs to the shore, misunderstood the point. Holding up their paddles they replied *yap* – which was their word for paddle. Ever since, the islands that the local residents call Wa'ab have been known to those outside its shores as Yap. ■

Concern over Yap's transpacific cable station, on line between the USA and Shanghai, led the USA to demand access to Yap as a precondition to recognising Japan's League of Nations mandate over Micronesia. Japan and the USA eventually came to an agreement and signed a treaty to that accord in 1921.

The Japanese then began to emigrate to Yap and set up stores, farms and sea-based industries. Their numbers were not as great as in other parts of Micronesia but they nonetheless came to vastly outnumber the dwindling Yapese population.

As WW II approached the Yapese were forced to build airfields and military fortifications for the Japanese. As punishment for non-cooperation the Japanese would smash pieces of Yap's highly valued stone money, sometimes using the broken pieces as road fill.

During WW II, US forces decided not to invade Yap Proper, although it was bombed by American air raids. Ulithi Atoll was captured and developed into a major Allied support base in 1944.

GEOGRAPHY

Yap Proper consists of the four tightly clustered islands of Yap, Tomil-Gagil, Map (pronounced 'mop', and also spelt Maap) and Rumung. All but Rumung are connected by bridges. The islands are 515 miles south-west of Guam.

Unlike other high islands in Micronesia which are volcanic in origin, Yap Proper was formed by land upheavals of the Asian continental shelf. Consequently the interior regions are not mountainous, but rather have gentle rolling hills. The highest point, Mt Matade on Yap Island, is 571 feet. Yap Proper has 38.7 sq miles of land, which accounts for 84% of the state's total land mass.

There are also a handful of small islands within Yap Proper's fringing coral reef. Three of these – Pekel, Bi and Tarang (O'Keefe's) – sit in the channel between Tomil-Gagil and Yap islands and total about 10 acres combined. Garim (Bird Island), off the south-east tip of Yap Island, is an uplifted 300-foot-long chunk of coral undercut by the sea.

Strung out some 600 miles to the east of Yap Proper are 134 outer islands, with a combined land area of 7.26 sq miles. Most are mere strands of coral and sand rising

Stone Money

Legend has it that the ancient navigator Anagumang set sail in search of the ideal stone to be used as Yapese currency. On Palau's Rock Islands he found a hard crystalline limestone that the Yapese then quarried into huge flat discs. Holes were carved in the centre so logs could be slipped through and the stones were then lugged down to barges and towed by canoe the 250 miles back to Yap.

With their weighty cargo, entire expeditions were sometimes lost in storms at sea. The most valuable stones were not necessarily the largest, but those that were transported at the highest cost of human lives. These stones commonly bore the names of the lost mariners.

Stone money, which the Yapese call *rai*, can range up to 12 feet in diameter and weigh as much as five tons. The Japanese civilian government counted 13,281 coins in 1929.

Although single pieces of stone money are commonly seen throughout Yap, most stone money is kept in 'banks' lined up along village pathways. The money is not moved, even when ownership changes. Stone money remains in use today for some traditional exchanges, although the US dollar settles most commonplace transactions. ■

David O'Keefe

The most colourful character of Yap's 19th-century history was David 'His Majesty' O'Keefe, a shipwrecked Irish-American who washed ashore in 1871. Near death, he was nursed back to health by the Yapese, and he spent the next 30 years of his life on the islands.

Where the Germans had failed in getting the Yapese to produce copra in quantity, O'Keefe saw a golden opportunity. He noted that the colourful cloth and trinkets that traders used to entice other Pacific islanders raised little curiosity among the Yapese, who stubbornly preferred traditional hibiscus clothing and grass skirts.

Realising that the enormous stone money the Yapese quarried in distant Palau offered more leverage as a medium of exchange, O'Keefe decided to get into the stone money trade. He went off to Hong Kong to buy a Chinese junk, then returned to Yap and began making runs down to Palau to pick up newly quarried stone money. Yapese chiefs paid for the stone money with copra and O'Keefe soon came to dominate the copra trade in Yap.

O'Keefe's Irish temper and penchant for feuding with colonial administrators made him legendary among the Yapese. In 1901 he disappeared at sea. His former homesite on Tarang Island in Tomil Harbor is now in the Register of National Historic Places, though only a couple of bricks and a stairway remain. ∎

precariously above the water. A major typhoon can easily sweep one of these islands clean of its coconut trees and occasionally wash an entire island into the sea.

Trade winds blow onto the north and east sides of the islands, leaving the south and west shores with good sandy beaches.

CLIMATE

Yap has an average year-round temperature of 81°F (27°C) with an approximate 10° variance between noon and night. The average annual rainfall is 121 inches.

The north-east trade winds prevail on Yap from November to May when the rainfall is lighter and the humidity lower. From June to October, the breezes falter, the humidity climbs, rainfall rises and the evenings are less comfortable.

Fully developed typhoons are uncommon near Yap, as most of them pass to the north. However, several of Yap's easternmost islands were severely damaged by Typhoon Owen in November 1990.

GOVERNMENT

In addition to an elected state legislature, Yap's constitution establishes two councils of traditional leaders. The Council of Pilung is made up of chiefs from Yap Proper and the Council of Tamol consists of chiefs from the outer islands.

The chiefs wield a lot of power and pretty much decide who runs and who wins in general elections. Although the Yapese can vote for whomever they like for political office, people still generally follow the advice and leadership of their chiefs. The councils have the right to veto any legislation that affects traditional customs.

If the governor is from Yap Proper, then the lieutenant governor must be from the outer islands, and vice versa.

ECONOMY

Yap's moneyed economy is largely reliant upon US funding, with government jobs accounting for the majority of Yapese wage earners.

Most Yapese continue to make a living in the subsistence economy of farming and fishing. Copra production is still important on the outer islands, with the copra traded for supplies brought by the field trip ship.

There's a garment factory on the western outskirts of Colonia, the first large-scale manufacturing facility in the FSM. A joint Taiwanese-Sri Lankan venture, it currently employs about 300 Chinese workers. The workers, who are in Yap on two-year contracts, work in sweltering conditions, live in barracks and earn about $175 a month. Most of the garments are shipped to the USA, which gives the FSM duty-free access.

The other big foreign operation in Yap is Ting Hong, which has a processing barge in Colonia Harbor and a fleet of nearly 50

YAP

Dress Code

In Yap, although bare breasts are the norm, it's considered vulgar for women to show their thighs. While men can wear regular shorts – or even a loincloth if they so opt – it's not acceptable for foreign women to wear shorts or skirts above knee-length. When swimming, it's OK for women to wear a swimsuit (but not a skimpy one!) but once out of the water you should put on a skirt. Otherwise, clothing in Yap is light and comfortable. In fact one of the acts of the first governor was an attempt to pass legislation that would make wearing ties illegal! ■

---

boats in Yapese waters. As elsewhere in Micronesia, the boats, which lack sanitation facilities, are a serious source of contamination.

Yap now has 70 hotel rooms and gets about 5500 visitors a year.

POPULATION & PEOPLE

The physical characteristics of the Yapese are of western Pacific origin, with traits that indicate Philippine, Palauan and Indonesian influences.

During the colonial era there was little intermarriage with Europeans or Japanese, which makes the Yapese unique among Micronesians. Attempts by the Japanese to assimilate the Micronesian peoples by offering privileges to the offspring of mixed Japanese-Micronesian parents had no impact on the Yapese. They continued to marry traditionally in accordance with their caste system and foreigners remained excluded.

For reasons that are still unclear, the Yapese population dropped by half under the Japanese administration. The entire population in 1945 was only 2582. With the birth rate among the world's lowest, there was serious concern that the Yapese as a people were on the verge of extinction. The Americans reacted by sending medical teams and a slew of anthropologists. Fortunately the latter needn't have made such haste, for the population slowly edged back upwards.

The current population is 11,500, with about 65% living on Yap Proper.

SOCIETY & CONDUCT

The Yapese, more than any other Micronesian peoples, have been reluctant to adopt Western ways. Despite four colonial administrations, their culture remains largely undiluted by outside influences and they still retain their own customs and traditions.

Caste

A complex caste system developed over time as a consequence of warfare between Yapese villages. The victors demanded land ownership rights and patronage of the defeated village. The defeated people retained rights to use the land in their village but were compelled to perform menial tasks for their new landlords, such as road construction and burial of the dead. In this manner the victorious villages climbed to the top of the caste system while the defeated ones sank to the bottom.

To this day, the village in which one is born determines one's name and caste. Members of a village belong to the same caste, although their rank within that caste varies. Every plot of land in the village has a name and a rank, with the highest ranked plot belonging to the village chief.

Depending on how you differentiate them, there are either seven or nine castes in Yapese society today. Each village has its own chief with the paramount chiefs of Yap coming from the three highest caste villages.

It's not really obvious where a village stands in the caste hierarchy just by looking at it. Caste has a more profound effect on people's status than upon their standard of living.

Women's Roles

Women have traditionally had subservient roles in Yapese society. They did the cooking and tended the fields, harvesting from one plot for male family members and from another for the females. The food then had to be prepared in separate pots over separate fires. Not only could men and women not eat together but neither could members of different castes share the same food.

Although such restrictions are not so strictly adhered to today, perhaps this has some bearing on why there are so few restaurants in Yap.

Traditional Community Houses

A *faluw*, or men's house, is a large thatched structure with a sharply pitched roof, supported by heavy wooden pillars and resting atop a stone platform. Traditionally the faluw served as a school for young boys, as quarters for bachelors and as a meeting place for the village leaders.

Pebai are community meeting houses. They often look much like men's houses, only they're larger and have open-air sides. Pebai are mostly built inland whereas faluw are usually by the water.

Once common throughout Yap, women's houses or *dapal* are now only found on the outer islands. When a girl reached puberty she was ushered off to a dapal for initiation and all women in the village went to women's houses to wait out their menstrual periods, using the time to weave, bathe and relax.

Traditional Dress

The cotton loincloth worn by men and boys is called a *thu* and most commonly is one of three colours: red, blue or white. Young boys wear just one thu, either red or blue. Upon reaching age 18 young men on Yap Proper switch to two layers of different coloured cloth and in their mid-20s they add a third layer. Older men affix strands of hibiscus fibre on top of their thus. Men on the outer islands generally wear just one layer of cloth.

Women have two kinds of traditional dress – grass skirts and *lava-lavas*. The latter is a wide strip of cloth woven from hibiscus and banana fibres or from cotton thread. The cotton ones are becoming more common, as they take only about a third of the time to make. Lava-lavas are wrapped around the lower body, extending from the waist to the knee.

Traditionally, neither men nor women wore clothing on their upper bodies, though today T-shirts are sometimes worn, to the chagrin of more traditional chiefs. Western-style clothing is more common than not in Colonia, but both Western and traditional dress are seen all around Yap.

Dos and Don'ts

Exploring Yap requires a grasp of Yapese etiquette. Once you step off the road anywhere in Yap (except for some parts of Colonia), you're on private property. Even some of the stone pathways through villages are private and walking along them is somewhat similar to cutting across someone's backyard. The Yapese themselves try to avoid entering a village other than their own once the sun has set. Once inside a village there are more rules of etiquette; some villages, for example, have areas that women are not allowed to enter.

The official line is that you need to get permission and sometimes a guide to visit most beaches, pebais or villages. Unofficially, the word is that because you're a foreigner and don't know the rules, the Yapese will understand as long as you're considerate and don't overstep the bounds.

The catch-22 is that if you have a guide with you, there are certain things you won't be able to see or do, because the guide knows precisely where he is and isn't allowed to take you.

In reality it's not difficult to go off on your own, asking people along the way for directions and permission when appropriate. Smiles go a long way in Yap. In a village you should greet everyone you see so it doesn't look as if you're sneaking around. Be prepared to back off when it's obvious you're intruding, and always ask permission before snapping someone's picture. Yapese don't like to be stared at or have things pointed at them, so video cameras are especially distasteful.

To the Yapese, not asking permission is an insult. But they're a very generous people and if you do ask, they'll probably let you go nearly anywhere and see almost anything you want. ∎

RELIGION

Most islanders are Catholic. There is also a Protestant Mission on the south side of Chamorro Bay and churches for Seventh-Day Adventists, Bahais, Baptists and Mormons.

LANGUAGE

The local languages are Yapese, Ulithian, Woleaian and Satawalese. The last three are the languages of outer islanders.

In Yapese, 'hello' is *mogethin*, though you're just as apt to be greeted with a cheery 'good morning'. 'Excuse me' is *siro*, 'thank you' is *kam magar* and 'goodbye' is *kefel*.

HOLIDAYS & FESTIVALS

Yap has the following public holidays:

New Year's Day
    1 January
Yap Day
    1st week of March
FSM Constitution Day
    10 May
FSM Independence Day
    3 November
Yap State Constitution Day
    24 December
Christmas
    25 December

Yap Day is the most colourful of these holidays and includes ceremonial dancing and sporting events.

Yap's big traditional celebrations are *mitmits*, all-out feasts accompanied by gift-giving and traditional singing and dancing. One village gives a mitmit for another village to reciprocate for one they received in previous years. The completion of a major village project such as a new community house is also a time for major festivities.

ACTIVITIES
Diving & Snorkelling

Yap has good diving, including virgin reefs with excellent coral, vertical walls, sea caves, channel drifts, schools of grey sharks and barracuda, sea turtles and a couple of shipwrecks.

The reef off Gilman at the southern tip of Yap Proper slopes gently with extensive branching corals, huge lettuce corals and spectacular coral heads.

Yap's most novel attraction, however, is its manta rays. In winter, divers go to Manta Ridge in Miil Channel, where a school of manta rays cruise about. These gentle creatures, which can have a wingspan of 12 feet, swim through the channel as divers cling to a ledge about 30 feet below the surface. The manta rays often come close enough to brush divers with their wingtips. The rays, which are cleaned by parasitic wrasses in the channel, are an awesome sight, especially when they open their wide mouths.

In summer the manta rays move to Gofnuw Channel at the north-east end of Gagil, an interesting site that often has sleeping sharks as well.

Dive Shops The rates at each of Yap's three dive shops include tanks, weights and lunch. BCs, regulators and other equipment can be rented for an additional cost. If you sign up in advance for a dive package lasting more than two days, enquire to find out if you'll be going to different sites, as there's a tendency to go back to the manta ray channel every second day.

Yap Divers (☎ 350-2300, fax 350-4567), Box MR, Colonia, Yap, FM 96943, at Manta Ray Bay Hotel, is Yap's largest dive shop. This five-star PADI operation offers two-tank dives for $95. Snorkellers can go out on the boat for $45, but as trips are generally geared for divers, ask in advance about destinations and water conditions. A choppy water surface that won't affect divers can make for less than ideal snorkelling. If you go to Miil Channel, it can be interesting watching the rays from above, even though it's a distant view, and you'll be close enough to the reef to swim over and do a little reef snorkelling as well.

Beyond the Reef Charters (☎/fax 350-3733), Box 609, Colonia, Yap, FM 96943, is a good alternative dive company that offers one-tank boat dives for $60 and two-tank boat dives for $80. They also have a half-day snorkelling tour, with the destination depending on the tides and customer preference, for $30 per person, lunch included. This small up-and-coming operation has an American divemaster and is located next to the Marina Restaurant, as is Nature's Way.

Nature's Way (☎ 350-2542, fax 350-3407), Box 238, Colonia, Yap, FM 96943, is a little Yapese-owned operation with an amiable Japanese dive instructor, Sue Yasui, who speaks English. Nature's Way charges $60/85 for one/two-tank boat dives and has a snorkelling tour for $40, lunch included.

Both Nature's Way and Beyond the Reef offer a one-day introductory scuba course and dive for beginners for $125, and all three operations offer night dives for $50 and dive certification courses.

All three shops rent snorkel gear; Manta Ray has the cheapest prices at $5 a set. If you want to buy a mask, Beyond the Reef has some quality ones for about $30.

Swimming

There aren't many good beaches in Yap and even fewer open to use by non-villagers. The most accessible beaches are Wanyan Beach in Tomil-Gagil and the beach at Bechiyal Cultural Center in Map. Women may wear a swimsuit in the water as long as it's not skimpy, but should cover up on the beach.

Fishing

Yap waters have marlin, yellowfin tuna, barracuda and trevally. Beyond the Reef Charters offers trolling, casting and bottom fishing from its 22-foot boat; half-day fishing charters cost $95 per person and full-day charters with lunch cost $130, equipment included. Nature's Way has rates that range from $35 for bottom fishing to $120 for a full-day charter. Yap Anglers at Manta Ray Bay Hotel, which has hosted the American TV programme 'Let's Go Fishing', specialises in whipping for giant trevally; its rates vary.

YAP PROPER

The major islands of Yap, Map and Tomil-Gagil are all tightly clustered and connected by bridges. Yap Island is the westernmost and largest island, with half of Yap Proper's land area and two-thirds of its people. Rumung is separated from the rest of Yap Proper by Yinbinaew Passage and can only be reached by boat. Rumung is not receptive to visitors, however, and outsiders need an invitation to go there. Yap Proper has 10 municipalities with more than 100 small villages.

The landscape of the main islands is mainly rolling hills with a green cover of grass interspersed with sparse pandanus and palm trees. In the south-west, the lowlands have thick growth and a marsh-like jungle floor. Yap Proper has some sandy beaches, but much of the coast is lined with mangrove swamps.

The most interesting sights by far are not WW II relics or scenic views, but glimpses into Yapese culture.

The sparsely populated villages outside the capital of Colonia are quiet, peaceful and tidy. On weekdays, when the children are at school and adults are off fishing or at work either in Colonia or in their taro patches, the villages can look semideserted. In a way, it's not a bad time to explore. You'll still see some people, but with fewer people around it's that many less whose permission you need to seek out.

Bechiyal, a traditional village on a sandy beach at the tip of Map Island, has opened itself to visitors as a living cultural centre. It offers the kind of experience you'd hope to find by journeying to a distant outer island, yet Bechiyal is only a $10 taxi ride away from Colonia. You can sleep overnight in a men's house, eat breadfruit and freshly speared fish, drink homemade tuba and learn from the villagers about Yapese culture.

COLONIA

Colonia, on Yap Island in Yap Proper, is the state capital, the business and administrative centre and the only part of Yap that is

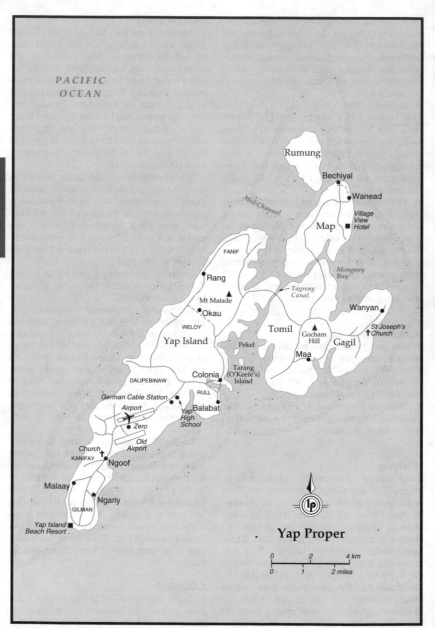

PACIFIC
OCEAN

Rumung

Bechiyal

Wanead

Mill Channel

Map

*Village
View
Hotel*

FANIF

Rang

*Munguiy
Bay*

Mt Matade

*Tagreng
Canal*

Okau

Wanyan

WELOY

Tomil

Gocham
Hill

Gagil

St Joseph's
Church

Yap Island

Pekel

Maa

Colonia

Tarang
(O'Keefe's)
Island

DALIPEBINAW

German Cable Station

RULL

Balabat

Airport

Yap High
School

Zero

Old
Airport

Church

KANIFAY

Ngoof

Malaay

Ngariy

GILMAN

Yap Island
Beach Resort

Yap Proper

0		2		4 km
0	1		2 miles	

the least bit modern. Even so the 'town' of Colonia, which is also called Donguch in Yapese, would be considered a village almost anywhere else.

Colonia wraps around Chamorro Bay, offering water views most everywhere. The bay, incidentally, got its name during the German era when the area was settled with Chamorro labourers who were brought in from Saipan to build the transpacific cable station. These days the south side of Chamorro Bay is home to a sizable Palauan community.

For all practical purposes Colonia's town centre is the YCA complex, a cooperative that was started by an expat Quaker in the 1950s. The old quaintly jumbled YCA department store embodied Yapese small-town character for nearly four decades before being torn down and replaced by a more modern building. While the charming sidewalk bamboo benches and thatched awnings are gone, the complex is still a meeting place of sorts and it's common to find Yapese men in *thus* standing around chatting.

There's quite a bit to see in the Colonia area and the best of it can be explored on foot: the stone footpath across town, the trail up Medeqdeq Hill, and a walk to the stone money bank and men's house in the nearby village of Balabat. These all make pleasurable strolls and you don't need special permission to do them on your own.

Information

Tourist Office The tourist office (☎ 350-2298), on the north side of the bridge in Colonia centre, is open from 7.30 to 11.30 am and 12.30 to 4.30 pm Monday to Friday.

Immigration The immigration office, on the 2nd floor of the Bank of the FSM building, is open from 8.30 am to 4.30 pm weekdays.

Money The Bank of Hawaii and the Bank of the FSM are near each other in Colonia centre. Both are open from 9.30 am to 2.30 pm Monday to Thursday and to 5 pm on

Fridays. The Bank of Hawaii is the place to change foreign currencies or get cash advances on credit cards. The only businesses on Yap that accept credit cards are the Manta Ray Bay Hotel (and dive shop) and Continental Micronesia.

Post Yap Proper's only post office, on the north side of Chamorro Bay, is open weekdays from 8.30 am to 4 pm. Mail goes off-island only twice weekly, on Wednesdays and Fridays.

Telecommunications Long-distance telephone calls can be made and telexes can be sent 24 hours a day from the FSM Telecommunications building in Colonia. Faxes can be sent for the cost of a phone call, plus a dollar. You can receive faxes at the office at 350-4115. There are no coin phones on Yap, but there are a handful of debit-card phones at stores in Colonia, where you can also buy the phone cards ($10).

The rate to call between FSM states is $1 a minute between 6 am and 6 pm on weekdays, and 50 cents a minute at all other times. Phone calls to all parts of the world except the FSM have a three-minute minimum charge – the per-minute rate is $2.50 to the USA or Guam ($2 on Sundays); $3 to the Marshall Islands, Palau, Saipan or Australia; $4 to Canada, the UK or Germany; $5 to most everywhere else.

Library Colonia's little public library, which is east of the Marina Restaurant, is open from 11.30 am to 4.30 pm Monday to Friday.

Laundry The coin laundry behind the YWA Handicraft Shop is open from 8 am to 8 pm Monday to Friday, 8 am to 4 pm on Saturdays and noon to 4 pm on Sundays. It costs 50 cents to wash, 50 cents to dry.

Books & Maps You can find a bookshop in the little white cement building near Yap Evangelical Church, which has a few books on diving, shells, and flora and fauna – not a large collection but worth a look. It's

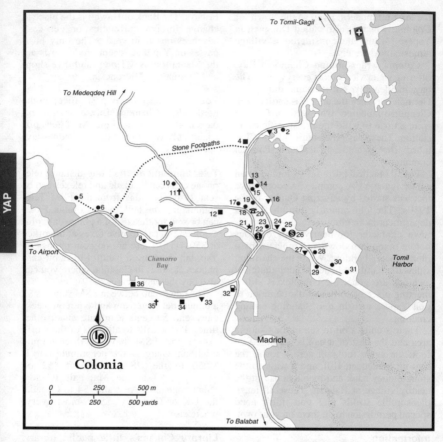

To Tomil-Gagil

To Medeqdeq Hill

Stone Footpaths

To Airport

Chamorro
Bay

To Balabat

Madrich

Tomil
Harbor

Colonia

0   250   500 m
0   250   500 yards

open from 9.30 am to 4.30 pm Monday to Friday. The Land Management office sells USGS maps of Yap for $5.

Media Yap has one radio station and a government-owned TV station, WAAB, which shows recorded programmes from the US mainland. YCA sells Guam's *Pacific Daily News* and the ESA Store, next to the ESA Hotel, sells Palau's local newspaper.

Airline Office The Continental Micronesia office (☎ 350-2127), in the YCA complex, has chequered hours, as the staff also handle flights at the airport. The office is

open from 8 to 10.30 am and 2 to 3 pm on Mondays; from 8 to 11.30 am and 12.30 to 3 pm on Tuesdays and Thursdays; from 7 to 8 am and 2 to 3 pm on Wednesdays, Fridays and Sundays; and from 8 am to 1 pm on Saturdays.

Emergency There's a public hospital (☎ 350-3446) at the north side of Colonia. For police emergencies, dial 350-3333.

Government Offices
The government administration building was constructed on the site of the old Spanish fort, of which only remnants of a

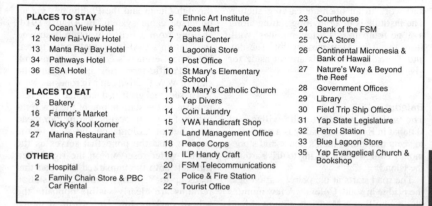

PLACES TO STAY		5	Ethnic Art Institute	23	Courthouse
4	Ocean View Hotel	6	Aces Mart	24	Bank of the FSM
12	New Rai-View Hotel	7	Bahai Center	25	YCA Store
13	Manta Ray Bay Hotel	8	Lagoonia Store	26	Continental Micronesia & Bank of Hawaii
34	Pathways Hotel	9	Post Office		
36	ESA Hotel	10	St Mary's Elementary School	27	Nature's Way & Beyond the Reef
		11	St Mary's Catholic Church	28	Government Offices
PLACES TO EAT		13	Yap Divers	29	Library
3	Bakery	14	Coin Laundry	30	Field Trip Ship Office
16	Farmer's Market	15	YWA Handicraft Shop	31	Yap State Legislature
24	Vicky's Kool Korner	17	Land Management Office	32	Petrol Station
27	Marina Restaurant	18	Peace Corps	33	Blue Lagoon Store
		19	ILP Handy Craft	35	Yap Evangelical Church & Bookshop
OTHER		20	FSM Telecommunications		
1	Hospital	21	Police & Fire Station		
2	Family Chain Store & PBC Car Rental	22	Tourist Office		

YAP

wall and the foundations remain. Among the offices here are those of the governor and of outer island affairs.

Yap State Legislature

The state legislature building is on the site of a former Japanese Shinto shrine. The main vestiges of the shrine are the cement torii (pillared gate) in the middle of the parking lot and a pair of stone lanterns flanking the steps leading to the front door.

Medeqdeq Hill

The 482-foot Medeqdeq Hill is topped with a light beacon and has a panoramic view of Colonia, the harbour and Yap's east coast. The top of the hill is about a mile up from Colonia on the road past St Mary's church. This Catholic church, incidentally, dates back to Yap's first Spanish Capuchin missionaries.

Although the walk starts out on pavement, the last half is along a rough dirt road that's not passable without a 4WD vehicle. Beware of a low-growing groundcover with fuzzy purple flowers and small razor-sharp thorns that draw blood at the slightest touch. The hike up and back takes about an hour from the church.

Stone Footpaths

There's a lovely traditional stone footpath that starts opposite the waterfront just south of Ocean View Hotel. The path is peaceful and shady, lined with flowering hibiscus and green ti plants much of the way. When the path splits, take the left fork and you'll come out to the paved road just above the Catholic school.

To continue on a second footpath that will bring you down to the north side of Chamorro Bay, turn right and go up the road for about 20 feet. The second path begins between a dumped car that looks like it'll probably be there forever and a pigpen. This path is not as well-lined with stones as the first, but it does offer some glimpses of taro patches and village houses.

The whole walk only takes about 15 minutes and is a very pleasant way to get across town.

Ethnic Art Institute of Micronesia

This new programme is attempting to preserve traditional art forms by serving as a place where local artists can create and sell their art, a bit like a mini-Ubed on Bali. To revive and expand the arts, village elders have been invited to teach their craftsmanship and techniques to younger artists. Part of the programme involves research to determine the exact form of original idols, discover what natural pigments were used before Western contact and the like.

The artists live on site in thatched homes

and work in an open-air carving shelter. The institute is in an inviting setting along a stone footpath just a few minutes' walk from the Aces Mart parking lot. Tuesday and Thursday afternoons are set aside for visitors.

Balabat

The mile-long walk to the village of Balabat in Rull Municipality is a good way to see a traditional men's house and stone-money bank without having to drive around the island.

The road starts at the petrol station near the bridge in south Colonia. A few minutes along, you'll pass **Madrich**, a point of land sticking out into the bay which is home to a settlement of outer islanders. Madrich, once the site of a Spanish trading station, was named after Madrid.

The walk continues along the waterfront until it reaches **Rull municipal office**, where the road is lined with an impressive collection of stone money. Just before you reach the municipal office you'll come to Sav-Way Mart where foreign tourists are expected to stop and pay $2.50 to enter Rull.

At the municipal office the pavement ends and the road curves to the right. Two-tenths of a mile past the municipal office, look on the left for a dirt road that is about as wide as the main road. It's just a couple minutes down that road to more stone money and a **seaside faluw** in a setting of coconut palms.

The main road ends at two raised **stone platforms** used for community gatherings. Traditional dances sometimes take place on the pathway between the platforms. The village of Balabat is neatly landscaped with betel nut trees, taro patches, hibiscus and lilies. You can usually spot bright-red cardinal honeyeaters in the trees along this walk.

AROUND YAP ISLAND
German Cable Station

In 1905, the German communications station in Yap completed a link to Shanghai through Guam and the Philippines via an undersea cable system. In August 1914, shelling from a British warship destroyed the station's 200-foot steel radio tower, breaking Germany's communications link to its Pacific territories and marking the start of WW I activity in Micronesia.

To see the graffiti-decorated concrete remains of the station, one of the few remnants of German occupation in Yap, head west out of Colonia on the road to the airport. Pass the pond that serves as the town's water reservoir on the right, then turn left onto the unmarked dirt road that leads up to Yap High School. The station remains are clearly visible opposite the school parking lot. The whole distance from the westside bridge in Colonia is 1.75 miles.

Japanese Zeros

To see the remains of some Japanese Zero planes, continue past the entrance to the new airport for exactly one mile and then turn left onto an unmarked dirt road. Continue on that road for half a mile, at which point you'll reach the old telecommunications station followed by the weather station.

The two planes that are best preserved and easiest to see are about 100 yards north of the weather station. To get to them, take the dirt road that runs back between the telecommunications and weather stations. You can visit them for free; however, if you want to photograph them, you're supposed to first see Martin at the weather station and pay $2.50.

The Zeros were destroyed on the ground by US aerial bombings during WW II. The planes are missing engines and other parts that were taken away by Japanese collectors, but the wings are still largely intact and they're interesting to see. The area around the planes is a good place to find low-growing, insectivorous pitcher plants.

There's a well-preserved Japanese anti-aircraft gun under a big mahogany tree on the weather station lawn about 20 feet from the road, just beyond the little chain-link enclosure. After you pass the gun, keep looking on the left to find a Yapese style tree house complete with a thatched roof.

The road continues on to an abandoned 5000-foot airstrip built by the Japanese. The old thatched-roof terminal still stands, but it's difficult to spot the remains of the 727 that landed short of the runway in 1980, lost a wheel and skidded off into the bush at the east end of the airstrip.

You can turn right onto the runway to get back to the main road that goes to Gilman.

Southern Tip of Yap

South of the old airport is the village of Ngoof, marked by St Ignatius of Loyola church and the adjacent cemetery. A mile beyond on the left is Nathan Store (no sign), where you can get a cool drink while checking out the store's old Spanish cannon, which is sandwiched by two pieces of stone money. The friendly proprietor is a school teacher who enjoys chatting and sharing insights.

After another 1.5 miles the road reaches the coast at Gilman, the southernmost end of the island. It's a neat community with much of the shoreline bordered by coconut palms and Yapese mahogany trees. There are some attractive traditional houses in this area, landscaped with stone money, hibiscus hedges and chenille plants with velvety red tails.

The road going up the west side skirts the mangrove-studded coast, in places narrowing to just one lane elevated a few feet above the swamps. Tiny lipstick-red fiddler crabs are easy to spot running around in the black mud between the sharp spikes of the mangrove shoots, and with a little luck you might also see mangrove crabs and monitor lizards. The lizards, which can reach a length of several feet, were introduced onto Yap and Ulithi by the Japanese both to control the rat population and to serve as a food source.

The road ends at Malaay Village, where an extensive moss-covered Japanese stone wall, part of WW II defence fortifications, runs along the side of the road. At Malaay,

turn east on the side road that's strung with power lines, to get back on the main Gilman-airport road. Just 200 yards along this side road look to the left to see a grassy stone money path.

Okau Village

The village of Okau in Weloy has one of Yap's best meeting houses and stone money banks at the end of a very pleasant stone footpath.

To get there from Colonia you take the road west, as if heading toward the airport, but instead of turning left with the main paved road take the right fork onto the wide dirt road, which is three-quarters of a mile from the westside bridge on Chamorro Bay.

When the road forks again, bear right, continuing on the wider road. The stone pathway, which is just over three miles from the airport road, starts on the right opposite a stone platform and just before two small houses and a bridge.

One section of the path meanders alongside taro patches and interesting mud flats, while another part is lined with hibiscus and lush variegated plants. Mosses grow in the cracks between the stones. It's very quiet and peaceful, almost like walking through a Zen garden.

The large pebai, about 10 minutes down the pathway, is built on a raised stone platform. The supports are made of mahogany, the inside floor planks are made of betel nut and the roof is nipa palm lashed onto bamboo.

Yap's most valuable stone money is generally thickest in the middle and thinner at the edges, with circular gouge markings across the face. You can see an example of this type of money in front of the pebai to the left.

Across a little footbridge that's opposite the pebai entrance is a *wunbey*, or meeting platform. There in the open air the elder men of the village have their meetings, sitting against stone backrests. Traditionally, a low stone table would be placed in the centre to hold food and betel nut which young men would then serve to the elders.

Fanif

From Okau, the road continues through Fanif Municipality around the northern end of Yap Island; en route it skirts extensive mangrove swamps, crosses little bridges and goes through a few sleepy villages.

Nearly two miles from Okau you'll enter the village of Rang. The chief's house is the first house on the left, surrounded by stone money – if he's on the front porch be sure to give a wave and if you're interested in using the beach, stop and ask for his permission. Rang Beach is a long brown sand beach; swimming might be good at high tide, but at low tide it's all sea grass and sand flats.

The dirt road continues another 12 miles, washboard-like in places but usually passable in a standard car, before coming out to Yap's main paved road. At this intersection, turn right to get to Colonia, left to go to Tomil-Gagil.

TOMIL-GAGIL ISLAND

Tomil-Gagil was once connected to Yap Island at the upper end of Tomil Harbor by mangrove flats. During the German occupation the shallow Tagreng Canal was dug between the islands to allow boat passage to Map and Rumung from Colonia.

Most visitors to Tomil-Gagil are on their way to the beach in Wanyan or to Bechiyal on Map Island. For the most part the interior is dry, with open rolling meadows and dusty red earth, while the coast is lusher with coconut palms, mangroves and bananas.

Shortly after crossing the Tagreng Canal you'll go by the Seventh-Day Adventist school. When the road forks a mile farther, veer left, continuing on the main road. The road north to Bechiyal will come in after a quarter of a mile, but to get to Wanyan continue straight ahead. The Wanyan road runs through the Micronesian Maritime & Fisheries Academy. The top of an inland hill may seem like an oddly landlocked location for a maritime academy, but it owes its location to the otherwise suitable facilities that were left at this site by the former US Coast Guard Loran Station.

Gacham Hill, south of the road near the academy, is a sacred place that is considered the centre of Yapese wisdom and the spot where Yap is said to have been formed.

Wanyan

To get to the coastal village of Wanyan, bear left at the fork three-quarters of a mile after the academy, on the road that parallels the power lines.

Yap's largest piece of stone money is on the island of Rumung, but since the people of Rumung have decided they're not ready for foreign visitors, you'll have to settle for number two, which is in the centre of Wanyan Village.

Upon entering Wanyan, you'll pass St Joseph's Catholic Church which is interesting for the mural painted above its door showing Yapese men presenting gifts of stone money, lava-lavas, food and storyboards.

Just a little farther on, you'll pass a meeting house and will then see two huge rai standing along the ocean side of the road. The piece on the left is Yap's second largest.

Wanyan Beach One of Yap's most accessible beaches is Wanyan Beach (also called Seabreeze Beach), at the end of the road. This brown sand beach is backed by lots of loaded coconut trees – if you're driving, be careful where you park! There are thatched picnic shelters, restrooms and showers. Pay the $1 beach use fee at the unmarked tin-sided store that's on the ocean side of the road a third of a mile before the beach. You can borrow a volleyball net there if you're so inclined; in the past they've also had a couple of kayaks for rent.

Swimming is best at high tide, as otherwise the water is shallow and there's lots of sea grass near the shore. About halfway out to the reef there are several circular drop-offs with good fish and coral. If you look straight out from the beach, you can identify these snorkelling holes by the water colour, which changes from dark blue to aqua. The closest is directly out from the beach at 11 o'clock and takes about 10 minutes to swim out to.

BECHIYAL CULTURAL CENTER

Bechiyal is a special place. This friendly seaside village at the northern tip of Map has not only decided to accommodate overnight guests, but has set itself up as a low-keyed cultural centre, providing visitors with an opportunity to more closely observe traditional Yapese village life.

Bechiyal is on a lovely beach, one of Yap Proper's best, though you'll usually need to wade out for about 10 minutes to reach water deep enough for swimming. Between the coastline and reef are two large V-shaped stone fishtraps of ancient origins. When the tide goes out the bigger fish get stuck in the narrow end of the traps, making it a cinch for villagers to go out and spearfish their next meal.

Visitors are welcome to use the beach in front of the men's house, though the beaches just beyond the village are even nicer, and as they're more secluded women can sunbathe without having to worry about offending anyone. There's a freshwater shower in the village. For $10 to $15, snorkellers can be taken out by boat to the channel, where the manta rays feed, and even do a scenic loop around the forbidden island of Rumung on the way back; however, advance planning is required.

Bechiyal's pebai is the largest on Yap, while its faluw, on a high stone platform above the beach, is one of the oldest on the island. The faluw is crafted in the centuries-old manner with openings that hinge in and out, and thatch that catches cool ocean breezes. Inside there are dried turtle skulls as well as a carved wooden figure that represents the *mispil*, which in times past was a woman captured from a neighbouring village and used as the mistress for the faluw.

The entrance fee to Bechiyal is $2.50 for adults, $1.25 for children, and includes a guided tour by one of the villagers. There's no extra charge for still photography, but previous negative experiences with video cameras makes their use frowned upon and there's a fee to use one. Taking shells is strictly forbidden.

Your guide can pick you a drinking coconut from a nearby tree and serve it up with a fresh-cut papaya-stem straw. Meals are available for $3 to $4 each, but should be arranged a day in advance. Dinner might well be a hardy Yapese meal of fish or crab, breadfruit, taro and fried banana, all from the village. Bechiyal's tuba has such a good reputation that Rumung islanders regularly come ashore to buy it, and those who spend the night at Bechiyal (see Places to Stay) commonly pass the evening sipping away.

There's a handicraft hut in Bechiyal that sells locally made woven bags, baskets, pandanus placemats, betel nut bags and toy bamboo rafts. Ask to see the little museum display stored here which includes shell money called *yar*, a pig's tooth necklace, shell adzes and other artefacts.

Getting There & Away

The nicest way to get to Bechiyal is on a delightful mile-long footpath that begins at the end of the Map road. To get started, drive or take a taxi ($10) to the end of the road (or, if you're overnighting, take the public school bus) and then walk across the log footbridge. The path passes through Wanead and Tooruw, two traditional villages of thatched houses spread along the coast, then leads through a jungle setting with lots of bird calls, dragonflies and scurrying lizards. There's also a bit of stone money along the way.

About 15 minutes along the route you'll reach a 4WD road. Turn right onto it for the simplest route into the village or continue on the old path straight ahead for the most scenic route. Either way, you're only about five minutes from Bechiyal.

If you have a real time crunch you could instead drive directly to Bechiyal on the 4WD road, which starts off the main paved road at the Maap Elementary School. However, not only is this a less interesting alternative to the footpath, but the road is not always passable in a standard car, especially if it's been raining.

PLACES TO STAY

Although Yap has fewer than 100 visitor rooms in all, they represent a surprisingly wide variance in both cost and type. Accommodation ranges from a $15 guesthouse in a traditional village at the north end of Yap to $150 luxury bungalows at the southernmost end. In Colonia itself, there are five small hotels: three straightforward budget types, one quintessentially Yapese and one of conventional tourist standards.

Yap has a 10% hotel tax, which is added to all rates.

Camping

Camping can be complicated on Yap as every speck of land is privately owned. If you do insist on communing with nature, you'll need to get permission from a landowner. The tourist office should be able to help if you aren't successful on your own.

For the most part people think camping is a bit odd and may insist you pitch your tent in their backyard where they can keep an eye on you. They'll need to explain it all to the neighbours and will most probably breathe a sigh of relief once you've gone.

The one notable exception is Bechiyal Cultural Center in Map, where arrangements have been made to accommodate campers. It costs $3 per person to pitch a tent and the location, near the men's house, is unbeatable.

Homestays

The tourist office maintains a list of Yapese families who are interested in taking travellers into their homes. The preferred way to arrange this is to write to the tourist office a month or so in advance to let them know when you're coming, how long you'd like to stay with a family and a little about yourself. When you arrive the tourist office can arrange for you to visit a home or two, allowing you and the families to check each other out. You should plan to stay in a hotel for one or two nights first until arrangements are complete. Rates are negotiable between you and the family, and there's no charge by the tourist office. Expect to pay about $15 per person; this generally includes meals. While most families prefer advance notice, homestays can sometimes be arranged on the spot as well.

These are not established guesthouses by any means so this is a good opportunity to experience authentic Yapese home life, while saving a bit on your travel expenses. Expect accommodation to be very modest, but warm and homey.

While it's best to go through the tourist office, if you should need a place on the weekend you might try Martin Tugchur (☎ 350-2437), who has a separate little guesthouse in Tooruw Village, about a 15-minute walk from Bechiyal.

Bechiyal Cottage & Men's House

Bechiyal has a wood-and-bamboo cottage for overnight guests; it's a suitably simple place, off the ground on stilts, with a loft and glass louvred windows all around. Guests are provided with futons on the floor, pillows, sheets, mosquito nets and lanterns. The cost is $15 per person, or the same price for a family.

Visitors can also stay overnight at the men's house, where a couple of village boys occasionally sleep. Despite the name, they will generally make exceptions for foreign visitors and allow women to stay as well. It costs $10 for mat space on the floor.

Reservations for overnight stays can be made through Chief John Tamag (☎ 350-2939), Bechiyal Cultural Center, Box 37, Colonia, Yap, FM 96943.

Hotels

The *New Rai-View Hotel* (☎/fax 350-2537), Box 488, Colonia, Yap, FM 96943, on a quiet hillside at the north side of Chamorro Bay, has tidy, straightforward rooms with fans, private bathrooms and either one double or two twin beds. Owner Lonnie Fread, an American expat who's been on the island for many years, is working hard to revamp the old Rai View Hotel into a quality budget accommodation. So far he's opened four rooms and has a half dozen more under construction. There's free coffee in the lobby. The cost is $40 for either singles or doubles. Lonnie meets arriving flights and provides free airport transfers.

The *ESA Hotel* (☎ 350-2139, fax 350-2310), Box 141, Colonia, Yap, FM 96943, run by a Palauan family, is an older place that overlooks Chamorro Bay. There are 16 plain but clean rooms with two comfortable twin beds, air-con, private bathrooms, refrigerators, phones and TVs. The rate is $45 for singles or doubles. It has a nice family atmosphere with a guest lounge on the 2nd floor. Airport transfers are provided at $6 per person return.

The *Ocean View Hotel* (☎ 350-2279, fax 350-2339), Box 130, Colonia, Yap, FM 96943, at the north-east side of Colonia, is a 17-room hotel with a decidedly local feel. Rooms have two twin beds, thermostat controlled air-con, ceiling fans, a small Japanese-style bathtub and a little table. There are free bananas and coffee at the counter. The cost is $50 for a room with a bay view, $40 without; there are discounts for monthly stays. Airport transfers cost $3 per person each way.

The *Pathways Hotel* (☎ 350-3310, fax 350-2066), Box 718, Colonia, Yap, FM 96943, consists of eight free-standing hillside cottages that nicely balance modern comforts and traditional Yapese aesthetics. Each is crafted from native materials, with nipa palm thatched roofs, split bamboo walls and mahogany beams tied with coconut fibre rope. There are pleasant sitting verandas, many with a clear view of Chamorro Bay. Although in town, the cottages are in a garden-like setting, connected by wooden walkways. Rooms have two single beds, ceiling fans, private bathrooms and a small refrigerator. There are screened windows that catch the breeze, as well as the early morning crowing of roosters. The management is knowledgeable and friendly and all things considered this is the most appealing traditional-style hotel in Micronesia. The rate is $85 for singles or doubles, plus $10 more if you want to use the air-con; for the best view request cottage 12. Airport transfers are free.

Catering largely to divers, the three-storey *Manta Ray Bay Hotel* (☎ 350-2300, fax 350-4567), Box MR, Colonia, Yap, FM 96943, has 23 large, comfortable rooms with rattan furnishings and modern conveniences. All have thermostat controlled air-con, room safes, VCRs, minibars and two queen beds, with waterbeds in the ground floor rooms. In-room TVs can be hooked up to satellite CNN and a few Asian stations for an extra $5. Singles/doubles cost $110/130 for street-side rooms and $130/150 for rooms with verandas facing the water. If you're paying this much, it's worth the extra $20 for the ocean view. For high rollers, there's a luxury suite with a king bed and a spiral staircase leading to a private rooftop Jacuzzi for $240. Airport transfers cost $10 return. The hotel has its own dock and dive shop.

The new *Village View Hotel* (☎ 350-3956), Colonia, Yap, FM 96943, is at the northern end of Map Island, about two miles south-east of Bechiyal. Run by Al Ganang, a former tourism officer, it comprises five duplex units, built Western-style of sheetrock construction and asphalt roof. The rooms have air-con, two twin beds and private bathrooms. It's on a nice, quiet (albeit sometimes windy) beach and could make an interesting getaway, though it's a pretty long haul into town if you want to dine out. There are plans to add a bar and restaurant. The rate is $65.

The *Yap Island Beach Resort* (☎ 350-4188, fax 350-4187), Box 34, Colonia, Yap, FM 96943, is a new up-market resort in the quiet village of Anoth in Gilman, at the southern tip of Yap Island. It currently has two bungalows open, but there are plans to add six more, as well as a central building with 15 air-con guest rooms, a restaurant and Yap's first swimming pool. There's a snack bar selling sandwiches, simple fare and drinks. The A-frame bungalows, which are on a little cove, are made of Indonesian hardwood and have thatched roofs and waterview decks. Inside they're studio-like and roomy, with a kitchenette, ceiling fans, bathroom with tub, two twin beds and two fold-out futons. Quality touches include hand-carved supporting beams and elegant coconut-wood furniture.

Some units will be accessible to disabled people. The rate is $150 for one to four people.

PLACES TO EAT

The best place for breakfast is at *Pathways'* little open-air courtyard, where you can get a plate of assorted island-grown fruits, juice, a pot of coffee and simple homemade muffins served warm. The whole thing costs $3.50 and is served between 6.30 and 9.30 am. Currently there are no other meals except for a Friday evening barbecue that attracts a nice mix of locals and expats.

Vicky's Kool Korner, on the 2nd floor of the Bank of the FSM building, is a favourite eating place of Colonia's workers. You can get a full breakfast for $4 to $5, a tuna sandwich for $2. It's open from 7 am to 10 pm on weekdays and from 8 am to 4 pm on Sundays (closed on Saturdays).

The *Farmer's Market*, open from 7.30 am to about 5 pm Monday to Friday, sells locally grown fruit and vegetables, including bananas, oranges and passion fruit. Cold drinking coconuts cost 45 cents. Until 4 pm food is served at picnic tables on a porch at the rear of the bayside market. Fried fish or a vegetarian meal cost $3, pork or fried chicken a dollar more; all include rice and local vegetables such as taro and yam. You can also get a bowl of ramen for $2.

The *ESA Restaurant* at ESA Hotel is unexciting but acceptable, with typical breakfast dishes with coffee for around $5. At other meals, a cheeseburger costs $3, a fish sandwich $4, yakisoba or oyako donburi $5.50. There are also various full dinner meals beginning at about double that. It's open daily from 7 am to 8 pm. Alcohol is not served, but drinking coconuts are.

A good place to eat is the *Marina Restaurant*, a casual, open-air eatery on the waterfront beside the marina. At breakfast, a waffle or French toast with an egg and bacon is $4, and throughout the day you can get a nice fresh fish sandwich for $3. A hearty fish or chicken dinner with taro, breadfruit, rice, fruit and a drink costs $7 at

lunch, $10 at dinner. The Marina is open from 7 am to 10 pm weekdays and from 5 to 10 pm on weekends.

The *Manta Ray Bar & Grill*, on the Manta Ray Bay Hotel's 3rd floor, has a bayside view with large windows that can be opened to catch the breeze. The food is standard American fare. At breakfast, you can get fruit and banana bread for $3.50 or eggs, bacon and toast for $6, both including coffee. At lunch, a cheeseburger or fish sandwich with onion rings costs $6. There's a decent cheese pizza ($9) that's big enough for two if you're not terribly hungry. Otherwise a la carte main dishes include the likes of vegetarian pasta, chicken coconut curry and pepper steak in the $10 to $17 range. Breakfast is from 6.30 to 10.30 am, lunch from 11.30 am to 2 pm and dinner from 6 to 9.30 pm.

There are no restaurants outside Colonia, though the outlying villages often have small stores. However, they're unmarked and usually look like private houses, so you'll need to ask around to find one.

YCA is Yap's biggest grocery/general store and is open from 8 am to 5.30 pm weekdays, 8.30 am to 2.30 pm on Saturdays and 8.30 am to 1 pm on Sundays. You can buy alcoholic beverages at *YCA* and in the *Liquor Shoppe* in the YCA complex. The nearby video shop sells soft-serve ice cream for 50 cents.

Other food stores are *Family Chain Store* and *Blue Lagoon Store*. There's a bakery on the road to the hospital selling cinnamon rolls and a few other simple items; it's open from 7.30 am to 4.30 pm daily except Saturdays.

Colonia's water is not safe to drink from the tap. A gallon of bottled water costs $1.50 at YCA.

ENTERTAINMENT

There's not much to do in the evening around Colonia in terms of standard entertainment. Yap has no movie theatre.

Colonia has three places with open-air bars and water views. The cheapest drinks ($1.75 for a beer) are at the *Marina Restaurant*, while the most atmospheric spot is the little thatched gazebo at the *Pathways Hotel*, where a Foster's costs $2 until 7.30 pm, $3 after that. The *Manta Ray Bar & Grill* has higher prices but the widest selection, including wines.

The drinking age is 21 and island residents need to get a liquor permit at the police station. At most places, including the bars listed here, foreign visitors can buy alcohol without the permit, though don't be surprised if clerks in smaller stores refuse to sell you beer without one.

Cultural Show

Maa Village, on Tomil-Gagil, opens up to tours a couple times a week, with traditional dancing by costumed boys and girls, a village stroll along a stone footpath and a sampling of local fruits. The tour is good fun,

---

Betel Nut

Everyone, but everyone, in Yap chews *buw*, as betel nut is called. Small stores do a good business selling zip-lock bags of betel nuts and pepper leaves for $2.50 for 'a plastic'.

Betel nut is split open while green, sprinkled with dry coral lime, wrapped in pepper leaves and then chewed. It produces a mild high that lasts about 10 minutes. Sometimes tobacco, or tobacco soaked in vodka, is added.

Betel nut turns the saliva bright red and stains the teeth red and eventually black. It's the lime that stimulates the flow of saliva. Once called 'a dentist's nightmare' by Westerners, recent findings indicate that chewing betel nut may actually help prevent cavities.

Not that this would sway the Yapese one way or the other. They start chewing buw at a very early age and continue as long as they are able to chew – perhaps even longer.

According to old timers, even ghosts chew betel nut. If a sailing canoe was to stop for no obvious reason in the middle of a lagoon the sailor would prepare a special betel nut mixture, wrap it in extra leaves and tie it up tightly with many knots. He would then throw it overboard and sail away easily, while the ghost who'd been holding his canoe was busy untying the knots. ■

---

offers an opportunity to see a traditional men's house and provides a rare chance to take photos of Yapese (no fee) without worrying about giving offense. The Wednesday tour takes place from 5 to 7 pm and costs $30, with the proceeds going to the Maa Youth Organization. This tour can be booked through ESA or Pathways hotels or Beyond the Reef Charters. Another tour is given on Saturday afternoons but it costs $50 (including a 'free' T-shirt) and can only be booked through the Manta Ray Bay Hotel.

THINGS TO BUY

Yap has some fine native handicrafts. Lava-lava skirts hand-woven of cotton or hibiscus and banana-tree fibres can make attractive wall hangings; they sell for $20 to $60. Other crafts are handbags or betel nut pouches woven of pandanus leaves, wood carvings of outrigger canoes and toy bamboo rafts.

The YWA Handicraft Shop in central Colonia, run by the Yap Women's Association, has a wide selection and good prices. It's open from 8 am to 4.30 pm Monday to Friday. The nearby ILP Handy Craft, open from 7.30 am to 8 pm daily, has lots of T-shirts with Yapese designs and some fine Ulithi-made pandanus purses.

YCA has stone-money design T-shirts for $15, tank tops for $12.50. The Lagoonia Store, a clothing store on the north side of Chamorro Bay, has a limited selection of lava-lavas.

The place to buy crafts directly from artists is at the Ethnic Art Institute of Micronesia, on the west side of Colonia. The Pathways Hotel has a little gift shop with a variety of items from lava-lavas to pencil sketches, photographs and watercolour postcards of Yapese scenes.

The Yap Institute of Natural Science, Box 215, Colonia, Yap, FM 96943, sells an annual calendar with sketches and short narratives on Yapese culture; it can be ordered for $5, postage included.

GETTING THERE & AWAY

Continental Micronesia is the only airline which services Yap and it flies on Sundays,

Wednesdays and Fridays. The flight originates in Guam, touches down on Yap on the way to Palau, and lands again on Yap on the return to Guam. There's also a Monday flight that bypasses Yap on the way south but goes from Palau to Yap and on to Guam on the northbound route.

The one-way fare between Guam and Yap is $208, while an excursion ticket which requires a three-day advance purchase costs $351. The one-way fare between Palau and Yap is $141, the excursion fare is $241. Micronesia residents can get a discount of 40% on the aforementioned one-way fares; for more information see the Getting There & Away chapter in the front of the book.

Many foreign visitors will find it cheaper to have Yap added onto their original ticket to Micronesia rather than buy a separate ticket to Yap from Palau or Guam. Also note that with excursions between Guam and Palau you can stop over for free on Yap in either direction.

Air
The airport is three miles from town. There are restrooms and a tourist information booth, but no car rental booths. The only pay phone at the airport is a debit-card phone; if you need to call for a ride, the Continental Micronesia desk might let you use their phone. At the west end of the terminal there's a reasonably priced gift shop selling baskets, pouches and bottles of Pohnpei pepper, as well as soda and beer.

Leaving Yap
Yap currently has no departure tax, though one is being considered.

GETTING AROUND
The island's main paved road begins at the airport, curves through Colonia, and continues through Tomil to the north-east end of Map. There are also a few paved roads around Colonia, but most other roads on the island are packed dirt. By Micronesian standards Yap's dirt roads are in very good condition.

To/From the Airport
Hotels provide airport transfers for their guests, and most meet each flight. There are no car rental booths at the airport; if you want to rent a car you can enquire with Lonnie of the New Rai-View Hotel or the ESA Hotel representative, both of whom have rental cars and meet all flights. There are usually no taxis at the airport, but you can call for one.

Bus
School buses run between Colonia and outlying villages transporting students and commuting workers, generally heading toward Colonia in the early morning and going back to the villages in the late afternoon. Visitors can use them on a space-available basis for 50 cents. If you're going to Bechiyal, buses usually leave Colonia around 3 pm carrying students and at 5 pm for workers. The buses return from Bechiyal (leaving from the log bridge at Wanead) at about 7 am. In Colonia, most buses park at the north side of the Bank of the FSM building.

Taxi
Yap's taxis are radio dispatched, not hailed down by the side of the road. Taxis don't have meters, but rides around the Colonia area are usually 75 cents. Fares quoted are per taxi, not per person.

The taxi fare from Colonia is $3 to the airport, $5 to Okau, $7 to Gilman and $10 to Wanyan or the beginning of the Bechiyal footpath.

The main taxi companies are:

Wanyo Taxi   (☎ 350-2120)
Mid-Land Taxi   (☎ 350-2405)
East-West Taxi (☎ 350-3676)

Car
ESA Hotel (☎ 350-2139) and PBC Car Rental (☎ 350-2266) rent sedans for $40 to $45 a day. The New Rai-View Hotel (☎ 350-2537) has a couple of well-maintained vehicles, including a 4WD, for $35 a day. There are no car rental booths at the airport. If you don't want to chase down

a car by yourself, the front desk at your hotel can generally make arrangements. There's a 10% tax on car rentals.

There are a number of small petrol stations around Colonia. Petrol costs $1.70 a gallon.

Hitching

There isn't enough traffic outside of Colonia to really depend on hitching, though if you're walking along the road you might get offered a ride. Sticking out a thumb is not a custom here.

Tours

Guided sightseeing tours can be arranged through the hotels or Wave Crest Travel Agency (☎ 350-2319) at the Manta Ray Bay Hotel. Wave Crest offers a half-day tour for $30 (minimum of two people) that takes in stone money banks and villages, and a longer full-day tour for $65.

Nature's Way (☎ 350-2542) provides half-day tours that include a sampling of local fruit for $45, full-day tours for $65; they also offer a mangrove boat tour of the Tagreng Canal for $35. The Pathways Hotel (☎ 350-3310) is beginning a series of ecotours; contact them for more information.

If you want to piece together your own little tour, you could also rent a taxi for the day and use the driver as your guide. Taxis can be chartered for $15 an hour or $65 a day.

OUTER ISLANDS

The outer islands are made up of 11 atolls and four single islands. Of these 15 outer island groups, 11 are populated.

Yap's outer islanders are some of the most isolated people on earth. Little is known of their origins although it's believed that their islands were settled quite independently of Yap Proper. Yap's easternmost islanders and Chuuk's westernmost islanders have more physical, cultural and linguistic similarities with each other than they do with either of their district centres.

Most outer islanders live the same way

they have for centuries, wearing thus and lava-lavas and living in thatched huts. Some of the elderly men still have elaborate body tattoos, though the practice has been all but abandoned by younger generations.

For the most part the outer islanders maintain a subsistence livelihood of fishing and farming. To earn a little money, many of the islanders produce copra which they load onto the field trip ship when it stops by.

Uninhabited islands are visited in outrigger canoes to gather turtles, turtle eggs and coconuts. On Lamotrek, for instance, turtle meat is the staple food between April and August.

Some of the smaller atolls have so little land that every spare bit is used for growing crops. During severe dry spells some islanders are forced to rely solely on drinking coconuts when they run out of catchment water.

Ulithian is the native language on Ulithi, Fais and Sorol. Satawal islanders speak Satawalese, which is closely related to the language of Chuuk's western islanders.

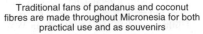
Traditional fans of pandanus and coconut fibres are made throughout Micronesia for both practical use and as souvenirs

The native language on Yap's other outer islands is Woleaian.

Permission to Visit

There's concern that Yap's more isolated outer islands may be very vulnerable, should the 20th century suddenly appear upon their shores clad in a bikini and grasping a video camera. It's largely because of this that visitors are screened.

In a government survey a few years back, outer islanders were adamant that visitors come only with prior permission and 99% thought visitors should be accompanied by a Yapese guide. The saving grace of all this is that 96% said they would like to share their knowledge of Yap's traditional culture and their present lifestyle with outsiders.

In response to this, the Governor's Office and the Council of Tamol (composed of chiefs from the outer islands) have established a formal set of guidelines for visiting the outer islands. The guidelines aren't meant to discourage 'appropriate' visitors, but rather to make the process smoother for everyone and assure that traditional ways are respected.

You should make a request to the Special Assistant for Outer Islands Affairs (☎ 350-2108), Office of the Governor, Colonia, Yap, FM 96943, at least a month before the date you're hoping to visit. The office will then take the request to the chief of the island you want to visit. Upon the chief's approval, the office will issue a pass authorising the visit and stating the length of stay. You can then purchase a ticket from either the field trip ship or PMA. Upon landing the pass needs to be presented to the island chief, along with a visitor fee of $20.

Ulithi Atoll

Ulithi Atoll, 100 miles north-east of Yap, has the most land and the most people of any of the outer islands. Its huge lagoon, which encompasses 209 sq miles, is the world's fourth largest. All in all, there are 49 islands with a total land mass of just 1.79 sq miles.

Ulithi played an important role in WW

II. The Japanese came in numbers that must have seemed enormous to the Ulithians – that is until the USA moved in with temporary population densities that rivalled those of major cities.

The Japanese had established a seaplane and naval base as well as a radio and weather station on Ulithi. When the Americans got close, the Japanese evacuated to Yap Proper taking most of the able-bodied Ulithians along with them.

In September 1944 the Americans landed on Ulithi unopposed. They quickly constructed an airstrip on Falalop Island, a hospital, and a recreation centre on Mogmog Island that eventually entertained as many as 20,000 soldiers a day.

Strategically located, Ulithi served as a major anchorage and supply and repair base for the final six months of the war. Its extensive lagoon held 617 Allied naval vessels prior to the Okinawa invasion.

Somehow folks on Ulithi survived these encounters with uninvited visitors from the 'civilised' world. These days if you want to visit the atoll you have to seek permission.

Ulithi is the most developed of the outer islands. It has the only outer islands high school, public electricity and even a little laundrette built with Australian aid. Concrete houses are more common than thatched houses. Partly because the US military left so much corrugated metal, there are more tin roofs on Ulithi than any of the other islands.

Ulithi's inhabited islands – Falalop, Mogmog, Asor and Fassarai – have a total population of 850. All have nice sandy beaches. The only airstrip is on Falalop and the terminal building has Yap's only outer island post office.

Flights between Yap and Guam often fly over Ulithi Atoll. It's quite an impressive sight from the air, with islands spread so far apart that they scarcely seem related.

Woleai Atoll

For many reasons Woleai makes a nice choice for an outer island visit – it has an appealingly simple lifestyle and friendly people and is serviced by both field trip

Picnic Island, Chuuk Lagoon

Outrigger canoe, Chuuk

Visiting the Japanese war ruins on Eten Isand, Chuuk

Weno Harbor, Chuuk

Balabat men's house, Yap

Village house with golden candles in Colonia, Yap

Yap's second largest piece of stone money

Stone money bank, Malaay Village, Yap

ship and plane. If you were to take the field trip ship from Colonia you could stay about a week and then catch the same boat back on its return leg.

Of the outer atolls, Woleai ranks a close second to Ulithi both in land size and population. About 800 people live on five of Woleai's 22 islets and the atoll has a junior high school. Several of the islands are clustered close together, some separated only by narrow mangrove channels and others joined at low tide by sand bars. Woleai has beautiful sandy beaches and canoes are favoured over motorboats.

Woleai holds onto its traditional ways more firmly than Ulithi does. At a recent community meeting it was decided to strictly enforce rules against wearing T-shirts, pants, baseball caps and other Western clothing. While foreign visitors are exempt, it aids your acceptance if you endeavour to wear traditional clothing – lava-lavas for women, thus for men. There aren't shops on Woleai that sell these items, but you can generally find someone willing to trade canned foods or other things for them.

During WW II the Japanese fortified Woleai, and wrecked ships and planes, old tanks, bunkers, field guns and monuments are all around the islands. Even the airfield used by PMA is a former Japanese fighter airstrip.

The runway and main village are on Falalop Island, the atoll's largest. In the village, at the south end of the runway, there are taro patches behind the school where you can find the remains of Japanese planes, including an intact Zero. From Falalop you can wade across to Paliau Island, where there's a sandy beach with a bunker and WW II guns. If you want to explore other war sights, it's usually possible to arrange for someone to take you by boat elsewhere around the atoll; you could even snorkel a US bomber that sits on the lagoon floor.

The governor's representative sometimes lets visitors sleep the first night in his office near the runway. If you want to camp, this can generally be arranged at a rocky beach on the ocean side of Falalop. If you prefer to stay with a family you may be assigned one of the small huts that rim extended family compounds.

Fais Island

Fais is a single island of raised limestone with just over one sq mile of land. It has a partial fringing reef, sandy beaches, cliffs and sea caves. With an elevation of 60 feet, Fais is the highest of Yap's outer islands and was once known for its agricultural production.

Both the Germans and the Japanese had phosphate mines on Fais that scarred the island. You can find the remains of a Japanese dock hit by US bombers during WW II, parts of a steel observation tower and the base of a shore defence gun. Fais has one village, a population of 250 and a 3000-foot crushed coral airstrip. The women are known for their skilled weaving of lava-lavas, many of which are created during their stays in the village menstrual house.

Satawal Island

Satawal, Yap's easternmost inhabited island, is home to some of the world's most skilled traditional navigators, who still sail vast expanses of ocean in outrigger canoes without charts or compass, relying on their knowledge of star positions, ocean swells and other natural phenomena. It was Satawal master star-path navigator Mau Piailug who was chosen to navigate the double-hulled sailing canoe *Hokulea* on its historic journey between Hawaii and Tahiti in 1976. Using traditional navigational skills preserved in Satawal but long forgotten elsewhere in the Pacific, the trip retraced the ancient routes of the early Polynesian seafarers who settled Hawaii.

Satawal is a single raised island of half a square mile of land. It has a fringing reef and is a difficult island to land on; the *Micro Spirit* cannot anchor close to shore and even its lighters cannot reach the island when the tide is low.

Satawal is rather densely populated, with 470 residents. Most live in the main village, which fronts a large sandy beach. After Typhoon Owen hit in November 1990, only nine of the island's 90 houses were left standing.

Lamotrek Atoll

Lamotrek Atoll is shaped a bit like a deflated triangle, with an island at each of the three points. At the south-east end of the atoll is Lamotrek Island, the largest and only populated island. The interior is swampy, while the lagoon side of the island has a lovely beach that's thickly lined with coconut palms. It takes only about 10 minutes to walk from one side of Lamotrek Island to the other and the total land area for the entire atoll is a mere 0.38 sq miles.

The population is about 300, and despite the surrounding reef and an abundance of land crabs and fruit, severe droughts occasionally cause famine conditions on the island. The Japanese occupied Lamotrek and the remains of WW II planes can still be found.

The 27-minute documentary *Lamotrek: Heritage of an Island* by Eric Metzgar focuses on the traditional skills of the Lamotrek islanders, including dancing, chants and crafts. The film is available on video cassette for $40 plus postage from Canyon Cinema (☎ 415-626-2255), 2325 Third St, Suite 338, San Francisco, CA 94107.

Ifalik Atoll

Ifalik Atoll has long white sandy beaches, lots of coconut palms and a lagoon in a near-perfect circle. The two inhabited islands were one island until a typhoon hit and broke a narrow channel through the middle. With a land area of just over half a sq mile, Ifalik is home to 485 people. The atoll is very traditional. There's a taboo area in the main village where no one may enter and the chief reportedly won't allow motorboats into the lagoon.

Faraulep Atoll

Faraulep Atoll has a small lagoon and five islets totalling just 0.16 sq miles, with most of the 200 residents living on Faraulep and

Pig. A large sand spit has built up on the south side of Faraulep islet and the field trip ship cannot enter the lagoon.

Eauripik Atoll

Eauripik Atoll has 140 people living on a mere 0.09 sq miles of land, giving it the highest population density of any of Yap's outer islands. Every speck of the island is used either for homesites or food crops. Copra is not made as all coconuts are eaten. Houses are built on raised stone platforms and the church is one of only two on the outer islands still of traditional-style construction.

Elato Atoll

Elato Atoll has seven islets, comprising 0.2 sq miles of land, in a lovely lagoon setting with a curving sandy beach. From its shores you can see Lamotrek, 13 miles to the east. There is a relatively large area set aside for copra production, though food is sometimes scarce. Elato has about 70 people.

Sorol & Ngulu Atolls

These two atolls have small land areas and only about 25 people each. Ngulu has a very large lagoon of 148 sq miles, with nesting areas for sea turtles and excellent commercial fishing.

Gaferut, West Fayu, Pikelot & Olimarao

These atolls have no permanent inhabitants and are nesting grounds for turtles and birds.

Places to Stay

None of the outer islands has established accommodation for visitors. Overnight visitors will probably end up staying at a men's house or with a host family. Where you stay and what it will cost will be the chief's decision, and won't necessarily be cheaper than staying on Yap Proper. Plan to bring enough food and supplies for the duration of your stay. Coffee, bread, canned meats or other food items unobtainable on the islands make welcome gifts.

Getting There & Away

A great way to start your journey is by chatting with islanders at the dock or airport counter. Yapese are curious about visitors and it's easy to strike up a conversation once people realise you're headed for their island. Not only will this help you gain insights into the place you're about to visit, but knowing someone generally smooths the way once you arrive.

Air Pacific Missionary Aviation (☎ 350-2360, fax 350-2539), Box 460, Colonia, Yap, FM 96943, flies a nine-passenger plane to Ulithi, Fais and Woleai. Its office is at the west side of the main airport terminal.

Scheduled flights are from Yap to Ulithi on Mondays and Fridays, from Yap to Fais and from Ulithi to Fais on Fridays, and from Yap to Woleai on alternate Wednesdays. When there are enough passengers, PMA sometimes schedules flights on the off-days as well, and flights are also made from Woleai to Ulithi or Fais on demand.

The one-way fare is $60 between Yap and Ulithi, $25 between Ulithi and Fais, $75 between Yap and Fais, $150 between Yap and Woleai, $110 between Woleai and Fais and $130 between Woleai and Ulithi.

Sea The field trip ship *Micro Spirit* runs between Yap Proper and all the populated outer islands. The full trip generally takes about 17 days, though it's not uncommon to be a day or two behind schedule. They go out almost monthly, averaging about 10 trips a year. Although the departure days vary, the boat tries to start each trip by leaving Colonia around 6 pm, arriving at 5 am the next morning in Ulithi.

Deck fares vary with the distance: from Yap Proper to Ulithi or Fais it's $6, to Woleai or Ifalik it's $12 and to Satawal, the most distant island, it's $18. Children aged four to 12 pay half fare, while younger children travel free.

There are also cabins. However, they're made available to travelling government officials first and can only be booked by visitors after it's been assessed that they're not needed by higher authorities. Cabin rates are calculated at 16 cents per mile and cost $17 to Ulithi, $60 to Woleai and $88 to Satawal. There's an additional berthing charge of $3 per night.

Meals can be purchased for $3 at breakfast, $4 at lunch and $4.50 at dinner but the food's pretty basic so you may want to bring your own.

The boat generally docks at each island for four to 12 hours, depending upon how much cargo needs to be loaded and unloaded. If you get a general permit from the governor's office in advance it's possible to disembark and visit the islands while the boat is in port and get back on when it's ready to leave. However, if you want to stay on the island for a few days until the boat returns, you'll need to get advance permission from the island chief (see the Permission to Visit section above).

Get permits from the unmarked Office of Outer Islands Affairs, the small blue and white metal shed at the north-west corner of the government offices complex. Book the boat through the Office of Sea Transportation (☎ 350-2403, fax 350-2267), Box 576, Colonia, Yap, FM 96943, the metal building with the blue roof marked 'SEA' that's at the back side of the complex.

YAP

Republic of Palau

Palau features Micronesia's richest flora and fauna, both on land and underwater. The islands are inhabited by exotic birds, crocodiles live in the mangrove swamps and orchids grow freely in people's yards.

Palau's waters contain an incredible spectrum of coral, fish and other marine life, including giant clams that weigh a quarter ton and many rare sea creatures found in few other places.

The scenic Rock Islands have some of Micronesia's finest snorkelling and diving just off their shores. Beyond them lie the sleepy southern islands of Peleliu and Angaur with their own special appeal to independent travellers.

The native name for the islands is Belau, though the new nation calls itself the Republic of Palau. Of all the political entities to come out of the Trust Territory, Palau is the smallest in terms of population. Koror has the bulk of the nation's 15,500 people and by Micronesian standards it's a busy town.

Palau, whose independence had long stalled over a conflict between its anti-nuclear constitution and the pro-nuclear compact of 'free association' with the USA, emerged as an independent nation in October 1994. In so doing it marked the end of the US-administered Trust Territory of the Pacific and the end of 50 years of direct US colonial rule.

Independence has brought renewed interest in Palau from overseas developers, and three international chains have already unveiled plans to build new hotels. The Hawaii-based Outrigger chain will construct a first-class hotel, while the Hilton and Hyatt corporations are preparing to break ground on luxury resorts – together they will more than double Palau's current inventory of hotel rooms.

Once the hotels open, direct flights from Japan are expected to follow and sleepy Palau, which now hosts only 40,000 visitors a year, will have awakened to surpass the entire FSM in tourism development.

HISTORY
Pre-European Contact

It is generally believed that the first inhabitants of Palau came from eastern Indonesia. Carbon dating of ancient sites of habitation has established that the Rock Islands were settled by at least 1000 BC.

Traditionally the women of Palau tended the taro swamps and the men fished the reef and harvested breadfruit and betel nut. With a fairly vast land area offering an abundance of vegetation, Palauans were not compelled to journey beyond their shores. They spent their leisure time working on projects such as the construction of *bai*, or men's meeting houses, with each village having its own skilled artisans to do the tasks of woodworking and thatching.

The Palauans developed fairly complex social systems. The culture was matriarchal and matrilineal, with property inherited by women, though owned by the clan. The

---

The Creation Myth

According to Palauan legend, in ancient times an island woman gave birth to a son named Uab who grew so quickly and had such an insatiable appetite that it soon became the primary chore of the islanders to keep the boy fed. The more they fed him, the more food he demanded and the larger he grew, until one day he was taller than the coconut trees and had eaten all the food on the island.

The villagers reluctantly decided they must destroy the giant boy in order to survive and one night set fire to the men's meeting house where he slept. Uab's bloated body exploded and parts of it were flung in all directions. Kayangel was created from his head, Babeldaob from his body, Peleliu from his legs, Angaur from his feet and all the little Rock Islands from his fingers and toes. The people then settled the new islands believing that as they had fed Uab, he would now feed them. ■

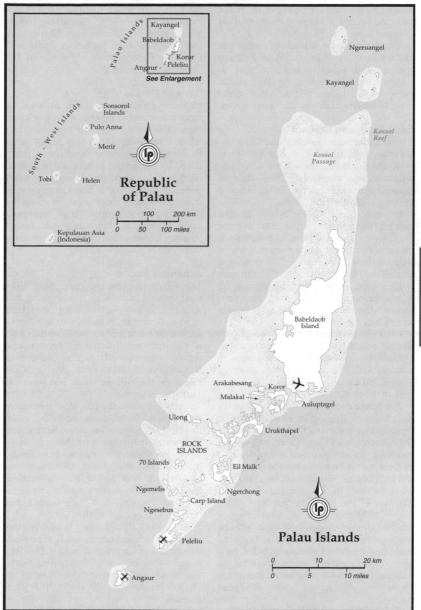

PALAU

women maintained the power of the purse and men needed to obtain their permission to spend money.

The accumulation of land and money has always been very important in Palauan society, with clans ranked according to their wealth. Villages were typically settled by seven to 10 clans and the chief of the highest-ranking clan was the village leader.

Early European Contact
The first European to sight Palau was probably the Spaniard Ruy Lopez de Villalobos in 1543. He named the islands Arrecifos, which means 'the reefs'. Spain claimed authority over Palau in 1686 but did nothing to develop the islands.

It wasn't until 1783, when English captain Henry Wilson wrecked his ship the *Antelope* on a reef off Palau's Ulong Island, that any significant contact began between Palauans and Westerners. The crew was treated well by Chief Ibedul of Koror, who helped them rebuild their ship from the wreckage and then sent his young son, Prince Lebuu (Lee Boo), back with Wilson to England for schooling.

Gifts from the Palauans, which the British called the 'Pelew Curiosities', included a bracelet made from a dugong vertebrate, a dagger made from a stingray stinger and tortoise-shell dishes. These are now in the British Museum.

The prince died of smallpox less than six months after arriving in London and the tragedy touched many Britons and piqued their interest in Palau. There was even a romantic melodrama called *Prince Lee Boo* that played on London stages at the time.

The story of Wilson and his crew was immortalised in the popular book *An Account of the Pelew Islands* by George Keate, published in 1788, which further whetted Britain's appetite for trade between the two nations. Unfortunately, favoured trade items for the Palauans included guns and other weapons, which served to increase hostilities among local tribes and at times were also turned against European traders.

The British were Palau's main trading partners until Spain finally moved in and expelled them in 1885. Spanish missionaries managed to introduce Christianity and a written alphabet before Spain sold Palau to Germany in the wake of the Spanish-American War.

German Period
Unlike the Spanish, the Germans were far more interested in making money in Palau than saving souls. By the time they had taken control in 1899 only about 4000 Palauans had survived the diseases introduced by Western explorers, a drastic drop from the estimated pre-European contact population of 40,000. The Germans took steps to contain contagious diseases by providing inoculations and instituting sanitary controls. They then used forced Palauan labour to start coconut plantations and other business ventures.

Japanese Period
The Japanese occupied Palau from 1914 until the end of WW II. It was during this time that Palauan culture went through its most radical transformation, as the Japanese attempted to replace local customs with a colonial administration. Free public schools were opened, teaching islanders in a subservient dialect of the Japanese language, and village chiefs lost power to Japanese bureaucrats.

Japan expanded the commercial ventures started by the Germans and developed many more. Thousands of Japanese, Korean and Okinawan labourers were brought in to work in phosphate mines, rice fields, pineapple plantations and other businesses that thrived under Japanese administration. Traditional inheritance patterns were shattered as Palauans lost their land, either through sale or confiscation.

After 1922 all of Japan's Pacific possessions were administered from Koror, which the Japanese developed into a bustling modern city complete with paved roads, electricity and piped-in water. Out of its 30,000 residents, only about 20% were Palauan.

In the late 1930s, Japan closed Palau to

Palauan Money

The early Palauans developed an intricate system of money that was used as a mode of exchange and as gift offerings at traditional events. Beads, called *udoud*, were the most common type of Palauan money. The beads were made of clay or glass and were usually yellow or orange in colour.

Common round beads were used for daily transactions, while beads which were oval, faceted or cylindrical were more prestigious and valuable. The beads were not made in Palau and although no one today knows exactly where they came from, it is thought they may have originated in Indonesia or Malaysia.

One legend, however, says they came from a mysterious Yapese island called Kablik. Kablik was said to be so magical that stones thrown from the island toward the sea never touched the water, but returned instead to the thrower.

The beads still have value but are in limited use today, exchanged mainly at times of birth, marriage and death. Strings of udoud are worn as necklaces (called *iek*) by high-ranking women on special occasions and it's common to see Palauan women wearing a single bead on a black cord as an heirloom necklace.

Another kind of traditional Palauan money is *toluk*, made by steaming hawksbill turtle shell and pressing it into a wooden tray-shaped mould. The shell is hardened into the shape of an oval plate; the larger and lighter coloured the toluk, the more value it has. ∎

the outside world and began concentrating its efforts on developing military fortifications throughout the islands.

WW II

During the final stages of WW II, as the Allied offensive moved westward across the Pacific, Japanese installations in Palau became a target for attacks. US aerial bombings of Malakal Island and Airai State in March and July 1944 destroyed numerous Japanese ships and planes, and set fuel tanks and military facilities ablaze. However, the real battles in Palau took place in September of that year on the islands of Peleliu and Angaur.

Before the USA's invasion of those two southern islands, most Palauans were rounded up by the Japanese and sent to central Babeldaob. The reason for the forced relocation is not entirely clear. Some islanders insist that the Japanese had plans to kill the Palauans and even had ditches dug to use as mass graves. Nonetheless, historians tend to credit the Japanese for getting the islanders out of harm's way and undoubtedly the action did save the lives of many Palauans who otherwise would have been caught up in major assault zones.

Despite the fierce fighting that took place on Peleliu and Angaur, the more heavily populated Koror and Babeldaob were never invaded and the 25,000 Japanese soldiers stationed on those islands remained there until the war's end.

Modern Palau

When the USA began to administer Palau after the war, it had hoped – in the grand design of expediency – to spin off Palau with the rest of Micronesia into a single political entity.

Palauans, however, voted in July 1978 against becoming part of the Federated States of Micronesia, opting instead to seek a separate political identity. In July 1980 Palauans adopted their own constitution; their first president, Haruo Remeliik, took office in January 1981.

Koror was named the provisional capital, though Palau's constitution requires that the capital eventually be moved to Melekeok State in Babeldaob.

Palau's struggle to emerge as a new nation has been a troubled one. President Remeliik was assassinated in June 1985. Although the son of his most powerful political opponent was convicted of the murder, he was later acquitted and the case still remains unsolved.

In August 1988 Remeliik's successor, Lazarus Salii, was found shot to death, an apparent suicide. His administration had been marred with accusations of bribery and corruption and the president himself was under investigation at the time for accepting huge payoffs involving a scandal-ridden power plant deal.

PALAU

Palau's next president, Ngiratkel Etpison, took office in January 1989. A successful businessman and part-owner of the Palau Pacific Resort, Etpison became the first Palauan president to serve out his term.

Etpison was followed by Kuniwo Nakamura, who took office in January 1993. The current president of the Republic of Palau, Nakamura presided over the final transition of Palau from a US-administered Trust Territory to an independent nation.

Nuclear Issues & the Constitution

In 1979, Palauans wrote into their constitution a provision which declared Palau nuclear-free. This nuclear ban, while hailed by environmentalists throughout the Pacific, was unacceptable to the US government, which saw Palau as part of a 'defensive arc', along with Guam and Tinian, to potentially be used in the event that the USA lost its bases in the Philippines.

Disregarding the Palauan constitution's anti-nuclear provision, the USA went ahead and drew up a Compact of Free Association that not only allowed it to bring nuclear weapons into Palau, but also gave the USA the right of eminent domain over virtually all Palauan territory. In exchange, the USA offered Palau millions of dollars in aid.

In eight heated referendums in as many years, a majority of the Palauan electorate voted in favour of the compact, but each time came up short of the 75% majority approval required to override the anti-nuclear provision in the constitution.

In response the pro-compact government finally amended the constitution itself, allowing the compact to be ratified with a simple majority vote. In effect, the government suspended the constitution's non-nuclear provisions for the 50-year duration of the compact.

In November 1993, under the amended constitution, Palauans voted 5193 to 2415 in favour of the compact, a 68% majority. Many of those that voted for the compact

argued that the end of the Cold War made it unlikely that the USA would build future military installations on Palau; they also worried that budget cutters in the US Congress would soon slice into the proposed compact funding if they didn't close a deal. In September 1994 the amendment vote cleared a review by the Palau Supreme Court.

On 1 October 1994 Palau officially became an independent nation, ending 47 years as a Trust Territory. In December of the same year it was admitted to the United Nations as its 185th member.

In its final version the compact was modified to limit US military access to 'just' a third of Palauan territory. In return for the USA's sweeping military rights in Palau, Palauans negotiated a hefty $450 million financial package for the first 15 years of the 50-year compact.

GEOGRAPHY

Palau, which is part of the western Caroline Islands, is the westernmost part of Micronesia, lying 470 miles east of the Philippines.

The tightly clustered Palau archipelago consists of the high islands of Babeldaob, Koror, Peleliu and Angaur; the low coral atolls of Kayangel and Ngeruangel; and the limestone Rock Islands, of which there are more than 200. The islands run roughly from north to south, covering about 125 miles. Except for Kayangel and uninhabited Ngeruangel in the north and Angaur in the south, all islands in the Palau group are inside a single barrier reef.

The nation's boundaries also encompass six other small, isolated islands: Sonsorol, Fana, Pulo Anna, Merir, Tobi and Helen. Known as the South-West Islands, they extend 370 miles south-west from the main Palau Islands, reaching almost as far as Indonesia.

The thickly jungled Babeldaob, the largest island in Micronesia after Guam, is 27 miles long and has a land area of 153 sq miles. All the other Palauan islands together total just 37 sq miles.

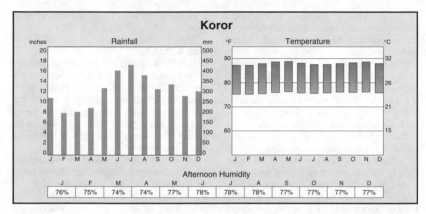

Koror

CLIMATE

In Koror, the average daily high is 87°F (30°C) and the average daily low is 75°F (24°C). Humidity averages 80% and the annual rainfall is 147 inches.

February and March are the driest months, averaging about eight inches of rainfall each, and June to August is the wettest period, averaging about 15 inches monthly. June is a month for thunderstorms, which have been known to drop as much as an inch of rain in 15 minutes. Although Palau lies outside the main typhoon tracks, it does occasionally get hit.

GOVERNMENT

The Republic of Palau has a democratic form of government headed by an elected president.

Palau's national congress, a 30-seat bicameral legislature, is called *Olbiil Era Kelulau*, which means 'meeting place of whispers'. The House of Delegates has 16 members, one from each state. The Senate, whose representation is based on district populations, has 14 members. Both branches of congress, as well as the president, are elected for four-year terms.

There's also a Council of Chiefs, composed of one traditional chief from each state, which advises the national government on legislation affecting Palauan customs.

The USA did a good job of introducing its style of government. Palau has a political framework similar to both the US federal and state governments – except that its population is not 250 million but a mere 15,500. Some of Palau's 16 states have fewer than 100 people, yet each has a governor, a legislature and a state office. It would be hard to find another nation where so few are governed by so many.

ECONOMY

Despite its greater political independence, Palau's economy remains heavily dependent upon US aid.

Under the terms of the new compact with the USA, Palau will receive $450 million in US funding over the next 15 years. In an effort to develop Palau's infrastructure and start up new enterprises, the funding is most substantial in the early years of the compact and narrows down at the end. Portions will be earmarked for development needs, ongoing government operations and long-term trust investments intended to continue providing income after US aid tapers off.

As one of the compact conditions, Palau was mandated to draw up an Economic Plan, charting how grant expenditures would be used to make the economy self-reliant – an effort to avoid the waste and haphazard spending that marked the final years of the US administration.

Palau's per capita GDP of $5750 is one

of Micronesia's highest. Government employment still remains the largest sector of the economy, while tourism is the fastest growing sector.

The number of tourist arrivals has tripled in the past decade and is expected to increase twofold in the next few years. Of the nearly 40,000 visitors who came to Palau in 1994, around 50% were Japanese, 20% American and 10% Taiwanese.

Two schemes to develop the economy, which have had dubious benefits on other islands, are now being looked at on Palau. One is the expansion of fishing by foreign long-line fleets in Palau's waters and the other is the development of garment industries to be operated by imported labourers.

POPULATION & PEOPLE

Palau's population is approximately 15,500. There are an additional 2500 foreigners living in Palau, the majority of them Filipino labourers.

Palauans place an emphasis on education and a large percentage of high school graduates continue their studies, often at overseas colleges and universities. They hold few qualms about travelling in search of economic opportunities and throughout Micronesia you'll find a scattering of Palauans who have gone farther afield.

SOCIETY & CONDUCT

On the surface, the people of Palau appear to be among the most Westernised of all Micronesians and for the casual visitor it's often challenging to find evidence of the indigenous culture.

However, Palauans still retain many traditional ways. Family and kinship ties are strong; traditional ceremonies, such as those for a first-born child, are commonly held in the home; age-old competition continues between clans; and chiefs still command an important role in the social hierarchy.

Although not as widespread as in Yap, many Palauans chew betel nut. The betel nut chewers, noted by their red teeth, tend to spit a lot, as the betel nut induces salivation and the juices are not swallowed.

Basketball and baseball are popular sports.

Dos & Don'ts

Palauans wear Western clothing and are quite casual in their dress, but scant clothing and short shorts are frowned upon, especially in villages outside Koror. Shoes are removed when entering a private home, and even a few public buildings, such as the library, have signs asking you to leave your shoes by the door.

In some areas of Palau there are prohibitions on fishing and camping; always check in advance with the governor's office or the village chief before doing either. The collection of live coral and seashells is prohibited everywhere.

RELIGION

Most Palauans are Christian, with both the Catholic and Protestant churches well established. Seventh Day Adventists have a strong following in Palau, while Jehovah's Witnesses and Bahai also have a presence.

Modekngei is a revived form of Palau's indigenous religion. Many Palauans still hold some form of traditional beliefs, based on nature spirits, clan-ancestral worship and village deities. Some Palauan homes leave a light on through the night to ward off unwanted ghosts.

LANGUAGE

Palauan is spoken at home and in casual situations, while English is more commonly spoken in business and government. Schools teach in both languages, so most Palauans are bilingual from an early age.

The South-West Islanders speak Sonsorolese and Tobian languages, which are more closely related to Yapese or Chuukese dialects than to Palauan.

In Palauan, 'hello' is *alii* and 'thanks' is *sulang*.

Many Palauan words begin with 'ng', which is a nasal sound, pronounced like the ending of the word 'bring'. The 'ch' spelling is pronounced 'uh'.

Islanders borrow the Hawaiian term *haole* to refer to Caucasian foreigners.

HOLIDAYS & FESTIVALS
Palau celebrates the following public holidays:

New Year's Day
   1 January
Youth Day
   15 March
Senior Citizens Day
   5 May
President's Day
   1 June
Constitution Day
   9 July
Labor Day
   1st Monday in September
Independence Day
   1 October
Thanksgiving
   4th Thursday in November
Christmas
   25 December

Youth Day features concerts and sporting events, while Senior Citizens Day features a parade with floats, handicraft exhibits and a dance competition. The Belau Arts Festival, which is held on Constitution Day, includes craft exhibits, dances and cooking contests. Some states celebrate a 'state constitution day', while Peleliu and Angaur have a 'WW II memorial day' coinciding with the day US forces landed on each island.

Koror

Koror, the economic centre and capital of Palau, is home to two-thirds of the republic's population. Many of the 10,500 people who live in Koror have been drawn from outlying villages by employment opportunities.

In prewar days Koror, with three times its current population, was jammed not only with homes, restaurants, office buildings and military facilities, but also with geisha houses, Shinto shrines, kimono tailors and public baths.

It's a more nondescript and less crowded Koror one sees today, with a pace more typically Micronesian and no particular penchant for hustle and bustle.

Despite Koror's modern overlay, if you look closely you'll often find remnants of a more traditional past sitting alongside its newer structures. One interesting juxtaposition is at the Koror State Office, which is fronted by an ancient platform with stone backrests in each corner where traditional leaders once sat in meeting.

The greater Koror area is good for maybe a day of exploration, but after that it's best used as a base for trips to the Rock Islands, Peleliu, Angaur and other islands.

Visitors should be aware that Koror has a curfew from midnight to dawn, largely an effort to control late-night rowdiness among heavy drinkers.

ORIENTATION
Koror State consists of the inhabited islands of Koror, Malakal and Arakabesang, all of which are connected by causeways. The island of Koror is also connected to the neighbouring island of Babeldaob via the impressive K-B Bridge. The airport is in Airai State, at the southern end of Babeldaob, a 15-minute drive from central Koror. The east side of Koror, between the town centre and the K-B Bridge, is called Topside.

INFORMATION
Tourist Office
The Palau Visitors Authority (☎ 488-2793, fax 488-1453) has its office at the west side of town and is open from 8 am to 4.30 pm Monday to Friday. The staff has a few handouts on tours, dives, hotels and the like and can answer general questions.

Money
The Bank of Hawaii and the Bank of Guam, both on the main road in central Koror, are open from 9.30 am to 2.30 pm Monday to Thursday, to 5 pm on Fridays. Credit cards are accepted at many hotels, car rental agencies, dive shops and larger restaurants.

PALAU

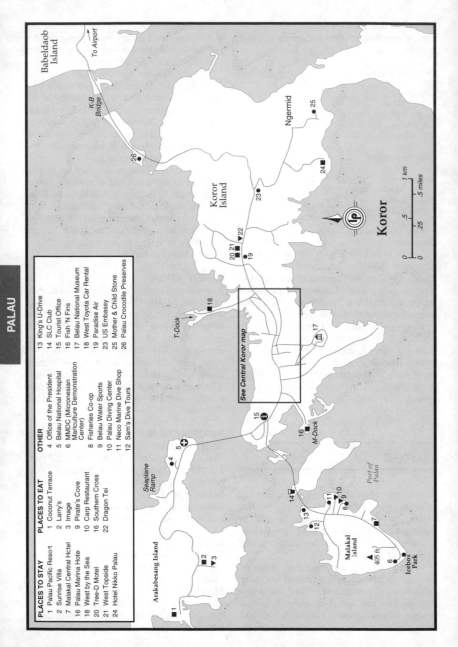

PLACES TO STAY
1   Palau Pacific Resort
2   Sunrise Villa
7   Malakal Central Hotel
16 Palau Marina Hotel
18 West by the Sea
20 Tree-D Motel
21 West Topside
24 Hotel Nikko Palau

PLACES TO EAT
1   Coconut Terrace
2   Larry's
9   Image
10 Carp Restaurant
16 Southern Cross
22 Dragon Tei

OTHER
4   Office of the President
5   Belau National Hospital
6   MMDC (Micronesian
    Mariculture Demonstration
    Center)
8   Fisheries Co-op
9   Belau Water Sports
10 Palau Diving Center
11 Neco Marine Dive Shop
12 Sam's Dive Tours

13 King's U-Drive
14 SLC Club
15 Tourist Office
16 Fish 'N Fins
17 Belau National Museum
18 West Toyota Car Rental
19 Paradise Air
23 US Embassy
25 Mother & Child Stone
26 Palau Crocodile Preserves

Post

Palau's only post office is in central Koror, open from 8 am to 4 pm Monday to Friday. Palau issues attractive postage stamps of tropical fish, flowers and shells as well as commemorative stamps of historic events.

Telecommunications

Most hotels and guesthouses have phones that can be used to make local calls free of charge. There are pay phones (25 cents for local calls) at some stores and larger restaurants.

International phone calls can be made 24 hours a day from the Palau National Communications Corporation (PNCC) office in the centre of Koror. Per-minute rates to other Micronesian islands and the USA are $3 from 7 am to 6 pm weekdays, $2 from 11 pm to 4 am and $2.50 at other times. Calls to most other destinations are about $4 a minute, though they also drop to $2 a minute between 11 pm and 4 am. There's a three-minute minimum charge on all calls.

Faxes can be received at the PNCC office (☎ 488-1725) free of charge and can be sent from the PNCC office for the same price as a phone call.

For directory assistance, dial 411. To reach an international operator, dial 0. You can make interstate calls, such as to Angaur and Peleliu, by calling 488-2435; the cost is 25 cents per minute.

Foreign Embassies

At present the only foreign embassy in Palau is the US Embassy (☎ 488-2920) in Topside, which issues US visas on Tuesday and Thursday mornings.

Immigration

The immigration office (☎ 488-2498) is on the 2nd floor of the courthouse, next to the library. It's open from 7.30 to 11.30 am and 12.30 to 4.30 pm Monday to Friday. For information on visas and visa extensions, see Visas & Documents in the Facts for the Visitor chapter in the front of the book.

Laundry

There's a self-service coin laundry on Lebuu St, another next to West Topside hotel and a couple of machines at the side of D W Motel.

Library

The public library has a section of books about the Pacific and is open from 7.30 to 11.30 am and 12.30 to 4.30 pm Monday to Friday.

Maps

Maps of the Palau Islands, Peleliu and the Rock Islands (1:25,000 scale), and some nautical charts, can be purchased for $10 each from Blue Line (☎ 488-2679), a business centre just south of the SLC Club on the road to Malakal.

Media

Koror has one private TV station and eight-channel cable TV, including Cable News Network (CNN) which broadcasts live 24 hours a day on Channel 11. Other channels are given over to pre-recorded US network TV, including California news broadcasts that are typically a week or two old.

The government radio station, WSZB, is on the air at 1584 AM from 6.30 am to midnight and broadcasts Voice of America and other overseas newscasts several times a day.

Guam's *Pacific Daily News* is flown to Palau daily, while the local paper *Tia Belau* comes out biweekly. Both are sold at the WCTC Shopping Center and other large stores.

Film & Photography

The best place to have slides developed is the photo lab at Palau Pacific Resort. One-hour print service and Kodak slide and print film are available at Palau in Prints, opposite Desekel Market.

Medical Services

Dr Yano's clinic, Belau Medical Clinic (☎ 488-2688) in Koror centre, is recommended for non-emergency medical attention. It's open from 9 am to 5 pm on

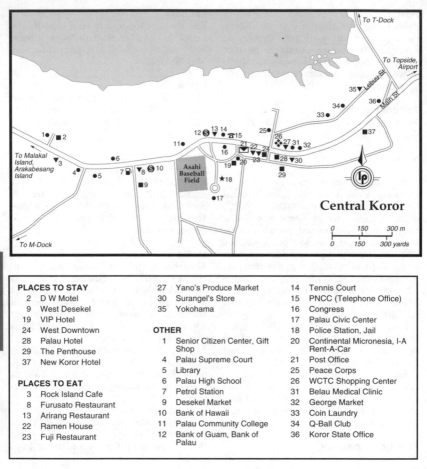

Central Koror

PLACES TO STAY		27	Yano's Produce Market		14	Tennis Court
2	D W Motel	30	Surangel's Store		15	PNCC (Telephone Office)
9	West Desekel	35	Yokohama		16	Congress
19	VIP Hotel				17	Palau Civic Center
24	West Downtown	**OTHER**			18	Police Station, Jail
28	Palau Hotel	1	Senior Citizen Center, Gift		20	Continental Micronesia, I-A
29	The Penthouse		Shop			Rent-A-Car
37	New Koror Hotel	4	Palau Supreme Court		21	Post Office
		5	Library		25	Peace Corps
PLACES TO EAT		6	Palau High School		26	WCTC Shopping Center
3	Rock Island Cafe	7	Petrol Station		31	Belau Medical Clinic
8	Furusato Restaurant	9	Desekel Market		32	George Market
13	Arirang Restaurant	10	Bank of Hawaii		33	Coin Laundry
22	Ramen House	11	Palau Community College		34	Q-Ball Club
23	Fuji Restaurant	12	Bank of Guam, Bank of		36	Koror State Office
			Palau			

Mondays, Tuesdays, Thursdays and Fridays and from 9 am to noon on Wednesdays and Saturdays. An office visit costs $11, plus charges for any additional tests or services.

The new government hospital (☎ 488-2558) is on Arakabesang Island, just over the causeway from Koror. Although there are sometimes long waits, the facilities are modern and it has a much better reputation than the old hospital had. There's a decompression chamber for divers who get the bends.

Emergency

The police emergency number is 911; the non-emergency number is 488-1422. For an ambulance or the fire department dial 488-1411.

ACTIVITIES
Snorkelling

The beach fronting the Palau Pacific Resort has some of Koror's best snorkelling. The water is calm, shallow and clear. Snorkellers will find colourful tropical fish, platter and mushroom corals, and giant tridacna clams with iridescent mantles. Breakfast in the open-air restaurant followed by a morning of snorkelling from the beach isn't a bad way to kick off the day. However, the resort officially charges non-guests a $15 fee to use the beach.

Snorkelling is also good off Icebox Park and the MMDC grounds on Malakal Island. There's no beach, but rather concrete retaining walls with steps leading into the clear water. The near-shore waters are deeper, dropping at the wall to 10 to 15 feet, and the fish are larger than at the resort. From Icebox Park, the best snorkelling is to the right toward MMDC where there are fairly calm waters and a beginners' reef for those comfortable with overhead depths. Expect to find clownfish hiding in anemone shelters as well as crown of thorns starfish. In front of MMDC, there are giant clams lined up in underwater cages just offshore. Watch out for the spiny urchins that cling to the sides of the wall, and also for motorboats that sometimes cut the corners sharper than they should.

If you're stuck in town, snorkelling is OK in the shallow water between the long breakwater and the Malakal bridge, half a mile from the tourist office. There are tiny tropical fish and some low thickets of coral.

On the other hand no one really comes to Palau to snorkel in Koror. The real action is in and around the Rock Islands – and it's worth whatever it takes to get yourself out there!

Information on diving in Palau, and on dive shops based in Koror, is in the Rock Islands section. Snorkel gear can be purchased at a few shops around town; a good place to start is Neco Marine on Malakal Island, where you can buy a good mask for $40, something cheaper for half that. Dive shops that rent snorkel gear include Palau Diving Center, Sam's Dive Tours and Splash; all charge around $10 a day.

Tennis
There's a tennis court next to Arirang Restaurant, with court lights available from 6 to 11 pm. The court can be reserved by paying $3 at the Bank of Palau, which is in the same complex as the restaurant.

Running
The local Hash House Harriers run every other Saturday (on payday weeks), meeting at the post office. For schedules, check the local paper or enquire at expat hangouts such as Rock Island Cafe.

Kayaking
The Rock Islands are ideal for ocean kayaking, a sport that is poised to take off soon in Koror. Some dive shops and tour companies are planning to stock rental kayaks; check with the tourist office for the latest.

KOROR ISLAND
Belau National Museum
A good starting place for understanding Palauan history and culture is the Belau National Museum. The sights begin at the door, which is intricately carved like a storyboard. Upon entering you'll be greeted by the mounted head of a 15-foot crocodile, the largest found in Palau since WW II. The museum has displays of bead and tortoise shell money, as well as local artefacts and crafts. The building that houses the museum once served as a Japanese weather station; the modern weather station is now next door.

To get there, turn south off Main St onto the side street west of the baseball field, curve to the left past the old hospital and then take the right-hand fork and continue on that road to its end; the museum is half a mile from Main St. It's open from 8 to 11 am and 1 to 4 pm Monday to Friday, and from 10 am to 2 pm on Saturdays. Admission is $2.

On the grounds of the museum is a beautiful wood-and-thatch bai, intricately carved and painted with depictions of Palauan legends, including one of Uab, whose body created the Palauan islands. Although this is a re-creation of an older bai that burned down in 1979, it's built in a traditional manner, constructed of rough

Above: Storyboard doors, Belau National
Museum
Below: Bai detail, Belau National Museum

planks with notched jointing and set off the ground on stone stacks – a splendid example of the old style of architecture.

The grounds also have a little lily pond, a few anti-aircraft guns and other Japanese-era artefacts, a small war memorial to Palauans who died during WW II and a bronze bust of Haruo Remeliik, Palau's first president, who was assassinated in June 1985.

There is no admission cost to visit the bai or stroll the museum grounds.

Next to the museum is a research library, with a good collection of books on Palau and Micronesia, which museum officials will open upon request.

Eastern Koror Sights

For a superb view of the Rock Islands head in the direction of the airport and when you get out of central Koror take the paved road to the right that winds down to the **Hotel Nikko**. The view from the hotel is worth catching at any time of day, but it's particularly nice at sunrise.

Follow the stairs up past the swimming pool to the top of the hill to see two anti-aircraft guns and get a sweeping view.

Near the beginning of the hotel driveway there's a rebuilt Japanese **Shinto shrine** that dates to prewar times.

You can continue on the road half a mile past the hotel into Ngermid, which despite its rather modern appearance is one of Koror's most traditional villages, having been settled by the same families for generations. The only 'sight' per se is the **Mother & Child stone**, which is said to be the Lot-like remains of a mother and child who were turned to stone after the mother took a forbidden peek inside the village men's house. Look for the small 'Mother & Child' sign on the left side of the road and follow the footpath. Within a minute or so you'll reach a corrugated tin house where you are expected to pay the landowner $2 to see the site.

If you want to see what native Palauan crocodiles look like, the **Palau Crocodile Preserves**, on a causeway island between Koror and Airai, has pens with three dozen crocs. It also has a few Angaur monkeys. Admission is $3 for adults, $2 for children, plus $5 for use of a camera or $10 for a video camera. It's open from 8 am to 4 pm Monday to Saturday.

MALAKAL ISLAND

Malakal Island, across a causeway from Koror, has the Fisheries Co-op, the deep-water commercial port, small boat docks and other marine businesses.

At the southern tip of the island is Icebox Park, so named because it was the site of an ice-making plant during the Japanese era. It's now a grassy public park and although there's no sandy beach there is access to the clear waters for swimming and snorkelling (see the Snorkelling section earlier).

Micronesia Mariculture Demonstration Center

The MMDC, at the end of the road on Malakal Island, is a research marine laboratory engaged in conservation and com-mercial projects. They have received international recognition for their success in cultivating the threatened giant tridacna clam.

The MMDC raises millions of seed clams to be planted in reefs around Palau and other islands in Micronesia, especially in places that can be guarded against illegal harvesting, and trains islanders in sea farming technology. After a few years, the clams have edible meat and these farm-raised 'baby giant clams' have now found their way onto menus around Micronesia, commonly as sashimi.

You can wander around the MMDC complex and peer into long shallow tanks of giant clams and view other tanks containing various species of sea turtles. There's a visitor centre that has a handful of small but nicely maintained saltwater fish tanks; the centre also sells a few souvenir items including shells, posters, postcards and T-shirts. MMDC is open to visitors from 8 to 11.30 am and 1 to 4 pm

---

Giant Clams

Micronesia's giant tridacna clams *(tridagna gigas)* regularly grow more than four feet in length and can weigh more than 500 pounds, making them the largest bivalve mollusc in the world. Their fleshy mantles have intriguingly mottled designs of browns, greens and iridescent blues. The largest of these creatures live more than a hundred years.

Unfortunately, the giant clams are listed as a threatened species under the Convention on International Trade in Endangered Species (CITES).

Palauans have long eaten the meat of the clams, sold the huge shells to tourists and ground up the smaller shells for lime powder to chew with betel nut. But it is not these particular practices that threaten the clams.

Rather it is outside poachers, mainly from Taiwan, who are wiping out the tridacna on coral reefs around the Pacific, overharvesting to a point where few are left for breeding. It's believed that tens of millions of adult clams have illegally been taken in the past two decades. The poachers often take only the profitable adductor muscle of the clam, which is prized as a delicacy and aphrodisiac in the Orient, while the rest of the clam is left to rot.

Giant clams would be largely unknown in the West, if not for their notoriety at the hands of science fiction writers, who like to portray them swallowing up unsuspecting swimmers. However, the probability of a giant clam clamping onto your leg while you're out diving is nil, as adult clams are generally slow to close and the mammoth ones cannot completely withdraw their mantles into the shells. ■

on weekdays. There's a $2 admission fee, with the proceeds earmarked for expansion of the visitor facilities.

Scientists or students interested in doing research at the centre may write for information to MMDC, Box 359, Koror, Palau 96940.

Malakal Hill

You can get an excellent view of the nearby Rock Islands by going halfway up Malakal Hill, where the road ends at a water tank. After leaving Icebox Park, take the dirt road to the left just past the green sewage plant. The road is steep and narrow, with sharp drops on both sides, but should be passable in a sedan. It also only takes about 10 minutes to walk up.

It's possible to continue hiking to the top of the 405-foot hill for even better views. It takes about 15 minutes of hard climbing from the water tank, though there really isn't much of a path and you may need a guide to show you the way.

ARAKABESANG ISLAND

Once a Japanese military base, Arakabesang Island is now a 'suburb' of Koror. On the south side of the island there's a village settled by people from Palau's South-West Islands, complete with traditional outrigger canoes.

After crossing over the causeway from Koror, the first road to the right past the PNCC satellite station leads to the Office of the President and other national government offices. If you're interested in WW II sites, make note of the concrete pillars flanking the entrance to this road, because the next road to the right with similar pillars is the turn-off to one of the Japanese-era seaplane ramps. Simply follow the road to the water. There's another seaplane ramp on the beach at Palau Pacific Resort on the west side of the island.

PLACES TO STAY

All of the top-end hotels are outside the town centre; consequently if you stay in one of them you'll need to take a taxi or rent a car if you want to go elsewhere for a meal or sightseeing. On the other hand, the low and middle-end places to stay are all in Koror, some near the centre, others on the outskirts of town.

Koror hotels can get booked out from around Christmas to mid-January and during the Japanese Obon holidays from late July through August. All hotels and guesthouses add on a 10% room tax.

Bottom End

The *D W Motel* (☎ 488-2641), Box 738, Koror, Palau 96940, has 17 simple rooms that are a bit tired but have refrigerators, air-con and private bathrooms. Avoid the room across from the lounge which has sheer curtains that offer little privacy and let the hall lights shine through all night long. There's free coffee and tea in the guest lounge. Complimentary transport is provided to and from the airport; after you clear customs ask for Wilfred Williams, the manager's son, who meets nearly every flight. Rates are a tad pricey at $35/45 for singles/doubles.

The new *Tree-D Motel* (☎ 488-3856), Box 1703, Koror, Palau 96940, in the Topside area, is a friendly family-run hostelry. The rooms are small and simple but clean, each with one double bed, a refrigerator, ceiling fan, air-con and private bathroom. Guests can use the office phone and free airport transfer is provided with advance notice. The rate is $35 for singles or doubles; credit cards are not accepted.

The centrally located *New Koror Hotel* (☎ 488-1159, fax 488-1582), Box 339, Koror, Palau 96940, has 26 very basic but adequate rooms with refrigerators, air-con and private bathrooms. Rates are $28/33 for singles/doubles. Airport transfers by taxi can be arranged for an additional $9.

The four-storey *Palau Hotel* (☎ 488-1703), Box 64, Koror, Palau 96940, in the centre of the business district, has 35 lacklustre rooms with air-con, refrigerators, telephones and private bathrooms. Singles/doubles cost $35/40.

Middle

The West Plaza Hotel group has four separate locations, all of which can be booked by writing to Box 280, Koror, Palau 96940, or by faxing 488-2136. All rooms have telephones with free local calls, and all West hotels provide complimentary airport transfers.

West by the Sea (☎ 488-2133) is a 34-room seaside hotel near T-Dock. It's a fairly good value if you request one of the rooms facing the lagoon, which have kitchenettes and balcony sitting areas – they're usually available for the same price ($60 single or double) as the more basic roadside rooms. The rooms are straightforward but comfortable enough with cable TV, air-con, a couple of chairs, a desk and either two single beds or one double. There's a Chinese restaurant and a Toyota Car Rental office on site.

More conveniently located is *West Desekel* (☎ 488-2521), which consists of 15 rooms above the Desekel Market grocery store. The hotel is the newest in the chain and consequently the rooms are the spiffiest and the most recommendable. Each has TV, air-con, a refrigerator, microwave and two twin beds. The rate is $50 for singles or doubles; there are also a couple of larger suites with kitchenettes for $80.

West Downtown (☎ 488-1781) is a 22-room hotel in the centre of town with adequate rooms at moderate prices. The rooms have two beds, a TV and a refrigerator. Rates are $55 for a standard room, $65 for a larger room with a partial kitchenette.

West Topside (☎ 488-2529), on the east side of town in the midst of a residential area, is a small, lacklustre apartment complex with a few units that are rented out by the week for $185 to $225.

The three-storey *Palau Marina Hotel* (☎ 488-1786, fax 488-1070), Box 142, Koror, Palau 96940, is on the water at M-Dock. The 27 rooms are standard but suitable with balconies, TVs, desks, refrigerators and phones. It's managed by Fish 'N Fins and geared for divers, who can practically step out of their rooms and into the dive boat. Rates are $65/80 for singles/doubles.

The Penthouse (☎ 488-1941, fax 488-1442), Box 6013, Koror, Palau 96940, is a quiet, centrally located 14-room hotel off the main road behind the Palau Hotel. The rooms are comfortable with modern amenities including TVs, VCRs, bathtubs, air-con, refrigerators and phones. A single room has two single beds and costs $79 for one or two people. Larger deluxe rooms with balconies cost $95.

VIP Hotel (☎ 488-1502, fax 488-1429), Box 18, Koror, Palau 96940, is a pleasant 22-room, owner-run hotel above the Continental Micronesia office in Koror. The rooms are spotlessly clean and the helpful owner, Rose Ngirarsaol, has created a personable guesthouse-like atmosphere. Free coffee and tea are available on each floor and there's a little reading lounge. There are no room phones but there's a guest telephone in the hall. Rooms are large, each with a single and a double bed, table and chairs, balcony, air-con, ceiling fan, TV and refrigerator. Singles/doubles cost $65/75; no credit cards are accepted.

The *Malakal Central Hotel* (☎ 488-1117, fax 488-1075), Box 6016, Koror, Palau 96940, by the dock on Malakal Island, has 18 rooms above a bar and restaurant. Each has a small oceanview balcony, air-con, TV and VCR, but though the rooms are only a few years old they're ageing fast. With rates of $140 during Japanese vacation times and $100 during the rest of the year, plus 5% service charge, they're overpriced.

Top End

In addition to the places listed below, a new 135-room *Outrigger Hotel* in central Koror and a 260-room *Hilton Hotel* on the road to the Hotel Nikko are both tentatively scheduled to open in 1997. The proposed *Hyatt Hotel*, which has yet to announce an opening date, will be built on Arakabesang Island, near the Palau Pacific Resort.

Airai View Hotel (☎ 587-3530, fax 587-3533), Box 37, Koror, Palau 96940, is a new hotel with an old-fashioned character. It has rich mahogany wood floors, a grand lobby decorated with the island's largest storyboard and a balcony restaurant and piano bar. The standard rooms ($80) are suitably straightforward with two double beds, air-con and a refrigerator, while the deluxe rooms ($120) have huge balconies looking across the jungle toward the ocean. There's a large pool. Located a few minutes' drive from the airport, the 87-room hotel is targeting Taiwanese tourists arriving on Continental Micronesia's new flights from Taipei.

The *Sunrise Villa* (☎ 488-4590, fax 488-4593), Box 6009, Koror, Palau 96940, on Arakabesang Island, has 21 poshly comfortable rooms and a friendly staff. All rooms have fine hilltop views of the lagoon, as well as carpeting, TVs, refrigerators and phones. Double rooms are huge with two queen beds. The single rooms, which are smaller but also good sized, are on the top floor and so sport the best views. Both cost $105. The executive suite costs $120 and has a main room with a king bed and a full kitchen and a separate second bedroom with a single bed. The presidential suite, at $180, may be the nicest room on Palau, with corner windows offering 180° views, a jacuzzi, VCR and a second bedroom. The hotel has a good moderately priced restaurant and a pool.

The *Hotel Nikko Palau* (☎ 488-2486, fax 488-2878), Box 310, Koror, Palau 96940, which is affiliated with Japan Air Lines, was once Palau's premier hotel. When the beachside Palau Pacific Resort opened a decade ago, that hotel became the darling of up-market tourists and the Nikko slipped into decline. Despite an air of neglect, the Nikko still has a gorgeous hillside setting overlooking Palau's northernmost Rock Islands. The 51 rooms are conventional and a bit worn, but adequate. They have central air-con, two double beds, a refrigerator and phone but no TV. Most rooms cost $110, but if you're spending this much it's well worth the extra $20 to stay in A-block, whose rooms have verandas with fantastic Rock Island views. The hotel has a swimming pool, bar and restaurant.

The *Palau Pacific Resort* (☎ 488-2600, fax 488-1601), Box 308, Koror, Palau 96940, on Arakabesang Island, is one of Micronesia's finest resort hotels. It's the only hotel in Palau located on a beach, a protected strand that's the finest in Koror. The 160 rooms have rattan furniture, block prints, tile floors, ceiling fans, air-con, private lanais and a queen or two twin beds. Room rates range from $215 for a garden view to $285 for an ocean view, while suites cost from $385 to $575. There's a beachside swimming pool, tennis courts, a fitness centre and a dive shop. Local events such as islander dance competitions and the presidential inaugural ball also take place at the Palau Pacific. Reservations can also be made through Pan Pacific Hotels (☎ 800-538-4040 in North America, 008-252-900 in Australia, 0120-001800 in Japan).

PLACES TO EAT

Seafood, especially fish, crabs and shellfish, is an important part of the Palauan diet. Crocodile, giant clam, pigeon and fruit bat are some of the more unusual local delicacies, though these are unlikely to appear on many restaurant menus. Most places in Koror serve both Japanese and Western dishes.

In Koror, be wary of drinking tap water as water and sewage lines lay side by side and when the water's turned off for rationing, cross-seepage can occur. Ice and water are OK in most restaurants. You can buy bottled water in grocery stores.

Budget

Yano's Produce Market, immediately east of the WCTC Shopping Center, is a great place to buy local produce and freshly cooked Palauan-style food. You could easily put together a meal from the fried fish, teriyaki squid, papaya bread, fried bananas and coconut candy, which are either pre-wrapped or sold by the piece from containers. Wash it all down with a cold drinking coconut (70 cents), which they'll chop open at the counter. Yano's market is open from 7 am to 8.30 pm Monday to Saturday.

The *WCTC Shopping Center* has a modern supermarket with reasonable grocery prices and fresh products. The nearby *Surangel's Store* can have cheaper prices on some items, but you'll need to check the expiry dates more carefully.

Ramen House, which is in the same complex and under the same management as Fuji Restaurant, has good inexpensive Japanese food. The gyoza makes a recommendable appetizer, while the seafood yakisoba or the miso ramen are nice main dishes. Nearly everything on the menu hovers around $5. It's open from 10 am to 2 pm and 5 to 9.30 pm Monday to Saturday.

Yokohama, on Lebuu St, is a popular local restaurant with generous portions of good food at honest prices. Sandwiches cost around $2, sashimi or ramen $3, and lunch or dinner dishes, including teriyaki chicken, grilled fish and beef curry, are $5 to $6. It's open Monday to Saturday from 5.30 am to 9 pm, on Sundays from 5.30 am to 2 pm.

The *Furusato Restaurant*, next to the Bank of Hawaii, is another popular eatery with good-value meals. At breakfast you can get a boiled egg, toast and coffee for $3.50 or a full breakfast for a couple of dollars more. At lunch and dinner, curry rice or oyako domburi are $5, while various beef, pork and fish dishes average $6 to $8. The kitchen opens at 6.30 am daily and the last order is taken at 9.30 pm.

The *Carp Restaurant*, beside the waterfront on Malakal Island, is a ramshackle little Japanese-run place with inexpensive homestyle food. Dishes include sashimi for $5, fried fish for $5.50 and fish and vegetable tempura for $6. The servings are generous and include rice, miso soup and fresh fruit. It's open from 11 am to 2 pm and from 3 to 9 pm.

The *Rock Island Cafe* (☎ 488-1010) is a favourite of expats because of its excellent pizza. A small pepperoni pizza costs $5, while a medium, which feeds two people, is double that. You can get pasta and Mexican food for around $7 and a big portion of fresh sashimi or a good burger with fries for $5. Full Western-

Magic Breadfruit Tree

A popular Palauan legend tells of a woman who owned a magic breadfruit tree that had a hollow trunk and roots that sank deep into the sea. Whenever the people of the island were hungry, they would call on the woman and a wave would come up through the trunk, bringing with it fish for everyone to eat. Over time, some of the islanders became jealous of the woman and cut down the tree. As a result, water gushed up through the hollow trunk and flooded the island, sinking it into the depths of the ocean. It is said the outline of the island can still be seen beneath the water off the coast of Ngiwal in Babeldaob.

A depiction of this legend is painted on the front of the Palau Civic Center in Koror, the building with the traditional high-pitched roof at the end of the driveway past the police station. ■

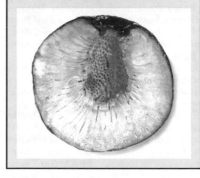

PALAU

style breakfasts with coffee also cost around $5. It's open from 6.30 am to 10 pm daily, except on Saturdays when it opens at 5 pm.

Middle

Pirate's Cove, near the Fisheries Co-op on Malakal Island, has a water view and well-prepared food. Dishes range from spaghetti in fish sauce for $6.50 to teriyaki steak with rice and salad for $9. On Friday nights there's often a special New Zealand T-bone steak for a few dollars more. Rachel, one of the owners, bakes excellent cheesecakes ($1.50 a slice). There's both indoor and balcony dining. Opening hours are from

9 am to 2 pm and 4 to 10 pm daily except Sundays, although the bar usually stays open a bit longer.

The restaurant at *Malakal Central Hotel* has a water view and half a dozen Japanese lunch specials with rice and soup for $6. While the food is only average, the atmosphere is a bit more up-market than at other similarly priced lunch spots. At dinner, prices range from $10 for sashimi to $18 for barbecued mix grill. Lunch is from 11 am to 2 pm, although they'll sometimes take orders a bit later than that. Dinner is from 5.30 to 9 pm.

Southern Cross, at the Palau Marina Hotel, has a fine view right on the water at M-Dock. Lunch is the best deal, with a grilled fish sandwich with fries for $6 and hot dishes such as spaghetti or shrimp gambas for around $8. Dinner features tempura, seafood and steaks priced from $11 to $14. They also have breakfast at moderate prices. It's open from 7 am to 11 pm.

Larry's at the Sunrise Villa, half a mile before the gate to Palau Pacific Resort, is a pleasant hotel restaurant with a fine hillside lagoon view and good food at surprisingly reasonable prices. You can get a full breakfast with a pot of coffee for $4 to $5. At lunch, grilled chicken or fried fish with rice or fries costs $6. Dinner ranges from spaghetti with meatballs for $7.50 to T-bone steak for $18. There's also a good-value meal of the day at both lunch and dinner. Breakfast is served from 6 to 10.30 am, lunch from 10.30 am to 5 pm and dinner from 5 to 10.30 pm.

Top End

The Arirang Restaurant (☎ 488-2799) is a Korean barbecue-style restaurant in the centre of Koror. The dinner menu features various meats that you cook on a small grill at your table; these are served with a nice array of spicy Korean vegetables and cost around $15. At lunch there are noodle dishes for about $5 and fish and meat specials for $6.50 to $8. Lunch is from 11 am to 2 pm, dinner from 5 to 10 pm; it's closed on Sundays.

The popular *Fuji Restaurant* (☎ 488-2774), in the same complex as West Downtown Hotel, is a good up-market place for seafood and Japanese dishes. Sweet and sour fish or a pork cutlet cost $8 while there's a set dinner with sashimi, land crab and various side dishes for $25. It's open for dinner only, from 6 to 10 pm daily except Sundays.

The Japanese-run *Dragon Tei* (☎ 488-2271), a new restaurant in the Topside section of Koror, serves some of the best food in Palau. Japanese, Palauan and Continental influences are combined in specialities that include land crab stuffed with coconut milk, baked local lobster ($15 a pound) and a tasty Napoleon fish sauteed in white wine. Dishes are served a la carte, but most are priced between $6 and $8, and rice is only a dollar more. There's a teppanyaki grill used to make huge okonomiyaki, which they dub 'Japanese pizza'. The interior has a pleasant decor, including tatami mats, and the service is excellent. It's open from 5 to 11 pm nightly except Wednesdays.

The open-air *Coconut Terrace* restaurant (☎ 488-2600) at Palau Pacific Resort has average food at higher-than-average prices. The restaurant has a breakfast buffet from 7 to 10 am for $13, and at lunch, served from 11 am to 5 pm, burgers or sandwiches with fries cost $7.50. At both lunch and dinner there are dishes such as nasi goreng or Thai prawn curry for $15.

A better bet for a top-end restaurant is *Image* (☎ 488-1881), which is down the same dirt road as Sunrise Villa and about a mile from Palau Pacific Resort. A favourite fine-dining spot with expats, this restaurant has an attractive setting with a superb veranda view and good food with Italian and Mexican accents. Starters are around $7, seafood main dishes around $15 and steaks a few dollars more. It's open on weekdays from 11 am to 2 pm and daily from 5 to 10 pm.

The *Hotel Nikko Restaurant* (☎ 488-2486) has a fine view of the Rock Islands, particularly from the tables at the back, but the food is not inspired. A full breakfast or a set meal

PALAU

at lunch costs around $10, while sandwiches are a bit less. A full-course dinner featuring crab or lobster costs $35, while a la carte dinner dishes range from $10 for fish meuniere to $25 for steak. Breakfast is served from 7 to 10 am, lunch from 11 am to 2 pm and dinner from 6 to 9 pm.

ENTERTAINMENT

The drinking age is 21. All bars close by midnight, when the town's curfew takes effect.

The beach bar at the *Palau Pacific Resort* makes a fine up-market place for a sunset drink.

Another popular waterfront spot is *Pirate's Cove*, a bar and restaurant that attracts a good mix of foreigners and locals. Occasionally there's music and dancing. The owner, Abby, is a burly Palauan with a calming presence, so the fights that occasionally break out in other bars around Koror are seldom an issue here.

The *SLC Club* (☎ 488-2915), on the road to Malakal, is a popular drinking and dance spot that has live bands; it's open daily from 4 pm to midnight.

Billiards players will find 10 pool tables at the new *Q-Ball Club* on Lebuu St. The cost is $6 per table per hour. It's open from 5 pm to midnight Tuesday to Sunday.

Palau has no movie theatres but free movies are shown weekly by the Seabees (☎ 488-1311), the US Navy division that helps with public works projects. To get there, take the side road to the airport, but rather than turning into the airport terminal, continue north about half a mile to the Seabees Camp, which is on the right.

Traditional dance shows can be arranged through the tourist office for about $100 to $150 a performance. Dancers in grass skirts usually perform in a line; the dances are typified by rhythmic movements and chanting in unison. The Belau National Museum sponsors one of Palau's best dance troupes, composed primarily of girls seven to 11 years of age; you can sometimes catch them practising after school on the museum grounds.

Palau Pacific Resort (☎ 488-2600) periodically has a 'Palauan Night', featuring a dinner buffet of Palauan foods and a dance performance by local children.

THINGS TO BUY

Palauan storyboards make excellent, albeit not inexpensive, souvenirs. A good place to find quality storyboards is at the shop in the entrance of the Koror jail.

Ben Franklin, in the WCTC Shopping Center, sells some rather simple storyboards for $50 to $125 and occasionally has a few quality pieces in the $500 range. It also carries other handicrafts of varied quality, T-shirts with Palauan designs, seashells and cassette tapes of Palauan music.

The gift shop at the museum sells storyboards, books about Palau, T-shirts, woven baskets and purses, commemorative stamps and posters. Other places to shop for storyboards and handicrafts are George Market, next to the Belau Medical Clinic, and the Palau Shop in Topside.

At the Senior Citizen Center, local craftspeople sit in an open-air shelter painted to resemble a traditional bai and weave hats, baskets and purses out of pandanus and coconut palm. The centre, opposite D W Motel, has a gift shop which is open weekdays from 7.30 am to 4.30 pm. Some of the most highly prized items sold here are the finely woven pocketbooks that are made from Kayangel pandanus and cost about $30.

The Palau Islands by Mandy Thyssen, a comprehensive 167-page book about the history and culture of Palau, has good colour photography and would make a fine souvenir. The book can be purchased at Neco Marine Dive Shop, which Mandy owns, for $20.

Keep in mind that sea turtles are endangered and the turtle shell jewellery which is sold in Palau cannot be brought into Guam, the USA, Canada, Australia, the UK or any other country that abides by the Convention on International Trade in Endangered Species.

PALAU

Storyboards

Palau's most unique art form is the storyboard, a smaller version of the carved legends that have traditionally decorated the beams and gables of men's meeting houses. A revival of this type of carving was initiated in 1935 by Japanese anthropologist Hisakatsu Hijikata, who suggested making the smaller boards as a way to keep both the art form and legends from dying out. Today, many of the scenes depicted on the storyboards have an element of erotica.

A good way to see what top-quality storyboards look like is to check out the collection on display in the Belau National Museum.

Some of the best storyboards are made by the inmates of the local jail, next to the police station in Koror. You can go and watch them at work during the day – usually one of the guards will escort you past the cells to the workshop area where the carving takes place. There's a gift shop near the entrance of the jail that sells the finished products.

A percentage of the proceeds from the sale of the storyboards goes to the jail as administrative costs, but the rest goes to the inmates, part as cigarette money and the remainder into a bank account that they can access upon release. ■

GETTING THERE & AWAY
Air

Continental Micronesia is the only international airline currently servicing Koror. It has daily flights from Guam with both early morning and early evening departures on most days. The one-way Guam-Koror fare is $320, while the return fare is $544. Both fares allow an en route stop in Yap.

Continental flies from Manila to Koror on Tuesdays, Thursdays and Saturdays for $210 each way. On Sundays Continental makes an en route stop in Koror on its Taipei-Guam flight.

The local airline, Paradise Air (☎ 488-2348), Box 488, Koror, Palau 96940, flies a six-seater Cessna from Koror to Peleliu and Angaur, passing over the Rock Islands along the way. Day trips are possible, as there are two return flights a day. Sometimes extra flights are added if there's a demand. Wednesdays are usually reserved for charter flights and there's only a morning flight on Saturdays. Paradise Air provides free transportation between the airport and its office in Koror. Planes can also be chartered for $300 an hour.

Airport As elsewhere in Micronesia, immigration officials at the airport usually ask you how many days you intend to stay and write that number in your passport. It's a good idea to ask for the maximum of 30 days, or at least give yourself a buffer, as visa extensions cost $50!

Koror's airport terminal has a Palau Visitors Authority booth that opens for weekday flights only, a row of car rental booths that open at flight times daily, several gift shops, a lounge and a snack bar.

Note that security commonly inspects every piece of carry-on luggage thoroughly, which is a tediously slow process, so it's wise to get in line early to make sure you make the flight!

Airline Office The Continental Micronesia ticket office (☎ 488-2448), which is behind the post office, is open from 8 am to 4 pm.

Consider reconfirming your flight before arriving in Palau, as the local office can be very difficult to reach by phone.

Boat
Because Koror is the nation's commercial centre, Palauans commonly commute by private speedboat between Koror and their home villages on other Palauan islands. You might be able to hitch a ride with someone by offering to help pay for petrol. Abby's Marine Shop near the Fisheries Co-op is where most of the speedboats fill up, so check there first. T-Dock and M-Dock are other possibilities.

Leaving Palau
There's a departure tax of $10 for non-Palauans.

GETTING AROUND
Koror is a sprawling town so it's not very convenient to get around solely on foot. As the town is crossed by only one main road, expect to encounter the occasional traffic jam, especially in mid-morning and late afternoon. For better or worse, the government has just allotted funds for Palau's first traffic lights, so the situation may change.

To/From the Airport
A few hotels provide airport transport for their guests. Neco Tours (☎ 488-1325) offers a shuttle bus service between the airport and any hotel for $7.50 per person, in either direction. There are taxis and car rentals at the airport.

Taxi
Taxis are plentiful and can be flagged down. Koror taxis are private, not the shared group kind, though they have no meters. Short trips around town are usually $2, while the fare between central Koror and Palau Pacific Resort is $5. Expect to pay about $15 from the airport to town, but ask around first and beware of overcharging. Taxis can be chartered for $20 an hour. Two of the island's larger taxi companies are City Cab (☎ 488-1394) and Koror Taxi 101 (☎ 488-1519).

Car
The following car rental agencies have booths at the airport as well as offices in Koror:

West Toyota Car Rental (☎ 488-2133), Box 280, Koror, Palau 96940
I-A Rent-A-Car (☎ 488-1113), Box 694, Koror, Palau 96940
King's U-Drive (☎ 488-2964), Box 424, Koror, Palau 96940

All three will also deliver cars to your hotel. Most rates begin at around $40 a day, although West has some Toyota Starlets for $35.

Check your car before driving away. We rented a Starlet at night without careful examination and after taking off found that it pulled sharply to the right, making for an unnerving ride over Koror's narrow causeways. The next morning we discovered that not only were the tyres bald, but one had only three lugnuts precariously holding it on!

Around town, watch out for dips and bumps and sharp V-shaped rain gutters that can tear up car bottoms. The maximum speed limit is 25 miles per hour and passing is not allowed. Go slowly over causeways, as most have no shoulders or guardrails.

Hitching
Hitching is not common, but if you start walking over the causeways to either Arakabesang or Malakal islands chances are good that someone will stop and offer you a ride. Likewise, it shouldn't be impossible to get a ride back to Koror from the MMDC or Palau Pacific Resort. The usual safety precautions apply, particularly for women.

The Rock Islands

The Rock Islands are Palau's crowning glory.

More than 200 of these rounded knobs of limestone, which are totally covered with green jungle growth, dot the waters for a 20-mile stretch south of Koror. The

PALAU

bases of the islands are narrower than the tops, having been undercut by water erosion and by grazing fish and tiny chitons that scrape at the rock. Because of their unique shape, the islands are often likened to emerald mushrooms rising from a turquoise-blue sea.

From the air they are an absolute knock-out! Even if you don't want to go anywhere, flights from Koror to Angaur or Peleliu are worth the airfare for the scenic overview of the Rock Islands alone.

But that's only half of it, for the waters that surround the Rock Islands contain some of the most abundant and varied marine life to be found anywhere.

The islands are also home to crocodiles and fruit bats and are rich with bird life, including kingfishers, reef herons, black noddies, white-tailed tropicbirds, black-napped terns and introduced cockatoos and parrots.

Most of the islands have been undercut all the way round and have no place for boat landings, but others have beaches where soft white sands have washed up and stayed. Ancient rock paintings can be found on Ulong Island and half-quarried Yapese stone money can be seen in a lime-stone cave near Airai Channel. Other islands have caves with dripping stalactites, rock arches and underground channels.

The Rock Islands are a superb place to lose the rest of the world for a while, hanging out on a speck of paradise and snorkelling the clear waters at whim.

ACTIVITIES
Diving & Snorkelling

Palau is one of the world's truly spectacular dive spots. If coral reefs, blue holes, WW II wrecks and hidden caves and tunnels aren't enough, consider the more than 60 vertical drop-offs.

Palau is the meeting place of three major ocean currents that merge with their abundant food supplies to support an enormous variety of marine life. The waters surrounding the Rock Islands are literally teeming with over 1500 varieties of reef and pelagic fish. There are four times the number of coral species in Palau than there are in the Caribbean, including immense tabletop corals, interlocking thickets of staghorn coral and soft corals of all types and colours.

Divers can see manta rays, sea turtles, moray eels, giant tridacna clams, grey reef sharks and sometimes even a sea snake, rare dugong or chambered nautilus. The sea temperature averages about 82°F (27°C) and visibility extends to well over 100 feet along drop-offs.

The **Ngemelis Wall**, also called the 'Big Drop-off', is widely considered the world's best wall dive. Starting in water just knee-deep, the wall drops vertically nearly 1000 feet. Divers can free float past a brilliant rainbow of sponges and soft corals whose intense blues, reds or pure whites form a backdrop for quivering nine-foot orange and yellow sea fans and giant black coral trees.

Blue Corner, Palau's most popular dive, is known for its sheer abundance of under-water life. You can expect to be totally bedazzled by the incredible variety of fish, including barracudas and schooling sharks, as well as hard and soft corals. Strong tidal currents nourish this chain of life, but also render it a dive for the more experienced.

Both the **German Channel** and **Turtle Cove**, near Peleliu, offer dives that novices can feel comfortable with. Snorkelling is also good from the beach at Turtle Cove.

Jellyfish Lake, popularised by the National Geographic TV special *Medusa*, is a different kind of experience. You'll need to hike up over a hill about 10 minutes through the jungle to reach this mangrove-bordered lake. Mark your entry point into the lake to avoid having a problem finding your way back out and be careful of slip-pery rocks around the shoreline where the water is murky and green. Farther out, the water clears up and millions of harm-less transparent jellyfish swim en masse following the sun. Snorkelling in this pulsating mass is an unearthly, somewhat eerie sensation.

Crocodiles are generally nocturnal crea-tures, but should you hear a low 'harrumph' you just might want to head in the opposite direction – unless you plan to test the theory that the crocodiles in Jellyfish Lake are more afraid of people than vice versa.

Dive Shops Most of Palau's dive shops offer similar packages, generally leaving Koror around 9 am and coming back around 4 pm, and breaking for a picnic lunch on a Rock Island between the morning and afternoon dives.

One thing worth checking out when you book a dive is the company's cancellation policy, as some shops charge steep cancellation fees even if the weather is rough on the day of the scheduled dive.

Belau Water Sports (☎ 488-2349, fax 488-1725), Box 680, Koror, Palau 96940, run by Swedish instructor Anna Fahlen, is a friendly personalised operation. The service is excellent; Anna gives a lot of attention to safety issues and to making her customers feel comfortable. A two-tank dive with lunch costs $85. In addition to standard dive tours, Anna can arrange diving/camping trips, which combine three dives a day with overnight camping on a Rock Island; the cost is $130 per person per day, with a four-person minimum. Rock Island tours, snorkelling trips or hiking outings can be arranged for around $40. Underwater camera rentals are available for $30 a day. Scuba certification courses in PADI can also be arranged.

Splash (☎ 488-2600, fax 488-1601), a PADI 5-Star Dive Center at the Palau Pacific Resort, Box 308, Koror, Palau 96940, is well regarded as a professional, safety-conscious operation. A night dive costs $70, while a two-tank boat dive with lunch costs $105. Full-day snorkelling trips are available for $55, plus $15 if you need

to rent snorkelling gear. For novices, there's a half-day Discover Scuba mini-course that includes a one-tank dive at the beach for $60 or a more elaborate Discover Scuba course that includes two beach dives at the Rock Islands for $130. A full four-day certification course costs $495.

The Neco Marine Dive Shop (☎ 488-1755, fax 488-3014), Box 129, Koror, Palau 96940, at a marina on Malakal Island, is one of Palau's largest operations and has a good reputation. It costs $65 for a one-tank dive, $98 for a two-tank dive and $133 for a three-tank dive, lunch included. Trips to Jellyfish Lake can sometimes be arranged between dives. Night dives cost $65. Dives to see the chambered nautilus or dives to Peleliu are available for $10 extra. Snorkelling tours, boat charters, PADI courses and introductory courses can be arranged. Free transportation is provided to and from Koror hotels. Diving gear and underwater cameras can be rented; there's a shop selling local books and dive supplies; and E-6 processing, personalised videos and camera repair work are offered.

Fish 'N Fins (☎ 488-2637, fax 488-1725), Box 142, Koror, Palau 96940, owned by local divemaster Francis Toribiong, is on M-Dock in Koror. A one-tank dive costs $65, while a two-tank dive costs $85, lunch included. Snorkellers pay $45 to go out with divers. Fish 'N Fins can certify divers in NAUI in four to five days for $500.

The Palau Diving Center (☎ 488-2978, fax 488-3155), Box 5, Koror, Palau 96940, is a Japanese operation next door to the Carp Restaurant on Malakal Island. One-tank dives cost $65 and two-tank dives $90, lunch included. Free hotel pickup is available. Palau Diving Center owns Carp Island Resort, which is a base for some of their divers, so the boat from Koror will stop there en route to

PALAU

dive sites. For information on Carp Island, see Day Trips below.

Sam's Dive Tours (☎ 488-1720, fax 488-1062), Box 428, Koror, Palau 96940, is a small dive operation run by American expat Sam Scott and his Palauan wife Felicia. Sam's tours are limited to eight divers. A one-tank dive either day or night costs $50, a two-tank dive $85. Sam's can also arrange snorkelling tours, land tours and camping expeditions.

Live-Aboard Dive Boats Two live-aboard dive boats ply Palauan waters.

The *Palau Aggressor* is a 110-foot diesel-powered boat that makes week-long cruises from Sunday to Sunday, which include 5½ days of diving. Each of the seven cabins has a queen and a single bed, toilet, sink, shower and individual climate controls. The boat has a hot tub and a photo/video centre with an E-6 processing lab. The cost is $1995, based on double occupancy, and includes meals and unlimited diving. There's a $200 discount for nondivers and for divers who book a back-to-back charter with the company's boat in Chuuk. Reservations are made through Live/Dive Pacific (☎ 808-329-8182, 800-344-5662; fax 808-329-2628), 74-5588 Pawai Place, Building F, Kailua-Kona, HI 96740. On Palau, information is provided by Neco Marine Dive Shop (☎ 488-1755).

The *Sun Dancer* is a 119-foot boat with eight double cabins. Each cabin has a private bathroom with shower and bathtub, picture windows, air-con and stereo. The boat has an entertainment lounge and a photo lab equipped to process E-6 slide film. The cost, based on double occupancy, is $1995 for a seven-day cruise, $2895 for a 10-day cruise – some of the tours go to Kayangel or the South-West Islands. Included are meals, all beverages, including alcoholic, all dives and accommodation on the final night at the Palau Pacific Resort. There's a $400 discount on some weeks from July to October. Reservations are made through Peter Hughes Diving (☎ 305-669-9391, 800-932-6237; fax 305-

669-9475), 6851 Yumuri St, Suite 10, Coral Gables, FL 33146.

Day Trips

For day outings, the dive shops can drop you off on a Rock Island beach in the morning and pick you up in the afternoon after their last dive, usually for the same price as a snorkelling tour.

Palau Diving Center and Neco Marine Dive Shop usually take you to their own islands, Carp Island and Neco Island respectively. If you just want to laze around for the day, Carp Island is a good choice and as it's quite far south you get a long, scenic ride through the Rock Islands coming and going. If you want to snorkel as well, Neco is the better bet, though you'll see only about half as many Rock Islands on the boat ride down.

Carp Island Ngercheu Island, more commonly called Carp Island, is primarily a divers' base camp for the Palau Diving Center.

A motorboat leaves Koror around 8 am, zips through the Rock Islands and arrives on Carp an hour later. There it picks up divers staying on the island and takes them out for the day, leaving you and a couple of friendly groundskeepers alone. When the boat brings the divers back in the late afternoon, it takes you back to Koror. The boat ride costs $30 return.

Carp Island is very peaceful, with a white sand beach lined with coconut palms, and hammocks tied to shady ironwood trees. At high tide the Rock Islands across from Carp seem to be floating on the sea, but as the water recedes they become encircled with beaches and linked by sand bars, and all around Carp Island beautifully rippled shoals of sand appear.

If the tide is right and the staff isn't busy, someone might give you a boat ride to a reef where there's good coral. Otherwise, snorkelling is not very good around Carp Island itself, as the water is shallow and about all you'll see is sea grass, goatfish and sea cucumbers. (If you want to go snorkelling with the divers instead of staying on the island, it costs an additional $30!)

Neco Island Neco Marine Dive Shop charges $50, including lunch, for an outing on the beach at Neco Island. As their divers usually have lunch on Neco Island, you can choose between staying on the island all day or spending half the day on the island and the other half out snorkelling with the divers, at no extra charge.

MARINE LAKES
The Rock Islands hold about 80 marine salt lakes, former sinkholes that are now filled with saltwater and have a limited exchange to the sea. Variations in algae give them different colours and some have soft corals, fish, sponges or jellyfish.

The heavily forested island of **Eil Malk** contains **Spooky Lake**, which has stratified layers of plankton, hydrogen sulphide and gases, and **Jellyfish Lake**, filled with jellyfish which have lost the ability to sting. Eil Malk also has a hot water lake that reaches 100°F (37.4°C) as well as Palau's largest salt lake, **Metukercheuas Uet**, which is 1.5 miles long and 200 feet deep.

Each lake harbours a unique ecosystem, providing habitat for specialised creatures that have evolved in their waters over the millennia. Travellers rarely get to see the lakes but they're a treasure to the marine biologists who study them.

70 ISLANDS (NGERUKUID)
Ngerukuid, also known as 70 Islands, is an extremely scenic part of the Rock Islands that's popular with aerial photographers. It is a nesting site for hawksbill turtles and seabirds and has been set aside as a wildlife preserve. Visits by divers, tourists and fishers are prohibited.

PLACES TO STAY
Camping
The Rock Islands are possibly the best place for camping in all of Micronesia and the star gazing is tremendous. Some of the islands have shelters and picnic tables (and some have enormous piles of Budweiser cans!), though none have water and you'll need protection from biting sand gnats. Also be aware that some of the islands have rat infestations, so it's a good idea to let whoever drops you off know that you prefer an island without rats. There are no fees to camp.

You can make arrangements for one of the dive shops to drop you and your provisions off on a deserted island and then pick you up later at an arranged time. Fish 'N Fins, for example, charges $40 for this service, though they'll usually drop you for free if you coordinate it with diving or snorkelling trips.

In this scenario, Fish 'N Fins picks you up on your Rock Island so you can join the dive group, at the same rate as if you got on the boat in Koror. They weave through the Rock Islands for most diving tours anyway, and on the return they can drop you back at your island. This is definitely one up on the free hotel pick-up service, and without any hotel bills the diving fees aren't nearly as painful.

For information on a chaperoned camping/diving outing, see Belau Water Sports under Dive Shops above.

Guesthouses
Carp Island Resort, booked through the Palau Diving Center (☎ 488-2978), has six rooms in duplex cottages, each with two single beds, a shared indoor toilet and a porch overlooking the beach. The cost is $55/65 for singles/doubles. There's also a divehouse with 40 beds in 10 rooms that costs $22 per bunk. Electricity comes on at night via a generator that is far enough away so as not to keep you awake. All accommodation is rustic but sufficient and clean. Showers are outdoors. There's an informal restaurant but choices are limited and meals cost $7.50 for breakfast or lunch, $20 for dinner. You can bring your own food and use the kitchen facilities at no charge. Staying on Carp Island instead of Koror allows much quicker access to dive sites and most of the guests are young Japanese divers.

The *Ngerchong Boat-el* (☎ 488-2691), Box 94, Koror, Palau 96940, on Ngerchong Island, is geared primarily for groups, with a large building that can accommodate up to 10 people and a smaller self-contained unit for up to four people. The latter rents for $40 a night, while rates on the larger place vary with the number of guests. Boat transportation can be arranged for about $80.

GETTING THERE & AWAY
Most visitors see the Rock Islands via boat trips run by the dive shops (see Diving & Snorkelling in this section). There are also non-dive tour companies that arrange boat tours through the Rock Islands.

Palau Island Adventures (☎ 488-1843), just south of the SLC Club, offers a few different tours of the Rock Islands. The shortest lasts two hours, costs $55, and includes a site where the Yapese quarried stone money, a bat cave and a bit of snorkelling. The longest takes all day, includes various snorkelling sites and Jellyfish Lake and costs $80. Children aged 6 to 12 are half price.

The Japanese-operated Rock Island Tour Co (☎ 488-1573), at the north end of Malakal Island, has a modern 'semi-submersible' boat that takes passengers on a cruise around the Rock Islands. There are underwater glass windows on a lower deck that allow passengers to view coral and tropical fish. The cost of $95 includes the boat ride, lunch, snorkelling and hotel transfers. Tours last from 9 am to 4 pm.

Babeldaob

Babeldaob, or Babelthaup, is the second largest land mass in Micronesia, three-quarters the size of Guam. It has 10 states but a total population of only about 3500, as many of the younger people have made an exodus to Koror in search of jobs.

Melekeok, a state with just 250 people, has been designated in the constitution as the future site of Palau's new capital. Plans

for a grandiose capital have been drawn up, though many people doubt the expensive complex will ever be built.

Although Babeldaob is a high volcanic island, the highest of its gently rolling hills, Mt Ngerchelchuus, has an elevation of only 713 feet. Babeldaob's Lake Ngardok, which is about 3000 feet long and 12 feet deep, is one of the few freshwater lakes in Micronesia. Parts of the island's dense jungle interior are virtually unexplored.

There are beautiful stretches of sandy beach on the east coast, particularly from Ngiwal to Ngaraard, while the west coast is largely mangrove-studded shoreline. Many

Babeldaob State Offices

The following are the phone numbers for each Babeldaob state office (governor's office). All these offices are in Koror, except for those of the southern states of Aimeliik and Airai, which are located on Babeldaob.

Aimeliik State	☎ 533-2967
Airai State	☎ 587-3511
Melekeok State	☎ 488-2728
Ngaraard State	☎ 488-1320
Ngarchelong State	☎ 488-2871
Ngardmau State	☎ 488-1401
Ngatpang State	☎ 488-1882
Ngchesar State	☎ 488-2636
Ngeremlengui State	☎ 488-2190
Ngiwal State	☎ 488-3254

of the villages are connected by ancient stone footpaths.

Ngarchelong State, at the northernmost point of Babeldaob, has an open field with rows of large basalt monoliths known as Badrulchau. Their origin is unknown, but according to one legend the gods put them there to support a bai that held thousands of people. There are 37 stones in all, some weighing up to five tons.

Many of Babeldaob's hillsides were once elaborately terraced into steps and pyramids. Although their purpose remains a mystery, archaeological research suggests they were probably started around 100 AD and abandoned around 1600. Quite mysteriously, few villages seem to have been located close to these terraced hillsides. Badrulchau is the only known exception.

AIRAI STATE

Airai, at the southern end of Babeldaob, has Palau's international airport. The state's relatively good roads and its proximity to Koror make it a good area for a bit of exploration. The most visited attractions are two bais, one old and one new.

Airai and Koror are connected by the 1272-foot cantilevered K-B Bridge, which at the time of construction was the longest bridge of its type in the world.

If you're returning a car to the airport,

Airai Bai

the last place to get petrol is at the Mobil station about a mile east of the airport.

To visit the bais, continue straight on the main road, rather than turning north to the airport. The bombed-out shell of a Japanese administration building is 1.25 miles farther, on the left just after the pavement ends. Behind the main ruins you can see another old wartime building which is now used as an auto repair shop. A Japanese tank and a few guns rust in union with a heap of car parts outside.

Continue down the main road for about 200 yards to a security gate; just past that the road splits. Take the road to the left to get to the new bai, which is on the right, 4.5 miles from the K-B Bridge. This bai is made mostly of concrete though it incorporates traditional features.

Just beyond, turn left at the T-junction and after a few hundred yards the road will end at Palau's oldest bai. The bai, which dates back a century, is 70 feet long and 20 feet wide with a steeply pitched roof reaching a height of 40 feet. It was constructed without nails using native materials of wood and thatch on a stone platform.

Chances are good that as soon as you start walking up the path, the keeper of the bai will appear. Expect to pay $5 to visit the bai, $10 if you want to photograph it ($50 for video cameras), though these fees have varied up and down a bit over the years.

While the most interesting is certainly the older bai, which is the last original structure of its type in Palau, both of the bais have legendary scenes and symbolic designs painted inside and out.

NGARAARD STATE

Ngaraard State has villages on both its east and west coasts and a road running across the state to connect them. Some of Babeldaob's prettiest beaches are on Ngaraard's east coast, as is the island's only established guesthouse. Though Ngaraard has only 310 people, that's enough to make it the third most populated state in Babeldaob (after Airai and Ngerchelong).

Ngaraard residents are used to seeing foreigners. Peace Corps volunteers train in this state and Bethania High School, a Christian girls school which takes students from throughout Micronesia, has some American teachers.

ORGANISED TOURS

Guided tours of Babeldaob can be arranged from Koror, but they tend to be expensive, averaging about $65 per person for a half-day tour and $100 for an extensive full-day tour. There's usually a two-person minimum. The following companies offer tours of Babeldaob: Neco Tours (☎ 488-1325), Island Adventures (☎ 488-1843), T-Ten Tour (☎ 488-1257) and Carp Corporation (☎ 488-2978).

Ngaraard Traditional Resort (☎ 488-1788) offers its overnight guests guided tours in northern Babeldaob. One that includes the stone monoliths of Badrulchau costs $25. A boat tour to Ngardmau, followed by an hour-long hike to Palau's largest waterfall, costs $30.

PLACES TO STAY

Camping can be a problem on Babeldaob as it's not a local custom and you'll need to first obtain permission from the village chief.

The Babeldaob state offices in Koror can sometimes help you make arrangements for places to stay, and it's advisable to make advance plans. However, if you just show up in a village often you'll find someone willing to put you up. Local school principals might let visitors stay in classrooms during school holidays. Appreciated gifts include bread, coffee and canned meat.

Guesthouses

Ngaraard Traditional Resort (☎ 488-1788 or 488-1077), Harson Shiro, Box 773, Koror, Palau 96940, has three cottages in a natural beach setting in Ulimang Village in Ngaraard. The cottages are built in traditional local style with thatched roofs and rough-hewn beams; each has two bedrooms with double beds and mosquito nets, an ice cooler and kerosene stove. Showers

View of the Rock Islands from the Hotel Nikko, Palau

Detail of bai at the Belau National Museum, Palau

Guide and WW II tank in Peleliu, Palau

Carp Island, Palau

Storyboard artist at work in Koror, Palau

Japanese post box, Palau

Aerial view of the Rock Islands, Palau

and toilets are outdoors. The cost is $25/45 for singles/doubles and $15 for each additional person.

You can bring your own food or, with a day's notice, local women will fix native dishes such as reef fish, mangrove crab, taro greens, fruit and coconuts. Meals cost $3.50 for breakfast, $5.50 for lunch and $10 for dinner. The resort has a bar with a pool table and there are small stores in the village that sell canned goods and basic supplies.

Hotels
The sole hotel in Babeldaob, the Airai View Hotel, is on the road between Koror and the airport and is listed under Places to Stay in the Koror section.

GETTING THERE & AWAY
Private speedboats, fishing boats and state motorboats going to Babeldaob generally leave from Koror's T-Dock or the Fisheries Co-op. Either check at the governor's office of the state you're planning to visit or simply go down to the docks and ask if anyone's heading in that direction. It usually costs about $5 to go anywhere on Babeldaob. Sometimes the boats go up and back the same day, and sometimes they stay overnight.

Ngaraard Traditional Resort can arrange a private speedboat from Koror to Ngaraard at a cost of $100 per boat for the round trip. The 25-mile ride takes a little over an hour each way.

GETTING AROUND
You can get from Koror to the bais in Airai in a sedan, but beyond that you'll probably be better off with a 4WD vehicle. It is possible to drive as far as Melekeok on the east coast, and Ngeremlengui on the west coast, on rough dirt roads (although rental companies may place restrictions on using their vehicles in these areas.)

Babeldaob has only a few vehicle roads, which generally follow the paths of the once-extensive road system constructed during the Japanese era. Some states have just a mile or two of roads which go through a main village and then stop. Because each state works on its own road projects, roads in one state don't always connect up with roads in the next. The road system into Babeldaob is expected to expand in the next few years, however, as compact monies begin to flow.

Peleliu

Peleliu was the site of one of the bloodiest battles of WW II. The island is small, only five sq miles in size, yet in two months of fighting on Peleliu there were over 20,000 casualties, more than the current-day population of all Palau. These days, many of Peleliu's visitors are survivors of that campaign.

In prewar days there were settlements scattered around Peleliu. During the final days of Japanese control of the island, however, the Japanese forced the islanders to evacuate Peleliu and move to Babeldaob. Upon returning to the battle-scarred island after the war, everyone resettled on the northern tip of Peleliu, where they are still concentrated today. The island's current population is about 600.

Several areas in Peleliu have been renamed in recognition of their military usage. Koska, at the southern end of Klouklubed, is not really a separate village, but is the area where the Coast Guard, or the *kos ka*, personnel once stayed. Ngerkeyukl, the former village north of Orange Beach, is now called Sina, which is the Palauan word for China, so named because of the Nationalist Chinese that came to that area to buy jeeps and other WW II surplus.

During the fighting Peleliu's forests were bombed and burned to the ground. Today the island is alive with the whistles and songs of tropical birds which thrive on the secondary jungle growth of vines and leafy foliage that have grown up to cover the battle scars. If there weren't the occasional pillbox, rusting tank or memorial to stumble across, there'd be no immediate sense of this island's place in war history.

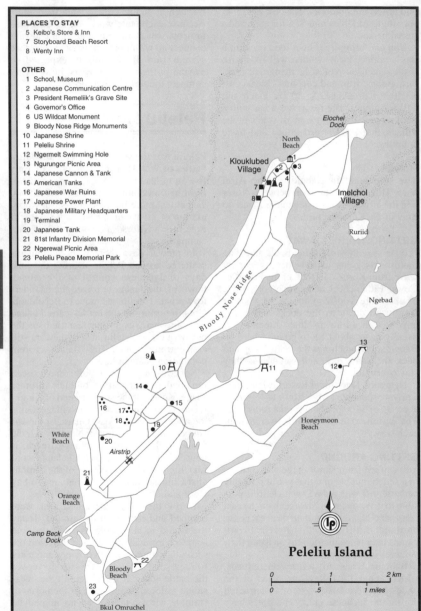

PLACES TO STAY
5   Keibo's Store & Inn
7   Storyboard Beach Resort
8   Wenty Inn

OTHER
1   School, Museum
2   Japanese Communication Centre
3   President Remeliik's Grave Site
4   Governor's Office
6   US Wildcat Monument
9   Bloody Nose Ridge Monuments
10 Japanese Shrine
11 Peleliu Shrine
12 Ngermelt Swimming Hole
13 Ngurungor Picnic Area
14 Japanese Cannon & Tank
15 American Tanks
16 Japanese War Ruins
17 Japanese Power Plant
18 Japanese Military Headquarters
19 Terminal
20 Japanese Tank
21 81st Infantry Division Memorial
22 Ngerewal Picnic Area
23 Peleliu Peace Memorial Park

PALAU

Elochel Dock

North Beach

Klouklubed Village

Imelchol Village

Ruriid

Ngebad

Bloody Nose Ridge

Honeymoon Beach

White Beach

Airstrip

Orange Beach

Camp Beck Dock

Bloody Beach

Bkul Omruchel

Peleliu Island

0   1   2 km
0   .5   1 miles

Peleliu is also known, in other circles, for its high-quality marijuana. Fertile soil is brought in from Babeldaob for pot planting in 50-gallon oil drums. Police raids, sponsored by US agents, occasionally swoop in and confiscate the harvest, much to the ire of locals, who consider it an attack on their economy.

Peleliu has much more to offer than just war relics. It's a fine place to kick back and take life easy for a while. The old name for Peleliu was Odesangel, which means the 'beginning of everything'.

ORIENTATION
The coral-surfaced 6000-foot airstrip, dating from WW II, is about five miles from the village. Sometimes there's a minivan that will give you a ride into town for about a dollar. If not, get a lift from one of the people meeting the plane.

Many remnants of the war are clustered north of the airport amidst a criss-cross of roads that can be confusing. It's helpful to have a guide, but if you don't care about seeing each and every war relic, you can explore on your own as the coral and concrete roads are in good condition. Peleliu is too big to thoroughly cover on foot, but bicycling is a good option if you don't want to rent a car. The island still has a scattering of live ammunition, so take care if you go off the beaten path. Don't be tempted to take 'souvenirs', no matter how small or insignificant they may seem; Palauan laws impose a $15,000 fine for the removal of war relics.

Most of Peleliu's best beaches are to the south.

ACTIVITIES
Diving & Snorkelling
The Peleliu Wall, south-west of Peleliu, is one of the world's finest dives, an abrupt 900-foot drop that starts in about 10 feet of water. It's a veritable treasure-trove of sharks, hawksbill sea turtles, black coral trees, mammoth gorgonian fans and an amazing variety of fish.

Many of Palau's best dive spots are in fact closer to Peleliu than Koror, but most people start from Koror because that's where the diving services are. However, Sam's Dive Tours (☎ 488-1720) of Koror has an arrangement with Storyboard Beach Resort to pick up divers in Peleliu and drop them back on the island at the end of the day.

Both White Beach and Bloody Beach have coral and good snorkelling.

KLOUKLUBED
The main village of Klouklubed is interesting more for its small-town atmosphere than for any particular sights, though there are a few.

Palau's first president, Haruo Remeliik, who was assassinated in 1985, was from Peleliu. The **former president's grave** is directly opposite the governor's office.

A small **war museum** containing war artefacts, munitions and period photos is adjacent to the school. If the door is locked, there's a key at the nearby governor's office.

A multi-storey bombed-out **Japanese communications centre** is right in the middle of the village, tangled with vegetation and encircled by homes. Kids play inside the building and its roof is now a forest floor.

There's a small **US military monument** opposite Keibo's Store. Heading toward the dock you can spot a cave and pillbox on the right, opposite a sandy beach.

AROUND THE ISLAND
WW II Ruins
North of the airport are the bombed-out shells of the Japanese power plant buildings, which are almost completely draped with vines hanging down from the upper ledges. Watch out for the wasp nests inside. The seemingly orchestrated chorus of birds in the background is amazing and the whole place has an eerie feeling of abandonment.

Nearby are two-storey buildings that served as Japanese military headquarters, now in a state of decay with concrete crumbling around the steel reinforcement rods.

PALAU

There are two rusting Quonset huts behind the main building.

Not far away, a small rusted Japanese tank sits at the convergence of three paths, all once paved roads. Other war wreckage in the general area includes a larger US tank with ferns and grass growing out the sides, two rusting US amphibs by the side of the road and a Japanese cannon guarding the entrance of a cave near a tiny Shinto shrine.

Bloody Nose Ridge
Below Bloody Nose Ridge, a sign points to a US Marine Corps monument in a clearing to the right, from where there's a nice view.

To get to the top of Bloody Nose Ridge, head uphill behind the sign, taking the path to the left. It starts as a rough road and soon changes to steep narrow stairs with a chain alongside to use as a handrail. The climb to the top takes about five minutes and the remains of some munitions can be seen along the way.

At the top of the ridge there's a monument, a machine gun and a spectacular 360° view that includes the Rock Islands to the north and Angaur to the south. There were once more than 500 caves dug into the limestone cliffs of Peleliu, many of them on this ridge.

Orange Beach
The first US invasion forces to land on Peleliu came ashore at Orange Beach on 15 September 1944. From concrete pillboxes the Japanese machine-gunned the oncoming waves of Americans as they hit the beaches. Despite the barrage, 15,000 US soldiers made it ashore on the first day.

Today Orange Beach is a quiet picnic spot with a sandy beach and waters that are calm and clear but too shallow and warm for swimming. The beach incidentally, is pronounced 'o-RAN-gee', not 'orange' like the fruit.

Just before the beach there are two grey coral monuments with plaques dedicated to the US Army's 81st Infantry

> ### The Battle for Peleliu
> The battle for Peleliu was conceived by US military tacticians who were worried that Japanese attacks from bases in Peleliu and Angaur might prevent a successful retaking of the Philippines. By mid-1944, however, US air bombings had reduced Peleliu to a negligible threat and it could have easily been bypassed, as was done with many other islands held by the Japanese. Instead Peleliu was captured at a terrible, unanticipated cost, with more than 8000 US casualties.
>
> At the time of the US invasion, some 10,000 Japanese soldiers were holed up in the caves that honeycombed Peleliu's jagged limestone ridges. Their goal was not to win, but to stall defeat. Far away from the beaches and the reach of naval bombardment, the Japanese tenaciously defended these caves to their deaths. In the bloody assaults that followed, the caves became mass coffins as American troops used flamethrowers, grenades and explosives to seal them shut.
>
> Rather than the expected quick victory, it took 2½ months for the Americans to rout out the last of the Japanese forces. In the end only 400 prisoners were taken alive and the majority of those were Korean labourers.
>
> In the late 1950s, a Japanese straggler who had been hiding in the jungle was discovered by an elderly woman as he entered her garden. Crouching low to see who had been stealing her tapioca, the woman froze and then screamed, thinking she was seeing a ghost. The man's uniform was torn into shreds, his hair matted and teeth streaked black. Police from Koror hunted the straggler down, bound him with rope and paraded him around for everyone to see. In that unglorious manner, the last WW II soldier left Peleliu. ∎

Wildcat Division. There's a striking sense of stillness at this site.

On the beach, look to the south to spot a Japanese defense bunker partially concealed by the rocks.

Camp Beck Dock
Behind Camp Beck Dock, where the water is a creamy aqua, you'll find a huge pile of mangled WW II plane engines, cockpits,

pipes, tubing, fuselages, anchors and who knows what, all compacted into blocks of twisted aluminium and steel.

South Beaches

At Bkul Omruchel, on the south-west tip of the island, the Japanese have constructed half a dozen chunky concrete tables and named the area **Peleliu Peace Memorial Park**. You can see Angaur to the south and when the surf crashes there are some small blowholes that erupt near shore.

Bloody Beach, despite its name, is a calm circular cove with a nice sandy strand. Just north of the beach is the Ngerewal picnic area.

North-east of the airport is **Honeymoon Beach**, a long stretch of beach with good seasonal surf.

At the eastern tip of the island is the **Ngurungor picnic area**, which has some mangroves and tiny rock island formations just offshore.

Heading back from Ngurungor, off a grassy road to the right, there's a refreshing little **swimming hole** of half-salt, half-freshwater that bobs up and down with the tides. A metal ladder hangs down the side of the tiny pit, but local kids just jump in from the top.

ORGANISED TOURS

An excellent tour of the island is given by Tangie, a very friendly man and Peleliu's resident historian of sorts. He shares lots of background info as he tours the sights. The cost is $40 (plus 10% tax) for one to four people, $10 per person for five or more. Tour arrangements can be made through Paradise Air.

PLACES TO STAY & EAT
Camping

Camping is easy and acceptable on Peleliu. Some of the beach picnic sites have open-air shelters, tables, barbecue pits and out-houses, but you'll need to take drinking water. You'll also need a close-knit screened tent or insect repellent to keep the bugs at bay.

While no permission per se is needed to

camp, you should first check in at the helpful governor's office. You can arrange in town for a car to drop you off at your camping site and pick you up later.

Ngurungor picnic area is a good choice for camping. It's close to the swimming hole and it usually has a refreshing breeze. Beware, though, that there have been reports of crocodile tracks on the shore!

Orange Beach is another possibility for camping, though the west coast doesn't catch many breezes, and it can be hot and muggy.

Honeymoon Beach is not recommended as it's littered and has a serious infestation of sand gnats that bite hard and can make for a totally sleepless night.

Guesthouses

The Wenty Inn, run by Emery Wenty, is a five-room guesthouse, each room with a double bed. The cost is $15 per person. Meals cost $6 for breakfast, $8 for lunch and $9 for dinner. There's a nice beach when the tide is in. Reservations can be made by writing to Wenty Inn, Peleliu State, Republic of Palau 96940.

The Paradise Air agent, Reiko Kubarii, rents rooms in her house a few doors down from the governor's office, and also in a small lodging house nearby. The cost is $15 per person. Meals are available for $7 at breakfast, $8 at lunch and $10 at dinner. Reiko can also drop you off for a day at the beach for $10 return.

At *Keibo Inn*, Mayumi Keibo rents three rooms next door to Keibo's Store. The rate is $15 per person, and meals are available for $7 to $12.

All three guesthouses can be booked through Paradise Air (☎/fax 488-2348) if you're flying in with them. They can also be reached from Koror via interstate radio by dialing 488-2435.

Storyboard Beach Resort (☎ 488-3280, fax 488-1725), Box 1561, Koror, Palau 96940, consists of six simple A-frame concrete cottages on the beach in the village just south of Keibo's Store. The cottages have hot showers, lanais and ceiling fans; some have queen beds, others have

PALAU

two twins. Meals can be prepared for about $5 for breakfast and $10 for dinner, depending upon what you want to eat. The main catch here is the room rate – steep at $75/85 for singles/doubles.

Peleliu has some small food stores but no restaurants.

GETTING THERE & AWAY
Air
Paradise Air (☎ 488-2348) flies to Peleliu from Koror for $24 and from Angaur for $15. Flights leave Koror at 9 am and 3.30 pm and arrive on Peleliu 20 minutes later. Flights leave Angaur at 9.45 am and 4.10 pm and take 10 minutes to get to Peleliu. There are usually no flights on Wednesdays and there are only morning flights on Saturdays.

Boat
The state boat runs between Elochel Dock in Klouklubed and the Fisheries Co-op on Koror. It generally leaves Koror on Mondays, Thursdays and Fridays and returns from Peleliu on Wednesdays, Thursdays and Sundays. Reservations are not necessary, but you should call in advance (☎ 488-1817) to verify departure times.

Departures are usually at noon, unless the tides necessitate a change. The two-hour ride costs $5 each way, and taking the boat gives you a nice opportunity to meet islanders on the way.

Private speedboats sometimes commute between Klouklubed and Koror, so you might be able to get a ride by asking around at the Fisheries Co-op.

Note that if you are diving in the area, some dive companies are willing to take their midday break on Peleliu and can provide guests with a land tour for an additional fee.

GETTING AROUND
Car
If you ask around where you're staying, you might be able to rent a pick-up truck or van for about $40 a day, although it's a rather hit-or-miss situation.

Bicycle
Wenty Inn rents bicycles for $10 a day. It would take a couple of days to see most of Peleliu's sights by bike. The road running down the east side of Bloody Nose Ridge is best for cyclists as it's shady and less frequented by cars.

Angaur

For the independent traveller looking to get off the beaten track, Angaur has a certain timeless South Seas charm. It's a low-keyed place with only one village and a population of just over 200.

Lying seven miles south-west of Peleliu, Angaur is outside the protective reef that surrounds most of Palau's islands. Open ocean pounds the north coast where the sea explodes skyward through small blowholes. The south end of the island is much calmer and fringed with sandy beaches.

As a result of the new compact, some capital improvement money has been earmarked for Angaur, including funds to eventually upgrade the power system. In the meantime the island's electricity and water are on for only six hours a day, from 5 to 11 pm.

ORIENTATION
Angaur's 'airport' is a 7000-foot paved airstrip that dates from WW II. You may be able to get a ride from someone meeting the plane, though the village is only a 10-minute walk from the airport.

The coastal road circling the island is mostly level and in good condition. Angaur is just 2.5 miles long, making it easy to get around on foot.

If you're on a day trip, however, you'll probably want to rent a vehicle or be content with walking around just a portion of the island. Although it's possible to walk the entire coastal road in a day, the heat and humidity don't make it tempting – at least not at midday. The hottest walking is around the village where the sun reflects off the crushed coral streets. Outside the

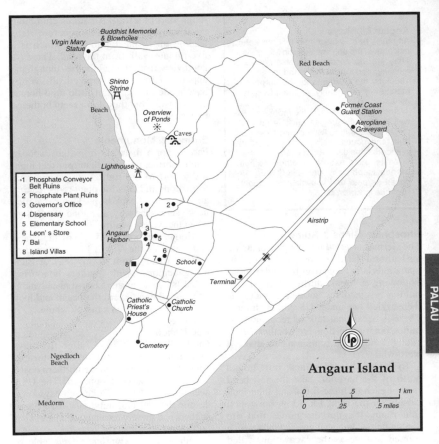

Angaur Island

Map key:

1 Phosphate Conveyor Belt Ruins
2 Phosphate Plant Ruins
3 Governor's Office
4 Dispensary
5 Elementary School
6 Leon's Store
7 Bai
8 Island Villas

Labels: Buddhist Memorial & Blowholes, Virgin Mary Statue, Red Beach, Shinto Shrine, Beach, Former Coast Guard Station, Aeroplane Graveyard, Overview of Ponds, Caves, Lighthouse, Angaur Harbor, Airstrip, School, Terminal, Catholic Priest's House, Catholic Church, Ngedloch Beach, Cemetery, Medorm

PALAU

village, tall trees and tropical growth close in, allowing for shady strolls.

ACTIVITIES
Swimming
On the south-west side of the village there's a quiet swimming cove near the Catholic priest's house. A concrete slab and rock under a large shade tree can be used to crack open tasty Palauan almonds, which are found scattered on the ground below. The beach that stretches from this cove to the southern tip of the island is called Ngedloch, though a few islanders whimsically dub it Waikiki.

Diving
There's good diving around Angaur between January and July, but the rest of the year the water's too rough. Diving arrangements must be made in advance in Koror, as there are no facilities on Angaur itself.

AROUND THE ISLAND
Angaur Harbor
Angaur's well-protected harbour is so nearly enclosed that the calm waters look like a big swimming pool. There's good swimming inside the boat basin and good snorkelling outside.

Angaur Monkeys

Angaur has about 600 crab-eating macaques, the only monkeys in Micronesia. They are the descendants of a couple of monkeys brought to the island in the early 1900s by the Germans for the purpose of monitoring air quality in the phosphate mines.

Accidentally released, the monkeys took well to Angaur's jungles, despite attempts to eradicate them. As the macaques like fruit, and occasionally raid crops, many islanders consider them a pest.

While their export to other Palauan islands is officially prohibited, they are prized as pets and you may occasionally spot one in Koror. ∎

Phosphate Mines & Ruins

The Germans started mining phosphate for agricultural fertiliser in 1909, with the operations later taken over by the Japanese. Following a break during WW II, the mining resumed for another decade, but then fizzled out under US administration. There is occasional talk of reopening the mines, but it's questionable whether there's enough phosphate remaining to make it worthwhile.

To get to the old mines, turn inland north of the harbour, take the left-hand road at each of three forks and then look closely on the right for a low horizontal iron ramp. It's not the mines that are visible below, but cool green ponds which formed in time as the excavations filled with water. Over the years, crocodiles have taken to the ponds, attracted by the brackish waters.

Back on the coastal road, look for the tall rusting iron girders of the conveyor belt that moved the phosphate down to the nearby harbour.

Japanese Lighthouse

North of town, there's an old Japanese lighthouse hidden by jungle on a hill to the left of the road. It takes a sharp eye to find it, but when the road nears a hill with dense vegetation, walk back toward the village about 50 yards and look for the rough start of a trail. A path of crumbling coral steps gives way to concrete steps leading up to the lighthouse, which is a five-minute walk from the road. There's a good view from the lighthouse, though the uppermost tower has toppled off. Wasps have made thousands of little mud homes on the inside, but they don't seem bothered by visitors.

Shrines & Monuments

Farther north there's a miniature wooden Shinto shrine, no more than four feet high. It's set off to the right, with jagged rock formations and twisting plant roots making an interesting backdrop. There's a nice beach across the way, and good snorkelling when the water is calm.

Around the north-west tip of the island is a statue of the Virgin Mary, erected to protect Angaur from stormy seas. A Buddhist memorial with markers honouring fallen Japanese soldiers is just ahead and if you walk down toward the ocean and look to the right you'll see a big blowhole.

Red Beach

On 18 September 1944, after five days of bombing, US Army troops stormed Angaur at Red Beach on the northern coast. The landings were unopposed. The USA declared the island secured two days later, despite the fact that hundreds of Japanese soldiers had merely retreated to caves in the north-west corner of the island.

Although the Americans were able to immediately move in and start building airfields, combat continued until 23 October. By the time the fighting had ended, 1500 Japanese and 240 US soldiers had been killed.

Aeroplane Graveyard

Look closely into the dense jungle left of the road about halfway between the former Coast Guard station and the northern end of the airstrip to find the aeroplane graveyard. In the woods here, pieces of wrecked WW II planes are blanketed with the soft needles of towering ironwood trees. A Corsair plane with both wings still

Spirit Respites

Beyond the Catholic priest's house is a cemetery with Palauan, Japanese and German graves and nearby, coincidentally, is an area where the souls of all Palauans are believed to go after death.

It's said that within one or two days after a death a small waterhole appears, so the spirit of the deceased can wash off all traces of earthly trappings and become totally free. The spirit then makes its way to Medorm at the south-west tip of the island, ascends a huge banyan tree and shoots off into the heavens. Palauans widely believe in spirits and people fishing in the area at night sometimes report seeing mysterious streaks of fiery light in the sky. ■

intact is the most recognisable; the incredible root structure of the trees and the dream-like setting are nearly as interesting as the planes.

PLACES TO STAY & EAT
Camping
Camping can be complicated; there are no developed facilities and, as most of Angaur's coastal areas are privately owned, you'll need to seek out permission from the landowner to set up camp. Make arrangements at the governor's office.

Guesthouses
Island Villas consists of two guesthouses managed by Leon Guilbert, the Paradise Air agent on Angaur. The choice one is a spacious, modern house on the beach with a kitchen, a wrap-around oceanview deck, two bedrooms and a couple of rooms capable of accommodating larger groups. If the beach house is full, a second guesthouse, on the south side of Leon's store in the village centre, also has a few bedrooms. The cost at either house is $15 per person. Meals are available at $7 for breakfast, $8 for lunch and $10 for dinner; the portions are generous, the food is good and you can request local delicacies such as land crabs in coconut milk for a few dollars more. Reservations are made through Paradise

Air (☎/fax 488-2348), PO Box 488, Koror, Palau 96940.

Angaur has a couple of small stores with basic provisions, but no restaurants.

GETTING THERE & AWAY
Air
Paradise Air (☎ 488-2348) flies between Koror and Angaur for $30 and between Peleliu and Angaur for $15. Flights leave Koror at 9 am and 3.30 pm, stopping on Peleliu en route. There are usually no flights on Wednesdays and only morning flights on Saturdays.

Boat
Unless the seas are unduly rough, a state boat usually makes the two-hour trip from Koror to Angaur on Fridays and Mondays and from Angaur back to Koror on Thursdays and Sundays. The cost is $5 and the boats leave Koror from the Fisheries Co-op. Departure times can vary, so call (☎ 488-2252) for current schedules.

Private speedboats sometimes commute between Koror and Angaur, but not nearly as often as between Koror and Peleliu. Because of the open seas the channel between Angaur and Peleliu can get very rough.

GETTING AROUND
If you don't want to explore on foot, Island Villas can arrange car rentals for $40 a day and sometimes can arrange mopeds ($15) and bicycles ($5). Bicycles could be quite a reasonable way to get around as most parts of the island are flat.

Guided land tours can be arranged through Island Villas for $40 for up to four people, $10 each for more than four. Snorkelling and fishing tours by boat can also be arranged at $50 an hour.

Kayangel

Kayangel, 15 miles north of Babeldaob, is a picture-postcard coral atoll. It has four islands fringed with sun-bleached beaches

PALAU

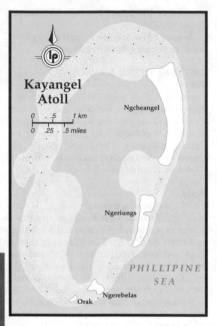

Kayangel
Atoll

0   .5   1 km
0   .25 .5 miles

Ngcheangel

Ngeriungs

PHILLIPINE
SEA

Ngerebelas
Orak

PALAU

ACTIVITIES
Diving
Splash Dive Center (☎ 488-2600) has recently begun day trips to Kayangel for divers, using a five-passenger seaplane operated by Paradise Air. The flight up takes about 35 minutes and the plane lands in the lagoon. The tour, which costs $245 per person, includes two dives, a land tour of Kayangel and a lunch of fresh fish and lobster. While diving Kayangel may not be on par with the Rock Islands, it does have virgin reefs and offers the opportunity to get well off the beaten path.

PLACES TO STAY
There are no hotels, but you can contact the Kayangel governor's office (☎ 488-2766) in Koror about the possibility of camping or staying with a family. You should be able to arrange a place for around $15 per person. The office is connected to the island by two-way radio.

Take rice, coffee, betel nut or other provisions to give to people who help you. Bread, sticky buns and other baked goods are particularly appreciated as there's no bakery on Kayangel.

GETTING THERE & AWAY
State diesel boats called *bilas* leave Kayangel for Koror every other Thursday, returning to Kayangel from T-Dock the following Saturday.

Another possibility is Kayangel's fishing boat, which travels to Koror about every five days. The schedule is irregular but the governor's office should know when it's in.

Both take seven to eight hours and charge $7. Private speedboats, if you can find one, take about three hours.

South-West Islands

The South-West Islands comprise half a dozen small islands scattered 370 miles beyond Koror and 100 miles north of Indonesia. Each of the islands covers less than one sq mile of land. The six islands are

and a well-protected aqua-blue lagoon. The main island, Ngcheangel, is barely 1.5 miles long and takes only a few minutes to walk across, yet there are two chiefs – one for each side.

Kayangel has just one quiet village of about 140 people, with a predominance of tin houses. There are a couple of small stores, a little ice-making plant and a few mopeds, but the island has no cars, phones or airport.

Although Kayangel is fairly traditional, it welcomes culturally sensitive visitors. Dress is particularly important – women should plan on wearing a T-shirt and shorts over their bathing suit when swimming and neither men nor women should wear shorts in the village.

Woven handbags and baskets from Kayangel are in demand as they're made of a high quality pandanus leaf. An average handbag costs $35 and lasts a couple of years.

Sonsorol and Fana (collectively known as the Sonsorol Islands), Pulo Anna, Merir, Tobi and Helen.

People from the South-West Islands are related culturally to people from the central Caroline Islands and have more in common with Yapese and Chuukese outer islanders than with people from the main islands of Palau. Their native languages are Sonsorolese and Tobian, which are similar to Yapese. They have a very traditional island lifestyle with thatched houses, carved canoes and fishing as a livelihood.

The South-West Islands were once heavily populated as most of them were used for phosphate mining during the period of Japanese occupation. Today, these islands are lightly populated. At last count, Tobi had 27 people, Sonsorol and Pulo Anna each had 18, Merir had five and Helen had four. While the island of Fana has remained uninhabited since WW II, the Sonsorolese visit Fana to fish and capture coconut crabs, turtles and birds.

Helen Island has nesting lesser crested terns and green sea turtles. South-West Islanders have long sailed to Helen Reef to hunt the turtles and harvest giant clams, as do occasional government supply ships and illegal Indonesian poachers. Merir Island also has nesting green sea turtles.

Other than the occasional researcher, there are virtually no foreign visitors to the islands, but the people are friendly and most speak some English. All of the islands have a radio, so communication is possible with Koror.

While there are no guesthouses in the South-West Islands, it would be possible to camp; best avoid Merir Island, which has a terrible mosquito infestation. You'll have to bring all your own food and supplies.

GETTING THERE & AWAY

Supply ships visit the South-West Islands at least every three months or so, and sometimes as frequently as once a month. Research vessels and a Palauan fishing patrol boat also make their way to the islands occasionally. For information on the boats, contact the Sonsorol governor's office (☎ 488-1237) in Koror.

PALAU

Guam

Guam is the metropolis of Micronesia. It's the region's largest island, covering 212 sq miles, and with about 145,000 people it also has the largest population. In appearance and in style it's not unlike a 'little Hawaii' mixed with the Americanised Hispanic flavour of East Los Angeles.

Guam has traffic jams, fast food restaurants, large shopping centres, a university, busloads of package tourists, a line of resort hotels and a substantial US military presence.

It also has tropical forests, sleepy villages, a mountainous interior, good sandy beaches and an abundance of butterflies and rainbows.

The way you view Guam usually depends on the direction from which you're coming. If you've just been island hopping through the less developed FSM then Guam is big time, and perhaps spoiled and overdeveloped. It's a consumer playground and a place for a salad fix for those expatriates visiting from the outer islands.

On the other hand, if you've just flown in from New York, Sydney or Tokyo, Guam is likely to appear slow, rural and laid-back.

Guam's prolific tourist bureau promotes the island both as 'Where America's Day Begins' and as the 'Gateway to Micronesia'.

HISTORY
Pre-European Contact
The ancient Chamorros inhabited the Mariana Islands at least as early as 1500 BC. Believed to have migrated from Indonesia, they shared language and cultural similarities with South-East Asians. The Chamorros were the only Micronesians to cultivate rice prior to Western contact.

Their society was stratified and organised in matrilineal clans. Most farming, construction and canoe building was done by men while the cooking, reef fishing, pottery and basket making was done by women.

The social system had three main classes. The *matua* and *achoat*, or the nobles and the lesser nobility, owned the land while the *manachang*, or lower class, worked it. Only members of nobility were allowed to be warriors, sailors, artists and fishermen. The manachang had to bow down in the company of nobles and were not allowed to eat certain foods including such basics as saltwater fish.

The island was divided into districts, each made up of one or more villages, which were mainly scattered along the coasts. The highest-ranking district noble, the *chamorri*, was in charge of local affairs but there was no island-wide leader. As a consequence the districts often fought against each other over petty squabbles, the villagers armed with slings and spears.

Chamorros were a handsome, well-built people. Before the arrival of Europeans the men wore no clothing at all, except occasionally hats or sandals made of palm leaves. When women wore anything, it was only a waist cord with a thin grass skirt attached.

Spanish Period
The first Western contact in the Pacific islands was on 6 March 1521 when the *Trinidad*, captained by Ferdinand Magellan, sailed into Guam's Umatac Bay. As Magellan's ships dropped anchor, they were greeted by a flotilla of outrigger canoes.

The Spaniards noted that the triangular lateen sail design used on the Chamorro canoes was superior in efficiency to the conventional European sails of the day. Magellan named the chain of islands *Islas de las Velas Latinas*, Islands of Lateen Sails. He retained the local name *Guahan*, meaning 'we have', for the island of Guam.

The Chamorros provided the crew with food and water but in return they took whatever they could find on the ships, prompting Magellan to quickly rename the

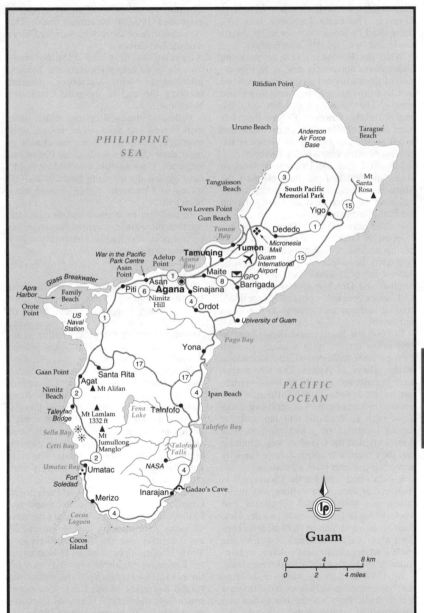

PHILIPPINE SEA

Ritidian Point

Uruno Beach

Anderson Air Force Base

Taragena Beach

Tanguisson Beach

Two Lovers Point
Gun Beach

Tumon Bay

Mt Santa Rosa

③

South Pacific Memorial Park

Yigo

⑮

①

Dededo

Micronesia Mall

⑮

War in the Pacific Park Centre
Adelup Point

Tamuning

Tumon

Asan Point

①

Maite

Guam International Airport

Agana Bay

Asan

Piti

⑥

Agana

Sinajana

⑧

GPO

Barrigada

Apra Harbor

Glass Breakwater

Family Beach

Orote Point

Nimitz Hill

④

Ordot

US Naval Station

①

University of Guam

Pago Bay

Yona

Gaan Point

⑰

Santa Rita

Agat

▲ Mt Alifan

PACIFIC OCEAN

Nimitz Beach

②

⑰

④

Ipan Beach

Taleyfac Bridge

▲ Mt Lamlam 1332 ft

Fena Lake

Talofofo

Sella Bay

▲ Mt Jumullong Manglo

Cetti Bay

Talofofo Bay

②

Umatac Bay

Umatac

Talofofo Falls

NASA

Fort Soledad

④

Merizo

Inarajan

Gadao's Cave

④

Cocos Lagoon

Cocos Island

Guam

0   4   8 km
0   2   4 miles

GUAM

islands *Islas de los Ladrones* – Islands of Thieves. The name Ladrones was still being used by sailors to refer to the Mariana Islands well into the 20th century.

What the Europeans saw as theft the Guamanians apparently saw as an expression of the traditional reciprocity practiced in Chamorro society between hosts and guests. The Spaniards did not take the matter lightly, however. Before they left three days later, Magellan's crew had killed seven people and burned 40 houses in the process of retrieving a stolen rowboat.

Miguel Lopez de Legazpi arrived in Guam in 1565 and officially claimed the Marianas for Spain before going on to establish the lucrative trade route between the Philippines and Mexico.

For the next 250 years Spanish galleons stopped at Guam to take on provisions during annual runs between Manila and Acapulco. In addition to galleon layovers, there were occasional visits by Spanish, English and Dutch explorers. Yet almost 150 years passed between Magellan's landing and any real attempt at European settlement.

In 1668 the Jesuit priest Diego Luis de Sanvitores arrived with a small Spanish garrison and established a Catholic mission in the village of Agana. The Chamorros were initially receptive to the missionaries, but as the Jesuits gained influence they became more outspoken in opposing traditions such as ancestor worship and the sexual initiation of young women. The priests insisted the islanders wear clothing and they blurred traditional caste lines by accepting converts from all classes.

It didn't take long for the Chamorros to realize that their very culture was under attack and this sparked rebellions and warfare that lasted for nearly two decades. Sanvitores was killed in 1672 after he baptised a chief's infant daughter against the chief's wishes. Spain sent soldiers to reinforce the missions and the battles escalated.

By 1690 the fighting was over, in large part because there were few Chamorro men left to fight. Between the bloodshed and epidemics of smallpox and influenza, the Chamorro population had dropped from an estimated 100,000 to around 5000. The vast majority of those who survived were women and children.

Spanish soldiers and Filipino men, brought in to help repopulate the islands, intermarried with Chamorro women, marking the end of the pure Chamorro bloodline.

Following the local custom at that time, men moved into their wives' houses after marriage, giving the women the chance to raise their children with some Chamorro influence. If not for this, the children would have grown up speaking Spanish and all traces of Chamorro culture would have been lost.

In addition to religion and disease, the Spanish introduced a written language, set up schools and taught construction and farming skills.

US Period

Although whale ships visited the Mariana Islands as early as 1798, it wasn't until 1822 that any stopped at Guam. Some of the whalers were British, but most were American; during the peak whaling years of the 1840s, hundreds of ships passed through Guamanian waters.

In April 1898 the USA abruptly declared war on Spain. Two months later US captain Henry Glass sailed into Guam's Apra Harbor with guns firing. He was greeted warmly by the Spanish authorities who, having no idea that their two nations were at war, apologised for not having enough ammunition to return the salute. The next day the Spanish governor officially surrendered.

In August 1898 the Treaty of Paris ceded Guam (as well as Puerto Rico and the Philippines) to the USA, which for the next 40 years maintained a largely unfortified naval control over the island. In February 1941, US president Franklin D Roosevelt, by Executive Order 8683, set Guam off limits to all visitors except those authorised by the Secretary of the Navy; that travel restriction, dubbed the 'Coconut Curtain', would not be lifted until August 1962.

Latte Stones
Latte stones are the most visible remains of early Chamorro culture. The upright posts were quarried from limestone and the rounded top capstones were of either limestone or brain coral. The stones are of such antiquity that at the time of the first Western contact the islanders no longer knew what their purpose had been. Historians now believe the stones were used as foundation pillars for men's houses and the homes of nobility. Latte stones vary from a few feet high to as tall as 20 feet. ■

Japanese Occupation

Japanese bombers attacked Guam from Saipan on 8 December 1941, the same day as the Pearl Harbor attack across the International Date Line. Guam was an easy and undefended target. On 10 December, within hours of 5000 Japanese invasion forces coming ashore, Guam's naval governor surrendered.

In anticipation of such an event, many Americans on Guam had been sent home just two months earlier. Those that remained were taken prisoner and sent to labour camps in Japan.

The Japanese administration in Guam immediately began the task of teaching the Chamorros the Japanese language. They renamed the island *Omiyajima*, which means 'Great Shrine Island'. Guam became part of an empire that the Japanese said would last for a thousand years. They held it for just 31 months.

In the beginning the Chamorros were largely left alone. Food supplies were rationed, but islanders could still live where they liked and workers were paid low wages for their labour.

Toward the end of Japanese control the military rule became quite harsh. Guamanians were placed in work camps to build fortifications and forced into farming to provide food for Japanese troops.

On 12 July 1944 the Japanese military command ordered all Guamanians be marched into concentration camps on the eastern side of the island. The people didn't know where they were going or why but, alarmed by a number of recent atrocities, many feared the worst. Particularly for some of the elderly and the sick it did indeed become a death march.

As it turned out, the move saved many lives by concentrating the Guamanians away from areas, such as Agana and the south-west coast, where the US pre-invasion bombing and subsequent combat was most intense.

Still, in the final hopeless days there were several incidents of massacres. The Japanese, hoping to kill as many Americans as possible before dying themselves, also took the lives of the Chamorros who they thought might compromise that aim.

In one infamous incident, 40 Chamorro men were taken abruptly at night from their camp to carry provisions as the Japanese retreated to the north. After arriving in Tarague, rather than allow the men to go back to their camp and give away their positions to the advancing US forces, the Japanese tied them to trees and beheaded them.

Americans Return

Pre-assault bombings by the USA began on 17 July 1944. The US invasion came on

GUAM

21 July, when 55,000 US troops hit Guam's beaches at Agat and Asan. The USA secured Guam on 10 August after fierce fighting which resulted in 17,500 Japanese and 7000 US casualties.

Agana was a city in ruins and many smaller villages were also destroyed. In the weeks that followed the population of the island swelled tenfold, as 200,000 US servicemen moved in to prepare for the invasion of Japan.

Large tracts of land, comprising roughly one-third of Guam, were confiscated by the US military at the time. When the war ended the military kept the land and settled in, turning the bases into permanent facilities. These bases played a role in the Korean War and again in the Vietnam War, when Guam's Andersen Air Force Base was a take-off point for B-52s that staged bombing raids over Indochina.

Although a 1986 class action lawsuit for dispossessed landowners won a multi-million dollar settlement from the US government, it is only in more recent times, with the closing and consolidating of US military bases worldwide, that Guamanians see the possibility of having any sizable tracts of land returned. The US Naval Air Station, adjacent to the international airport, is in the process of closing, but it won't necessarily be returned to displaced landowners – the Guam government is pressing to have the base transferred to its administration for future expansion of the airport.

GEOGRAPHY

Guam, the southernmost island in the Marianas chain, is about 30 miles long and nine miles wide. It narrows to about four miles in the centre, giving it a shape that resembles a bow tie.

The northern part of Guam is largely a raised limestone plateau, sections of which have steep vertical cliffs. The south is a mix of high volcanic hills and valleys containing numerous rivers and waterfalls.

Reef formations surround much of the island. The beaches on the west side tend to be calmer, while those on the east coast have heavier seas. The southern tip of the island has a number of protected bays.

CLIMATE

Guam's climate is uniformly warm and humid throughout the year. Daily temperatures average a low of 72°F (22°C) and a high of 85°F (30°C).

Guam's annual rainfall averages 98 inches. The most pleasant weather is during the dry season from January to the end of April when the dominant trade winds, which blow year round from the east or north-east, are strongest. The humidity is also slightly lower in the dry season and during that period the rainfall averages just 4½ inches monthly.

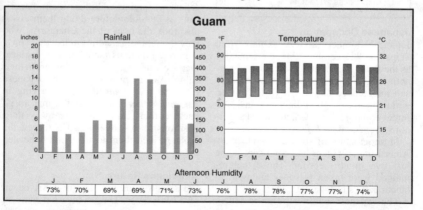

The Big One

On 8 August 1993 Guam was rocked by the worst earthquake to hit the region in nearly a century. Measuring 8.2 on the Richter scale, the minute-long seismic jolt resulted in 60 injuries but fortunately caused no deaths.

Guam's frequent typhoons were partially responsible for protecting the island, as housing codes require all structures to to be able to withstand 150 mile-per-hour winds, which in turn shored up many houses against the quake action. In addition, all multi-storey buldings must meet more stringent building codes for seismic zone 3 earthquake activity, which is just one notch below San Francisco's. Nonetheless, parts of the Royal Palm Resort and the Grand Hotel collapsed, requiring both to be demolished. A few island bridges were damaged; in a couple of cases, cars tumbled into rivers.

The quake originated deep in the Mariana Trench where seismic activity is common, but because that activity is buffered by the world's greatest ocean depth, its effects are seldom felt on the islands. This certainly was a jarring exception. ■

Guam lies in the path of typhoons and strong tropical storms, which are most frequent in the last half of the year but can occur in any month.

GOVERNMENT

Guam is an Unincorporated Territory of the United States of America. The Organic Act of Guam in 1950 installed a civilian government and granted all Guamanians US citizenship.

Guam's government structure resembles that of a US state. There's a 21-seat legislature, a governor and a lieutenant governor. Still, Guam does not have a voice on par with the 50 states. The islanders cannot vote in national elections; in 1972 they were finally given the right to send a representative to the US Congress, but that representative sits on the sidelines without being able to vote.

Many Guamanians feel that the newly established Commonwealth of the Northern Marianas has brokered a much better deal with the USA – both financially and in terms of self-government – than has Guam. In an effort to redefine its relationship with the USA, Guam is attempting to change its status from an Unincorporated Territory to a US Commonwealth. The Clinton administration is sympathetic but Congress, reluctant to give Guamanians more control over the island's federally held lands, has been stalling on the issue.

Guamanian politics haven't always been squeaky clean. Graft and payoffs were so widespread in the late 1980s that a federal investigation of local government resulted in more than 100 indictments, including many against department heads and Governor Ricardo Bordallo himself. In January 1990, just hours before he was to fly to the US mainland to begin a prison sentence on corruption charges, Bordallo chained himself to the Chief Quipuha statue in Agana and shot himself dead.

ECONOMY

Despite the ending of the Cold War, Guam continues to have a heavily militarised economy. The US pullout from bases in the Philippines has at least temporarily spurred

Guam Flag

Designed in 1917 from a sketch by Helen Paul, the wife of a US naval officer, the Guam flag features a sailing canoe, a coconut tree and the bay beneath the cliffs of Two Lovers Point. The oval shape of the flag's central emblem represents the slingstones that ancient Chamorros used as weapons. This emblem was adopted as Guam's official seal in 1930. On the flag it has a red border and is set on a background of deep blue. ■

an increased flow in defence spending on Guam. The military currently chalks up $750 million in annual expenditures and maintains 10,700 active duty military personnel on Guam; 70% are with the navy, most of the remainder with the air force.

Surprisingly, the biggest employer on the island is not the military, but rather the local government. A bloated bureaucracy dubbed GovGuam, it employs 13,500 people – more than 25% of the total civilian workforce. When you add on federal employees, Guam ends up having the highest concentration of government employees of any political entity under US jurisdiction.

The tourism industry is also a key element of the economy. In 1968, six years after the military lifted a security clearance on Guam, commercial jet service opened the island to tourism. Neighbouring Japan, then emerging as an economic power, provided a ready flow of tourists. Today Guam gets about 800,000 tourists annually, with more than 75% of those coming from Japan. The past few years have also seen a growing number of tourists from Korea and Taiwan.

POPULATION & PEOPLE

Guam's current population is 145,000.

Although the 55,000 Chamorros are still the largest ethnic group, their percentage as a total of the population continues to slip and indigenous rights groups are concerned that Chamorros will end up losing control of their island to outsiders.

The next largest ethnic groups are Filipinos (32,000) and Micronesians (7000). Guam is also home to sizable numbers of Koreans, Chinese and Japanese as well as a smattering of other Pacific peoples.

Of the 33,000 residents from the US mainland, 22,000 of them are active-duty military personnel or their dependents.

SOCIETY & CONDUCT

Present-day Chamorro culture is heavily influenced by the island's Spanish colonial past. Over 90% of Guam's Chamorro population remains staunchly Roman Catholic and Catholicism has a powerful sway on

island culture, from Guam's unyielding anti-abortion laws to village fiestas that still centre around the church.

Spanish influence can also be seen in the colourful *mestiza*, which is comprised of a full loose-fitting skirt and a frilled sleeveless blouse made of lightweight cotton; it's commonly decorated with a pattern of tropical flowers. The mestiza is still worn by Chamorro women on special occasions and for festive events.

LANGUAGE

Spanish never completely replaced the Chamorro language, even though more than 75% of modern Chamorro words are derived from Spanish. Although it has more guttural and repeated rhythmic sounds, Chamorro sounds a lot like Spanish too.

Chamorro was first written by Spanish missionaries who, using their own language as a base, used 'y' for the Chamorro article 'the'. Western scholars later started writing it as 'i'.

Chamorro also has a unique sound that's something like 'dz', which is spelt 'y' in the Spanish style and 'j' in the Western style. These two systems for spelling Chamorro words are still in use, so you can expect to see both.

In theory Chamorro and English are both official languages as both are taught in schools and used in government documents. In practice, however, English is taking over as the language of choice.

Many common Chamorro phrases are the same as in Spanish. 'Good morning' is *buenas dias* and 'goodbye' is *adios*.

The common Chamorro greeting is *hafa adai* (pronounced 'half a day'). Literally, it means 'what?' but it's sort of a 'hello', 'what's up?' and 'how are you?' all combined. *Hafa adai* is sometimes shortened to *hafa* or *fa*. 'Thank you' is *si yuus maasi*.

HOLIDAYS & FESTIVALS

Guam's public holidays are:

New Year's Day
    1 January

Martin Luther King's Birthday
   3rd Monday in January
President's Day
   3rd Monday in February
Guam Discovery Day
   1st Monday in March
Good Friday
   Friday before Easter, in March or April
Memorial Day
   Last Monday in May
US Independence Day
   4 July
Liberation Day
   21 July
Labor Day
   1st Monday in September
Columbus Day
   2nd Monday in October
Veterans Day
   11 November
Thanksgiving
   4th Thursday in November
Our Lady of Camarin Day
   8 December
Christmas
   25 December

Guam Discovery Day, which marks Magellan's landing, is celebrated at Umatac, where festivities include a re-enactment of the landing, cultural dances, sports competitions, arts and crafts and *tuba* making.

Liberation Day celebrations include feasts, fireworks and the largest parade of the year, which proceeds along Marine Drive.

New Year's Eve is wild. Some Guamanians sit in their backyards with their own fireworks, which in some cases include shooting off guns, and there's a public fireworks display at Ypao Beach Park at Tumon.

The Guam Visitors Bureau publishes a free calendar of events, including fiesta dates.

Fiestas

Nowhere is the Spanish influence so evident as in Guam's Catholic traditions, particularly in its fiestas and celebrations.

Each village has an annual fiesta honouring its patron saint, a community affair that commonly begins with a Saturday evening mass in the local church, a procession around the village carrying a statue of the saint and a buffet feast in the church hall. The festivities usually continue on Sunday.

Fiestas are celebrated on the weekend closest to the saint's feast day so the dates vary slightly each year. The idea is to attract as many people as possible to the festivities, so everyone is welcome.

Guam's largest fiesta is held in Agana on 8 December, a public holiday that honours Our Lady of the Immaculate Conception, the patron saint of the island.

Fiestas are held in the following villages:

January
   Asan, Tumon, Chalan Pago, Mongmong
February
   Maina, Yigo
March
   Inarajan
April
   Barrigada, Merizo, Agafa Gumas, Inarajan
May
   Malojloj, Santa Rita
June
   Tamuning, Chalan Pago, Toto, Ordot
July
   Agat, Malojloj, Agat, Tamuning
August
   Piti, Barrigada, Agat
September
   Canada-Barrigada, Agana, Talofofo
October
   Mangilao, Yona, Umatac, Sinajana
November
   Agana Heights
December
   Dededo, Agana, Santa Rita

ORIENTATION

Most of Guam's main tourist and business facilities are centred in the adjacent areas of Tumon, Tamuning and Agana.

The airport is in Tamuning about a mile up from Route 1, which is also called Marine Drive. From the intersection of the airport road and Route 1, Agana is to the left. Tumon Bay, Guam's main resort area, is immediately below you, though you must first turn onto Route 1 (either way) before heading down to the bay.

The four-mile stretch of Marine Drive

from Tamuning to Agana has four-lane roads that get jammed with rush hour traffic.

A 50-mile road circles the lower half of the island, which is the most scenic and historic part of Guam.

Most of the driving around Guam is on excellent paved roads, but tourist attractions are often marked poorly or not at all, and street signs and highway markers are scarce. It's more common to see signs pointing the way to 'Maria's Christening Party' or 'Roasting Pigs 4 Sale' than to a viewpoint or village.

INFORMATION
Tourist Office
The Guam Visitors Bureau (☎ 646-5278, fax 646-8861) at 401 San Vitores Rd in Tumon (mailing address: Box 3520, Agana, Guam 96910) has helpful staff and free brochures and maps. It's open from 8 am to 5 pm Monday to Friday.

Money
Bank of Guam, Bank of Hawaii and First Hawaiian Bank are the island's biggest banks and together have about 20 branches around Guam – a list of locations can be found in the yellow pages of the Guam phone book.

All 12 Bank of Guam branches on the island are open from 10 am to 3 pm Monday to Thursday, from 10 am to 6 pm on Fridays and from 9 am to 1 pm on Saturdays; foreign currencies are exchanged only at the Tumon and Agana branches.

Branches of the Bank of Hawaii and the First Hawaiian Bank are open from 9 am to 3 pm Monday to Thursday, from 9 am to 6 pm on Fridays.

Major credit and charge cards are widely accepted on Guam.

Post
On Guam, all mail sent General Delivery (even mail marked Agana) must be picked up at the less-than-central General Post Office (GPO), on Route 16 in Barrigada. Hours are 9 am to 5 pm Monday to Friday and 1 to 4 pm on Saturdays. Most mail is held 30 days, but express mail is held only five days. Mail should be addressed to General Delivery GMF, Barrigada, Guam 96921.

The branch post office in central Agana is on Chalan Santo Papa and open from 8.30 am to 4.30 pm on weekdays and 9 am to noon on Saturdays. The one in Tamuning is behind the ITC Building and open from 8 am to 4 pm weekdays and 9 am to noon on Saturdays. You can get inexpensive boxes and padded envelopes at any post office.

Telephone
International calls can be made from pay phones by using a credit card or reversing the charges. To use IT&E (which connects worldwide through the AT&T system) dial 013; to use MCI dial 002.

Calls to Australia cost \$8.50 for the first three minutes, \$2.40 for additional minutes. Calls to the USA and Canada cost \$8 for the first three minutes and 70 cents to \$1 for each additional minute, depending on the time of day. Three-minute calls cost \$2.50 to the Northern Marianas and \$11.75 to Palau, the Marshalls or the FSM.

Travel Agency
Travel Pacificana (☎ 472-8884), Guam's American Express Travel Service representative, is a recommendable travel agency; ask for Jhun Navarro, who keeps on top of the best deals. The office is at 207 Martyr St in central Agana and open from 8 am to 5.30 pm weekdays, 9 am to noon on Saturdays.

Bookshops
Guam has only a few bookshops, but the two best shops, I Love Books and Faith Bookstore, are conveniently side by side in the Agana Shopping Center. Both have comprehensive Micronesian and Guam collections and good travel sections; I Love Books has the better general interest sections and the longer hours, from 10 am to 10 pm daily (to 8 pm on Sunday). Bestseller in the Micronesia Mall has the island's widest variety of magazines and

sells the Sunday edition of *The New York Times* for $5.50.

Libraries

The Agana public library (☎ 472-6417), on the corner of Route 4 and West O'Brien Drive, is open from 9.30 am to 6 pm on Mondays, Wednesdays and Fridays, from 9.30 am to 8 pm on Tuesdays and Thursdays, from 10 am to 4 pm on Saturdays and from noon to 4 pm on Sundays. There are other public libraries in Barrigada, Dededo, Agat and Merizo.

There's also a good general library at the University of Guam as well as a more Pacific-oriented research library at its Micronesian Area Research Center.

Media

Most hotels are hooked up to cable TV, which on Guam connects with 35 channels, including the three major US networks, CNN and MTV. Local news comes on at 6 pm on KUAM, channel 8.

Guam has several radio stations, ranging from a Christian music station (92 FM) and easy listening (95.5 FM) to rock (98 FM).

Guam's main newspaper and only daily is the *Pacific Daily News*, which costs 60 cents on weekdays, $1 on Sundays. The *Guam Visitors Guide*, a monthly magazine in Japanese and English, contains lots of ads and a bit of useful tourist information; it can be picked up free at the tourist office or major hotels. *USA Today* is available from vending machines at the airport.

Laundry

There's a coin laundry on Hospital Rd in Tamuning between the Guam Shopping Center and the Golden Motel.

Weather Recording

To get the latest pre-recorded weather forecast, including wind, wave and tide updates, dial 117.

Medical Services

The main civilian hospital is the Guam Memorial Hospital (☎ 646-5801) in Tamuning; the emergency room number is 646-8104. For more routine medical issues, the Seventh Day Adventist Clinic (☎ 646-0894) on Ypao Rd in Tamuning is a better choice.

Divers with the bends are sent to the SRF Guam Recompression Chamber (☎ 339-7143). The Crisis Hotline is 477-8833; the AIDS Hotline is 734-2437.

Emergency

For police, fire or ambulance emergencies, dial 911. The non-emergency police number is 472-8911.

ACTIVITIES
Diving & Snorkelling

Guam's waters provide habitat for more than 800 species of fish and 300 species of coral. In addition to its rich marine life, Guam also has numerous war wrecks.

There are a couple of dozen popular dive spots on the west coast alone, many in or south of Apra Harbor. One of the best known, for advanced divers, is the Blue Hole at the end of Orote Peninsula. At about 60 feet a perpendicular hole in the reef can be descended by divers in a free fall. At about 125 feet there's a window that allows divers to exit. The area is known for its large fish and sea fans, and has good visibility.

One of the more unusual wreck dives is to the *Tokai Maru*, a Japanese freighter bombed during WW II in Apra Harbor. As it sank it landed on top of the *Cormoran*, a German cruiser scuttled during WW I, which rests upside down on the ocean floor. At about 95 feet you can have one hand on each war. The uppermost part of the *Tokai Maru* is only 40 feet underwater, so it can make a good beginner dive.

Some of the better snorkelling spots are Gun Beach in the Tumon Bay area, Family Beach on the north side of Apra Harbor, the Piti Bomb Holes in Piti and Shark's Hole to the north of Tanguisson Beach.

Dive Shops MDA, the Micronesian Divers Association (☎ 472-6321, fax 477-6329), 855 Marine Drive (Route 1), Piti, Guam 96925, is a popular five-star PADI

GUAM

operation geared to English speakers. Located opposite the Piti Bomb Holes, MDA offers free guided shore dives at 9 am and 1 pm on Saturdays and Sundays (gear can be rented for $28). MDA offers a wide range of boat dives, most priced at $40 for two tanks, plus gear rental.

The Coral Reef Marine Center (☎ 646-4895), behind the Tamuning post office, no longer does dives, but it still sells, services and rents equipment at reasonable rates and fills tanks for $3. A regulator or BC can be rented for $5, tanks for $4, mask and snorkel for $3, fins for $3 and weight belts for $2.

Bob Odell at Real World Diving Co (☎ 646-8903, fax 646-4957), Box 2800, Agana, Guam 96910, which operates at the side of the Coral Reef Marine Center in Tamuning, offers some of the most exciting dives on the island and is a master at finding manta rays and dolphins. Two-tank boat dives cost $80, but ask about the local rate which is $15 cheaper. Real World offers half-day boat tours that include snorkelling, dolphin watching and trolling for $65, gear included.

For Japanese-speaking visitors, a recommendable dive operation is Kitagawa Sensui Midsummer (☎ 649-9870, fax 649-8525), Regency Hotel, No 109, San Vitores Rd, Tumon, Guam 96921.

Swimming
The calmest waters for swimming are usually along the west coast, with the greater Tumon Bay area having the busiest beaches. There are no fees at any of the island's 20 beach parks, many of which have showers, toilets and picnic tables. Before entering the water, check for jellyfish which occasionally float in, especially when the trade winds pick up.

There's a large public swimming pool in Agana (☎ 472-8718) opposite the Agana Shopping Center. It's open from 11 am to 8.30 pm Tuesday to Friday, from 11 am to 7.30 pm on weekends, and admission is 50 cents.

Surfing
While Guam is not a prime surfing locale, surfing is possible; the best conditions are between December and June. Beginners

STRONG CURRENT   MAN-OF-WAR   SHARP CORAL

HIGH SURF   DANGEROUS SHOREBREAK   WAVES ON LEDGE

Beach hazard warning signs

generally prefer Talofofo Bay, while the more experienced surf the channel near Agana Boat Basin. Surfboards can be rented at Primo Surf (☎ 472-2053) on Route 4 in Agana, next to Winchell's.

Other Water Sports

Windsurfing is popular in Tumon Bay and in Cocos Lagoon off Merizo.

The Marianas Yacht Club (☎ 477-3533), Box 2297, Agana, Guam 96910, at Apra Harbor sponsors several races throughout the year. These include the Guam-Japan Goodwill Regatta in February, the Rota and Return Race on Memorial Day weekend and the Round the Island Race in December. The club also has information about charter boats and sailing lessons.

There's an upsurge of interest in traditional outrigger canoeing. The Marianas Paddle Sports Racing Association sponsors numerous races in six-person outrigger canoes in Tumon Bay and Apra Harbor.

Some of the larger Tumon Bay hotels, such as the Hyatt, have beach huts that offer outrigger canoe rides, windsurfing lessons and rent Hobie Cats and other water sports equipment, though prices tend to be high.

Fishing

Deep sea fishing boats leave from Agana Boat Basin and Apra Harbor on the search for marlin, wahoo, yellowfin tuna, sailfish, barracuda and mahimahi. A 1153-pound Pacific blue marlin, caught off Ritidian Point by a Guamanian in 1969, broke the world record at the time. For information on chartering a fishing boat, contact the Guam Visitors Bureau.

Hiking

Guam has a number of hikes, ranging from short trails at Asan Park and up to the Piti guns to hardier hikes to Sella Bay and Mt Jumullong in southern Guam. Details are given under these respective sites elsewhere in this chapter.

The Department of Parks & Recreation sponsors guided 'boonie stomps' on most Saturdays, meeting at the Paseo Recreation Building in Paseo de Susana in Agana and usually departing at 12.30 pm. Hikes are rated according to difficulty; children under age 12 are not allowed on the more strenuous hikes. The cost is $2 and hikers are asked to provide their own transportation to the trailhead. Destinations include remote jungle war sites and secluded waterfalls; call 477-8280 or 477-8197 for the current schedule.

Running

The Athlete's Foot (☎ 472-1514), in the Agana Shopping Center, has information on the Guam Running Club and upcoming road races. There's a jogging track around the stadium at Paseo de Susana.

Tennis

The Agana Tennis Center (☎ 472-6270), next to the public pool in Agana, has four lighted courts open to the public on a first-come, first-served basis. There's no fee and the gates are never locked – last players out at night turn off the lights!

GUAM

Traditional outrigger canoe

There are other public tennis courts scattered around the island, but most of those outside Agana are not well maintained. Some of the larger hotels have tennis courts for their guests.

Golf

Guam currently has seven public golf courses and a driving range; the prices that follow include green fees and cart:

Country Club of the Pacific in Yona; 18 holes, $100/130 on weekdays/weekends (☎ 789-1361)

Guam Municipal Golf Course in Dededo; 18 holes, $110/150 on weekdays/weekends (☎ 632-1197)

Guam Takayama Golf Club in Yona; 18 holes, $80/97 on weekdays/weekends (☎ 789-1612)

Hatsuho International Country Club in Dededo; 27 holes, $110/150 on weekdays/weekends (☎ 632-1111)

Leo Palace Resort Country Club in Yona; 27 holes, $150/190 on weekdays/weekends (☎ 888-0001)

Mangilao Golf Club in Mangilao; 18 holes, $120/170 on weekdays/weekends (☎ 734-1111)

Talofofo Golf Resort in Talofofo; 18 holes, $130/170 on weekdays/weekends (☎ 789-5555)

Tumon Golf Driving Range in Upper Tumon; $4 for a bucket of balls (☎ 649-8337)

Bowling

Guam has two bowling alleys: Central Lanes (☎ 646-9081) and Royal Lanes (☎ 646-8847), both on Marine Drive in Tamuning. The cost to play a lane is $3; expect them to be packed on weekends.

Other Activities

The *Atlantis* submarine (☎ 477-4166) runs 10 dives a day to Gab Gab Reef II in Apra Harbor; the first tour is at 8 am, the last at 4.15 pm. The 65-foot sub carries 46 passengers and has 26 viewport windows. Passengers spend about an hour on the sub, which goes to a depth of 50 to 90 feet, depending on water conditions. The regular cost is $94, including hotel pick-up; there's also a local rate of $50.

The more moderately priced *Nautilus*

Guam (☎ 646-8331) is a semi-submersible boat that has an underwater lower deck with port windows. It goes out from Apra Harbor for 45-minute cruises and charges $25, if you avoid the inflated Japanese-tourist rate.

For something more local, the Adventure River Cruise (☎ 646-1710) takes a catamaran riverboat up the Talofofo River to an ancient latte stone site where craft demonstrations are given. The outings begin at 9 am and 1 pm, last two hours and cost $52 for tourists, including pick-up at Tumon hotels. However, if you get to Talofofo Bay yourself, you might be able to join the tour from there at the local rate of $15.

AGANA

The capital city of Agana (pronounced a-GHAN-nya) has been the centre of Guam since the Spanish period. With its parks and historic sites it's a pleasant place to spend a few hours sightseeing. If you have a car, it's easiest to park in the public lot by the museum; from there you can visit most of the sights on foot.

Plaza de Espana

Plaza de Espana, in the heart of Agana, is a peaceful refuge of Spanish-era ruins, old stone walls and flowering trees.

The plaza was the centre of Spanish administration from 1669 and served as the hub of religious, cultural and government activities. US naval governors who replaced the Spanish administrators in 1898 continued to use it as a seat of government, as did the Japanese during WW II.

Buildings once completely surrounded the central park area and included schools, a hospital, priests' quarters, governor's residence, military compound, arsenal and town hall. Most were constructed of ifil wood and a concoction of lime mortar and coral called *manposteria* and were roofed with clay tiles. Only a few of these buildings survived the US pre-invasion bombings in July 1944.

Among those that remain is the **Garden House**, which once served as a storage shed and servants' quarters and is now the site of the Guam Museum.

A minute's walk north of the museum brings you to the **Chocolate House**, the small white circular building with the pointed tile roof. It's so named because it was used by the wives of Spanish governors to serve afternoon refreshments, most commonly hot chocolate, to their guests.

Immediately west of the Chocolate House are the remains of **Casa Gobierno**, the Governor's Palace. The house itself is long gone but a raised, open-air terrace that once served as its foundation remains

intact. Also notable are the three stone arches that are used as an entrance into the adjacent garden; the arches date from 1736 and were originally part of the arsenal.

There's a roadside **statue of Pope John Paul II** north of the plaza on the site where he held Mass on a visit to Guam in 1981. Don't get disoriented if you find that each time you go by the statue it's facing in a different direction – this pope revolves, making one complete turn every 24 hours. Near the statue is a **war memorial** honouring Guamanians killed during the Japanese invasion of 10 December 1941.

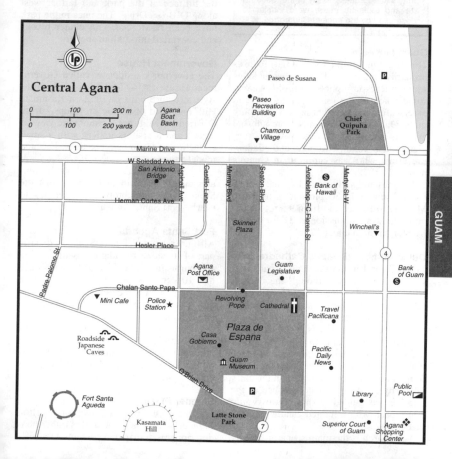

Central Agana

The Last Straggler

WW II straggler Shoichi Yokoi was a corporal in the Japanese army who managed to evade capture until 1972, when he was finally discovered hiding in the rugged interior of southern Guam. Cut off from the Japanese-speaking world, he held out for an amazing 28 years, simply because no one had told him the war was over!

Yokoi's tools of survival are now on display in the Guam Museum. They include a skilfully woven jacket and a pair of pants made from wild hibiscus fibre, a rat trap made from wire (rat liver was his favourite food) and a frying pan cut from a discarded army water canteen. Many of the foods he ate and tools he made were similar to those used by the ancient Chamorros. ■

Guam Museum

This small museum (☎ 477-8320) focuses primarily on the WW II years and includes some interesting photos of old Agana, some taken at the onset of the war and others after the devastating US bombing raids. One of the museum's more unusual displays is dedicated to the WW II straggler Shoichi Yokoi, a corporal in the Japanese army, who was captured in Guam's jungles in 1972.

The museum, in Plaza de Espana, is open from 9 am to 12.30 pm and 1 to 4 pm Monday to Friday and from 9 am to 2 pm on Saturdays. Admission is $1 for adults, free for children under 12.

Dulce Nombre de Maria Cathedral

The cathedral in the Plaza de Espana was first built in 1669, although the current building dates to 1958. Chief Quipuha and other Chamorro chiefs and church leaders are buried beneath the cathedral floor.

Above the main altar is a 12-inch statue of Santa Marian Camarin, which is carved of ironwood and has human hair and a face made of ivory. Local lore says that it was found in the waters off Merizo in the early 1800s by a fisherman who watched as the figurine was guided to shore by two gold crabs, each with a lighted candle between its claws.

The church is the main scene of activity during Agana's two annual fiestas, honouring the 'Sweet Name of Mary' in early September and the 'Feast of the Immaculate Conception' on 8 December.

Latte Stone Park

The latte stones in Latte Stone Park, at the base of Kasamata Hill, are thought to be house pillars dating from about 500 AD. They were moved to this site from an ancient Chamorro village in the south-central interior of Guam.

There are a number of Japanese-era caves, built by forced Chamorro labour, in the hillface at the park and farther west along O'Brien Drive. The ones in the park have been reinforced with cinder blocks and converted into fallout shelters.

Government House

The governor's residence, called Government House (☎ 477-9850), is a Spanish-style structure built in 1952 on Kasamata Hill, one-third of a mile up Route 7 from O'Brien Drive. It has a panoramic view of Agana and a visitors gallery with a small collection of Chamorro beads, baskets and model canoes.

If you're on foot, it takes about 10 minutes up to Government House from Latte Stone Park, and another 10 minutes to nearby Fort Santa Agueda.

Fort Santa Agueda

All that remains of Fort Santa Agueda is part of its stone foundation, built of coral and burnt limestone. The fort, which once had 10 cannons, was built in 1800 as a lookout, which is the best reason to visit it now – the view of Agana and the turquoise bay is unbeatable!

This is also the site of Guam's first mission, established in 1668, though nothing remains to be seen from that cra. The fort is on the first road on the right, after heading uphill from Government House.

Skinner Plaza

Guam's first civilian governor, Carlton Skinner, lends his name to this rather nondescript grassy strip that contains a few memorials to Guam's war heroes, including a statue of General Douglas MacArthur.

San Antonio Bridge

The San Antonio Bridge, also known as the 'Old Spanish Bridge' or *To lai Achu*, was built of cut stone in 1800 to cross an artificial branch of the Agana River. The bridge survived WW II bombing raids but during the reconstruction of Agana the canal it spanned was filled and the river diverted. The San Antonio Bridge now crosses just a shallow pool, though the park-like setting with its seasonal flame trees is attractive. A stone plaque on the bridge honours St Anthony of Padua.

Paseo de Susana

Paseo de Susana, north of central Agana, sits upon an artificial peninsula that was created during the Agana reconstruction. The military, needing to dispose of the rubble and debris of the levelled city, opted to bulldoze it here as coastal landfill.

Today it's a popular park and recreation centre, as well as the site of Agana's public market. Known as **Chamorro Village**, the market has kiosks with food vendors, produce sellers and a few handicraft artists. The park's **baseball stadium** is used by Guam's league teams and as a winter training camp by the Yomiuri Giants, a top Japanese major league baseball team.

The **Agana Boat Basin** is along the

Statue of Chief Quipuha

Sirena the Mermaid

Overlooking the pool at San Antonio Bridge is a statue of the mermaid Sirena. According to legend Sirena, a young girl from Agana, went swimming instead of gathering coconut shells as her mother had asked. When she didn't return on time the mother cursed her daughter saying, 'If the water gives Sirena so much pleasure I hope she turns into a fish!' Sirena's godmother overheard the curse and intervened in time to add, 'Let the part that has been given to me by God remain human.' Sirena thus became a mermaid – half fish, half human. ■

west side of the park. At the park's northern tip there's a tacky miniature replica of the **Statue of Liberty** and beyond that a breakwater where you can walk out and watch local surfers challenge the waves.

In the south-east section of the park, a statue of **Chief Quipuha** stands forever condemned to survey Agana's congested traffic on Marine Drive. Quipuha was Agana's highest ranking chief when the first mission was built on Guam and he was

GUAM

the first Chamorro adult to be baptised. Under Jesuit persuasion, Quipuha donated the land for Guam's first Catholic church, the site of the present Dulce Nombre de Maria Cathedral.

TUMON BAY

Tumon Bay, the tourist centre of Guam, has all the usual trappings of resort life. Its fringing white sand beach is lined with hotels, clubs and restaurants. Duty-free shops, shooting galleries and other tourist-targeted businesses prevail along the inland side of the road.

As the most developed resort area in Micronesia, Tumon Bay is often likened to Hawaii's Waikiki, but in terms of both density and variety the analogy is over-blown. Although Tumon's hotels are multi-storey, they're not packed together and the tourist strip is essentially just one road deep.

While Tumon is appealing enough, it's largely geared for Japanese package tourists, which translates to high prices – there's a dearth of affordable places to stay, inexpensive restaurants are few, and water sports equipment rents by the hour at prices that surpass daily rates elsewhere.

Tumon Bay is quite shallow at low tide

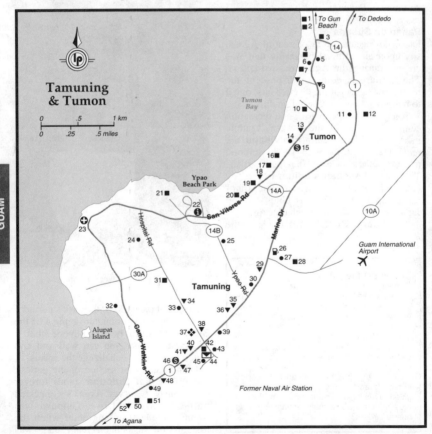

and it's commonly possible to wade clear out to the reef. If you're not a strong swimmer be cautious, as it's possible to unwittingly get stuck on the reef by incoming tides – a situation made all the more precarious by the fact that there are no lifeguards stationed along the beach.

Ypao Beach Park

Ypao Beach is a large public beach park along the south-west side of Tumon Bay. It was once the location of an ancient Chamorro village and in the late 1800s was the site of a penal and leper colony.

The park has playground equipment, picnic facilities and an expansive beachfront with white sand and turquoise waters. It's not only a popular weekend place for local families but it's also a well-used venue for festivals and other celebrations.

Zoo

Jimmy Cushing runs a small, funky zoo and aquarium on Tumon Bay, opposite the Church of the Blessed Diego. Tourists largely bypass it, as it's geared more toward local kids, but it's a good place to see animals resident in Micronesia, including monkeys and a saltwater crocodile from

Palau, brown tree snakes, monitor lizards, coconut crabs, Guam deer, small sharks, moray eels, tropical fish and a carabao. It's open from 10 am to 5 pm daily. Admission costs $3 for adults, $1.50 for children.

Gun Beach

Gun Beach is one-third of a mile down the washed-out, but generally passable, coral road that goes by the Hotel Nikko. It's named for the rusted Japanese gun that is half-hidden in jungle growth at the foot of the northside cliff, just behind the remains of a beachside pillbox.

Straight out from the centre of the beach, there's a cut in the reef that was made for the placement of underwater cables. It's convenient for divers and snorkellers who can follow the cable run out to deeper waters, where conditions are quite good when the water's calm.

The sand at Gun Beach is quite fascinating as it's largely comprised of tiny orange grains with little star-shaped points. Known as star sand, it's actually the calcium carbonate shells of a common protozoan found on Guam's reefs.

Gun Beach is pleasant enough, but past the gun and around the point to the north is

PLACES TO STAY		PLACES TO EAT		11	St John's School
1	Hotel Nikko Guam	8	Wet Willie's	14	Zoo
2	Guam Hotel Okura	9	7-Eleven	15	Bank of Guam
3	Regency Hotel	13	Kentucky Fried Chicken	22	Guam Visitors Bureau
4	Guam Reef Hotel	18	Tony Roma's	23	Guam Memorial Hospital
7	Hyatt Regency Guam	29	McDonald's	24	Guam Greyhound Track
10	Fujita Tumon Beach Hotel	34	Pim's Place	25	Seventh-Day Adventist
12	Pagoda Inn	35	Winchell's		Clinic
16	Sotetsu Tropical Hotel	36	Denny's Restaurant	26	Exxon Petrol Station
17	Guam Dai-Ichi Hotel	38	Marianas Trench	27	Thrifty Car Rental
19	Pacific Star Hotel	40	Fiesta's Buffet	30	Korean Airlines
20	Pacific Islands Club	41	Marty's Mexican	33	Coin Laundry
21	Guam Hilton		Restaurant	37	Guam Shopping Center
28	Hotel Mai'Ana	47	Taco Bell	39	Northwest Airlines
31	Golden Motel	48	Pizza Hut	42	ITC Building
32	Onward Agana Beach	52	Caravelle Vietnamese	43	Hafa Adai Theatre
	Hotel		Restaurant	44	Tamuning Post Office
42	ITC Plaza Hotel			45	Coral Reef Marine Center
50	Tamuning Plaza Hotel	**OTHER**		46	Bank of Hawaii
51	Mid-Town Hotel	5	DFS	49	Continental Airlines
		6	SandCastle & Onyx Disco		

GUAM

an even nicer crescent of white sand. At low tide it's possible to wade around the point and at high tide you can swim or snorkel around it. There was once an old Chamorro village in this area and latte stones can be found by following an overgrown trail that leads inland.

NORTHERN GUAM
Two Lovers Point

Two Lovers Point, or Puntan Dos Amantes, is a scenic coastal lookout at the top of a sheer 410-foot limestone cliff just north of Tumon Bay.

Heading north on Route 1 toward Dededo, turn left on the road across from the Micronesia Mall, continue down nearly a mile and turn left at the little blue cinderblock building. Beware of the unmarked speed bumps as you drive down to the point!

As the story goes, two young Chamorro lovers entwined their hair and jumped to their deaths from this jagged cliff while being hunted down by the Spanish captain who had been promised the girl in marriage.

A giant gilt statue on this site that graphically showed the two lovers entwining more than just their hair was knocked down by a typhoon a few years back. A recast was planned, but controversy has thus far kept the statue from being re-erected.

The top of the cliff is a good vantage point for views of Tumon Bay and the coral gardens below. Another attraction at the point is a very deep basalt cave which drops steeply to the ocean; it's enclosed by protective fencing but you can look down into it.

Northern Beaches

Two of Guam's best beaches are **Tarague Beach** and **Uruno Beach**, on the northern tip of the island. However, although these beaches are public the only land access to them is through Andersen Air Force Base and without a visitor's pass non-military types can't get to them. On the other hand if you approach from the sea you're allowed to land.

One of the few stretches of northern coastline with public access is **Tanguisson Beach**, also known as NCS Beach. To get there, take the turn-off from Route 1 toward Two Lovers Point but instead of taking the final turn-off to the point follow the main sealed road, which passes a sewage treatment plant and then winds down to the shore.

Tanguisson is a popular place for local picnics but a huge power plant at the south end of the beach mars the view.

You can reach more appealing beaches by heading north from Tanguisson Beach along a dirt road that runs parallel to the ocean. You can drive at least partway down, though how far depends on recent rain and road conditions. You could also park at Tanguisson Beach and walk, which is probably safer for your car. There are good sandy beaches en route, the nearest just a few minutes' walk away. The final one, which is about two miles north of Tanguisson and is called **Shark's Hole**, has a turquoise hole with very good snorkelling. There are two channels into the hole so beware of currents.

South Pacific Memorial Park

This park in Yigo is a memorial site for those who died during WW II. The main monument is a 15-foot abstract sculpture of large white hands folded in prayer, which is surrounded by personalised memorial plaques in Japanese script. A small chapel called the Queen of Peace is staffed by Japanese priests and nuns.

Steps lead down the hill from the monument to four caves which served as the last Japanese Army command post. On 11 August 1944 US soldiers detonated 400-pound blocks of TNT at the opening of the caves. When the caves were reopened a few days later more than 60 bodies were removed, including that of the Japanese commander, Lieutenant General Hideyoshi Obata, who had taken his own life. The caves are surrounded by a bamboo forest which creaks in the wind and is spooky enough to conjure up images of restless spirits.

The park, on Route 1 in Yigo, is open from 8 am to 5 pm daily.

University of Guam

The University of Guam, which is in Mangilao on the east coast, offers both undergraduate and graduate programmes. It is noted for its work in marine biology. The university's Micronesian Area Research Center (☎ 734-2921) has an excellent collection of books, maps and documents on the Pacific region and the library staff are very helpful if you're interested in research.

Guam's two-year community college is just to the north of the university.

SOUTHERN GUAM

If you had only one full day on Guam, you couldn't do better than to rent a car and circle the southern part of the island, taking time to stroll through historic sites and catch the scenery along the way. Southern villages such as Umatac and Inarajan give a glimpse of a more rural Guam whose character remains unaffected by tourism.

If you start in Agana and go down the west coast in the morning and up the east coast in the afternoon you'll keep the sun at your back for photography and views.

GovGuam at Adelup Point

South of Agana on the western coastal road is Adelup Point, which was once heavily fortified by the Japanese and is now the site of a Spanish-style complex that houses government administration offices.

Both the east and west side of the complex have little beach parks with picnic tables. There's a new museum (☎ 477-3325) perched at the north end of the point that has a splendid view of Agana and Tumon bays and a collection of pottery, stone adzes and other displays on Chamorro culture. Admission is $3 or free for children under 12.

Route 6 Side Trip

At another time you might want to take the five-mile Route 6 loop from Adelup Point through the Nimitz Hill area to Piti. You'll get some views of the west coast as well as glimpses into the island's interior.

About 1.5 miles up Route 6 there are two bunkers in the hillside, visible on the right side of the road, which once served as a Japanese command post. Nimitz Hill, incidentally, takes its name from US Admiral Chester Nimitz, the first Commander of Naval Forces Marianas to take up residence on the hill.

War in the Pacific Park

War in the Pacific National Historical Park has its visitor centre and WW II museum in Asan, almost a mile south of Adelup Point on Route 1. The centre's main displays combine period photos and military paraphernalia to give an engaging chronological history of Guam during the war years.

Movies are shown continuously in the centre's theatre, most commonly a 30-minute footage film of the US retaking of Guam. You can also request to see anything in the extensive tape library; subjects include Guam's brown tree snakes, Chamorro history and culture, environmental issues and war battles around the Pacific.

The centre is open from 9 am to 5 pm Monday to Friday and from 10 am to 5 pm on weekends. Admission is free, as are brochures that map out the various battle sites around Guam.

Seven separate parcels of land that were battlefield sites during WW II are part of the park's historical holdings and some of them are easily visited.

The park's Asan Beach Unit includes the visitor centre as well as **Asan Point**, a big, grassy beach park a mile farther south which has guns, torpedoes and monuments on the grounds. Asan Beach was one of the major sites of the US invasion in July 1944 and just off the beach a couple of landing craft that never made it ashore can be seen at low tide. On the south-west side of the park, a 15-minute loop trail takes in a cave and a couple of Japanese gun emplacements.

GUAM

Piti Bomb Holes

The Piti bomb holes, which are about 100 yards offshore and within the reef, are ideal for beginner divers as they bottom out at around 30 feet. Seen from Tepungan Beach, the holes look like dark blue circles surrounded by the aqua shades of shallower water. It's just local lore that the holes are bomb craters – they're actually natural sinkholes.

Snorkellers might enjoy the hard yellow corals around the edges of the holes, but the water is deep enough in the centres to make it difficult to see the bottom. Closer to shore you'll see bright blue starfish, zebra damsels, pufferfish and other small tropicals. If you want to snorkel out to the holes rather than wade, the best time is high tide, as otherwise the nearshore waters can be quite shallow. Watch out for strong currents around the holes farthest out.

Although public access to the site will continue, the area is undergoing some major changes as an unusual underwater observatory, connected by a walkway from the beach, is being constructed in the largest bomb hole.

The parking area is on the right about one-quarter of a mile after Asan Point, across the street from a metal warehouse.

Piti Guns

On a hill behind the Catholic church in Piti are three Japanese coastal defence guns, now part of the War in the Pacific National Historical Park holdings.

To get there, turn left off Route 1 onto J M Tumcap St, just past the Mobil Station in Piti, and at the stop sign turn right onto Assumption St. Park under the big monkeypod tree to the left of the church social hall, the building with the white cross on the front, and then take the concrete steps that lead up the hill. The path is fairly well defined, although slightly overgrown with hibiscus bushes. It's only five minutes up to the first gun, which is amazingly well preserved. The second gun is a couple of minutes farther along the same path while the third is at the end of a side path.

Apra Harbor & Beaches

Apra Harbor, Guam's huge deepwater harbour, was named San Luis de Apra by the Spanish who developed it in the 1700s as a port of call for their Manila galleons.

The US Naval Station encompasses all of the land surrounding Apra Harbor, including Orote Peninsula to the south. In addition to home-ported US Navy vessels, Apra Harbor has extensive commercial operations, a small boat harbour and space for cruise ships. The harbour also contains a number of sunken ships which makes it a popular diving spot.

The north side of the harbour is marked by a peninsula, called Cabras Island, which is extended by a long breakwater. About halfway out, along the harbour side of the peninsula, is a **recreational dock** used by glass-bottom boats and the Nautilus semi-submarine. Just beyond the dock, look for a grove of ironwood trees on the left side of the road; they mark **Family Beach**, a sandy harbourside strand that's locally popular for weekend outings.

Dogleg Reef, fronting Family Beach, is a good place for snorkellers to see both soft and hard corals as well as anemone colonies with clownfish. The waters are protected and the top of the reef, which starts just a few feet underwater, is visible from shore.

When the seas are calm, **Luminao Reef**, which stretches along the north side of the peninsula, can also be snorkelled. It has good coral and small fish in waters five to 15 feet deep and can be accessed in several places along the road by short paths.

To get to Family Beach, turn right onto Route 11 at the traffic lights, go past the commercial port and at the oil tanks continue straight ahead on the lower road, which is sealed; to get to Luminao Reef take the upper road to the right at the oil tanks.

Back on Route 1, an artificial (we hope!) Polaris missile guards the entrance to Polaris Point, part of the naval station.

To continue south around the island, turn left at the traffic lights just past the US Army Reserve Center; there's a Taco Bell

Fort Soledad sentry post overlooking Umatac Bay, Guam

Beach at Tumon Bay, Guam

Latte stone in Agana, Guam

Riding carabao, Guam

A basket-making demonstration at the Chamorro
Cultural Village in Inarajan, Guam

Mural in Utamac, Guam

on the corner, followed by a Pizza Hut. This is not well marked and if you miss the turn you will wind up at a guarded US Navy gate. South of the harbour, Route 1 briefly becomes Route 2A and then turns to Route 2.

The bright yellow flowers growing tall along the roadside are *Cassia alata*, more commonly called golden candles, and the pink flowers winding amongst the trees are known as chain of love, as each tiny flower on the vine is shaped like a heart.

Gaan Point

The park at Gaan Point, on Route 2 in Agat, was one of the main landing sites for the US invasion of southern Guam. On 21 July 1944, US marine and army combat divisions came ashore here to battle with the heavily fortified Japanese infantry.

From their coastal caves and pillboxes the Japanese cut down the Americans as they jumped from their landing crafts. In the first hours of the assault there were more than 1000 US casualties and it wasn't until the third day of fighting, after US tanks made it ashore and managed to knock the Japanese out from behind, that the beachhead was finally secured.

Known also as the War in the Pacific National Historical Park's Agat Unit, Gaan Point has a large 20-centimetre naval coastal defence gun, an anti-aircraft cannon and intact bunkers that can be explored.

There's a US WW II amtrac underwater about 400 yards out and 50 feet down, popular with divers.

Much of the reef off the Agat area can be snorkelled or dived. Agat is also the site of a new small-boat marina, Nimitz Beach Park and the Taleyfac Bridge.

Taleyfac Bridge

In the late 1700s the Spanish built a bullcart coastal road to link Agana with Umatac and other southern villages. The road, known as the Camino del Real, was connected by several stone bridges.

The best preserved bridge is in Agat at Taleyfac, just a little beyond Nimitz Beach Park, on the ocean side of the road. It's a few hundred feet back from Route 2 just before The Last Market store; look for the roadside sign that marks the spot. The picturesque bridge, which is 36 feet long, has twin stone arches that span a narrow river.

Sella Bay Vista Point & Trail

A couple of miles south of Agat, the road rises up the coastal hills and you'll reach a roadside lookout with a fine view of Sella Bay and the surrounding coast. If it's been raining recently, be sure to also glance inland to the north-east for a view of a cascading waterfall.

From the lookout parking lot a well-defined red clay trail leads down to Sella Bay, the site of an ancient Chamorro village. The whole walk is wonderfully scenic but watch out for slippery mud and trailside sword grasses that can cut. An old Spanish bridge that dates to the 1790s still crosses the Sella River close to the coast. There are also a few other overgrown remnants of earlier habitation, including an old beehive oven and some latte stones. Give yourself about 1½ hours to make the hike down and back.

Some people prefer to make a day of it, continuing south from Sella Bay along the shore to Cetti Bay and then up the Cetti River Valley. The valley dead-ends at Cetti Falls, but before that point there's a trail to the left that goes up to the main road.

Cetti Bay Vista Point

The most panoramic roadside vista on the south-west coast is from the Cetti Bay Vista Point. It's just a two-minute walk up the steps to the lookout, which offers a commanding view of the palm-lined Cetti River Valley and picturesque Cetti Bay. You can also see Cocos Island, the Merizo Barrier Reef which encloses Cocos Lagoon and the whole south-west coastline.

Mt Lamlam & Mt Jumullong Manglo

Inland from the Cetti Bay Vista Point and topped with large wooden crosses is Mt Jumullong Manglo, or Humuyung Manglu, the final destination of cross-bearers during the island's annual Good Friday procession.

GUAM

The starting point for a trail that goes up the 1282-foot Mt Jumullong Manglo is across the road from the Cetti Bay Vista Point. You begin by heading up an eroded hill and continue along the mostly well-defined trail. At the divide, go to the right to get to the crosses. There are excellent views of both the coast and the interior forests on the way and the hike should take about an hour. A more difficult and more obscure trail continues left from the divide to the 1332-foot Mt Lamlam, Guam's highest point. Lamlam means 'lightning' and legends call it the source of the winds.

Memorial Vista

Memorias Para I Lalahita, a Vietnam War memorial about one mile north of Umatac, is in a small roadside park graced with two latte stones and a hilltop view of Umatac Valley.

Umatac

Umatac is an unspoiled, friendly village, steeped in history.

Magellan's 1521 landing in Umatac Bay is celebrated in the village each March with four days of activities, including a re-enactment of the event. There's a tall concrete **monument to Magellan** in the village centre.

The Spanish 'Reduction'

The villages of Merizo and neighbouring Inarajan were founded in 1695 largely as resettlement sites for Chamorros who were forced to abandon their homes in the Northern Marianas and migrate to southern Guam. The relocations were made under a Spanish policy known as 'reduction' that intended to more effectively convert and 'Hispanicize' the natives by centralising them on one island. In the new villages, which had populations of about 400, the Chamorros were obliged to live in clustered thatch homes that were built around a central church. To this day many inhabitants in Merizo and Inarajan can trace their lineage to the still uninhabited islands of the Northern Marianas that their ancestors were forced to abandon. ■

The Spanish used Umatac Bay for more than 200 years as a major port of call for their galleons, though little remains of the four forts that once protected the bay.

Opposite the Magellan monument are the ruins of the **Saint Dionicio Church**, which was originally built in the 1690s, reconstructed in 1862 and destroyed by an earthquake in 1902. All that remains today are rubble and a few stone pillars.

The rusting skeleton of a Japanese midget submarine used to be visible offshore at the river mouth but it's now buried under the sand bar. There's a **Japanese Zero** fighter plane in the bay about 150 yards from the beach and 50 feet underwater that makes a good dive.

On your way out of town you'll see the decorative **Umatac Bridge** with its spiral staircase towers that are intended to symbolise Guam's Chamorro-Spanish heritage.

Fort Soledad

Fort Nuestra Senora de la Soledad offers a lovely hilltop view of Umatac Bay and the coastline to the north. To get there take the ironwood-lined road on the right after crossing the Umatac Bridge.

The fort was built by the Spanish in the early 1800s to protect their treasure-laden Manila galleons from pirates roaming the western Pacific. Today the main remnant of the fort is a small hillside sentry post.

If you have a keen eye you can see the remains of Fort Santo Angel which was built in 1742 on a rock jutting out on the north-west side of the bay.

Merizo

In the courtyard of San Dimas Church, in the village of Merizo, there's a **monument** to the 46 Chamorros who were executed by the Japanese in the Merizo hills in July 1944, one week before the US invasion of Guam.

Next door you can see the ruins of **Merizo Conbento**, which was built by the Spanish in 1856, soon after the smallpox epidemic which killed almost two-thirds of the population. The conbento (convent) was constructed of ifil wood and manposte-

A Meeting of Chiefs

According to legend, Tumon's Chief Malaguana, weary of hearing exaggerated rumours about the strength of Gadao, a rival chief in the southern part of Guam, set out in his canoe for Inarajan determined to kill Gadao.

When Malaguana reached Inarajan a stranger invited him to dinner but unknown to him, that man was Gadao. When Gadao asked his guest to get a coconut for dinner, Malaguana shook a coconut tree and the coconuts fell like rain. Gadao then picked up one of the coconuts and crushed it open with one hand.

After a few more such contests, Malaguana became worried – if this common Inarajan man was so strong, what would his chief be like? So Malaguana asked the man to take him back to Tumon by canoe. Both chiefs got in the canoe but paddled in opposite directions. The canoe broke in half but Malaguana, in his urgency to leave, was paddling so fast that he didn't even notice until he was back in Tumon. ■

ria (burnt limestone mixed with coral rocks) and was still being used as a parish house until it was heavily damaged by Typhoon Russ in December 1990.

Directly across the street is Kampanayun Malessu, the **Merizo Bell Tower**, built in 1910 under the direction of Father Cristobal De Canals. It was restored in 1981.

Route 4 continues to follow the coast around the southern tip of Guam, offering ocean views and glimpses of nearshore islands.

Cocos Island

About 1.5 miles offshore from Merizo is Cocos Island, which sits within a huge barrier reef. The island has good beaches and the lagoon's calm waters are ideal for many water sports.

Cocos Island Resort, occupying the east side of the island, is a day-trip destination catering mainly to the younger Japanese set, offering jet-skiing, parasailing, kayaking, banana boats and other activities.

Boats go to the resort (☎ 828-8691) from Merizo Pier half a dozen times a day between 9 am and 3 pm. The cost for tourists, which includes the 10-minute boat ride, the day-use fee and lunch is $40. Locals pay $10, without lunch – as long as you're not getting off a tour bus you might pass as a local, but an ID such as a Guam driving licence is commonly required. Once on the island, water sports cost extra. Visitors are not allowed to bring food or beverages to the resort; there's a snack bar with burgers and plate lunches for about $7.

While most of Cocos is privately owned, the west side of the island, formerly the site of a US Coast Guard station, is part of the territorial park system. To get to the public side, called Dano, you either have to hike over from the resort dock or find someone with a private boat to take you over from Merizo. Dano Park has restrooms, picnic tables and barbecue pits; camping is allowed with a permit from the Department of Parks & Recreation.

Inarajan

Inarajan is another sleepy village with a smattering of Spanish-era influence.

Along the roadside, just before reaching the village, you'll see **Salugula Pool**, a natural saltwater pool with diving platforms and arched bridges that are now in disrepair as a consequence of the harsh storms that have whipped the south coast in recent years. Jagged grey lava rocks separate the calm pool from the crashing ocean surf beyond, and there's an interesting coastal view.

The body of Chamorro priest Jesus Baza Duenas is buried beneath the altar of Inarajan's **Saint Joseph's Church**. Duenas, his nephew and two other Chamorros were beheaded by the Japanese near the end of the war for failing to reveal the whereabouts of US Navy radioman George Tweed, who had survived the Japanese occupation in hiding. The church, which was damaged in the 1993 earthquake, is currently closed to the public.

Along the waterfront is the **Chamorro Cultural Village**, a publicly funded complex of bamboo and thatch shelters where traditional Chamorro crafts are demonstrated every morning between 10 am and noon. It's a simple concept that's delightfully presented and admission is free. You can see cookies being baked in an old beehive oven, watch coconut fronds being woven into hats and baskets and even ride a

carabao. The best time to visit is on Wednesday mornings when Inarajan students put on a traditional dance performance.

Just beyond the cultural village are the crumbling ruins of a concrete **Baptist church**, built in 1925. Next to it a **bronze sculpture** depicts a local legend about an encounter between two powerful Chamorro chiefs, Malaguana of Tumon and Gadao of Inarajan.

Gadao's Cave

From the statue of Gadao in Inarajan, you can see some caves in the cliffs across the bay, not far from the point. One of them is Gadao's Cave, which has ancient pictographs said to be the canoe story drawn onto the wall by Gadao himself.

To get there, drive north out of town on Route 4. Just across the bridge take the first sealed road to the right and park at the far end of the beach just before the road turns inland.

Walk along the beach and then take the trail across a meadow and up a cliff to the caves. The walk takes about 15 minutes. Some of this land may be private property, so if you see anyone along the way ask their permission to continue.

Talofofo Falls

Talofofo Falls is a two-tier cascade, with pools beneath each waterfall. There's a 30-foot drop on the top one, though it's usually gentle enough to stand beneath. The deeper and larger pool is at the base of the second fall, where the water flows gently over a very wide rockface. This is a popular swimming and picnicking spot.

To get there, take the marked turn-off to the left about 2.5 miles past Inarajan. About 1.5 miles down, just before the NASA Tracking Station, turn right onto a dirt road. The falls are about a mile farther.

Talofofo Falls is open from 9 am to 5 pm on weekdays, to 5.30 pm on weekends. Admission is $4 for adults, $1 for children under age 12. You can either park in the lot above the falls and walk from there or brave the steep, winding one-lane road down to a lower parking area. If you walk, it will take less than 10 minutes to get down but probably double that to walk back.

Talofofo Beaches
Back on Route 4, **Talofofo Bay Beach Park** is about two miles ahead. This is one of Guam's prime surfing spots. Guam's longest and widest river, the Talofofo, runs out into the bay and the sand is chocolate brown.

A couple of miles down the road is **Ipan Beach Park**, another popular swimming place with calm shallow water and iron-wood shade trees. Just north of Ipan is Jeff's Pirates Cove, a casual beachside restaurant that has moderately priced burgers and sandwiches, drinks and occasional live music.

Pago Bay Vista Point
An unmarked viewpoint just past the town of Yona looks over the Pago River as it empties into broad Pago Bay. There was once a Spanish village at the mouth of the river but its inhabitants were wiped out in the 1856 smallpox epidemic.

The area between Pago Bay on the east coast and Agana Bay on the west is the narrowest part of the island.

According to legend a giant fish who wanted to divide Guam in half used to visit the island and nibble away at this neck of land. Guam was saved by the women of the island who cut off their long hair, wove a big net from their locks and scooped up the fish with the net.

PLACES TO STAY
Camping
Camping information is available from the Department of Parks & Recreation (☎ 477-7825), 490 Chalan Palasyu in Agana Heights, up the hill from Fort Santa Agueda. The office is open from 8 am to 5 pm Monday to Friday. The staff will sell you a $2-per-day camping permit, but beyond this they seem completely at a loss as to why you might want to camp or which places are safer than others.

The truth is, camping is not that common on Guam – except by extended families or other large groups who also book the park pavilions for birthday parties and picnics. If you do camp alone or with just a couple of people it's advisable not to choose a roadside park as there's apt to be a few rowdy drinkers cruising the roads at night. Guam's crime rate is high enough for potential campers to think twice.

Dano Park on isolated Cocos Island is one of the eight approved camping locations in the park system and is one of the more frequently recommended spots.

Hotels
The majority of Guam's 6000 hotel rooms are in the high-rises lining Tumon Bay. These resorts are geared for Japanese package tourists and are generally not good value for independent travellers, who pay inflated rack rates. However, some of the international chain hotels, such as Hilton and Hyatt, offer periodic promotions that provide substantial discounts from their published rates.

It can be difficult booking a room in Guam, particularly during peak Japanese vacation periods from late December to early March and from June to September. Generally the farther you go from Tumon Bay, the easier it gets to find a room during those times.

Outside of Tumon Bay, there are a number of small hotels that bill themselves as business-oriented. The majority are on or near Marine Drive in Tamuning, Upper Tumon and Agana. Although the prices are reasonable by Guam standards, you shouldn't expect anything resembling a holiday hotel – most are quite utilitarian and not terribly well maintained.

All rooms in Guam hotels have private bathrooms. A 10% room tax is added onto all rates.

Bottom End The *Hotel Marina* (☎ 477-6701, fax 477-2709), 470 West Soledad Ave, Agana, Guam 96910, is an older hotel that's a bit tired but nonetheless adequate considering that it's the cheapest hotel on the island. A former business hotel near the centre of Agana, its 44 rooms have TVs, air-con and refrigerators and cost $35 for singles or doubles. The staff are friendly and there's a good coffeeshop-style restaurant off the lobby.

The *Harmon Loop Hotel* (☎ 632-3353, fax 632-3330), 1900 Harmon Loop Rd, Suite 107, Dededo, Guam 96912, is a newer hotel with a few dozen rooms above a small shopping centre on Route 16, about two miles east of the airport. Rooms are straightforward but modern with thermostatic air-con, cable TV, refrigerator and a double or queen bed. The location's not special but if you're just there to sleep it's good value at $45 for one or two people. Ask for a room away from the road. There's free morning coffee, an Asian restaurant on site and a McDonald's across the street. It's a popular place with Micronesian travellers so it often books solid, but you can occasionally get a room simply by calling from the airport courtesy phone.

The three-storey *Mid-Town Hotel* (☎ 649-9882, fax 946-7575), Box 1263, Agana, Guam 96910, behind the Ben Franklin department store in Tamuning, has straightforward rooms with refrigerators, phones, TVs and two twin beds. While the place could be cheerier it's otherwise fine for the price: $40/45 for singles/doubles.

The *Pagoda Inn* (☎ 646-1882, fax 646-9065), Box 4285, 801A N Marine Drive, Agana, Guam 96910, opposite St John's School on Route 1 in Upper Tumon, has 41 rooms that are very small and a bit lacklustre but otherwise OK. Each has a TV, refrigerator and phone and costs $45 for singles or doubles.

The 18-room *Golden Motel* (☎ 646-9118, fax 646-9628), Box 10328, Tamuning, Guam 96911, on Hospital Rd in Tamuning, promotes itself as a romantic hotel, which means, among other things, that you can pay by the hour. Overnight rates are $45 for rooms with a regular double bed or from $50 for the VIP rooms with a round double bed and a jacuzzi.

Guam Garden Villa (☎ 477-8166), Mrs Herta Laguana, Box 10167, Sinajana,

Guam 96926, is a pleasant B&B in a family setting in Ordot, about three miles from Agana. The house is large, with a porch and garden, and has three guest rooms with a shared bathroom. The rate of $40/50 for singles/doubles includes a hearty breakfast. Mrs Laguana can provide airport transfers for $10 each way and the public bus stops nearby, but overall it could be inconvenient without a car.

The *Plumeria Garden Hotel* (☎ 472-8831, fax 477-4914), Box 7220, Tamuning, Guam 96911, is on Route 8 in Maite, one-quarter of a mile inland from Route 1. The 78 rooms are in a series of motel-style two-storey cinderblock buildings. Rooms are worn with stained carpets and the like, but have TVs, refrigerators and phones. There's a large swimming pool and free coffee and doughnuts in the morning. Although renovations seem overdue, the hotel remains popular with repeat business travellers. Singles or doubles cost $55.

Middle The *Tamuning Plaza Hotel* (☎ 649-8646, fax 649-8651), 960 S Marine Drive, Tamuning, Guam 96911, near the Ben Franklin department store in Tamuning, has 40 large rooms, each with refrigerator, cable TV, air-con, a small table and two double beds. It's better maintained than most other hotels in this price range and is one of the more recommendable options. As it's on Marine Drive it makes a fairly convenient base, yet it's set back far enough from the road to be quiet. There are a number of restaurants within walking distance. Rates are $60 for singles or doubles.

The *Cliff Hotel* (☎ 477-7675), 178 Francisco Javier Drive, Agana Heights, Guam 96910, built in 1975, is one of Guam's oldest hotels. Once a favourite of business-people, it now shows its age without grace, but it does have a swimming pool, health club, tennis court and a cliffside locale overlooking Agana. Rooms have TVs, phones, tables and small verandas for a pricey $77/93 for singles/doubles. There are also some studios with kitchenettes for $93.

The *Cliff Condo Guest House* (☎ 477-

7276, fax 477-3420), Box 2925, Agana, Guam 96910, manages 40 privately owned condo units in the same building as the Cliff Hotel. Rooms have air-con, cable TV, refrigerator and phone. The decor varies with the owner and for the most part they're not very well maintained. Still, if you're not overly fastidious this can be a reasonable low-end option when they're running one of their frequent $45 room specials. Skip the $70 oceanview rooms – it's a distant view and if the mountain view rooms book out you may well be upgraded to an 'oceanview' anyway. Guests have use of the pool and health club.

The *Hotel Mai'Ana* (☎ 646-6961, fax 649-3230), Box 8957, Tamuning, Guam 96911, is on the airport road, half a mile west of the airport. Rates begin at $63 for a studio and $84 for a two-bedroom unit. All have kitchens, air-con, TVs and phones; there's a pool and a free airport shuttle. Overall it has the impersonal ambiance common to airport hotels, but most of the rooms have been renovated and it's a reasonably good value, particularly if you're just looking for a place to crash for one night between flights.

The *ITC Plaza Hotel* (☎ 646-3500, fax 646-3502), 590 Marine Drive, Tamuning, Guam 96911, has 28 standard rooms with cable TV, phones and a view of the town. The regular rates are high at $73/86 for singles/doubles, but if it's slow or if you're staying a few days you can usually negotiate a more reasonable 'local rate' of $50. The location, on the 8th floor of the commercial ITC Building, may seem a bit odd, but it is central to a number of services.

Although it's a 10-minute walk to the beach, the *Regency Hotel* (☎ 649-8000, fax 646-8738), 1475 San Vitores Rd, Tumon, Guam 96911, is good value for the Tumon Bay area. The 126 rooms are pleasant and fairly large, each with cable TV, phone, refrigerator, microwave oven, bathtub and balcony. There's a 24-hour convenience store, a jacuzzi and a free shuttle to the beach and airport. The rate is $85 for one or two people.

The *Fujita Tumon Beach Hotel* (☎ 646-

1811, fax 646-1805), 153 Fujita Rd, Tumon, Guam 96911, was the first hotel built at Tumon Bay. This sprawling lowrise Spanish style complex has some nice touches including tile murals on the exterior walls that depict Guamanian history and legends. There's a pool, tennis courts and a coin laundry. The 283 rooms have TVs, room safes, minibars, phones and bathtubs. While the hotel is older, most of the rooms have been renovated and they're as nice as you'll find in some of the newer high-rises, making this a relatively good deal at $125/135 for singles/doubles. Discounts of 20% are given to military, local and 'regular' customers.

Top End The *Guam Hilton* (☎ 646-1835, fax 646-6038), Box 11199, Tamuning, Guam 96911, is at the quieter end of Tumon Bay, beside Ypao Beach. The hotel, which has long been a favourite among international visitors, took a hard hit in the 1993 earthquake and all 695 rooms have either since been renovated or are in a newly built wing. Each has cable TV, a verandah and the other expected resort amenities. Standard rooms in the renovated section begin at $165/190 for singles/doubles, although if you're spending that much you might as well splurge on the new executive floor which at $200/225 has larger rooms and a cosy oceanview lounge with free cocktails, snacks and breakfast. There's a swimming pool and lighted tennis courts.

The new 455-room *Hyatt Regency Guam* (☎ 647-1234, 800-228-9000; fax 647-1235), Box 12998, Tamuning, Guam 96911, is the swankiest of the high-rise hotels along Tumon Bay. It has a grand pillared lobby, nicely landscaped grounds and a fun series of pools and interconnecting waterways. The rooms each have a large oceanfront balcony, heavy shade curtains, marble vanity, a soaking tub and separate shower, minibar, room safe and voice mail. A non-smoking floor and king beds are available. The staff are friendly, the hotel has good restaurants and there's often live

GUAM

ic. Rates begin at $210/225
ables.

Hotel Okura (☎ 646-6811,
fax   )3), 185 Gun Beach Rd, Tumon,
Guam 911, has a classic but subdued elegance that sets it apart from other large Japanese hotels on Tumon Beach. Rooms in the Tower Wing, which cost $220, have all the expected resort amenities as well as deep soaking tubs, an armoire to conceal the TV and refrigerator, and balconies with clear-on ocean views. Rooms in the South Wing are smaller and some don't have ocean views, but they have a similar decor and start at $130. When it's not busy, quoted walk-in rates are about 20% less.

Other first-class high-rise hotels on Tumon Bay are:

Sotetsu Tropicana Hotel, 825 San Vitores Rd, Tumon, Guam 96911; 200 rooms, from $135 (☎ 646-5851, fax 649-9342)

Guam Dai-Ichi Hotel, Box 3310, Agana, Guam 96910; 337 rooms, from $130/140 for singles/doubles (☎ 646-5880, fax 646-6729)

Guam Reef Hotel, Box 8258, Tamuning, Guam 96911; part of the Nikko Hotels chain, 297 rooms, from $150/180 for singles/doubles (☎ 646-6881)

Hotel Nikko Guam, Box 12819, Tamuning, Guam 96931; part of the Nikko Hotels chain, 492 rooms, from $200/210 for singles/doubles (☎ 649-8815, fax 649-8817)

Pacific Islands Club, Box 9370, Tamuning, Guam 96931; 502 rooms, from $246 (☎ 646-6109, fax 649-2434)

Pacific Star Hotel, Box 6097, Tamuning, Guam 96911; owned by the Republic of Nauru, 436 rooms, from $195/205 for singles/doubles (☎ 649-7827, fax 646-9335)

PLACES TO EAT

Guam's multi-ethnic population and thousands of tourists support more than a hundred restaurants in the Agana-Tumon area. There are a lot of cuisines to sample, including Japanese, Chinese, Korean, Mexican, Indian, Italian, Vietnamese, Filipino and Thai.

A tip of 10% to 15% is commonly expected at restaurants other than the fastfood type.

Guam's tap water is treated and safe to drink.

Budget

Chamorro Village, Agana's new public market, is a fun place to get a cheap local meal. Numerous tidy kiosks sell fixed plate lunches of local favourites such as spicy chicken kelaguen or barbecued spareribs with red rice for $3 to $5 – depending upon how high you want to heap your plate. Worth checking out is *Pagoda Fastfood* at the east end of the complex, which has good quality Chamorro and Asian food. There are a couple of dining courts where you can sit and eat. The market is open from about 9 am to 5.30 pm daily, though most kiosks sell out by 3 pm. There are also a few produce huts selling fruits, vegetables, betel nut and tuba.

Simply Food, adjacent to the Adventist church and opposite the turn-off to Agana's Fort Santa Agueda, is a small health-food store with a snack bar serving vegetarian food. The store is open from 9 am to 5 pm Monday to Thursday, from 9 am to 3 pm on Fridays. The lunch counter, open from 11 am to 2 pm weekdays, has smoothies, soups, salads and build-your-own sandwiches for under $4 as well as a daily lunch special for $5.75.

The *Mini Cafe*, near the police station in the centre of Agana, serves a full range of standard Chinese dishes, most around $7. The best deals are the lunch specials, which average $5. It's open from 11.30 am to 3 pm and 5.30 to 10 pm daily.

Sizzler Steak House in the Agana Shopping Center has a great all-you-can-eat salad buffet that includes not only green salad with all the fixings, but also soups, a taco bar, spaghetti and a good variety of fresh fruits. As a meal in itself it costs $7.50 at lunch, $9 at dinner. Sizzler also has standard steak and seafood meals from about $6 at lunch, $10 at dinner. It's open daily from 10.30 am to 9.30 pm.

Fiesta's Buffet on Marine Drive in Tamuning has a buffet that includes pizza, spaghetti, fried chicken, a taco bar, soups

GUAM

and salad. It's not on par with the one at Sizzler, but it's cheaper and will fill you up. It costs $6 from 11 am to 4 pm, $7 from 5 to 9 pm, except on Saturdays and Sundays when it's $8 and is served until 10 pm.

Caravelle Vietnamese Restaurant on Marine Drive in Tamuning, in the complex next to the Cinema movie theatre, offers up a decent pho (beef soup with bean sprouts, noodles, mint and lettuce) for $7 and fresh lumpia for $4. Most other dishes cost $7 for meat, $10 for fish or shrimp. It's open from 11 am to 2 am daily and doubles as a karaoke bar at night.

You can get reasonable Thai food at *Marianas Trench*, opposite the Guam Shopping Center in Tamuning. This hole-in-the-wall is basically a quiet bar with a couple of billiard tables, a jukebox and dining tables off to the side. Dishes include the likes of hot and sour beef salad or eggplant with chicken, both served with jasmine rice for $8. It's open from 5 to 11 pm Monday to Saturday.

Wet Willie's, an open-air beach bar on Tumon Bay, is not only popular for its singles scene but also serves reasonably priced food; a half-pound burger with fries is $5.50, fried chicken $6.50. It's pretty low keyed at lunch but the pace picks up as the day rolls on, with volleyball in the sand, happy hour specials and live music. Tumon Bay's other nod to inexpensive eats are a *Kentucky Fried Chicken* and a *7-Eleven* convenience store that has muffins and snacks.

The *Micronesia Mall* on Route 1, a mile north of Tumon, has a small food court with stalls that serve Hawaiian, Korean, Chinese, Japanese and American food. Most have plate lunches with combos chosen from steamer trays for around $5. There's a similar, though smaller, food court inside Gibson's store in the *Guam Shopping Center* in Tamuning.

Fast food enthusiasts will find branches of *McDonald's, Wendy's, Burger King, Pizza Hut, Subway, Winchell's* and a host of others; they're particularly thick on Marine Drive in Tamuning. *Denny's*, a family-style restaurant that's open 24 hours a day, is on

---

Chamorro Food

Chamorro food is a rich mix of Spanish, Filipino and Pacific dishes.

Ahu is grated coconut boiled in sugar water
Bonelos aga is banana dipped in a sweet flour batter and deep fried
Cadon guihan is fish cooked in coconut milk with onions and sweet peppers
Escabeche is fresh fish marinated in vinegar and soy sauce
Golai hagoin sumi is taro leaves cooked in coconut milk
Kelaguen is minced chicken, fish, shrimp or Spam mixed with lemon, onions, pepper and shredded coconut
Lumpia is similar to an egg roll, but dipped in garlic sauce or vinegar
Pancit is a mix of shrimp, vegetables and garlic over noodles
Poto is a ricecake of tuba, sugar and rice-meal

Other local delicacies include whole roast pig, tropical fruits, yams, coconut crabs, red rice made with *achiote* (annatto) seeds and anything barbecued. To turn ordinary dishes into a Chamorro meal ask for *finadene*, a hot sauce made from fiery red peppers, soy sauce, lemon juice and chopped onions.

Although the best Chamorro food is generally found at village fiestas and private feasts, the Chamorro Village in Agana is also a good place to sample local dishes. ∎

Marine Drive in Tamuning, at the Micronesia Mall and on Route 2 in Agat.

There are a few *Baskin Robbins* ice cream shops on the island, including one at the Micronesia Mall. Another option for ice cream enthusiasts is to simply visit the nearest grocery store, as most stock Haagen Dazs ice cream bars and sell them individually.

Middle

Marty's Mexican Restaurant, in the Royal Lanes bowling alley opposite the ITC Building in Tamuning, serves reasonable Mexican dishes at moderate prices. At dinner you can get a two-item combo plate with rice, beans and salad for $10. The lunch menu begins around $5. It's open

GUAM

from 11 am (noon on Sundays) to at least 10 pm. If you just want a quick, cheap burrito, there's a *Taco Bell* across the street.

Tony Roma's, with branches on Marine Drive in Tamuning and San Vitores Rd in Tumon, is part of a mainland chain specialising in barbecued baby back ribs. A full plate of ribs, or ribs and barbecued shrimp, costs $14. Lunches start around $6. Both restaurants are open daily from 11.30 am to 10 pm.

The popular *Pim's Place* on Hospital Rd in Tamuning is a pleasant restaurant serving good, authentic Thai food. Noodle and soup dishes cost $7, most meat and chicken dishes $8 and seafood dishes $10. It's open from 11.30 am to 3 pm Monday to Friday and nightly from 5 to 11 pm.

The *Garden Terrace Coffee Shop* in the Guam Reef Hotel has a good-value business lunch buffet on Tuesdays and Thursdays from 11 am to 2 pm. It costs $9.50 and has a salad bar, half a dozen hot dishes including fish and red meat, pastries, ice cream and coffee or tea. There's also a decent champagne brunch on Sundays from 10.30 am to 2 pm for $17.

Top End

La Premier (☎ 647-7714) in the Onward Agana Beach Hotel on Agana Bay has an all-you-can-eat soup and salad bar for $6.50 and a full lunch buffet for $10 from 11.30 am to 1.30 pm Monday to Saturday. On Thursday and Friday nights the restaurant features an Indian dinner buffet for $20, half price for children ages eight to 12, free for those under eight.

La Mirenda, a cafe-style restaurant at the Hyatt hotel, has a good buffet lunch spread that includes a dessert table of fresh fruit and tempting cakes and pies. The full buffet is from 11.30 am to 2 pm Monday to Saturday and costs $15.50. Sweet-tooths could also just eat their fill from the dessert table, open from 11 am to 11 pm, for $7.50 – avoid late afternoon as the desserts are replenished at around 5 pm. The La Mirenda also does a more elaborate Sunday champagne brunch for $22 from 10.30 am to 2 pm.

If you're only going to have one splurge night out on Guam, you couldn't do better than *Roy's Restaurant* (☎ 646-1835) in the Guam Hilton, which serves superb Pacific Rim cuisine. The goat cheese with gingered eggplant salad makes a nice starter at $6. Main dishes include a crispy Thai chicken for $15 and grilled shrimp in lobster nage for $17, both excellent. Meals begin with complimentary hot nan served from a clay oven; for dessert the hot souffle is a treat. Roy's also has a lunch special on weekdays, from 11.30 am to 2 pm, that includes appetizers, a choice of main dish, dessert and coffee for $16.50. Dinner is from 5.30 to 9.30 pm nightly.

ENTERTAINMENT

The large Tumon Bay hotels have a variety of live music nightly, ranging from jazz or hard rock to karaoke, and also have 'Polynesian' dance shows geared for package tourists.

For free hotel entertainment, the *Hyatt* often has live afternoon music in its beachside lounge; it also puts on a cultural show on Friday afternoons in the hotel lobby.

Wet Willie's, a large beachside bar, is the hottest scene at Tumon Bay and attracts a pleasant mix of locals and foreigners. There's live rock or reggae music most nights and on weekend afternoons, the drinks are big and there's never a cover charge. Happy hour ($2 beers) is from noon to 3 pm daily and from 5 to 7 pm on weekdays.

There's a great sunset view from the wrap-around windows at the *Salon del Mar* in the Guam Hotel Okura. During happy hour, from 5 to 7 pm, beer costs $2, tropical drinks cost $3.25 and there's complimentary popcorn and hors d'oeuvres.

A bellwether for Tumon Bay's future may well be the glitzy *SandCastle* (☎ 649-7263) entertainment complex on San Vitores Rd, which has pricey Las Vegas-style cabaret and dinner shows. It also houses the *Onyx* disco, which holds 750 people, has a $6 cover charge and is open from 9 pm to 2 am (to 4 am on weekends);

it features techno, rave, hiphop, reggae and alternative music. *TJ's*, a Mexican restaurant at the Hyatt, is another popular dance spot; the $10 cover includes a drink and there's usually live music.

Guam's main movie complex is the multi-screen Hafa Adai Theatre (☎ 646-4834) near the ITC Building in Tamuning.

There are also several shooting galleries that round up Japanese tourists. In part because of strict gun controls back in Japan, this has become one of Guam's most popular side attractions, with visitors dishing out $50 to shoot off a round of shells. Many shops add a Wild West facade to it all, with tourists donning cowboy costumes and Indian headdresses to videotape their own shoot-outs.

For more local flavour, Guam has a greyhound racing track, automobile raceway park and legalised cockfights.

THINGS TO BUY

Guam, with its modern shopping centres, is the best place in Micronesia to buy supplies you may need on other islands. The largest centre is the Micronesia Mall in Dededo, which has a branch of the Hawaii-based Liberty House department store, a Payless Supermarket and about a hundred other shops. The Guam Shopping Center in Tamuning and the Agana Shopping Center in Agana are also large shopping centres.

The Tumon Bay area has lots of stores selling imported designer items with labels by the likes of Gucci, Hermes and DKNY. The largest is DFS, a 'duty-free shop' that resembles an up-market department store.

Guam isn't noted for its handicrafts and most of what passes for local souvenirs, including tacky coconut-husk carvings and shell items, are made in the Philippines. Best bet for finding an island-made souvenir is at the new Chamorro Village in Agana, which has a goldsmith and a few other craftspeople.

Although more expensive than in the USA, print and slide film is cheaper in Guam than elsewhere in Micronesia and can be picked up at a number of places,

including Kimura Camera in the ITC Building in Tamuning. Regardless of where you buy it, check the expiry dates.

US citizens returning to the States from Guam are allowed a higher than usual duty-free exemption on articles acquired abroad. They are permitted $1200 worth of duty-free items ($600 is usual), but no more than half of that total is supposed to have been acquired outside Guam.

GETTING THERE & AWAY

For those coming from Asia, Guam is the main gateway to the rest of Micronesia. There are direct flights to Guam from Honolulu, Japan, Australia, Indonesia, the Philippines, South Korea, Hong Kong and Taiwan.

For complete information on getting to Guam refer to the Getting There & Away chapter at the start of this book.

Air

Airport The busy Guam International Airport in Tamuning has a foreign exchange booth, restrooms, pay phones, hotel courtesy phones, car rental booths, a taxi stand, a duty-free shop and a coffee shop.

If you have a long layover, the Hafa Adai VIP Lounge on the 3rd floor of the terminal offers an alternative to the crowded airport departure lobby. It costs $5 to use the VIP Lounge for up to two hours, $7.50 for four hours, including complimentary baggage storage, beverages, fruit and simple pastries.

Airline Offices The following airlines have offices on Marine Drive in Tamuning:

Continental Micronesia	☎ 647-6453
Japan Air Lines (ITC Building)	☎ 646-9195
Korean Air	☎ 649-3301
Northwest Airlines	☎ 649-8380

Leaving Guam
Guam has no departure tax.

GETTING AROUND
It's challenging getting around Guam without a car, especially if you want to tour the

whole island, and hitchhiking is not a common practice. The public bus can get you between many areas but it isn't extensive or frequent enough to be practical for most sightseeing purposes.

To/From the Airport

There are car rental booths and taxis at the airport, but the public bus does not serve the airport. Only a couple of hotels provide airport transport.

Bus

Guam Mass Transit Authority operates a limited public bus system that primarily serves central Guam. The most useful route for visitors is the Blue Line which runs from the Micronesia Mall in Dededo through Tumon, Tamuning, Agana and Piti before turning around at the Naval Station gate at the south side of Apra Harbor. One bus heads south on the hour every hour from 6 am to 5 pm and north on the hour from 7 am to 6 pm.

While the long-term outlook for the bus may be doomed by low ridership, a consequence of Guamanians' well-entrenched love affairs with their cars, in the meantime it's certainly a cheap, if limited, mode of transportation.

The fare is $1 for a single ride or $3 for a day pass. There's no service on Sundays or holidays. For schedule information call ☎ 475-7433.

Shuttle Bus The Micronesia Mall in Dededo has a private shuttle bus that runs between the mall and Tumon Bay hotels. The cost is $3 return. The service is about twice an hour from 9.30 am to 9 pm (to 6 pm on Sundays); call 632-8881 for pick-up times at specific hotels.

Taxi

Taxi fares, which start at $1.80 at flagdown, are $3 for the first mile and 60 cents for each quarter-mile after that, plus $1 for each piece of heavy luggage. From Tumon

Bay it costs about $10 to get to the airport or the Micronesia Mall and $20 to the Agana Shopping Center. A 10% tip is customary.

Outside the airport, you'll probably have to phone for a taxi. Some of the larger companies are Hafa Adai Taxi Service (☎ 477-9629), City Taxi (☎ 646-1155) and Guam Taxi (☎ 649-6842).

Car

Budget (☎ 646-0366), Hertz (☎ 649-6283), Nissan (☎ 646-0110) and Islander Rent-A-Car (☎ 646-8156) have rental booths at the airport while Thrifty (☎ 646-6555), located a mile below the airport, has a free airport shuttle. Budget usually offers the best walk-up rate, around $35 a day with unlimited mileage, but all the companies tend to negotiate a bit when extra cars are available.

On reservations booked in advance from overseas, Thrifty often offers the best rate at around $35, while the other companies generally hover closer to $40.

Optional collision damage waivers (CDW) are available for an additional $13 a day. A 5% fee is added onto car rentals picked up at the airport.

Avoid renting from the smaller Japanese companies found in the lobbies of resort hotels as they charge much steeper rates and some also tack on per-mile charges. Most of the major companies, including Budget, will deliver cars to your hotel at no extra cost.

Road Rules As in the rest of Micronesia, driving is on the right. The speed limit is 35 miles an hour unless otherwise posted. All cars must stop for school buses whenever the bus lights are flashing. Foreign drivers must be at least 21 years old to drive on the island. US and foreign driving licences are valid for 30 days after arrival on Guam.

Bicycle

Bicycles can be rented for $15 a day at the T-Shirt House (☎ 646-2328), opposite the Guam Reef Hotel at Tumon Bay.

Tours

A score of tour companies provide all sorts of sightseeing tour options, though most are in Japanese only. Discover Guam (☎ 649-8687), Box 2860, Agana, Guam 96910, is a local company that has tours for English-speaking visitors, including half-day circle-island tours, tours of WW II sites, 'jungle adventures' and even a night-time bar-hopping tour.

Commonwealth of the Northern Marianas

The Northern Marianas, which has opted for closer political ties with the USA than other Micronesian island groups, is now a US Commonwealth, similar in status to Puerto Rico.

The main islands of the Northern Marianas are Saipan, Rota and Tinian. Saipan, the largest island, is the centre of commonwealth activities. It has 90% of the population, dominates in economic development and political strength and gets most of the tourist trade. Both Tinian and Rota remain unspoiled, quiet and friendly. Rota, the more developed of the two, is about to open its first Japanese golf resort. Tinian's tourism is largely limited to a trickle of day visitors, though that may soon change, as there are now plans to build the island's first casino.

The Northern Marianas, the scene of some of the Pacific War's most devastating battles, woos the Japanese back these days by turning war ruins into sightseeing spots, erecting peace monuments and encouraging the development of resort hotels.

With new US passports in hand, the people of the Northern Marianas are hurtling headlong after the American dream, and in the rush to look, eat and act American, much of their cultural heritage is being lost. Yet the traveller who chances upon a village fiesta or christening festivities can still get a glimpse of the more traditional Chamorro life.

HISTORY
Pre-European Contact
The Northern Marianas were settled around 1500 BC by Chamorros who shared cultural ties with Guam's indigenous people. (See the Guam history section for details on early Chamorro culture.)

Spanish Period
First named the Islas de los Ladrones (Islands of Thieves) by Ferdinand Magellan in 1521, the Mariana Islands were renamed Las Marianas upon the arrival of the Spanish priest Luis Diego Sanvitores, in honour of the Spanish queen Maria Ana of Austria. In 1668 Sanvitores and five other Jesuit priests established the first mission in the Marianas. From the onset the missionaries received a hostile welcome and the next two decades were marked by sporadic uprisings that cost the lives of a dozen priests and scores of Chamorros. By the late 1680s the Jesuits, and the Spanish troops that they relied upon to secure their missions, had clearly gained the upper hand and the uprisings ceased.

In the 1690s the Spanish, initiating a new policy termed 'reduction', swept down through the Marianas, rounded up the Chamorros and brought them to Guam in order to more effectively convert them to Christianity. On Rota several hundred Rotanese managed to hide in the hills and avoid capture. Consequently some of the purest Chamorro blood in the Marianas today is in Rota.

The other Northern Marianas were left uninhabited. Explorers who landed on the abandoned islands (including the British captain Samuel Wallis in 1768, soon after 'discovering' Tahiti) sometimes took advantage of the wild cattle and chickens found there, but most went instead to Guam to stock up on provisions.

Around 1820 the Spanish allowed islanders from the western Carolines to move to the larger Mariana islands. The Carolinians managed Spanish cattle herds and maintained a presence on the Marianas at a time when Spain was skittish over German intentions in the area.

After Pope Leo XIII declared Spain's sovereignty over the Marianas in 1885, the now Hispanicized Chamorros were encouraged to move back to the Northern Marianas from Guam. They were given land for farming, but by that time the Carolinians had already settled much of the best coastal land.

German Period

Germany bought the Northern Marianas from Spain in 1899 as part of its Micronesia package deal. Germany's primary interest in the islands was in copra production.

Although colonial administrators and a handful of teachers and priests came to the islands, the Northern Marianas were not heavily settled by foreigners during either the Spanish or German administrations.

Japanese Period

When the Japanese took the Northern Marianas from Germany at the beginning of WW I, there were fewer than 4000 Chamorros and Carolinians on the islands.

The Japanese had little interest in copra but had great expectations for sugar cane. They chopped down groves of coconut trees and cleared tropical forests and jungles to create level farmland. When latte stones from ancient villages got in the way, they were cast aside.

In the mid-1920s, after Saipan's sugar industry was determined a success, plantations were also set up on Tinian and Rota. On all three islands sugar cane was loaded from the fields onto bullcarts and hauled to little narrow-gauge railroads where steam-powered trains carried the cane to mills for processing. Both sugar and alcohol made from the cane became major export items.

By the mid-1930s, sugar operations in the Marianas were providing the Japanese with more than 60% of all revenues generated in Micronesia.

Many of the people who worked the cane fields came from Okinawa, where poor tenant farmers were recruited to work for low wages. The high influx of foreigners and the tendency of the colonisers to turn villages into miniature Japanese-style towns overwhelmed the native culture.

At the outbreak of WW II there were

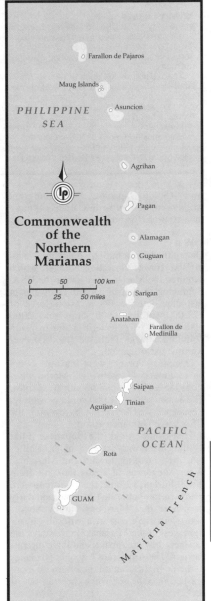

PHILIPPINE SEA

Farallon de Pajaros

Maug Islands

Asuncion

Agrihan

Pagan

Commonwealth
of the
Northern
Marianas

Alamagan

Guguan

| 0 | 50 | 100 km |
| 0 | 25 | 50 miles |

Sarigan

Anatahan

Farallon de Medinilla

Saipan

Aguijan   Tinian

PACIFIC OCEAN

Rota

GUAM

Mariana Trench

Military Leases

In the early 1970s, the US Defense Department was focusing attention on the Northern Marianas. Strategically positioned between Japan and the Philippines, where some of the USA's largest overseas military bases were located, the Marianas were seen as a potential back-up should bases in those neighbouring countries become too politically or financially expensive to maintain.

To keep the islands close to the fold, the USA lured the inhabitants of the sparsely populated Northern Marianas with a heavy flow of greenbacks. Many islanders saw US Commonwealth status as the best option for maintaining that cash flow – and they calculated correctly. Following passage of the commonwealth covenant, Saipan had the distinction of receiving more federal funding per capita than any of the 50 US states.

In exchange, the Northern Marianas turned over access to 28.4 sq miles of land to the US military, mostly in terms of 50-year leases. The biggest chunk of this land is in Tinian, where the USA leases two-thirds of the island, but the deal also involves smaller tracts of land, including such prime real estate as Saipan's Micro Beach. ■

over 45,000 Japanese and immigrant workers in the Northern Marianas – more than 10 times the number of Micronesians.

WW II

One of the largest military operations in all of WW II was Operation Forager, which captured the Mariana Islands for the USA. Beginning in Saipan and attacking Guam just days later, a US invasion force of 127,000 soldiers, 600 ships and 2000 planes took part. American pre-invasion bombing attacks included the first-ever wartime use of napalm.

Operation Forager went into full swing on 15 June 1944, as two US Marine divisions landed on Saipan's south-west coast. The Japanese had 31,000 soldiers waiting. Resistance was fierce but by evening the USA had 20,000 men ashore.

That same night the Japanese First Mobile Fleet was detected in the Philippine Sea heading toward the Marianas. When squadrons of Zeros took off from those ships on 19 June, the US forces were ready. In the battle that became popularly known as the 'Marianas Turkey Shoot' both sides took part in a wild all-out air fight west of the Marianas. In two days the Japanese lost 402 planes and three aircraft carriers. The Americans lost only 50 planes in the dogfights, but on the return 80 more crashed into the sea when they ran out of fuel.

With the defeat of their fleet, Japanese forces in the Marianas lost any chance of rescue or reinforcement. On Saipan the Americans advanced northward and into the island's mountainous interior.

Garapan, the Japanese administrative centre, fell on 3 July. When the battle for Saipan was declared over on 9 July, 3500 Americans, 30,000 Japanese defenders and 400 Saipanese were dead.

After the fall of Saipan, the Japanese had no hope of holding onto Tinian. Still, the 9000 Japanese soldiers on Tinian chose to fight to the death rather than surrender.

The Americans made their first beach landing on Tinian's north-west shore on 24 July 1944. They secured the island after nine days of heavy combat and the loss of 400 American and more than 5000 Japanese lives. US troops immediately began extending the Japanese airbase on Tinian, using it to stage air raids on Japan, including the atomic bomb drops on Hiroshima and Nagasaki.

US invasion forces bypassed Rota. The USA bombed the northern airstrips, but the Japanese held the island till the war's end and Rota came through the conflict relatively unscathed.

Postwar Period

The fierce fighting had reduced whole towns to rubble and in the years following the war there were no attempts to rebuild the sugar industry. The USA administered the islands by providing hand-outs rather than by encouraging economic development.

In 1948 the CIA closed off half of Saipan to islanders and outsiders alike, using the northern part of the island for covert military manoeuvres. When the CIA moved its operations out of Saipan in 1962, the Northern Marianas was finally opened to visitors. The Trust Territory administration then moved its headquarters to Saipan, taking over the former CIA offices.

In 1961 Saipan and Rota petitioned the US government, asking to become integrated with Guam. The requests were made nearly every year until 1969, when Guam voters were allowed to vote in a referendum on the issue and rejected the idea. One reason cited for the rejection was that many Guamanians still harboured ill feelings toward those Saipanese who had acted as interpreters during Guam's occupation by the Japanese.

In June 1975 the people of the Northern Marianas voted to become a US Commonwealth, and in so doing became the first district to withdraw from the Trust Territory. Under the terms of the commonwealth agreement, which began to take effect in January 1978, the Northern Marianas retain the right to internal self-government, while the USA retains control over foreign affairs. In November 1986 the new commonwealth covenant became fully effective and the islanders became US citizens.

GEOGRAPHY

The Mariana Islands mark the dividing line between the Pacific Ocean and the Philippine Sea.

The Commonwealth of the Northern Marianas is made up of 14 of the 15 islands in the Marianas archipelago, which stretches 400 miles northward in a slightly curved line from Guam, the chain's southernmost island.

All the islands are high types of either volcanic or limestone formation. The total land mass of the Northern Marianas is 184 sq miles; Saipan has an area of 47 sq miles, Tinian has 39 sq miles and Rota has 32 sq miles.

Northern (Outer) Islands

Except for Aguijan, which is just south of Tinian, the smaller Mariana islands run north of Saipan. From south to north they are Farallon de Medinilla, Anatahan, Sarigan, Guguan, Alamagan, Pagan, Agrihan, Asuncion, the Maug Islands and Farallon de Pajaros. All are rugged volcanic islands. The highest point in all of Micronesia is in the Marianas – 3166 feet on the remote island of Agrihan.

Pagan, which is 18.5 sq miles, is the largest of these outer islands and one of the most beautiful. The Maug Islands and Sarigan are protected nature preserves. Farallon de Medinilla is used on occasion as a bombing and gunnery target by both the US Navy and Air Force.

Micronesia's only active volcanoes are among these islands. Following weeks of earthquakes, Pagan's volcano erupted in May 1981, shooting up flames, rocks and clouds of ash as high as 60,000 feet. Almost half of all the arable land was covered with lava. All 54 residents were evacuated to Saipan and although the island has temporarily been re-inhabited since then, ongoing seismic activity – including another eruption in 1988 – has kept permanent settlements from being re-established.

Ironically, while the eruptions have left the islands largely uninhabitable, the volcanic ash that spewed out has proven ideal for use as a cement additive and is now

Mariana Trench

The Mariana Trench is an underwater canyon that extends 1835 miles along the floor of the Pacific to the east of the Mariana Islands. At 38,635 feet, the trench contains the world's greatest known ocean depth.

The Mariana Islands, which are but the emerged tips of massive underwater mountains, can also make claim to another record. If measured from their bases deep in the Mariana Trench, the islands, which rise from the ocean floor more than 10,000 feet higher than Mt Everest, would constitute the highest mountains in the world. ∎

being mined and shipped to Saipan, Rota and Guam for use in new condo and resort developments.

In April 1990, all 21 residents of the island of Anatahan were evacuated to Saipan following an earthquake that measured 7.4 on the Richter scale and signs that a volcanic eruption was imminent.

The 1000-foot peak on Farallon de Pajaros and Asuncion's 3000-foot mountain sometimes send up smoke and steam as well.

CLIMATE

Saipan, which is listed in the *Guinness Book of World Records* as having the world's most equable temperature, averages 81°F year-round. The rainy season is from July to October, when rainfall averages about 12 inches a month, while from December to May monthly rainfall averages only about four inches.

The climate of the Northern Marianas is very similar to Guam's and, also like Guam, the islands lie directly in the typhoon track. The most common months for typhoons are August to December.

GOVERNMENT

The Commonwealth of the Northern Mariana Islands (CNMI) elects its own governor, lieutenant governor and a legislature with nine senators and 15 representatives. Each main island has its own mayor.

Although the people of the Northern Marianas are US citizens, they don't vote in US elections, and are exempt from paying US income taxes. Representation in the US Congress is limited to non-voting observer status, although CNMI representatives are allowed to lobby and make presentations.

ECONOMY

Since the commonwealth covenant took effect, the USA has provided over $300 million in funds for capital development, government operations and other programmes in the Northern Marianas. The government is the largest single employer, providing about 2200 jobs.

Still, the mainstay of the economy is tourism. Approximately 550,000 visitors, 70% of them from Japan, come to the Northern Marianas each year. The number of hotel rooms on Saipan has tripled in the past decade to 3200 and the local visitors bureau projects it will triple again by the year 2000, though downturns in the Japanese economy make that prediction seem excessively bullish.

The CNMI minimum wage, just $2.45 an hour, is the lowest of any place under US jurisdiction.

Shady Labour Practices

As a condition of its commonwealth covenant, the CNMI government retains its own controls over immigration. As a consequence, the Marianas imports a large number of low-paid Asian labourers, the majority from the Philippines and China. All told, there are 27,000 foreign contract workers in the CNMI, a disproportionately high number of them young women.

Filipino women are often recruited by shady employment agencies in Manila, who promise them hotel work but often end up placing them in private homes or all-night bars. Charges of rape, forced prostitution and non-payment of salaries abound.

To take advantage of Saipan's duty-free access to the USA, several foreign-owned garment factories set up shop on the island in the 1980s. Currently there are 23 of them employing 6800 workers, mostly from mainland China. On paper, workers are paid the minimum wage, but because they live in factory barracks their rent, food and other expenses are taken out of their pay, leaving them only a fraction of that. The factories export an estimated $300 million a year in duty-free clothing to the USA, all tagged with 'Made in the USA' labels. For hosting the factories, Saipan receives about $2 million annually in taxes.

In late 1994 the US government, under criticism for not intervening to stop 'slave-labour' practices, announced plans to triple the presence of federal law and labour officials in the CNMI, with the $7 million expense to be deducted from the annual infusion of grant money that the islands receive. ■

POPULATION & PEOPLE

The Northern Marianas is the fastest growing area in Micronesia. There were 9640 residents in 1970, 16,780 in 1980 and 43,555 in 1990.

The current population is estimated to be 53,000, with approximately 47,900 people on Saipan and 2550 each on Rota and Tinian. Slightly more than half of the total population is made up of resident aliens, mostly from the Philippines, China and Korea.

Of the native population, roughly 75% is Chamorro, while the remainder are Carolinian.

SOCIETY & CONDUCT

The local Chamorro culture is a hybrid of native and Spanish colonial influences, with a powerful overlay of popular American trends. As with the Chamorros on Guam, most cultural activities centre around the Catholic church and religious festivities.

RELIGION

The predominant religion in the Northern Marianas is Roman Catholic, especially among the Chamorro population and Filipino immigrants. There are also Baptist, Methodist, Mormon, Korean Presbyterian, Evangelical and Seventh-day Adventist churches.

LANGUAGE

English is the official language, Chamorro and Carolinian are native tongues and Japanese is spoken in most hotels and some shops. *Hafa adai* is the traditional greeting, as it is in Guam, although the slang term *howzit* is becoming nearly as common.

HOLIDAYS & FESTIVALS

Public holidays in the Northern Marianas include:

New Year's Day
    1 January
Commonwealth Day
    9 January
President's Day
    3rd Monday in February

Covenant Day
    24 March
Good Friday
    Friday before Easter, in April or May
Memorial Day
    Last Monday in May
US Independence Day
    4 July
Labor Day
    1st Monday in September
Columbus Day
    2nd Monday in October
Citizenship Day
    4 November
Veterans Day
    11 November
Thanksgiving
    Last Thursday in November
Constitution Day
    8 December
Christmas Day
    25 December

Most villages have an annual fiesta in honour of their patron saint, which is the big village bash of the year. Rota and Tinian have one fiesta each, while Saipan has six. See the individual islands for more details.

GETTING THERE & AWAY

For information on travelling to and from the Northern Marianas see Getting There & Away in the Saipan section later in this chapter.

Saipan

Saipan has only Guam as a rival in the crush of Japanese tourists that flock to its shores. Over the past decade Saipan has had the dubious distinction of being the fastest growing island in Micronesia, with new golf courses and resorts popping up all around the island. Tourists and alien workers now outnumber the Saipanese and the island has lost much of its Micronesian character.

Still, Saipan has gentle beaches on its west and south coasts, a rugged and rocky east coast, a hilly interior and dramatic

SAIPAN

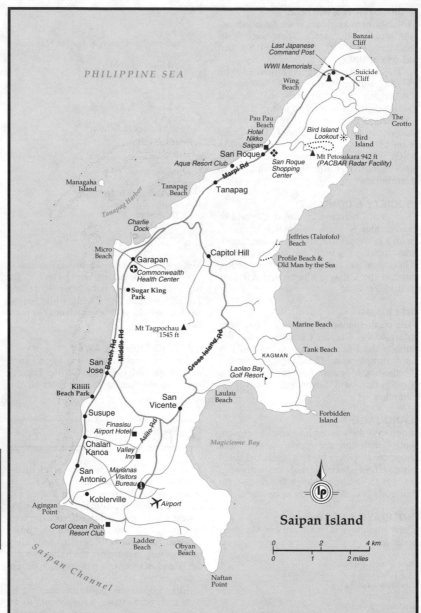

PHILIPPINE SEA

Banzai
Cliff

*Last Japanese
Command Post*

WWII Memorials

Wing
Beach

Suicide
Cliff

The
Grotto

Pau Pau
Beach

*Bird Island
Lookout*

Bird
Island

*Hotel
Nikko
Saipan*

San Roque ·

Aqua Resort Club

*San Roque
Shopping
Center*

▲ Mt Petosukara 942 ft
(PACBAR Radar Facility)

Managaha
Island

Tanapag
Beach

Tanapag

Marpi Rd

Tanapag Harbor

*Charlie
Dock*

Jeffries (Talofofo)
Beach

Micro
Beach

Garapan ·

Capitol Hill

Profile Beach &
Old Man by the Sea

*Commonwealth
Health Center*

· **Sugar King
Park**

Mt Tagpochau ▲
1545 ft

Marine Beach

Cross Island Rd

KAGMAN

Tank Beach

**San
Jose**

Beach Rd

Middle Rd

*Laolao Bay
Golf Resort*

**Kiliili
Beach Park**

**San
Vicente**

Laulau
Beach

Forbidden
Island

Susupe

*Finasisu
Airport Hotel*

Aslito Rd

Magicienne Bay

**Chalan
Kanoa**

*Valley
Inn*

**San
Antonio**

*Marianas
Visitors
Bureau*

· **Koblerville**

✈ *Airport*

Agingan
Point

*Coral Ocean Point
Resort Club*

Ladder
Beach

Obyan
Beach

Saipan Channel

Naftan
Point

Saipan Island

0   2   4 km

0   1   2 miles

cliffs on the north coast. The island is about 14 miles long and five miles wide.

The main tourist sights are in the west coast town of Garapan and in the Marpi area at the northern end of the island. By car, most sights can be touched on in just a few hours, though a more leisurely exploration would take a full day.

ORIENTATION

Orientation is simple. The airport is at the southern end of the island. Most of the major hotels and services are on Beach Rd, which runs along the west coast.

INFORMATION
Tourist Office

The Marianas Visitors Bureau (☎ 234-8325) is just outside the airport in a fortified concrete building that once served as a Japanese communications station. If you want tourist literature in English, it's best to get it here, as the free tourist magazines found at hotels are only in Japanese. It's open from 8 am to 5 pm Monday to Friday and from 8 am to noon on Saturday.

Money

Both the Bank of Guam and the Bank of Hawaii have offices in Garapan. The Bank of Hawaii also has a branch in the Nauru Building in Susupe. Banking hours are from 10 am to 3 pm Monday to Thursday, 10 am to 6 pm on Friday.

If you have a major credit card, or a Plus or Cirrus system bank card, you can withdraw cash at any time of the day from the Bank of Hawaii's ATM in the lobby of the Dai-Ichi Hotel in Garapan. Credit cards are widely accepted in Saipan.

Post

The main post office, in Chalan Kanoa, is open from 8.30 am to 4 pm Monday to Friday and from 9 am to noon on Saturday. On Capitol Hill, there's a branch office in the government complex that's open from 9 am to 3 pm Monday to Friday and 9.30 am to noon on Saturday. There's another branch on the main road in San Vicente, next to Lau Lau Market, which is open

from noon to 5.30 pm on weekdays and from noon to 3 pm on Saturdays. All mail to Saipan uses the zip code 96950.

Telephone

Local and long-distance calls can be made from pay phones and most hotels. Dial 411 for local directory assistance. It costs 25 cents a minute to call from one CNMI island to another.

International calls can also be made via IT&E (☎ 234-8521), a locally owned long-distance telephone company, which has phone booths in numerous shops around the island and an office in San Jose. Calls can be placed at some of the booths 24 hours a day and at the office from 8 am to 9 pm Monday to Friday, to 7 pm on Saturday and to 5 pm on Sunday.

Per-minute rates for direct-dialled calls are 70 cents to Guam, $1.60 to the USA, $1.95 to Japan and $2.50 to Australia. Calls to Palau, the FSM or the Marshalls are $2.50 a minute.

Faxes can be sent from the IT&E office in San Jose for the price of a phone call plus $2, and can be received (at ☎ 234-8525) for 50 cents a page.

Consulates & Immigration

Japan has a consulate office (☎ 234-7201) on the 5th floor of the Horiguchi Building in Garapan and the Philippines has a consulate office (☎ 234-1848) off Beach Rd in San Jose. Nauru has a local representative (☎ 234-6941) on the 6th floor of the Nauru Building in Susupe.

The CNMI Immigration Office (☎ 234-6178) is at the airport.

Bookshops

Saipan's two small bookstores both carry a limited selection of books on Micronesia. Bestsellers, in the Joeten Shopping Center in Susupe, has the better magazine selection, while Sablan Bookseller, in the Sablan Building in Chalan Kanoa, is the only one with a travel book section.

Library

The island's public library, at the north side of the Joeten Shopping Center in Susupe, is one of the most modern in Micronesia and has good periodical and travel sections. Opening hours are from 10 am to 6 pm weekdays and from 10 am to 4 pm on Saturdays.

Newspapers

There are four newspapers published on Saipan: the *Marianas Variety*, which is published Monday to Friday; the *Marianas Observer* and the *Pacific Star*, both published on Fridays; and the *Saipan Tribune*, published on Wednesdays and Fridays. The latter is free, the others are 50 cents. Guam's *Pacific Daily News* is flown in daily. You can pick up newspapers at most island grocery stores and at larger hotels.

Emergency For police, fire and ambulance emergencies, dial 911. Saipan's modern hospital, the Commonwealth Health Center (☎ 234-6115), is on Middle Rd in Garapan.

Other Information

There's a coin laundry a few minutes' walk east of the fire station in Garapan. For 24-hour recorded weather information, including marine conditions, dial 234-5724.

ACTIVITIES

One noteworthy quirk in Saipan is the observance of a tiered pricing system – customised to fit everyone's wallet. Especially for activities, there is often one price quoted for locals, a second price for American tourists (generally a euphemism for non-Asians) and a third for Japanese tourists. Sometimes there are just two rates: local and tourist. 'Local' commonly covers those who have been living in Micronesia for any period of time – including foreign expats, Peace Corps volunteers etc.

Diving & Snorkelling

Saipan's most unusual and exciting dive is the Grotto, a natural cavern with waters 50 feet deep and tunnels to the open sea. Although it's a popular spot for locals to swim and for divers with a guide, the tricky currents can be dangerous for the uninitiated. You'll also have to be in good physical condition to do the dive, as it involves carrying your tanks up and down a long, steep set of stairs.

Other popular dives are war wrecks in Tanapag Harbor, caves and garden eels at Obyan Beach and a huge coral head offshore from the Saipan Grand Hotel.

Saipan's best snorkelling is at Managaha Island. Pau Pau, Laulau and Wing beaches have reasonably good snorkelling, as does Bird Island, though it requires a hike. You can also snorkel out around a couple of US Army tanks which rest in the shallow waters off Susupe's Kilili Beach, where US invasion forces first came ashore in June 1944. It's best to stick to the tank nearest the beach, as jet skiers commonly race around the tank farther offshore.

Dive Shops Saipan has a score of dive operations, but most are geared exclusively for the Japanese market.

Ben & Ki Water Sports (☎ 235-5063, fax 235-5068), Box 5031 CHRB, Saipan, MP 96950, on the beach fronting the Dai-Ichi Hotel, is locally owned by Ben Concepcion. Two-tank boat dives cost $95, including gear and hotel pick-up. Two beach dives, one of which is usually the Grotto, cost $80. One-tank dives (beach or boat) cost $50, as does an introductory dive. Snorkel sets rent for $10 a day.

Seashore Dive Shop (☎ 234-5549, fax 233-5901), Box PPP 292, Saipan, MP 96950, near the Hyatt, offers one-tank beach dives for $50, and two-tank dives for $90, including tanks and weight belt. If you need full equipment rental, add on another $35. Boat dives are $20 more.

Marine Fantasia (☎ 235-5990, fax 235-5991), PPP 188, Box 10000, Saipan, MP 96950, is a PADI-affiliated dive shop next to the Big Dipper ice-cream store on Beach Rd in Chalan Kanoa. It offers two-tank beach dives for $70, two boat dives for $100 and an introductory dive for $60.

Other Water Sports

Windsurfing is popular on Saipan, the only island in the Northern Marianas with a large lagoon.

Windsurfing Saipan (☎ 234-6965), inside the old WW II bunker on Micro Beach in front of the Hyatt, is run by a friendly expat from Japan who speaks English. Windsurfing equipment costs $10 an hour or $30 for four hours. Windsurfing lessons are also available and cost $30 an hour, including equipment. The shop also rents snorkel sets for $8 and one-person kayaks for $10 an hour.

There are more beach stands in front of the Dai-Ichi Hotel that rent various water sports equipment, including windsurfing gear, kayaks and catamarans. They can also make arrangements for water skiing, parasailing and trolling.

Hiking

Saipan has a number of options for getting in a hardy walk, including the jogging trail that begins at the north side of Micro Beach. Most of Saipan's better forest trails are in the northern part of the island; one that stands out is the Laderan Tangke Trail, an interpretive loop through the Marpi Commonwealth Forest.

Saipan has a Hash House Harriers group that gets together on Saturdays and covers a different route each week. They meet at the Bank of Guam in Garapan at 3.30 pm; a $5 donation covers beer and snacks. It's a nice way to socialise with some of the island's more energetic foreign residents.

Golf

Saipan has four golf courses.

At the local nine-hole Saipan Country Club (☎ 234-8718) near San Jose, green fees are $15/50 for locals/tourists. There's also a $25 intermediate fee for 'foreigners' that should cover most English-speaking visitors. Electric carts cost $15, pull carts $5.

The Laolao Bay Golf Resort (☎ 256-8888), the island's newest and most exclusive golf course, in the Kagman area,

officially charges $150 for 18 holes, though American tourists are generally quoted $70 and locals pay only $25.

Coral Ocean Point Resort Club (☎ 234-7000) has an 18-hole golf course on the coast at Agingan Point, at the south side of the island. The cost for a round of golf, cart included, is $100 for American tourists, $150 for Japanese tourists.

The 18-hole golf course at the Marianas Country Club (☎ 322-2211) in Marpi charges a local rate of $20 and a tourist rate of $130.

There also Dan Dan Driving Range, on the airport road about a mile north of the airport. A bucket of balls costs $4.

Tennis

The American Memorial Park maintains four public tennis courts at the north end of Middle Rd. The courts, which are lit for night play, are currently free. However, because of the high cost of electricity, the introduction of a fee system is under consideration.

A number of Saipan's 1st-class hotels have tennis courts which are free to their guests.

Bowling

Saipan Bowling Center (☎ 234-6420), on Beach Rd in San Jose, has 12 lanes and is open from 9 am to midnight. It costs $1.25 per game.

Other Activities

A 48-passenger submarine goes out half a dozen times a day in the lagoon between Saipan and Managaha islands. Because the lagoon is fairly shallow, the sub descends only to about 45 feet. Underwater sights include the ruins of a Japanese freighter and an American B-29. It costs $89 when booked through a tour agent, but you should be able to get the local price of $50 if you book direct by calling 322-7734.

Sightseeing tours by land or air are detailed under Tours in the Getting Around section at the end of this chapter. Information on sporting events is in the following section.

SAIPAN

FESTIVALS & EVENTS

Village fiestas are held in San Vicente in early April, in San Antonio in mid-June, at the Mt Carmel Cathedral in Chalan Kanoa in mid-July, in San Roque in mid-August, in Tanapag in early October and in Kobler-ville in late October.

The week-long Liberation Day Festival celebrates the American liberation of the islands and ends on 4 July, US Independence Day. Festivities include a beauty pageant, nightly entertainment, games and food booths.

As for sporting events, Saipan hosts a half marathon and a 10-km fun run along Beach Rd in late January, the Tagaman triathlon in mid-May and a five-mile run up Mt Tagpochau on Thanksgiving. The Tagaman consists of a two-km swim, a 60-km bike ride and a 15-km run and attracts international competitors. The annual Micronesian Open Boardsailing Regatta and the Saipan Laguna Regatta are international windsurfing and Hobie Cat competitions held at Micro Beach in mid-February. A fishing tournament is held in August, during the marlin season. The Kintetsu Buffaloes, a pro-baseball team from Japan, has its spring training on Saipan during the first two weeks of February.

GARAPAN

The Japanese developed Garapan, their administrative centre in the Marianas, into one of the most bustling towns in Micronesia. Home to 15,000 residents, its streets were lined with neat rows of houses and its central area looked like a little Tokyo, with public baths, sake shops, Shinto shrines and Japanese schools and office buildings. Garapan was completely leveled by US bombers during WW II and it wasn't until the 1960s that the Saipanese began to resettle the area.

These days Garapan is booming, thanks again to the presence of the Japanese – this time as tourists. The streets are lined with signs in Japanese announcing sushi shops, souvenir stores, karaoke clubs and the like. Walking around the Micro Beach area it would be easy to imagine you were in Okinawa.

Micro Beach

Micro Beach, Saipan's most attractive white sand beach, is travel poster material. In fact, it's not that uncommon to find Japanese film crews out shooting TV commercials on the shore. The broad beach has brilliant turquoise waters, a good view of Managaha Island and a fine angle for catching one of Saipan's lingering sunsets. It's also a popular venue for windsurfers.

It's a long walk out through Micro Beach's shallows to get to water deep enough for swimming but, except for a few sea cucumbers that can be squishy underfoot, the wade is pleasant enough as the bottom is sandy.

There are public toilets and showers on the beach between the Dai-Ichi and Hyatt hotels and at the north side of Micro Beach at American Memorial Park.

American Memorial Park

The 133-acre American Memorial Park, under the auspices of the US National Park Service, stretches north along the coast from the Hyatt hotel, encompassing the north end of Micro Beach and the Smiling Cove harbour area. To the east the park extends all the way to Middle Rd, and takes in a swamp forest that serves as an important bird habitat.

With the exception of public tennis courts on Middle Rd, all of the park's facilities are on the west side of Beach Rd. The park has beachside picnic grounds, restrooms and a popular ironwood-shaded **jogging path** that runs 1.5 miles up the coast.

Inland from the beach is Saipan's one-room **WW II Museum**, easily recognised by the two tanks that sit rusting in the parking lot. The museum has a small collection of war paraphernalia, including weapons, uniforms, gas masks and period photos. As it's run by volunteers, opening hours are a bit tentative but it's generally open from 10 am to 2 pm Monday to Saturday.

Along Beach Rd the park has erected two large **memorials** honouring Americans who died in the US invasions of Saipan and Tinian. One of these, the Court of Honor, is ringed by plaques inscribed with the names of the 2840 marines and 1824 infantry men killed during the invasions, as well as the names of 505 navy

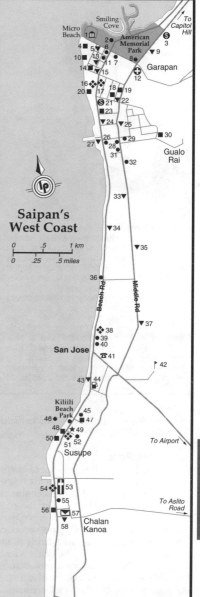

Saipan's West Coast

PLACES TO STAY		3	Bank of Hawaii
4	Hyatt Regency Saipan	6	Fire Station
10	Dai-Ichi Hotel	7	Coin Laundry
14	Remington Club	8	Public Tennis Courts
18	Holiday In Saipan	11	Saipan Scooters
19	Oriental Hotel	12	Commonwealth Health Center
20	Hafadai Beach Hotel	16	Hafadai Shopping Center
23	Saipan Ocean View Hotel	17	DFS Galleria
30	Sugar King Hotel	21	Bank of Guam
47	Sun Inn	26	Horiguchi (Federal) Building
48	Saipan Diamond Hotel	28	Old Japanese Hospital
50	Saipan Grand Hotel	29	Sugar King Park
56	Pacific Gardenia Hotel	31	Old Japanese Jail

PLACES TO EAT

5	Coconut-Tei	32	Saipan Game Club
9	Supanna Hong	36	Japanese Tank
13	Chamorro House	38	Hakubotan (Duty-Free Shop)
15	Winchell's Donuts, Bobby Cadillacs	39	Continental Micronesia (Airline Office)
22	Mom's Round II	40	Saipan Bowling Center
24	Canton Restaurant	41	IT&E
25	Poon's	42	Saipan Country Club
27	Thai House Restaurant	44	24-Hour Petrol Station
33	J's Restaurant	45	Philippine Consulate
34	China House Restaurant	46	American tanks
35	Pizza Hut	49	Police Station & Library
37	McDonald's	51	Joeten Shopping Center
43	Oleai Beach Bar & Restaurant	52	Nauru Building
58	Saipan Farmers' Market	53	Mt Carmel Cathedral
		54	Town House Shopping Center

OTHER

1	WW II Museum	55	Sablan Bookseller
2	Court of Honor Memorial	57	Post Office

SAIPAN

Amelia Earhart

Rumours persist that famed aviator Amelia Earhart was held in the Garapan jail after being shot down by the Japanese over the Marshall Islands in 1937. According to the theory, the Japanese military, who suspected her of being on a spying mission, sent her to Saipan for interrogation and eventually executed her as a spy. While this play of events has its followers, most scholars assume she simply ran out of fuel, crashed into the Pacific and died at sea. Still there are a few older Saipanese who insist they saw Amelia on the island and the mystery of her demise adds an element of intrigue as you look around the old jail. ■

personnel who died in the related battle of the Philippine Sea.

Sugar King Park

Sugar King Park is a hodgepodge of historical and memorial sights on the east side of Middle Rd. A bright red railroad engine on the roadside grassy knoll makes the park easy to spot.

The **steam-powered engine** was once used to haul sugar cane from fields in the Marpi area to a factory in Chalan Kanoa where Mt Carmel Cathedral now stands. The route was along the current Middle Rd, although none of the train tracks remains.

The **bronze statue** in the centre of the park is of Haruji Matsue, head of the Nanyo Kohatsu Kaisha (South Seas Development Company), responsible for developing the sugar industry in the Marianas. The statue was erected in 1934 and survived the wartime bombings.

The rear section of the park is called the **Commonwealth Botanical Garden**. While it's not as extensive as the title might imply, there are some nice old trees and flowering bushes that make for pleasant strolling.

At the far end of the park a red, riverless bridge leads to a **Japanese shrine** called the Katori Jinja. Originally built in 1911, it was destroyed in 1944 and rebuilt in concrete in 1985. Steps behind the shrine lead to a 15-minute loop trail that climbs around the hill in back, stopping along the way at a **hexagonal prayer temple** dedicated to WW II Japanese soldiers.

Old Japanese Hospital

The ruins of the old Japanese hospital are on Middle Rd directly across from Sugar King Park. The hospital entrance is at the back of the building, but beware of the two temperamental watchdogs in the yard next door. The interior of the hospital is a popular spot for budding graffiti artists.

Old Japanese Jail

The old Japanese jail stands largely intact and makes for an interesting sight. You can walk down the corridor past the damp concrete cells, some of which still have their barred steel doors attached. The main cell block row was for male civilian prisoners, while geishas who stole from their customers' pockets and women who didn't complete their employment contracts were held in a smaller building.

To get there continue south on Middle Rd from the old Japanese hospital and take the signposted dirt road to the right. The jail is just 100 yards down on the right.

NORTH OF GARAPAN

North of Garapan are Tanapag and San Roque, once sleepy seaside villages that are being invaded by new resort developments. San Roque now has a large shopping centre, La Fiesta San Roque, where you can stop and get a meal, and there are grocery stores in both Tanapag and San Roque.

The northern tip of the island, called Marpi, has most of Saipan's WW II tourist attractions and some of the island's prettiest scenery. It's easy to explore as the roads are well paved. Still, it's an undeveloped area, with much of the roadside lined with papaya trees and *tangan-tangan* bushes.

The defoliation of Saipan during WW II was so complete that the quick-growing tangan-tangan was aerially seeded to keep parts of the island from washing into the sea. Today this pervasive shrub is the most prevalent plant on Saipan. Although it has prevented major erosion, it has also choked out native flora and upset the natural prewar ecosystem.

Pau Pau Beach

Pau Pau Beach in San Roque has the splashy Hotel Nikko at its south end, but its north end remains in a pleasantly undeveloped state. It has soft sand, a picnic shelter, fairly shallow waters and good snorkelling and swimming during high tide.

Suicide Attack

The quiet village of Tanapag was the site of one of the most fanatical attacks of WW II. On the night of 6 July 1944, 4000 Japanese soldiers, many emboldened by sake, hurled themselves in a *banzai* attack upon US forces, which were lined up along Tanapag Beach. Some of the Japanese had guns, but most were armed just with clubs, bayonet sticks, bamboo spears and grenades.

The Japanese, honour-bound to die one way or another in the face of defeat, were intent on taking as many Americans with them as possible. As wave after wave of Japanese soldiers rushed down in the surprise attack, the Americans were pushed out into the water, across Tanapag Harbor and all the way back onto the reef, firing all the while at the unrelenting enemy. By the next morning it was all over and 5000 men were dead. ∎

Originally named Papau, meaning 'bitter root', the beach name was inadvertently changed to its present form by Americans, and Pau Pau is now used by everyone except older Saipanese.

A paved road just north of the Nikko leads down to the beach.

PACBAR Radar Facility

In 1989, the US Air Force constructed a radar facility (called PACBAR) at the top of the 942-foot Mt Petosukara in the Marpi Commonwealth Forest. The radar tracks foreign satellites and other resident space objects.

A 2.25-mile paved road leads up to the facility. There are ocean views and a couple of roadside WW II bunkers along the way. The best reason to take this road, however, is to hike the Laderan Tangke Trail, which the US Air Force developed and maintains as part of its land-use agreement.

To get there, turn off Marpi Rd onto the road immediately north of the San Roque shopping centre and then veer right at the water tank. The marked trailhead is 1.5 miles up, on the left.

Laderan Tangke Trail This 1.8-mile loop trail through the Marpi Commonwealth Forest is one of the most pleasant in Micronesia, as it's a well-maintained public trail crossing the sort of dense jungle that's generally not easily accessible to hikers .

The trail begins over a soft bed of ironwood needles as it passes through a raised limestone forest of tall trees, tangan-tangan and lots of ferns. It continues along the Laderan Tangke Cliff, from where there's a distant ocean view. The last half-mile, along an overgrown dirt road, brings you back to the starting point. As parts of the terrain are steep and rocky, proper footwear is recommended.

Fifteen interpretive markers identify flora, fauna and geological features. The first marker, placed beside a WW II foxhole, identifies pandanus, which traditionally has provided islanders with both fibre for weaving and a source of food.

The forest is a habitat for numerous

Vanikoro swiftlet

species of birds, including the rufous fan-tail, which is brown with a russet belly and has a tail that spreads like a fan, and the bright red cardinal honeyeater; both are easily spotted. There are also three endangered species residing here: the Vanikoro swiftlet, the Micronesian megapode and the nightingale reed-warbler.

As you walk along the trail you'll probably notice the shells of giant African snails scampering around – they're occupied by hermit crabs which are born in the ocean and, rather amazingly, climb up to the forest!

Wing Beach

Wing Beach was named after the US Navy aircraft wing that lay half buried in the sand for decades before falling victim to an aluminium recycling programme.

The south end of the beach has a shoreline coral shelf, but the north end is sandy and has good snorkelling.

Wing Beach is a mile north of Pau Pau Beach. Turn left off Marpi Rd just beyond the country club swimming pool. This unmarked road changes from packed coral to dirt after a third of a mile. You should be able to make it down in a car though it

might get a bit rough if it has been raining heavily. The beach sand is a pleasant mix of white shells and coral bits; vines of white and purple morning glory add a splash of colour.

Memorials

A series of WW II memorial parks are neatly lined up along the road starting about 7.5 miles north of Garapan. The first is the Korean Peace Memorial, the second park is dedicated to Okinawans and the Last Japanese Command Post is straight ahead.

Banzai Cliff

Waves crash onto the jagged rocks below Banzai Cliff, one of the places where hundreds of Japanese civilians jumped to their deaths as the Americans were taking over the island in 1944.

Whole families lined up in order of age. Each child was pushed over the edge by the next oldest brother or sister, until the mother pushed the oldest child and the father pushed his wife before running backwards over the cliff himself. Although US soldiers dropped leaflets and shouted through loudspeakers that those who surrendered would not be harmed, the mass suicides were deemed preferable to the shame of capture and to the torturings the Japanese had been convinced the Americans would inflict upon them.

Over the years the Japanese have put up a number of plaques and memorials to commemorate the spot, including a large statue of Heiwa Kannon, the Peaceful Goddess of Mercy.

The turn-off to Banzai Cliff is off Marpi Rd opposite the Okinawa Peace Memorial.

Last Command Post

It was at the spot now known as the Last Command Post that troops of the Japanese Imperial Army readied themselves for their final desperate battle against US invasion forces.

Lieutenant General Yoshitsugo Saito, acknowledging defeat, asked his remaining soldiers to each take seven American lives for the emperor, triggering the banzai suicide attack at Tanapag Harbor. Saito then faced north-west toward Japan and committed hara-kiri, thrusting his sword into his stomach while his aide shot him in the head.

Guns, torpedoes and tanks have been placed on the lawn below the concrete bunker which served as the command post. The bunker, which was built into the rock face, is cleverly concealed. You can climb up inside and scramble around.

Banadero Trail The Banadero Trail runs from behind the Last Command Post bunker up to the top of Suicide Cliff. The trail, which is marked with orange ribbons, leads through a thick forest with large trees and lots of birds. One native you're apt to spot is the golden white-eye, a small bright yellow bird. When the trail is properly maintained it takes about 45 minutes to reach the summit, but you might want to consider hitching back as the trail is very steep in places and you have to climb over some rocks and roots, which makes for a rougher climb down than the climb going up. There's also a fair amount of sword grass, so knee-high socks or long pants are a good idea.

Suicide Cliff

Half a mile beyond the Last Command Post, you'll come to a fork where you should bear right. At a second fork, which is a mile farther on, continue straight ahead to get to the Grotto and Bird Island, or bear right to get to Suicide Cliff.

From this turn-off, it's two miles up to Suicide Cliff; follow the paved road all the way, following the signs that read 'Laderan Banadero', the Chamorro name for this area.

The 820-foot sheer rock face of Suicide Cliff was another site for Japanese suicides, similar to those that took place on Banzai Cliff.

The cliff provides an excellent view of the northern tip of the island. Below the lookout you can see the remains of the North Field runway, an old Japanese fighter strip. White-tailed tropicbirds and fairy terns swoop and soar in the wind drafts along the cliffside.

A monument at the lookout reads:

The purpose of the Peace Memorial is to console the spirits of those who died, irrespective of nationality in this historic area, as well as to remind our posterities of the tragic futility of war, with our sincere hope that everlasting peace and friendship may prevail amongst all mankind.

The Grotto

The Grotto, Saipan's most unique diving spot, is a collapsed limestone cavern with a pool of cobalt-blue seawater filled by three underwater passageways. Sometimes the Grotto is calm and at other times powerful surges of water come whooshing in and out.

Once, locals who wanted to swim in the Grotto had to shimmy down a rope but there are now steep concrete stairs down to the water. Tiny stalactites drip from above and massive spider webs hanging overhead make interesting photographs if caught in the right light. The glowing blue light at the bottom of the rock wall comes from the tunnels which lead to the open sea. There's a viewpoint looking down into the Grotto at the top of the stairs to the left.

To get to the Grotto, turn left a quarter of a mile past the Suicide Cliff turn-off and follow the road to the end.

Bird Island Lookout

Bird Island, a rocky limestone islet close to shore, is a wildlife sanctuary that provides

Nightingale reed-warbler

a habitat for brown noddies and other seabirds.

The windy lookout affords a scenic view of Bird Island, whose east side is battered by open ocean while the inland side is protected by a calm reef. The purple beach morning glory which grows around the lookout cliff is known as *alalag-tasi* in Chamorro.

Bird Island Trail You can hike down to Bird Island but not from the lookout. Instead, head back the way you came and look for the start of the trail three-quarters of a mile on the right, shortly before the turn-off to the Grotto.

The beginning of the dirt footpath, which looks like an eroded driveway, leads down the hill through tall grass and a canopy of tangan-tangan.

At the bottom there's a coral sand beach. The water is clear and coral formations provide good snorkelling between Bird Island and the beach. Currents are rough beyond the reef.

CROSS ISLAND ROAD

The Cross Island Rd heads north from Garapan, turns inland to Capitol Hill, circles around Mt Tagpochau, goes south through San Vicente and then heads back to the west coast, passing the Northern Marianas College on the left and ending up on Beach Rd in San Jose.

From various spots around Capitol Hill, and on the drive up from Garapan, there are excellent views of Tanapag Harbor, Managaha Island and the brilliant turquoise waters of the lagoon.

Capitol Hill

Capitol Hill is the site of most government offices for the Commonwealth of the Northern Marianas, including those of the governor and the legislature.

The complex of houses and office buildings that make up Capitol Hill was built in 1948 by the CIA as a base camp for secretly training Nationalist Chinese guerrillas to fight against Mao Zedong. The soldiers were trained in the Marpi area.

After the CIA moved out in 1962, Capitol Hill became the headquarters for the Trust Territory government. In the 1980s, as the Trust Territory was dismantled, the buildings were turned over to the emerging commonwealth government.

Mt Tagpochau

You can drive right to the top of Mt Tagpochau which, at 1545 feet, is Saipan's highest point. To get there take the crossroad opposite the convention centre on Capitol Hill, drive a short way up through the housing project and turn right up to the former Congress of Micronesia buildings, now marked as civil defence and energy agencies. Continue a few hundred yards beyond the buildings and take the dirt road heading down to the right. If it's been raining heavily you may need a 4WD vehicle from this point, but otherwise a sedan takes about 10 minutes to get to the top.

Mt Tagpochau is the destination each Easter for hundreds of Saipanese who hike up carrying a heavy wooden cross to plant at the top. There are excellent views of most of the island from the summit.

East Coast Beaches

Heavy seas beat against a rugged shoreline along much of Saipan's east coast although there are some protected areas. Most of the east coast beaches can be challenging to reach, as they are at the end of dirt roads that are subject to washouts after heavy rains. This may well change, though, as this part of the island is beginning to be developed for both residential and tourist use.

Profile Beach is an isolated little beach with a limestone islet called Old Man by the Sea, which looks remarkably like the laughing head of an old man. To get there turn off Cross Island Rd at Esco's Bake House (which has good homemade papaya turnovers) at the south end of Capitol Hill. Take a left at the Y-intersection and park about 100 feet down. The trailhead is on the right side of the road and it's about a 20-minute hike to the beach.

If you were instead to follow the road past Esco's Bake House to its end you'd reach Jeffries (Talofofo) Beach, which has a small pocket beach and some nearby natural arches and blowholes.

Tank, Marine and Laulau are other east coast beaches that can all be reached by dirt roads. Laulau Beach, on the north side of Magicienne Bay, is one of the more popular and protected beaches on the east coast and is good for beach dives.

Another popular remote beach is Forbidden Island, which has a long stretch of beach, a grotto and a swimming hole. It's on an island-like peninsula south-east of the Laolao Bay Golf Resort and requires a 20-minute hike to reach.

SOUTH OF GARAPAN
San Jose, Susupe, Chalan Kanoa and San Antonio were once distinct villages on Saipan's south-west coast until a decade of development turned Beach Rd into a nearly continuous strip of nightclubs, restaurants and shopping centres.

Susupe has the police station, courthouse and library. Chalan Kanoa has the main post office, the island's only remaining movie theatre and the picturesque Mt Carmel Cathedral. San Antonio, though it's being developed, is still the quieter end of it all.

Sunken Treasure
In 1638, in the midst of rough gales, the Manila galleon *Nuestra Señora de la Concepción* went down east of Agingan Point, scattering its rich treasure along the shallow reef that now borders the Coral Ocean Point golf course.

In 1987, after searching through archives in Seville, Mexico City and Manila to research the location and cargo, an international crew of 30, including historians and archaeologists, began a two-year salvage operation. Some 10,000 dives later they had recovered scores of cannonballs and ballast stones, 1300 pieces of gold jewellery, many inlaid with precious gems, and 156 storage jars, some still filled with fragrant resins. Some of the pieces were recovered in as little as two feet of water. ■

Southern Beaches
Ladder and Obyan are two south coast beaches that get a few local picnickers, but are well off the tourist track. To get to them, go around the south-west tip of the airport runway. The road to Ladder Beach will come in on the right a quarter of a mile after passing the turn-off to Koblerville.

Ladder Beach is a rounded cove backed with 30-foot limestone cliffs. Most of the beach is covered with chunky coral pebbles, and the water is generally too rough for swimming. There are large caves in the cliffs which are used as picnic shelters, complete with picnic tables.

More appealing is Obyan Beach, a pretty white sand beach with calm waters protected by Naftan Point. The expansive beach is good for shelling and snorkelling. At the head of the parking area is a large WW II concrete bunker, and about 75 yards east, just inland from a grove of coconut trees, are the remains of eight latte stones that have been carbon dated to around 1500 BC. The stones, which are easy to find, are in two parallel rows and are thought to have once supported a beachside structure.

The turn-off down to Obyan Beach is 1.5 miles beyond Ladder Beach.

MANAGAHA ISLAND
Managaha, the island 1.5 miles north-west of Micro Beach, is an old patch reef which geological forces lifted above sea level some 10,000 years ago. It's now covered with a fringing white sand beach and has Saipan's best snorkelling. The clear waters surrounding the island have lots of colourful tropical fish and there's also abundant coral, although much of the near-shore coral shows signs of being trampled on – a consequence of the beach's heavy use.

This uninhabited island is small and only takes 20 minutes to walk around. The island has the rusting remains of a few war relics, including a pair of coastal cannons along the beach near the boat landing. On the other side of the island is a colourful statue and a small monument marking the burial site of the Yapese chief Aghurubw, who in 1815 led a group of settlers from the Satawal atoll in the Yap chain and established a Carolinian settlement on Saipan.

Managaha, once the domain of Saipanese picnickers, is now packed with Japanese tourists on day trips. Consequently the food and beach gear equipment are costly: $15 will get you use of a beach mat or snorkel set, $2.50 buys a soft drink and $20 a barbecue lunch. Your best bet is to bring your own or look for the stand that's sometimes set up by a local family at the end of the dock, where rentals and soft drinks are about half the price charged by the Japanese concessionaires.

There are covered picnic tables and free changing rooms with toilets, showers and coin lockers.

Getting There & Away
All regularly scheduled boats to Managaha leave from the north side of Smiling Cove. The crossing takes about 15 minutes.

The *Sounds of Saipan* leaves at 9 and 10.30 am and 1 pm and returns from Managaha at 12.30, 2.30 and 4 pm. The regular tourist price is $43, however Tasi Tours (☎ 234-7121) in the Dai-Ichi Hotel sells last-minute unsold tickets for the next day's trip for $15; you can stop by around 5.30 pm the day before, but note that the office closes at 6 pm.

The *Sounds of Coral* has a submerged lower deck with two rows of benches facing a series of windows and is a better choice if you want to see a bit of the underwater world on the way to Managaha, as it takes a more scenic route, passing over a sunken Japanese Zero. It leaves four times a day and costs $49. Reservations are made through Tasi Tours.

PDI (☎ 234-6210) has a glass-bottom boat which also passes over the Japanese Zero and some coral heads on the way to Managaha. The cost is $43.

Another way to get to Managaha is from the water sports concession stands at Micro Beach, which charge $25 to zip passengers over by speedboat and pretty much provide the service on demand.

PLACES TO STAY
Most hotels on Saipan, including the listings that follow, accept major credit cards. Add a 10% hotel tax to all room rates.

During the Japanese holiday season, particularly Christmas through January and mid-July through August, it can be very difficult to find accommodation, and advance reservations are recommended.

Bottom End
Camping There are no developed camping grounds in Saipan and rip-offs and crime are issues that need to be seriously considered by anyone intending to camp.

Uninhabited Managaha used to be a good spot for overnighting, but with hundreds of tourists now going over for day trips, it's no longer ideal for that purpose. These days, Saipan's largely undeveloped east coast, such as the isolated Profile and Jeffries beaches, may be the best bet.

Hotels If you don't mind being inland, the *Valley Inn* (☎ 234-7018, fax 234-7029), Box 1120, Saipan, MP 96950, is the best low-priced option in Saipan. The staff are cheery and helpful, the rooms are pleasant, and there's a central courtyard that's ideal for meeting other guests. All units have remote-control TV, phones and thermostatic air-con. The lowest priced studio rooms ($45) are compact but cosy and have a separate kitchen area with a refrigerator, hot plate and toaster. There are also roomier deluxe studios for $65 and a few large two and three-bedroom, two-bath suites with full kitchens for $110. The studios can be rented by the month for $550, utilities included. There's free morning coffee, a coin-operated laundry and a barbecue grill; a grocery store is within walking distance. The Valley Inn is a five-minute drive from the airport, but well beyond aircraft noise. Free airport transfers are available but the location is really only practical if you plan to rent a car.

The *Remington Club* (☎ 234-5449; fax 234-5619), Box 1719, Saipan, MP 96950, is an 18-room pension-style hotel in Garapan, just a minute's walk from Micro

Sunset on Saipan's east coast

Old Japanese communications building, Tinian

Statue to Yapese chief Aghurubw on
Managaha Island, Saipan

Snorkeling at Pinatang Park, Rota

Goofing around after school, Rota

Beach. The rooms are straightforward but quite adequate and have been recently renovated, each with air-con, a refrigerator and a phone. Considering its location in the midst of Garapan's resort area, the hotel is quite a good value at $45/55 for singles/doubles. There are also a few twin rooms with kitchenettes and TV for $70 and a two-bedroom suite that costs $90 for up to four people.

The *Sugar King Hotel* (☎ 234-6164), Box 1939, Saipan, MP 96950, in a quiet area above Sugar King Park, has two dozen basic rooms in concrete duplex cottages. Rates are $48 for one or two people in a room with a platform-style double bed, refrigerator, air-con and TV, but as the quarters are cramped and a bit rundown you won't want to spend much time hanging around inside. Also, bed coverings are skimpy so you may need to ask for an extra blanket. On the plus side is the large, uncrowded swimming pool with its distant ocean view. Rooms can also be rented by the month for $350 to $550, the higher price being for larger rooms in a separate hillside building.

The *Sun Inn* (☎ 234-3232; fax 235-6062), Box 920 CK, Saipan, MP 96950, behind the baseball field in Susupe, has 36 rooms with TV, refrigerator, air-con and phone. The cheapest, which cost $40/50 singles/doubles, are spartan and a little musty but the newer, deluxe rooms at $10 more are quite comfortable.

Middle

The *Oriental Hotel* (☎ 233-1420, fax 233-1424), Box 809, Saipan, MP 96950, on Middle Rd opposite the Commonwealth Health Center, is a good choice for a mid-range hotel. Unlike many hotels that have lower rates for locals and groups, and steeper rates for independent travellers, the Oriental charges everyone the same $60 rate. This three-storey hotel has very nice rooms for the money, each with cable TV, air-con, one twin and one double bed, phone, table and two chairs, minibar and bathtub, as well as a VCR upon request. It's

a 10-minute walk to central Garapan and Micro Beach.

Saipan Ocean View Hotel (☎ 234-8900; fax 234-9428), Box 799, Saipan, MP 96950, is a 73-room two-storey hotel on Beach Rd in Garapan. Its modern rooms, which have phones, mini-refrigerators, room safes and cable TV, are nearly of the standard of some of the beachfront hotels but cost just half the price. Rates are $65 for either singles or doubles in a regular room, or $100 for a suite. There's a pool, and free airport transfers are provided.

The 26-room *Holiday In Saipan* (☎ 234-3554, fax 235-5023), Box 5308 CHRB, Saipan, MP 96950, a couple of blocks inland from Beach Rd in Garapan, has rooms that are modern and reasonably pleasant, with cable TV, phones, carpeting, refrigerators and bathrooms with tubs. Rates are a bit steep however, costing $65/85 for singles/doubles. There's also a pool.

Finasisu Airport Hotel (☎ 235-6524, fax 235-8013), PPP 521, Box 10000, Finasisu Rd, Saipan, MP 96950, near the college, is a large apartment complex with one wing converted for daily rentals. The units each have a full kitchen, a living room with cable TV and two bedrooms, one with two single beds and the other with a queen-size bed. The regular rate is $66, but the management will sometimes discount it to $50 if there are only one or two guests using the unit. It's good value if you're looking for a lot of space and condo-like accommodation. There's a small coffee shop on site. Free airport transfers are available but it's not a terribly practical place to be without a rental car.

The locally owned *Pacific Gardenia Hotel* (☎ 234-3455, fax 234-3441), Box 144, Saipan, MP 96950, is on Beach Rd at the north end of Chalan Kanoa. Despite being in a rather built-up area, there's a nice white sand beach in back of the hotel. The 14 rooms, which are all on the 2nd floor along an atrium-like hallway, are large and well furnished, with cable TV and phone; all but two of them have kitchens. The rate is $89. The helpful staff can provide cribs, ironing boards and the like upon request. There's also a coin laundry and free airport transfers.

Top End

Saipan's larger hotels, thriving on the package-tour trade, have less need to be receptive to independent travellers and room rates are typically high. With few exceptions, the atmosphere is more Tokyo than Micronesia.

The seven-storey *Hyatt Regency Saipan* (☎ 234-1234; fax 234-7745), Box 87 CHRB, Saipan, MP 96950, is right on Micro Beach. All 183 rooms have balconies with sunset and ocean views. The rates start at $210 for rooms on the 2nd floor, with prices going up as the floors do. While the Hyatt is the oldest of Saipan's resort hotels, it's been refurbished over the years and has the most international clientele and the best beach location. The grounds are pleasantly landscaped and there's a pool, lit tennis courts and a fitness centre. If money is no object, this is the place to be.

The *Aqua Resort Club* (☎ 322-1234, fax 322-1220), Box 9, Saipan, MP 96950, on the beach in Tanapag, is the best of the Japanese-oriented resorts. It has a casual yet classy ambience, with a pleasant open-air lobby that incorporates some Micronesian touches, a good beachfront setting, large swimming pools, a good restaurant and friendly staff. All 91 rooms have verandas (most with ocean views), ceiling fans, air-con, TV, desks, room safes, refrigerators and separate bathing and toilet areas. Rates start at $170 to $190, depending upon the season.

Other first-class hotels in Saipan include the following:

Saipan Grand Hotel, Box 369, Saipan, MP 96950, in Susupe (☎ 234-6601, fax 234-8007); 224 rooms, from $130
Pacific Islands Club, Box 2370, Saipan, MP 96950, in San Antonio (☎ 234-7976, fax 234-6592); 220 rooms, from $130
Hafadai Beach Hotel, Box 338, Saipan, MP 96950, on the beach in Garapan (☎ 234-6495, fax 234-8912); 280 rooms, from $155
Saipan Diamond Hotel, Box 66, Saipan, MP 96950, in Susupe (☎ 234-5900, fax 234-5909); 264 rooms, from $160
Dai-Ichi Hotel, Box 1029, Saipan, MP 96950, in Garapan (☎ 234-6412); 425 rooms, from $160
Coral Ocean Point Resort Club, Box 1160, Saipan, MP 96950, on a golf course south of San Antonio (☎ 234-7000, fax 234-7005); 102 rooms, from $160
Plumeria Resort, Box 228 CHRB, Saipan, MP 96950, in Tanapag (☎ 322-6201, fax 322-6217); 100 rooms, from $180
Marianas Resort Hotel, Box 527, Saipan, MP 96950, adjacent to the Marianas Country Club in San Roque (☎ 322-0770, fax 322-0776); 50 cottages, from $200
Hotel Nikko Saipan, Box 5152 CHRB, Saipan, MP 96950, in San Roque (☎ 322-3311, fax 322-3144); 313 rooms, from $210

PLACES TO EAT

Tipping is now a common practice in Saipan and a tip of at least 10% is expected at most restaurants.

Budget

The booths at Garapan's *Winchell's Donuts* are a popular place to start the day. Doughnuts cost 50 cents and you can get a decent cup of coffee for 65 cents, which is about half the price of most other places.

Herman's Modern Bakery, on the way to the airport, is a local eatery with cheap breakfasts, sandwiches and lunch specials. Herman started his bakery in 1944 to bake bread for American GIs. By the time the GIs had moved out, the Saipanese had developed a taste for bread and Herman's continues to supply most of Saipan's bread and pastries, including the buns for the new McDonald's. The bakery is open daily from 6 am to 4 pm (to 3 pm on Sundays).

The *Hafadai Deli & Bakery*, in the Hafadai Shopping Center in Garapan, has plate lunches from steamer trays for around $5, deli foods and bakery items.

Canton Restaurant on Beach Rd in Garapan has good, cheap weekday lunch specials. From 11 am to 2 pm you can select from a number of dishes, including standards like beef with vegetables or sweet & sour pork, served with rice and soup, for just $4. At dinner, from 6 to 10.30 pm, there's an extensive menu, with most items priced from $8 to $10.

Supanna Hong is a small, unpretentious Thai restaurant at the north end of Middle Rd. There are just eight tables. Soups, curries, pad Thai and chicken dishes are around $5, seafood dishes $8. It's open from 11 am to 2 pm Monday to Saturday and daily from 5 to 10 pm.

There are a slew of authentic Japanese restaurants in the Micro Beach area, though many are overpriced. One good-value place is *Coconut-Tei*, a hole-in-the-wall on a back street, one block inland from the Hyatt. Set lunches, including yakiniku, sashimi or fried fish, cost $6, beverage included. Prices at dinner begin around $10. It's open from 11 am to 1.30 pm for lunch and 5.30 to 10.30 pm for dinner (closed on Wednesday).

Kentucky Fried Chicken in the Town House Shopping Center in Susupe has the standard fried chicken, but where else does the Colonel serve it up with red rice cooked with achiote seeds?

There's a *McDonald's* on Middle Rd with the typical US menu and prices (69-cent hamburgers); it's open until at least midnight daily.

About a mile north of McDonald's is a *Pizza Hut* with a daily all-you-can-eat buffet of pizzas, pasta and salad for $6 from 11.30 am to 1.30 pm and $7 from 5.30 to 8.30 pm. The salad bar, which is simple but fresh, is available at other times for $2.29 a serving. Regular pizzas begin around $7 for a small size, with an optional second pizza available at half price. It's open from 10.30 am to 11.30 pm daily.

J's Restaurant on Middle Rd in Gualo Rai, is a 24-hour diner-style place with standard fare such as bacon, eggs and pancakes or a cheeseburger with fries for $3.75 and lunch specials for around $5. It's also popular for its back-room poker machines.

Bobby Cadillacs on Beach Rd in Garapan is another popular place for pizza, though prices are a bit higher than at Pizza Hut. It also makes decent sandwiches, has a small deli and serves $1 Budweisers. It's open from 10 am to 11 pm daily.

Mom's Round II, a few blocks inland from the Hafadai Beach Hotel in Garapan, is a bar with dart boards and inexpensive Mexican food. You can get a taco, burrito or enchilada with rice and beans for $5.50, a cheeseburger with fries for $6.50.

There are a couple of *Lappert's* ice cream shops, a fairly good Hawaiian chain, in the Micro Beach area, including one inside the DFS Galleria on Beach Rd.

Saipan Farmers' Market, the 'Co-op of the Hardworking People', is a simple fruit and vegetable market opposite the post office in Chalan Kanoa. They sell local papaya, betel nut and taro, but much of the other produce is imported so prices are still on the high side.

Supermarkets in Saipan are modern and well stocked, at least by Micronesian standards. The *Payless Supermarket* in the Town House Shopping Center and *Joeten*, a local chain with branches around the island, are among the largest and sell reasonably priced wine and general items as well as food. Most grocery stores are open until 10 pm.

Middle

Chamorro food is basically the same in Saipan as in Guam, except it's harder to find. One shining exception is *Chamorro House*, a popular restaurant in the Micro Beach area, which has been serving quality local food for years. Their best deal is at lunch, when Chamorro dishes such as tinaktak katni (beef strips in coconut milk) and kelaguen mannok (a tasty dish of grilled chicken and fresh shredded coconut in a light lemon sauce) cost just $7. Dinner prices are about double. At both meals these dishes are served with red rice, soup and salad. It's open daily from 11 am to 1.30 pm and from 5.30 to 9.30 pm.

The friendly *Coffee Care*, on Beach Rd in Garapan, just north of DFS Galleria, is the place to go for a caffè latte, cappuccino or espresso. You can also get light meals such as sandwiches, soups, salads and desserts at reasonable prices. At dinner there are often specials, such as pasta or Thai food, for around $10. It's open from 7 am to 10.30 pm, with lunch from 11.30 am to 2.30 pm and dinner from 6 pm (closed on Sundays).

Poon's on Middle Rd has a mix of Chinese and Indonesian food, including satays and curry dishes, mostly priced from $7 to $10. The food is all right if you're looking for something different, but otherwise isn't worth going out of your way for.

Rudolpho's (☎ 322-3017), on Marpi Rd opposite the turn-off to Capitol Hill, has good, reasonably priced Mexican and Italian food. The bar is a favourite hangout for expats and there's both indoor and outdoor dining. You can get a taco, burrito or enchilada with rice and beans for around $7 or lasagna with garlic bread for the same price. There are also seafood, chicken and steak meals from $10 to $17, as well as good pizza and hearty sandwiches. Rudolpho's serves a varied breakfast menu from 10 am to 1 pm on weekdays and 7.30 am to 1 pm on weekends. Everything else is available from 11 am to 11.30 pm daily, and free home delivery is available.

Thai House Restaurant on Beach Rd at the south end of Garapan has good Thai food at moderate prices. There are weekday lunch specials for $6.50 or you can order off the menu. Pad Thai, red or green curries and other dishes are priced at $7 for chicken or pork versions and $9 for shrimp. The spring rolls make a great appetizer. If you're not used to hot food, order mild, as the moderate is quite fiery and the Thai-hot is strictly for the initiated. Frosty 18-ounce mugs of Steinlager on tap cost $3. It's open for lunch on weekdays from 11 to 2 am and for dinner daily from 5 to 10 pm. There's a happy hour from 4 to 6 pm.

The hottest place on the island is the new German-run *Brewhouse Pub & Restaurant* (☎ 322 7662) on the road to Capitol Hill, about a mile east of Marpi Rd. Centred around Micronesia's first microbrewery, it has plate-glass windows that make it possible to view the operation while you sit back at the bar and down the freshest brew in the islands. Lager, pilsner and light beer are all brewed in strict accordance with German beer-purity laws. The pub serves rotisserie chicken, authentic German sausages and various other snack items. The restaurant dining room has good, moderately priced Italian-style dishes with home-made pasta. Both brew and food are served from 10 am to 10 pm daily.

For mid-range Chinese food, the *China House Restaurant* on Beach Rd in Gualo Rai has a local following.

Top End

The Aqua Resort Club's *Terrace Restaurant* (☎ 322-1234) has an Austrian chef and Saipan's best-value buffets. On Friday nights it features fresh oysters, shrimp and other seafood; on Saturdays there's Black Angus prime rib. Both buffets are served from 6.30 to 9.30 pm, cost $20 and are accompanied by an extensive spread of hot dishes and appetizers, including sashimi, tempura and salads. There's an impressive dessert table and excellent service. Sunday features a champagne brunch with prime rib, suckling pig and an array of other foods for $19 from 10.30 am to 2 pm. On other days, from 11 am to 2 pm, there's a sandwich board for $11 that includes luncheon meats, soup, salads, desserts and iced tea.

The Hyatt's *Kili Terrace* has a reasonably good, though somewhat overpriced, lunch buffet from 11 am to 2 pm Monday to Saturday. You can sit out in the pleasant open-air terrace and eat your fill of such dishes as mahimahi, sushi, soba, spareribs, breads, soup, salads and desserts; the cost is $15. There's also an á la carte menu with lunch or dinner main dishes priced from $13 for spaghetti to $19 for steak.

The Hyatt's *Oceana House* (☎ 234-1234) has a grand Sunday buffet brunch (10.30 am to 2 pm) in an up-market setting, complete with live piano music. The spread includes suckling pig, teppanyaki grill, sashimi, seafood and dessert tables, and waffle, crepe, omelette and tempura stations. It's a favourite place among well-to-do islanders for a Sunday splurge. The cost is $26.

The *Dolphin Restaurant* (☎ 234-6495),

on the 10th floor of the Hafadai Beach Hotel tower, has an excellent ocean view but prices are high. At lunch there are a few fixed meals for $15, otherwise the à la carte menu ranges from $12 to $24; at dinner, prices are triple that. The best deal is the Sunday brunch, from 10.30 am to 1.30 pm, which costs $18, includes a glass of champagne and is accompanied by piano music.

Sango (☎ 234-7000) at the Coral Ocean Point Resort Club has an ocean view across the golf course and a good-value weekday bento box lunch from 11 am to 1 pm that costs $9 and includes three Japanese dishes, rice, miso soup and iced tea. At other times there are various set meals priced from $15 to $25.

ENTERTAINMENT

The open-air *Sunset Bar & Grill*, behind the Pacific Gardenia Hotel in Chalan Kanoa, has a great sunset locale right on a white sand beach. There's a happy hour from 5 to 8 pm with $2 beers and free popcorn, and sometimes live entertainment. If you settle in you can also have dinner here, as there's a beachside barbecue grill with chicken and steaks for $15 to $20.

The beachfront patio at *Oleai Beach*, a bar and restaurant in San Jose, is also a nice place to be at sunset. At happy hour, which is all afternoon until 6.30 pm Monday to Friday, beers are $2.

A good sunset spot in the Garapan area is on the upper deck of *Ship Ashore*, an old boat that's permanently docked behind the Thai House Restaurant. There's a daily happy hour from 4 to 7 pm with $1 cans of Budweiser and free popcorn.

The *Remington Club* in Garapan has half-priced drinks from 4.30 to 7.30 pm. There are live bands on Friday and Saturday nights, anything from cha cha music to Jawaiian (an upbeat mix of reggae and contemporary Hawaiian music).

Gilligan's in the Hyatt has a dance floor; on Fridays there's live reggae and the $5 cover charge is waived for women. It's open on weekends from 9.30 pm to 2 am.

Many of the large hotels have 'Polyne-

sian' dance shows and other high-priced tourist entertainment.

There are lots of flashy nightclubs, dance spots and seedy massage parlours in the Micro Beach area. Most of the signs are in Japanese and have names like Club Passionate Love and Folk Pub Massage Services. The most flamboyant dance club in the Micro Beach area is Discoteque Gig, which is flanked by two large Sphinxes and charges $25 admission.

There's a movie theatre in Chalan Kanoa on the west side of the post office and cockfights at the Saipan Game Club on Middle Rd in Garapan.

THINGS TO BUY

Virtually none of the carvings, woven wall hangings or other handicrafts in Saipan's shops is made on the island. Most are imported from the Philippines and generally the prices are high and the quality is low. Postcards, T-shirts and plastic knickknacks bearing the island's name are just about the only souvenirs 'unique' to Saipan.

A fair amount of shopping goes on in Saipan nonetheless, largely by the Japanese who are obligated to take souvenirs home. Duty-free shops with high-priced designer products are a big hit. The largest are DFS Galleria in Garapan and Hakubotan in San Jose, which resemble up-market mainland department stores. There's also a large, fledgling mall-like shopping centre, La Fiesta San Roque, opposite the Hotel

Nikko, which has speciality clothing and gift shops as well as restaurants.

GETTING THERE & AWAY
Air
Airport Saipan's modern airport, eight miles south of Garapan, has car rental booths for Hertz, Budget, Thrifty and Dollar, a small handicraft shop, a simple restaurant, restrooms, phones, a duty-free shop and a separate commuter air terminal.

Airline Offices The Continental Micronesia ticket office (☎ 234-6491), in the Oleai Center in San Jose, is open from 9 am to 5 pm Monday to Saturday. Reservations can be made by phone daily between 7 am and 6 pm. Other airlines centre their operations at the airport.

To/From Japan There are daily flights to Saipan from Tokyo on Japan Air Lines, Northwest Airlines and Continental; from Osaka to Saipan on Japan Air Lines, Continental and United Airlines; and from Nagoya to Saipan on Continental and Japan Air Lines. There's also regular but less frequent service from other ports in Japan, including Sapporo, Sendai and Fukuoka.

Return fares from Japan begin around $700 for midweek travel with a 14-day advance purchase and a 30-day stay. The one-way fare with no restrictions is $686. Travel in the opposite direction is much cheaper – $331/430 one way/return from Saipan to Tokyo, Osaka or Nagoya.

To/From Korea There are flights between Seoul and Saipan on Continental, Asiana and Northwest airlines, the latter via Tokyo. The one-way fare in either direction is from $329; the return fare is $586 in the low season, $633 in the high season.

To/From the Philippines Continental flies four times a week between Manila and Saipan. The one-way fare is $457; the return fare, valid for a 45-day stay, is $551.

To/From Hong Kong Continental flies three times a week between Hong Kong

and Saipan. The one-way/return fares start from $424/672.

Within Micronesia Pacific Island Aviation (PIA) and Continental fly numerous times daily between Saipan and Guam; one-way fares are $55. If you have an international flight with Continental you can usually add on the Guam-Saipan sector for an extra $20 to $30. Freedom Air also has a couple of flights a day between Saipan and Guam for $65/98 one way/return.

All FSM and Palau connections to Saipan go through Guam, as do connections from Bali, Taipei and Honolulu. For more details see the Getting There & Away chapter in the front of the book.

Freedom Air and PIA fly to Tinian and Rota; see details under Getting There & Away in those island sections.

Leaving Saipan
Saipan has no departure tax.

GETTING AROUND
Saipan has a good road system and traffic is light in most areas, but you can expect to see bumper-to-bumper traffic on busy Beach Rd. The traffic between San Jose and Chalan Kanoa, in particular, can slow to a crawl at any time of the day, and at rush hours it's usually jammed.

To/From the Airport
Taxis and car rentals are available at the airport. Many hotels will provide airport transport for their guests, either free or for a fee.

Shuttle Buses
Saipan has no public bus system. However, La Fiesta San Roque (☎ 322-0998) in San Roque and Hakubotan (☎ 234-0979) in Chalan Kanoa both have regularly scheduled shuttle buses to and from their shopping centres, with pick-up service at major hotels around the island approximately every 30 minutes. Look for printed schedules in tourist handouts and at hotels. The Hakubotan bus is free, the La Fiesta bus charges $3.

Taxi

Taxis on Saipan are metered and privately owned. It typically costs $18 to $20 to get from the airport to Garapan and Micro Beach, $30 from the airport to San Roque and $12 from Garapan to Susupe. Taxis are clearly marked and usually easy to find at the airport and around larger hotels. If you need to call one, Manuel Muna (☎ 234-6277) is a good choice, as he has a few cars.

Car & Moped

The phone numbers and cheapest posted daily rates of the car rental agencies at the airport are: Hertz (☎ 234-8336; $43), Thrifty (☎ 234-8356; $41), Dollar (☎ 288-5151; $47) and Budget (☎ 234-8232; $40). These rates include unlimited mileage; collision damage waivers (CDW) are available for $9 to $13 more a day.

If you don't have a reservation, the best bet is to just walk up to each window (they all share a single hut) and ask for the best rate – if business is slow there's often a bit of room for negotiating the price down. Last time we were there Dollar was willing to knock $10 off the rate if we took an older car; Budget gave us an even better deal of $33 a day for a current-year Toyota Tercel.

In addition to the airport, there are also car rental agents in a few of the larger hotels and many companies will pick you up anywhere on the island.

Saipan Scooters (☎ 233-7433), next to the gun club in Garapan, has moped rentals for $10 an hour, though you may well be able to work out a more reasonable daily rate of around $30. It's open from 10 am to 6 pm daily.

Hitching

Saipan's main routes are reasonably good for hitching, although we don't advise doing so, as the island's not totally crime free. Be especially wary of accepting one-way rides to secluded areas, both for the usual safety reasons and because it can be a very long time between vehicles when you want to come back.

Tours

A number of tour companies with offices at the larger hotels offer land tours, sunset cruises and trips to Rota and Tinian.

Most land tours of Saipan are geared for Japanese package tourists and they don't take you anywhere you can't easily explore on your own. Gray Line (☎ 234-7148) charges $40 for a three-hour tour that includes Sugar King Park and the Marpi area sites. Saipan Koresco Tour (☎ 288-6001) and MMC Tours (☎ 234-6976) both advertise similarly priced tours. When you book with any of these companies, it's wise to confirm that an English-speaking guide will be available on your tour.

For an alternative, consider Roger Ludwick Tours (☎ 322-3717), which covers more sights, adds local insights, includes lunch and lasts five hours. The cost is $50.

Macaw Helicopters (☎ 234-7000) does flightseeing tours of Saipan, operating out of Coral Ocean Point Resort Club in Koblerville. A 15-minute spin costs $65 and a 30-minute ride costs $95.

Freedom Air (☎ 234-8328) has Piper Cherokee six-seater planes that can be chartered for sightseeing at $180 an hour.

Tinian

Tinian, a peaceful one-village island just three miles south of Saipan, has a notorious place in history as the take-off site for the aircraft that dropped the atomic bombs on Hiroshima and Nagasaki.

It's an attractive island with ancient latte stones, ranchland with grazing cattle, secluded sandy beaches and scenic vistas. The sleeper of Marianas tourism promotions, Tinian has an insufficient number of hotels and restaurants to support package tourism, which makes the island a nice destination for individual travellers.

Tinian is the second largest island in the Northern Marianas, about 12 miles long and five miles wide, and is the least mountainous, with a top elevation of 690 feet.

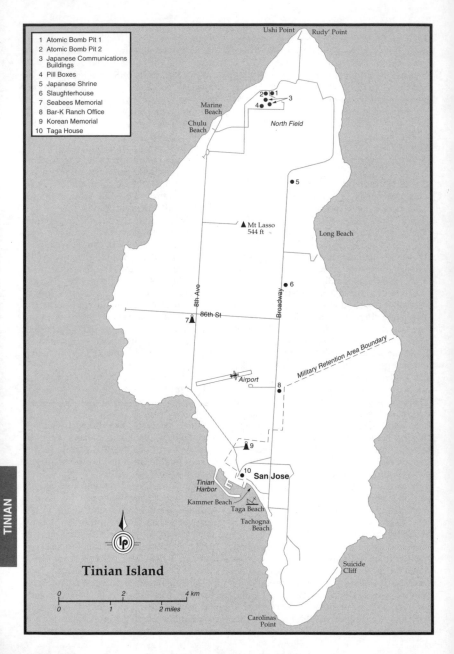

1 Atomic Bomb Pit 1
2 Atomic Bomb Pit 2
3 Japanese Communications
   Buildings
4 Pill Boxes
5 Japanese Shrine
6 Slaughterhouse
7 Seabees Memorial
8 Bar-K Ranch Office
9 Korean Memorial
10 Taga House

Ushi Point   Rudy' Point

Marine
Beach

Chulu
Beach

North Field

5

Mt Lasso
544 ft

Long Beach

6

8th Ave

86th St

7

Broadway

Military Retention Area Boundary

Airport

8

9

10 San Jose

Tinian
Harbor

Kammer Beach

Taga Beach

Tachogna
Beach

Suicide
Cliff

TINIAN

Tinian Island

0   2   4 km

0   1   2 miles

Carolinas
Point

Tinian's fertile soil was used to advantage by the Japanese, who levelled the forests and turned the island into a chequerboard of sugar cane fields. Its level terrain was also ideal for the airfields which were built later. Only a few Chamorros lived on Tinian during the Japanese occupation and they were greatly outnumbered by the nearly 18,000 Japanese, Okinawans and Koreans, most of whom were farm labourers.

Homesick Americans who captured the island in 1944 and quickly developed it into a huge airbase decided the shape of Tinian was not too different from New York's Manhattan Island. They named the roads they constructed Broadway, 42nd St and 8th Avenue and called one section of the island Harlem and another Central Park. Some of the road names are still used today, though having an 86th St seems a bit out of place on an island that now has little traffic and only a few paved roads!

After the war Tinian reverted to pastoral ways and ranching took hold. The island became known for its beef and dairy products which were exported to neighbouring islands.

A few years back Tinian voters, eager to pick up on some of the overseas money pouring into Saipan, approved the development of casinos, but then became tepid on the issue and stalled. However, Tinian seems to be re-embracing the gambling concept and local officials have recently announced a plan to build the island's first casino, a 50,000-sq-foot structure overlooking Kammer Beach. A second phase of this scheme would eventually add a 300-room hotel – should it materialise.

In the meanwhile Tinian remains a tranquil getaway, retaining an unhurried small-island charm long since lost on neighbouring Saipan.

ACTIVITIES
Diving
Tinian has clear waters, an ocean bottom that slopes rapidly from the shore and a number of good dive sites a short distance from San Jose. One of the most popular is Dump Coke , which was a huge dumping ground for WW II junk and where small Japanese tanks, jeeps, trucks, shell casings and other munitions can be easily spotted.

Suzuki Diving (☎ 433-3274), Box 100, San Jose, Tinian, MP 96952, across from the Fleming Hotel, is Tinian's only dive shop. They offer one beach dive for $40 or one boat dive for $80. Introductory beach dives for beginners cost $60 and two-hour snorkelling tours by boat cost $40.

Snorkelling & Other Water Sports
The best snorkelling from shore is at Tachogna Beach.

Tinian Marine Sports (☎ 433-0648), a fledgling operation in a hut at Kammer Beach, rents snorkel sets for $15 a day. A short snorkelling outing by boat costs $20 and includes all-day gear rental. They also have 'banana boat' rides ($25 for 30 minutes), water skiing ($60 an hour) and jet skis ($70 an hour).

Other Activities
Tinian's new gym has a basketball court, volleyball and table tennis. Visitors can use the facilities on weekdays from 6 to 10 pm for 50 cents.

Military Presence

Should the USA again build up its presence in the western Pacific, Tinian could become the next US military base in the region. The northern third of the island has been leased to the US military for its sole control and use. The middle third is also leased to the military, though it includes some areas in joint use with the Tinian government (such as the airport and harbour) and other areas such as pastureland that are being leased backed by Tinian residents.

Though there aren't yet any permanent military facilities, Tinian is sometimes used by US forces for training and military exercises. These maneuvers have been more frequent since the closure of bases in the Philippines, especially by the US Navy's special warfare SEALS unit.

Access to the northernmost part of the island is restricted whenever military exercises are taking place. ■

TINIAN

Micronesia Development Corporation's Bar-K Ranch has plans to offer horse riding; check with the Marianas Visitors Bureau (see below) for the latest information.

FESTIVALS & EVENTS

Tinian's fiesta is held during the last weekend in April or the first weekend in May in honour of San Jose, the island's patron saint. Everyone is welcome to join in the feasting, dances and cultural events, although finding accommodation at that time can be a challenge.

Tinian holds a fun run in late September and a cliff fishing competition in early November. Tuna weighing a good 60 pounds have been caught from Tinian cliffs. Both activities are open to anyone who wants to participate.

SAN JOSE

The quiet village of San Jose, where most of Tinian's 2100 residents live, was once the site of an ancient village of 13,000 Chamorros. The current population is partly comprised of a group of Chamorros who had been living on Yap since the German era and who were resettled in San Jose by the Americans after WW II.

The town is fronted by a big deepwater harbour that was constructed by US Seabees for the purpose of unloading the scores of bombs that were dropped on Japan in the final months of the war.

San Jose is a small village and easy to walk around, although streets are not marked.

Information

Tourist Office The Marianas Visitors Bureau (☎ 433-9365), on Broadway, is open from 8 to 11.30 am and 12.30 to 4.30 pm Monday to Friday.

Money The Bank of Guam is open from 10 am to 3 pm Monday to Friday. Most businesses on Tinian do not accept credit cards.

Post & Telecommunications Tinian's post office is open from 9 am to 3 pm Monday to Friday. There are pay phones (25 cents for local calls) and debit-card phones in several places, including the Fleming Hotel and Tinian Center.

Laundry There's a small coin-operated laundry next door to the Fleming Hotel and a larger one behind the Bank of Guam.

Library A new public library has opened at the Tinian branch of the Northern Marianas College, open from 8 am to 5 pm Monday to Saturday.

Newspapers LPS: What's In Tinian, a very small local paper, is published periodically. The mayor's office publishes a free monthly newsletter, The Tinian Observer, and there's a well-used notice board at the post office.

Guam's Pacific Daily News and Saipan papers are sold at grocery stores.

Emergency In case of an emergency, call 911. The police and fire station can be reached at 433-9222, the Tinian Health Center at 433-9233.

Taga House

San Jose's most notable attraction is Taga House, an impressive collection of latte stones said to be the foundations of the home of Taga the Great, legendary king of the ancient Chamorros.

The grassy park contains a dozen or so pitted limestone shafts with capstones, some as large as five feet in diameter and 15 feet in height. One latte stone is still standing upright in its original position, while the others now lie horizontally. The site is on the US National Register of Historic Places.

There are some small Japanese memorials on both sides of Taga House.

Taga Well

A few minutes' walk east of Taga House is the Taga Well, which in ancient times supplied spring water to the island. However the water has long since disappeared and

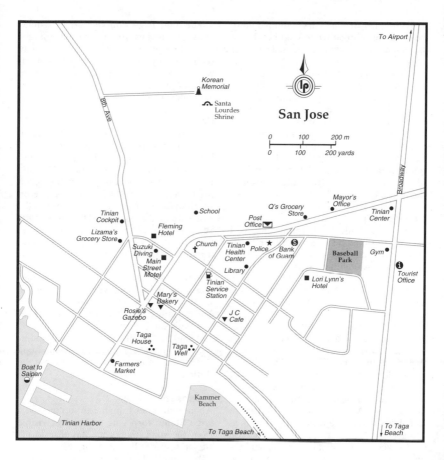

these days there's nothing to see other than a small pit surrounded by stones.

Kammer Beach

Kammer Beach, also called Jones Beach, is a nice white sand beach east of the harbour and an easy walk from the centre of town. It has coconut palms, half a dozen pavilions, picnic facilities, restrooms, showers, a water sports hut (see "Snorkeling & Other Water Sports" in the Activities section for equipment rental details) and a view of Aguijan Island to the south.

During WW II, Americans staged a fake diversionary landing at Kammer Beach just hours before the actual invasion on the north-west shore.

SOUTH OF SAN JOSE
Taga & Tachogna Beaches

Taga Beach Park is one mile south of town on Broadway. From the cliff above the beach there's a striking view of San Jose and some of the most brilliant turquoise waters you can ever expect to see. Stairs lead down the cliff to a small sandy beach. The water gets deep fairly quickly, which makes for good swimming.

TINIAN

Tachogna Beach Park, immediately beyond, has a broad white sand beach and is another good swimming area. The water may be a bit choppy at high tide, but at low tide snorkellers can wade right out to the shallow coral patch visible just offshore.

In addition to getting to the beaches by car, both beaches can also be reached on foot from San Jose by following a coastal walkway (known as the jogging trail) that starts past the easternmost pavilion at Kammer Beach. Taking this route, it's only about a 10-minute walk to Taga Beach, and another five minutes from Taga Beach to Tachogna Beach.

Suicide Cliff

To get to Suicide Cliff, follow the road inland from Taga Beach another four miles, bearing right first at the crossroads and then at the fork. Along the way there are excellent views of the south-west side of the island looking back toward San Jose. The grassy road to Suicide Cliff is usually negotiable in a sedan.

In the hills above the cliffs are the natural and soldier-dug caves that were the last defence position and hide-out for the Japanese military. Though Tinian was secured by the USA after nine days of combat, it took an additional three months to rout out the Japanese from the caves in these cliffs. Most of the 4000 Japanese defenders never accounted for are assumed to have committed suicide inside the caves.

A peace memorial at the site remembers the Japanese civilians who leapt from the cliffs in a smaller version of the suicidal jumps that took place on Saipan. The jump site along the cliff is now barricaded by a fence.

Cow patties (step lightly!) attest to the grazing done in the area, Polynesian rats hop across the road, and on a clear day you can see Rota.

NORTH OF SAN JOSE

You can make an interesting tour of the island by heading north from San Jose along Broadway and then returning via 8th Avenue.

The route begins through green pastureland and makes for a pleasant country drive. Broadway, a divided highway, may seem out of proportion for tiny Tinian – it was built by Americans during WW II to connect the harbour with bustling airstrips at the north end of the island.

Ranches

Although Tinian has a number of small, local ranches, the island's ranching is dominated by the Bar-K Ranch of the Micronesian Development Corporation (MDC), the largest cattle operation in Micronesia. MDC grazes over 1000 head of cattle on 11.72 sq miles of leased land, mostly on the east side of the island. MDC still exports beef to supermarkets in Guam and Saipan, though it has long ceased its dairy operations. The offices are opposite the airport turn-off.

Farther north, the former Japanese communications building with its heavy metal window grates is now a slaughterhouse for Tinian cattle and, when needed, also serves as a typhoon shelter.

About half a mile north of the slaughterhouse a dirt road leads east to scenic Long Beach; if you take it, be sure to close the cattle gate behind you.

Japanese Shrines

About four miles from the airport turn-off a large Shinto *torii* gate on the left, visible from the road, marks the entrance to the site of a former Japanese shrine.

Just ahead, the road circles a roundabout which has another old Japanese shrine in its centre. A little past this, Saipan comes into view. Along the rocky north-east coast, waves crash against the cliffs, in places bursting up through spectacular blowholes.

North Field

The main road loops around North Field, a massive network of landing fields and criss-crossing roads that once comprised the largest military airbase in the world.

At the outbreak of the battle for the Marianas, the Japanese already had two 4700-foot runways completed and three other airstrips under construction. After Tinian was taken, the US Seabees quickly built four new airstrips, each 1.5 miles long. These strips were take-off sites for fire-bomb raids on Japan's home islands and later for the planes that carried the atomic bombs.

Once inside the field, there's a confusing maze of roads, airstrips and overgrown crossroads that can all look the same. It's easy to get lost – more than 29 miles of airplane taxiways alone were built at North Field!

The abandoned runways that once held rows of planes now have only lazy monitor lizards basking in the sun.

Ushi Point

A road to the right, about eight miles past the airport turn-off, goes to Ushi Point, the northern tip of Tinian. A cross and memorial stand on the point in remembrance of Tinian islanders who have died at sea.

If you follow the cliff road east it will take you to another memorial marker, known locally as Rudy's Point and dedicated to a fisherman who lost his life near here in 1989. It has a good view of Saipan.

Atomic Bomb Pits

Back on the main road circling North Field, a dirt road leads to the loading pits for the atomic bombs that were dropped on Japan.

The road to the pits is on the left, about three-quarters of a mile beyond the turn-off to Ushi Point and 4.5 miles from the Japanese shrine roundabout. The pit sites are neat and sterile, marked with signs, plaques and plumeria trees.

Japanese Communications Buildings

There are some Japanese WW II installations nearby in the overgrown brush. Go south a few hundred yards from the loading pits until the road splits and turn to the left, then take the first right and the first right again onto a runway. Continue on the runway until you notice a small overgrown road to the right which goes straight in to the complex.

The reinforced concrete building at the right is the easiest to spot, but hidden, straight ahead, is a larger two-storey former communications building. It was once used in conjunction with an underwater cable system which connected Tinian to Saipan. Low concrete pillboxes with gun holes are concealed in the brush to the left as you face the main building.

Invasion Beaches

From the Japanese buildings turn right, back onto the runway, and at the end of the road turn left, then take the next right to get to Chulu Beach. A little to the north of Chulu Beach is Marine Beach. Both are attractive white sand beaches.

Chulu and Marine beaches, which were dubbed White Beach I and II by US forces, are the invasion beaches where more than 15,000 US troops landed in July 1944.

The Chulu Beach area is undergoing one of the largest archeological excavations ever undertaken in the Mariana Islands.

Little Boy & Fat Man

In the early evening of 5 August 1945 a uranium bomb code-named 'Little Boy' was loaded aboard the *Enola Gay*, an American B-29 aircraft. The four-ton bomb had been brought to Tinian from San Francisco aboard the heavy cruiser *Indianapolis*.

The *Enola Gay* and its 12-man crew took off from Tinian at 2.45 am on 6 August and headed for Hiroshima, 1700 miles away. The bomb was dropped at 9.15 am Tinian time. It exploded in the air above the city, forming a fireball that quickly mushroomed into a dark-grey cloud three miles wide and 35,000 feet high. More than 75,000 people perished that day from the explosion, beginning the age of atomic warfare. Because of the lingering effects of radiation, the final death toll in Hiroshima has now reached an estimated 200,000.

The second atomic bomb loaded on Tinian was a 4.5 ton plutonium bomb named 'Fat Man'. It was dropped on Nagasaki on 9 August 1945, immediately killing 75,000 of the city's 240,000 residents. It's estimated that another 75,000 people have since died from the effects of that bombing. ∎

Although the excavations, which were contracted by the US Navy, are not yet complete, they have already uncovered three layers of Chamorro civilisation, ranging from 1500 BC to the Latte Period of 1000 AD to 1500 AD.

Mt Lasso

About 1.3 miles south on 8th Avenue, a side road leads east to the 544-foot Mt Lasso, northern Tinian's highest point. At the top of the mountain there's a Japanese shrine and a very scenic view of the island.

Seabees Memorial

A memorial on the corner of 86th St and 8th Avenue has a plaque and a map of wartime Tinian. The plaque reads:

To the men of the 107th United States Naval Construction Battalion and all the Seabees who in 1944-45 on Tinian, Mariana Islands, participated in the largest engineering feat of WW II. Seabees constructed four runways and created the world's largest air base, enabling the US Armed Forces to end the war in the Pacific. We of the ex-107th Seabees consecrate this ground to our fallen comrades. May God help us to avoid WW III.

Korean Memorial

Seven miles south of Chulu Beach on 8th Avenue (just under half a mile north of Lizama's Store in San Jose), turn inland onto a grassy path lined with palm trees. Not far from the road is a memorial, built on the back of a carved stone turtle, honouring Koreans who died during WW II. Through the grass, to the left of the turtle, is a brick oven which served as a crematorium for Koreans who died before the war.

Honeycombed into the nearby hills are caves where the Japanese hid from invading US forces. One huge cave to the right of the memorial has recently been turned into the Santa Lourdes Shrine, with a statue of the Virgin Mary and a few candles.

AGUIJAN ISLAND

Aguijan is an uninhabited island less than five miles south of Tinian. During the Spanish and Japanese administrations it was sporadically inhabited but now it is nicknamed Goat Island after its current residents. Goat and coconut crab hunting takes place in season.

Aguijan is part of Tinian's political district and it's necessary to get a permit from the mayor of Tinian before visiting the island. From Tinian, it takes about 20 minutes to reach Aguijan by boat, but there are no beaches and landings are usually made by jumping ship close to shore and wading in. Thorns can be a deterrent to exploring the interior.

PLACES TO STAY
Camping

Tinian is one of the better islands in Micronesia for camping and no permission is needed to camp on public beaches.

Kammer Beach, at the edge of town, has a sandy beach, toilets, outdoor showers, barbecue pits, electricity and picnic tables.

Taga and Tachogna beach parks, about a mile from town, both have picnic tables, barbecue pits and showers. Tachogna is the better bet for camping as it has shady trees and a sandy beach.

If you want someplace more remote, try the white sands of Chulu Beach on the north-west coast, but take drinking water with you.

Hotels

Tinian has three small hotels, all in San Jose. Rooms in all three have private bathrooms, cable TV, air-con and small refrigerators, but no phones or ceiling fans. A 10% tax is added to room rates.

Lori Lynn's Hotel (☎ 433-3256), Box 50, San Jose, Tinian, MP 96952, is owned by Vicente and Rita Manglona, a friendly local couple who work at the post office. The 14 rooms in this two-storey hotel cost $40/55 for singles/doubles. There's a restaurant on site and airport transfers can be provided on request.

The older, two-storey Fleming Hotel (☎ 433-3232), Box 1268, San Jose, Tinian,

MP 96952, has 13 good-sized rooms, a bit run down but with balconies, two double beds and bathtubs. The cost is $50/60 for singles/doubles. Fleming's (which is officially named the Meitetsu Fleming Hotel) caters largely to Japanese tourists. There's a restaurant and store on site.

The smaller *Main Street Motel* (☎ 433-9212), Box 92, San Jose, Tinian, MP 96952, a few doors down from the Fleming Hotel, has five rooms with either two twin beds or one double bed. The cost is $42 for either one or two people.

PLACES TO EAT

All restaurants on Tinian are in San Jose.

Mary's Bakery, tucked back in a residential area, is a friendly place with inexpensive options. Freshly made baked items, hot from the oven, are a good choice at breakfast. At lunch there's a good-value special which changes daily but usually includes a meat dish, rice, salad and fruit for $4.75. The regular menu has such dishes as sweet and sour pork, beef curry or fried chicken for $6, rice included. It's open from 7 am to 9 pm Monday to Saturday.

J C Cafe has a varied menu and is open from 7 am to 4 am daily. At breakfast, served from 7 to 9 am, an omelette or a plate of rice, egg and bacon (or Spam) costs $6.50. At lunch, sandwiches average $4, while a variety of chicken, beef, fish, squid and mussel dishes average $8. At happy hour, from 4 to 9 pm daily, beer costs $1.75.

Fleming Restaurant (at the Fleming Hotel) serves full American or Japanese breakfasts for $8 between 7 and 9 am. Cheeseburgers and salads are good and reasonably priced, while Japanese dishes are a bit expensive, with the likes of tempura or fried shrimp for $15. It's open until 7.30 pm on Sundays and to 8 pm on other days, although the last dinner order is taken an hour earlier.

Lori Lynn's Restaurant, at the hotel of the same name, serves local, Western and Japanese dishes. Breakfast averages $5 to $8, lunch and dinner $7 to $12. It's open

from 6.30 to 9.30 am, 11.30 am to 1.30 pm and 5.30 to 9.30 pm.

Rosie's Gazebo has a pleasant outdoor dining area, a bar and good food. A variety of western-style breakfasts cost $5. There are beef or chicken dishes for $7 and fancier 'cook's specials', such as prawn thermidor or pepper steak flamed with brandy, for around $12. It's open from 10.30 am to 2 am daily.

Kerida's, a fast food stand adjacent to Q's store, has cheap burgers, hot dogs and milkshakes, and offers a daily hot plate lunch such as pork menudo or fried fish for $3.50.

The island has several small grocery stores, including *Q's*, *Tinian Center*, *Fleming* and *Lizama's*. The *Farmers' Market*, near the harbor, sells local produce such as corn and beans, but doesn't often have fruit.

In recent times, Tinian has had some difficulties with its water system, so you should avoid drinking unboiled tap water. Bottled water is readily available in stores.

ENTERTAINMENT

Evening entertainment is very limited. *Rosie's Gazebo* has a billiards room. *J C Cafe* has karaoke, 25-cent poker machines and will put on disco music if anyone wants to dance. For some local flavour, the Tinian Cockpit has cockfights on weekends and holidays.

THINGS TO BUY

Tinian, a 92-page softcover souvenir book by Don Farrell (1992, Micronesian Productions, Box 5, Tinian, MP 96952), is loaded with photographs and detailed information about Tinian past and present, with an emphasis on the war years. It sells for $10 and is available at Q's, the Fleming store and other places.

GETTING THERE & AWAY
Air
All flights to Tinian leave from Saipan, a hop that takes just 10 minutes.

Freedom Air (☎ 234-8328 in Saipan, 433-3288 in Tinian) flies about a dozen times daily between Saipan and Tinian. The first flight leaves Saipan at 6.45 am and the last returns from Tinian at around 5.30 pm. The schedule is a bit flexible, as the airline essentially shuttles back and forth as passengers show up. The fare is $25 one way.

Pacific Island Aviation (PIA) departs from Saipan daily for Tinian hourly on the half hour from 7.30 am to 4.30 pm and returns from Tinian on the hour, from 8 am to 5 pm. In an effort to compete with the boat, ticket prices have been lowered to $15 one way, $30 return. There's also a booklet of eight one-way tickets for $96; these are transferrable and could be used by a party of four to make the return trip. Reservations can be made on Tinian by calling 433-3600 and on Saipan at 288-0770.

Airport Tinian's modern airport is 2.5 miles from San Jose. It has airline and car rental counters, restrooms and a snack bar.

Sea

The *Super Emerald* (☎ 234-9157), a 65-foot high-speed passenger vessel, leaves Saipan's Smiling Cove at 8 am daily except on Mondays, arriving in Tinian Harbor about 1½ hours later. The boat is scheduled to return from Tinian at 2.45 pm, though it sometimes takes off a few minutes earlier. Reservations are not usually needed, but you should call in advance to verify departure times, as the boat occasionally gets chartered out. The cost is $20 one way, $35 return.

Even though the *Super Emerald* is a comfortable boat, the channel between Tinian and Saipan is generally rough (locals call it the 'washing machine') and those easily prone to seasickness may prefer to go by plane.

Leaving Tinian

Tinian has no departure tax.

GETTING AROUND
To/From the Airport

The Fleming Hotel provides airport transfers to town for $10 (free to its guests). There's no taxi service on the island.

Car

Tinian's main roads are paved and in good condition.

Budget (☎ 433-3104) has a booth at the airport. The cheapest car, usually a manual-transmission Toyota Tercel, rents for about $35 a day. Make reservations through the Budget office on Guam or Saipan to get the best rates. Credit cards are accepted.

Tinian Rental Service (☎ 433-3390), based at the Tinian Service Station in San Jose, rents four-door automatic Toyota Corollas with air-con for $39 a day.

Other companies located in San Jose are Han's Rent-A-Car (☎ 433-9412) and Islander Rent-A-Car (☎ 433-3025).

Bicycle

Suzuki Diving (☎ 433-3274) has bicycle rentals for $15 a day. If they're out diving there may not be anyone around, so it's a good idea to call first.

Hitching

It's often possible to hitch from the airport to San Jose; ask the airline staff if they know of anyone going to town. San Jose itself is OK for lifts, but outside the village there isn't enough traffic to count on hitching – to get to Suicide Cliff or North Field you really need a vehicle. People on Tinian are hospitable and the island has very little crime but, as elsewhere, the usual safety precautions apply.

Tours

M&F Corporation at the Fleming Hotel (☎ 433-3232) offers sightseeing tours of the island for around $25 to $50, depending on the length of the tour.

Several Saipan tour operators arrange day-long sightseeing tours of Tinian that start and end in Saipan, but they're geared to Japanese package tourists and tend to be overpriced, starting at $125.

TINIAN

WW II armaments at the Last Command Post, Saipan

WW II tank at the Last Command Post, Saipan

Old Japanese jail in Garapan, Saipan

WW II gun on Managaha Island, Saipan

Latte stone at the Taga Stone Quarry, Rota

Rota

Rota, about halfway between Guam and Saipan, is just beginning to get an overflow of tourists from those larger islands. Nevertheless, the island retains a distinctively slow pace – the main village, Songsong, still gets by without a single traffic light or shopping centre.

Rota is roughly oblong, measuring three miles by 10, and has a hilly interior. The island has small farms, good spring water, enough deer to have a hunting season and fiery orange sunsets that light the evening skies. Locals call the island Luta.

It's surprising that Rota has never been nicknamed 'The Friendly Island'. Without fail, Rota drivers wave to each other in passing, a tradition so strongly entrenched that those who don't wave are immediately recognised as not being from the island.

Songsong, which means 'village' in Chamorro, is the island's business centre, while the newly established homestead development of Sinapalo, just south of the airport, has rapidly grown into the island's second village.

Throughout the 1980s, Rota was spared the kind of resort development that flourished on Saipan and Guam, leaving the character of the island pleasantly local, low-key and friendly.

In the 1990s Rota changed course and approved plans for three resorts with 18 hole golf courses, all on leased government land. The first of the developments is expected to open in late 1995 just north of the airport. Another development is being constructed on the road to Mt Sabana, while a third is planned for the island's north shore.

The scale of construction has required hundreds of workers to be brought in from off the island (mostly from the Philippines) and, as on Saipan, the Rotanese are grappling with the changing demographics and the prospect that they could eventually find themselves a minority on their own island.

While the island may be in flux, Rota's laid-back character is still its leading attraction. Where else can you swim right in town and still have the beach all to yourself?

ACTIVITIES
Diving & Snorkelling
A highlight of diving Rota is the excellent visibility. One popular area is Coral Gardens, in Sasanhaya Bay, known for its huge platter corals. Rota also has interesting cave and tunnel dives.

The wreck of the *Shoun Maru*, a Japanese freighter sunk by an aerial torpedo during WW II, lies offshore about 90 feet underwater in Sasanhaya Bay. The wreck contains trucks and assorted paraphernalia, such as bathtubs, bicycles, and motorcycles, all encrusted with coral.

Dive Rota (☎ 532-3377, fax 532-3022), Box 941, Rota, MP 96951, is a small personalised dive operation owned and operated by Mark and Lynne Michael. A single boat dive costs $50, two dives cost $75 and night dives can be arranged for $60. Dive Rota also operates a 1½-hour snorkel trip (gear include   to the Coral Gardens for $25, rents filled tanks or snorkel sets for $5 and takes fishing enthusiasts trolling for $200.

For snorkelling from shore, Teteto Beach has large coral formations just below the surface, but you'll have to time your snorkelling with high tide as the coral is in shallow water. Closer to town, the entrance to Sasanhaya Bay boat harbour has soft corals and a good variety of tropical fish.

The small island at Pinatang Park, at the north end of Songsong, has rather sparse marine life, but swimming and snorkelling between the rock formations can be interesting and the water is clear and calm.

FESTIVALS & EVENTS
The largest and most popular fiesta in the Northern Marianas is held on Rota on either the first or second weekend in October. The celebration, which honours San Francisco de Borja, the patron saint of Songsong, attracts people from throughout the Marianas. Events include a luau-like

ROTA

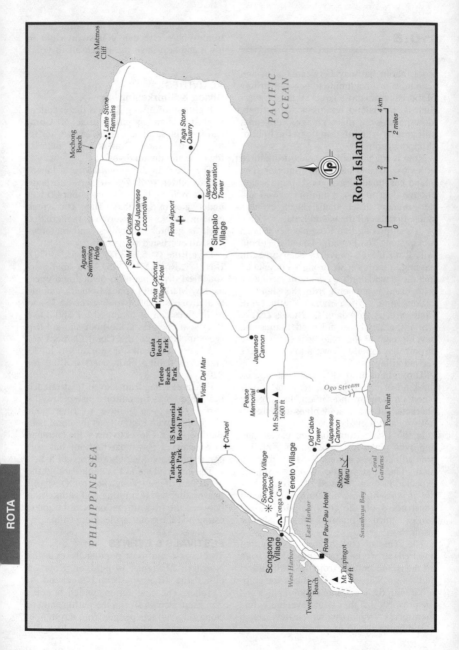

Rota Island

PACIFIC OCEAN

PHILIPPINE SEA

As Matmos Cliff

Mochong Beach

Latte Stone Remains

Taga Stone Quarry

Agusan Swimming Hole

SNM Golf Course

Old Japanese Locomotive

Rota Airport

Japanese Observation Tower

Sinapalo Village

Rota Coconut Village Hotel

Guata Beach Park

Teteto Beach Park

Vista Del Mar

Japanese Cannon

Ogo Stream

Peace Memorial

Mt Sabana 1600 ft

US Memorial Beach Park

Tatachog Beach Park

Chapel

Old Cable Tower

Japanese Cannon

Pona Point

Songsong Village Overlook

Teneto Village

Tonga Cave

Coral Gardens

Shoun Maru

East Harbor

Rota Pau-Pau Hotel

Susanhaya Bay

West Harbor

Songsong Village

Mt Ta·pingot 469 ft

Tweksberry Beach

0   1   2 miles
0   2   4 km

feast of Chamorro food, religious processions, music and dancing.

Rota also annually hosts a 10-km fun run in late June and a cliff fishing derby on Labor Day weekend in early September.

SONGSONG VILLAGE

Songsong Village extends along a narrow neck of land on the island's south-west peninsula. The village itself is not particularly distinguished, but it has a scenic backdrop in the 469-foot Mt Taipingot, which is nicknamed Wedding Cake Mountain because of its layered appearance.

Songsong boasts an abundance of latte stones, some adorning public buildings such as the library, others simply landscaping front yards. The most notable building in town is the San Francisco de Borja Church, whose church bell dates to the period of German occupation, though the present church was built in the 1940s.

You can get a good view of Songsong Village by taking the rough dirt road that leads to the hilltop above Tonga Caye. The road, which begins behind Dean's Mobil Station at the north end of Songsong Village, makes a nice hike, though it could also be negotiated in a 4WD.

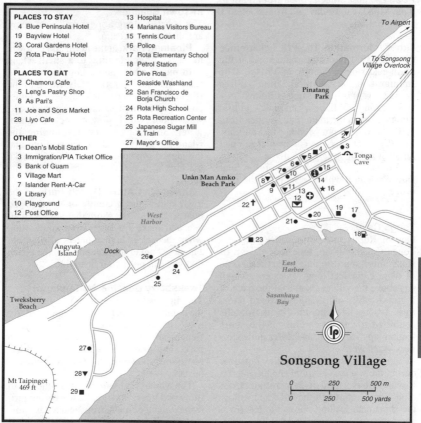

PLACES TO STAY
4 Blue Peninsula Hotel
19 Bayview Hotel
23 Coral Gardens Hotel
29 Rota Pau-Pau Hotel

PLACES TO EAT
2 Chamoru Cafe
5 Leng's Pastry Shop
8 As Pari's
11 Joe and Sons Market
28 Liyo Cafe

OTHER
1 Dean's Mobil Station
3 Immigration/PIA Ticket Office
5 Bank of Guam
6 Village Mart
7 Islander Rent-A-Car
9 Library
10 Playground
12 Post Office

13 Hospital
14 Marianas Visitors Bureau
15 Tennis Court
16 Police
17 Rota Elementary School
18 Petrol Station
20 Dive Rota
21 Seaside Washland
22 San Francisco de
   Borja Church
24 Rota High School
25 Rota Recreation Center
26 Japanese Sugar Mill
   & Train
27 Mayor's Office

Songsong Village

ROTA

Information

Tourist Office The Marianas Visitors Bureau (☎ 532-0327) is up the hill a couple of blocks south of the Blue Peninsula Hotel, in the building with the latte stone motif. Hours are 7.30 to 11.30 am and 12.30 to 4.30 pm Monday to Friday.

Money The Bank of Guam, in the same building as the Blue Peninsula, is open from 10 am to 3 pm Monday to Thursday and from 10 am to 6 pm on Fridays.

Note that other than for car rental, credit cards are not very widely accepted on Rota.

Post The post office is open from 6 am to 3 pm Monday to Friday and from noon to 1 pm on Saturdays.

Other Information The PIA ticket office (☎ 532-0397) is on the main road at the north-east side of Songsong Village. The Immigration & Naturalization office (☎ 532-9479) is in the same building.

Songsong Village's modest public library, also on the main road, is open from 7.30 am to 4.30 pm Monday to Saturday. The *Pacific Daily News* can be picked up at larger stores in Songsong Village.

You can do laundry at the coin-op Seaside Washland, which is south of the post office.

Tonga Cave

One of Rota's most impressive sights is Tonga Cave, a damp, limestone cavern of stalagmites and dripping stalactites, some of them eight feet long. The cave, which sits above the village, begins at the back of a grassy park with orange-flowered flame trees. It's just a few minutes' walk from the centre of town. Be careful on the stairs leading up to the cave, as they're quite slippery when wet.

Tonga Cave was used by the Japanese during the war as a hospital shelter and the Rotanese have used it as a refuge from typhoons. Go through the cave and follow the short path leading out to the left for a good view of Songsong and Mt Taipingot.

Japanese Sugar Mill & Train

Down near the West Harbor are the remains of a Japanese sugar mill, most of which was dismantled after the war.

Although Rota's soil was not as good for growing cane as the soil on Saipan or Tinian, there was enough sugar to support two refineries, as well as distilleries for making whisky and port wine from molasses. In the mid-1930s Rota's sugar industry employed nearly 800 Chamorros and 5000 Japanese and Koreans.

A tiny locomotive once used to haul sugar cane from the fields is on display in front of the mill.

In-Town Beaches

The beaches along Songsong's west shore are sheltered and calm.

Pinatang Park, at the north end of town, has a footbridge leading to a small island with picnic tables and a couple of small, sandy beaches. Unfortunately, much of the island has been buried in concrete in a misconceived attempt to create a grand saltwater pool, which now collects stagnant water. Still, the waters surrounding the island are fairly good for snorkelling and the jagged offshore rock formations make the area a picturesque place to catch the sunset.

Unain Man Amko Beach Park, in the town centre, has a couple of large rusted boats right near the shore that attract small fish and make for interesting snorkelling when the tide is high. There's also an old Japanese bunker just inland from the beach that you can poke your head into.

Tweksberry Beach & Mt Taipingot

The dirt road that runs south of town past the commercial dock leads through orderly rows of coconut trees to Tweksberry Beach, an attractively landscaped beach park. The grassy park has picnic tables, restrooms, showers and lots of red hibiscus bushes.

The white-coral sand beach is lined with ironwood trees. Though the waters are protected, much of the narrow beach has a low rocky shelf that can make it less than ideal for swimming. Sunbathers, however, will find a nice ribbon of white sand along the shore when the tide is low.

A trail made by the Youth Conservation Corps starts up Mt Taipingot about 50 yards before the beach parking lot, between the first two coconut trees on the inland driveway. The trail is periodically cleared and re-marked with orange ties. The climb is steep but not too difficult, takes about two hours up and back, and ends near the edge of a cliff at a grove of ironwood trees. Along the way beware of bees that can get a bit aggressive; you may want to wear long pants and long sleeves for added protection. The hike offers nice views of Mt Sabana, Songsong Village, Pona Point and Sasanhaya Bay.

CENTRAL & NORTHERN ROTA

The remains of a two-storey Japanese building that once served as an observation tower are on the left side of the road a quarter of a mile east of the airport. After continuing another half-mile, a road to the right leads to the Taga Stone Quarry.

If you don't turn down to the quarry, the dirt road circles around the airport, past fenced-off farms, pastures and an old Japanese locomotive and continues around to the main paved road.

Taga Stone Quarry

The Taga Stone Quarry has nine latte shafts and seven capstones still sitting in the trenches where they were being quarried before they were inexplicably abandoned. Mosses, grasses and tiny ferns have grown up around them.

The early Chamorros were able to quarry the latte stones without the benefit of metal tools. It's believed they built fires in trenches around the stones and then used basalt stone adzes to cut into the softened limestone.

For anyone interested in Chamorro culture, this is an impressive sight. The road into the quarry is signposted and easily negotiable in a car. The quarry itself, which is half a mile from the turn-off, is in a grassy park alongside the road.

According to legend, the ancient Chamorro king Taga the Great jumped from Guam to Rota to establish a kingdom here. He then put the island's inhabitants to work quarrying these latte stones, which he used as foundation pillars for royal buildings.

Sinapalo

The village of Sinapalo, south of the airport, was created a decade ago to provide homestead property for Rota's landless.

When the government failed to follow through with promises to extend power lines and water to the village, many homesteaders who had already built houses hooked up their own water catchment tanks and generators and settled in. Utilities were finally brought to Sinapalo in 1990 and the settlement began to boom. Although it's largely a residential community, in addition to the homesites there are also a new courthouse, a grocery store, a bar and restaurant and a few other small businesses.

Sinapalo 2, a second area of homesteads, is currently being developed on the north side of the airport road – all of which will eventually make the Sinapalo area Rota's biggest village.

Sabana Peace Memorial

Japanese peace memorials abound in Micronesia. Rota's was erected in 1973 near the top of the 1600-foot Mt Sabana. The coral road up to the memorial, which is marked, starts two miles west of the airport.

Though the road is in fairly good condition most of the way, this 5.25-mile drive can be rather disappointing as the memorial itself is nondescript and there's no real view of the island from the mountain plateau.

More interesting than the memorial is a camouflaged Japanese cannon that sits inside a cave in a park-like setting about two miles in from the paved road. The cannon site is also one of the most likely places to spot fruit bats, a species that has been hunted nearly to extinction on the other inhabited Mariana Islands. About 1000 fruit bats remain on Rota.

Tatachog

In the 1930s there was a resettlement of Rotanese in the Tatachog area and the ruins of some of their homes can still be seen near the main road.

On the slopes above Tatachog is a tiny chapel built during the German era. To get there, take the coral road leading inland just south of Tatachog Beach Park and bear right when the road forks (the left fork goes to the dump). One mile up, turn left onto a grassy dirt drive. The chapel is in a clearing that looks deserted, but don't be surprised if you find burning candles or fresh orchids at the altar.

North-West Coast Beaches

There are sandy coves and beach parks all along Rota's north-west shore.

Tatachog Beach Park, 2.5 miles north of Songsong Village, has shallow water and is lined with jagged rocks, a combination that makes it uninviting for water activities, but attractive for picnics.

A half-mile to the east is **US Memorial Beach Park**, which has a little roadside monument and a small beach with some snorkelling potential.

Teteto Beach Park, five miles north of Songsong Village, has a pretty white sand beach and good snorkelling. Waves crash just outside the reef but inside it's calm and protected and snorkellers will find a variety of fish. You'll need to watch the tides however, as the water is not deep enough for swimming or snorkelling when they're low. As the Japanese hotels generally shuttle their guests to Teteto Beach in the early afternoon, it can get a bit busy at that time, but if you visit in the morning you may well have the beach to yourself.

The hut across the road from Teteto Beach, which opens when the shuttle vans drop off tourists, sells cold drinks (soda for $2, Budweiser for $2.50) and rents snorkel gear for a steep $12.

Guata Beach Park, midway between Teteto and the turn-off to the Rota Coconut Village Hotel, has picnic shelters and a beach which is a mix of white sand and rocks.

Natural Swimming Hole

A nice place for a dip is the swimming hole at Agusan, a large, bowl-shaped, natural basin in the shoreline rocks north of the new golf course. Unless the tide is high or the seas unusually rough, the deep waters here are almost as calm as a swimming pool. Incoming waves trickle in over the top and outgoing water returns to the sea through small cracks in the rocks below. It can also make an interesting place to snorkel, as there are often small schools of captive fish.

To reach the swimming hole, turn off the main road onto the dirt road that leads to Rota Coconut Village and go 2.25 miles north-east.

Mochong Beach

Mochong Beach, at the north side of the island, is a lovely white sand beach that's nearly always deserted. To get there continue north beyond the swimming hole until you reach a side road that leads east; continue on that side road through the gate, which is usually kept open and is marked for beach access. As it is on private property there's a $5 fee for use of the beach. Inland from the beach are the remains of some latte stones and the site of an ancient Chamorro village that's been carbon dated to 640 BC.

EAST OF SONGSONG VILLAGE

The packed coral road that heads east of Songsong Village edges along Sasanhaya Bay. Along the way there are scenic views looking across the bay's brilliant turquoise water to Mt Taipingot. In places the road cuts along the coastal cliffs and in other places it goes through jungle, shaded with a canopy of tropical vegetation.

Beware of very steep drops along the edge of this road, which are not always obvious as sections tend to get camouflaged with foliage. Going over the edge could be fatal.

Old Cable Tower

On the east side of Sasanhaya Bay the Japanese once had a phosphate mill and ceramic factory. If you look up the hillside about two miles east of Songsong Village, you can still see the rusty remains of an old cable tramway tower that carried the phosphate from the Sabana plateau down to ships in the harbour.

Japanese Cannon

A Japanese cannon points straight out to the harbour and to Mt Taipingot from its concrete shelter on the road 2.5 miles east of Songsong Village. The gun barrel can be moved from side to side but don't leave it sticking straight out or the next car going by could get whacked. Also, don't park your rental car too close to the barrel, as once it starts moving it's hard to stop.

Pona Point & Ogo Stream

Just over a mile past the cannon, there's an open grassy field on the right side of the road which slopes down to Pona Point, a wind-whipped rocky outcrop that offers a good view of the area's rugged coastal cliffs. There is also excellent cliff fishing from Pona Point. Although you may be able to drive all the way down to the point, it's only a three-minute walk from the field.

Half a mile farther down, the main road passes above Ogo (also spelled Okgok) Stream, which features some small waterfalls. If you want to visit them you must first get permission from the landowner; inquire in advance at Joe & Sons market in Songsong Village.

After this point the road deteriorates and if it's been wet lately it may not be negotiable in a rental car.

PLACES TO STAY
Camping

Although it's not a common practice, many of Rota's public beach parks will allow camping. Most of the parks are easily accessible if you have your own transportation, but this accessibility is a mixed blessing as strangers can also cruise by and the island is not as crime free as it was in days past.

In addition to public parks, you may be able to camp on secluded Mochong Beach at the north side of the island for $5 a night; contact the landowner, Mr Mendiola (☎ 532-5065).

Hotels

A 10% tax is added to all room rates in Rota.

The *Coral Gardens Hotel* (☎ 532-3201, fax 532-3204), Box 597, Rota, MP 96951, has 22 rooms in Songsong Village, most of which are in a new, two-storey building facing the bay. These rooms are neat and compact with whitewashed walls, cable TV, air-con, refrigerators, oceanfront balconies and either two single beds or one double bed. It's good value at $40/45 for singles/doubles.

The *Bayview Hotel* (☎ 532-3414, fax 532-0393), Box 875, Rota, MP 96951, is a bit older and doesn't have as good a view, but it's also a reasonable option at $40/48 for singles/doubles. The nine rooms have cable TV, air-con, refrigerators and ceiling fans; various bed combinations are available. There's a small restaurant and a travel agency on site.

The 21-room *Blue Peninsula Hotel* (☎ 532-0468), Box 539, Rota, MP 96951, is a rather cheerless place in the centre of Songsong Village. You may have a difficult time being understood if you don't speak Filipino. The rooms are simple but have mini-refrigerators, air-con and showers. The cost is $35/50 for singles/doubles.

The *Rota Pau-Pau Hotel* (☎ 532-3561, fax 532-3562), Box 503, Rota, MP 96951, on a hillside at the south-western outskirts of Songsong Village, has 55 rooms in a couple of motel-like, two-storey wings. Overpriced and geared to packaged tourists, it has an expensive restaurant, gift shop and dive operation. There's also a swimming pool. The 50 rooms start at $145/165 for singles/doubles. A better upper-end choice is the *Rota Coconut Village Hotel* (☎ 532-3448; fax 532-3449), Box 855, Rota, MP 96951, which has 10 duplex cottages with an island motif of peaked roofs, rattan furnishings and small Japanese-style soaking tubs – although there may not always be enough hot water

ROTA

to fill them. There's a swimming pool and restaurant. Singles/doubles cost $85/95. While the hotel, which is north-east of Guata Beach, has an idyllic setting, it's also out of the way, so you'll probably need a car to get around. The staff will ferry small groups to the swimming hole or Teteto Beach for $5 return and to the airport or Songsong Village for $12 return.

In addition to the aforementioned places, two new up-market hotels are expected to open by late 1995. The *SNM Rota Island Resort*, at the north side of the airport, will originally open with 40 rooms and a nine-hole golf course, but the hotel plans to add another 60 rooms and the course will later be expanded to 18 holes. The *Vista Del Mar*, opposite the beach 3.25 miles north of Songsong Village, is more low-key, with just 30 units and a Mediterranean design. Both developments will cater to Japanese tourists and the latter is expected to be timeshare style. For the latest information on either place, contact the Marianas Visitors Bureau (see Information in the Songsong Village section above).

PLACES TO EAT

Restaurants in Rota tend to be more expensive than you might expect and in many cases the quality depends on the latest cook, which is usually someone with a work visa from the Philippines. Although this can add some nice accents to the food, it's not great for consistency.

As *Pari's* restaurant and bar, on the main road in Songsong Village, near Unain Man Amko Beach Park, is a perennial favourite. It's comfortable, with well-prepared food, reasonable prices and music that's at a lower decibel than most places. A variety of full breakfasts are available for around $6. Noodles, spaghetti and fish dishes average $8, while an extensive selection of meat dishes with rice cost around $10. It's open from 6 am to 2 pm and 6 to 10.30 pm.

Another good choice is the new *Chamoru Cafe*, a modern spot at the north end of Songsong Village where you can get a doughnut and coffee for $2, pancake and

eggs for $4.50 and some good-value lunch specials with rice and soup for around $8. Dinners are a couple of dollars more. The food, a mix of Chamorro and Filipino influences, is good and the service is efficient.

The restaurant and bar beneath the *Blue Peninsula* is open from 6 am to 2 am daily. Full breakfasts cost about $6, sandwiches or yakisoba around $5, and various Chinese, Filipino and Thai dishes are priced from $10. The interior is dark and not terribly inviting. There's karaoke music at night and people playing the poker machines in the back room at any time of the day.

Leng's Pastry Shop & Restaurant is open from 6 am to 2 pm and from 6 pm to 2 am daily. Leng's bakes pies and frosted cakes and serves full breakfasts for about $5, hamburgers with fries for $3 and beef or chicken meals for about $8.

The *Liyo Cafe*, out near the Rota Pau-Pau Hotel, opens at 7.30 am with Chamorro breakfast (fried rice, eggs and Spam) for $5. Lunch is simple, with sandwiches averaging $3 to $4. Most dinners are $8 to $10.

In the restaurant at the *Rota Pau-Pau Hotel*, a breakfast of eggs, bacon and coffee will set you back $10. At lunch, a club sandwich costs $11. At dinner, starters are priced around $10, main courses around $20. Considering the prices, neither the food nor the setting are particularly distinguished.

The restaurant at the *Rota Coconut Village Hotel* is a bit pricey but serves good Japanese food. Breakfast averages about $10, lunch $12 and dinner from $25 to $50 for a full-course meal. Hours are 7.30 to 9.30 am, 11.30 am to 1.30 pm and 6.30 to 8.30 pm.

The *Mayflower Restaurant* at the airport is open from 7 am to 6.30 pm daily, with breakfasts, burgers and sandwiches for $4 to $5. It's adequate if you're waiting for a plane.

One of the best stocked of the numerous stores selling groceries in Songsong Village is *Joe & Sons* market. Open from 6 am to 10 pm, it sells a nice fresh Chamorro bread ($2) that resembles Indian nan but is sweet, and has a simple deli selling cheap hot dogs and burritos.

In Sinapalo you can buy groceries at *Sirena's Mart* or get a sit-down meal at the adjacent restaurant and bar. Both are beside the village petrol station, a quarter of a mile south of the airport turn-off.

Rota's drinking water comes from a spring in a natural water cave and may be the best in Micronesia. There's even occasional talk of bottling it for export to other islands.

ENTERTAINMENT

The biggest entertainment hit around Rota is the laser karaoke, which consists of video renditions of pop songs with the lyrics written in English across the screen and a live microphone for would-be stars to croon along. *As Pari's*, the *Blue Peninsula* and a few other restaurants become late-night venues for karaoke.

The drinking age on Rota is 21.

Cockfights are held just north of the public market on Saturday evenings.

GETTING THERE & AWAY
Air

Pacific Island Aviation (PIA) flies to Rota from Guam and Saipan four times daily, with the first flight from either island leaving at 7.45 am and the last at 5.45 pm. The return flights leave Rota 45 minutes later. The fare is $55 one way.

Freedom Air, which has a friendly in-flight service and is highly regarded for safety, has flights at 9.45 am and 5.15 pm from Saipan to Rota and at 8 am and 3.30 pm from Guam to Rota. The return flights leave Rota 50 minutes later. The fare is $54 one way and $88 return.

Airport The airport is nine miles north-east of Songsong Village. Upstairs in the Mayflower Restaurant there are a few interesting old photos from the Japanese administration period that are worth a look if you have time to spare.

Leaving Rota

Rota has no departure tax.

GETTING AROUND

Rota has a good paved road between the airport and Songsong Village, but beyond that most of the island's road system is packed coral and dirt. Depending on recent rains and how long it's been since the roads have been graded, you may not be able to manage some of Rota's more remote and rutted dirt roads in a sedan without bottoming out. Getting to most of the main sights, however, usually isn't a problem. If you want to do a lot of exploring it's best to avoid a low-slung compact car in favour of something that rides a bit higher.

To/From the Airport

As there are no taxis or other public transport on Rota, you'll either have to rent a car, make arrangements for your hotel to pick you up or hitch a ride with someone leaving the airport.

Car

Rota has three car rental agencies with booths at the airport. All take credit cards and offer optional collision damage waivers.

Islander Rent-A-Car (☎ 532-0901), which also has an office in Songsong Village, rents sedans from around $40 a day.

Paseo Drive Car Rental (☎ 532-0406) has cars for $45 and 4WD jeeps for $80.

Budget (☎ 532-3535) generally has the lowest prices, with sedans beginning around $35. Make reservations in advance at the Budget counters in Saipan or Guam to guarantee the best rates.

Hitching

It's possible to get lifts around the main parts of the island, such as between the airport and Songsong Village, though traffic is likely to be too infrequent in other areas to make hitching practical. The usual safety precautions apply.

Tours

The commentary for any sightseeing tour is likely to be given in Japanese; if that's not a language you understand, inquire in advance to find out if a bilingual guide will be available.

The Rota Coconut Village Hotel has full-day sightseeing tours for $55, which includes lunch, and a half-day tour for $35.

The Pau-Pau hotel also has sightseeing tours but they are more expensive and geared for a more timid Japanese package-tour market.

A better option, if you're not renting a car, may be to ask around Songsong Village to find someone with a pick-up truck who is willing to take you around the island.

Glossary

achiote – the annatto seed, from a small tropical tree, used to colour food; in the Marianas, it's used to make rice red

bai – a traditional men's meeting house in Palau

banzai attack – a mass attack by troops without concern for casualties, as practised by the Japanese during WW II

beche-de-mer – a type of sea cucumber (also called trepang) with an elongated body, leathery skin and a cluster of tentacles at the oral end. They burrow in sand or creep on the sea bed and were gathered by early traders and sold in China and South-East Asia as a delicacy and aphrodisiac.

betel nut – the fruit of the Areca palm tree which is commonly split open, sprinkled with dry coral lime, wrapped in a pepper leaf and chewed as a digestive stimulant and mild narcotic

breadfruit – a tree of the Pacific Islands, the trunk of which is used for lumber and canoe building. The fruit is cooked and eaten and has a texture like bread.

Chamorro – the indigenous people of the Mariana Islands

copra – dried coconut kernel, used for making coconut oil

dapal – a women's meeting house in Yap

dugong – a herbivorous mammal, similar to the manatee of Florida, which inhabits shallow tropical waters around Palau

faluw – a Yapese meeting house for men

finadene – a fiery hot sauce used to enliven food in the Marianas

iroij – traditional Marshallese chief

jambos – Marshallese picnics or trips

kahlek – night fishing, using burning torches to attract flying fish into hand-held nets, as practised in Pohnpei

kelaguen – minced chicken, fish, shrimp or Spam mixed with lemon, onions, peppers and shredded coconut

korkor – a Marshallese dugout fishing canoe made from a breadfruit log

lagoon – a body of water that is bounded by an encircling reef

lanai – a Hawaiian word commonly used in Micronesia to refer to a veranda

latte stones – the stone foundation pillars used to support ancient Chamorro buildings in the Marianas. The shafts and capstones were carved from limestone quarries.

lava-lava – a wide piece of cloth of woven hibiscus and banana fibres, worn as a skirt by women throughout Yap and in Chuuk's outer islands

lumpia – a fried food, similar to an egg roll, which is usually dipped in garlic sauce or vinegar

mangrove – a tropical tree that grows in tidal mud flats and extends looping prop roots along the shoreline

manposteria – a building material, used in the Marianas, made from burnt limestone mixed with coral

Modekngei – the traditional religion of Palau

muu-muu – a long, loose-fitting dress introduced by the missionaries

mwaramwars – head wreaths of flowers and fragrant leaves worn throughout the FSM

nahnmwarki – a district chief in Pohnpei

nahs – a traditional ceremonial house on Pohnpei

nipa palm – a palm tree common to the tropics whose foliage is used for thatching and basketry

noddy – a tropical tern, or aquatic bird, with black and white or dark plumage

omung – a perfumed love potion used in Chuuk

oyako domburi – a Japanese dish of sweetened chicken and egg served over rice

PADI – Professional Association of Dive Instructors, the world's largest diving association

pancit – a dish of shrimp or meat, vegetables and garlic served over noodles

pandanus – a plant common to the tropics whose sword-shaped leaves are used to make mats and baskets

pebai – a Yapese community meeting house

purse seine – a large net generally used between two boats that is drawn around a school of fish, especially tuna. Boats that use this method are called purse seiners.

rai – Yapese stone money

sakau – a mildly narcotic Pohnpeian drink made from the roots of a pepper shrub

sake – Japanese rice wine

saudeleur – a member of a tyrannical royal dynasty that ruled Pohnpei prior to Western contact with the islanders

seka – a narcotic, ceremonial drink (similar to *sakau*) of Kosrae

sennit – a hand-twisted rope formed from coconut fibre

tangan-tangan – a shrub that was mass-planted in the Marianas to prevent erosion

taro – a plant with green heart-shaped leaves, cultivated for both its leaf and edible rootstock; the latter is commonly boiled and eaten like a potato

thu – a loincloth worn by Yapese males and by outer island Chuukese

trade winds – the near-constant winds that dominate most of the tropics and in Micronesia blow mainly from the north-east

Tridacna clam – the giant clam, *Tridagna gigas*. The largest known bivalve mollusc, it is collected and farmed in Palau for its edible flesh, and is poached throughout the Pacific for its valuable adductor muscle, which is considered a delicacy and aphrodisiac in Asia.

trochus – a shellfish commercially harvested for its shell and flesh

tuba – an alcoholic drink made from coconut sap

udoud – traditional Palauan money, either beads of glass or fired and coloured clay

wunbey – a Yapese meeting platform

Index

PLANET TALK

Lonely Planet's FREE quarterly newsletter

We love hearing from you and think you'd like to hear from us.

When... is the right time to see reindeer in Finland?
Where... can you hear the best palm-wine music in Ghana?
How... do you get from Asunción to Areguá by steam train?
What... is the best way to see India?

Every issue is packed with up-to-date travel news and advice including:

• a letter from Lonely Planet founders Tony and Maureen Wheeler
• travel diary from a Lonely Planet author – find out what it's really like out on the road
• feature article on an important and topical travel issue
• a selection of recent letters from our readers
• the latest travel news from all over the world
• details on Lonely Planet's new and forthcoming releases

To join our mailing list contact any Lonely Planet office (addresses below).

LONELY PLANET PUBLICATIONS
Australia: PO Box 617, Hawthorn 3122, Victoria (☎ 03-9819-1877, fax 03-9819-6459)
USA: Embarcadero West, 155 Filbert Street, Suite 251, Oakland, CA 94607
(☎ 510-893-8555, toll-free 800-275-8555, fax 510-893-8563)
UK: 10 Barley Mow Passage, Chiswick, London W4 4PH (☎ 0181-742 3161)
France: 71 bis rue du Cardinal Lemoine, 75005 Paris (☎ 1-46 34 00 58)

Also available: Lonely Planet T-shirts. 100% heavyweight cotton (S, M, L, XL)

Guides to the Pacific

Australia – a travel survival kit
The complete lowdown on Down Under – home of Uluru (Ayers Rock), the Great Barrier Reef, extraordinary animals, cosmopolitan cities, rainforests, beaches... and Lonely Planet!

Bushwalking in Australia
Two experienced and respected walkers give details of the best walks in every state, covering many different terrains and climates.

Bushwalking in Papua New Guinea
The best way to get to know Papua New Guinea is from the ground up – and bushwalking is the best way to travel around the rugged and varied landscape of this island.

Islands of Australia's Great Barrier Reef – Australia guide
The Great Barrier Reef is one of the wonders of the world – and one of the great travel destinations! Whether you're looking for the best snorkelling, the liveliest nightlife or a secluded island hideaway, this guide has all the facts you need.

Melbourne – city guide
From historic houses to fascinating churches and from glorious parks to tapas bars, cafés and bistros, Melbourne is a dream for gourmets and a paradise for sightseers.

New South Wales & the ACT – Australia guide
Ancient aboriginal sites, pristine surf beaches, kangaroos bounding across desert dunes, lyrebirds dancing in rainforest, picturesque country pubs, weather-beaten drovers and friendly small-town people, along with Australia's largest and liveliest metropolis (and host city for the 2000 Olympic Games) – all this and more can be found in New South Wales and the ACT.

Sydney – city guide
From the Opera House to the surf; all you need to know in a handy pocket-sized format.

Outback Australia – Australia Guide
The outback conjures up images of endless stretches of dead straight roads, the rich red of the desert, and the resourcefulness and resilience of the inhabitants. A visit to Australia would not be complete without visiting the outback to see the beauty and vastness of this ancient country.

Victoria – Australia guide
From old gold rush towns to cosmopolitan Melbourne and from remote mountains to the most popular surf beaches, Victoria is packed with attractions and activities for everyone.

Western Australia – Australia guide
This is the most detailed and practical guidebook to Australia's largest state. It's full of down-to-earth information and reliable advice for every budget. Whether you've got a spare weekend or a month, there are hundreds of tips to help you make the most of your trip.

Fiji – a travel survival kit
Whether you prefer to stay in camping grounds, international hotels, or something in-between, this comprehensive guide will help you to enjoy the beautiful Fijian archipelago.

Hawaii – a travel survival kit
Share in the delights of this island paradise – and avoid some of its high prices – with this practical guide. It covers all of Hawaii's well-known attractions, plus plenty of uncrowded sights and activities.

New Caledonia – a travel survival kit
This guide shows how to discover all that the idyllic islands of New Caledonia have to offer – from French colonial culture to traditional Melanesian life.

New Zealand – a travel survival kit
This practical guide will help you discover the very best New Zealand has to offer: Maori dances and feasts, some of the most spectacular scenery in the world, and every outdoor activity imaginable.

Tramping in New Zealand
Call it tramping, hiking, walking, bushwalking or trekking – travelling by foot is the best way to explore New Zealand's natural beauty. Detailed descriptions of over 40 walks of varying length and difficulty.

Papua New Guinea – a travel survival kit
With its coastal cities, villages perched beside mighty rivers, palm-fringed beaches and rushing mountain streams, Papua New Guinea promises memorable travel.

Rarotonga & the Cook Islands – a travel survival kit
Rarotonga and the Cook Islands have history, beauty and magic to rival the better known islands of Hawaii and Tahiti, but the world has virtually passed them by.

Samoa – a travel survival kit
Two remarkably different countries, Western Samoa and American Samoa offer some wonderful island escapes, and Polynesian culture at its best.

Solomon Islands – a travel survival kit
The Solomon Islands are the best kept secret of the Pacific. Discover remote tropical islands, jungle-covered volcanoes and traditional Melanesian villages with this detailed guide.

Tahiti & French Polynesia – a travel survival kit
Tahiti's idyllic beauty has seduced sailors, artists and travellers for generations. This book provides full details on the main island of Tahiti, the Tuamotos, Marquesas and other island groups. Invaluable information for independent travellers and package tourists alike.

Tonga – a travel survival kit
The only South Pacific country never to be colonised by Europeans, Tonga has also been ignored by tourists. The people of this far-flung island group offer some of the most sincere and unconditional hospitality in the world.

Vanuatu – a travel survival kit
Discover superb beaches, lush rainforests, dazzling coral reefs and traditional Melanesian customs in this glorious Pacific Ocean archipelago.

Also available:
Pidgin phrasebook, *Australian* phrasebook, *Fijian* phrasebook, & *Papua New Guinea* phrasebook.

Lonely Planet Guidebooks

Lonely Planet guidebooks cover every accessible part of Asia as well as Australia, the Pacific, South America, Africa, the Middle East, Europe and parts of North America. There are five series: *travel survival kits*, covering a country for a range of budgets; *shoe-string guides* with compact information for low-budget travel in a major region; *walking guides; city guides* and *phrasebooks*.

Europe

Baltic States & Kaliningrad
Baltic States phrasebook • Britain
Central Europe • Central Europe phrasebook
Czech & Slovak Republics • Dublin
Eastern Europe • Eastern
Europe phrasebook • Finland
France • Greece • Greek phrasebook
Hungary • Iceland, Greenland & the Faroe
Ireland • Italy • Mediterranean Europe
Mediterranean Europe phrasebook
Poland • Prague • Russian phrasebook
Scandinavian & Baltic Europe
Scandinavian Europe phrasebook
Slovenia • Switzerland • Trekking in Gree
Trekking in Spain • USSR • Vienna
Western Europe • Western Europe phraseboo

North America

Alaska • Backpacking in Alaska • Baja California
Canada • Hawaii • Honolulu • Mexico
Pacific Northwest • Rocky Mountain States

Central America

Central America • Costa Rica
Guatemala, Yucatán & Belize: La Ruta Maya
Eastern Caribbean • Latin American
Spanish phrasebook

Africa

Africa • Arabic (Moroccan) phrasebook
Central Africa • East Africa
Kenya • Morocco • North Africa
South Africa, Lesotho & Swaziland
Swahili phrasebook
Trekking in East Africa • West Africa
Zimbabwe, Botswana & Namibia

South America

Argentina, Uruguay & Paraguay
Bolivia • Brazil • Brazilian phrasebook
Chile & Easter Island • Colombia
Ecuador & the Galápagos Islands
Peru • Quechua phrasebook
South America • Trekking in the
Patagonian Andes • Venezuela

Mail Order

Lonely Planet guidebooks are distributed worldwide. They are also available by mail order from Lonely Planet, so if you have difficulty finding a title please write to us. US and Canadian residents should write to Embarcadero West, 155 Filbert St, Suite 251, Oakland CA 94607, USA ; European residents should write to 10 Barley Mow Passage, Chiswick, London W4 4PH; and residents of other countries to PO Box 617, Hawthorn, Victoria 3122, Australia.

North-East Asia

Beijing • China • Mandarin Chinese phrasebook • Hong Kong, Macau & Canton • Cantonese phrasebook Japan • Japanese phrasebook Korea • Korean phrasebook • Mongolia Mongolian phrasebook North-East Asia • Seoul • Taiwan Tibet • Tibet phrasebook • Tokyo

The Middle East

Arab Gulf States Arabic (Egyptian) phrasebook Egypt & the Sudan Iran • Israel • Jordan & Syria • Middle East Trekking in Turkey Turkey • Turkish phrasebook • Yemen

South-East Asia

Bali & Lombok • Bangkok • Cambodia Ho Chi Minh • Indonesia Indonesian phrasebook • Jakarta Laos • Lao phrasebook Malaysia, Singapore & Brunei Myanmar (Burma) • Burmese phrasebook Philippines • Pilipino phrasebook Singapore • South-East Asia Thailand • Thai phrasebook Thai Hill Tribes phrasebook Thailand travel atlas Vietnam • Vietnamese phrasebook

Indian Subcontinent

Bangladesh • India India travel atlas Trekking in the Indian Himalaya • Hindi/Urdu phrasebook • Karakoram Highway • Kashmir, Ladakh & Zanskar Nepal • Nepali phrasebook Trekking in the Nepal Himalaya Tibet phrasebook Pakistan • Sri Lanka Sri Lanka phrasebook

Islands of the Indian Ocean

Madagascar & Comoros Maldives & Islands of the East Indian Ocean Mauritius, Réunion & Seychelles

Australia & the Pacific

Australia • Australian phrasebook Bushwalking in Australia • Fiji • Fijian phrasebook Islands of Australia's Great Barrier Reef • Melbourne Micronesia • New Caledonia • New Zealand Tramping in New Zealand • New South Wales Outback Australia • Papua New Guinea Bushwalking in Papua New Guinea Papua New Guinea phrasebook Rarotonga & the Cook Islands • Samoa Solomon Islands • Sydney • Tahiti & French Polynesia Tonga • Vanuatu • Victoria • Western Australia

The Lonely Planet Story

Lonely Planet published its first book in 1973 in response to the numerous 'How did you do it?' questions Maureen and Tony Wheeler were asked after driving, bussing, hitching, sailing and railing their way from England to Australia.

Written at a kitchen table and hand collated, trimmed and stapled, *Across Asia on the Cheap* became an instant local best seller, inspiring thoughts of another book.

Eighteen months in South-East Asia resulted in their second guide, *South-East Asia on a shoestring*, which they put together in a backstreet Chinese hotel in Singapore in 1975. The 'yellow bible', as it quickly became known to backpackers around the world, soon became *the* guide to the region. It has sold well over half a million copies and is now in its 8th edition, still retaining its familiar yellow cover.

Today there are over 160 Lonely Planet titles in print – books that have that same adventurous approach to travel as those early guides; books that 'assume you know how to get your luggage off the carousel' as one reviewer put it.

Although Lonely Planet initially specialized in guides to Asia, they now cover most regions of the world, including the Pacific, South America, Africa, the Middle East and Europe. The list of *walking guides* and *phrasebooks* (for 'unusual' languages such as Quechua, Swahili, Nepali and Egyptian Arabic) is also growing rapidly.

The emphasis continues to be on travel for independent travelers. Tony and Maureen still travel for several months of each year and play an active part in the writing, updating and quality control of Lonely Planet's guides.

They have been joined by over 50 authors, 110 staff – mainly editors, cartographers and designers – at our office in Melbourne, Australia, at our US office in Oakland, California, and at our European office in Paris; another six at our office in London handle sales for Britain, Europe and Africa. Travelers themselves also make a valuable contribution to the guides through the feedback we receive in thousands of letters each year.

The people at Lonely Planet strongly believe that travelers can make a positive contribution to the countries they visit, both through their appreciation of the countries' culture, wildlife and natural features, and through the money they spend. In addition, the company makes a direct contribution to the countries and regions it covers. Since 1986 a percentage of the income from each book has been donated to ventures such as famine relief in Africa; aid projects in India; agricultural projects in Central America; Greenpeace's efforts to halt French nuclear testing in the Pacific; and Amnesty International.

Lonely Planet's basic travel philosophy is summed up in Tony Wheeler's comment, 'Don't worry about whether your trip will work out. Just go!'.